THE NEW ARCHEOLOGICAL
DISCOVERIES

AND THEIR BEARING UPON THE NEW TESTAMENT AND
UPON THE LIFE AND TIMES OF THE PRIMITIVE CHURCH

*"I believe in the spade. It has fed the
tribes of mankind. It has furnished them
water, coal, iron and gold. And now it is
giving them truth—historic truth—the mines
of which have never been opened till our
time."*

—OLIVER WENDELL HOLMES.

(London Academy XXV: 422)

A WOMAN TEACHER

A GLADIATOR (?)

From Dr. W. M. Flinders Petrie's "Hawara Portraits" (First to Second Century)

NERO AS A YOUTH

A LADY OF THE FIRST OR
SECOND CENTURY

A GENTLEMAN OF THE FIRST OR
SECOND CENTURY

From Thomas Graf's Collection of Roman-Egyptian Mummy Portraits (First to Second Century)

THE
NEW ARCHEOLOGICAL DISCOVERIES

AND THEIR BEARING UPON THE NEW TESTAMENT AND UPON THE LIFE AND TIMES OF THE PRIMITIVE CHURCH

By

CAMDEN M. COBERN, D.D., Litt.D.

James M. Thoburn Chair of English Bible and Philosophy of Religion, Allegheny College; Honorary Secretary for Pennsylvania and Member of the General Executive Committee (American Branch) of the Egypt Exploration Fund, etc., etc.

INTRODUCTION BY

EDOUARD NAVILLE, D.C.L., LL.D., F.S.A:

Foreign Associate of the Institut de France; Professor of Archeology in the University of Geneva, Switzerland.

SECOND EDITION, REVISED

ST. PROCOPIUS PRIORY,
1641 Allport Street
CHICAGO, ILL.

FUNK & WAGNALLS COMPANY
NEW YORK AND LONDON
1917

DEDICATED TO

MY CO-WORKER AND
BEST CRITIC
ERNESTINE CRAFT COBERN

PREFACE TO FIRST EDITION

THIS book has no competitor, for it is the pioneer work in this field.

Specialists have written many ponderous volumes touching limited areas of the general subject, but no one has previously attempted to give a summary of all the discoveries in all lands, so far as these in any important way have cast light upon the New Testament writings or the life of the Primitive Church.

The aim has been to make this work a "corpus" of all the more fascinating facts and all the most beautiful and worthy sayings that have floated down to us from those opulent centuries in which the earliest Church was trained. The mass of new information comes from the buried hoards of Greek and Coptic papyri, recently unearthed; but for the sake of vividness a certain amount of supplemental material has occasionally been introduced from the classics and early Fathers, such additions, however, being carefully marked in the context or notes.

It is perfectly evident that no one could write of all these varied discoveries with exhaustive first-hand knowledge. While the writer has had some experience in excavation, and has been forced by his college duties to obtain a somewhat comprehensive knowledge of the general field and a special knowledge of certain parts of the field, yet slips of statement and errors of judgment are inevitable when one ventures—as in this case one was necessarily compelled to venture—into domains where personal, first-hand knowledge was impossible.

The writer can only hope that it will be clear to scholars that he has written with a keen desire to state truthfully the facts, and that in cases where he felt himself unable to form a personal judgment he has, in most instances, been able to have direct access to the best authorities.

Credit for each new fact or conclusion has been given when possible; yet so much of the material has been used over and over again in the classroom that some few references can not be located and some scholar may thus, wholly unintentionally, fail to get his proper credit for some original discovery or novel phrase. It may be added that the forms of personal address and the occasional emphasis of personal experience, which have proved effective with students, have been preserved, so far as practicable, in these published lectures.

It is only because the writer has had rather an exceptional opportunity not only to see in the field the work of many of the masters in modern excavation, but has also had their cordial cooperation, that he has been able to complete satisfactorily this much-needed work.

It will be noticed that many of the texts utilized in this volume are here translated into English for the first time, and a number of my, as yet, unedited papyri have also been used. Dr. Edgar J. Goodspeed of the University of Chicago has kindly deciphered certain of the Greek papyri which had proved baffling, and Dr. H. Hyvernat of the Catholic University of America has done the same with some of my Coptic texts.

To Professor Naville, who is known in every continent for his original contributions to the science of Egyptian archeology, I am especially grateful for reading this book in manuscript and for writing the introduction to it. Dr. Victor Martin of Geneva, Switzerland, associate editor of *The Greek Papyri in the John Rylands Library* (Vol. II, 1915), also read the entire work in manuscript and made a number of important suggestions.

Professor Stanley S. Swartley, of the Allegheny College faculty, has read the entire work as it came from the press, correcting, so far as was possible, its faulty English, for which work of love he has my hearty thanks; these are also due in a very special way to my honored colleague Professor William A. Elliott for his constant sympathy and frequent assistance in the interpretation of the more difficult papyri.

Of the generosity of the publishers of this work too much can not be said. I will always remember the kindness shown by my friend Professor Geo. W. Gilmore, whose breadth and minuteness of learning have been a constant protection.

The following specialists have read such limited sections of the proof sheets as most appealed to them, and in some cases have added invaluable information: Drs. W. M. Flinders Petrie, Agnes Smith Lewis, Adolf Deissmann, A. A. Vaschalde, A. T. Robertson, Wallace N. Stearns, John R. Crawford and Professor Howard Crosby Butler.[1]

This does not mean, however, that these scholars are in any degree responsible for the general argument

[1] I am indebted to Sir William M. Ramsay and Professor George H. Richardson for the loan of several photographs which I could not get elsewhere; to Professor Butler for full permission to use the very valuable photographs obtained by the American Expedition and the Princeton Expedition to Syria; and to Houghton Mifflin Company for the photograph of Rodolfo Lanciani (from *Wanderings in the Roman Campagna*). Other illustrations in this book, unless otherwise stated, were ordinarily photographed by or for the author.

or for the final form of any section of the work. If this semi-popular summary of important results, written primarily for Bible teachers and ministers, shall be accounted of any special value by technical scholars, this will be chiefly due to these friends, just mentioned, who have so generously encouraged the enterprise. To them belongs the praise; the mistakes are mine.

CAMDEN M. COBERN.

Meadville, Pa., April 19, 1917.

PREFACE TO SECOND EDITION

THE popular favor given to this work has made a second edition necessary within less than six months of its original publication.

The author hereby extends his thanks to the scholars who have pointed out various verbal errors in the previous edition. Such errors are corrected here. Fortunately, none of our statements of fact or general judgments seem at present to need revision. A few additional new discoveries brought to light during the present year are referred to in the footnotes.

C. M. C.

INTRODUCTION

By Edouard Naville, D.C.L., LL.D., F.S.A.
Foreign Associate of the Institut de France
Professor of Archeology at the University of Geneva,
Switzerland

INTRODUCTION

It is most remarkable to see the great changes which have been brought about in the study of antiquity by the archeological discoveries made at the end of last century and the beginning of this.

I need not recall here the discovery of the Ægean civilization, which has revealed to us that for several centuries a culture, which originated at Crete, had ruled over the Eastern Mediterranean. A vast, rich field has thus been opened to our researches, and we can now see and often admire the remains of a time, on the history of which we have to-day certain data. These data will undoubtedly be increased when its script is deciphered and when the numerous inscriptions unearthed no longer remain a sealed book.

These archeological discoveries have entirely changed the views we had before on Homer, the author to whom was due the only description preserved of the dawn of Hellenic culture. We see how faithfully he pictured a state of things which lasted for centuries, and that his work can no more be considered as mere fable, as the product of his imagination. The Homeric poems are now studied in quite another light, their conformity with what really existed having been vindicated in the most remarkable way.

Greek civilization and history have not alone profited by the work of the pick and spade. A great deal has also been added to our knowledge of Scripture and of the history of Israel, not so much by the scientific exploration of Canaan, which is being carried out with untiring zeal by various societies like those of the English or the German Funds for the exploration of Palestine, but chiefly by what has come from outside. Mesopotamia and the remains of the mighty cities of Assyria and Babylonia, have helped us considerably in the understanding and interpretation of some parts of the Old Testament. But, curiously enough, the country which has furnished the most valuable documents, the bearing of which on the knowledge of Scripture is not completely realized, is Egypt.

The history of Israel as a nation begins in Egypt, and the most important discoveries in reference to the Old Testament have been made in the valley of the Nile: I refer to the Tel-el-Amarna tablets in Babylonian cuneiform, and the Aramaic papyri of the Jewish colony settled at Elephantine.

But a new and unexpected light has also been shed on the New Testament by the work of the explorers in Egypt. The thousands of Greek papyri written before and in the first centuries of the Christian era, that vast literature so admirably described by Dr. Cobern, the greater part of which comes from the old city of Oxyrhynchus, the present Behnesa—that enormous collection of documents of all kinds—is a philological and archeological treasury on which we shall be able to draw for a better understanding of the sacred text. Its language will be our dictionary, where the true sense of many words is recorded. From the great variety of documents, secular as well as sacred, letters, legal deeds, contracts, accounts, and others having a decidedly religious character, we shall derive a more correct view of the peoples for whom the gospels and the epistles of St. Paul were written.

For the New Testament there is another country whose exploration has given first-rate historical evidence: Asia Minor, a field of excavation which would certainly rival Egypt if it were under other than Turkish rule, where also Sir William Ramsay's researches have shown what is still to be expected. If we add to this manuscripts like the Sinaiticus discovered by Tischendorf last century, and more recently the Freer manuscript and the Syrian Codex found by Mrs. Lewis and Mrs. Gibson at Sinai, we have the chief bases on which will rest henceforth the exegesis of the New Testament.

We have to thank Dr. Cobern for having given us, with a great deal of learning, a vivid account of all these mines of scholarly research, which are still far from having been thoroughly worked. Especially their bearing on the books of the Bible has not been adequately shown, the reason being that most Biblical scholars are still tied down to the methods of the destructive criticism. A book of Scripture is taken, a minute philological analysis is made of it, with often a great amount of scholarship, but this analysis necessarily leads to the discovery of apparent inconsistencies, of disconnections, of repetitions, which have been interpreted as showing the hands of different writers. The whole process has been one of disintegration of the books, resulting in the creation of a great number of authors, for the existence of whom no historical proofs whatever can be adduced.

The archeological discoveries, to which we may add also the help drawn from anthropology (for very often the difficulties we meet in antiquity are easily solved by what we hear or see at the present day), have greatly furthered another method which Sir William

Ramsay calls that of the twentieth century, a designation which is not quite correct, since it existed before, chiefly in France. It is not mainly negative, like much of the higher criticism, but is marked by "a growing power of insight and the power of belief that springs therefrom." Its main principle consists in replacing a book amid its environment. For whom was it written? What was the character of the readers to whom it was dedicated? Do the new discoveries give us an insight not only into their material circumstances, but also into their way of thinking or speaking? It is obvious that the surroundings amid which author and readers move, their conditions of life, their intellectual capacities and their moral condition will rule the language of the writer, the plan of his book, and the meaning which he gives to his words.

As I said, let us put a book into its proper environment, where and when it was originated; let us judge it from what we know of the people who lived at the time it was brought out, to whom it was probably dedicated and who understood it. In this respect it was an invaluable boon when the readers of the New Testament were put in possession of the thousands of papyri discovered in Egypt, of this vast literature, part of which is of the time when the books of the New Testament, gospels and epistles, were written.

The first result which came out of the study of these documents was to show exactly what was the language employed, and where we are to look for its interpretation. According to Dr. Cobern, it is first to Professor Deissmann that we are indebted for setting forth clearly the nature and the characteristics of the language of the New Testament. The language and

style are those of the "vulgar tongue" of the first century, the vernacular of the home and shop, used by
the middle class and the working man, the Κοινή of
the day, the language of every-day life and not that of
the school. It had spread throughout a considerable
part of Egypt, as we know from the numerous papyri
unearthed in that country.

And this fact agrees remarkably well with the
nature of the books of the New Testament. One may
even say that it was commanded by the doctrine which
these books contained. The gospel was not the sacred
book of a chosen people, like the Hebrews; it was not a
book written for priests or for the learned, and of
which they alone had a right to know the mysteries.
"Go ye and make disciples of all the nations," said the
Lord to His disciples (Matt. 28: 19). "There is no distinction between Jew and Greek, for the same Lord is
Lord of all" (Rom. 10: 12); "The Gentiles are fellow-
heirs and fellow-members of the body, and fellow-par-
takers of the promise in Christ Jesus through the gospel"
(Eph. 3: 6), says the great apostle of the Gentiles.

The gospel was for all nations and for all conditions of men. "The poor have good tidings preached
to them," says the Lord (Luke 7: 22). The "small,"
"those of low degree" and the "little ones" were the
first disciples of the gospel, and, as Paul wrote to the
Corinthians, "not many wise after the flesh, not many
mighty, not many noble are called." Therefore, the only
language which would be used for preaching the gospel, and for the books that contained its doctrine, was
the Κοινή, that popular form of the Greek language
which after the conquest of Alexander had spread over
the whole of Western Asia, and particularly in Egypt,

where, owing to the fact of the kings being Greeks, it had become the idiom of a great part of the population, the language of trade and of transactions in every-day life. And this we know from the enormous literature which has been discovered.

And it is only a small part of what existed in Egypt. At Tmei el-Amdid in the Delta, the site of the old Thmuis, I have dug in a series of rooms which contained thousands of papyri absolutely carbonized. Here and there plants had grown in them, finding them a good soil. One could see that they were Greek; one or two of them have been rescued. But it was in vain that I attempted to send some of them to the British Museum; they arrived there as mere ashes. Certainly, as regards size, the archives of Thmuis could well compare with those of Oxyrhynchus.

Greek had become in Egypt a language commonly used by the middle and lower classes, therefore it is in these texts that we are now to look for the interpretation of certain words which seem to be peculiar to the New Testament and were thought to be translations from Hebrew or Aramaic. The papyri will teach us their proper sense, and not the elegant Attic prose of Plato or Isocrates.

But it is not only as regards language that we derive more information; we now know better the conditions of life of the people of that time, their occupations, their family intercourse and the interests toward which their thoughts and their activity were daily directed. We see now that Paul, in his epistles, did not forge new words for his teaching; he did not invent new expressions. He used those with which his contemporaries were familiar, giving them a Christian sense; for instance, the titles by which the emperor was addrest are the words applied to God himself, or to Jesus Christ. Following Deissmann, Dr. Cobern shows in a very interesting way that the title "Lord" given to Jesus is seen from the papyri to have had a deeper meaning than we had ever supposed. Since the title Κύριος "Lord" could only be used after Cæsar had been acknowledged as God, and implied, therefore, that the emperor had been deified, the term Κύριος Ἰησοῦς (Lord Jesus) was a distinct ascription of deity to Christ, and its use must almost have been accounted an act of direct antagonism to the claims of the Roman emperor.

The Christians did not go out of the Roman world; they used and appropriated whatever they could adapt of it to their belief and to their way of living. In art they gave new interpretations to old and familiar symbols. De Rossi showed this, years ago, in his works on the catacombs; for instance, the representation of the Good Shepherd was identical with that of Ἑρμῆς Κριοφόρος; and Orpheus, who attracted even animals by the harmony of his music, was frequently taken as a symbol of the attraction which the new preaching exerted over the hearers.

The holy oracles were communicated, not in a language miraculously originated or artificially perfect, "a language of the Holy Ghost," but in a speech which was in a peculiar and universal sense the language of the people. This fact, which comes out in such a striking way as we study the papyri, is also the leading feature of one of the most ancient translations, the Coptic.

One often speaks of the Coptic language. In one sense

this expression is not correct; there is no classic Coptic like classic Greek; there are only Coptic dialects. Until a few years ago there were three of them known; there is now a fourth, and it is quite possible that the discovery of some papyri among ruins which have not yet been completely explored may reveal a fifth dialect, because these dialects were originally the local speech of a certain region. Coptic shows what might have been suspected, that the spoken language of the people differed from the book language written in hieroglyphs or even in demotic.

When the Christian missionaries came to Egypt they had to do nearly the same as the missionaries of the present day coming to a country where there is no writing. They could not use hieroglyphs; they applied the Greek alphabet to note what they heard, what was the common language of the people, and, since the Greek alphabet was not sufficient to express all the sounds which struck their ears, they added to it six new letters. Coptic is the vernacular of the different parts of Egypt written in Greek characters.

"The language of the people" does not mean a vulgar speech, incapable of beauty, and choosing in preference prosy and commonplace expressions. The people's language, when it is the voice of the heart, the undisguised utterance of deep feeling, can attain remarkable beauty. The total absence of artificial ornamentation, the simplicity of the descriptions, is precisely what produces the most vivid picture of a scene, or gives it the strongest emotional effect. Let us look at the parables— how brightly everything comes out in what might often be called a child's language. Refined art could hardly appeal more strongly to our intimate feelings than the few strokes which describe the prodigal son or the good shepherd.

Dr. Cobern says rightly that Paul's language is often lifted to an unusual elevation of style, which has excited the admiration of experts in Greek language and literature like Von Wilamowitz. Paul's contemporaries called his letters weighty and strong. For Paul, unlike the disciples, was a man of education; he had received a Greek training in the learned city of Tarsus, and tho he also used the language of the people, nevertheless in his epistles, in his way of reasoning, one recognizes that he had been under the influence of teachers.

It is remarkable that the three men in the Bible who are said to have had the most intense literary activity, Moses, who wrote the law; Ezra, who revived it after the captivity; and Paul, who gave a concrete form to the Christian doctrine—who, it might be said codified it—were all men who had received a complete education in the country which they inhabited. Moses was instructed in all the wisdom of the Egyptians, Ezra was a ready Mesopotamian scribe, having gone through the teaching of this class of men, who were the learned of the country; besides, he was "the scribe of the words, of the commandments of the LORD." Paul had not only received a Greek education at Tarsus, where he was born, but he was also brought up in Jerusalem at the feet of Gamaliel. Thus all these were men of the Hebrew law, and at the same time imbued with the knowledge and wisdom of the people among whom they lived.

I can not go over the various fields of archeology or literature which have a bearing on the New Testament: the manuscripts, some of which have been discovered quite recently; the numerous religious writings which are contemporary with the beginning of the Christian Church; and what is properly archeology, the inscriptions or the monuments found in excavations, whether these monuments be temples, constructions, or small objects like coins. This part of archeology is intimately connected with geography; it implies traveling in the country and exploring the spots concerned. This might be called the practical research, which often not only modifies, but even upsets the results obtained in the library from mere literary evidence.

The reader who follows Dr. Cobern in his elaborate description of all the means supplied to us by archeology for a better knowledge of certain epochs of antiquity can not fail to be struck by the change which the discoveries have brought about in the methods and in the ruling principle of historical research. This change might rather be called a return to sound historical principles. History has to rest on documents such as they are, in their plain sense, and not on theories said to be inferences from those documents and which are based more or less on preconceived ideas. At the same time, these documents have to be tested as much as possible from archeology, from the actual remains of what the ancients have made, have touched, or have seen.

Truth will best be reached by the concurrence and the mutual help both of literary and archeological evidence. Considering only what is within the limits of this book—the New Testament—the recent discoveries compel us, as we said, to replace the authors of its different parts in the time when they are said to have lived, and among their readers or the hearers to whom they spoke. This seems to the present writer the best answer to the radical criticism and the most telling way of showing how insufficient and often misleading are its results, which are generally brought forward as being above discussion.

If we put side by side the gospels, the epistles of Paul, and the writings which have been discovered of the first century, we shall find in those "as it were a new autographic commentary," the explanation of many expressions showing that "the New Testament writings were not theological treatises, but were mostly composed in the now technical and rather careless language of the street and home." This comparative study has led Dr. Milligan to declare that "in view of all the new light coming upon the question from recent discovery, it is safe to conclude that "with the probable exception of 2 Peter, all our New Testament writings may now be placed within the first century," tho the collection called the New Testament may be of much later date.

This goes a long way to disprove many of the critical theories, attributing parts of a book like the gospel of John to a later epoch, and cutting it up between various authors, some of them quite unknown and mere literary creations.

Archeology has already done a great deal to modify the ideas or systems based on mere literary or philological evidence. Here we may confidently look forward to new discoveries. We can hardly admit that the soil of Egypt, which has already restored to us such invaluable treasures, is exhausted. We can not say what may be recovered from the ruined mounds of another Oxyrhynchus. For instance, there is no impossibility that some day a fortunate explorer, or perhaps a fellah digging for manure among the decayed bricks of ruined houses, may come upon a deposit of papyri in which there will be a copy of the Septuagint of a time not very remote from that when the translation was made. One may fancy what a prodigious effect such a find would produce in the studies of the Old Testament, and especially as regards the radical higher criticism.

If we think how much light the documents which we now possess have thrown upon the interpretation of Scripture, we may well hope that further excavations will bring out fresh material and new help for the understanding of the Holy Books, which are the spiritual food of a considerable part of mankind.

EDOUARD NAVILLE.

CONTENTS

PART I

THE GREEK PAPYRI AND OTHER MANUSCRIPTS STUDIED WITH ESPECIAL REFERENCE TO THEIR BEARING ON THE NEW TESTAMENT WRITINGS

PART II

THE MONUMENTS, INSCRIPTIONS, AND OTHER ANCIENT REMAINS STUDIED WITH ESPECIAL REFERENCE TO THEIR BEARING ON THE LIFE AND TIMES OF THE PRIMITIVE CHURCH

LIST OF ILLUSTRATIONS

[xxxi]

PART ONE

THE GREEK PAPYRI AND OTHER MANUSCRIPTS

STUDIED WITH ESPECIAL REFERENCE TO THEIR
BEARING ON THE NEW TESTAMENT WRITINGS

I

THE STORY OF MODERN DISCOVERIES OF PAPYRI

1. The Origin, Nature, and Value of Papyrus Documents

IT would be difficult to overestimate the effect upon civilization of the invention of a writing material made from the papyrus plant. Previous to that epochal event the Egyptians had engraved their records upon stones, and perhaps in some parts of the world clay tablets were already being used to record the thoughts of men; but rock monuments and little clay bricks, tho not easily destroyed, can bear no comparison with the delicate yet firm and portable papyrus as a medium for preserving a nation's literature and encouraging a people's correspondence.

The oldest papyrus known just as we have it, was written over 4500 years ago; but even this is merely the copy of a treatise a thousand years older. At least as early as 1500 B. C. tanned skins were used as writing material in Egypt as in Western Asia; but while this material could produce luxurious specimens of book-making, and altho even yet the Jews write the sacred synagog rolls upon this material, yet almost as soon as Egyptian history opens, the papyrus became universally popular and its use continued uninterruptedly for nearly four thousand years. The history of the world's languages can be read from the papyri; for these contain records written in hieroglyphic, hieratic, and demotic Egyptian, Coptic, Aramaic, Hebrew, and Arabic, as

[3]

well as in the oldest Greek and Latin script in existence, while some of the most valued ancient documents
in almost every European language were preserved
upon this imperishable material.

What was the process by which this papyrus paper
was prepared in the days of Moses and the patriarchs,
and in the days of Jesus and the apostles? It was made
by cutting the white pith of the papyrus into long strips,
which were laid down vertically, over which other
strips were placed horizontally, the two layers being
either pasted together, perhaps with the aid of Nile
water, as Pliny tells us, or else prest together into a
single sheet, which was dried in the sun, hammered
and rolled into flat layers, and then rubbed thoroughly
with some smooth substance until it was ready for use.
The sheets made in this way were then pasted together
to form a roll of any length desired, some specimens
over a hundred feet in length being yet in existence.

The papyrus book (*codex*) does not come into
use before the first century of our era and does not
become common until two or three centuries later. It
was a direct copy of the parchment or vellum codex
which had been made possible by the new process of
preparing these skins (197-158 B.C.) so that they could
be written upon on both sides. By the third century
of our era these two processes of book-making were
both being used freely, altho, for the finest work,
the vellum codices stood unrivaled.[1] Indeed, there has
been nothing equal, even in modern times, to the fine
purple skins written in gold and silver which come to

---

[1] The technical distinction between parchment and vellum is that the
former is made from sheepskin, and the latter from calf. Vellum and
parchment are still used for legal documents in Egypt and elsewhere.

us, especially from the third to the sixth centuries. But while the parchment and vellum manuscripts continued to be used for church Bibles and legal documents for many centuries, some of the latter even appearing as late as the middle ages, yet for the private New Testaments of the early centuries and for ordinary letter writing and business purposes the tough but inexpensive papyrus was almost universally used. The ordinary size of a papyrus sheet in the days of the apostles was about five by ten inches, and the ordinary grade was often sold in rolls of perhaps twenty sheets, the price of a sheet being a little more than twenty-five cents. While the width of the cheaper papyri was only about six inches, a better quality called *Charta Livia,* after the Emperor's wife, reached a width of eight inches or more; and the highest grade, called *Hieratica* (or *Augusta,* in honor of the Emperor), ran about nine and a half inches in width. In the days of Claudius an even better grade was introduced, which averaged from twelve to eighteen inches wide. It is doubtful whether any New Testament writer had ever in his life used the higher grades of papyrus, and it can be counted absolutely settled that every book of the New Testament was written upon the medium or poorer qualities. But in all the years since linen paper came into common use—in the eighth or ninth century of our era—it has never been honored as was the humble papyri of that first century which received the autographs of the apostles and evangelists as they told the story of the Man of Nazareth,

"A poor man toiling with the poor." [2]

[2] As the reader's eye must not, in a popular work, be burdened with numerous footnotes, the author desires here, once for all, to record his con-

2. The Earliest Finds of Greek Papyri Dating
   from the Apostolic and Adjoining Centuries

No one discovery for a thousand years has equaled
in importance that of Grenfell and Hunt when, in
1897, they excavated for the Egypt Exploration Fund
the now famous site of Behnesa, the ancient Oxyrhynchus (situated in the Nile Valley some 120 miles
south of Cairo), and discovered literally tons of Greek
papyri, hundreds of which were written in the language of the New Testament. When it is remembered
that no one previous to this time had ever read even
one autograph manuscript which had been written by
a scribe of the first century in the language which the
common people of Palestine and Egypt used in that
era, the sensational nature of this discovery may be
more easily realized.

To be sure, many papyri had been found previous
to this time. The use of this writing material must
have begun in Egypt nearly 4000 B.C., and up to the
time of Alexander the Great it was carried on as a
government monopoly, the ancient scribes of Egypt
being almost as voluminous writers as the scholars
of to-day. These papyri were well known from the
days of the earliest visitors, but had not been counted

---

stant and inestimable indebtedness in every chapter of the present work, to
the great encyclopedias and Biblical dictionaries. Hereafter, such references will be made only in exceptional cases or where differences of
opinion are involved. See for further particulars *Encyclopedia Britannica*,
"Papyrus," "Manuscripts," "Parchment"; *International Standard Bible
Encyclopedia*, "Papyrus"; Milligan's *The New Testament Documents*, and
Wessely's brilliant summary in the opening section of his *Aus der Welt
der Papyri*; also Breasted's article, "The Physical Processes of Writing in
the Early Orient and Their Relation to the Origin of the Alphabet," in
the *American Journal of Semitic Languages*, 1916; 249ff.

of any great importance. About the middle of the eighteenth century a number of charred rolls in Greek, which proved to be of a literary character, were found during excavations at Herculaneum but were not regarded as of value.[3] In 1778, some Arabs found 40 or 50 papyrus rolls in an earthen pot, and tho most of these were destroyed, one was brought from Egypt to Europe; but there was no particular disappointment when it became known that these documents were so abundant along the Nile that the natives were using them for fuel or burning them for their pleasant fragrance. Who cared what the Ptolemies were writing to their friends or what kind of barbarous Greek they used? For over forty years nothing more appeared in the field of papyrus discovery worth mentioning, but in 1820, on the site of the Serapeum at Memphis, a group of documents was found dating from the second century B.C. It was chiefly with the help and under the inspiration of this discovery that George Ebers composed his fascinating Egyptian novels. The next year a book of the Iliad, many centuries older than any previously seen, was bought near Elephantine and brought to England; shortly after a roll containing the Lycophron and other orations of Hypereides was discovered; in 1856 the funeral oration of this celebrated writer was obtained, while in 1855 the Louvre had acquired a long-lost work by Alcman. By this time so many Ptolemaic documents had accumulated that one or two progressive thinkers began to use them in explanation of some words in the Septuagint —that most valuable translation of the Old Testament which was published in Ptolemaic times (250-100 B.C.),

[3] These papyri are only now being worthily edited and published.

which the apostles and most other Jews of the first century used as Sacred Scripture.

The first discovery on a large scale, after papyri were seen to be worth preserving, took place at the site of Arsinoë in 1877, but these were of a non-literary nature and in a very fragmentary state and were all late in date, being of the Byzantine time, and there- fore aroused very little interest until long afterward, when those in the possession of the Archduke Rainer of Vienna began to be published. As it has been estimated that there are over a million papyri in this collection, it goes without saying that many, even yet, remain unedited. In 1892, on the site of a village named Socnopaei Nesus, very near to Arsinoë, an extensive series of documents in much better condition, dating from the first to the middle of the third cen- tury of our era, was discovered, and found by the German scholars to be full of interesting material, tho no one had yet caught the stupendous truth that these were written in the colloquial language of the first century, i.e., in Biblical Greek.

In 1890, the famous work of Aristotle on the Con- stitution of Athens was discovered, and the edition of the text, when published the following year by Dr. F. G. Kenyon of the British Museum, produced a veritable sensation. The work had been lost for at least twelve hundred years and its discovery ranked "as the most striking event in the history of classical literature for perhaps the last three centuries" (Kenyon). It had been considered outside the bounds of possibility that this much quoted work should ever be recovered in its original form. It was written from 325-322 B.C., either by Aristotle's own hand or at least by his orders and under his own eye. From classical references scholars had been sure that it treated of the history and growth of this most famous of ancient "Constitutions," giving also the great philosopher's comments on the laws of his own day as compared with the past, and one of the fondest hopes, when Herculaneum was excavated, was the prospect of finding this work or at least some considerable fragment of it. But this expectation had not been fulfilled, nor had the monasteries afforded any new knowledge of this, or indeed any other of the more important works of classical literature—and then suddenly this greatest discovery of all was made! The text was written on the back of four rolls of papyrus nearly a foot wide and extending to a length of nearly nineteen feet, thus giving to scholars the work almost complete. Its unusual size may be seen from the fact that its translation, as given by Sir F. G. Kenyon in 1912, covers 116 solid pages.

This precious document was written in several different hands upon the back of papyri which had been used for recording the daily accounts of the manager of a small Egyptian farm A.D. 78-79. It contained over 63 chapters, practically complete. The first part of this noble work consists of 41 chapters treating most carefully the provisions of the original Constitution of Athens and the changes through which it had passed. The second part describes the constitution of Aristotle's day and its regulations concerning citizenship, training of the youth, functions of the Council (Βουλή), archons, military officers, law courts, etc.

To the surprize of classical scholars it was found that this ancient original document takes a very different view of the course of Greek history, particularly of the legislation of Draco and Solon, from that which modern critics had favored. In fact, the newly discovered history, which is absolutely authoritative for the first quarter of the fourth century B.C., differs so radically from many modern reconstructions of that period that, as Sir F. G. Kenyon says, it tends to make us almost skeptical as to the value of most conjectural restorations of historic facts, either in Greek or in Hebrew history. "So many eminently reasonable theories and conjectures are scattered to the winds by this slight addition to the ancient testimonies that considerable caution seems to be imposed for the future alike on the propounding and the accepting of similar and equally plausible imaginations."[4] The museums and great libraries had by this time begun to realize in some degree the value of these papyrus documents which they had previously disregarded. As early as 1839, the British Museum had published a little volume of 44 papyri, including the Serapeum records found some twenty years before, and in 1891 and 1893 other important volumes followed.

An additional word will perhaps be welcomed concerning the unique temple records which had so much influence in rousing popular attention to these strange discoveries. These documents were concerned with the temple of Serapis at Memphis where two girls who were twins, Thaneas and Thaus, petition through a friend named Ptolemy for certain rights of which they had been deprived. Ptolemy was a Macedonian who lived the life of a recluse in the temple where he had twice been violently assaulted because he was a Greek

---

[4] *Aristotle on the Athenian Constitution,* transl. by F. G. Kenyon, 1912, p. xix.

—which reminds us forcibly of the attack upon Trophimus in the temple at Jerusalem which led ultimately to Paul's arrest and final martyrdom (Acts 21:29).

The girls had been accustomed to offer libations to Isis, Serapis, and Asclepius, for which services they were paid regularly for six months, after which the account fell into arrears. When the king and his queen visited the temple the twins presented a petition to him, but nothing came of it; and it is suggestive to see how many petitions were sent before anything was paid, the minor officials putting the matter off as long as possible and never, so far as we know, paying in full.

Another volume of British Museum papyri contained many magical texts written in gibberish, but attempting to show how one could succeed in love or hate and keep good health and beauty under all circumstances; a ring, an emerald, and a beetle play important parts in this magic; and also a boy, who by looking into a magic bowl was, it seems, able to forecast the future just as well as any modern Oriental fortune teller. The volume also contained spells by which to control the various deities at favorable hours during favorable days, and what would seem even more valuable, prescriptions for cleaning houses of bugs and fleas and restraining old women from drunkenness and garrulity.

Among the public accounts was a tax register of the second century, and among the private documents the day book of a farm steward of the first century by the name of Didymus. These farm records of the apostolic age discuss weeding, rush-picking, irrigation, harrowing, dyke-making, and the free distribution of beer to laborers. On the back of this document was written the large and important work on the Constitution of Athens, which has previously been described. The "Classical Texts from the Papyri," edited by Dr. F. G. Kenyon in 1891, called especial attention to the newly discovered poems of Herodas (third century B.C.) and to the new light which they threw upon our thought of ancient times. Herodas represented a class of poetry never seen before except in small fragments. The newly discovered manuscript, however, contained seven poems, each one of which threw a flashlight into that long forgotten and far-off world. Let us try in a few brief phrases to epitomize a few of these.

1. The Matchmaker or the Go-Between.

This old woman, after complaining of the mud which "is nearly up to one's thighs," gives extravagant sympathy to her friend because her husband had been ten months in Egypt and had never written back:—in Egypt the land of wealth and wine and of women who rival in beauty the three goddesses! "Cheer up," she says in substance, "do not moor your ship with one anchor alone; consider the famous athlete Gallos and have a good time while your husband is gone!"

2. The Pander.

This poem tells the story of a stranger who had come to this man's house and abused one of his girls. It is worse than Balzac.

3. The School Master.

The mother brings her boy and urges the pedagog to flog him within an inch of his life, for he is the "terror of the home." "He associates," she says, "only with the lowest characters and he will not study at all. Everything he is told to remember runs through him like a sieve. When his teachers or parents scold him he either runs away or climbs on the roof of a house and makes faces at them like a monkey and ruins the tiles of the roof."

It is a pleasure to add that the school-master rises to the occasion and uses the cowhide. The poem closes with a series of howls and promises to be good.

4. A Visit to Asclepius.

This poem is most remarkable for its description of the wonderful art treasures in the temple. No church of to-day is as rich in gifts as those ancient heathen sanctuaries.

5. A Jealous Woman.

In this poem a lady who is evidently in love with her slave sends him off to receive a thousand lashes on his back and stomach, because in her jealousy she thinks he has paid attention to another woman. Before the order can be executed, however, she calls him back, saying she has decided instead of that to have him branded on the face with a hot iron. The probability is that she forgave him before the poem concluded.

Such poems as this open up the social conditions and the base immorality of the second century of our era in a rather startling way.

It is noteworthy that this one little volume of British Museum papyri contained three manuscripts of classical works hitherto unknown and collations of seven manuscripts of works already extant, thus representing all such papyri at that time in the possession of the British Museum with the exception of six previously published. Other museums had, meanwhile, been making some fine purchases, the most important being the acquisition by

the Louvre, in 1892, of the greater part of the long-lost
masterpiece of Hypereides, his oration against Athen-
ogenes; which, however, was balanced by the British
Museum's securing four years later the Odes of Bac-
chylides, a contemporary of Pindar. Soon, Berlin was
able to announce another great discovery, The Persae,
a poem of Timotheus of Miletus (446 B.C.), which had
been discovered by Dr. A. Wiedemann in 1902 at Abusir
and sent to the German capital. This was found in a
wood coffin still containing the corpse, together with a
pair of sandals, leather bag, etc. It represented the oldest
book known, antedating the founding of the library of
Alexandria. But we must return to Egypt and watch
some of the leading explorers engaged in the practical
field work which was giving these wondrous treasures to
the European libraries.

Dr. Edouard Naville, that prince of scholars, excavating in 1892 under the auspices of the Egypt Exploration Fund, made a most remarkable discovery
when he recovered the carbonized papyri of Thmûis.
The reference which my distinguished friend makes to
this discovery in his introduction to this volume
(p. xviii) is entirely too modest.

In a ruined building at this site he found an entire
library of decayed rolls, the burned contents of which almost choked its chambers.[5] Following his lead, Mr. C.
C. Edgar again cleared this building in 1906, tho
the papyrus was of the poorest quality and seemed
completely undecipherable in its decayed and carbonized condition, and he obtained little more than an interesting collection of clay seals.[5a] Some other unofficial

---

[5] *Egypt Exploration Fund, Archeological Report*, 1892, pp. 4ff; cf. *Ahnas
el Medineh*, p. 21.
[5a] Cf. *Annales du Service des Antiquité*, pp. 154-57.

digging between the above dates yielded only other bundles of seemingly worthless documents—but it has just been discovered that even these burned papyri can be read! Up to 1915 only about twenty of these documents had ever been deciphered; but in that year the editors of the Greek papyri, in the John Rylands Library, Manchester, succeeded in publishing about eighty fragments of these carbonized papyri in such a splendid way that they can now be easily translated. Altho the rolls were crusht by the weight above them, yet the fragments were gummed to cards in such a careful manner that one side of each document could be examined, tho the writing on the back was necessarily destroyed. These documents were written by trained scribes and treated of many diverse subjects, tho uniformly official in character. The ruined building which Dr. Naville discovered was a government office containing the registration files of the district, these files showing the leases of government lands, apportionments of surpluses and deficits in revenue, taxes in money and grain, and considerable private correspondence. All date from the last half of the second to the beginning of the third century and give a valuable picture of the administration of the district.[5aa]

Thmûis was the capital of one of the nomes of the Delta, and reached the zenith of its power under Roman occupation. The taxation accounts are elaborately classified, being arranged in well-defined divisions and indexed with headings and subheadings. The bookkeeping is modern in its thoroughness.

[5aa] Petrie made the first great "find" of carbonized papyri at Tanis in 1884. He so carefully wrapt and packed the two baskets full which he recovered that they reached England with little loss (see *Two Hieroglyphic Papyri from Tanis,* 1889).

A new enthusiasm in papyri research began, however, with the finds of manuscripts by Dr. W. M.
Flinders Petrie in the cemetery at Hawara, 1888-1890,
where he made the spectacular discovery of Ptolemaic
mummies whose faces were covered with casings made
of papyri pasted together. This greatest of all modern explorers appreciated the richness of this find and
invented new ways of separating and restoring the old
fragments, which proved to be some of the most important documents for the history of Greek paleography
ever found, including ancient wills and other legal documents of the third century B.C., but especially several
papyri containing large fragments of the Phaedo and
Laches of Plato, the lost Antiope of Euripides, and
other classical works which filled scholars everywhere
with delight.

Prof. J. P. Mahaffy *(The Petrie Papyri)* has told
the fascinating story of how Professor Sayce and
himself, during a college vacation in 1890, pored over
the seemingly undecipherable fragments of the torn
and mutilated papyri which Dr. Petrie had sent them,
until finally the Phaedo emerged, then the leaf of a
tragic poem and then the names of Roman emperors
began to appear out of these tattered and dirty scraps
that for over 2,000 years had been hidden in the dust
heap. It was on one of these warm and happy days that
Professor Mahaffy guessed the meaning of the abbreviation always mysteriously appearing at the beginning of all wills:

"Being of sound mind and clear understanding."

The original finding of these papyri in the mummy
cases at Gurob (near the Fayum) was just as strange
and unexpected as any discovery could be.   These

coffins and mummy cases were not very attractive. The only decoration upon any coffin was a carved wooden head of marvelous rudeness, almost grotesque, the nose being simply a long, triangular ridge, while the eyes were marked with two scars in the board, and the mouth by another scar. Within these grossly rough cases were comparatively fine painted cartonnages, ornamental coverings, made usually of pasteboard. The separate pieces of the cartonnage were the head-piece coming down with a spread on the chest; the pectoral or collar plate, semicircular; the open work on which were figures of the gods about the breast; and the foot case. The earliest heads were tolerably well made of folds of linen pasted together and molded on a block. Over the cloth was a coat of stucco painted dark blue, and often the face was gilt and burnished very skilfully. In later times, about the era of Ptolemy Philadelphus (284-246 B.C.), papyrus was substituted for cloth, and several layers of Demotic or Greek papyri were glued together, covered with stucco and painted, and thus developed into the massive plaster head-pieces of the Hawara cemetery. In this stage they did not glue the papyri together but merely soaked them and plastered them one on the other, trusting to crossing them and a good coat of plaster and glue to hold them together. The papyri recovered from the glued cases were mostly in a bad state, but the cases made with plain wetting were by far the best source of papyri, and when a document had been used whole, being spread out on the breast or down the back, it could be taken out "none the worse for its burial for over 2,000 years" (Petrie).

Among the other works specially deserving of mention coming from this site, was a petition of a prisoner who urges freedom, "in the name of God and of fair play"; a correspondence of Kleon and Alexander, in which the latter advises that repairs to a conduit be paid for by putting an extra tax on salt; a complaint of Petosiris, a tanner, who declares that Dionysios, "tho not even an official tax-gatherer," had rushed into his house and carried off various valuables, including "two pillows, a Cyprian drinking-cup, and a box of tools"; and the personal narrative of a royal party which had marched to Ephesus and Laodicea, the writer describing in a most fascinating way how, when they had arrived at Seleucia, the royal party had been met and entertained by the magistrates, priests, citizens, and soldiers, all crowned with garlands!

As the present writer visited Dr. Petrie, both at Hawara and Gurob, at the critical moment when this initial and most startling discovery was being made, he may be pardoned, perhaps, for having dwelt upon it so long, especially as Messrs. Grenfell and Hunt, who have won the greatest fame as papyri hunters, were, in part, trained by Dr. Petrie and it was under his direction that they went to Oxyrhynchus, he himself opening the site and leaving it only because the ruins were not more ancient. As early as 1894 Mr. B. P. Grenfell had been in Egypt working with Dr. Petrie, who subsequently obtained from a native dealer a remarkable papyrus roll over 40 feet in length containing the revenue laws of Ptolemy Philadelphus, which he unrolled and handed to Dr. Grenfell to edit. Mr. Arthur S. Hunt had also been in Egypt during this same period, securing papyri for a great English library. In 1895 these two men, the oldest being but

26 years of age, joined together in excavations for papyri in the Fayum and were extraordinarily successful.

But it was in 1897 that the new era of papyri discovery began. When, in that year, these two young scholars started to dig at Oxyrhynchus neither of them could possibly have dreamed that the most far-reaching discovery in its bearing upon the New Testament which had ever been made in Christian history was about to be accomplished. Nor, indeed, did they imagine this even after they had begun to uncover from the *afsch* (rubbish) of the mounds these masses of papyri. They found some of these the first day of their digging at Behnesa, and almost continuously—day after day, and week after week—these ancient documents were upturned. How many thousands of papyrus scraps these young men took to England the writer does not know, but so many that it will yet be a generation before they can all be thoroughly examined.[5b] When the store boxes, in which these treasures were packed, came to London from Oxyrhynchus, they were so heavy that they were weighed by the ton when billed by the freight agent. In 1897 these men gave their first official report, having examined at Oxford the contents of some 1,300 of these documents. This first volume contained 158 texts, tho four-fifths of the whole collection had not yet been unpacked, and the best part of what they had obtained had been left at the Cairo museum. Perhaps no published work in our generation ever aroused more curious interest than this, and the volumes which followed fully sustained the expectation.

[5b] See *Journal of Egyptian Archæology*, April, 1914, pp. 82, 91.

The Greek texts in Vol. I date from 200 B.C. to A.D. 600. They comprise new manuscripts with new and important readings in a vast number of the classics, such as Homer, Herodotus, Xenophon, Sophocles, etc., a good many new works by authors formerly known, and some quite important works by authors previously almost unheard of. The editors were able to publish a new ode by Pindar, singing the praises of the simple life, and also a poem by Sappho, beautiful enough to sustain fully the literary reputation of this remarkable woman. This first poem of Sappho, written in the Aeolic dialect and assigned to the third century, commences with an invocation to Aphrodite, and is one of the vain appeals from Sappho to her brother Charaxus, whom she had permanently estranged by her bitter reproaches because of his devotion to Rhodopis, a slave at Naucratis, whom he ransomed. Portions of twenty lines are preserved, of which we quote a few in translation:

> "And may he have the will
> To me his sister some regard to show,
> To assuage the pain he brought, whose cruel blow
> My soul did kill,

> "Yea, mine, for that ill nam
> Whose biting edge, to shun the festal throng
> Compelling, ceased awhile; yet back ere long
> To goad us came."

We add here a few verses from a more recently discovered love song of this same famous woman, which has been put into English verse by Joyce Kilmer:

"Unto some a troop of triumphant horsemen,
  Or a radiant fleet, or a marching legion,
Is the fairest sight—but to me the fairest
    Is my beloved.

"Every lover must understand my wisdom,
  For when Helen looked on the whole world's beauty
What she chose as best was a man, her loved one,
    Who shamed Troy's honor.

"Then her little child was to her as nothing,
  Not her mother's tears nor her father's pleading
Moved her. At Love's word, meekly she surrendered
    Unto this stranger."

Other treasures discovered were a new comedy by
Menander, in which he makes the statement which
sounds very modern: "No honest man ever grew rich
quickly"; an interesting work resembling the "Al-
manack" of our own Benjamin Franklin, in which were
practical maxims like "Every thing grows old except
the love of gain"; and a new rhetorical treatise whose
author asserts that he is able to give to every speaker
on every subject an epigram which will just fit his needs.
This rhetorician, altho most of his work is gone, leaves
one injunction which might even yet be remembered
with profit in some theological schools: "Do not be
stiff or artificial in your speaking. It is better to show
hesitancy [rather than fluency], for it gives a better
impression when everything does not seem cut and
dried beforehand."

It is also interesting to find here a legal decision
of the second or early part of the third century, in
which the doctor lays claim for immunity for some kind
of public service on the ground of his being a physician,
while the court demands scientific proof that he is a

physician by having him answer certain technical questions.

Another official document (A.D. 173) is "from a public physician" named Dionysus, who hands in his coroner's report that Heraclides came to his death by hanging. There are orders of arrests, denial of money claims, complaints of robberies made to the police court, property returns, emancipation papers, official tax lists, meat bills, nurses' receipts, invitations to dinner, and everything else connected with the life of the ordinary citizen of that town in the first, second, third and fourth centuries of our era. The invitation to dinner has not been much improved upon by modern society. It reads:

> "Chaeremon requests your company at dinner
> At the table of the Lord Serapis in the Serapeum
> To-MORROW, the fifteenth, at nine o'clock."

The wedding invitations are precisely as ours.

Many documents from the guilds of workmen and trade unions were found. Corporations, and even individuals, were, about the era of St. Paul, found engaged in business plans which seem strikingly up to date. For example, an egg-seller (A.D. 32-37) binds himself under oath not to sell eggs privately at a discount, but only in the public market at the fixt price.[6]

Many private letters were published from the ordinary business men of those early centuries, and some from slaves and women and even a few from boys. It was a perfect surprize to find how freely the people who lived 2,000 years ago were accustomed to express

---

[6] This explanation of the text seems to me the most reasonable, altho such an affidavit may have been required also because of a possible attempt to avoid taxation or for other reasons.

themselves in this way. Letter writing was not confined to rare occasions and important subjects, but
dealt with the most trifling matters of every-day life.

Perhaps the most famous letter published by Grenfell and Hunt in their first volume was that of little
Theon, who some time in the second or third century
of our era sent a letter to his father, Theon, who had
gone off to Alexandria without taking him along. The
letter is printed out in school-boy fashion instead of
being written in ordinary cursive form, and the spelling
and grammar are quite original: "It was a fine thing
of you not to take me with you to the city!" says the
little fellow immediately after his greeting. "If you
won't take me with you to Alexandria [next time] I
won't write you a letter or speak to you or say good-by
to you." Dr. Deissmann thinks this letter to be very
impertinent; but when we remember the supreme
power which parents had over children at that time—
which must certainly have put outward respect, at least,
at a premium—I am inclined to believe that in this
case father and son were chums and that the boy knew
he could take liberties with such a father without fear.
The spirit of love and mirthfulness crops out when at
the close of his letter he begs his father to send him a
lyre and adds, "If you don't, I won't eat, I won't drink;
there now!"

The greatest treasures revealed in this first publication of the papyri consisted, however, in some Biblical
texts, dating to a period at least a hundred years
earlier than any other known texts of the New Testament, and some "sayings of our Lord," together with
some Christian letters and some certificates of sacrifice
which had evidently been required of persons suspected

of being Christians. All of these we will consider later.

The question must arise with every one why these papyri are found only in or near the Fayum in Egypt, and how perishable papyrus, which is merely the ancient paper, could be preserved for all these centuries without rotting. As to the latter point, the dry climate of Egypt and the sand, which covers every dead thing with its protecting shroud, must be credited with preserving these and many other tender and delicate objects which would certainly have perished in any other country. The writer has actually seen flowers taken from the tomb, where they had been buried for 3,000 years, still retaining their color, and in some cases it almost seemed that they still preserved a little portion of their fragrance. All sorts of cloth, even the most delicate linens, could remain hidden in the sand for centuries, or even millenniums, without injury; often looking as fresh when taken from the tomb as when first buried. Papyrus, like paper, is very easily preserved if it happens to be buried in a dry place; and even when a house is burned, if a great quantity of paper or papyrus is piled close together, only the outer sheets are harmed, while the inner sheets are perfectly safe. And since the ink-makers for the Pharaohs seem to have been more able or more honest than most modern dealers, such papyri can very generally be easily deciphered, tho written two or three thousand years ago, unless, indeed, the worms have been attempting to digest the contents of the library, or the abbreviations and orthography prove too much for us.

A few remarkable facts not usually known will

show clearly why the papyri have mostly been recovered from a few villages buried in the sand along the former shore of Lake Moeris in the Egyptian Fayum. About 1,000 years before the Trojan war a Pharaoh took advantage of a natural depression in this part of Egypt and by the construction of several vast dams, parts of which still remain, he formed an artificial reservoir nearly one-seventh as large as Lake Erie, if some critical calculations are correct, making this the basis of an irrigating project stupendous enough to startle almost into incredulity our modern engineers; tho probably the original purpose of these dams was to save the country from inundation because of the rise of the Nile. The fact seems to be that for many years previous to the reign of Senwosri I, who first began these improvements, the entire Fayum had been a lake with only one high ridge or plateau which could be inhabited. Amenemhat III and the Pharaoh just mentioned, by means of these great dams and powerful locks, succeeded in keeping the maximum level constantly below that of the towns which were on the plateau—the same plateau on which the modern capital of the district, Medinet el Fayum, is now situated. He also diverted the surplus water from the Fayum, thus reclaiming considerably more land, establishing in this district won from the lake a famous summer resort, where he built splendid monuments, including the famous Labyrinth, which was really his palace, and the pyramid of Hawara, which was his tomb. The wonderful colossi at *Biahmu,* standing on the edge of this second plateau which he had reclaimed, were really statues of the king and his wife at the landing-stage of the lake. The lake continued in this condition even down to the days of Herodotus, altho by very little effort more surplus water might have been kept out and the inflow of the *Bahr Yusuf* might have been so regulated as to reclaim more land.

During the two centuries, however, between the visit of Herodotus (*cir.* 450 B.C.) and the reign of Ptolemy Philadelphus (*cir.* 260 B.C.) the Fayum again became the object of royal attention in order to provide settlements for Greek veterans. New dykes and canals were constructed and again the lake shrank in size, a large number of new villages springing up along the new lake front.

Still later a third plateau was put above water and the lake margin again changed, a new line of towns being built. From the reign of Philadelphus to early in the third century of our era the prosperity of the Fayum was at its height, but upon the decline of Egypt and the destruction of the regular irrigation system this prosperity suddenly ceased and the desert took possession of the Fayum as nowhere else in Egypt, thus making this district, because of its stranded villages buried in the desert, the pre-eminent source of all our supplies of ancient papyri.[7] In the piles of rubbish (*afsch*) which often rise to a height of 20 or 30 feet about these ancient towns, and in the deserted houses themselves, have been found most of the literary wealth which has compelled the rewriting of much ancient history and even the rewriting of our Bible grammars and lexicons. At Oxyrhynchus, which was located south of this lake district on the canal upon which the Fayum depended for its entire water supply, no documents were found in the ruins of houses, for

[7] See especially *Fayûm Towns and their Papyri,* 1900.

every house had completely disappeared. All of these vast quantities of papyrus scraps came from the rubbish heaps which are so characteristic of every oriental town. The desert sand was in this case God's angel sent to bury these waste papers and preserve them through the centuries as perfectly as if deposited in the steel safe of a modern bank.[8]

When we remember that no autograph letter or legal document of the first century had ever been seen until these towns were uncovered, it may be appreciated with what thrilling excitement Greek scholars examined these fragments dug up at Oxyrhynchus and the towns of the Fayum. Here were found imperial edicts and tax collector's reports and legal documents of all kinds. Here was a death notice (A.D. 37), a receipt for bath tax (A.D. 36), a tax on beer (A.D. 61), and poll-tax receipts from all periods. Here was a dedication of a banqueting hall (A.D. 69-78), and another (A.D. 109), the latter being the dining-hall of the "elders" (πρεσβυτέρων) of the Alexandrian corporation of weavers. Here were questions to the oracles written with pathetic eagerness in the same century in which the Christian teachers were interfering with heathen magic:

"To Socnopaeus, the Great, Great God. Answer me.
Shall I remain? Shall I meet (him)? Answer me."

Here were many, many letters. In one package of

---

[8] The presence in these rubbish heaps of torn fragments of certain greatly prized documents, such as the "Holy Scriptures" of the Hebrews and Christians, may possibly point to some tragedy of persecution (cf. 2 Kings 10:27; Ezra 6:11; Dan. 2:5). So were the sacred books of the Hebrews treated during the Maccabean and other persecutions; and nothing pleases a Mohammedan better to-day than to be able to "defile" the sacred book or worshiping place of a Jew or Christian.

fourteen all the letters were wholly concerned with the private affairs of one family, mostly written by Gemellus, an old soldier who had reached his sixty-seventh year and wrote one letter about the time St. John was dying (A.D. 100), in which he gives directions concerning the hoeing and plowing, complaining of his nephew in no measured terms because of his delay in harvesting. Ten years later, when 77 years old, he writes in a shaking and almost illegible hand to the same relative, Epagathus, about manuring the land properly, and scolds him roundly about his mistakes in caring for the land as he had previously scolded another young farmer for being cheated in his purchase of a bundle of hay which was below weight and so rotten that it was "no better than dung." In almost every letter he writes, "Do not neglect these instructions"; he is evidently quite sure that the modern generation is quite incapable of farming as well as the young folk could when he was a boy.[9]

It makes a Bible student quiver to read the report of a law suit (A.D. 49) in which Pesouris "in the seventh year of our sovereign Tiberius Claudius Caesar picked up from the gutter a boy foundling," or the petition of Tryphon to the prefect in the same year when Pesouris, after the above foundling died, tried to "carry off into slavery" a neighbor's "infant son." Here are sales, mortgages, registration of cattle, loans, contracts of apprenticeship, marriages, divorces, emancipation of slaves, and all manner of legal documents from this suddenly recovered first century. Here is the horoscope of a person born 10 P.M., Sept. 28, A.D. 15; a village scribe (A.D. 37) swears "by Tiberius

[9] All the above examples are taken from *Fayûm Towns*.

Cæsar, son of the deified Jupiter, Liberator Augustus," that he does not know of any extortion on the part of the soldiers; but a dozen years later we have several papyri concerning the extortions of tax collectors, bringing vividly to mind the feeling against Matthew and Zacchaeus.

One young reprobate in this same century laments the death of his fighting cock, saying: "For his sake have I been called great in my life and deemed happy . . . I am at a loss where to go"—and actually threatens suicide! One husband, Sarapion, has a complaint lodged against him (A.D. 20-50) by his wife because he has squandered her dowry, ill-treated her, and left her in poverty; while another husband complains that his wife Demetrias has left him after stealing many valuables (A.D. 30-35). One man writes to his brother (A.D. 22):

"I am not so much as anointing myself until I hear from you. . . . Let me hear about our baldheaded friend, how his hair is growing again on the top. Be sure not to forget."

The letters are about every conceivable subject. Horus (first century) writes concerning "Lampon, the mouse-catcher," and Indike writes to a relative concerning the bread basket she has sent her, closing her note with remembrances of friends, just as St. Paul so often closes his letters:

"Salute my friend Theon and Nicoblus and Dioscurus and Hermocles who have my best wishes." [10]

[10] All the above from *Oxyrhynchus Papyri*, parts 1 and 2, 1898-99.

3. Dr. Deissmann's Epoch-making Discovery
Concerning the Papyri

At first the chief value of the papyri seemed to lie in the new light which they threw upon the first century, and in the multitude of ancient classics they had revealed, and in the Christian fragments of the first four centuries preserved. But in 1895 Mr. Adolf Deissmann, tho not a university professor or even a clergyman, but a young candidate for the ministry, a privatdocent at Marburg, published a discovery which he had made in the examination of the papyri, which is, without doubt, the greatest single discovery of an interpretative principle ever made in New Testament archeology.

Deissmann was the first to recognize that these papyri were written exactly in the language of the New Testament, and to draw the conclusive inference that Biblical Greek could not any longer be regarded as an esoteric, sacred language, or as a language to any considerable degree Hebraized by its Jewish authors.

How it ought to curb the pride of specialists to find that the original discovery which opened to the world the Egyptian language, the Babylonian language, and the New Testament language, was in each case made, not by a world-renowned expert, but by a shrewd young man of good sense and insight unbiased by the trammels of scholarly tradition.

It was Deissmann who caught the revolutionary truth that the gospels were a "people's book" written in the dialect of the middle classes in the vernacular of the home and the shop; written in a style which no literary man of that day would have permitted himself to use, but which did appeal to the masses. An examination of the papyri written contemporaneously with the New Testament proved, according to Deissmann, that the New Testament books, with perhaps the exception of two or three, were written to working men in the tongue of the working man, the Bible authors freely using the colloquialisms and even the solecisms of the market-place. This was a theory which at first seemed too good to be true. It meant that Wycliffe only did for England what Matthew and Mark did for the Roman world. Christianity from its beginning spoke the tongue of the peasant. Its crooked grammar and mixed orthography and peculiar syntax, upon which have been built so many theological castles in the air, are all found paralleled exactly in the letters and other familiar documents of that first century. This common Greek (the κοινή) was spoken everywhere throughout the entire Roman empire, and even our early church titles, such as "bishop," "presbyter," "deacon," etc., were well-known official names used in the trade unions and other corporations, religious and civil, of that era. This contention, which seemed at first utterly unbelievable, has now inside of twenty years gained the adhesion of almost every great living Greek scholar and has caused the re-writing of the New Testament lexicon and grammar.

Deissmann's first work was his *Bibelstudien* (1895), followed by his *Neue Bibelstudien* (1897), both translated into English in 1901. Dr. Deissmann —tho to be sure he was not a "Doctor" then—in his first volume divided the subject into two parts. In the first part he gave a "Prolegomena to the Biblical Letters and Epistles." He showed first that Paul's writings ought not to be called epistles, but letters. An epistle is literature written for a literary purpose, but a letter is personal and, however carefully written, exposes the private feelings and lays bare the heartbeats as no merely literary production could do. He translated a large number of the new papyri, especially the letters, and showed that the New Testament collection as a whole, and especially the publication of the letters of Paul in one package or volume, was indirectly influenced by the custom in ancient times of making just such collections of letters. He showed by a multitude of examples that the style of Paul's letters exactly agreed with the style of the letters just recovered from the first century, and pointed out that the contents of Paul's writings, especially their contradictions or unexplained suggestions, would be utterly impossible in a worked-out treatise, but were exactly what must be expected in any real letter.

In the second part of the book he makes his contribution to the language of the Greek Bible. He shows that the Septuagint, which was "translation-Greek," was more stately, but also more clumsy than the vernacular represented by the New Testament and the papyri. Most of the alleged Hebraisms of the Septuagint were probably merely popular Greek expressions common to the vernacular. The real language of the Septuagint was the spoken Greek language in Egypt under the Ptolemies. This, according to Deissmann, explains many of the supposed errors of the Hebrew text as revealed by its Greek translation. Often when it has been inferred by modern critics that the Septuagint translators had before them a text different from our own, it is now seen that they were

Dr. Adolf Deissmann

Dr. B. P. Grenfell

Dr. Caspar René Gregory

Dr. Arthur S. Hunt

© Elliott & Fry

Dr. James Hope Moulton

Dr. W. M. Flinders Petrie

Dr. A. T. Robertson

Dr. Edouard Naville

simply striving to make the ordinary Hebrew text intelligible to the Greek-speaking Egyptians. They often substituted a colloquial word for a literary term instead of making a direct translation, and the actual meaning of the substituted word can only now be known since the Egyptian sources have been so strangely opened to us.

When we come to the New Testament we find that its quotations from the Septuagint "stand out merely by the sound." "The Hellenistic Jews spoke Greek, prayed in Greek, sang psalms in Greek, wrote in Greek, and produced Greek literature; further, their best minds thought in Greek." Purely verbal comparison of terms is always dangerous; for religious terms especially are always altering and getting a richer or a poorer content with each generation. Therefore, an exact quotation may express a different meaning at different eras, as shown, for example, by the word "spirit" as used by Paul, Augustine, and Luther. So "angels," "God," "faith," "flesh," "hell," "judgment," "sacrifice" "righteousness," "love," etc., might not change in form, but might change considerably in current usage and meaning between the era when the Septuagint was written and that of the Christian fathers.

For the first time contemporary documents, written in the language of the early Christian authors and at the same era, are in our hands; and just as we must set the printed Septuagint side by side with the Ptolemaic papyri in order to get the exact meanings of the words used, so we must read the New Testament in the light of the contemporaneous inscriptions and other documents. Deissmann also pointed out that as the

papyri had given a new linguistic meaning to the New
Testament Greek, so the inscriptions in Asia Minor,
Syria, and Egypt had thrown new light on the times,
while both papyri and inscriptions had given a new view
of the theology of the early Christian centuries and of
the spirit of the primitive Church and its thought of the
Bible. The conclusion was that a practical exegesis
of the New Testament was necessary, since the New
Testament writings were not theological treatises but
were mostly composed in the non-technical and rather
careless language of the street and the home. He also
called attention to the curious fact that many of the
titles ascribed to Jesus, such as Saviour (σωτήρ) and
Son of God (υἱὸς Θεοῦ) were to be found on votive
inscriptions dedicated to heathen gods or to the emperors. Indeed, it was evident that St. Paul had
selected his honorable adjectives describing Jesus with
special reference to the titles of deity given in that
first century to the Roman emperors, forcing the de-
cisive issue that it was not the imperial Caesar but the
imperial Christ who was to receive honor as God.

Deissmann catalogued sixty-seven words from
the New Testament and Septuagint upon which
the papyri threw new light. The word brother
(ἀδελφός) ascribed to a member of the Christian community was exactly the term used for the members of
the Serapeum of Memphis and other religious associations of the first century. The term "writing"
(γραφή) used for the Old Testament was the common
legal term for a royal decree which could not be altered.
The word "propitiation" could not be used for a person
or propitiatory sacrifice, but in the sense of "propitiatory gift"; thus Christ is set forth in view of the cos-

mos as the "votive gift of the divine love for the salvation of men." The strange word (λογία) used in 1 Cor. 16: 1, 2 was now found for the first time outside of the Bible in connection with the "collection" or "tax" which the labor guilds or the government had a right to make. The word "little" or "less" ὁ μικρός (Mark 15: 40) refers in the papyri invariably to age, not stature, so that the question of Jesus means "Can one add anything to the length of his life?"

So the title "friend" (φίλος), given by Jesus to the disciples and found so often in the Bible, was a title of honor given at the court of the Ptolemies to the highest royal officials—a title correctly translated "prince" by the Septuagint (Esther 2: 18).

Many of the terms used by St. Paul describing the atonement were found to be legal terms used in multitudes of the papyri; so the particles and prepositions upon which theologians had relied chiefly in making many of their minute distinctions, were not used in this critical sense in the papyri. Several very striking new interpretations of well-known Bible phrases were made possible by this study of the papyri. For example, the phrase "in the name" of Christ (εἰς τὸ ὄνομα) received unexpected illumination from the many inscriptions in which slaves are mentioned as being bought by the temple "into the name" of a certain deity, meaning that the slave mentioned now belongs to God; so that baptism "into the name" or belief "into the name" meant, according to an ancient and well-known sacred formula, that he was thus officially marked as belonging to God.

Altho Deissmann's revolutionary view, that the New Testament was written in the common vernacular of the first century as contrasted with the literary language, was at once opposed by the greatest Greek authority, Friedrich Blass (*Grammatik des neutestamentlichen Griechisch,* 1896), yet it immediately gained respect, and after the publication of his *Neue Bibelstudien* (1897) it was almost universally received with favor, and even Blass soon abandoned his opposition. In his new book Deissmann gave multitudes of instances from the papyri to prove that a consistent New Testament orthography ought not to be demanded since variations in spelling were as common in the papyri as in the New Testament. He showed more fully also that the so-called "Hebraisms" of the Bible could, in almost every instance, be paralleled in the secular non-Jewish papyri, *e.g.,* "name" (ὄνομα) occurring with the meaning of "person"; "Lord's Day" finding its exact parallel in "Emperor's Day"; "place of prayer" (προσευχή) being used for heathen assemblies, etc., etc. Those who had tried to correct the New Testament text in order to make each passage conform with every other, supposing that the text had been mutilated in transmission, were shown to have made their argument on a false basis. Even ἐάν was used for ἄν in the papyri as in the New Testament, and εἰς and ἐν were constantly interchangeable. "Presbyter" was an official title of pagan priests in Egypt, and so also was the term "prophet." To be "sealed" (σφραγίζω) (Rom. 15:28), meant in the papyri to be imperially protected and retained for the imperial use.

Seals were set on sacks of grain to guarantee the correctness of the contents and there was a mark (χάραγμα), containing the Emperor's name and the year of his reign, which was necessary upon documents relating to buying and selling, and this mark was technically known as the "seal" (comp. Rev. 13: 16, 17; 14: 9, 11; 19: 20, etc.). It was the credential of the royal document making it legal. If the "beast" (Rev. 13) refers to the Roman emperor, as most scholars acknowledge, then we can now in these ancient documents look at the very technical sign referred to by St. John, as in his vision he sees the imperial stamp imprest on the forehead or hand. This also gives to the "number" of the beast a new and vivid meaning. It would not have been unusual for an apostle thus to use a local technical symbol, for the papyri prove that many of the well-known phrases of Scripture are quotations of popular formulæ; indeed, St. Paul (Gal. 3: 10) makes an intentional change in a quotation from Deut. 27: 26, in order to adapt it to a well-known legal phrase, and this was not an unusual custom.

Many previously rare words having doubtful meanings were clearly explained; e.g., the word translated "spiritual" milk (1 Pet. 2: 2) was found in the papyri with the meaning "unadulterated," and the word translated "the proving" or "proof" of your faith (James 1: 3; 1 Pet. 1: 7) was seen to have the meaning "proved," "standard," "genuine"; so that James 1: 3 means that true "proved" faith worketh patience, and 1 Pet. 1: 7 should read "what is genuine in your faith may be found more precious than gold"—proved genuine by fire, unto praise and glory and honor at the revelation of Jesus Christ.

Such are a few of the many strange and beautiful suggestions illuminating the meaning of the Bible phrases which Dr. Deissmann discovered from the common contemporaneous usage of these words at the time when the New Testament was being written. So, carrying this comparison further, we find that Paul's famous companion Bar-nabas had a name originally meaning "Son of Nebo," so that the name was changed in its ending probably to remove its pagan appearance, just as Nebo was changed to Nego (Dan. 2:49); so Manaen (Acts 13:1) is now seen not to have been necessarily the "foster brother" of "Herod," but perhaps rather "companion" or playmate, *i.e.*, intimate friend.[11]   When Paul says he bears branded on his body the "stigmata" of the Lord Jesus (Gal. 6:17), he refers to a common practise of branding the servants of a temple with the sacred sign which put them under the god's protection; and when he speaks of the "large characters" in which he writes to the church which he had so roundly criticized (Gal. 6:11), this may be "amiable irony" or perhaps may be a distinct act of respect, since in writing to distinguished persons it is now seen that the chirography was expected to be larger than in ordinary writing.[12]

This large synopsis of these two books of Dr. Deissmann's has been given because of their epoch-making importance. It was a stroke of genius rarely surpassed when this young scholar reached this original conclusion so vastly important, bringing as it were a new autographic commentary upon the Bible out from the very generation in which the apostles lived, and by one noble effort interpreting results in such a way that

[11] Sir William Ramsay, however, objects to applying the secondary and official meaning of this term to Manaen, since "foster-brothers," in the ordinary sense, are often spoken of in the inscriptions.

[12] Dr. Deissmann in his *St. Paul*, 1912, p. 50, takes the position that he wrote in large script because he was awkward and clumsy with the pen, but I prefer the explanation given above, which, tho not affirmed, was suggested by Dr. Deissmann's remarks in his earlier work.

those who have followed him have done little more than supplement his results, notwithstanding the enormous increase in the material now at the disposal of Greek scholars.

4. Most Recent Discovery and Publication of New Material

Dr. Deissmann was limited in his Greek texts almost wholly to the volumes of the Oxyrhynchus papyri which we have already described. But, as we have seen, the publication of those initial volumes by Grenfell and Hunt hurried on the scholars of all lands to seek for new treasures out of the rubbish heaps and to search diligently the museums for manuscripts hitherto neglected. Good work began in Egypt under the auspices of all the great European nations, and soon five collections began to be published of newly found papyri; but none of the new workers could equal in success the original explorers who continued their work at Oxyrhynchus during 1903 and 1906-7. Just as the century opened (1899-1900) Grenfell and Hunt had made a most amazing "find" at *Umm el-Baragat,* the ancient Tebtunis, situated in the south of the Fayum. They had been digging here for papyri, but for many weeks could find nothing but crocodiles. Crocodiles are no good substitute for papyri. When Dr. Petrie a few years before had found a cemetery of sacred crocodiles near Hawara, there had been some curiosity and pleasure in such a novel discovery; but one such cemetery is surely enough, and the diggers at Tebtunis were thoroughly disgusted when day after day crocodiles and nothing but crocodiles appeared. Finally one workman was so overcome with stupid anger at his disappointment in finding a baby crocodile in a tomb which he had hoped might contain a princess robed in jewels, that he flung the mummy of this crocodile upon a rock and broke it to pieces—and then the discovery was made!

The crocodile was stuffed with papyri! It may be imagined how rapidly the value of these formerly despised creatures increased. There was a rush for the other bodies which had been thrown upon the rubbish pile and it was found that a very large proportion of these contained deposits of the most remarkable character. Some, to be sure, were stuffed with reeds or sticks and merely covered with layers of cloth arranged in the check pattern recently made so familiar in opening the sacred Ibis cemetery at Abydos; but others had rolls of papyrus stuffed in their mouths, and others still were wrapt in layer after layer of this most precious material. If they had been laid to rest clothed in garments more glorious than those of Solomon, these sacred animals could not have aroused more devout admiration on the day of their resurrection than they did when these young explorers found literary fragments of ancient classics, perfectly preserved, royal ordinances, petitions, land surveys, contracts and accounts, and private letters which had formed the strange shroud of these deities when they were reverently laid to rest 2,000 years ago.

It took immense labor to edit these papyri, and much material gathered by Grenfell and Hunt during the opening years of the century was not edited till long afterward; but these young Oxford scholars soon proved themselves as careful editors as they were brilliant excavators. In 1900 they published the

Amherst Papyri, to which we will often refer in the future, containing, as it does, many Biblical and some very rare apocryphal texts, perhaps the most important specimen of the latter being a large fragment of the Greek recension of the long lost *Testament of Hezekiah,* an early Christian work originating near the close of the first century and giving us most valuable insight into the worldliness and selfishness of many of the chief ecclesiastics at that time, as well as of the growing heresies in the Church, just as 2 Peter and 2 Timothy describe them. Two other non-Biblical texts in which Bible students have a direct interest, and which may be mentioned here, are seven papyrus leaves preserved from a sixth century "The Shepherd of Hermas," and an account of the correspondence between Christ and Abgar, king of Edessa. Down to 1859, the "Shepherd," influential as it was in early Christianity, had been known only through translations, but Tischendorf discovered about one-fourth of this work in connection with the Codex Sinaiticus, and in 1888 Professor Lambros found twelve leaves more. "The Shepherd of Hermas" was written in the second century and vividly shows the life and thought of the Christians in Rome at that obscure period (A.D. 110-140). It was the earliest Pilgrim's Progress, and had an enormous vogue. It shows the "Holy Church" under the similitude of a noble building in process of erection, and pictures the great tribulation near at hand as a devouring beast. It is a call to repentance and righteousness, and makes perfectly plain the duty of the Christian "shepherd" to preach his message faithfully. It emphasizes Christian experience as strongly as any Methodist exhorter, and declares in the name of the

Lord that the highest and most spiritual ideal of Christianity is practicable to one who "keeps the Lord in his heart." Holiness is the command of the holy God who could not command what man could not obey:

"Believe, therefore, in Him, and fearing Him have self-mastery. For the fear of the Lord dwelleth in the good desire."

"The Epistles to Abgar" were written about A.D. 200, and while they were plainly apocryphal, yet it caused deep satisfaction to get an ancient copy of this influential Syriac document. Eusebius gives this correspondence between Christ and Abgar (*Hist. Eccles.* 1 : 13), and as early as the fifth century the portrait of Christ is mentioned, which, according to the legend, our Lord presented to the king at his request. The latter was once supposed to be incredible, as no portraits were known coming from that era; but the discovery in the Fayum that oil paintings were very common, even in middle-class houses of the second century after Christ relieves the legend of positive absurdity; tho of course it in no degree establishes its truth. We must be content not to know how Jesus looked. His portrait almost certainly was never painted. The orthodox Jews of the first century had a religious objection to pictures; so its natural origin is as unlikely as its supposed supernatural origin is unbelievable. Yet what a mistake it was that no one of the artists of Pilate's court was willing to take a few minutes from his frivolous and paltry engagements to paint the face of the youthful claimant to David's throne and thus seize his one chance to make his name immortal.[12a]

In 1903 Grenfell and Hunt published another

[12a] For ancient portraits see *Revue Archéologique*, V. Ser., Tom. I., 1.

volume of Oxyrhynchus texts, and in 1906 *The Hibeh Papyri,* which they had obtained in 1902 from the Ptolemaic Necropolis at *el Hibeh* or bought from the natives there. The latter were obtained from mummy cartonnages and were all of the third century B.C. Among the new classical fragments was a gnomic poem by Epicharmus (b. 540 B.C.), in which he gives a collection of epigrammatic maxims to use on any occasion or in any assembly, humorously describing the rascal, gentleman, bully, drunkard, and politician; also scraps of Sophocles and Euripides, including the maxim: "Evil communications corrupt good manners" (Gk. "good character"), quoted by St. Paul (1 Cor. 15: 33), which was here shown probably to have come originally from Euripides instead of Menander; and a discourse on music by Hippeas, ridiculing a man who pretended to be a musical critic tho he had no musical ear or voice and tho his musical skill consisted only in "doing everything worse than any one else!"

Here was also a work discussing the atomic theory of Democritus, and a book of practical philosophy which sagely declared that "some men are frugal because they dislike to spend more than to save." Here also were packets of legal documents and royal ordinances and—infinitely more important than either—a fine edition of Homer's *Iliad* containing a list of various and new readings. Perhaps most interesting, if not most important, was a bundle of ancient letters which had been cast into the waste-basket and thus preserved. In this private and semi-official correspondence we find references to "the horse doctor's tax," a strike on the part of workmen employed in a stone quarry who were therefore to be arrested, and many references to the

government monopoly on oil, the weaving industry, etc.
Because of a monopoly on food products it appears that
the price of grain had been recently considerably
raised. It was proved quite clearly by these discoveries
that the postal registration of that period was very
thoroughly worked out since "the day book in the
registered letter department of a modern post office
can hardly be more methodical and precise."

But meanwhile the British Museum had been ac-
cumulating vast quantities of Greek papyri. The earlier
volumes published by the Museum have already been
mentioned; but in 1898, 1907, and 1910, other volumes
of much greater intrinsic value, tho not perhaps containing so much novel material, were published. Many of
these texts will be used later in this work, but we may
now mention a few curious things brought to light
here. Does it not, for example, throw light on the
early Christian era to find Eulogius writing to the
Roman prefect, Abinnæus, asking him to use his influence in Rome to procure him the position of tax
collector? and to find a servant in Alexandria complaining to his master, Athenodorus, that he has been left
without either work or food for two days? The latter
note was written in such haste that it was folded before the ink was dry. It is interesting to notice that
these collections contain several petitions in which the
name of the reigning Emperor is misspelled. It gives
one a strange sensation to see on the back of one of
these petitions the red official stamp of the government
officer who first received it. In another official paper
the temple at Heraclea leases a mill at a voluntary rent
for five years, after which period the rent is to be
120 drachmae annually, a certain amount of produce

being added. The method of signature shows that these heathen priests were quite illiterate, tho any broad inferences from this fact must be drawn with caution, since in a number of the Christian documents here- after to be mentioned, and especially in those recently discovered at Syene, the Christian officials show an equal illiteracy.

The extraordinary value of the texts found in the volume published by the British Museum in 1898 may be seen from the fact that it contained over 200 docu- ments dating from the apostolic age (10 B.C.—A.D. 75). It is almost startling to notice that in the Christian texts coming from the early centuries abbreviations are just as common as in secular writings, and especially for such names as God, Christ, Church, salvation, and other sacred names which were held in reverence. In the volume referred to we dare mention among the more curious things only a fragment of a medical treatise which seems to relate especially to the opera- tions of dentistry, and a few of the financial papers.

It is enough almost to take away one's breath to read the specifications connected with the contracts of the first and the second century made through the bank of Didymus which was located on the street *Phremei,* which was evidently the Wall Street of Arsinoë at this era. One per cent. a month for quick loans was not at all unusual, some notes even running at 18 per cent. and 22 per cent. per annum, and even at higher rates of interest. Many papyri mention, in very modern phraseology, burglars, kidnappers, and thieves. One receipt is for fourteen drachmae which Thaeses paid as "earnest money" for a part of a house. This was in the year A.D. 166, and as the purchaser bought only one forty-second part of the house it seems at first sight as if flats were no new thing under the sun; but, as we will see later, this would be an incorrect inference. Many events are recorded at special dates running from Nov. 20, A.D. 11, to Mar. 22, A.D. 90; especially interesting to Bible students are the bank registrations and other accounts dated A.D. 17 and 23, during the lifetime of our Lord; the sale of an ass's colt A.D. 52; and a death report in the twelfth year of Nero, September, A.D. 66. Was St. Paul alive when the latter was written?

One of the most important documents published in this volume established for the first time the regularity of the Roman census which was connected with the poll tax during a fourteen-year period, the men being liable to this poll tax from the age of 14 to 60, and women from 12 to 60. The earliest census of which any direct evidence had previously been found dated from the eighth year of Nero, A.D. 61; but by the proof found in this document of the fourteen-year period the census was carried back to 9-6 B.C., the birth year of our Lord, thus explaining the previous puzzle concerning the enrolment of Quirinius. Previous to this it had been thought necessary by scholars to affirm either that this ruler had been several times governor of the province of Syria, or else to admit an inaccuracy in St. Luke's account (Luke 2:2); but these new census reports suggested a better interpretation of the above text in which the earlier or "first" enrolment is perhaps referred to rather than the first governorship of Quirinius. Sir W. M. Ramsay [12a] was the first to see the importance of this new document; but since then a

[12a] *Was Christ born at Bethlehem,* 1898.

large number of these tax enrolments have been found, the earliest yet discovered being in A.D. 20. If, as now seems fairly certain, Augustus began this system of a periodic census once in every fourteen years, and if this is what Luke refers to, we are able for the first time to reconcile all previous "contradictions" concerning the date of our Lord's birth—which must now be placed somewhere between 9 B.C. and 6 B.C. The exact year can not be named, as such general enrolments would necessarily be prolonged, especially in the outskirts of the empire. In order that the reader may see the exact nature of the edict mentioned in connection with the journey of Joseph and Mary to Bethlehem, we append in full one of these documents:

"Gaius Vibius Maximus, prefect of Egypt, saith: The enrolment by household being at hand, it is necessary to notify all who for any cause soever are outside their homes to return to their domestic hearths, that they may also accomplish the customary dispensation of enrolment and continue steadfastly in the husbandry that belongeth to them" (A. Deissmann, *Light from the Ancient East,* pp. 268-269).

The next two volumes of British Museum papyri (1907, 1910) furnish less material concerning the times in which Bible students are most interested; yet there is one letter addrest to Demetrius (A.D. 113), and another in faint ink dated probably in the very year in which Jesus, as a boy, went up to the Temple; a tax receipt (A.D. 11); a most novel diploma of membership in a famous athletic club; a rhetorical composition dealing with friendship; a curious Egyptian romance in demotic written on the back of an official document dealing with the land revenue; a receipt from a livery stable keeper; a deed of divorce after less than a year of marriage; a number of comic poems and various legal documents concerning the guild of ironworkers which supplied iron for the public service, signed by the president, Aurelius Severus; others from the guild of bakers, the guild of masons, and from Aurelius Irenæus, president of the guild of carpenters, etc. There are also certain orders for wheat guaranteed to be delivered A.D. 65-66, and a letter considerably earlier than this from Menon to Hermocrates, complaining about certain actions of a Jew named Daniel.

The Aphrodite papyri, published by the British Museum in 1910, consist of several hundreds of documents, all coming from the same village and all written within twenty years of one another. Altho these are considerably later than the period in which we are specially interested, they are of great value since they give a vivid picture of the conditions in Egypt immediately after the Moslem conquest (A.D. 698-722). It is here strikingly illustrated that altho the Moslems were exempt from taxation and the Christians heavily taxed and otherwise handicapped, yet comparatively few Christians apostatized, and they even succeeded, because of their superior trustworthiness or cleverness, in retaining a large number of important posts under the government, some Christians being employed even in the governor's household. We refer to this as being a fair exemplification of what happened in the first century and as a good parallel to the statements— which some scholars have found it so difficult to believe—that some even among the first generation of Christians might have become members of Caesar's household.[13]   It is a thrilling indication of the firmness

[13] Phil. 4:22; compare especially papyri 1373 and 1447.

and loyalty of these conquered Christians to their divine Master that even the governor's private secretary would not use in his official correspondence any of the distinctive Mohammedan formulæ, and it also speaks well for his recognized efficiency that he was allowed to do this and keep his position. The office of secretary was laborious as well as honorable, since official documents were quite generally written in both Greek and Arabic.

One of the greatest libraries of papyri in England, just made available to scholars, is the John Ryland's Library in Manchester. There are at least 7,000 MSS. in this collection, the nucleus of which was obtained by Mrs. Rylands in 1892 from the late Earl Spencer, 6,000 additional rolls being purchased nine or ten years later from the Earl of Crawford. Mr. A. S. Hunt, of whom we have heard so much, purchased most of these papyri for Lord Crowford and Mrs. Rylands in 1892 and later. In 1911 Dr. Hunt began to edit the Greek papyri in this collection, the demotic and Coptic MSS. having been edited by other scholars earlier. In the first volume, which contained only literary texts, there were many papyri from the classical period, including a very abstruse and learned astronomical treatise dating from the third century after Christ, and a treatise on physiology dating from the first century B.C. The latter deals particularly with the nervous system of the human body, and it is satisfactory to note that the distinction between motor and sensory nerves is stated clearly and with almost scientific accuracy. A number of medical recipes for various ailments (third century) were also found, in which the medicine was put up in the form of lozenges or pastilles; there was also a recipe for tooth powder. It sounds very modern also to find in a political treatise of the first century B.C., an argument urging that the army be put in a state of preparedness, and that it be supported not by sporadic requisitions from the war office, but by regular levies.

Some of the lyrics brought to light in this publication are very curious; for example, in one second century poem we have the following lament of a maiden whose lover has been carried off to fight as a gladiator, whose release she has not been able to obtain by the heaviest bribe she could offer.

MAIDEN'S LAMENT

"You, it is you I call! Terrible things are happening to our boy,
They have persuaded him to fight alone with evil beasts.
O Zeus, may my voice reach thee and not be unheard!" [14]

One sumptuous papyrus contains a comedy of the second century, but it is difficult to get any good appreciation of the jokes involved if, indeed, it was necessary to have real wit in these ancient plays. Some of the "limericks" that have been preserved show no more humor or novelty than those made in modern times, as may be seen from the following lines, written in St. Jerome's day, to a newly wedded couple:

"Bridegroom, the sweet Graces and glory attend thee. . . .
Dear bride, great and abiding joy be thine!"

The classical texts in this volume are particularly valuable, especially one large vellum book written about A.D. 300, which contains a considerable part of Homer's Odyssey (books xi-xxiv). It is written in brown ink, easily decipherable, and gives a mixed text

---

[14] The word for beasts used here is not the same as in 1 Cor. 15:32.

which does not fall in line with any other manuscript extant. Its size may be indicated from the fact that it fills solidly over seventy folio pages in the printed publication.

Far more interesting, however, to ordinary people, than any of the classical texts are some curious school-boy note-books, or examination papers, coming from the third and later centuries. Demosthenes "On the Crown" seems to have been a favorite exercise for the boys to practise on at that time. In one exercise, which was probably a primary copy-book, the first line of this oration is copied over and over again. In another of these ancient school-boy papers the student has written at the end of his assignment:

"Good luck to the writer and to the reader."

Evidently, this little rascal was either on very good terms with his teacher or else felt reasonably certain, as it is rumored some modern high-school students do, that the work done would not be very thoroughly examined.

The chief value of this great collection is its religious texts. We will use these constantly in later chapters of this work, but we may mention, as a matter of exceptional interest, that among the Samaritan MSS. there is one very early vellum codex of the Pentateuch (copied A.D. 1211); among the Syriac texts there is a vellum codex of the gospels coming from the sixth century, this being probably the oldest complete Syriac copy of the four gospels in existence; there is also a copy of the Nicene Creed dating from the sixth century. This is the oldest known copy of this famous creed; but while it does not coincide exactly with any other version, it differs only slightly from these. At the end of this MS. the scribe has written his own confession of faith:

"This is my creed. With this language I shall approach without fear the terrible judgment seat of the Lord Christ in that dread day when he shall come again in his own glory to judge the quick and the dead and to reign with the saints for ever and ever, Amen."

From what may be a private book of devotion, dating from the fifth century, we take this passage:

"Suffer the little children to come unto me; of such is the kingdom of heaven. On thee do I wait all the day. Remember thy tender mercies O Lord. . . . Saviour keep me, O Lord, as the apple of thy eyes. . . . Create in me a clean heart, gracious God, and save me."

One of the most curious things in the whole collection is a little papyrus book of magic, coming from the fourth century, so small that it could have been easily carried in the pocket. Eight leaves of this book are preserved, with the string that held them in place yet unbroken. It is exactly the kind of book which the Christian Church always repudiated (Acts 19: 19), but which was very popular with the heathen and, doubtless, with the more superstitious among the Christians. It gives the prognostications to be derived from involuntary twitchings of various parts of the body, and is almost certainly a part of the celebrated work of Melampus, thus dating back to the first century.

"If the abdomen quiver, it denotes something good with adverse talk. If the right part of the hips quiver, the person will have grief for the time being, and afterward gladness on his own account or that of a friend. If both parts of the hips quiver, a person so affected will stand in the grip of a two-fold trouble. . . . If the groin of an unmarried person quiver it denotes marriage.

. . . If the left knee quiver it denotes changes and troubles from females. . . . If a woman's right leg quiver, it denotes loveliness; pray and sacrifice to Aphrodite! If a man's right shin quiver it denotes that he will be very wealthy; pray to Hermes. . . . If the left leg bone quiver, it denotes that he will go on a long and unexpected journey. . . . If the left calf quiver he will have pain over a woman or a friend; pray to Fortune. . . . If the great toe quiver, it signifies for a slave that he will become a master and be freed from all pain; if the fourth toe quiver, he will be lord of much wealth and many slaves, and a slave will be his heir," etc.

The second volume of this remarkable work appeared in 1915.[15] As these texts date from the Roman period or earlier, we shall use them constantly in the next section of this work, and we shall, therefore, only now mention an Astrological Dialog (third century), in which various parts of the body are connected with the sun, moon, and planets, and signs of the Zodiac—a fortune-teller's chart, which ought to be read in connection with that given above—and a letter of the second century which, tho containing no Christian phrase, sounds very Christianlike. The astrological piece reads in part:

"The Sun is the right eye, the moon the left; the tongue, smell, and hearing belong to Mercury; the viscera to Jupiter; the chest to Mars; the spleen to Venus; the kidneys to Saturn; the buttocks to Libra; the nails to Capricorn," etc.

The letter referred to was written by two women to their steward, and is very different from most letters on similar subjects.[15a]

[15] *Catalog of the Greek Papyri in the John Rylands Library,* Manchester, Vol. II; Ed. by J. de M. Johnson, M.A., Victor Martin, Docteur es Lettres, Genève, and Arthur S. Hunt, D. Litt., F.B.A., Prof. of Papyrology in University of Oxford.

[15a] Dr. Victor Martin writes me that internal evidence disproves my first impression that this was a Christian letter.

"Demarion and Irene to their dearest Syrus, very many greetings.

"We know that you are distressed about the deficiency of water; this has happened not to us only but to many and we know that nothing has occurred through any fault of yours. We now know your zeal and attentiveness to the work of the building and we hope that with God's help (σὺν Θεῷ) the field will be sown. . . . We pray for your health."

This volume should not be dismissed without mentioning the large group of petitions dating from Euhemeria, A.D. 28-48, and the addition to our knowledge concerning taxation in the first century which other texts, with the editorial comments, have given.

It will be remembered that the first publications which stimulated critical interest in these papyri were the earlier volumes of the Oxyrhynchus texts put out by Grenfell and Hunt. While all this other work, which we have just narrated, was being accomplished, these scholars kept sending out, from time to time, additional volumes from the ruins of this city, each volume rivaling the last in interest. Between 1908 and 1915 six large volumes appeared, upon which we shall now draw for certain illustrative material, too interesting to be omitted and yet not naturally falling into our future argument. In all of these volumes many classical fragments appear; the MSS. often are written with beautiful care, and accents, breathings, and marks of quantity and elision occur freely in some papyri, even as early as the second and third centuries of our era. Many of these productions, such as the first or second century Menander, were also punctuated rhetorically, a high dot representing a long pause and a low dot a short pause. In the dramas a change of speakers was sometimes marked by double dots. One of these texts, a commentary on Thucydides written soon after the beginning of the Christian era, actually contains critical textual notes and exegetical comments.

Some of these ancient literary works occasionally give to us very curious information, as, for example, when in some fragments recovered from a new play of Euripides we read how the women at one time, in their advocacy of "woman's rights," massacred all the men of a certain island and seized the government— and what happened afterward! This newly recovered work was written just a little before the "Frogs" of Aristophanes, which was doubtless intended to parody this play. So, in a little papyrus book of seven leaves, containing a story by Callimachus of a girl sleeping with her affianced suitor, we obtain some very good epigrams, such as "Verily, much knowledge is a grievous ill for one who controls not his tongue; how truly is he a child possest of a knife."

Numbers of legal documents give the formula and conditions of "adoption," which St. Paul knew so well and upon which he based some of his rabbinical arguments; and numbers of others have to do with the "making free" of slaves, which was one of the great apostle's favorite figures, illustrating the way in which freedom came to the Christian. The customary formula in such an emancipation read something like this:

"In .... year of our Emperor .... the most illustrious Cæsar, I ...., son (or daughter) of .... my mother, being of the city of ...., have set free my slave .... aged ...... years, of middle height, fair, having a long face and a scar on the right foot, his mother being ...., for .... drachmae of coined silver. I hereby agree voluntarily and of my own free will and irrevocably to the freedom of said ...... under sanction of Zeus, Earth, and Sun (the deed being drawn up in the street) and said ...... can henceforth have and hold himself to be a free man since I have here freed him unto this liberty wherewith I have made him free." (Compare Gal. 5: 1.) [16]

Two articles of apprenticeship also ought to throw a vivid light upon the era in which ·Christianity, the "religion of the Carpenter," made its successful entrance into the thought of artizans throughout the world.

APPRENTICESHIP TO A WEAVER (A.D. 183)

"Ischrion, son of Heradion and ...... of Oxyrhynchus and Heraclas son of Sarapio, also called Leon ...... agree with each other as follows. ...... Thonis, a minor, to be taught the art of weaving for a period of five years. ...... his stipulated period of work being every day from sunrise to sunset. ...... For the first two years and seven months ...... Heraclas shall pay nothing for the boy's wages, but for the remaining five months of the third year he shall pay him twelve drachmae a month, for the fourth year, sixteen drachmae a month, and for the fifth year twenty-four drachmae."

Each year Heraclas agrees to furnish his apprentice with a new tunic, which shall the first year cost sixteen drachmae and the following years twenty drachmae, twenty-four drachmae, twenty-eight drachmae, and thirty-two drachmae, respectively. The contract continues:

"The boy shall have twenty holidays in the year on account of festivals without any deduction from his wages, after the payment of wages begins."

Arrangements are finally made that if through idleness or ill health he exceed the number of holidays, his

---

[16] Greek scholars will notice that I have here imitated in a free way the redundancy of language shown in the *Papyrus Edmondstone, Oxyrhynchus Papyri*, Vol. IV, p. 202.

guardian, or master, shall be responsible for his serving an equal number of extra days beyond his allotted apprenticeship, feeding him during this period. Each party is held to this agreement by a fine of one hundred drachmae to the party abiding by the contract, "and to the treasury an equal sum."

APPRENTICESHIP TO A SHORTHAND WRITER (A.D. 155)

"Panechotes ...... to Apollonius, writer of shorthand, greeting.

I have placed with you my slave Chaerammon to be taught the signs which your son Dionysius knows, for a period of two years ...... at the salary agreed upon between us, 120 silver drachmae, not including feast days; of which sum you have received the first instalment amounting to forty drachmae, and you will receive the second instalment (forty drachmae) when the boy has learned the whole system, and the third you will receive at the end of the period when the boy writes fluently in every respect and reads faultlessly."

Among the classical texts, new and old, brought to light in Vol. VIII of the Oxyrhynchus texts, we ought to mention especially the Meliambi of Cercidas the Cynic, an author who had previously been represented only by about a dozen lines gleaned from scattered citations. This large manuscript, dating from the second century B.C., discusses how the facts of life can be reconciled with the view that the so-called gods are at once just and all-powerful. If Zeus is Father, "why are some of us treated in such a step-fatherly fashion?"

He ridicules the deities who have neither hearing nor sight. If they really exist, he says, it ought to be easy for them to take the "swinish wealth" away from the "dirty usurer" and give it to the one "who takes his bite in season and shares his cup with a neighbor." He utterly repudiates the fictitious gods of the astrologers, preferring himself the three earthly divinities,

Healing, Giving, and Retribution. This poem shows very well the attitude of the better classes with reference to polytheism and their tendency to agnosticism at this era. The second poem is on "Love," and Cercidas, like Diogenes, decries marriage and describes love as the occupation of the idle.

There was also published in this volume an anonymous satyric drama, formerly unknown, and also a new commentary on the Iliad (first century B.C.), on the back of which were medical recipes of the first century after Christ, including local applications to induce sneezing (for good luck); an application to cure leprosy; potions for fever, liver complaint, dropsy, etc. To men of sedentary habits it may be of interest to know that anise, opium, and henbane are among the prescriptions to cure insomnia. A number of wills are given, one of these showing how a rich man (A.D. 237) was able, by a legal trick, to leave his inheritance of 200,000 sesterces to his heirs free from the customary income tax of 5 per cent. It looks as if capitalists have had shrewd lawyers to advise them in every age.

In Vol. IX (1912) there are various new classical texts, but especially a "Life of Euripides," by Satyrus (circa 150 B.C.), in which he gives some spicy gossip concerning the philosopher's relation with women, saying that at one time the women joined together and came in a body to mob him. He, however, believes that Euripides has more of the flavor of life in his poetry than all other writers, as is proved by this recipe for poetry:

"Take some Sophocles and a little Æschylus but put in a whole Euripides."

In Vol. X (1914) are published some new texts of Sappho elsewhere given, some fragments of unknown comedies, a work of Alcæus (second century), urging men to forget their troubles in the wine cup; a critical literary work (second century), in which an outline is given of each play of Menander with an appraisement of its value; and, finally, a "Chrestomathy" (second century), in which a historic catalog of the great men of ancient times is made, including sculptors, painters, grammarians, soldiers, and inventors.

We have given this extended outline of these latest Oxyrhynchus "finds" because they were the richest of all; yet many treasures have been reported by these and other explorers which well deserve mention, e.g., the "Pæans of Pindar" (first or second century); a Greek history "worthy to be compared to that of Herodotus"; four comedies (1,300 lines) of Menander; the Idyls of Theocritus (who was the originator of the idyl), seven centuries older than any other copy; an illustrated botanical work, probably by Dioscorides; a treatise on ethics by the Stoic Hierocles; a grammatical work containing among other valuable things a list of words with their shorthand equivalents; various so-called "erotic" fragments, a farce and mime of the early Roman period "which look like survivals of a local music hall"; a fragment of a book of fables by Babrino—who is now proved by this to have lived in the second or first century, not the third; a romance by Achilles Tatius, who is thus proved to have lived about A.D. 300, instead of in the fifth or sixth century, as previously argued by the critics; and a splendid papyrus roll over twelve feet long, containing a large part of Plato's "Symposium."

Perhaps the only one of these works which would greatly interest the general reader is the new poem by Pindar, only small fragments of which had ever been seen before. As translated by the editor, one verse of this reads:

"Ere the pains of old age draw nigh let a man clothe his mind with cheerfulness and be content in due measure, seeing the power that is set in his house.

"Oh joy! Now the consummating year and the Hours, children of Themis, have come to the horse-loving city of Thebes bringing Apollo's garlanded feast;

"May he long crown the generations of the citizens with the flowers of sobriety and good governmen⸱ "

The most recently published volume of Oxyrhynchus texts (Vol. XI) reached American subscribers in 1916; but even a hasty examination shows that it almost equals the best of its predecessors in the novelty of its contents. It contains discoveries made chiefly in 1905-6. Among the classical texts reported is a large fragment of Thucydides (968 lines), and a romance from the third century relating the adventures of Glaucetes who, during a ride, sees the ghost of a youth who points out where he and a maiden lie buried after being foully murdered. Such stories were very popular among the middle classes of the early centuries, as were also stories of miraculous cures and escapes. A sailor's chant, in which he prays to the Rhodian winds for a calm voyage (third century), is probably the reproduction of a song so ancient that it may have been heard, just as we now have it, by Luke, when he and Paul sailed over these dangerous waters (Acts 21:1):

"I said to the seaward parts that the sea should not be smitten. Make the ocean obedient to seafarers! Suddenly a whole tempest arises. Shut off the winds and night. Grant that the waters be smooth!"

But the chief wealth of this volume consists of three remarkable religious texts, two of which are heathen and one Christian. The latter papyrus gives us "one of the most interesting documents concerning the early Egyptian Church that have been discovered." It is a calendar of church services at Oxyrhynchus. Altho this town had suffered a collapse, seemingly, at the end of the third and in the fourth centuries, it had begun to recover its lost activity in the fifth century, and by the sixth century it had become a "veritable stronghold of Christianity," as this document proves. This public placard of services, just recovered, gives the list of meetings to be held at various churches in the town on Sundays, and festivals during an almost continuous period of five months, beginning with October 21, A.D. 535.

These series of special services were in honor of the visit of the patriarch—either Timotheus, the patriarch of Alexandria, or Severus of Antioch, who was, as Dr. Crum has pointed out, the Monophysite patriarch *par excellence*. We know that the bishop of Oxyrhynchus the year previously was Abba Peter, so that he may have conducted these "stations," probably celebrating the eucharist in the churches named. Sixty-two services were held in twenty-six different churches, which proves how greatly these buildings had multiplied since the preceding century, when there were twelve churches in the town and, as the learned editor points out, at least one church must have continued in existence, even during the terrible persecution of Diocletian. Some of the churches bear names which are yet common in Egypt, such as "St. Mary," "St. Justus," "St. Menas," etc., while Michael, Gabriel, Jeremiah, and Zacharias also have churches named after them, and it seems exceedingly modern to read of the "Church of the Evangelist" (probably St. John), the "Church of the Baptist" and the South and the North Church—the last two evidently being named either from their relative location in the city, or from the name of the streets on which they were situated. One name not now common bears a pathetic reference to the sufferings of this Oxyrhynchus church during the early persecutions, the "Church of the Martyrs."

In an "Invocation to Isis," preserved from the second century, we get an original document showing us, for the first time, with certainty, the words of ritual or private worship used by an initiate of this faith. Altho written in the second century, it almost certainly was composed as early as the first (p. 191). As the Isis worship was popular in Rome, and even in the small Italian towns in the apostolic era, it is absolutely certain that the faith represented here was almost as well known to all Christian teachers as that of Mithra (the most popular religion of all), not only in Egypt but throughout the Roman world. Isis was the particular protectress of sailors and travelers, so that the apostles on all their voyages would hear her hymns sung or witness the adoration of her worshipers. She was the special friend of woman, offering to her a power equal to man's, was joint inventor of writing with Hermes, and was interested in music and all learning; but especially, in the popular mind, she was the goddess of immortality. Outside of Egypt and Italy, as the editor shows, she was worshiped in

Arabia, Asia Minor, Cyrene, Crete, Chalcedon, the
Ægean Islands, Cyprus, and Palestine, and even in
India and Persia. Her worshiper here gives her
"name" in each of these places, thus, perhaps, attempting to teach her universal nature and essential "one-
ness," notwithstanding her different names. Her titles
show rather a noble ideal and concept of deity:

"Many-shaped Aphrodite, gentle, affectionate, immortal, ruler,
saviour, almighty, holy, divine, . . . by whose command images
and animals of all the gods are worshiped . . . the lady of war
and rule, easily destroying tyrants by trusty counsels."

The lotus was her flower, probably because it was the
symbol of immortality,[17] and the cow was her animal.

On the back of this unique papyrus was written a
poem in praise of Imouthes-Asclepius, a deity whose
worship in the early Christian centuries connects
through Hermes with that of Isis. The writer recounts
that he had for a long time wished to translate the
ancient praises of the god but felt himself unworthy;
but having at a certain time been cured of an "ungodly
quartan ague" by seeing the god in a vision, he was
finally constrained to attempt to "recount his marvelous
manifestations, the greatness of his power, the gifts of
his benefits." So he begins his song of praise by
crying:

"Assemble hither, ye kindly and good men; avaunt, ye malignant and impious! Assemble all ye who by serving the god have
been cured of disease!"

And then, most unfortunately, the papyrus breaks off
and the song itself is lost.

[17] Yet see article "Lotus" in *Encyclopædia of Religion and Ethics.*

The thousands of papyri from which we have selected the above specimens of the non-literary products of the first and adjoining centuries of the Christian era are all written in the language of the New Testament, and each shows some turn of expression or peculiarity of grammar or vocabulary familiar to the student of New Testament Greek, or else throws some unexpected light upon the circumstances surrounding the early Christians. By selecting these concrete examples of the ancient literature from the overwhelming mass of material examined, the author has sought to give the reader a true and clear vision of the new data upon which scholars are now building and to make it possible for him to follow, with independent judgment, the modern conclusions from such data. There has been no attempt to mention everything that has been found, but only to disentangle from the disorganized mass of ancient documents certain typical and certain strange forms, together with some new illustrative material, that ought to be useful to Bible students.

It must not be imagined that the above collections of papyri used by the author exhaust the material available. We have confined ourselves almost entirely to discoveries made by English explorers; but, while these have indeed carried off the chief honors in this field, a number of great Continental scholars, like Wilcken and Jouquet, have dug for papyri in Egypt; and it was Rubensohn, in 1908, who brought to light at Abusir the only considerable body of Alexandrian papyri which has ever been found. The learned excavators of the Societa Italiana have also gleaned at Oxyrhynchus, since 1906, with surprizing success.

Since the beginning of the century Berlin, Vienna,

Florence and Paris, either by excavation or purchase, have gathered thousands of papyri and published them in many volumes, which contain some rich fruits of research; including many ancient Bible texts, especially a third century Genesis; some new orations of Hypereides; a lyric by Timotheus of Miletus (fourth century) ; and a commentary on the Theætetus, the oldest extant literary papyrus in Greek.

Smaller but valuable collections, especially of non-literary papyri, have been made by the cities and learned societies of Europe, and by American colleges, while the celebrated Tebtunis papyri, described above, are owned by the University of California, and the great Amherst collection was brought to America by the late Mr. J. Pierpont Morgan.[17a]

5. A General View of the District Where Most of the Papyri Were Found

(1) THE FAYUM

The Fayum is a sunken oasis, crossed by several ridges, situated in the Libyan desert, west of the Nile, beginning about forty miles S.S.W. of Cairo and extending southward some thirty miles. The district covered from four hundred to nine hundred square miles at different eras. In ancient time this depression was largely occupied by the famous Lake Moeris, the two chief towns on the lake being Socnopaei Nesus on

[17a] Recent excavations at Theadelphia, Karara, and El-Hibeh have brought to light few papyri (*Revue archéologique,* 1915, pp. 181-188; *Klio,* 1914, p. 121). But the discoveries at Kôm Ishgau have yielded rich spoil (*Journal of Egyptian Archæology,* 1916, pp. 288-293).

the extreme northwest, and Crocodilopolis (Arsinoë), the capital city, which was more centrally located. Oxyrhynchus, which is ordinarily spoken of as a Fayum town, was really some little distance south of the oasis, but was doubtless in very close touch with it, as it was built on the Bahr Yusuf which supplied the Fayum with water. An enormous mass of papyri has come to us from these three cities and the adjoining villages, Oxyrhynchus being the most important site, not only because of its location—lying within nine or ten miles of the Nile, and so close enough to enjoy some of the privileges of the Nile traffic as well as that of the oasis—but also because it was an important Christian center, and from the dust heaps of its ruins most of the Christian papyri of the early centuries have come.

From the third century before to the third century after Christ the entire Fayum, as we have seen, was prosperous; but it then lost its prosperity "as nowhere else in Egypt," and the desert took possession of this former fertile district. Beginning with the fourth century the monks flocked in crowds into this desert district and soon well-fortified monasteries were found in many places to which, in time of danger, the people were accustomed to flee. The stretch of desert sand from six to fifteen miles in width, which separated the Fayum from the Nile valley, must have rendered it a comparatively hidden and secluded retreat. The revolt of the native Egyptians against the Romans, A.D. 175, undoubtedly affected the Fayum population, as this marked the beginning of a rapid agricultural decline throughout Egypt. It must also have been seriously affected by the persecutions of the Christians under Severus (A.D. 202), Decius (A.D. 250), and by the

famine, panic, and persecution during the reign of Diocletian (A.D. 301-303). It is significant that the Coptic
era of the martyrs dates from Diocletian's accession.
The above facts and dates ought to be borne in mind
as one studies the Fayum papyri in their bearing upon
early Christianity.

The architecture of the cities of the Fayum in the
Roman period was not simply inferior to that of Italy,
but was in a marked degree inferior to North African
towns such as Timgad, and to many towns of the
Roman era in Palestine (*cf.* the author's *Recent Explorations in Palestine,* pp. 77, 127). Of the many
Fayum towns which have been dug up, very few covered more than eight or ten acres, the temples were generally quite small and built of brick or native limestone—
very little resembling the elegant temples of the Delta,
—the ordinary houses were constructed of unbaked
brick one or two stories high, the roofs were made of
reeds plastered with mud laid on palm logs, the furniture was a negligible quantity, and even cellars were
uncommon (*Fayûm Towns,* pp. 10-16).

The better class of residents was of Greek extrac-
tion, and the Greek influence was always strong
because the best land of the province had been
given by the Emperor to his veteran Macedonian soldiers. Doubtless, the native Egyptians constituted the
mass of the population, however, and many Jews were
to be found; the Greeks and natives intermarried
freely and therefore the Fayum always remained
Egyptian in its customs and tone of thought as contrasted with the Greek spirit of the Delta.

In the third century the Fayum suffered greater
encroachment from the desert than any other nome in

Egypt. Socnopaei Nesus was the first town to be deserted. At this point no papyri have been found later than the third century, while many other towns were practically abandoned in the fourth century, and even Karanis and Tebtunis, on the edge of the cultivated district, shrank to much smaller size (*Fayûm Towns,* pp. 10-16). Oxyrhynchus continued to thrive, but the papyri suggests that it, too, was seriously affected by the collapse in trade.

The contrast between the elegance of Alexandrian life and that of the Fayum was quite noticeable. It is true that at least one second century papyrus speaks of a "four-story house" just built in Hermopolis, and there are a few other evidences of occasional wealth; but the difference is, nevertheless, very marked in every era between this country district and the splendid and luxurious life of the Delta. The collection of Alexandrian laws contained in the papyri of Dikaiomata, at Halle, and in others in Berlin, show vividly, as Wessely has pointed out, the ordinary life of Alexandria—the Alexandrian waitress who insists on having a regular "day off" mentioned in her contract, the Alexandrian widow who goes about destroying all remembrances of her recently deceased husband, and the Alexandrian literary man who, in the vast libraries there, was drawing a good salary from the treasury of the government. Two centuries before Christ, one of these scholars had received a salary of as much as 270 drachmae, but it was left for the emperors of the second century of our era to elevate a mere flattering rimester to high office in the library and university at the enormous salary of 200,000 sestertii, and to advance a favorite soldier, who had no claim to learning, to an

Temple of Artemis (Diana), Sardis

Temple at Pergamum

Wall-painting on Tomb, Marissa,
Palestine (2d Century B.C.)

Capitol and Propylaeum at Timgad,
North Africa

Ancient Ruins at Cæsarea,
Palestine

Columbarium from Beit Jibrin,
Palestine

SOME RESULTS OF EXCAVATION AT SARDIS, ETC.

EQUESTRIAN STATUE OF NERO

A POMPEIAN NOBLE

THE EMPEROR TIBERIUS AND A WOMAN

A STATUE OF A CHILD

A FAMOUS POMPEIAN BANKER
OF THE APOSTOLIC AGE

WORKS OF ART FROM THE FIRST CENTURY OF THE CHRISTIAN ERA

equally influential position in this famous Academy of Science.[18]

The best cities of the Fayum seem like pitiable villages when compared with the capital of the Delta, and the common life of the Fayum and of the towns bordering it on the Nile appears at best simple and frugal. There were no great manufacturies of glass and paper in the Fayum as in the Delta, almost its sole manufacture being the weaving of linen cloth, which was carried on in the simplest way in almost all the villages. Even its coinage was imported, excepting, perhaps, certain small leaden pieces which may possibly have been used as money. In the great hoard of coins from the Constantine era found in 1905, it is suggestive to note that 1,592 were minted at Alexandria, 1,611 at Antioch, 845 at Cyzicus, 698 at Constantinople, and 285 at Rome.[18a] This indicates how "neutral" was this little island in the desert, no controlling influences reaching it from any of these political and ecclesiastical centers. Alexandria always seemed a foreign town to native Egyptians, and, as a great scholar has recently pointed out, the terms "Alexandrian" and "Egyptian" were in some ways antithetical, altho this contrast must not be prest too far, since the *Gospel to the Egyptians* certainly shows the influence of the Alexandrian philosophy. Yet whatever influence may have come indirectly from the Delta to the Fayum and to

[18] For these and other details given below I am indebted to Wessely, *Aus der Welt der Papyri*, p. 64*ff.*; for much other illustrative material see my article "Alexandria" in *The International Standard Bible Encyclopædia*. Dr. Petrie writes me that 270 drachmae must be regarded as a small salary even for teachers, being only equivalent to about $75 in our money, representing, when compared with current prices, a salary equal to about $750 now.

[18a] *Fayûm Towns*, p. 16; *American Journal of Archæology*, October, 1915, p. 69.

upper Egypt, it certainly was not controlling. The religious papyri of this region show very little kinship with the writings of Clement of Alexandria and the other great Delta theologians; even the symbols on the Christian graves, as we shall see later, are very different. The native Christians of the Fayum were ascetic, contemplative, and mystical in spirit, and had comparatively little sympathy with the philosophic, disputatious, and ambitious churches in Alexandria. The Egyptian theological controversies which compelled the Council of Nicæa, A.D. 325, found their leaders and chief battle-ground in the Delta.[18b]

In both its literary output and in its artistic products the Fayum also differed widely from the Delta. The pottery and terra-cotta products, when compared with those of Alexandria, show a very "low level of achievement." [19] It is perfectly clear that wealth and luxury must have been a novelty in this district. While, doubtless, there were some rich men in the Fayum who owned or at least controlled most of the land and its products, yet, from the very numerous business and private documents, it is evident that the trade carried on was just such as a poor country district would demand, and there was ordinarily no such distinction between classes as was found farther north. This comparative democracy of spirit is shown from the fact that even the ordinary *fellaheen* and slaves can sometimes make their voices heard in protest against oppression. From a certain Hermopolis, for example, comes a series of documents (third century B.C.) in which some quarrymen complain of their boss (Σεκά-

---

[18b] See W. M. Flinders Petrie, *Personal Religion in Egypt,* p. 61.

[19] See Milne in Petrie's *History of Egypt,* Vol. V, pp. 162*ff.*

ταρχος), concerning Apollonius, saying that they are much overworked by him, and in response to this petition these men are given wedges to lighten their labor. Demetrius, too, who distributed bread to these slaves, was badly assaulted by them, and altho he complained concerning this, we find him in prison a month or two later, a fact suggesting that the slaves may have convinced the head manager that he deserved all that they had given him, and more. Another complaint comes from the workmen in the copper mines, setting forth that they have been kept at work for ten months steadily without rest, and from certain cavalry soldiers who petition the *strategus,* asking that they be given as much pay as similar troops elsewhere. Not only the transactions carried on through the bank of Anubion in Antinöopolis (third century A.D.), but also the private accounts of Heronimus, who was chief steward of private properties located in Theadelphia, giving the daily record of work done, money received, and the payments to workmen in cash, food, and wine—all impress us with the conviction that these ancient southern towns were very much like the small Egyptian villages to-day, in the same part of Egypt. One pathetic proof of the poverty of the district is shown by the pawn-broker's record, in which he gives the value of the hoes, baskets, shirts, etc., which he had received in pawn. At Hermopolis a mill, in the first century, could be leased for seven months at twelve and a half silver drachmae a month, and a house and court are given for security for a loan of 220 drachmæ. The poll tax here at this time was only twelve drachmæ, and the pig tax, of which we hear much, only about two drachmae. The most famous residence in this town, in the third century of our era, was that of the Moros brothers. We have a multitude of business contracts which belong to this family, from which we learn much of their family life. These were evidently the aristocrats of the city, tho Herminus Moros, who comes to view as early as September 12, A.D. 194, was originally a "boxer" who, for his prowess, was given at the above date honorary membership in the athletic club of the city. Some thirty years later (A.D. 226), two of the Moros boys make a declaration under oath in court that they have recently inherited from their uncle two-thirds of a house and court in Hermopolis. In December of this same year one of these brothers sells a house and court for 300 drachmae, the actual payment on the property being delayed, however, until January 12 of the next year— as we find from the banker's certificate, attached to the document; July 31, A.D. 227, one of these same brothers buys one-third of a house from the other, and August 11, A.D. 231, a sister buys this same property from him, probably in connection with a loan she had made him of six hundred drachmae some four years before. The prices of these houses show their inferiority. Abinnaeus, commander of the camp at Dionysias, on the southern edge of the Fayum, not far from Oxyrhynchus, perhaps occupied the most conspicuous place of any man well-known to us in this district during the fourth century of our era. Twenty letters connected with this military officer are now in Geneva and thirty-seven more in the British Museum, all of these coming from the period A.D. 341-351. We shall have something to say of these letters later, but merely call attention to them at this time to record the fact that they bear out our conclusion of the general poverty of the district and its particularly desolated condition at this era. One of these letters, for example, speaks in an emphatic way of the hyenas which had been devastating the crops, and of the nets which must be used to protect the growing grain from antelopes.[20]

Beginning, as we have said, with the early fourth century, the condition of the farmers and middle classes kept getting more and more pitiable, and the suffering population soon fled in multitudes to the religious houses on the edge of the desert. This section had never been celebrated for its good order and observance of law, but broils and injustice seem to become more marked after this date. Several records exist in which seemingly entire villages, including the priests, attack each other. As early as the second century a man accuses his mother of wrongfully appropriating the property left him by his father and even of assaulting him, tearing his garments, and offering him physical violence; but in the fourth century many such cases are recorded, or worse. Syrus reports to the police that his wife, tho born a free woman, has been carried off as a slave, together with her children, by certain parties who entered his house to commit this crime, beating him when he protested. Even in the most sacred duties due to the dead, men were proving themselves to be unmoved either by superstition or religion, for Melos is forced to complain that altho he has paid Serapion and Silvanus for removing his brother's dead body, instead of this they have only removed his effects. The civil courts were known to be flagrantly guilty of receiving bribes, but the military courts were worse, and it became so notorious that men

[20] See especially *Archiv für Papyrusforschung,* Wilcken, I, 57-65.

were getting unjust vengeance upon their enemies in this way that in A.D. 307 the Prefect of the Oxyrhynchus nome was forced to threaten confiscation of property in the case of any person appealing from the civil to the military tribunals.

More and more after the second century the Fayum became isolated from the outside world. It had never been on the trade route and now it lost its little place in the route of tourists. Tourists during the first two centuries of our era came in multitudes from all lands into the Delta, scratching their names on the Great Pyramid, gaping at the strange Apis ceremonies at Memphis, and making votive offerings at Naucratis— as Herodotus is just proved to have done.[21]

Doubtless quite often these tourists would visit the edge of the Fayum to see the Hawara Pyramid and Labyrinth, and possibly to visit the sacred crocodile at Arsinoë on their way to the more fashionable "show places" at Thebes and beyond; but few, even then, would go, as Germanicus did, to Lake Moeris, and fewer still would travel into the Fayum.

But toward the end of the second century, because of internal and external troubles, the general tourist travel, even in the Delta, stopt abruptly, and even such occasional visits to the Fayum must have ceased; while the towns of Upper Egypt, presumably including Oxyrhynchus, were rendered unsafe for peaceful travel for a considerable period thereafter because of raids of tribes dwelling farther up the Nile.[22]

These facts should be borne in mind in estimating the value of our later conclusions concerning the proven-

---

[21] *Journal of Hellenic Studies,* Vol. XXV, 116.
[22] *Cf.* J. G. Milne, *Journal of Egyptian Archæology,* April, 1916, pp. 76-79.

ance of the newly discovered New Testaments and other papyri touching the life of the early Christians.

(2) THE COMMON LIFE OF SOME EGYPTIAN TOWNS IN
THE FIRST CENTURY OF THE CHRISTIAN
ERA, AND LATER

Standing to-day among the ruined buildings of any one of these ancient Egyptian villages, an archeologist who possesses a spark of the historic imagination ought to be able, with the help of the many funereal and other inscriptions, to reconstruct a good portion of the history of the place.

Unfortunately, few students of the ancient past possess this rare gift; yet, confessing our limitations, we will attempt to give now, not an imaginary picture, but the real life history of one or two of the most conspicuous of these Egyptian towns during the first century of the Christian era.[23]

Life in Socnopaei Nesus in the Apostolic Era

Socnopaei Nesus is the name of the village with which we shall first concern ourselves. It is an island town situated in the northwestern corner of the Fayum, and represents probably the most populous city of that most fertile part of Egypt from the first to the third century.

This town, together with Karanis, Philadelphia, and several others that are well known, were on the northern border of Lake Moeris, while Alexandrou

---

[23] The chief authorities upon which we depend for our facts will be Dr. Carl Wessely—*Aus der Welt der Papyri* (1914) ; the *Catalog of the Greek Papyri in John Ryland's Library.* Vol. II. (1915) ; and scattered texts found among the *Greek Papyri in the British Museum,* Vol. II. (1898).

Nesus, Magaidus, and many more were on the southern border. Oxyrhynchus lay some miles farther south.

Socnopaei Nesus was a town dedicated to the crocodile-headed god, and boasted a temple so famous that branch temples were established in various cities, for example at Arsinoë. The chapel possest a holy of holies decked with gold, and the statues of the god were made of the richest metals. The sacrifice and incense, the sprinkling of the holy of holies with sacred water, and the ceremony of lighting the sanctuary lights were as elaborate as in Herod's temple in Jerusalem, and the prayers said were doubtless as carefully prepared. The life of the priests has been opened to us quite fully. They had no easy life. One class of priests had to master an entire division of literature in order to determine what was ceremonially pure and impure, while another priestly caste was expected to know fully the four books of Hermes. The administration of the temple was no small matter. One hundred and fifty-five annual feast days are mentioned in the festival calendar of the god, together with the minute specifications of requirements, financial and otherwise, for each occasion. The budget of the priests which has come down to us is of distinct interest. The prophet of the crocodile-headed god could draw an order upon the temple treasury for 344 drachmae and have it honored. The total expenditure for a year was over 11,000 drachmae besides 1,200 artabae of wheat, 2,000 measures of oil, and forty jugs of wine. Part of this expenditure was paid to the Roman government; for not only was the temple compelled to pay a certain annual tax because it was a place of worship, but government officers were constantly making an inventory of the votive offerings and taxing each small gift, even down to the silver-plated handles of the temple censers and the iron pans of the temple kitchen.

But no institution could pay taxes easier than the temple. As one has said, "If the god is a landowner, he should also pay taxes"—and the god was a land-owner. The temple of Edfu, as we know, possest nearly a square mile of fruitful land besides other revenues from manufactures of all sorts—linen, felt, etc. So at Socnopaei Nesus the temple had a brewery which must have been extensive, as the tax amounted to more than 200 drachmae; while its fishing industry must have been of considerable value, since the tax amounted one year to over 120 drachmae, and the right to pickle fish was taxed additionally. The priestly lands and houses were also taxed, and that these houses were the best in the city and situated in the finest loca-tion is perfectly evident from the court records. In one will a priestess gives to her daughter two "three-story houses with all their appurtenances"—one of these being bounded on the north by the house of Gallio and on the west by the Royal Highway.

The temple offerings were not wholly voluntary. The people were taxed according to their ability and sometimes the civil officers took part in collecting the temple dues. If it had not been for these dues the temple could not have carried on its work. Even as it was, the subordinate priests had a hard economic problem, and were compelled to farm or to train camels in order to make ends meet. Quarrels among the priests as well as dishonesty seem to have been com-mon. In one famous trial which took place A.D. 13, Nestäephis and Satabous accuse each other of stealing mortar out of the mill and brick belonging to the temple, and of manufacturing oil while evading the tax—Satabous even being accused of stealing the very lot on which he had built his house. It is difficult to tell the right and wrong of this legal contest; but we know that finally Satabous paid to the Roman official one-third of the value of his property in order to be left in possession, tho the evidence seemed to show that he had bought it from a higher priest or prophet and might not have been personally to blame.

There can be no doubt that in the first century the priesthood had fallen low in Egypt. There was probably no priest caste, for altho a son usually followed his father into the priesthood, yet any boy who could pass the physical and ceremonial examination and pay the initiation dues could become a priest.[23a]

The higher priestly offices were purchased from Rome very much as the Sadducees purchased the priestly offices in the Jewish temple. The Egyptians were so religious that the priesthood, tho generally quite ignorant, must have had a strong influence. In all the Fayum towns the chief streets were named after warriors or gods, tho Market Street and other familiar modern titles were common.

A magnificent sacred street nearly a quarter of a mile long was the peculiar pride, not only of the temple in Socnopaei Nesus, but of the whole country round about.

Every fourteen years a general house-to-house canvass was made in the interest of the government census. One of the census reports taken by Herakleides in this town shows 173 males living in his distric⁺

[23a] So Wessely; but Grenfell and Hunt are against this.

and the amount of their tax. Among these, four foreigners appear, three from Italy, and one from India.
There are in this district thirteen men over sixty years
old, who therefore are excused from the tax. But
very few are excused, and the investigation is rigid.
Not only are the manufacturers on this street, and the
private citizens taxed heavily, but a list of slaves and
freedmen is given, each being taxed according to the
social position of his master or mistress. It is noticeable that a difference in the tax rate is made in favor
of Fayum citizens as against those who come from
Rome or Alexandria.

It is interesting to find a Jewish quarter at Socnopaei Nesus in the first century of our era. It has long
been known that many Jews lived in the Delta in Egypt
and recently new traces of these have been found (*e.g.,*
Palestine Exploration Fund, *Quarterly Statement,* 1914,
p. 43); but it is now certain that as early as the third
century B.C., there was a Jewish colony in the Fayum
living in a town called Samaria. Even then the Jews
were bankers, tax-gatherers and police-officers, and were
enjoying the special prosperity which had come to them
in Egypt through Alexander's favor. The entire fourth
district in Alexandria was a Jewish quarter, and in
many of the Fayum towns they doubtless had houses
of prayer as at Athribis, and a special ghetto as at
Socnopaei Nesus. It need not surprize us, therefore, to
find that Herakleides, as the inspector of a ward (A.D.
72), devotes an entire section of his report to these
Jews of Socnopaei Nesus. The heading of his official
report—which was issued while "St. John the presbyter" was still alive—reads as follows:

"The Report of Herakleides, Inspector of The District of Apollonia Parembole, with Reference to Special Taxation and Census of the Jews."

He mentions the ages of men, women, and children, and gives their ancestry back to the third generation. In each house he gives the list of males of taxable age, together with the names of the children and women. Even in the case of children but one year of age, he gives the names of the mother, father, and grandfathers. Sample paragraphs from his report read:

"Tryphania, granddaughter of Kales, mother of Dosarion, 61 years of age, exempt from taxation."

"Dosarion, daughter of Jacob and granddaughter of Jacob, mother of Sambus, wife of Simon; 22 years of age, etc."

Each family had to pay a little over eight drachmae as a "home" tax, and added to this was the extra tax of 15 drachmae for the first registration. The excessive pedantry seen in these reports and the fact that the year of birth, age, and relationship had to be repeated with the same scrupulous minuteness each year, prove the severity of the government oversight.

From other neighboring places other equally remarkable reports concerning the Jewish population of the Apostolic Age have come to us. An ostrakon from Apollinopolis Magna has along side of such old-fashioned Hebrew names as Jacob and Simon certain Greek appellatives which seem to have been very popular among the Jews, such as Antipater, Demas, Jason, etc. Every one will at once recognize these as Bible names.

The most remarkable series of inscriptions which has appeared from this site [23b] consists of twenty ostraka concerning Jews who lived in the first century, six of whom

[23b] *Studien zur Palæographie und Papyruskunde von Dr. C. Wessely,* Leipzig, 1913.

were named Jesus, one Didymus and another Theophilus. It is indeed a startling thing to read these Biblical names upon inscriptions written during the apostolic age. Altho the subject matter may not be otherwise interesting, nevertheless every Christian must look with vital interest mingled with surprize at such records as these:

"Sambathion and Jesus ('Ιησοῦς) son of Papias, listed in the census taken in the twentieth year of the Lord (τοῦ κυρίου) Domitian .... drachmae."

"Census list of a block of houses belonging to .... of the Jews .... drachmae."

"Sambathion and Jesus, son of Papias, Jews .... year of our Lord Trajan .... drachmae." [23c]

But the population of Socnopaei Nesus did not consist chiefly of Jews, and we turn to the activities of these other contemporaries of the apostles with keen anticipation. Here are the certificate of sale of a house, November 20, A.D. 11, written in Greek and demotic, and a few years later the application by four fullers, who are descendants of the old Persian settlers, for the lease of a double laundry carried on at Socnopaei Nesus and Nilopolis by Satabous, 240 drachmae being paid for the current year. In A.D. 33 Tesenouphis, son of Demas, makes a loan of money, taking ample security, while at about the same time (A.D. 14-37), an old soldier of the third legion makes a repayment of a loan, the receipt for which has been faithfully preserved to us for nearly two thousand years. In A.D. 28, in the second year of "Tiberius Cæsar Sebastus, the god, son of the god," a divorce appears in which the decision of the court

[23c] The surprize at finding these pre-Christian "Jesus" records vanishes when we remember that the name Jesus is only Joshua in a Greek form and that Jesus b. Perahyah, who it is said learned magic in Egypt, at the end of the second century B.C., was one of the most celebrated Jews of his time.

is approved by both the parties to the separation, altho the wife receives, as part of the decree, a house "built with beams and doors and repeated in three stages," at the east end of the town on the street Pharaoh; the husband, Pa-anhuri, seeming to have been glad to obtain the decree even by paying thus liberally to get it. In this same year Herieus sells Hisarous two out of five parts of a two-storied house and court, and a little later Stotoatis sells Apunchis two of his five shares in a two-storied house and court, and two out of four shares of a fallen house, as well as one-twelfth share in the ownership of a mill. In the former transaction it is interesting to note that neither woman was able to write, so that their sons signed the document in their stead; while in both contracts there is a striking indication that apartment houses and the corporate ownership of buildings were not unknown in the apostolic era.

Many other documents prove that flats are not merely a modern iniquity.[23d] In the year A.D. 82, Tesenouphis sells to Panephimmis, son of Pame, two-fifteenths of a house and courtyard, and a month or two later this same Panephimmis buys from Papeis and Pasokis one-sixth (or one-tenth) of a house and yard. A little later (A.D. 71) Thasis sells to her son-in-law one-fourth part of a two-storied "priest's chamber and yard."

[23d] The use of modern terminology must not, however, blind the reader to the radical difference between oriental and western conditions. The "apartment houses" and "flats" were not buildings erected as investments, but were undoubtedly communal houses. It is still very common in Egypt among the better class natives to find the grandfather, father, and most of the married sons and grandsons living, with their families, in separate rooms of the same house. So the "branch laundries" must be visualized as merely a central wash house where the towels of the public baths from two nearby villages were washed.

The account book of one state granary has been preserved from the first century B.C., showing the amount
of seed corn loaned on account to small farmers; and
many documents of the first and second century B.C.
show the monopolies upon the sale of woolen goods by
the Crown, as well as upon bricks, eggs, and probably
natron and the public baths. These public baths must
have been an important institution, for in a contract
dated A.D. 42, a man receives 2,000 drachmae to furnish
firewood for one year for the baths connected with the
gymnasium. While the trade guilds were not as common in Roman Africa as in Italy, and while a general
organization by trades and occupations was to be
found in only a few cities of the East, as in Rome and
Pompeii or Philadelphia or Thyatira, yet signs of these
trade unions meet us in many papyri. The earliest
inscription relating to a trade guild was put out by an
association of foreign cooks [23e] in Sardinia. These
guilds of almost every trade and profession were probably to be found in every large town of the first century,
organized not so much for self-protection as for social
recreation and enjoyment and to insure to each member
a decent burial. They were not charitable societies nor
mutual benefit insurance associations, tho occasionally
a loan is mentioned in the papyri and mutual aid was
actually given on some occasions. The early Christians
made use of these funeral associations and trade
brotherhoods in order to organize their forces, and it
is for this reason, doubtless, that the Emperor Valerian
made such furious attacks upon these guilds (A.D. 275).[24]

[23e] *Corpus Inscriptionum Latinarum*, XI, 3078.

[24] See for further particulars concerning these "Unions," *Encyclopædia of Religion and Ethics*, VI., 219ff.

At Socnopaei Nesus, in the first century, we see the primitive working of this institution. In A.D. 14-37, e.g., the president and secretary of the guild of weavers, acting for the guild, became sureties for five weavers against whom a court proceeding is pending. The fullers must have had a large association, for we learn that the office of superintendent of this industry was farmed out in this town as the weaving business was farmed out in Archelais and the manufacture of bricks at Kerkethoëus, the retailing of oil at Heraclea, the goldsmith's industry at Euhemeria, and bird hunting in another district. The weavers, too, must have done a good business here, for in a badly written and ill-spelled receipt issued by the "receivers of public clothing" (A.D. 128), nineteen tunics and five cloaks are mentioned. These were, we discover, military cloaks bought for soldiers serving in India, and this was the tax levied on this town for the support of these local volunteers. That the weavers could contribute corporately to pay this tax is a new proof that this trade was here organized into a guild. This receipt reads as follows:

"We, Dionysius son of Socrates, and the associate collectors of public clothing for the Guards, have received from the weavers of the village of Socnopaei Nesus nineteen. . . . tunics . . . and for the needs of the soldiers serving in India five white cloaks. The thirteenth year of the Emperor Caesar Trajanus. . . . (in another hand) Received by Diogenes."

It is evident that taxes are no modern invention. In the days of Jesus everything and everybody was taxed. The custom house receipts from Socnopaei Nesus show that there was a heavy rate upon both exports and imports, while individual merchants and tradesmen of all kinds, as well as the boatmen who carried the god's images in ceremonial processions, had to pay heavily for the business. Taxes on land and farm stock, on goats and pigs of the temple, and especially on the temple pigeon cotes—in fact upon every item of wealth or industry—meet us in every pile of ancient documents excavated. The day book of one of the revenue officials at Oxyrhynchus has come to us, and many official reports from Socnopaei Nesus.

A very heavy force of collectors and government police must have been constantly maintained in every town. The chief of police had a rank (Στρατηγός) equal to the modern "general" or Bey, and his duties and temptations to "graft" were quite as numerous as now, as we know from a "politician's drawer" preserved from the Arsinoïte nome and from innumerable references in many documents. We know, for example (*Greek Papyri in the British Museum,* II: cccvi), that Stotoëtis, of Heraclea, August 28, A.D. 145, sold one-third of his office of tax collector for two years to Satarnilus for 252 drachmae a year. From the police records of a neighboring village (Euhemeria) the following are selected as typical of the whole:

A.D. 28—While the wife and mother of Hippalus were bathing in the public baths, two men and two women attacked them, beating them badly and stealing a gold earring, etc.

A.D. 29—Senthus, identified by a scar on his left wrist, presents information against Papantos, a former brewer, for breaking into his house "by way of the beer shop on the north," and stealing considerable silver, a clock, shovel, basket of bread containing fifty loaves, two tin drinking-cups, etc.

A.D. 30—A woman worker at an oil mill ran off with the cloak of the manager and forty silver drachmae—so affirms Hatres, identified by "a scar on the middle of his forehead."

A.D. 34—Lysanias is notified of the theft of thirty bundles of hay which had been "boldly carried away on donkeys by the thief."

A.D. 36—Orsenouphis is caught in the act of stealing at night five rakes, six hay sickles, fifteen measures of wool, etc. Another charge in this same year is that of stealing a pig "worth eight drachmae."

A.D. 37—A similar charge was made when six hundred bundles of hay were thus carried off.

A.D. 38—Ision, slave of Chaeremon, who had loaned some money to another man, was beaten seriously by him when he spoke to him of the debt. In this same year, Dictas complains of Chaeremon, a former brewer employed by him, who had beaten and robbed Artemidorus, the man put in his place when he had been discharged.

A.D. 40—A woman burglar entered a house, beat the owner's daughter who was at home, tore her purple tunic, and carried off a hundred drachmae.

Some official documents from Socnopaei Nesus are bi-lingual (demotic-Greek), and many private letters in Greek exist, showing that the population was interested in the same things as interest the common people to-day, and that they were writing freely about these daily happenings. We give a typical instance dating between A.D. 38 and 40:

Ammonius to his dearest Aphrodisius, greeting.

"I wrote a letter to the herdsman Heracleus that he should supply you with a donkey, and I bade Ophelion also to supply you with another, and to send me the loaves. . . . As to the pigs' fodder and the rest of the price for the hay, make provision until I come. Urge your wife from me to look after the pigs, and do you also take care of the calf. Be sure and send me the loaves and the relish. . . . Good-by."

A letter written to Ammonius by this same agent (A.D. 40) shows the intimate relation at this time between employer and employed in these little country towns.

"I will send the donkeys without fail. Please do your utmost to procure me the unguent of lentils; do not neglect this last. We think you have become all at once estranged toward us."

Innumerable private letters, some of them written in great haste, about the pickling of olives, the pressing of grapes, the care of children, the building of new houses, and all the minute details of business have now come into our hands from men who lived at the very time when Luke was writing the Acts and while the other literature of the New Testament was being produced. One man gives an intensely interesting description of his trip up the Nile, and another describes the new house which the carpenters were just finishing. It must have been an especially fine house for a country village of that day, for he mentions the "smaller and larger dining-rooms," and states that the "second water refrigerator is to be roofed to-morrow." These letters constantly mention the names of the children of the correspondents, and contain many reproaches because of the failure of their friends to write oftener.

There seems to be no perceptible difference between the style of the private letters from the first to the early fourth century, but there are remarks made occasionally which throw a brilliant light on the great

change in financial conditions.   The fact that a brother
writing to his sister in the third century remarks that
"everything has risen in price" might not in itself
prove much, but there is convincing corroborative evidence of the truth of this complaint.   February 6, A.D.
149, a woman at Socnopaei Nesus wants money so much
that she borrows 1,200 drachmae at 1 per cent. a
month, and at Oxyrhynchus (A.D. 381) a man goes
surety for a friend who has borrowed 42,000,000 denarii.   Of course these documents are not in themselves
conclusive, for there are always people in every age
who will give any kind of interest for ready cash, and
so far as borrowing 42,000,000 "shillings" or going
security for the man who has done this, there are some
examples in modern America of even greater extravagance and folly.   But the cumulative evidence is absolutely convincing that the whole district of the Fayum
suffered a serious collapse in the third century, and
that by the early fourth century the money of Egypt,
as elsewhere, had become almost as valueless as the
wild-cat issues of certain banks in America about a
century ago.   This may not seem to be a matter of
much concern to the reader, but as we shall see it may
have some little bearing, at least, upon the value of the
New Testament texts which come to us from this district
in the third or fourth century.

Life in Oxyrhynchus in the Early Christian Period

Oxyrhynchus is to us the most important of the old
Egyptian towns, because it is from this site that almost
all of our ancient fragments of the newly discovered
New Testaments have come.   Its life story ought to

be at least equal in thrilling interest to that found in the "Anthology of Spoon River."

Oxyrhynchus (Behnesa) was located on the Bahr Yusuf, the leading canal of the Fayum, about ten miles from the Nile and about two hundred and sixty miles from Alexandria. A number of granite columns and shattered temple altars show the importance of this city in early times, tho this importance dwindled greatly in the third century of our era. Indications of this partial collapse of the business life of the city may be found in the proportion of the papyri that have come to us from the various eras, e.g., of the 960 dated texts published in the eleven volumes of the Oxyrhynchus papyri, over 740 belong to the first three Christian centuries, a trifle less than a hundred certainly belong to the fourth century; and of the dated fourth century texts only twenty come from the seventy-five years following the Council of Nice (325). In the fifth century the city began to recover its lost activity, the town and the desert around it being filled with monks and nuns, and by the sixth century it seems to have fully regained its old prosperity and to have been regarded as one of the leading Christian cities of Egypt.

Oxyrhynchus was a self-governing city, boasting several "senators" and other civil dignitaries, and was the chief town of the nome. This did not mean, of course, that it was ever a large and wealthy city in the modern or even in the Alexandrian sense; but it had corn mills and bakeries with a "superintendent of food supplies" constantly on duty to see that people could get bread at a moderate price; it must have had a weekly market and large bazaar, and was probably in almost all respects very like the modern Medinet el-Fayum or any other large Egyptian town that is away from the ordinary tourist route.

The amusements of the town never ceased at any era, the gymnastic games even in the fourth century being vastly popular, the victors being granted special privileges by the municipality. Doubtless, in Oxyrhynchus, just as in Rome, the lower classes were kept in subjection and made to forget their poverty and their wrongs by these games provided at senatorial or government expense. The placards yet in existence show that these exercises were regarded as part of the ancient "tradition" of the place. The excitement incident to such occasions is well illustrated from some texts of the sixth century when, evidently through the influence of Christianity, horse racing had taken the place of the brutal gladiatorial shows. From these contemporary accounts it is perfectly clear that the Derby never created more excitement than these races did.

The whole population was divided into two factions, called the Blues and the Greens, each shouting, and presumably betting, on their own horses. It is interesting to notice that each side had a "starter" and provided certain funds for maintaining their favorite stud.

The public baths also always continued to be kept up at some expense, fifty talents of silver being spent in repairs (A.D. 303), and 10,000 denarii being expended in painting some of these baths a little later (A.D. 316); while twenty years later an additional wooden bath was built. But, as we have seen, 10,000 denarii at that date did not mean a very large amount of silver, and other texts show conclusively the comparative poverty of the place. Even the amusements may not have represented any great extravagance, as a contract for the hire of two dancing girls by the president of the town in the third century shows that they were paid only thirty-six drachmae a day.

The official records and private correspondence in this city in the first and adjoining centuries are so personal and minute that one almost feels ashamed to repeat some of the disclosures of human frailty and business complications coming from this far-away country town. One father, in a public placard, thrashes his son Castor for "riotous living," and warns the community to lend him no money; while a little later Trophimus writes to his father a letter in the most injured tone because his parent had suggested that he was "boastful" and was wasting his money on a paramour instead of sending it home. A mother writing to her husband about a much-loved boy of quite different character, says, "It quite upset him for you to go away and leave him behind." How close it brings us to the apostolic age to read in these newly discovered papyri the horoscope of a man born 10 P.M. September 28 (A.D. 15); of the hire of a mill (A.D. 17); of the bail offered for a prisoner (A.D. 28); of a promise to attend court (A.D. 59); or of a complaint against a husband (A.D. 20-50), by Syra, who says her husband squandered her dowry, mistreated her, and finally left her wholly without support. Zois (A.D. 30) writes about the bread she has ordered but not received; in another first century text we find made out in due form the valuation of a bakery; and it is noteworthy that in some other business account books, tho not in this, a method is used much like our own "double entry."

One man swears "by Cæsar" that he does not know of any extortion on the part of a soldier mentioned; another, January 31 (A.D. 52), makes out a deed of sale for an ass's colt, while a death report is dated the twelfth year of Nero, September, A.D. 56, and a sale of wheat is made A.D. 81-96.

It makes one feel that he is touching very closely the private actions and common gossip of that time to pick out from a blurred papyrus a whispered secret concerning Pheros, "contractor for the beer and nitrate tax," and about Menches, who "bribed" the village to secure reappointment to his office of royal scribe; or to read a private letter from a husband to his wife, giving directions about his tools and "the old cushion that is up in the dining-room"; or to read a love letter written A.D. 22, in which the wife says, "I am not so much as anointing myself until I shall hear from you!"

The temple and its services are much in evidence. When a Roman senator visits a certain temple (first century) we have a private note from one priest to the other telling of the sacrifices which must be prepared for the occasion, and of the "titbits" to be made ready for the sacred crocodiles. It is evident that the ancient Egyptians were even ready to exploit their most sacred religious customs for the sake of the backshish.

Here is a list of articles for sacrifice (second century)—a calf, wine, wafers, garlands, cakes, palm branches, oil, honey, milk; here is also a contract in which musicians are engaged for a five days' festival to receive transportation, board, and 140 drachmae; and here are others where the partners in a pigeon-house arrange for the division of the dung; and here again Hermogenes gives an order for a hundred empty jars and "the wheel of the machine." Here is a deed of divorce (A.D. 45) in which both husband and wife are identified by scars; and several law court records (A.D. 50) in which it is charged that women have been receiving wages for nursing foundlings "picked up from the dung-hill" after these children had died. It is noticeable that the men who cared for these cast-off children are called here "benefactors" (cf. Luke 22: 25).

That boys were boys nineteen centuries ago is shown by a contract of apprenticeship dated A.D. 66, in which Pryphon, who was born A.D. 8, and was a weaver by trade, binds his son to a neighboring weaver for a small recompense, with the agreement that if the boy plays truant he must make up the time and his father must in addition pay forfeit for each day thus lost.

It throws a vivid light upon the common superstitions of the day to read as the characteristic expression in many letters:

"Above all I pray that you may be in health, unharmed by the evil eye."

Several letters mention dreams and their influence, and one son is represented in a sort of circular letter as saying to his father:

"I have been deceived by the gods trusting in dreams. All things are false and your gods with the rest."

From a mass of papyri of the second century we select for mention as illustrating the conditions of society at Oxyrhynchus a letter from a man of family who writes to the lady Didyme, saying:

"Do not lose heart about the rent, for you will certainly get it."

In a will probated A.D. 123, a mother aged seventy-eight, leaves all her property to her daughter on condition that she discharge her debts and give her a good funeral. A registration of paupers (A.D. 149) raises the question whether there could have been a "poor-rate" in Roman Egypt by means of which the well-to-do were forced to contribute to the support of those lacking means. A complaint against a priest (A.D. 159) charges him with letting his hair grow too long —not a strange charge, since short hair at this time must have been commonly considered the mark of a Christian teacher as contrasted with the usually unshorn locks of the heathen philosophers.

While the fourth century texts are, as we have said, few and generally unimportant, some of these show the terrific financial strain to which the country was subjected after Diocletian established an imperial absolutism, blotting out freedom and making the spirit of militarism rampant. Wessely has pointed out that while in A.D. 267 a house at Socnopaei Nesus cost 2,000 drachmae, forty years later a mortgage on this same house was taken for 3,840,000 drachmae; and that while (A.D. 255) a measure (about a peck) of wheat cost sixteen drachmae, in A.D. 314 the same amount cost 10,000 drachmae.[24a]

So at Oxyrhynchus in A.D. 306 a man paid 720,000 denarii (about $120,000) for five hundred pounds of meat. We transcribe this curious document:

From Ptileminus Thonius, steward of Nigrius, Greeting.
"Measure out to my Brother Dorotheus, who is about to collect

[24a] Wessely, *op. cit.*, p. 73.

payments on my accounts through Hieronichus for the price of 500 lbs. of meat, 40 artebae of aracus, 72 myriads of denarii" (*Oxyrhynchus Papyri;* XI, 367).

Two years later there is a record even more sur- prizing than this, of a man's paying 75,000 denarii for a hide. The rentals of land about this time went up to impossible prices, and food became so dear that a leg of antelope is recorded as having been sold for 50,000 drachmae and four chickens for 30,000 drachmae (Wessely). Altho wages had gone up correspondingly—grooms receiving from 3,000 to 6,000 drachmae a month, even pedagogs receiving almost as much—yet conditions were feverish and dangerous, and fraud, blackmail, and graft were the order of the day.[25]

From the first to the middle of the third century of our era, Oxyrhynchus enjoyed its highest prosper- ity. Even the classics were studied; more fragments of these ancient works having been found here than in any other town. The city contained several heathen temples dedicated to Serapis, Isis, Thoeris, etc.; and a Cæsarium, theater, gymnasium, capitolium, and a few other municipal buildings, besides several public baths. There was, without doubt, a Jewish synagog, and there were also at this time, as recently proved, several Christian churches, two of which, tho not public buildings, were important enough to be mentioned in an ancient official report of city edifices. It is thrilling to get even this transient glimpse of those early fol- lowers of Jesus as an organized body, having well-

[25] In the earlier days respectable teachers would not take wages, but lived upon the voluntary gifts of their students. One man, mentioned by Suetonius, boasted that he received 400,000 denarii annually from his scholars. Vespasian was the first emperor to establish state-paid profes- sorships.

known meeting-houses in which they conducted worship. Burial associations had official existence at Oxyrhynchus at least as early as 67 B.C., and the Christians in the first and second centuries of our era may have organized themselves at times under some such name, but by the third century their churches were, as we have seen, well known. These churches must not be visioned as large and elegant buildings, but rather as much resembling the oldest Coptic churches of Cairo, such as Mâr Mina or Al-Muallakah.

Oxyrhynchus and the villages of the Fayum had always been isolated to a degree because of their geographical location; but with the collapse of business in the Fayum—upon which the trade of Oxyrhynchus largely depended—this isolation must have become more marked. It was a long row against the stream if one ventured the long trip from Old Babylon to Oxyrhynchus (120 miles), and a three-hour ride by camel or two by donkey from the Nile to the town. If he came all the way by camel it could scarcely take him much less than a week from Old Babylon, and twice as long coming from Alexandria. It was not likely that the rich politicians and ecclesiastics of Alexandria should be much interested in these poor towns in the Fayum and Upper Egypt, especially after financial misfortune had befallen them. That intercourse between these two widely separated sections of Egypt was exceedingly limited is further suggested by the fact that no native was allowed to go from one district to another without a permit.[26]

We leave this discussion for the present with the final statement that the linguistic, religious, and social

[26] *Greek Papyri of the British Museum, IV., XV.*

atmosphere of Oxyrhynchus was that of the Fayum, not that of Alexandria.[27] This fact has an important bearing upon the value of the newly discovered New Testament texts—but that is another story which must he told in another chapter.[27a]

[27] The "Blessed Pachomius" (A.D. 292-346) makes it perfectly clear in the *Paradise of the Holy Fathers* that Oxyrhynchus, tho he speaks of it as "a great city," could not have had a population much above 20,000, for he says that 5,000 monks lived in the city, and as many more round about it, and that "the monks are not much fewer in numbers than the ordinary inhabitants of the city." The poverty of Oxyrhynchus is additionally shown by the few orders to silversmiths as compared with some other towns (*cf. Archiv. für Papyrusforschung,* 1909, p. 382; *Hawara Papyri,* No. 68). On the crudity and poverty of the churches in Lower Egypt and Nubia see Somers Clarke, *Christian Antiquities in the Nile Valley* (1912); and Geoffrey S. Mileham, *Churches in Lower Nubia* (1910).

[27a] Those who wish to keep in close touch with the latest discoveries in this field should become members of the Egyptian Exploration Fund ($5.00), and thus receive regularly *The Journal of Egyptian Archæology,* which is by far the best publication in English touching these matters. Those who desire to help the work of exploration and keep informed on this subject can send their names to Mrs. Marie N. Buckman, secretary of the Egyptian Exploration Fund for the United States, 527 Tremont Temple, Boston, Mass., who will furnish literature and further information.

II

NEW LIGHT FROM THE PAPYRI UPON THE LANGUAGE OF THE NEW TESTAMENT

1. NEW LIGHT UPON THE ORIGIN AND TEXTUAL FORM OF THE NEW TESTAMENT

THE writer appeals to Sir F. G. Kenyon, of the British Museum,[1] and to Dr. George Milligan, of the University of Glasgow,[2] for the latest expert judgment in regard to this. According to these scholars, the new discoveries have not only made all former results of Greek paleography out of date, but have really for the first time established the science on a solid basis. The old division of manuscripts into uncials and minuscules is now of little use, the real division being between literary and non-literary manuscripts; the cursive script being used in common matters even in the earliest centuries. While few, if any, dated papyri come from the first century B.C., great numbers come from the two centuries preceding and from the first, second and third centuries after Christ, so that for the first time undated documents can now be generally assigned with considerable certainty to their proper century. The formation of the letters and the character of the abbreviations and other changes in handwriting and orthography make it as easy to decide between a first century and a third century Greek manuscript

[1] *Textual Criticism of the New Testament,* 1912.
[2] *New Testament Documents,* 1913.

98

as between a sixteenth century and a nineteenth century English manuscript. The grammar and popular phraseology show equal changes, so that a new argument inexpressibly strong has suddenly arisen, compelling skeptical scholars almost irresistibly to date the New Testament documents in the first century. Thus paleography adds its weight to the former strong internal argument.

In the lifetime of our Lord there was a "widespread habit of writing among all classes of the population," and no doubt the leading facts were written down and circulated "almost as soon as they took place"—tho doubtless at first in fragmentary form—so that probably the first account of the death of Jesus "must be presumed to be written in the year he died" (Milligan). As soon as the converts became so many that the original apostles could not easily carry authoritative facts personally to all Christian communities, a need of records would be felt which, because of this general habit of note taking and writing, could be readily supplied.

We now know exactly how those first records of the Lord's life looked in the middle of that first century. They were written on papyrus sheets which ordinarily measured five by eleven inches, with twenty sheets usually to the roll, the columns being generally two or three inches wide with small margins. Mark's gospel would make a roll about nineteen feet long and Romans eleven and one-half feet; while 2 Thessalonians could be written in a five column roll fifteen inches in length. They were written with a reed pen (*cf.* 3 John 13), with an ink made out of soot and gum, which was very legible except when "blotted out" or "washed out" (*cf.* Col. 2:14). The roll was bound with a thread and sealed (Rev. 5:1), a will often being sealed seven times and authenticated. For preservation rolls were fastened together in bundles and laid in arks or chests, "a practise which enables us to understand how unsigned rolls laid up in the same place and dealing with cognate subjects would come, in some instances, to be joined together as if they formed parts of one work, while in the case of others, errors regarding authorship and destination might readily arise" (Milligan).

The ordinary practise in letter writing was by dictation, as is true yet in Palestine and Egypt, tho the writer might sign his name himself and add a postscript (*e.g.,* 1 Cor. 16:20; Col. 4:18). In emergencies almost everybody could write, tho probably not in such good penmanship as the official letter writers and in a somewhat different style from what he would customarily use when simply talking out what he wanted to say.

It is quite plain that the old argument which would deny to St. Paul certain letters, believed by the early Church to be his, because these were written in a different style from others, loses most of its force. It may be remembered just here that St. Jerome explained the stylistic difference between 1 Peter and 2 Peter as a difference in scribes. Doubtless at different times these amanuenses were allowed different degrees of liberty in taking the dictation. It is perfectly clear that there would be great differences in results if they made only a rough draft of what was to be said and then carefully rewrote it, or if they took it in shorthand—which, however, was not common among the middle classes—or if they took down the dictation word for word as spoken.

Certain it is that the papyri were usually written in one hand and signed in another. What would naturally happen can be seen from contemporaneous autograph letters of the first century, and from the average newspaper report of the modern sermon. This has been very brilliantly illustrated by Prof. James Hope Moulton in his *New Light from the Egyptian Rubbish Heaps* (1916), in which he explains the fact that Ephesians contains more "Semitisms" than any other letter of St. Paul, by the simple theory that Timothy, or some other close Hebrew friend, was Paul's scribe in writing that epistle. Paul, according to this view, wrote Colossians with his own hand, and then let Timothy, after hearing it read, turn it into a circular letter which would be suitable for all the churches of the valley. Timothy was with Paul as helper, and "from a child" had been steeped in the sacred writings (2 Tim. 3: 15), never having been Hellenized as Paul had. Dr. Moulton believes that it needs only this very natural supposition to remove entirely this serious argument against the Pauline authorship of Ephesians.

Dr. Moulton also believes that the papyri prove tnat such a theory is not far-fetched, for two ancient letters written upon the same day by different persons have come to us, which are almost as near alike as Colossians and Ephesians, one being written by a wife to her husband, Hephaestion, and the other written to the same man by his brother—the similar phrases and sequence of thought being evidently due to the fact that the wife and her brother-in-law had talked the matter over and then independently written within a few hours of each other.

So also many of the grammatical mistakes, the broken constructions and lapses of connection in St. Paul's letters, as well as the changes of style, seem to be quite fully and satisfactorily explained by the ordinary method of letter writing which is now proved to have existed at that period. A break in the change of tone in the same letter would naturally occur if the dictation had been interrupted. It is also now known that there was generally no punctuation, little if any separation of words, many abbreviations, and no quotation marks in the first century letters—all of which must be remembered in criticizing the present text.

Even the pastoral epistles, tho greatly differing in style and language from the other letters of Paul, are now accepted by many scholars of international reputation as embodying "genuine Pauline material, tho showing such an advanced state of ecclesiastical organization that they may have been put in their present form after the apostle's death." [3] The new discoveries have considerably relieved the defense of the Pauline authorship of the pastoral epistles, for the amanuensis may merely have been a man of wider culture and have been left a freer hand than usual.[4] At any rate, the new discoveries show that the Pauline and other New Testament epistles, if they originated like similar material of the same era, were probably written to dictation and always with a definite audience before the eye of the author and were therefore almost as

[3] *New Testament Documents,* p. 85; *cf.* Bartlett, *London Expositor,* 1913, p. 347*ff.*

[4] Milligan, *op. cit.,* p. 103; but see against this view Moffatt, *Introduction to the Literature of the New Testament,* 1914, p. 407.

much speeches as letters, this speech-form being molded by contemporary rhetoric and by local and racial methods of expression and reasoning.

So far as textual criticism is concerned, Dr. Milligan is certainly entitled to give an expert opinion, and he declares that in view of all the new light coming upon the question from recent discovery it is safe to conclude that "with the probable exception of 2 Peter all our New Testament writings may now be placed within the first century" (*ibid.*, p. 172). If Professor Harnack is right in saying that it is "in the highest degree probable" that the book of Acts was written "at a time when St. Paul's trial had not yet come to an end," [5] then he and Dr. Milligan can not be far wrong in placing the composition of the Acts about A.D. 62, and the synoptic gospels could not have been much later; tho it was nearly three centuries before all the separated documents of the New Testament were gathered together as we now have them. [6]

It is surprizing how few can now be found to defend the late dates so popular two generations ago. The encyclical nature of many of the epistles would necessitate copies, and even private churches would be likely to send to other churches any rare apostolic message which they possest—travel being easy, as is illustrated from a recently discovered document which shows that one merchant had journeyed from Asia to Rome over seventy times. In the main these copies would probably be made faithfully, tho breaks might occur and the *lacunae* afterward restored from memory. It must be remembered that copies would at first be made

[5] *Date of Acts and Synoptic Gospels,* 1911, p. 99.

[6] The views of other scholars may be noted in Moffatt's *Introduction to the Literature of the New Testament,* 1914, p. 213.

hurriedly and with no thought of the need of verbal accuracy, so that a copyist might try in love to remove what looked like some blemish of language or meaning. It must also be remembered that the hardest usage for a roll would come naturally at the beginning and end, as is illustrated by the shorter and longer endings added later to Mark's gospel. This is wholly in accordance with the facts as observed in the documents preserved to us from the first and following centuries. Parts of a letter might also be easily displaced (as Rom. 16), and different letters from the same person might be copied into the same roll but not in chronological order (*e.g.*, 2 Corinthians 10-13).

Papyrus books were not so common in the early Christian centuries as papyrus rolls. The book represented a more elaborate literary product. It was always from the pen of some celebrated author or was made up of a collection of writings gathered together after these writings had become so sufficiently celebrated that a large demand for them had become common. Parchment was not limited in its source, as papyrus was, and being stronger and more flexible it came into use for literary purposes at least as early as the second century B.C., and by the fourth century of our era had become popular for the better class of Christian literature. From this century comes one of the most beautiful editions of the Apocalypse written, on vellum, each leaf being of miniature proportions.[7] One discovery such as this is quite sufficient to annihilate the eccentric theory of Nikolaus Morosow that the book of Revelation was written as an astrological exercise by

[7] *Oxyrhynchus Papyri*, Vol. VIII, 14.

John Chrysostom on or about September 30, A.D. 395![8]

The new discoveries have enabled us to get to the original New Testament with more certainty than in the case of any other ancient book. "For our knowledge of Sophocles, for example, we are mainly dependent on a single manuscript written about 1,400 years after the poet's death, and tho in the case of Vergil we are fortunate in possessing one nearly complete manuscript belonging to the fourth century, the total number of Vergilian manuscripts can be numbered only by hundreds, as compared with thousands in the case of the New Testament writers." Dr. Milligan dares to add concerning the New Testament: "We may take it that in all substantial particulars the words of the autographs have been recovered." And Caspar René Gregory suggests that the early changes in the text were no more marked than those introduced by recent critics, such as Griesbach, Tischendorf, Tregelles, and Westcott and Hort.[9] This does not mean that there were not varieties of text, marginal glosses, and "interpolated adscripts," even in sub-apostolic times —these occur in every classic;[10] but it does mean that all the mass of new discovery has only made more certain the antiquity and essential integrity of the New Testament text, as all the great text critics admit.

[8] *Die Offenbarung Johannes,* 1912, pp. 100-110.

[9] *Textcritik des Neuen Test.,* 1909, p. 1,008; see also Milligan, *New Testament Documents,* pp. 196-199; also Von Soden, *Die Schriften des Neuen Test.,* Band I., Abt. II., passim; Kenyon, *Handbook,* 1901, chap. VIII.; Scrivener, *Plain Introduction,* I : 4-8, II : 259-273; Gregory, *Canon and Text of New Test.,* pp. 126, 501-508; Zahn, *Introduction to New Test.,* pp. 178-194.

[10] See Rutherford, *Fourth Book of Thucydides,* pp. xxxiff.

2. NEW LIGHT UPON THE GRAMMAR OF THE NEW TESTAMENT

In the last twenty years New Testament grammar has become a new study because of the papyri. Even as early as 1841, Thiersch pointed out the value of the papyri for the study of the Septuagint.[11] Lightfoot, in 1863, saw the advantage which would come to us in explaining the New Testament if we could have the letters of ordinary people from that era; but it was Deissmann who first attempted to examine extensively the grammar of the New Testament in the light of the new discoveries of papyri.[12] In 1901, Thumb published a great book on the *Koine*,[12a] and five years later Dr. J. H. Moulton gave to the English-speaking world his *Introduction to the New Testament Greek;* but no one has treated the entire grammatical field in the light of the new discoveries with such fulness and thoroughness as A. T. Robertson in his *Grammar of the Greek New Testament in the Light of Historical Research,* 1914.

The remarkable increase of interest in this field, due chiefly to the new discoveries, may be seen from the fact that within the last eight or nine years at least eight or nine notable Greek grammars have been published. Some of these deal with the grammar of the papyri directly;[13] others deal with the modern Greek, which is now seen to be far more closely connected with the

[11] *De Pentateuchi versione Alexandrina.*

[12] *Die sprachl. Erforschung der griech. Bibel,* 1898, and *Bibelstudien,* 1895-1898.

[12a] *Die griechische Sprache im Zeitalter des Hellenismus.*

[13] Mayser, *Grammatik der griech. Papyri,* 1906.

New Testament language than classical Greek;[14] still others deal with the Greek of the Septuagint.[14a]

The best recent grammars which have to do directly with the New Testament Greek are named below.[15]

Innumerable smaller works and important contributions on the New Testament in the light of the papyri have appeared and also several new lexicons.[16]

This shows the unprecedented interest which has been aroused by these new discoveries. Without the Greek learning of the sixteenth century the Reformation could not have been accomplished. Since that day until now there has never been a revival of Greek learning equal to that which is stirring the whole world at the present moment. And the influence of these discoveries has produced an eager enthusiasm for Greek grammar and the Greek New Testament,

[14] Thumb, *Handbuch der neu-griech. Volkssprache*, 1910; Thumb-Angus, *Hand Book of the Modern Greek Vernacular*, 1912.

[14a] Conybeare and Helbing, *Grammatik der Septuaginta*, 1907; Stock, *Selections from the LXX: a Grammatical Introduction*, 1905; Thackeray, *A Grammar of the O.T. in Greek*, Vol. 1, 1909.

[15] Abbott, *Johannine Grammar*, 1906; Blass, *Grammatik des neutest. Griechisch*, 1902; Gerth-Blass, in *Ausführliche Grammatik der griechischen Sprache*, 1890-1904; Thackeray-Blass, *Grammar of the New Testament*, 1905; Moulton, *Grammar of New Testament Greek*, Vol. I, *Prolegomena*, 1906; Radermacher, *Neutest. Grammatik*, 1911; A. T. Robertson, *Short Grammar of the Greek New Testament*, 1908 (translated into Italian, 1910; French and Dutch, 1911; German, 1912); Brugmann-Thumb, *Griechische Grammatik*, 1913; Blass-Debrunner, *Grammatik des neutest. Griechisch*, 1913; Robertson, *Grammar of the Greek New Testament in the Light of Historical Research*, 1914, (2d ed. 1915).

[16] Among the latter should be mentioned Nägeli, *Der Wortschatz des Apostels Paulus*, 1905; the Cremer-Kügel Lexicon of New Testament Greek, 1912; the revision of Passow's Lexicon by Crönert, 1912; the supplementary Greek Lexicon by Herwerden, 2 vols., 1910; the great Greek Lexicon begun at Athens in 1901; and Preuschen's *Vollständiges griechisch-deutsches Handwörterbuch*, 1908-1910; Souter, *A Pocket Lexicon to the Greek New Testament*, 1916. Lexicons are also announced by Deissmann, and by Moulton and Milligan, the latter of whom have been publishing for ten years in *The Expositor* important contributions to Lexicography from the Papyri and at this writing have issued Parts I and II of their exhaustive *Vocabulary of the Greek Testament*, covering all New Testament words from Alpha to Delta.

such as has not been known for four hundred years. The grammar of the *Koine* (which was the vernacular of the first century, spoken and written all over the civilized world) and the grammar of the New Testament are essentially the same, as the great grammarians referred to above have shown.[17] There was an ancient Attic vernacular corresponding to the literary Attic, and upon this as a base there were deposited various influences from other dialects; yet the *Koine* was practically homogeneous, notwithstanding local variations, tho in remote districts it became Doric-colored or Ionic-colored. So far as phonetics and orthography are concerned, we find that there were no settled rules, probably, in the *Koine*. There never was a fixt orthography in Greek, and we do not know certainly how the ancient Attic or the *Koine* were pronounced, tho we can approximate it because the pronunciation of the modern Greek vernacular is known. It is of value to discover that we must not insist too strongly in Bible study on "hair-splitting differences hinging on forms which for the scribe of our uncials had identical value phonetically."[18] As rough breathings and the accent came into use only in late Christian times, our phonetic reconstruction of the ancient tongue must be by guess. No doubt there were local variations in the pronunciation of the *Koine,* and as many Bible manuscripts were written from dictation instead of from reading, it is natural that there should be much variation in spelling, even in the earliest New Testament manuscripts; yet there is a marked difference between

[17] See also the masterly article by Thumb in *The Dictionary of the Apostolic Church,* 1916, on "Hellenistic and Biblical Greek."

[18] Angus, *The Koine,* p. 79.

the papyri of the first and the fourth centuries. Here
we possess a new proof that our fourth century Bible
texts were copied from ancient originals. In the *Koine*
of the first century, as contrasted with the classical
Greek, old suffixes were dropt and new suffixes
coined, and the number of words compounded by juxta-
position greatly increased. The *nominativus pendens*
is much in evidence. The neuter plural is used with
either a singular or a plural verb. The accusative is
regaining ascendency. The comparative often does
duty for the superlative adjective. The use of the personal pronoun becomes more frequent, but that of the
possessive pronoun decreases. In the verb there is a
marked tendency toward simplification, the two con-
jugations blending into one. The cases with prepositions are changing. The optative is disappearing. The
instrumental use of ἐν is common. The future parti-
ciple is less frequent. The growth of the passive over
the middle is marked, as is also the later use of participles. In the vocabulary words from town-life
(the stage, the market-place) come to the front, and
there is a marked increase in the number of diminutive forms. Thus we find both in word formation and
accidence, as well as in the vocabulary and orthography, clear tests by which the age of the texts can
now be discriminated—showing by a new line of argument not possible to our fathers the antiquity of the
originals of the New Testament manuscripts. Professor Robertson in his great *Grammar of the Greek
New Testament in the Light of Historical Research*
has pointed out minutely and voluminously these changes
from the classical usage found in the papyri and in the
New Testament. We have used above his authorita-

tive conclusions and we now venture to borrow from him further on a most important phase of this subject.

The New Testament writers were once supposed to have used prepositions so freely because of the Hebrew and Aramaic, and it was counted equally certain that every preposition had some divine meaning in the sacred text, so that to interchange one for the other would amount almost to sacrilege. This old and well-established opinion has been badly damaged by the newly discovered facts; for we find the new prepositions which were supposed to be Semitic used freely in the vernacular of the early centuries by a non-Jewish population, and we fail to find the inflexibility in the use of such prepositions which the theologians and grammarians of a generation ago assumed. ἀπό παρά, ὑπό and ἐκ are used in the papyri without exactness of distinction, and ὑπέρ is often only a colorless "about" or used in the sense of "to" without any reference to the deeper original meaning.[19] The interchange of εἰς and ἐν is frequent in the papyri, and only the context can determine whether εἰς means "into," "unto," "in," "on," or "upon." This, of course, does not prove that prepositions in the New Testament are mere synonyms; but it does suggest that theological conclusions from such premises must be drawn with care, since the New Testament was practically the spoken language of the first century, and minute distinctions are not to be expected in colloquial use.[20] The New Testament writers used the language common upon the

[19] Moulton, *op. cit.*, pp. 105, 237.

[20] It should be noted, however, that the New Testament writers are from the middle class, not the lowest class, and that both Moulton and Robertson recognize the nice discrimination ordinarily shown in the use of prepositions by Bible writers. See particularly Robertson, *op. cit.*, pp. 556-557, 885ff, 902.

street, and this language was changing in their very lifetime; so that we find a new usage of περί, beginning in Paul's letter with Philippians.[21] So the weakened use of ἵνα is one of the characteristics of the *Koine* and is richly illustrated in the New Testament, particularly in the writings of St. John.

From the study of the grammar of the *Koine* it is perfectly clear that many of the supposed blunders and solecisms of the New Testament writers and their supposed errors in transcription of the text are merely grammatical forms common among the middle classes of the first century. This is one of the greatest discoveries that have been made. The two genders found with the same word in Rev. 14: 19 are also found with this same word in the papyri.[22] So Blass needlessly wished to amend the text in 2 Tim. 2: 14, and both Blass and Moulton hesitated to accept -αν in the present perfect instead of the usual -ᾶσι—regarding it as "a vulgarism due to the occasional lapse of an early scribe"; but the papyri prove that while these are loose constructions, they were not uncommon in the apostolic era and were not marks of an uneducated person.[23]

The accuracy and age of the New Testament documents are thus confirmed by the new discoveries in a striking way; for altho the great New Testament uncials of the fourth and later centuries were changed slightly in vocabulary and grammatical idiom to conform to the customs in those centuries, yet these retain the ancient and peculiar forms of the first and second centuries to such an extent that their origin is

[21] Robertson, *ibid.*, p. 620.
[22] Moulton, *Prolegomena*, p. 60.
[23] Robertson, *ibid.*, pp. 336, 945.

now undoubted. It does not need a "redactor" any longer to explain the different spellings and changes in orthography, and in every direction these modern studies have increased the authority of the great uncial MSS. of the New Testament.[24] The textual problem is, however, complicated somewhat by the fact, now finally settled, that the earliest Bible texts, near the Constantine era, while essentially the same as our Greek text, did not fall so constantly into the two general types which later. became universal ("Eastern" and "Western"); but were rather "neutral" texts which related the gospel story before the verbal phraseology had become stereotyped. It was, seemingly, only in later times that the adoration of the "letter" of the New Testament began. The early Christians were more interested in repeating the substance of the gospel story and getting the spirit of the narratives than in remembering the exact phraseology.

3. New Light Upon the Style of the New Testament

The style of the New Testament was the style of the *Koine*. As Moulton well says: Biblical Greek did not "lie in a backwater"; it was in the "full stream." No literary man of the day would have used this local dialect. The Holy Ghost spoke in the vernacular. The very grammar and dictionary cry out against men who would allow the Scriptures to appear in any other form than that understood by the people.

Each New Testament writer had individual characteristics, but, with the exception of Luke, the author

[24] Moulton, *op. cit.*, pp. 42-38.

of the Hebrews, and Paul in a few of his epistles, these
were all written in the "vulgar tongue" of the first
century. Mark often uses the "dramatic present" just
as servant girls do now in their talk; but Luke
changed these tenses to suit literary proprieties. Luke
was quite familiar with the Greek Bible (LXX) and
consciously imitated it.[25] He was a Gentile and the
most literary of the gospel writers. His vocabulary
illustrates his breadth of culture, for he uses 750
words, very many of which are technical medical terms
not occurring elsewhere in the New Testament in the
same sense (Hobart). While he has a fine command
of the popular diction there is a literary touch about
him not found in the papyri. Blass has even suggested
that his prolog was imitated from the opening of
Dioscorides' great work on *materia medica,* which he
probably had in his library.[26] The author of the Epistle
to the Hebrews shows a quality of studied literary
style above all the other Bible writers. This book was
written by one who, tho he apparently knew no
Hebrew and used only the LXX, was filled with the
Semitic spirit. The vocabulary, like the style, is less
like the vernacular *Koine* than any book in the New
Testament. Of 87 words which are found in the LXX
and in this book alone in the New Testament, 74 belong
to the ancient literary works and only 13 to the vernacular.[27] Paul, especially in Romans and Ephesians,
shows at times an almost classic perfection; yet this is
due to intellect and passion rather than to studied
effort. There is not space here to quote in full Pro-

[25] Moulton, *Prolegomena,* p. 131; *Camp. Bibl. Essays,* p. 479.
[26] *Philology of the Gospels,* 1898, p. 34.
[27] Robertson, *Grammar of New Test. in the Light of Hist. Research,* p. 132.

fessor Robertson's keen analysis of Paul's style; but perhaps a few quotations may show him in his relation to the common language of his day:

"He disclaims classic elegance and calls himself ἰδιώτης τῷ λόγῳ (2 Cor. 11:6); yet this was in contrast with the false taste of the Corinthians. But Deissmann (*St. Paul,* p. 6) goes too far in making Paul a mere tent-maker devoid of culture. He is abrupt, paradoxical, bold, antithetical, now like a torrent, now like a summer brook; but it is passion, not ignorance nor carelessness. . . . Paul's style is unhellenic in arrangement, but in Romans 8 and 1 Cor. 13 he reaches the elevation and dignity of Plato. . . . The grammar shows little Semitic influence. . . . He is noted for his varied use of the particles and writes with freedom and accuracy, though his anacolutha are numerous, as in Gal. 2:6-9. He uses prepositions with great frequency and discrimination. The genitive is employed by Paul with every variety of application. The particle appears with great luxuriance and in all sorts of ways . . . but even in a riot of language his thought is clear, and Paul often draws a fine point on the turn of a word, or a tense, or a case. . . . He thinks in Greek, and it is the vernacular κοινή of a brilliant and well-educated man in touch with the Greek culture of his time though remaining thoroughly Jewish in his mental fibre" (pp. 128-131).

"Luke was not an artificial rhetorician nor was Paul a mere bungler. When Paul's heart was all ablaze with passion, as in 2 Cor., he did pile up participles like boulders on the mountain side, a sort of volcanic eruption (*cf.* 2 Cor. 3:8-10; 6:9*f;* 9:11*ff.*); but there is always a path through these participles. Paul would not let himself be caught in a net of mere grammatical niceties. If necessary he broke the rule and went on" (*Ibid.* p. 1136).

It is evident that even Paul, genius as he was and educated as he must have been, wrote in the common, middle-class language of his day, lifting it, however, to an unusual elevation of style and occasionally coining a new word to fit his new and noble thought. Professor Souter notes three such probable originations on the part of Paul, and Moulton notes one, "double-minded," on the part of James. The other New Testament books are undoubtedly examples of the vernacular, both in grammar, vocabulary, and style, unless it be the gospel of John. The latter contains Hebraisms and a mystic cast of thought and expression which are unusual either in the New Testament or out of it. Yet in the formal grammar the Greek is "much like the vernacular," and certain newly discovered Jewish or early Christian documents, to be mentioned later, show that its style and theological thought were not entirely unknown in the first Christian century. The vernacular, however, both in vocabulary and grammatical idioms, is "far more in evidence in the Apocalypse than in the gospel and epistle" (Robertson). It is also an interesting fact that the two New Testament authors whose Greek jars upon us most (Rev., and 2 Peter) are the very two who are called in the New Testament "ignorant and unlearned" (Acts 4: 13).

The result of the most careful study of the papyri during the last twenty years in their connection with the New Testament proves that, while a certain Semitic influence was felt by the New Testament writers, this was chiefly due to the Septuagint, since most of the grammatical forms previously supposed to be distinctly Semitic are proved by the new discoveries to have been common to the non-Jewish population of the apostolic era. Jews would undoubtedly show their Semitic "birthmarks"—which Deissmann was at first inclined to forget—especially if they were brought up in the teaching of the synagog; yet the fact remains that this Semitic influence affected the thought and spirit of their writings more largely than either the grammar, style, or vocabulary. Dr. C. C. Torrey is alone among experts in his strong statement that the spoken Greek of the first century did not "even remotely" resemble the language in which the gospels were written; but he is right, I think, in seeing a Semitic idiom underlying much of the Greek text, tho this Semitic tinge is probably due more to ancestry and the Septuagint than to any other causes named by him.[28] Nevertheless, the synoptic gospels and Paul's letters are related more closely in grammer and style to the papyri of the first and second centuries than either to the classical Greek or to the Septuagint. Many of Paul's "jumbled phrases," and the piling up of negatives by other New Testament writers (*e.g.*, Mark 5: 3; John 15: 5; Luke 23: 53; Heb. 13: 5; Rev. 18: 14, etc.) can not be ascribed any longer to Hebrew influence, but to the uncouth, unrevised vernacular which was commonly used by the common people at that era. Luke, tho a Gentile, used these supposed Semitisms almost as freely as Matthew.

Even when Mark says "Beware of the scribes" (12: 38), this must not be regarded as a Hebraism, since in a letter A.D. 41, a man counsels a friend who is in money difficulties, "Beware of the Jews!"—this evidently coming from the pen of an enemy, and being, so far as the writer knows, the first reference to this race as money-lenders in the early Christian era.

Generally speaking, the language of the New Testament, like that of the papyri, is the language of life and not of books; it is the language of nature, not of the schools. Clearness is more desired than elegance.

[28] *Studies in the History of Religions,* 1912, pp. 264-317.

There usually is no effort at rhetorical embellishment.[29] The Greek of the New Testament compares with classical Greek as the English of *Pilgrim's Progress* and *Robinson Crusoe* compares with the English of Macaulay and Browning and Emerson. It compares in style and vocabulary with the papyri as the modern magazine of the better class compares in style and vocabulary with the spoken language. This permits in the Bible writers a beautiful simplicity and an occasional sublimity of expression, never found in other papyri, while excluding the artificiality and affectation so often present in first century "classics." Instead of saying bluntly, as has been common of late, that the New Testament literature was written in the vernacular, it might be more accurate to say with Wellhausen that in the gospels the spoken Greek became literature.[30] The New Testament does not contain the vulgarities common in the papyri, but lifts this spoken language to a new dignity. No letter even from the most cultured Roman has been found equaling in beauty Paul's note written to the owner of the slave Onesimus, where the play on this man's name—"his name is Helpful and he has been helpful to me"— adds a literary charm to the peculiar Christian teaching of the missive.

It may be profitably noted that a comparison of the New Testament letters with the private correspondence of contemporaries recently discovered shows that St. Paul used the customary polite form which was universal among the middle classes at that period. There is an opening address or greeting followed by a

[29] Robertson, *op. cit.,* pp. 71-74.
[30] *Einleitung in die drei ersten Evangelien,* p. 9.

thanksgiving and prayer for the one to whom he writes, followed by the special message which is the subject of the letter, the whole being closed by salutations and perhaps a word of prayer. It is now known for the first time that this current epistolary phraseology was so common as to be almost stereotyped.

One other point in regard to New Testament style can only now be fully appreciated. The letters of the New Testament and of the papyri were usually written to dictation and therefore must be read aloud to be best appreciated.[30a] This is one reason for the vividness of the New Testament language. Paul expected his letters to "be read aloud to the brethren" (1 Thess. 5: 27), and any letter of special interest to be passed from church to church (Col. 4: 16); this was without doubt in accordance with the expectation of other religious teachers at that time. Even when a private letter was written the writer knew that if he stated anything of unusual interest the neighbors would be called in to hear it read, so that even in private correspondence an audience was in mind. At the end of a most unimportant private note just discovered, the writer, Serapion, says: "Copy my letter and give it to N. N. Do not forget it. I pray you to do it well." [31]

[30a] *Cf.* Milligan, *New Test. Documents,* p. 103.

[31] For a most interesting general discussion of the style of St. Paul and other writers of the New Testament, see further Jülicher, *Introduction to the New Testament,* pp. 49-51; and Jacquier, *The History of the Books of the New Test.,* pp. 27 *ff.*

4. New Light Upon the Vocabulary of the New Testament

Of the 5,000 words or more in the Greek New Testament about 3,000 are found in ancient Attic writers. The remainder are almost all taken from the *Koine* or popular language of the first century. Only about twenty Hebrew words appear in the New Testament, altho it has not been many years since hundreds of such words were acknowledged by scholars. These supposedly Hebrew words have been found, however, in the non-Jewish papyri and early inscriptions. A few years ago Professor Kennedy [32] found about 550 words of a form or used in a manner which he believed to be peculiar to the New Testament; but to-day Deissmann and others will admit only about fifty such words. [33] Robertson in his *Grammar of the Greek New Testament in the Light of Historical Research* (1914) gives a list of some forty words which were supposed to be "Biblical" until they were found recently in papyri, and another list of over 150 words which, tho they had been thought to possess a meaning peculiar to the Septuagint or the New Testament, have recently been found in the inscriptions or papyri. Thayer in Hastings' *Dictionary of the Bible* [34] gives some twenty-five other words common to the New Testament and the vernacular, but not found in classic Greek. This all proves convincingly that "the vocabulary of the New Testament is practically the same as that of the vernacular in the Roman empire in the first century after Christ" (Robertson).

[32] *Sources of New Testament Greek*, p. 62.
[33] *Light from the Ancient East*, p. 72.
[34] "Language of the New Testament."

Even some slang words were used by the New Testament writers in order to give force to their statements among the "common people." While this was recognized even before the new discoveries in the case of certain colloquialisms like σκύλλω "worry" (Matt. 9: 36) and ὑπωπιάζω (Luke 18: 5)—which really means "punish" in the slang of the prize-ring, as also the kindred word in 1 Cor. 9: 27, where Paul speaks of "giving it to" his body (*Expositor,* 4: 29-35)—yet the papyri have opened up a large new field where this popular phraseology can be for the first time fully appreciated.

The abbreviation of personal names, which has long been recognized in the Bible MSS., finds a constant equivalent in the newly discovered papyri, pet names being as commonly used then as now. Such examples in the New Testament occur in Tit. 3: 12, 13; Rom. 16: 7; 8, 14; Rev. 2: 13, etc. It gives a touch of life seldom connected with the New Testament writings to think of Apollos (Acts 18: 24), Epaphras (Col. 1: 7), Cleopas (Luke 24: 18), Silas (Acts 15: 22), and Luke (everywhere in Paul's letters), appearing in this familiar abbreviated form.

It must not be imagined, however, that there is nothing original in the vocabulary or content of words in the New Testament. While it is a great surprize to find that many of the supposed new words in the New Testament, such as "love-feast," "baptism," "Logos," "anathema," "presbyter," "bishop," "church" (ἐκκλησία), etc., are used in the papyri without Christian implication, showing that the names of Christian rites and church officers grew up naturally out of the existing conditions and were copied from existing forms; yet it is equally clear that many Christian terms, altho used in the papyri, receive a new technical or spiritual sense in the Biblical writings. Christianity, the greatest religious movement which ever affected civilization, produced also an effect upon language by the formation of new ideas and the modification of old ones.[34a]

The New Testament is as different from the papyri in its charm and spiritual elevation as from the ancient classics. It used the common language of its day, but it glorified and spiritualized it. Our latest and greatest New Testament grammarian gives a list of sixty-five words and phrases which, tho Greek, were the symbols of quite other than Greek ideas, having in the New Testament a totally new connotation (Robertson, *op. cit.*, p. 115). Among these the following well-known terms are conspicuous: "Charity" or "love," "holy," "sanctified," "brother," "recompense," "redemption," "damnation," "apostle," "kingdom," "baptism," "justify," "righteous," "peace," "the Church," "elect," "hope," "converted," "gospel," "life," "death," "liberty," "priest," "the called," "atonement," "the world," "fellowship," "ransom," "repentance," "the Way," "comforter," "faith," "to believe," "the Spirit," "spiritual," "stumbling-block," "the flesh," "the cross," "conscience," "salvation," "Savior," "humility," "Son of God," "Son of Man," "adoption," "grace," "natural" (*vs.* "spiritual"), etc. To this list others might be added such as the "Word," "minister," "the parousia," "mystery," "eucharist," etc., representing either new words or old words with a new meaning when found in the New Testament. It has been well said that these

---

[34a] So even Deissmann states, *Ency. Bib.*, article "Papyri."

words with their new meanings contain in large part "the history of Christianity."

No one, unless he has had the same experience, can even imagine the excitement which comes to the student who, when looking over a mass of blurred and broken papyri, suddenly catches sight of some well-known Biblical term. Such excitement came to the writer not an hour ago, when as he examined certain ancient scraps which he had recently obtained in the Fayum and which likely no one had ever glanced at before except the fellaheen, he caught sight of the word μισθόν ("wages"). This word is found three times repeated by Jesus in the phrase "they have their reward" (Matt. 6: 2, 5, 16). Now the verb (ἀπέχω), used here in connection with this term, is found scores of times in the papyri in the sense of "receipt in full." It is a technical expression which Deissmann first recognized as giving a new and most vivid meaning to the words of Jesus. He was speaking of the long prayers which the Pharisees made on the corners of the streets "to be seen of man," and with quiet irony he says of them: "Verily they have received in full their reward"—that is, they need not expect any answer to their prayers from God, since they pray to be seen of men. They have "received in full" the answer to their prayer when men look at them as they pray! Paul also uses this verb in the same sense (Phil. 4: 18), saying: "I give you a receipt in full for all things" and "abound" because of your kindness.

Another instance in which the new light cast upon the exact local meaning of a word has made more vivid the New Testament text can be found in the reference to Jesus Christ as having been openly "set

forth" as crucified before the Galatians (Gal. 3: 1);
for in one papyrus a father uses this same term (προ-
γραφῆναι) when he speaks of having "placarded" or
caused a notice "to be posted up," declaring that he
would no longer be responsible for his son's debts seeing he had squandered his own goods in "riotous living." [35]

Another term long ago explained by Professor
Mahaffy,[36] but recently illustrated by the papyri, which
gives a new and important meaning to a Scripture passage is παιδαγωγός, translated "school-master" (Gal.
3: 24). This well-known individual was not the head
master, but at best an inferior instructor, often being
merely a faithful slave whose chief duty was to bring
his master's sons safely to and from school, guarding
them from mischief on the way. When St. Paul said
the "law was the pedagog" to lead us to Christ, it was
Christ of whom he thought as the true "teacher," the
Old Testament law being only the Father's trusty
servant to bring the world to him. Multitudes of such
suggestions of a more vivid meaning in the original
Bible terms might be mentioned, as for example, when
we find St. Paul counting up the honors and hopes of
his youth and declaring that he counted all these things
which he had given up to be "loss" for Christ (Phil.
3: 8). How it strengthens this expression when we
find that a papyrus uses this same word (ζημία) for
the bones thrown out on the street to the dogs!

Another important term (μυστήριον) which occurs
a score of times in the New Testament meets us often
in the papyri. Jesus speaks of "the mystery of the

---

[35] The word used is ἀσωτευόμενος, corresponding exactly to that used
in Luke 15: 13.
[36] *Greek Education*, p. 29.

kingdom of God" (Mark 4: 11), and Paul again and again of "the mystery which was kept secret," "the wisdom of God in a mystery" (*e.g.*, Rom. 16: 25; 1 Cor. 2: 7). We usually think of a mystery as something hidden; but in the New Testament it means something revealed. It had been "kept secret" and was still hidden to the world in general; but this mystery of God's nature and God's will had now been "made known" (Eph. 3: 3; 6: 19). The full meaning of these expressions can hardly be understood unless we bear in mind that the best religious force in the first century was found in the mystery cults, which sought to bring the ancient world out of its materialism and debauchery into a serious consideration of these "mysteries" of God—the unity of the worshiper with deity; salvation and the future life. These matters were absolutely dark to the pagan world in general; but they were supposed to be revealed to the "initiated." Paul again and again uses symbols and terms connected with these mystic rites. He does not, of course, accept the doctrine of these heathen fraternities; but he represents the Christian Church as being also a mystery-fraternity in which the profoundest secrets of God are made plain to the initiated through the revelation of the head master, Jesus; and the terminology which he uses was a mystic terminology which the new discoveries have found in the contemporary mystery documents, the meaning of which would be easily grasped, therefore, by his hearers and readers, most of whom were accustomed to them. It is to be noted that ten of the twenty-six times in which this word "mystery" is used in the New Testament, it is found in Ephesians and Colossians. These mysteries encour-

aged purification by lustration, a "new birth," and sacramental communion with the deity.   Gold tablets
found in tombs in widely separated districts show the
same aspiration on the part of these devotees:

"I am the son of earth and heaven . . . I came
from the pure . . . I have paid the penalty of unright-
eousness . . . I have flown out of the weary, sorrowful circle of life. . . . Oh, blessed and happy are those
who have put off their mortality and become divine."

Notwithstanding recent criticisms,[37] the researches
of Reitzenstein,[38] with the enormous mass of documents which he produces, must be accepted as conclusively proving the close relation between the Pauline
and mystery vocabularies.   St. Paul was sensible
enough to use with discretion this point of contact with
the Greek people who had grown up in the atmosphere
of these mystic cults, the nature and process of the
salvation through Jesus the Christ being put in striking contrast with that proclaimed by the Isis or Mithra
mystics.   He used the current religious vocabulary to
teach a new doctrine.   Salvation and immortality is not
reached by magic or ritual or deification; but by regeneration of the spirit and unity, not with a mythical
personage, but with the living Christ, this "new birth"
leading on to a new life of holiness utterly unknown,
so far as the evidence shows, to initiates of any other
religion.[39]

Some striking illustrations of New Testament
usages have come from the papyri, thus approving
translations of the New Testament texts which previously had been doubtful.   Thus in 1 Cor. 16:1. a

[37] E.g., Kennedy, St. Paul and the Mystery Religions, 1913.
[38] Die hellenistischen Mysterienreligionen, 1910.
[39] See this point well stated by Kennedy, op. cit., pp. 211-218, 280-299.

unique Greek word (λογεία) was translated "collection"; this same word has recently been found with the same meaning in some papyri. So also another word (ἐλλογάω) used by St. Paul when he bids Philemon "put down to his account" any loss he may have suffered at the hands of Onesimus (verse 18), has been found in several papyri with exactly the same meaning. When Paul speaks of those who are "unsettling" his converts (Gal. 5: 12) he uses a word very common in the papyri, where a man who is being driven to the wall in money matters pleads with a creditor, "Do not upset me"; and in another case a mother complains of her naughty boy, "He is upsetting me!" (cf. Acts 17: 6). An even more impressive illustration of the new meaning given by the papyri to New Testament expressions may be found, Mark 6: 8, where Jesus sent out his apostles telling them to take "no bread, no wallet, no money." The wallet mentioned is now seen not to have been a mere traveling bag, as was formerly supposed, but almost certainly a beggar's "collecting bag," such as peripatetic religious teachers were accustomed to carry at that time, for it is called by this same name (πήρα). Our Lord means to teach that his disciples are to go out as laymen not in any special ministerial garb or making any special claim of mendicant piety, but nevertheless dependent for their living upon those who "receive" the word.[40]

Deissmann, after a careful study of the papyri, shows the depth and originality of the term "in Christ Jesus" as used by Paul. Here we find the mystic indwelling of God in man unmistakably and constantly

[40] For very many of the above suggestions I am indebted to Deissmann, as also for those which immediately follow. See *Light from the Ancient East*, chapters ii. and iv.

declared in a sense utterly inscrutable to the heathen.

The title "Lord" as given to Jesus is also now seen from the papyri to have had a deeper meaning than we had ever supposed. The fact that the Emperors, when they became deified, as began to be common in the first century, were addrest as "God," "Son of God," "Lord," "Saviour of the world," etc., gives a new point to the common use of these titles for Jesus. For the first time we possess a new argument for the deity of Jesus Christ, since the title Κύριος "Lord" could be used only after the Cæsar had been acknowledged as God. We now see that the term Κύριος, Ιησοῦς (Lord Jesus) was a distinct ascription of deity to Christ, and that its use must almost have been accounted an act of direct antagonism to the claims of the Roman Emperor. Indeed, the exact phrase by which deity was ascribed to Jesus—"Great God and Saviour" (Tit. 2:13; 2 Peter 1:1)—appears letter for letter in an inscription 2 B.C., in which the Emperor is given this title; tho of course the difference in meaning as read by a Christian and by a heathen was heaven high. It must not be forgotten in this connection that ὁ Κύριος is constantly used in the Septuagint as a title of God.

St. Paul's confession of our "Lord" Jesus Christ, like the complemental thought that the worshipers were "slaves" of the Lord, was understood in its full meaning by everybody in the Hellenistic East. This becomes still clearer if we compare, for instance, St. Paul's expression, "the table of the Lord" (1 Cor. 10:21), with the analogous Egyptian expression concerning their chief deity, "the table of the Lord Serapis," recently discovered in a papyrus. So when a number of

papyri and ostraca recently discovered speak of Nero as
"the Lord," this is exactly synonymous with the inscriptions calling him "the God." This is the reason St. Paul
insists that Jesus Christ is "our only Master and Lord"
(1 Cor. 8: 5, 6). No one can confess Jesus Christ as
"Lord" (Κύριος), but by the Holy Ghost (1 Cor.
12: 3); yet every tongue shall "confess that Jesus
Christ is Lord" (Phil. 2: 9, 11). This claim of deity
wrapt up in the word explains why Polycarp went
to martyrdom rather than to say "Lord Cæsar." [41]

All of this, as Deissmann shows, throws a brilliant
light upon the adjective, "the Lord's," that is, "belonging to the Lord" (κυριακός), as used in the New Testament. So ordinarily used, the "Lord's Day" meant
"Emperor's day." So "Christian" (Χριστιανός) meant
originally an imperial slave (Deissmann), or soldier
(Souter), belonging to the divine Christ, just as
"Cæsarian" (Καισαριανός) meant slave or soldier of
the Cæsar. In the same way "freedman of the Lord"
(1 Cor. 7: 22) corresponds to "freedman of the emperor" (cf. John 15: 14), and the phrases so common
with the early Christians, "friend of Christ" and "acquainted with God," correspond exactly to the words
in the inscriptions "friend of the Emperor" and "acquainted with the Emperor." So the Biblical word
used for the ransomed sinner is used for manumitted
slaves. This manumission was always accompanied
by the blood of sacrifice (the law allowed slavery for
debts); therefore remission of debts was "blotting out
of the bond" (Col. 2: 14), and this was accomplished

---

[41] See Deissmann, *op. cit.*, pp. 355, 360; *cf.* Moulton, *Prolegomena*, p. 84*ff*;
Robertson, *Grammar*, p. 786; J. Weiss, *Urchristenthum*, p. 330*ff*; Case,
Evolution of Early Christianity, pp. 109-116; 195-239.

in the first century by marking a cross over the writing (Deissmann, *op. cit.,* pp. 332, 337).

This is only a hint of what the papyri have done for us in giving new shades of meaning to New Testament language. To be sure, many of the proper names and technical terms used in the New Testament are Semitic, and a number of words common in the gospels, but rare in the papyri, were evidently derived directly from the Septuagint; yet as we turn the pages of Moulton and Milligan's *Vocabulary of the Greek Testament* (Parts I and II, 1914-1916), there is not a leaf which does not show some new light from the papyri on some well-known Biblical word. For example, selecting instances quite at random, Jesus is said not merely to have been "slain" but actually "murdered" (Acts 10: 39) ; the men who raised a riot against Silas and Paul at Thessalonica (Acts 17: 5) were not merely lewd fellows of the baser sort, but "market-place agitators"; Peter and John (Acts 4: 13), and Jesus also (John 7: 15), were actually declared by their calumniators (according to the common meaning of the word) to be unable to write; John Baptist was not counted worthy to "take off" his Master's sandals (Matt. 3: 11) ; Paul was not only beaten "uncondemned" but also "untried" (Acts 16: 37; 22: 25) ; he is called not simply an architect, but rather "chief engineer" (1 Cor. 3: 10) ; Mnason was not an "aged" disciple, but an "original" disciple (Acts 21: 16) ; Jesus is not called the "captain" but the "originator" of our salvation (Heb. 2: 10) ; God is not an "austere" but an "exacting" employer (Luke 19: 21) ; Judas not only "bare" but "bare off" (*i.e.,* stole) the "bag"—*i.e.,* as the papyri show, the "money bag" (John 12: 6) ; Jesus is set forth as an "example" in the sense of "sample" or "pattern" (Jude 7); Paul's prayers (Phil. 1:4) become "strong entreaties"; "doubting" (1 Tim. 2:8) becomes "debating"; "I have kept the faith" (2 Tim. 4:7) is changed to the very strong statement, "I have guarded my trust"; while the apostle's "thorn" in the flesh becomes a "stake"; tho the "beam" in the eye of the Pharisaic critic (Matt. 7:3) now becomes the less dangerous but more irritating "splinter."

These changes may seem small, but they are not inconsequential if they actually give more perfectly the sense of the inspired Word; and there are many other changes more significant, *e.g.,* the "immutability" of God's counsel (Heb. 6:17) gains strength when we notice that the word used is the technical term common in wills which could not be altered; our "calling and election" is made "legally secure" (2 Peter 1:10); and the word spoken to angels is "guaranteed" to us (Heb. 2:2); the "fruits of the earth" (Matt. 26:29; Mark 14:25), the orthography of which was universally accepted as a blunder of the New Testament manuscripts, is now attested by a multitude of papyri; while the injunction, "Let him have thy cloak also" (Matt. 5:40), gets a new force when we find a pawnbroker disposing of one of these outer garments for 2,700 drachmae of copper; Thomas Didymus "the twin" (John 11:16) appears to us in a new light when we notice the custom of naming boys "twin" with direct reference to Castor and Pollux, the patron saints of heathen sailors in the first century of our era; while the scornful reference of our Lord to the "vain repetitions" (the "blather") of the praying hypocrites (Matt. 6:7), becomes more marked when we notice that this very

Greek root occurs in the sneering nickname of Demosthenes as the "babbler" (βάτταλος).

This list could be immeasurably increased, but perhaps we have given a sufficient number of instances to illustrate the value of the papyri in illuminating the New Testament vocabulary. Many others will appear later in the course of the discussion.[42]

[42] Greek students who may not feel able to purchase the incomparable "Vocabulary" of Moulton and Milligan (Hodder & Stoughton, 1914, *ff.*), with its detailed references to the papyri, will find it much to their advantage to obtain Prof. Alex. Souter's little *Pocket Lexicon* (Oxford, Clarendon Press, 1916), which constantly makes use of the new knowledge.

III

ANCIENT NEW TESTAMENTS RECENTLY DISCOVERED

1. Greek New Testaments

THE writer was working in London University when the first sensational discovery was made of a leaf from a pocket Bible which had been carried by an Egyptian Christian of the third century. This leaf was a hundred years older than any other fragment of Scripture previously known. It was written on poor papyrus in a fairly good hand and well represented the New Testaments which were being used by poor men in the days of the martyrs. The book must originally have been composed of twenty-four or twenty-five sheets of papyrus.

Only those who have come personally into close touch with supremely important discoveries can understand with what eagerness this discolored leaf was examined by every one interested in the authenticity of the New Testament writings. It had been written generations before the great council of Constantine—was it the same Biblical text as that which in uninterrupted succession continued to be used from the fourth century onward? The whole tone of modern New Testament criticism was changed for the better when it was found that, with the exception of a slightly different spelling of three proper names, David, Zerah, and Amminadab, and the omission of two articles before proper names, this oldest extant manuscript of the New Testament agreed exactly with the Westcott and Hort Greek text which formed the basis of our Revised Version—having even the same abbreviations and one wrongly placed rough breathing. It looked as if the Church of the martyrs possest the same New Testament as our fathers revered.

(1) ANCIENT NEW TESTAMENTS PREVIOUSLY KNOWN

Previous to this discovery the oldest Greek manuscripts known to be in existence were those now to be described.

Codex Sinaiticus.

It was just fifty-two years before this discovery at Oxyrhynchus that Dr. Constantine Tischendorf discovered in the Convent of St. Catharine at Mt. Sinai this most famous of all manuscripts. The discovery as he himself told it was most picturesque:

"I perceived in the middle of the great hall a large and wide basket full of old parchments; and the librarian who was a man of information told me that two heaps of papers like this mouldered by time had been already committed to the flames. What was my surprise to find amid this heap of papers a considerable number of sheets of a copy of the Old Testament in Greek which seemed to me to be one of the most ancient I had ever seen. The authorities of the Convent allowed me to possess myself of a third of these parchments or about 45 sheets all the more readily as they were destined for the fire. But I could not get them to yield up possession of the remainder." [1]

In 1853 a second journey was made, but no further traces of the treasure of 1844 was found. But on Feb. 7, 1859, having again reached the convent through the favor of the Emperor of Russia, he was shown a bulky volume wrapt in a red cloth.

[1] *Narrative of the Discovery of the Sinaitic Manuscript,* 1866, p. 28.

"I unrolled the cover and discovered to my surprise not only those very fragments which fifteen years before I had taken out of the basket, but also other parts of the Old Testament, the New Testament complete and in addition the Epistle of Barnabas and a part of the 'Pastor of Hermas.' . . . I knew that I held in my hands the most precious Biblical treasure in existence, a document whose age and importance exceeded that of all the manuscripts which I had ever examined during twenty years of study of the subject. . . . On the 27th of September I returned to Cairo. The monks and archbishops then warmly expressed their thanks for my jealous efforts in their cause and the following day I received from them, under the form of a loan, the Sinaitic Bible to carry to St. Petersburg and there to have it copied as accurately as possible. I set out for Egypt early in October and on the 19th of November I presented to their Imperial Majesties in the Winter Palace at Tsarkoe-Selo my rich collection of old Greek, Syriac, Coptic, Arabic, and other manuscripts in the middle of which the Sinaitic Bible shone like a crown."[2]

Dr. Tischendorf well considered this discovery greater than that of the "koh-i-noor of the Queen of England." The manuscript still remains as, perhaps, the greatest Biblical treasure of Europe; tho the present writer can testify that the monks at Mt. Sinai have no words too bitter for the man who carried it off. It should be remembered, however, that the Czar in 1869 sent to the monks of St. Catharine 7,000 rubles and various decorations in return for this manuscript, and no written protest against this settlement is known to exist.

This most important manuscript is accepted by all competent authorities as dating from the fourth century and is practically complete. It can now be examined by scholars in a photographic edition taken in St. Petersburg in 1908 by Helen and Kirsopp Lake with the help of Dr. Kenyon, Dr. Hunt, etc. It is a

[2] *Ibid.*, pp. 29-35, 40.

vellum manuscript written in four columns, forty-eight lines to each page. It contained originally the entire Bible, and the New Testament is still complete. Some time between the fifth and seventh century after Christ the manuscript lay in the library at Cæsarea, which was one of the three great libraries of the Christian world as early as the third century, the other two being at Jerusalem and Alexandria. This library was famous in the day of Eusebius and was used by St. Jerome (b. A.D. 345), who said that the original Biblical papyri preserved here were wearing out in his time and were being recopied in parchment. This library was probably destroyed by the Arabs A.D. 630, and it is very likely that this precious manuscript was at that time carried from Cæsarea to Mt. Sinai by refugees. It was not written by the same scribe as wrote the Codex Vaticanus, tho they probably belonged to the same *scriptorium*; neither was it one of Constantine's copies made for Constantinople. It is possible that it was originally written at Cæsarea, tho it is almost certain that it came from Egypt, probably Alexandria; its date is between A.D. 340-367, the earlier year being the more probable date.[3] The manuscript is a fine parchment made from the skin of some rather large animal, perhaps an antelope as Tischendorf suggested. The original text was written by three or four scribes, a few notes and corrections being made later.

Codex Vaticanus.

An uncial manuscript of the fourth century, being practically of the same age as the Codex Sinaiticus, tho it is now generally held by textual critics to be a

[3] *Codex Sinaiticus,* by Helen and Kirsopp Lake, 1911, p. xv.

little older.[4] It originally contained the whole Bible, but is now lacking in the Old Testament, Gen. 1-46, Ps. 105-137, and in the New Testament, Heb. 9: 14 to end; 1 and 2 Timothy; Titus; Philemon and Revelation. It was written by three scribes, the text being corrected by two, one of these being a contemporary of the original writer, and the other of the tenth or eleventh century. The latter probably re-inked the manuscript, unless this was done by a monk of the fifteenth century. It is first mentioned in the catalog of the Vatican in 1481. Pope Sixtus V made it the basis of an edition of the Greek Old Testament in 1580, thereby determining the "received text" of that portion of the Bible. Tho used by Rome it was not published to scholars until 1828-38 (5 vols.), and then very inaccurately. A better edition followed (1868-81), and new phototypic editions were published 1889-90, 1905.

The manuscript is of parchment, three columns on each page, and much resembles Codex Alexandrinus in its form. It was reckoned as the chief authority among MSS. for the Greek Testament of Westcott and Hort. It is the best example of the so-called "Neutral" text, except in the Pauline epistles, where it has a strong "Western" element.

Codex Alexandrinus.

This is another most famous New Testament manuscript. It contains almost the entire Bible and at the foot of the first page of Genesis is a note written in Arabic:

"Made an inalienable gift to the Patriarchal Cell in the City of Alexandria. Whosoever shall remove it thence shall be accursed and cut off. Written by Athanasius the humble."

[4] Kenyon, *Handbook*, 1912, p. 77.

AUGUSTUS 27 B.C.	NERO A.D. 54	VESPASIAN A.D. 69
TITUS A.D. 79	DOMITIAN A.D. 81	TRAJAN A.D. 98
HADRIAN A.D. 138	MARCUS AURELIUS A.D. 161	CONSTANTINE A.D. 311

ROMAN EMPERORS

Busts more or less recently discovered, of some Roman Emperors who were in some way vitally connected with the development of early Christianity

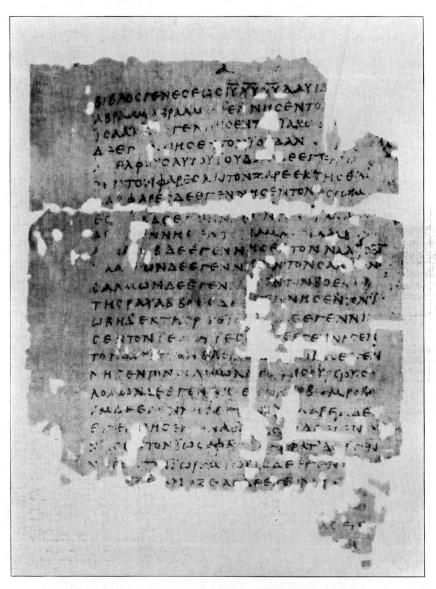

LEAF FROM ST. MATTHEW'S GOSPEL (THIRD CENTURY)

From "The Oxyrhynchus Papyri," Part I, Plate 1.   (Egypt Exploration Fund)

This "humble" scribe was probably the Melchite patriarch who died A.D. 1308. Another note in Arabic of the thirteenth or fourteenth century, written back of the Table of Books, records the fact that the manuscript was written by the martyr Thecla, but this is probably inaccurate.

The manuscript is on very fine vellum and consists of 773 leaves, measuring 12⅞ x 10 inches. The text is written in double columns and the opening lines of each book and also the titles of the Psalms are written in red. The first letter of each paragraph is enlarged and stands in the margin. Some of the Greek letters have Egyptian forms; quotations are marked with an arrow-head in the margin. There are numerous corrections generally written over erasures, but single letters are struck out with the pen or marked for omission "with a fine oblique stroke resembling an acute accent." No accents or breathings occurred in the original text, tho some were added later.[5]

This manuscript is an uncial not later than the "middle or end of the fifth century" (Nestle). It originally contained the whole of the Old and New Testaments, including the Psalms of Solomon in the former and 1 and 2 Clement in the latter; but it has suffered mutilation in a few places, the beginning of Matthew's gospel being absent (chaps. 1-24); and also John 6: 50, 8: 52; 2 Cor. 4: 13, 12: 7. We shall not describe it further as the new discoveries do not require it, since the codex came to Europe early in the seventeenth century. It represents essentially the text of the King James version.

[5] *Facsimile of the Codex Alexandrinus,* 4 vols., pub. by British Museum 1881, with critical introduction by E. Maude Thompson Most of the above statements were taken from this work.

Codex Bezae (Cantabrigiensis).

This manuscript is not later than the sixth century and perhaps considerably earlier. It is a Greek-Latin manuscript of the New Testament containing 409 leaves, and represents the oldest and best form of the Western text. It was presented to the University of Cambridge by Calvin's friend, Theodore Beza, in 1581, having been obtained by him after the sack of Lyons in 1562. Its early history is doubtful. It never contained the Old Testament, but contains the Four Gospels with a few lacunæ, the Acts, and the concluding verses (in Latin) of 3 John. At least nine later hands worked upon it. It is unique among the Biblical manuscripts. It alone contains the incident of the man working in the field on the Sabbath day (following Luke 6: 4), to whom Jesus said: "Oh man, if thou knowest what thou doest, blessed are thou; but if thou knowest not, thou art cursed and a transgressor of the law." It alone renders Luke 11: 2, "When you pray use not vain repetitions as the 'others' (λοιποί) do"; and it also stands alone in a number of other readings and in certain omissions (*e.g.*, Luke 22: 20; 24: 12, 36, 40, 51). The text of this manuscript differs widely from any other Greek manuscript, but finds affinities with the Old Syriac and the Old Latin versions. The variations in the text of the Acts are so frequent that these have given rise to the theory that this represents a different edition of the book issued by St. Luke himself (F. Blass, Nestle, Salmon); but such a theory would not account for similar variants of the Western text in other Bible books.[6] Sir F. G. Kenyon believes that this and other Western texts represent private rather

[6] See Kenyon, *Handbook*, pp. 79, 301.

than church copies of the Bible, and were, therefore, written less scrupulously. It was written in two languages, because near Byzantium where it, like other Greek-Latin texts, probably originated, the inhabitants spoke Latin, while the invaders spoke Greek. A bilingual Bible was, therefore, a necessity for church services.[7] Hoskier and others rank this text above either the Sinaiticus or the Vatican Codex.[7a]

Such were all the oldest New Testament MSS. of the first class known in the world up to the end of the nineteenth century. Among particularly valuable New Testament manuscripts of the second class known previously to 1896 might be mentioned the *Codex Claromontanus* for the Pauline epistles; the *Codex Laudianus* for Acts; the *Codex Dublinensis* for Matthew's gospel; the *Codex Nitriensis* for Luke's gospel, all of which were of the sixth century. Perhaps particularly interesting to most readers would be the four silver lettered purple manuscripts of the Four Gospels, all made after the pattern of Codex Nitriensis, the first of which was found in 1879, and the last in 1896, when 182 leaves of these beautiful MSS. came to light. .

(2) NEWLY DISCOVERED FRAGMENTS OF ANCIENT NEW TESTAMENTS (4TH-5TH CENTURIES) WRITTEN UPON SKINS AND CATALOGUED BY GREGORY

In 1909 Dr. Caspar René Gregory, a celebrated scholar born in America, but since 1889 a professor in the University of Leipzig,[7b] catalogued all the known

[7] See the illuminating statement by Alex. Souter in *Journal Theol. Studies,* 6: 240*ff*.

[7a] *Codex B. and its Allies,* H. C. Hoskier, 1914.

[7b] He was killed in the Great War on April 9, 1917.

manuscripts of the New Testament in all lands. Among these, if I count correctly, he listed between thirty-five and forty fragments of parchment and vellum New Testaments dating from the fourth to the sixth century, inclusive; at least sixteen or seventeen of these representing discoveries which had been made within less than twenty years of the publication of his great work.[8] We will now give the most important of these newly discovered texts, listed by Gregory.

Matthew 1:21; 2:2 (5th or 6th Century)—This text, which was first published by Grenfell and Hunt (*Oxyrhynchus Papyri*, III, No. 401), contains the account of the virgin birth of Jesus and the visit of the Magi. It is a leaf from a vellum book, written in very small characters. A letter is occasionally inserted by mistake and in one case an omitted letter is placed above the line (2:2); but on the whole it is well written and agrees with the regular text.

Matthew 6:5, 6, 8, 9, 13-15 (4th Century)—This was first published in 1901 and gives us the beginning and end of the Lord's Prayer.

Matthew 7:7, 22; 11:5, 12, 13; 7:47, 54; 14:4, 13, 20; 15:11, 16, 18; 17:2, 24; 18:4, 9; 19:3, 10, 17, 25; 20:9; 21:5, 12; 22:7, 15, 24, 32; 23:35; 24:3, 12, 16, 30 (6th Century)—This is a beautiful purple, gold-letter manuscript of forty-three leaves, which was found in 1899 at Sinob. The original text contained pictures of Herodias asking for the head of John the Baptist, the feeding of the five thousand, and also of the four thousand, the healing of the blind man at Jericho, and the cursing of the fig tree. The text, without the pictures, is given by Gregory with critical notes.

Matthew 18:18, 19, 22, 23, 26, 28, 29 (4th or 5th Century)—This text has recently been published by Wessely.[9] It is a much broken parchment leaf of thirty-six lines, beautifully written in narrow columns. There is one misspelled word to which an observant reader has called attention by writing

[8] *Textkritik des Neuen Testaments*, Dritter Band, 1909.
[9] *Griechische und koptische Texte, Inhalt*, III, 89, text 24.

"sic" in the margin. The passage contains a portion of the parable of the man who owed 10,000 talents; and some notable expressions stand out in the text, "Whatsoever things ye shall bind on earth shall be bound in heaven"; "if two of you shall agree . . . it shall be done for them," etc.

Mark 6:28, 29; Luke 2:1, 8 (4th or 5th Century)—This text was brought to light in 1899. It tells of the burial of John the Baptist and the birth of Jesus.

Mark 6:30b—41 (6th Century)—This is a vellum fragment recorded by Deissmann in *Die Septuaginta-Papyri und andere altchristliche Fragmente* (Heidelberg, 1905). The eleven verses preserved are marked by thirty variations from the *Textus receptus,* in many of which the fragment agrees with the Westcott and Hort text.[9a]

Mark 15:29-33-38 (4th Century)—Gregory gives this entire text with critical notes (*op. cit.,* pp. 73-74), and it has been re-edited by Wessely in a very beautiful manner (*op. cit.,* III, No. 186, text 21). It is a parchment leaf excellently preserved and written on both sides. It contains only five verses to a page, so that it must have represented a very small "Diamond Edition" of the New Testament. The word "cross" is so abbreviated as to make the cross literally appear in the word itself, and this has been done also in writing the word "crucifixion." The most curious and interesting reading is the expression put upon the lips of the priests who mocked Jesus: "He saved others; he *can* save himself." Was the "not" omitted from the last phrase through mistake or because of the reverence of the scribe?

Mark 10:50, 51; 11:11, 12 (5th or 6th Century)—A leaf from a vellum book now preserved in the Chicago University. It agrees with the ordinary Greek text and has no peculiarity deserving of attention. It tells of the blind man who, casting away his garment, came to Jesus and was healed; and of our Lord's visit to Bethany.

Luke 12: 15; 13:32; John 8:33, 42 (5th Century)—This text is of little importance excepting as it represents a volume

[9a] I am indebted to Prof. Wallace N. Stearns, Fargo College, Fargo, N. Dak., for this reference.

in which the four gospels were bound together with Coptic and Sahidic translations. It closes with the verse in which Jesus declares, "I proceeded and came from God, neither have I come of myself, but he sent me."

John 2:11-22 (4th Century)—First published in *Oxyrhynchus Papyri,* VI, No. 847. It is a vellum leaf practically entire, containing a dozen verses in a text more closely resembling that of the Vatican than of the Sinaiticus. It mentions the "manifestation of his glory" at Cana of Galilee, and then describes the equally glorious act of the Messiah in driving out the money-changers from the worshiping place of the Gentiles in the temple.

Acts 2:11, 12, 13, 14, 16, 17, 20 (5th or 6th Century)—This important text, first published in 1900 (*Amherst Papyri*), is given in full by Gregory with critical notes. It deals with the outpouring of the Holy Spirit upon the day of Pentecost.

Acts 3:24—4:13, 17-20 (4th Century)—This text preserved in Berlin, gives the end of Peter's speech at Pentecost and describes the consternation of the rulers at the "boldness" of these "unlearned and ignorant" men.

Acts 13:28-31 (5th Century)—First appeared in 1894 in *Studia Sinaitica.* It gives a few words from Paul's speech at Antioch, where he refers to the death and burial of Jesus, tho Pilate had "found no cause of death in him."

Acts 24:22-26, 27; 1 Peter 2:22—3:7 (6th Century)—This text was first published by Charles Taylor in his *Genizeh Palimpsests,* in 1900. It represents fragments taken from a volume which contained, probably, the entire New Testament. The first quotation represents a portion of Paul's speech before Felix; the second begins with Peter's statement concerning Christ, "who did no sin, neither was guile found in his mouth," and who "his own self bore our sins in his body on the tree."

Acts 28:30—31:1a (late 5th Century)—A vellum fragment listed by Deissmann in *Die Septuaginta Papyri.* It shows a few minor unimportant variants.[9b]

[9b] I am indebted to Professor Stearns for this reference.

Revelation 16: 17-20 (5th Century)—Published in *Oxyrhyn-chus Papyri*, VI, No. 848. It is a leaf from a vellum book of remarkably small size, the written surface being only four inches in height. The text agrees most closely with the Codex Alexandrinus. It contains a description of the pouring forth of the seventh bowl of God's wrath upon the earth.

Dr. Gregory catalogued and briefly criticized the newly found *Washington Codex,* to be mentioned later, and gave a list of a dozen papyri dating from the third to the sixth century, which list is the basis of later catalogs. The study of the New Testament has been splendidly advanced by this notable work.[10]

(3) RECENTLY DISCOVERED PORTIONS OF NEW TESTA-MENTS (3RD-4TH CENTURIES) WRITTEN
UPON PAPYRUS AND CATALOGUED BY
GREGORY AND KENYON

The startling discovery in 1897 of a leaf from a papyrus New Testament over sixteen hundred years old (see above) was followed very rapidly by others, until Sir F. G. Kenyon, of the British Museum, in his *Hand-book to the Textual Criticism of the New Testament* (1912), and Dr. George Milligan, of the University of Glasgow, in his *New Testament Documents* (1913), could add eight more to the list given by Gregory (1909), thus cataloging and describing some fifteen leaves from twelve or thirteen different papyrus Bibles or lectionaries which were being used by the early Christians from the third to the sixth century, and seven or eight fragments from rolls of Scripture

[10] Gregory's numbers for the texts referred to above are: O71, O152, O23, Tt, Evl. 1043, O149, Tu, O69, Twoi, O162, O76, O165, O77, O93, O163. There are several others among Gregory's texts which probably were discovered as early as those recorded above; but the writer has not been able to find proof of this.

equally early. We give below this remarkable list, merely classifying the texts differently, and adding comments of our own.

ANCIENT PAPYRUS NEW TESTAMENTS CATALOGUED BY
SIR F. G. KENYON [11]

Fragments of Ancient Papyrus Books Containing Portions of St. Matthew's Gospel.

Matt. 1: 1-9, 12, 14-20 (3d Century)—This is the leaf from a papyrus book referred to above. It is written in capital letters (uncials). When discovered it was the "oldest known manuscript of any part of the New Testament." In a very clear way it supports the Eastern text represented by Westcott and Hort's Greek Testament. It gives the genealogy and birth of Jesus.

Matt. 10: 32-37a, 39-42; 11: 1-5 (5th Century)—This gives us probably the oldest authority for reading αὐτόν (10: 32). It contains the great discourse of Jesus in which he says, "He that loveth father or mother more than me is not worthy of me," and "He that doth not take his cross and follow after me is not worthy of me."

Fragments of Ancient Papyrus Books Containing Portions of St. Luke's Gospel.

Luke 1: 74-80; 5: 3-8; 5: 30—6: 4 (4th Century)—Here in the midst of the broken text one can still see standing out in characters written over 1,500 years ago the eternal message "I am not come to call the righteous but sinners to repentance."

Luke 7: 36-44; 10: 38-42 (6th Century)—This is written in a cursive hand and tells of the Mary who hath "chosen the good part," and of the woman that was a sinner who broke the box of ointment over our Lord and ceased not to kiss his feet.[12]

[11] Based on Gregory's list given *Die griechischen Handschriften des Neuen Test.* (1908), pp. 45-47, and *Textkritik des Neuen Test.* (1900-1909), III., pp. 1084-1092.

[12] Both this and the text above are catalogued by Gregory as *Liturgies* (Nos. 943, 348), rather than leaves of New Testaments.

*Fragments of Ancient Papyrus Books Containing Portions of
St. John's Gospel.*

John 1 : 23-31, 33-41 ; 20 : 11-17, 19-25 (3d or 4th Century)—
This is a long and very important text which agrees generally
with the Codex Sinaiticus and in several instances supports it
with readings not found elsewhere. This leaf from one of
the most ancient fragments of the New Testament in existence contains the testimony of John the Baptist to Jesus, and
here in plain Greek, as it was written over 1,500 years ago, we
can read the world-shaking announcement concerning the
Lamb of God "that taketh away the sin of the world," and
also the narrative of the resurrection of Jesus.

John 12 : 12-15 (5th or 6th Century)—This text the writer
has not seen and does not know whether it is a roll or a leaf.
At any rate it contains the passage which reads : "Hosannah!
. . . . . the king cometh."

John 3 : 14-18, 31, 32 (6th Century)—These texts are written
on fragments of two leaves of a papyrus book which com-
menced with St. John's gospel. Tho left undated by Sir
F. G. Kenyon, it is probably to be dated to the sixth century
(see *Publicazioni della societa Italiana—Pap. greci.* V. 1,
No. 3). In verse 18 "in the name" (of the only begotten
Son of God) is twice repeated probably by a copyist's error,
and the last half of verse 31 is wanting. But these slight
scribal errors are forgotten when one sees the statement,
"for God so loved the world that he gave his only begotten
Son," etc.

*Fragment of an Ancient Papyrus Book Containing a Portion of
the Acts of the Apostles.*

Acts 4 : 31-37; 5 : 2-9; 6 : 1-6, 8-15 (4th Century)—This is
one of the most important and one of the best preserved of all
the texts given by Drs. Milligan and Kenyon, showing no
break excepting an occasional word at the end of a line.
It was found in 1903 and represents two good leaves from
one of the most ancient New Testaments in existence. It
begins with the statement that the disciples were "all filled
with the Holy Spirit . . . and with great power gave the
apostles their witness of the resurrection of the Lord Jesus,"
continues by giving the story of Ananias and Sapphira and

the appointing of the seven deacons, and ends with the thrilling account of the death of Stephen.

Fragments of Ancient Papyrus Books Containing Portions of the General Epistles of St. Paul.

Rom. 1:1-7 (Early 4th Century)—Altho included in Kenyon's list, this appears in such rude penmanship that Grenfell and Hunt think it to have been a school-boy's exercise, but Deissmann thinks it was a gospel amulet. In any case, out of that far-distant century we get in the rough chirography of this peasant the declaration that Christ Jesus "was declared to be the Son of God with power ($\overline{YY\Theta YEN\Delta}$-YNAMEI)by the resurrection of the dead."

Rom. 12:3-8 (Late 6th or 7th Century)—This passage was probably copied out in this form to be read in the church. It contains the famous passage which describes Christians as members of Christ's body.[13]

I Cor. 7:18-8:4; Phil. 3:9-17; 4:2-8 (Second half of 4th Century)—Two leaves from a papyrus book containing the Pauline argument that love is greater than knowledge, for "knowledge puffeth up, but love buildeth up"; also his teaching concerning the "power of his resurrection and the fellowship of his sufferings," and the heroic expression of the apostle's determination to press on "unto the prize." A comma is sometimes used to separate the syllables. To indicate long pauses a blank, coronis, or other mark to catch the eye is used.

I Cor. 1:17-20; 6:13-18; 7:3, 4, 10-14 (5th Century)—Five fragments written in large letters declaring: "Christ sent me not to baptize but to preach the gospel . . . for the word of the cross . . . unto us who are saved is the power of God," etc.

I Cor. 1:25-27; 2:6-8; 3:8-10, 20 (5th Century)—Seven small fragments very much mutilated but containing those great passages which speak of "God's wisdom in a mystery," "we are God's fellow workers," etc.

---

[13] This is, however, probably a fragment of a lectionary rather than of a New Testament, as the marks usually used to catch the eye in public reading are still plainly visible.

Fragment of an Ancient Papyrus Book Containing a Portion of a Pastoral Epistle.

Titus 1:11-15; 2:3-8 (3d Century)—A leaf from a papyrus book in which Timothy is urged to show himself an example not in "uncorruptness" (ἀφθορίαν), as our A. V. reads (2:7), but in "freedom from envy" (ἀφθονίαν).

Fragments of Ancient Papyrus Books Containing Portions of Hebrews.

Heb. 1:1 (3d or 4th Century)—Altho included in the list of Kenyon and Milligan, this is not properly designated as a "leaf" from an ancient New Testament, for, altho it is among the earliest known Biblical fragments, it is really written on the margin of a letter: "God having of old time spoken unto *our* fathers," etc.

Heb. 2:14-5:5; 10:8-11:13; 11:28-12:17 (Early 4th Century)—This is a very large manuscript containing about one-third of the epistle to the Hebrews. It was written on the back of a papyrus containing the new epitome of Livy (*Oxyrhynchus Papyri,* 4:668). Eleven broad columns of the text remain, filling eight quarto pages when printed. The numbers on the ancient leaves prove that other books of the New Testament preceded the book of Hebrews in this very ancient collection. The text is good, but the spelling is poor. The form of punctuation used is that of a double point. It contains the entire argument concerning the "great salvation" which had been confirmed by "signs and wonders . . . and gifts of the Holy Spirit." It is a very valuable contribution to text criticism.

Heb. 9:12-19 (4th Century)—The same system of punctuation mentioned above is found here. In the text one reads about the "blood of Christ" and the "eternal spirit."

Fragment of an Ancient Papyrus Book Containing a Portion of the Epistle of St. James.

James 2:19-3:9 (Late 3d Century)—This leaf containing a text in general agreement with that of the Vatican Codex gives the argument that if a man has faith he must have works also; a man's tongue must be pure if his heart is pure.

*Fragment of an Ancient Papyrus Book Containing a Portion of
I John.*

1 John 4: 11-12, 14-17 (4th or 5th Century)—This text has
been carelessly copied, but one can still read: "Behold if God
so loved, we also should love . . . the Father hath sent the
Son to be the Saviour of the world. Whosoever shall confess
that Jesus is the Son of (God) in him God abideth."

*Fragments of an Ancient Papyrus Roll Containing Portions of
the Book of Revelation.*

Rev. 1: 4-7 (4th Century?)—This text is written on the back
of a roll containing the book of Exodus, dating from the third
or fourth century, in which Jesus Christ is spoken of as the
"faithful witness . . . ruler of the kings of the earth . . .
who cleansed us of our sins by his blood." The text is whole
with the exception of two letters. The name Jesus Christ is
abbreviated in rather an unusual way ($\overline{\text{ιη}}$ $\overline{\text{Χε}}$).

The discovery within twenty years of the above
twenty fragments from some twenty different ancient
New Testaments or lectionaries was a wonderful surprize, and proved the integrity of the ancient texts in
a manner entirely satisfactory to believers. Sir F. G.
Kenyon omitted, however, from his survey the newly
discovered texts written on parchment and vellum, and
even since the above list of Biblical papyri was tabulated by Kenyon and Milligan (1912-13), a few other
equally surprizing discoveries have come to light; so
that the writer is now able to give an additional list
of twenty-eight ancient New Testaments (seventeen on
skin and eleven on papyrus) to supplement the notable
catalogs given above.[13a]

[13a] Several of the Papyrus fragments listed by Gregory (such as P[7] and
P[16]), are omitted from the above list because they are undated or are
certainly not pieces of New Testaments.

(4) OTHER MORE RECENTLY DISCOVERED ANCIENT NEW
TESTAMENTS ON PAPYRI, PARCHMENT OR VEL-
LUM DATING FROM THE THIRD TO THE SIXTH
CENTURIES.[14]

*Fragments of Ancient New Testaments Containing Portions of
St. Matthew's Gospel.*

Matt. 6:5, 6, 8, 9, 13-15, 17 (5th or 6th Century)—A vellum
leaf published in *Oxyrhynchus Papyri* (IX: 1169). It contains the remarks of our Lord concerning prayer: "Thou,
when thou prayest, enter into thine inner chamber, and having
shut thy door, pray to thy Father who is in secret; and thy
Father who seeth in secret shall recompense thee," etc. This
was evidently a fine Bible, originally measuring over six
inches high by five inches wide. The text is divided into
paragraphs and a new line with an enlarged initial letter commences each paragraph.

P.—Matt. 12: 24-26, 32-33. (5th Century). This papyrus leaf
(*Oxyrhynchus Papyri;* X: No. 1227), written in large uncials
by a good penman, follows the Codex Bezae in one variant:
"This (fellow) does not cast out demons but by Beelzeboul
prince of the demons. But knowing their thoughts he said
to them . . . whosoever shall speak a word against the Son
of Man (υυ του ανου), it shall be forgiven him; but whosoever speaketh against the Holy Spirit, it shall not," etc.

*Fragments of Ancient New Testaments Containing Portions of
St. Luke's Gospel.*

Luke 1:74—2:7 (6th Century)—Text published by Wessely
(*op. cit., Inhalts* II, 1911, No. 55 B). This is a parchment
leaf on the opposite side of which is Luke 1:59-72 in
Coptic. The importance of this bi-lingual text and those
which are to follow is great. It proves that in those early
centuries the Church believed in giving the gospel to the
people in their own language. While on one page the Greek
text was given, on the opposite page a translation of the Greek
into Coptic was given also. The particular Greek text given
here consists of 72 lines, not a word being lost. One syllable

[14] Examined and catalogued by the author. In order to facilitate quick
reference the texts on papyri are marked **P.**

in verse 75 is repeated by mistake and there are two or three slight errors in spelling; otherwise this ancient text agrees letter by letter with our modern critical editions. The passage given contains the hymn of Zacharias and tells of the birth of Jesus, the "dayspring from on high."

Luke 9: 59-62; 10: 1-14 (4th or 5th Century)—Greek text given by Wessely in work cited, No. 185, text 20. This is a parchment leaf containing over fifty lines very beautifully written on both sides in remarkably wide columns. It is evidently one of the few elegant church Bibles that have come from this very ancient time. There are a very few transpositions of words, and in verse 62 a word is left out; otherwise the text is that of Westcott & Hort almost letter for letter. This leaf contains the wonderful message of Jesus concerning the harvest being great but the laborers few; he sends out his disciples "as lambs in the midst of wolves."

Luke 16: 4-12 (6th Century)—Text published by Wessely (*ibid,* No. 56 C). This is a parchment leaf containing 63 narrow lines of Greek text in rather a bad state of preservation. The chief variants are found in verse 8, where "sons of the light" is changed to "son of the light"; and in verse 11, where a negative appears before the word "faithful" and the text reads, "If therefore ye have not been found unfaithful in the unrighteous mammon, who will commit to your trust the true (riches)?" The ancient New Testament which contained this text contained also a Coptic translation in the same volume, the text on the back of this leaf being Luke 15: 27—16: 3.

Luke 19: 17, 22-24 (5th or 6th Century)—Given by Wessely, *op. cit.* No. 188, text 23. This is a well-written parchment leaf, containing almost all the parable of the pounds. The only unusual change in the text is a note of insolence, which appears in verse 20, where, instead of saying "Lord, behold here is thy pound," by a very slight verbal change the slothful servant is made to say: "Lord, here is the thing I have kept laid up in a napkin." This might be a liturgical text so far as the verses are concerned (Gregory, *Textkritik des Neuen Testaments,* 1: 357).

Luke 21: 30-22:2 (6th Century)—Published by Wessely (*ibid.* No. 57 B). This is a parchment leaf, the Greek half of which contains 74 lines very well preserved; on the other side in Coptic is written Luke 21 : 21-30. Very few mistakes are to be noted in this text, when the itacisms common in all ancient manuscripts and a few other misspellings due to mispronunciation are not counted. In verse 36 a syllable is omitted, and in verse 34, after ἡμέρα the word διέλθωσειν is inserted. I cannot conjecture why this insertion was made, and my colleague, Dr. W. A. Elliott, who has given me much valuable help in this section of my work, is equally at loss.

Luke 22 : 44-56, 61-63 (4th Century)—Published in *Publicazioni della Societa Italiana; Papyri greci e latini* (II., 124). I take this to be the same text as was published in this same work in shorter form a year or two previously, which Schubart dates in first half of fourth century (I, No. 2). This rather rare manuscript was found at Eshmûnên, about 175 miles south of Cairo. Either the scribe had before him an unusual text, or he is exceedingly careless or he is more particular about giving the exact thought than the exact language of his copy.. In verse 47, instead of writing (λεγόμενος) "he that was called" Judas, he uses the more common form for the same thought (καλούμενος), and adds to Judas his ordinary title "Iscariot," which the New Testament manuscripts usually omit. In verse 49, instead of saying that those about Jesus saw "what would follow," he writes "what had followed"; so in verse 51, "answered" is omitted; and in verse 55, instead of saying when they had kindled a fire they "sat down together" (σύν), he says they sat "around" it (περί). His spelling is also sometimes rather original. The probability is that the copyist trusted his memory of the text too fully and, therefore, his text is a little less verbally accurate than others; but this speaks well for his previous Bible training. He knew the facts perfectly; but he was not as careful as some to write the Greek letters correctly. It looks as if this scribe did not think of the Bible text as a magical thing. It was the spirit and meaning that gave it life.

Fragments of Ancient New Testaments Containing Portions of St. John's Gospel.

John 7 : 3-12 (6th Century)—This is an uncial fragment (published by Wessely, *op. cit.* XI, p. 12) written on vellum. The text shows abbreviations, and the ten verses here preserved contain fourteen slight variants from the *Textus Receptus,* thus lacking marked agreement with the Westcott and Hort text.[15]

P.—John 10: 1, 2, 4, 7, 9, 10; 11: 1-8 (?), 45-52 (5th Century)—In an Akhmim papyrus now at Strassburg University, published by Roesch, *Bruckstucke des ersten Clemensbriefes* (Strassburg, 1910). This is a bi-lingual codex containing also, 1 Clement (1—26: 2). It was probably a church reading book. The portions given in Coptic (Akhmimic) are St. John (10: 1—12: 20; 13: 1, 2, 11, 12) ; St. James (1: 13; 5: 20). This fragment is badly mutilated only seven letters of one verse remaining (10: 4), and little more in one or two other verses, so that it is not very valuable for critical purposes; yet a few changes from the ordinary text may be noted, *e.g.,* interchanges of letters, ph (φ) for th (ϑ), and t for g, in many places; o to a, and e to ē. It is interesting to ask whether these changes are not in several instances due to mispronunciation (*cf.* ϑ for φ 11: 52), rather than to mistakes of the eye. It seems a mere careless slip of verbal memory when, instead of the phrase "of strangers they know not the voice" (10: 5), this scribe writes "they know not the voice of strangers." In the midst of the broken lines some good words can be made out: "Verily, verily, I say he that entereth in through . . . sheepfold . . . but climbeth up . . . the same is a thief . . . but a stranger [they will not follow]" (John 10: 1-10). There is given the beautiful story of "that Mary" who anointed the Lord with ointment and wiped his feet with her hair and it was told him. . . . His sister sent unto him saying, "Lord, behold . . . [this sickness is not unto] death, but for the glory of God that the Son . . . might be glorified. Now Jesus loved Mary . . . when he had heard therefore (that he was sick) he abode two days where he was." The last section tells how "many of the Jews which came to Mary and had seen the things which he did, believed on him. Men gathered the chief priests . . . [and said] if [we let him alone] all men [will believe] and . . . Caiaphas . . . said, . . . it is expedient that [one] man [should die] for the people." One of the beautiful personal touches which render the examination of these ancient docu-

[15] This reference obtained from Prof. Wallace N. Stearns, of Fargo College, N. Dakota.

ments so fascinating is found at the close of John (10:45), where this ancient scribe, or some early reader, over 1,400 years ago, added in the margin "Amen" (PΘ) after the statement, "Many . . . believed on him."

John 15: 25-27; 16: 1, 2, 21-31 (Late 3rd Century)—This is a roll (*Oxyrhynchus Papyri*, X, No. 1228) containing a neutral text with the usual abbreviations and no punctuation marks. It is a long fragment, and as one glances at the Greek text certain words and phrases stand out clearly, notwithstanding the mutilations of age: "When the Com[forter] is come . . . from the Father . . . which proceedeth from the Father [he shall testify] of me . . . ye now therefore have sorrow . . . your hearts shall rejoice [and your joy] no man taketh from you. And in that day ye shall ask me nothing . . . whatsoever . . . in my name . . . ye shall ask in my name . . . the Father loveth you because ye . . . have believed that I . . . came forth from the Father . . . we believe," etc. The early Christian who wrote and used this ancient Bible lived about as near to St. John as we are near to the boyhood of George Washington.

Fragments of Ancient New Testaments Containing Portions of the Acts of the Apostles.

Acts 2: 1-5 (6th Century)—Published by Wessely (*op. cit., Inhalts* II, No. 59 C). This is another of the bi-lingual New Testaments and contains Acts 1: 15-20 in Coptic. The only difference between this and Bibles of this type formerly mentioned is that the two languages, instead of being on different pages, are in parallel collumns on the same page. The Greek text is the same as the modern critical text with only a very few trifling changes in spelling and the insertion of a particle that does not change the meaning in verse 3. The passage contains the account of the day of Pentecost when the disciples spoke with tongues and were filled with the Holy Spirit ($\overline{\pi\nu\varsigma}$).

P. Acts 6: 7-10, 11-15 (5th Century)—Published in *Publicazioni della Societa Italiana; Papiri greci e latini* (II, No. 125). This large leaf is well preserved, needing restoration of text in only a very few places. Excepting in verse 9, it follows the Westcott and Hort text. It is written in uncials, half on one side of the leaf and half on the other. It preserves for us the trial and death of Stephen, closing with the statement that all that sat in the council saw his face as if it were the face of an angel.

P. Acts 15: 22-24, 27-32 (6th or 7th Century)—Published by Wessely (*op. cit., Theol. Inhalts,* III, No. 190, Text 25). This is a leaf of a papyrus codex containing 30 lines of elegant writing, only one broad column to a page. It was probably a church Bible. This particular fragment tells of the choice of Barsabas and Silas to go to Antioch with Paul and Barnabas, and of the famous letter sent by the Jerusalem church declaring that no burden of the Jewish law was to be laid upon Gentile Christians. The only notable variant is in verse 22, where, instead of Barsabas, this scribe has written Barnabas.

Fragments of Ancient New Testaments Containing Portions of the General Epistles of St. Paul.

P. Romans 1: 1-16 (6th or 7th Century)—First published in 1915 by Grenfell and Hunt (*Oxyrhynchus Papyri,* Vol. XI, No. 1354). This is a papyrus leaf from a very large church Bible which originally must have been at least eleven inches high by seven inches broad. It is written in red-brown ink, in an upright script, large and very heavy. It contains the ordinary text with a very few exceptions, as *e.g.,* in verse 10, where by a mistake, ἐπὶ is changed to ὑπὲρ. Some of the abbreviations are interesting, *e.g.,* Δας for David; προς for πατρος ("of the Father"), and (probably) α for πρῶτον ("first"). This passage contains St. Paul's famous declaration, "I am not ashamed of the gospel, for it is the power of God."

P. Romans 1: 27-2: 2 (5th Century)—Published in *Pap. greci e latini,* I, No. 4. This papyrus gives without the variation of a letter the Westcott and Hort text. It begins with the last word of verse 27 and ends with the first word in 2: 2. It contains St. Paul's terrific indictment against the sinfulness of the Roman world of the first century, an indictment which the discoveries have amply vindicated.

P. Romans 8: 12-27, 33-39; 9: 1-3, 5-9 (3d Century)—First published by Grenfell and Hunt in 1915 (*Oxyrhynchus Papyri,* Vol. XI, No. 1356). It is a leaf from a papyrus book, the height of which was about four and one-half inches and the width less than two. It is written in very small characters, in an upright, informal hand, and is unpunctuated, excepting where a paragraph is indicated. The leaf is badly mutilated, yet from what remains it is clear, as the learned editors point out, that it is in "general agreement with the Codex Vaticanus, altho it occasionally corrects its vulgar spelling. There are occasional interchanges of letters as ε and εα with ϑ and π with φ. In verse 20 a later hand replaces the ordinary reading, "The creature shall be delivered" by the new reading, "is delivered." This is probably a mere freak of memory on the part of the copyist; yet it is an attractive suggestion that there may be a theological reason for the present tense here, since elsewhere in the letter (6:18, 22; 8:2) Paul speaks of the freeing process in the past tense.[15a] While in the great passage at the end of the eighth chapter half of the lines are broken, we can yet make out in this oldest of all Bible texts the precious words: "As many as are led by the Spirit of God, they are the sons of God . . . children of God . . ., and if children . . . joint heirs . . . I am persuaded that neither death . . . nor powers . . . nor height nor depth . . . shall be able to separate us."

P. 1 Cor. 16:4-7, 10; 2 Cor. 5:18-21; 10:13, 14; 11:2 (6th or 7th Century)—This large text of 112 lines was published by Wessely in 1912 (*op. cit., Inhalts* III, No. 191, text 26). It is part of a papyrus book which originally contained the entire New Testament or perhaps was confined to Paul's epistles. The text is beautifully written in narrow parallel columns; it is essentially intact and agrees exactly with Westcott and Hort, except in a few cases of poor spelling and one rather remarkable variant (2 Cor. 11:4), where the adjective "different" is omitted: "If he that cometh preacheth another Jesus . . . or if ye receive a different spirit . . . or a gospel which ye did not accept," etc.

Gal. 2:5, 6 (5th Century)—This uncial text, which was first published in 1913 (*Pap. greci e latini*, II, No. 118), gives but the last two words of verse 5, and shows the same defects of

---

[15a] I am indebted to Dr. E. J. Goodspeed, of the University of Chicago, for the suggestion of this possibility.

transcription as many of the other passages previously given;
e.g., in verse 6 there is a slight transposition of words.

P. Gal. 3:16-24 (Late 5th Century)—Two pages almost
complete of a small parchment leaf (cir. 4½ x 2¼ in.) with
narrow margins, published in 1915 (*Pap. greci e latini*, III,
No. 251). It contains 37 lines, written in straight and accurate
uncials, punctuated by two hands. In two readings it agrees
with the Western text, but otherwise with Westcott and Hort,
except for one or two unimportant verbal mistakes in transcription, such as in verse 24, where the perfect tense is used
instead of the present. It contains the great argument of
St. Paul concerning the promise "not of seeds [as of] many;
but as of one . . . to thy seed . . . Christ." The covenant
of Abraham cannot be annulled by the law which came centuries later; rather the law was our schoolmaster (παιδαγωγός) to bring us to Christ that by faith we might be
justified. In line eleven "Jesus Christ" is abbreviated to
ιυ Χυ.

*Fragments of Ancient New Testaments Containing Portions of
the Epistle of James.*

P. *James* 1:10-12, 15-18 (4th Century)—This is a leaf (*Oxyrhynchus Papyri*, X, No. 1229), from a papyrus Bible over
1,500 years old. It gives the ordinary Westcott and Hort
text, but has a grossly ungrammatical form in verse 17. The
numbers of the pages marked on the leaf prove that the
ancient book began with the first chapter of James. It probably contained only this one Bible book. The ancient Christians evidently believed in the very modern custom of publishing the New Testament in handy editions. Our text contrasts the blessedness of the poor with the rich, declares the
man that endureth temptation "shall receive the crown of
life," and points out that every good gift cometh from the
Father of lights, who "of his own will brought us forth by
the word of truth." There is some ornamentation occasionally
attempted, and the height of the leaf was over 7½ inches, so
that this probably was a church Bible, altho the writing is
rather coarse and irregular.

James 1:25-27 (5th Century)—This text was published recently by the Italians (*Pap. greci e latini*, I, No. 5). It agrees

with the Westcott and Hort text; the fact that one Greek word is split into two might, however, suggest that the copyist did not understand the language very well. The pages have the numbers 17 and 18 on the margin.

Fragments of Ancient New Testaments Containing Portions of the First General Epistle of Peter.

I Peter 2: 21-25; 5: 1-5. (6th Century)—This large leaf was published by Wessely (*op. cit., Theol. Inhalts*, II, No. 60 B). It represents another of the ancient bi-lingual New Testaments, the Coptic translation being found on the same page with the Greek text. There are sixty-seven lines of Greek well preserved. It is not very carefully written. In 2: 20 the scribe inserts "and"; in verse 23 τὸν τόπον; in verse 24 he omits "in"; in 5: 1 he inserts "the" before elders and leaves out "therefore"; in the second verse he not only interchanges some words but also inserts "according to the will of God" and "exercising oversight," which the best texts omit; and he succeeds also in various places in misspelling several words.

I Peter 5: 5-13. (4th Century.)—This text was first published in 1915 (*Oxyrhynchus Papyri*, Vol. XI, No. 1353). It is a thin vellum leaf, broken and worm-eaten and very small, measuring only about five by four inches in size. The scribe writes in abnormally large characters, thus proving himself to be untrained at such work. As the page of this particular leaf was numbered 229, it is evident that the book was of considerable size. If the New Testament books were then in the same order as now, this volume probably began with Romans. In that case this was near the end of the second volume, the first volume containing the four gospels and the Acts. The text is decidedly unique, not agreeing with any of the main authorities, the slight variations being too many to notice here. There is no change, however, in the exalted teaching which shines gloriously from the broken sentences of this very ancient pocket Bible: "Casting all your care upon him, for he careth for you. . . . The God of all grace who hath called into his eternal glory in Christ . . . to him be glory forever and ever."

Fragments of Ancient New Testaments Containing Portions of Revelation.

Rev. 3:19—4:1-2. (4th Century)—This vellum leaf (*Oxyrhynchus Papyri*, VIII, No. 1080) represents the ordinary critical text, tho there are several minute marginal corrections by a second hand—one at least of which (4:7) is incorrectly made. It contains the beautiful words to the church in Laodicea: "Behold I stand at the door and knock; if any man hear my voice and open the door I will come in to him and will sup with him and he with me," etc. This also contains the curious reading "He that hath hearing beyond his ears let him hear." The most interesting thing about this miniature edition of the Bible is that its form proves conclusively that this volume did not contain all the New Testament but only the Apocalypse.

P. Rev. 5:5-8; 6:5-8. (Early 4th Century)—Published *Oxyrhynchus Papyri*, X, No. 1230. This is a leaf from a papyrus book containing no special features. It speaks of the elders falling before the Lamb, and the opening of the seals. So far as it goes the text "agrees with the Codex Sinaiticus" (Hunt). Each line is broken, both at the beginning and the end. It is interesting to note that ς is used for ἑπτά in the expression "seven spirits of God" (verse 7). The text reads: ς π̅ν̅α του Θ̅υ̅.

An Ancient Fifth Century New Testament Containing Portions of All the Four Gospels.

Matt. 3:7-17; 4:23-25; 5:1-12; 7:13-25; 10:37-42; Mark 6:18-29; Luke 2:1-20; 11:27-32; 24:36-38; John 20:1-18, 24-27.—Catalogued by Gregory as W032, and beautifully edited by Wessely in 1912 (*Griechische und koptische Texte; Theol. Inhalts,* III, No. 184, Text 19). Fragmentary as these gospels are as here given, they still make ten solid pages of the Greek text, seventy lines to a page. With but perhaps one exception to be mentioned later, no greater New Testament discovery, so far as the text is concerned, has been made since the days of Tischendorf. We have here not merely a single leaf of an ancient book snatched by the ravages of time out of its proper connection, but we possess in substantial shape a considerable part of the four gospels which were bound together into one volume nearly fifteen hundred years ago. The manuscript is beautifully written, but with the same slight variations in spelling, etc., from the classical forms, which were universal in ancient manuscripts written by the middle classes in the early Christian centuries. The same rather startling abbreviation of the word "cross" (c⳨ϒ) is used which we have seen previously in other manuscripts, the cross itself being shown in the middle of the word. The Sermon on the Mount is given with almost absolute verbal perfection—better than any senior class in a modern theological seminary would be likely to copy it. This shows that the copyist knew that portion of the Scripture word for word. In many other places there are slight variations in spelling and an occasional change in the order of words, and in one or two cases a change in case, due evidently to the copyist reading the sentence and then repeating it from memory as he wrote it; but in no case is there any change in doctrine or any contradiction of the gospel facts. In Matt. 3:7 the scribe uses a synonym for "warned." In Matt 4:24 he repeats a syllable, and in 5:2 he by accident makes a wrong letter and turns it into an ornament; but the Beatitudes he knows so well that he writes them correctly word for word and letter for letter.

In Luke 2:2 the name of the governor Quirinius is misspelled, and in verse 11 "Christ the Lord" is abbreviated curiously. In John 20:7 instead of the napkin "that was upon his head" this copy, by a slight change, reads "which had been provided for the head"; and in verse 17 the text reads "He saith" instead of "Jesus saith," while in verse 16 the customary "Rabboni" became "Rabbounei." In still another place "therefore" is omitted; in verse 25 a particle is inserted and in verse 10 the reading is "so they then went back to the disciples."

The only variation in sense in any passage is in Matt. 7:18, where instead of writing "neither can a corrupt tree bring forth good fruit," this ancient copyist has written "neither can a good tree bring forth good fruit." The early Christian's love for his Bible is seen from the fact that instead of mutilating the text some reader far back in that ancient world has put in the margin—"sic!"

Many great texts are preserved in this manuscript copy of the gospels which is over 1,400 years old. In the Matthew fragments we have the preaching of John the Baptist; the statement that Jesus was "healing all manner of disease"; the entire list of Beatitudes; the great teaching concerning the narrow gate and the broad way and the judgment of a tree by its fruit; and the passage centering in the doctrine, "He that findeth his life shall lose it, and he that loseth his life for my sake shall find it." In the Mark passage we have the entire story of Herodias and the murder of John the Baptist. In the Luke passages we possess the narrative of the birth of Jesus and the song of the shepherds—which reads "on earth peace and good will among men"; Christ's statement that no sign shall be given to an evil generation, but "the sign of Jonah"; and the appearance of Jesus to his disciples after his resurrection saying, "Peace unto you!" The remnants of John's gospel are even more important, including the visit of Mary Magdalene and Peter to the sepulchre on the morning of the resurrection, the meeting of the Savior with Mary, and finally the refusal of Thomas to believe in the resurrection until Jesus appeared to him personally. Our fragment reads:

"And after eight days again his disciples were within, and Thomas with them. Jesus cometh, the doors being shut, and stood in the midst and said, Peace be unto you. Then saith he to Thomas, Reach hither thy finger," etc.

THE MOST VALUABLE OF ALL THE NEWLY DISCOVERED MANUSCRIPTS

An Ancient Fourth or Fifth Century New Testament Containing the Entire Four Gospels and Fragments of the Pauline Epistles. (Washington Codex, 1908-9.) [16]

Never since the startling discovery of Tischendorf has there been greater joy than came to the hearts of textual critics when Prof. Henry A. Sanders, of the University of Michigan, announced that Mr. Charles L.

[16] While Dr. Gregory briefly mentioned this discovery, it was impossible properly to estimate it previous to its publication in full with critical notes in 1912. Cf. *New Testament Manuscripts in the Freer Collection*, Part I., 1912, by Prof. Henry A. Sanders.

Freer, of Detroit, Michigan, had obtained in Egypt a New Testament manuscript which, in its completeness and age, could rank with the three great MSS. of the world, being certainly not later than the sixth century and being probably as old as the Sinaitic Codex. Not only its venerable antiquity, but the fact that its readings often sustained the Western (Bezae) text as against the usually accepted Eastern text added to the unique value of this discovery, while adding at the same time to the difficulties of text criticism. It determined once for all the fact that as early as the third, or perhaps the second century, there were at least two or three independent types of New Testament texts, all of these being alike in their statement of essential facts and doctrine, but differing considerably in their verbal form. It seemed to settle the question that there was no settled and stiff form of the New Testament text necessary to orthodoxy at that time, as came later to be the case, both with the Greek and Hebrew Bibles; but that several verbal types existed peacefully together. This adds greatly to the apologetic value of this early document, but complicates the question concerning the "original" text. The manuscript, which was also accompanied by three others containing the books of Deuteronomy, Joshua, and the Psalms, was bought by Mr. Freer of an Arab dealer named Ali, in Gizeh, near Cairo, December 19, 1906. Professor Sanders saw the manuscript for the first time in October, 1907, and at once recognized its value. The dealer from whom it was bought first declared that it had been obtained at Akhmim, but later denied this. Certainly a very unusual treasure of manuscripts about 1906 was discovered near Akhmim; and Carl Schmidt,

Edgar J. Goodspeed and others feel that it is incredible to think of two such unique and vast finds of Biblical manuscripts being made in the same year in two separate localities, no other such discovery of large Biblical MSS. having been made for at least half a century. Professor Sanders, however, is very sure that it was found among the ruins of some monastery in the Delta, probably that of the Vinedresser, the site of which was close to the Third Pyramid, instead of coming, as Schmidt and others supposed, from the White Monastery near Sohag, opposite Akhmim.[17]

In 1910 Professor Sanders dated this manuscript in the fifth century (*op. cit.*, p. 13), but in 1912 he changed this to the early fifth or second half of the fourth century, and a little later dated the main part of the manuscript without any reservation to the fourth century,[18] having the approval of the great expert, Dr. B. P. Grenfell, in this more mature dating. Granting this, we have here a manuscript equal in importance to any now in existence. This would place the writer of this manuscript as near to the traditional date of Saint John as we are to the father of John Alden.

Two early owners of the manuscript, as shown by the notes, lived in the fifth century, and a third owner in the sixth century. The subscription in diminutive uncials, written presumably by one of the earliest owners, but dating from the fifth century, reads:

"Holy Christ, be thou with thy servant Timothy and all of his."

[17] See on the general controversy *Bib. World*, 33:201-6; *Am. Journal of Theology*, 13:597-603; 15:112, 115; *Am. Journal of Archæology*, XIII.; *Old Test. MSS. in the Freer Collection*, Part I., Henry A. Sanders, 1910, Introduction. Full list of discussions given in *Old Test. MSS. in Freer Collection* (1917), p. 1.

[18] *New Test. MSS.*, Part I., pp. 135-139; *Facsimile of Wash. MSS.*, Introduction, 1913; *cf.* Goodspeed, *Freer Gospels*, p. 6.

The manuscript is written on parchment of excellent quality, which has, however, suffered exceedingly from age, wear, and exposure. It is not so elegant as the Codex Sinaiticus, but was undoubtedly intended for a magnificent copy. The edges of the leaves are badly decayed, but the body of the manuscript is well protected by painted board covers, which were put on the manuscript probably in the ninth century. These covers are very curious, containing pictures of the Evangelists, John and Mark, both being represented as white-haired, and Mark being slightly bald after the Pauline type. The parchment is mostly made of sheepskin, tho some goatskin leaves occur. The ink is dark brown, but that of the first quire of John is darker. The writing is in one column, 30 lines to a page. At present there remain 374 pages (187 leaves), two blank pages appearing at the end of John's gospel. The usual abbreviations occur and a few unusual ones; for example, Κυριος (Lord) in Matthew appears in five different forms (Κς, Κυ, Κω, Κν, Κε), each case receiving its appropriate abbreviation. This name is always abbreviated when referring to God, otherwise not. Punctuation is rare; a single dot is regularly used, a double dot occasionally; phrases are separated by small blank spaces. "The remarkable variations in paragraphing in the different parts of the MS. indicate quite plainly the care of the scribe in following his patchwork copy." The scribe actually seems to copy mistakes in the original parent papyrus, even continuing the gross misspelling of certain common words. The manuscript once contained the whole of the four gospels in the order Matthew, John, Luke, Mark (Western order). Two lacunae now occur (John

14: 25-16: 7; Mark 15: 13-38), caused by the dropping out of two leaves. "The remainder of the MSS. is so perfect that there is rarely a letter missing or indistinct." That it was much reverenced in the early centuries is proved by the blots on it when in ancient time the tallow dropt from candles while it was being shown to visitors, or the early saints were studying it. The peculiar value of this MS. consists in its affiliation with the old Latin and Syriac, the so-called Western text. The only spectacular reading, however, is found in an extra passage which follows Mark 16: 14:

And they defended themselves, saying: This world of lawlessness and of unbelief is under Satan, which does not suffer those unclean things that are under the dominion of spirits to comprehend the true power of God. On this account reveal thy righteousness now. They said (these things) to Christ. And Christ replied to them:There has been fulfilled the term of year. of the authority of Satan, but other dreadful things are drawing nigh (even to those) for the sake of whom as sinners I was delivered up to death in order that they might return to the truth and sin no more; in order that they might inherit the spiritual and incorruptible glory of righteousness which is in heaven, but go . . .

The style of this addendum is so different from the other portions of Mark's gospel that it seems to the writer impossible to think of it as an original reading. It was perhaps a marginal note which came from very early time and crept into the text.

Other Fragments of Ancient New Testaments—One Written on Pieces of a Broken Pot

In addition to the above twenty-eight ancient New Testaments recently discovered—to which must be added the fourteen MSS. written on skin, catalogued by Gregory in 1909, and the twenty written on papyrus

reported by Drs. Kenyon and Milligan in 1912-13—
multitudes of other Bible texts have come down to us
from the fourth, fifth, sixth, and later centuries, some
of which almost certainly must originally have belonged
to entire gospels, but which are so mutilated that this
can not certainly be proved. There must also be a number of other bi-lingual texts known to scholars—such
as those used by Horner in his study of the Coptic version of the New Testament, and others reported elsewhere (*e.g., Le Muséon N. S.,* XII: 2, 3; XIII (1912),
pp. 175-365; *Jour. of Egypt. Arch.,* 1917, p. 68). The
writer has not examined these Greek texts and, therefore, can not describe and estimate them. One of the
most curious collections of these early Bible texts is that
which was made by three poor Christians during the
time of the Arab conquest, the Greek text of the gospels
being written on pieces of broken pottery because they
were unable to afford papyri. Twenty of these ostraca
have come down to us covering Matt. 27: 31, 32; Mark
5: 40, 41; 9: 17, 18, 22; 15: 21; Luke 22: 13-15, 16,
40-71; John 1: 1-9, 14-17; 18: 19-25; 19: 15-17.[19] Each
ostracon is numbered, the series being written either
to form "a cheap gospel lectionary . . . for private or
public reading consisting of extracts from the gospels
or perhaps even a continuous text" (Lefebvre), or
perhaps by candidates for deacon's orders or by some
monk or school-boy, or possibly by some ignorant
layman, or some "simple woman—some soul forgotten
among the myriads that perish" (Deissmann). If,
indeed, these twenty written scraps represent, as they
may well do, a seventh century copy of the gospels,
they stand for the most unique volume ever writ-

[19] See further, Deissmann, *Light from the Ancient East,* pp. 49-52.

ten. A New Testament written on potsherds! If this is indeed true, then we ought to have given this the place of honor in our catalog of newly discovered ancient New Testaments. Dr. Deissmann publishes one of these in facsimile, and it gives one a thrill to spell out of this rough scrawl on a piece of a broken pot written over twelve centuries ago the words:

"And they all said, Art thou then the Son of God? And he said unto them, Ye say that I am. And they said, What further need have we of witness, for we ourselves have heard from . . . mouth."

The unexpectedness of the discovery of valuable Biblical texts written on broken pottery may be seen from the fact that up to within a decade and a half no one ever regarded these potsherds as important, and excavators as well as the fellaheen had usually thrown them away as useless rubbish. The first appreciation of their importance came from Ulrich Wilcken in his work, *Greek Ostraca in Egypt and Nubia,* in 1899, followed by W. E. Crum's *Coptic Ostraca,* in 1902.

(5) SPECIAL IMPORTANCE OF THE NEWLY DISCOVERED NEW TESTAMENT FRAGMENTS FOR TEXT CRITICISM[21]

No one would be likely to deny the importance of the larger manuscripts such as the last two described above, but it may seem as if many of the others are too small to be considered of any special value. This is a mistake. While Gregory's list, given above, totals only a little more than one hundred verses, and our own

[21] This argument was first given by the writer in December, 1915, before the Society of Biblical Literature and Exegesis at Columbia University, and can only be summarized here.

list is not much larger, yet in Gregory's list thirty verses from three different New Testaments date from the fourth century, and in our list over forty verses come from two New Testaments dating from the third century (a century earlier than any MSS. known previous to these discoveries); while Kenyon's list contains some forty verses from three New Testaments of the third century and several hundreds of verses from seven or eight other New Testaments dating from the fourth century.

But it is not the large number of verses discovered, or even their early date, which alone gives these manuscripts their remarkable value; but rather the unusual character of many of these texts and their *provenance*. The unique importance of these new discoveries can be properly apprehended only when one notes that practically all of them came from Egypt, and almost all from a distant country province, presumably much less influenced by the official Church texts of Alexandria, not to speak of Antioch, or Cæsarea, or Rome, than if they had been found in the Delta (see pp. 65-97). Besides, there is a strong probability that a considerable number of these New Testaments were private property, not official texts—church Bibles written by church officials with possible ecclesiastical tendencies —but poor men's Bibles written on poor material by poor men, who were also poor penmen, for private use.

If this be accepted as true these discoveries ought almost to mark a new epoch in New Testament criticism. Our great codices from which come our A.V. and R.V., represent church New Testaments written by trained scribes, and come from great centers of ecclesiastical influence, but in these earliest texts just de-

scribed, we, for the first time, can see how the New
Testament of the poor man in a country district differed
from that of the rich man and the priest, and here we
have our first opportunity to see how the primitive New
Testament looked before it became stereotyped into the
authorized versions of the East and the West.

We have previously shown that the Fayum, so intimately connected with the towns in which most of
these texts were found, was separated in a marked way
from the financial, social, and ecclesiastical centers of
Egypt. The whole district had practically gone to ruin
toward the end of the third century. The villages were
stranded. Even the celebrated Moros brothers lived in
a house that did not cost much more than a camel, and
the poverty of these villages as well as their distance
from Alexandria insured little travel to this devastated
district by any church officials who might have been
interested in the minute orthodoxy of the New Testament text used by the Fayum Christians. The papyri
prove that most of these towns had a bank or two,
and that there were a few three-story houses, certainly a chain of laundries, a number of pawn-brokers'
establishments, and certain other supposedly infallible
signs of civilization, such as easy divorce, monopolies
of farm products and manufactured goods, and loans
at 1 per cent. a month; but the churches of the third
and fourth centuries in the Fayum were very poor.
Even at Socnopaei Nesus, whose ruins cover forty acres
and which must be ranked as one of the most important and populous of these southern towns, there are
few evidences of luxury and no suggestions up to the
date of its destruction (end of the third century) that
hierarchical authority from Alexandria was dominating

the Christian population. That the entire Fayum was isolated from the Delta is shown not only by the frequent misspellings of the names of reigning emperors and by the mistakes in the regnal year, but by the local dialect used and by the fact that the monks and anchorites chose this neighborhood as their hiding-place. That the church censorship was not very rigid, either here or in adjacent towns like Oxyrhynchus, is clearly indicated by the fact that this was the special home of the non-canonical gospels. The poverty of the population has been illustrated in almost every text excavated and is strikingly shown by multitudes of unmistakable signs, among which may be noted, in passing, that in all the papyri there is scarcely a mention of silversmiths, while even in the fourth century, when the cost of material had risen to a preposterous height, the "Guild of Coppersmiths" at Oxyrhynchus could report that the full value of all their stock remaining on hand at the end of the month amounted to only 1,000 denarii (*Oxyrhynchus Papyri*, I, 85). There are evidently additional reasons, therefore, beyond any previously appreciated, why we are compelled to decide that such splendid volumes as the Codex Sinaiticus and the Codex Vaticanus were not likely to have been produced at Oxyrhynchus,[22] and that such poor New Testaments as were written there would not have the same ecclesiastical censorship as might have been exercised at Alexandria.

All of this shows the importance to be attached especially to the small and worst-written copies of these ancient New Testaments, which presumably represented the Bibles of the poor coming from unofficial sources

[22] *Cf.* Kirsopp Lake, *Codex Sinaiticus,* 1911, p. 13.

(out of a culture which must be ranked, I think, not only lower than that of Herculaneum, but much lower than that of Pompeii or Timgad), and which, at least occasionally, give us types of New Testament texts differing both from that which was approved by Constantine and that which was favored by the Alexandrian scribes. Very few of these third and fourth century New Testaments are well written. While the chirography is usually better than that of ordinary letters and legal documents, yet even some of the wills and deeds and registrations of cattle were written more carefully. The script is coarse and irregular, and the general impression very inferior to that given by any one of our great uncials or by the scraps of Old Testament texts which have been preserved from the same period; while these rudely written Testaments, almost always with little or no punctuation or ornamentation, are in striking contrast to the beautifully engrossed works of Homer and Plato, Menander and Pindar, the Commentary on the Iliad, the new History of Greece by Cratippus, and most of the other classics coming from the same or an earlier time. They are even surpassed generally by the uncanonical gospels and the "Sayings of Jesus." Some of them are written on the poorest kind of material and several are written on the back of earlier literary works. It goes without saying that these texts, besides omissions of words and lines and blunders of transcription due to the misreading or mispronunciation of words, show the usual grammar of the *Koine* and the ordinary mistakes of the non-literary papyri— interchange of vowels, letters improperly inserted; above all, misspellings quite equal to any a modern workingman would be likely to make. When one looks at the crooked grammar, mixed orthography, and peculiar syntax of these ancient New Testaments, and notices also that the "readings" in many places are strikingly independent of the "standard" text, it would not be strange if he thought, at first glance, that they could be of no possible importance in text criticism. But such a decision would be unsound.

Previous to these discoveries all leading textual critics rested confidently on two or three great manuscripts representing fundamentally the Eastern text, believing that the Western text (typically represented by the Bezæ Codex) must be considered "foul." But these new papyri discoveries, as Dr. Turner and other distinguished Bible critics have fully shown, carry back the Western text at least to the third century.[23] Von Soden in his massive work has made it perfectly clear, tho his preference for Western readings may be deprecated, that as early as the third and perhaps as early as the second century there were at least three distinct types of national texts emanating respectively from Palestine, Syria, and Egypt. It is not to be supposed, as was once universally thought, that these various types of texts grew up through deliberate intention to alter the original Scriptures.[24] Instead of this it now becomes plain that these are mere local verbal variations of the Bible story, all giving the same facts but with local differences which date back probably to apostolic times.

It is evident that the value of these early texts is

[23] Of course the standard work in this field is Von Soden's *Die Schriften des neuen Testaments* (Berlin, 1902-15; but compare F. C. Burkitt, *Texts and Studies*, V. (1899), p. XVIII.).

[24] Von Soden affirms that excepting the influence from Tatian's *Harmony of the Gospel*, there is no evidence whatever of any extensive alteration of the text (*cf. Am. Journal of Theology*, 1916, p. 410; *The Interpreter*, July, 1915). Of course, local changes were not at all uncommon (*cf.* J. Rendel Harris, *Sidelights on New Test. Research*, pp. 5-60).

immeasurably increased because they were written before what Von Soden well calls "the mechanical Jewish dogma of inspiration" had been introduced. There is no counting of words or letters, and no settled or stiff form of text such as seemed a little later so necessary to orthodoxy. Let it again be emphasized that the earliest of these newly discovered Egyptian New Testaments, especially those which by their poor writing and small size evidently represent private rather than church Bibles, very generally differ from all the national texts which became stereotyped as early as the third century. They represent a really neutral text—in a sense different from that in which the Vatican MS. can be called neutral—a text which has come to us unexpectedly and which shows us contemporaneous copies of the kind of New Testaments used by the early Christians of Egypt in the pre-Constantine era.

It may be thought that I am making too much of this, as so few of these manuscripts come from the third century; but it will be remembered that the early fourth century texts were pre-Constantine, and that even late fourth century, or early fifth century texts, when written for private use in this far-away province, would very naturally represent an older MS., and a text much less official than if written in Alexandria or Carthage or Antioch or Rome for church use.

It is true that trained scribes having access to especially fine archetypes had, no doubt, better advantages for getting at the primitive text and correctly copying it than these rather ignorant countrymen; yet it is something to get in these newly discovered fragments a contemporary check upon our great uncials, being now able to examine quite a number of the New

Testaments which were actually in use in Egypt at least a generation before Constantine's royal influence was exerted toward text standardization, and even before the Antiochian or Alexandrian revision had obtained general acceptance.

Having said this, it must be frankly acknowledged that nothing very spectacular or strange has been brought to light in these sixty, or more, new texts. The results are surprizingly negative. Tho quite a number of these were in use some time before the Eastern or Western standard texts became "fixt," yet, as we have seen, very few variants of importance occur. However, what could be better than just such a negative result? Let us once more state the general facts.

No man had ever seen a page from any pre-Constantine New Testament previous to these discoveries. Many supposed that if such Bibles ever came to light they would be very different from ours. Some skeptics frankly exprest their opinion that the present New Testament was either originated by Constantine or much changed by him. But now these New Testaments are in our hands. We now know the kind of New Testament which the poor Christians of the martyr period were using and reverencing. It was the same as ours.[25] It is now certain that there was noth-

---

[25] Scholars generally agree that the papyri substantially support the Westcott and Hort Greek text lying at the basis of our Revised Version. A few, like Hoskier, strongly disagree with this, believing that they support the Bezae type of text. See the detailed argument in *Codex B, and Its Allies,* by H. C. Hoskier, 1914. Certainly the papyri show a pleasing independence, possibly more in harmony with Von Soden's eclectic text than with Westcott and Hort's. But this does not involve any material change, as may be seen by comparing Moffatt's new translation of the New Testament, which followed the Von Soden text, with the Revised Version. Since writing this footnote, I am pleased to find this decision confirmed by Dr. A. Savary, after a careful study of the New Test. Papyri fragments, *Rev. Or. Chret.,* XVI, 396.

ing of importance left out by Constantine. There was nothing put in. There are enough verbal changes among these many New Testaments from the third and fourth centuries to prove the independence of the scribes and their freedom from ecclesiastical censorship, but not even one very important change in the readings was found, and no change whatever in the teaching. The results confirm surprizingly the ancient text as worked out by the scholarship of the last century.

It must not be forgotten that these very ancient new MSS. just discovered constitute but a very small proportion of the text material which scholars have before them in determining the Bible text. In addition to the versions to be mentioned later it may be said— speaking only of Greek MSS.—that Von Soden in 1902 catalogued 2,328 New Testament manuscripts. Of these about forty contain in whole or part all the books of the New Testament. Some 1,716 MSS. contain portions of the gospels, 581 of the Acts, 628 of the Pauline epistles, and 219 of the Apocalypse. The text of no other ancient book is so certain as that of the New Testament.

While at first sight it might seem strange that so few third and fourth century Bible texts have come down to us, yet when we consider the perishable nature of the papyrus and the comparatively few texts of any kind which have been uncovered from that far-distant past, it becomes, as Wessely somewhere exprest it, a matter contrary to all expectation and almost "bordering upon the miraculous" that, by some happy accident, these many fragments of ancient New Testaments should have been preserved.[25a]

[25a] Sir. F. G. Kenyon in 1903 knew only 109 MSS. of Homer, 11 of Plato, and 20 of Demosthenes.

2. SYRIAC NEW TESTAMENTS

Aramaic was the native language of the Jews in Palestine in the first century. It has long been noticed that our Lord, at least in times of excitement, spoke his native tongue. Dalman and others have made this perfectly clear.[26] It is very likely that all the disciples were not only bi-lingual but also tri-lingual just as the modern Palestinians are. Syriac was a dialect of Aramaic and "the first language into which the New Testament was translated; and as the Greek text itself was written by men who habitually thought in Syriac, the early versions in this tongue have a closer affinity with the original text than those of any other can possibly have, not excepting the Old Latin" (Agnes Smith Lewis). While this statement seems to affirm a too close kinship between the Syriac written at Antioch and Edessa and the Aramaic spoken by Matthew and Paul, yet it vividly suggests the value of this ancient version. Dr. Lewis points out that various Aramaic phrases embodied in the Greek text, such as "Epphatha," "Talitha cumi," and the last despairing cry of our Lord on the cross, "Eloi, Eloi, lama sabachthani," are not translated in the Old Syriac version, "for the very good reason that they are part of the text itself."[27]

At the present time over forty manuscripts representing forty different Syriac New Testaments of the fifth or sixth century are known to exist. These manuscripts come from widely separated districts, Syria, Sinai, Mesopotamia, and Armenia. Up to within the last fifty years scholars have been wholly dependent

[26] See especially *The Words of Jesus*, G. H. Dalman (1902); and *The Messiah of the Gospels*, C. A. Briggs (1894).

[27] *The Four Gospels*, translated from the Sinaitic Palimpsest, p. xv.

upon the Peshito, which was a Syriac text of the common type and has been known to European scholars
since 1552;[28] but in 1842 Cureton discovered another
type of text in a fifth century MS. (published 1852),
and later several other types were found, the last notable discovery being the Apocalypse of St. John, representing the "Philoxenian" text, written by Polycorpus
(A.D. 508), and published in 1897 by Dr. John Gwynn.
It is now known, especially through the researches of
Dr. F. C. Burkitt, that the Peshito is not "the queen"
of all Syriac versions, as had always been supposed,
but is rather a late type appearing first in A.D. 411 to
take the place of older versions, the most important of
which is represented by Tatian's *Diatessaron* ("Harmony"), to be discust later, and by the Sinai gospels
discovered on Mt. Sinai by Mrs. Lewis• in 1892 and
edited by Professor Bensly, etc., in 1894.[29] There is
such romantic interest connected with the discovery of
the Sinai gospels that we tell the story in detail.

(I) NEWLY DISCOVERED SYRIAC NEW TESTAMENT FROM THE CONVENT OF ST. CATHERINE

It is one of the divinely foreordained synchronisms
of history that the mountain which gave to the Israelites
and, therefore, to all modern nations the "law," should
in these last times have given to the world the gospel.
When St. Sylvia journeyed to Mt. Sinai during the

[28] The later copies of the Peshito MSS. number 125 of Gospels, 58 of
Acts and Catholic Epistles, 267 of Pauline Epistles.

[29] See especially Burkitt, *Evangelion da Mepharreshe*, 2 vols. (1904);
Studia Sinaitica, No. VI.; *Text and Studies*, VII., 2; *Journal of Theol.
Studies*, II, 174-185; *The Four Gospels in Syriac* by R. L. Bensly, etc.,
1894; *Palestinian Syriac Lectionary* by Lewis and Gibson, 1899. A. Min-
gana believes the Peshito translation to have been made by Christian Jews
in Mesopotamia (*Jewish Quar. Rev.*, January, 1916).

reign of Theodosius between A.D. 385 and 388, she
speaks of the "little church" which, tho so small, "has
of itself great grace." When this woman traveler
visited the monastery, over 1,500 years before Mrs.
Lewis and Mrs. Gibson made their memorable visit, it
was less than three centuries since John the Apostle
died and she was nearer to the beloved disciple than
we are to Henry VIII. or Luther or Shakespeare. The
manuscripts of the gospels then on Mt. Sinai may have
been translated from the originals.

It was on Mt. Sinai in February, 1892, that Mrs.
Agnes Smith Lewis and her sister, Mrs. Margaret
Gibson, made their sensational discovery. Both of
these twin sisters could speak modern Greek with
fluency, and Mrs. Lewis, who had previously studied
Arabic and Hebrew, made special preparation for this
trip by studying Syriac, and became thoroughly acquainted with the oldest Syriac manuscripts at Cambridge, thus being providentially prepared for the discovery which was made possible only by this recent
study. Having reached Cairo in January, 1892, they
won the good will of the Greek archbishop of Mt. Sinai,
who gave them permission to examine the Sinaitic
library, together with his blessing—even promising
them immunity from the Khamseen winds! We can
not describe their journey across the desert and their
first sight of the Mount of God which, Dean Stanley
has well said, "rises like a huge altar, . . . visible
against the sky in lonely grandeur from end to end of
the whole plain." At length they came in sight of the
massive walls of the stately convent of St. Catherine.
Undoubtedly many unknown manuscripts in Greek,
Slavonic, Syriac, Arabic, and Iberian lie hidden behind

those walls—do they contain any treasure for these two adventurous Christian women? The kindness of the librarian, who can be forgotten by no one of us who have ever visited this ancient sanctuary, opened everything in the convent to their inspection, and on February 8, 1892, they began their work, examining, copying, and photographing such works as appeared to them especially valuable.

The most ancient of these manuscripts were kept in dark closets, and the damp leaves, which "had evidently been unturned for centuries," could often be separated only by manipulation with the fingers or by the steam of the kettle. One day in this month of February, as they were searching through the rare, old, unbound parchments which had probably not even been looked at for centuries, they came across a Syriac palimpsest of 358 pages whose leaves were glued together by time and so old that "the least force used to separate them made them crumble." The overwriting in this case bore the date A.D. 778, and proved to be a very entertaining account of the lives of female saints. The preface to this read:

"By the strength of our Lord Jesus the Christ (the Son) of the Living God, I begin, I the sinner, John the Recluse of Beth-Mari Kaddisha, to write select narratives about the holy women, first the writings about the blessed lady Thecla, disciple of Paul the blessed apostle. Brethren, pray for me."

Later the author treats of the "Blessed Eugenia" and of Philip her father, of Pelagia the harlot of Antioch, of the blessed Onesimus, of Theodosia the virgin, of Theodota the harlot, etc., ending: "Let every one who reads . . . pray for the sinner who wrote it."

The under and more ancient writing was greatly

blurred, some of the words being wholly obliterated, yet Mrs. Lewis detected the words "Evangelion," "Mathi," "Luca," and jumped to the correct conclusion that this older writing must be an ancient Syriac text of the four gospels. They photographed this work entirely, and left the convent on the eighth of March. Having reached home, they developed their thousand photographs and showed them to various scholars, but without finding any one who could make out the blurred writing or saw that it was of any special importance until Mr. F. C. Burkitt, a young scholar of Cambridge, took the photographs and showed them to Prof. R. L. Bensly, who was just finishing a new edition of the oldest Syriac version of the four gospels (the Cureton). He recognized at once that this was another copy much like the Cureton, but very much more complete and probably older. Almost immediately it was arranged that Professor Bensly, Mr. Burkitt, and Prof. J. Rendel Harris should accompany the discoverers back to Sinai where they would accurately transcribe the manuscript word for word. Arriving at the convent February 8, 1893, they found to their great delight that the experienced experts could easily trace the words in the underwriting, and after forty days of steady labor they were able to return to England bearing with them an almost complete copy of this precious document. The copy was completed in 1895.

We have given long space to a description of this discovery because of its picturesque interest and its great and generally unappreciated value. Its importance will be recognized as soon as one remembers that scholars of all schools believe that the Greek Testament was translated into Syriac—a branch of the language

used by the Jews of Palestine at the time of our Lord—
at least as early as the middle of the second century of
the Christian era, and that some of the very greatest
scholars, like Merx, of Heidelberg, and Hjelt, of Hel-
singfors, as well as Dr. Lewis, believe that this newly
discovered text is a copy of that primitive Syriac version which was in use by the Church in Palestine not
later than A.D. 150—nearer to the crucifixion than we
are to the Revolutionary War. These Syriac gospels
which must have been written in Antioch (Lewis)
within fifty or sixty years of the death of St. John,
being the earliest translation of the four gospels into
any language, were a translation of the earlier Greek
gospels, proving that those four gospels, in almost the
exact form in which we now have them, were then the
accepted standards of the Church. Dr. Lewis points out
forcibly that this Antioch text is older than Tatian and
holds very nearly the same relation to the Greek of
the gospels as the Septuagint does to the Hebrew of
the Old Testament.[30] The special thing that makes this
Syriac text so valuable is not the fact that it proves the
existence of these Greek gospels within fifty years of
the apostolic age—no intelligent person denies that
now—but because it gives the version of the New Testament used in Palestine at that early age, being written in the Eastern branch of the very language which
our Lord and the apostles spoke.

This Syriac text gives us the real Aramaic forms of
names rather than those which have been transferred
into our translation from the original Greek text. Especially is this noticeable in proper names; e.g., we read
Halfai for Alphæus, Juda Scariota for Judas Iscariot,

[30] *The Old Syriac Gospels,* 1910, pp. vi., xiii.

Cepha for Peter, Ramatha for Aramathea, Beni-Rogschi for Boanerges, Hannan for Annas, *Ain Nun* (*i.e.,* the "fish spring") for Nain, Shiloah for Siloam, Beth Zaita (*i.e.,* "mount of the house of olives") for Mt. Olivet, etc. The fact is that these Syriac names, in most cases, probably represent the local pronunciation better than the Greek, which was itself a translation or modified transcription of these native names. Some plays on language found here may represent the original words of Jesus; *e.g.,* John 8: 34, "He who doeth sin is the slave of sin." Other changes which may possibly be due to this thorough acquaintance with the language spoken by Jesus are: "Blessed . . . who hunger and thirst for justice"; "We have seen his star from the East"; "My yoke is gentle, my burden is small"; "Put these sayings in your ears"; "There are not two or three gathered together in my name and I not with them"; "You hold the key of the kingdom of heaven before men; for you neither enter in yourselves, nor those that are coming do you suffer to enter"; "This is my blood, the New Testament"; "I do that which I have seen of my Father"; "Let not your heart be troubled. Believe in God, and in me ye are believing"; They murmured against her "in their teeth"; "He rolled up the book"; "Thou art not fifty years old and hath Abraham seen thee?"; "Now we know that thou knowest all things and needest not that thou shouldst ask any man." A discrepancy is removed by having John 18: 13 followed by verse 24; and by omitting "more than these" and "Thou knowest that I love thee" (John 21: 15-17), and "Father forgive them" (Luke 23: 34).

Judas, not Iscariot, is called in this version Judas Thomas; but the most striking change in names is found in Pilate's question: "Which will ye that I release unto you, Jesus Bar Abba or Jesus that is called Christ?"—a reading which makes Pilate say, "Which Jesus will you have, Jesus the son of Abba (*i.e.,* the malefactor) or Jesus the king?" This may really represent an original reading; yet if so I can hardly think it would have been omitted without cause from our other manuscripts and versions, and therefore it seems rather to be a sign that this text, old as it is, is not as old or pure as that of the great Greek manuscripts from which our English translation was made. Indeed, there are many indications amounting to proof that the Syriac reading is a later explanation or paraphrase of the Greek text. When the Greek text says "good" fish, the Syriac says "very good"; when the Greek says "sick," the Syriac says "very sick"; when the Greek says "Not I, Lord," the Syriac says "Not I surely, Lord"; when the Greek says "two mites which make a farthing," the Syriac says "two mites which make two farthings, which make an eighth"; when the Greek says that the woman "wet" his feet with her tears, the Syriac says "bathed"; when the Greek says, "Thou hast nothing to draw with," the Syriac says "not even a pitcher"; when the Greek has simply "Master," the Syriac almost always has "Our Master." On the other hand, Lazarus is called a "poor man," not a "beggar," and "son" is omitted in Abraham's reply (Luke 16: 25); in Luke 17: 10 we read "servants" instead of "unprofitable servants," and in Luke 19: 22 "fruitless" not "wicked" servant; and in John 3: 13 the Son of Man, not "in" but "from" heaven.

Certain other interesting readings are "If (two of you) shall agree upon earth about everything"; Anna

was "seven days with a husband after her virginity";
Joseph went to Bethlehem with his "wife" (Luke 2: 5);
"And all the people and the publicans that heard justified themselves to God" (Luke 7: 29); "Thou shalt
have glory"; "Love your enemies . . . and do
not cease hope of men"; "The disciple is not perfect as
his master in teaching"; "The Pharisees derided him
because they loved silver"; "Rebuke the disciples that
they shout not"; "They that have authority and do good
are called benefactors"; "Woe to us, what hath befallen us! woe to us for our sins"; "That which is born
of the spirit is spirit, because God is a living Spirit";
"I was blind and because of him, lo! I see"; "I am
the vine of truth"; "Peter warmed himself, for it was
freezing"; "Peter cast himself into the lake and was
swimming"; "Feed my lambs, feed my sheep, feed my
flock." It is plain from this that, altho the Syriac form
is beautiful, it can hardly be the primitive text, for in
that case there could be no explanation of the change
into the present text. On the other hand, in many cases
certain variations in the Syriac seem to make it certain
that this was derived from our Greek text; e.g., Luke
4: 29, where the people of Nazareth took Jesus to the
brow of the hill that they might "throw him down
headlong," the Syriac text has so that they might "hang
him," which is plainly a misreading of the Greek word.
So in John 11: 31, where the Greek says Mary "rose
up quickly," the Syriac says she was "amazed," which
is almost certainly a misreading, as the two Greek
words are very nearly alike. It also seems to me probable that the curious reading, "and seven days only was
she with a husband" (Luke 2: 36), may be due to a
scribe's blunder, who perhaps mistook ἔτος "year" for

ἔτι "yet" and guesses at the meaning "seven (days) only." [31]

Having now seen that old as this text is, it is not as pure or old as the Greek text, we are ready to look steadily and intelligently at what is supposed to be a very unorthodox reading: "Joseph to whom was betrothed Mary the Virgin begat Jesus who is called the Christ." "And she bore to him a son, and he called his name Jesus" (Matt. 1: 16). In considering this it must be remembered that our Lord was legally and socially the son of Joseph, and that this fact is indeed the only logical ground for the incorporation of Joseph's genealogy in the evangelist's narrative. The editor of this text also points out that the word "begat" is used here in a purely conventional sense, for in the eighth verse we have it stated that Joram begat his own great grandson, and in the twelfth verse the childless Jechoniah is said to have "begat" Shealtiel. The Christian system does not hang upon the miraculous birth of Jesus, altho certain metaphysical and theological conclusions may seem to require it; but it must be added, nevertheless, in all fairness, that there is even in this new Syriac text the usual distinct statement that the birth of Jesus was supernatural (Matt. 1: 18-20). These Syriac gospels are not rivals of our Greek texts any more than a very early French translation of Shakespeare would be a rival of the English text of Shakespeare, but they do offer a new proof of the remarkable integrity of our Greek text. These Syriac translations, dating back al-

[31] See especially *The Four Gospels Transcribed from the Sinaitic Palimpsest,* Agnes Smith Lewis, 1894; *The Four Gospels in Syriac,* by R. L. Bensly, J. Rendel Harris, F. Crawford Burkitt, with an Introduction by Agnes Smith Lewis, 1894; *Some Pages of the Four Gospels Retranscribed from the Sinaitic Palimpsest,* 1896; and *The Old Syriac Gospels,* 1910, by Agnes Smith Lewis, D.D., LL.D.

most if not quite to apostolic times, are translations of our four gospels, and contain not a single extract from the gospel of Peter or any other private memorandum of events. Even the mistakes of this text, as we have seen, prove the existence of the earlier authoritative Greek texts. In this Syriac version, Mt. Sinai has given us a new proof of the age and integrity of the Greek originals.

Dr. Agnes Smith Lewis has made five trips to Mt. Sinai since the discovery mentioned above, and has made several other "finds" of especial interest. Among these we should probably give first place to the fragments of a beautiful sixth century Palestine (Syriac) text of the four gospels and Pauline epistles obtained on her sixth visit in 1915.[31a] This discovery consisted of eighty-nine leaves of a palimpsest, the upper script mostly dating from the ninth century; but part of the Syriac text, according to Mr. G. Margoliouth, dates from the sixth century. The Greek underwriting, according to Nöldeke, represents a Palestine Syriac version originating in the fourth century (*ZDMG*, XII, 525), tho Dr. Burkitt would date it two centuries later (*Journal of Theological Studies*, II, 183). This Syriac text, according to the learned editor, was not a lectionary, but a translation from the Greek New Testament, and contains: Matt., chaps. 24, 25, 27; Acts, chaps. 19, 20, 24, 27; Romans, chaps. 4, 5, 7, 9, 10; 1 Cor., chaps. 3, 4, 13-16, and scattered portions of 2 Corinthians, Galatians, Colossians, Thessalonians, 2 Peter and 1 John.[31b] One of the most interesting of Dr. Lewis's recent discoveries is that of a "Harmony of the Gospels," containing Matt. 5: 30-37; 6: 1-2;

[31a] See *Horæ Semiticæ*, No. VIII., *Codex Climaci Rescriptus*, 1906.
[31b] The writer has not been able as yet to get access to this Greek text.

8: 8-17, 20, 21; 9: 7-13, 36; 10: 5; John 12: 1-3, 6, 9, 14, 15-18; 20: 19, 20, 25, 28-31; 21: 1, 2.[31c] This "Harmony" is now in Dr. C. R. Gregory's care in Berlin for examination, and the writer, because of the war, has not been able to learn anything further concerning this text either from Dr. Lewis or Dr. Gregory.[31cc]

3. COPTIC NEW TESTAMENTS

In 1883, nine thousand leaves of Coptic manuscripts were discovered in the White Monastery between Assiut and Thebes, 250 miles south of Cairo. Among these leaves were some of the oldest and most valuable Coptic Bibles ever seen. The first Coptic manuscript of any considerable part of the Bible reached the British Museum in 1896; by 1905 the Museum possest fifty-nine fragments of Coptic Old Testaments and eighty-three pieces of as many Coptic New Testaments, and it has been gathering such manuscripts ever since.[31d]

There are at least five or six Coptic dialects now known to scholars, but they fall into three general divisions: the Sahidic, which was the dialect of Upper Egypt; the Bohairic, the dialect of Lower Egypt; and Middle Eygptian, the dialect of Akhmim and the Fayum. Of these the Bohairic is the most literary and artificial, being still used in the ritual of the Coptic church. All of these various dialects are well represented in late manuscripts of the New Testament; but for-

[31c] See *Horæ Semiticæ Climaci* 5.
[31cc] See note 7b, p. 139.
[31d] *Catalog of Coptic MSS. in the British Museum*, 1905, and for a further list of extant Coptic Biblical texts see especially Hyvernat, *Catholic Encyclopedia*, Index Vol., articles, "Coptic Literature" and "Versions of Bible, Coptic"; *Revue Biblique*, 1896-7, and *Muséon* XIII., 275-362; XV., 49; Chabot in *Journal des Savants*, X., 174ff., and Schleifer, in *Revue Critique* XLIX.

tunately the Sahidic, which was probably the earliest and most important in Scripture translation, is represented in a great number of New Testament MSS., many of which go back to the fourth and fifth centuries. In 1904 a good edition of many fragments, with forty full-page collotype specimens, was issued at Rome by P. J. Balestri, O.S.A., and in 1911 an almost exhaustive edition of all these Sahidic texts was published by Oxford University. Altho this latter work did not include some valuable material from the Rainer collection, later published by Wessely,[32] it was an enormous work in which 751 MSS., mostly dating from the fourth to the eighth century, were collated with the Greek, Old Syriac, Old Latin, etc., and all important variants noted.

Of these fragments of 751 Coptic New Testaments only one "appears to have suffered any systematic correction," even the MSS. as late as the tenth or twelfth century showing very few variants.[33] All the fragments omit the story of the woman taken in adultery (John 7: 53—8: 11), as do all the oldest Greek texts. While the texts in general showed a Western influence they were, in fact, "neutral" in tendency, thus indicating their translation from very early Greek originals. The distinguished author recognizes that the history of the Egyptian Church begins with the accession of Demetrius to the Patriarchate in A.D. 188, and expresses his conviction that this Coptic version arose in Egypt as early as the second century, probably about A.D. 150.[34]

[32] *Studien zur Paläographie und Papyruskunde,* IX.-XII.
[33] *Coptic Versions of the New Test. in the Southern Dialect,* 3 vols., Oxford, 1911, Vol. I., p. 374.
[34] *Ibid.,* pp. 398, 399; a second century date is accepted also by Hyvernat, *Revue Biblique,* 1897, pp. 67*ff.*; and Kenyon, *Textual Criticism of the New Testament;* all of these *vs.* Hastings, *Dict. of Bible; Ency. Brit.,* and *Ency. Bib.* Leipoldt dates the completion of the version A.D. 350, *Gesch. der christlichen Literatur, VII.,* 2, Leipzig, 1907, pp. 139*ff.*

It is evident that as a confirmation of the authenticity of the present Greek text of the New Testament, these most recent researches into a language which no text-critic of the last century was able to explore, have proved very satisfactory. While the Bohairic version has not previously been counted so important as the Sahidic, yet the multitude of new discoveries has permitted practically the entire new Testament to be reproduced in this dialect.[34a] A new manuscript of great value has just been discovered containing a large part of the Four Gospels. It is much older than any previously known gospel manuscript in this dialect, the earliest previously known being the *Curzon Catena,* dated A.D. 889. The newly found Bohairic gospels, thought by some to represent an older text than even the Vatican manuscript, contains Matthew and John and a good part of Mark; and, in Sahidic, all of St. Paul's epistles and those of Peter and John. This discovery is from all points of view, "Biblical, critical, paleographic and artistic . . . by far the most important event of recent years."[35] Hoskier even believes that the writer of the Sinaitic MS. had before him several ancient texts, of which the Bohairic was one. This shows, at least, the new and great importance of this newly found version.

The Fayumic version is not represented by any such enormous collections of ancient fragments; yet a sufficient number of these have been obtained to show that the dialect of this district had been used as a medium for New Testament translation very early in

[34a] *The Coptic Version of the New Testament in the Northern Dialect,* by George Horner, 4 vols., 1898-1905.

[35] *Journal des Savants,* X., 179.

the Christian history.[36] The first text was brought to
the British Museum in 1879, and dates probably from
the sixth century. This version is of special importance because our earliest Greek fragments were found
in the Fayum (see pp. 166-173). The study of the
Akhmimic dialect of the New Testament has been
pushed forward greatly during the last fifteen years.
Among the discoveries, high rank must be given to the
entire papyrus book containing the Proverbs of Solomon and to the important fragment of a book containing a portion of the gospel of St. John in Greek and
Akhmimic. The Greek text of the latter we have
already commented upon (p. 152). The Coptic contains St. John 10: 1—12: 20; 13: 1, 2, 11, 12; James
1: 13—5: 20.[37]

The famous parchment codex of the twelve lesser
prophets in the Rainer collection is still unfortunately
unpublished at this writing, but a sufficient number of
New Testament scraps have been found to make
this dialect, which flourished midway between the Delta
and ancient Thebes, of considerable interest, tho not
of great textual value.[38]

The recent discovery of a very ancient copy of the
book of Acts and book of Revelation in Sahidic, the text
of which has just been published to the world by the
British Museum (ed. by Dr. E. A. Wallis Budge, 1912),
may well close our review of these Coptic New Testaments. This codex of Acts, which was discovered in

[36] See E. Chassinat, *Bull. de l'Inst. Franc. d'arch. au Caire* II.; *Frag-
menta Bassurica*, I.-III.; especially Wessely, *Sitzungsberichte der kais.
Aked. der Wissensch. in Wien. philos. hist. Klasse*, Vol. 158 and Joseph
David, *Revue Biblique*, 1910.

[37] Roesch, *Bruchstücke des ersten Clemens-Briefes, Strassburg*, 1910.

[38] See Lacau, *Bulletin de l'Inst. française d'arch. orient*, VIII. (Cairo,
1911).

1901, and which must be dated, according to the editor, not later than the middle of the fourth century, marks a distinct advance by putting in our hands "the oldest known copy of any translation of any considerable portion of the Greek Bible."[39] This translation is, in fact, as old as our oldest large Greek MSS., and fortunately, with the exception of a few mutilated verses, the only portions of the manuscript absent are chapters 24: 17— 26: 31; 27: 7, 8, 9, 18, 19, 20, 28, 29. It is well written in a good hand, tho there are many mistakes in spelling and omissions of entire lines, due either to the carelessness of the writer or "because he was copying from an old and partly obliterated text." He evidently did not understand always what he was writing, as he copied "destruction" for "healing" (Acts 2: 6); "thy disciples" for "thy sins" (22: 16), etc. In a few passages the readings differ from the later MSS. of the Sahidic versions; e.g., "God of our fathers" instead of "God of Glory" (Acts 7: 2); "the voice answered" instead of "the voice was against me" (11: 5). Often the readings are more correct than those of the later texts. A little sermon at the end of the Acts in cursive script written about the middle of the fourth century contains some remarks which it might be profitable to repeat:

"Why do ye commit sin? Ye add sin to your sin, ye make to be wroth the Lord God who hath created you. Love not the world nor the things which are in the world, for the glory of the world belongeth to the devil and the destruction thereof . . . for many times the devil wisheth to prevent the sun from rising on the earth . . . he wisheth to swallow up men . . . for this reason God hath showed compassion on us in sending (!) his Son into

[39] Wessely, however, dates his Sahidic Acts (ii-xxvi.) to cir. A.D. 400 (*Muséon* XV, 40).

the world that he might deliver us. . . . Fasting is nothing and God did not ordain it, and (those who practise it) [*i.e.*, as a saving ordinance] make themselves strangers to the covenant of God.[39a]

There are a few very interesting readings:

Acts 8: 10—"This is the great power of God" (or) "This man is the great one of the power of God."

10: 36—"For his word he sent it to the children of Israel. He preached peace by Jesus the Christ. This is the Lord of everyone."

11: 20—"And having come to Antioch they spoke with the Greeks; they preached the Lord Jesus."

16: 13—"On the day of that Sabbath we came out outside the gate on the river to a place wherein we might pray."

18: 5—"Paul was persevering in the word; he was testifying to the Jews that Jesus was the Christ."

20: 28—"Church of the Lord which he hath acquired through his own blood."

21: 16—"The disciples who were in Cæsarea took us to an old disciple a Cyprian, Mnason, that we might sojourn with him."

The Codex of the Apocalypse published with the Acts is almost equally important, and the various readings equally curious, *e.g.*:

Rev. 9: 20—"The demons of gold and silver."

11: 18—"To judge the living and the dead."

13: 18—"He who hath understanding, let him count the number of the name of the beast; for it is the number of a name; it maketh 600, 6, 60."

[39a] Dr. A. A. Vaschalde, of the Catholic University of America, calls my attention to the fact that this translation is not critically exact. "Sin" (fourth word from end of first line) should be "sins"; "wisheth" (fifth line) should be, "wished"; "he wisheth" (sixth line) should be "wishing"; while instead of "and the destruction thereof" (fourth line) we should read (following "world"), "and its dissoluteness"; while the passage beginning, "Fasting is nothing" may be omitted, as the text is badly mutilated here and Budge's interpretation somewhat uncertain.

17:5—"There was a name of mystery written upon her fore-head."[39b]

It should be noted that this great codex was not used as a service book, but was the property of some private individual, perhaps a monk. It had been used till it was nearly worn out and the back of it had to be strengthened.

This discovery brings another proof that the Coptic version must hereafter be reckoned with as one of the important authorities for the text of the New Testament.

4. Ancient New Testaments in Latin and Other Languages [40]

The Latin versions of the Scriptures can be traced back into the second century, altho, naturally, no second century copies of this translation now exist. We know, however, that the martyrs at Carthage in the year A.D. 180, had in their case of Latin rolls the

[39b] Dr. Vaschalde in a personal letter points out some critical corrections to these renderings of Dr. Budge. Acts 8:10, the second rendering "is certainly false," and the first is in complete harmony with the Greek. Acts 10:36, 11:20, 20:28 agree with the Greek. Acts 16:13, read "on the day of the Sabbaths"; Act 18:5, translate: "Paul was persevering in the word, testifying to the Jews that Jesus is the Christ." Acts 21:16 should be translated " . . . the disciples, who were in Cæsarea; they took us to an old disciple, etc." Dr. Vaschalde points out that none of the readings in Revelation, (excepting perhaps 11:18) are peculiar to this codex, the same readings being found in Goussen's or Wessely's texts. That is, these readings, while they may be peculiar to the Sahidic Version, are not peculiar to Budge's Codex. "It must also be borne in mind that the Sahidic version is, as a rule, not as literal as the Bohairic."

[40] Almost all of these new discoveries have been made in monasteries. The Egyptian papyri have yielded comparatively little Latin material, altho Wessely has recently given fifty examples of Roman script (three from the first century and six from the second), and has described in a fascinating way the peculiarities of the early Latin script at the time when Vergil and Horace were writing. One of the most interesting secular documents is a bundle of letters dated 21-18 B.C. by Macedo, a citizen of the Fayum (*Aus der Welt der Papyri,* pp. 45*ff.*).

"Epistle of Paul, the just man." Cyprian, also, in the middle of the third century, quotes the Latin text of the New Testament constantly. By the middle of the fourth century so many different translations of the Greek text had already appeared that the Latin MSS. exhibited a most confusing variety of text, and this lasted till Jerome's version (A. D. 384-400) supplemented all others.[41]

Within the last two decades the Latin versions have advanced to a place of primary importance in determining the original text of the New Testament. It has long been acknowledged by textual critics that the Vulgate of Jerome represented in many places a better text than our Authorized Version; for in the year 1611 no scholar was able to consult such ancient Greek texts as Jerome used in the fourth century. Jerome attempted to produce a critical edition, and did the work well so far as the gospels were concerned, altho not so well in the epistles. There now exist some 8,000 MSS. following Jerome's revision. These prove that Jerome's translation was much modified by later revisers, especially from the ninth to the twelfth centuries; the original Vulgate being quite different from the authorized edition of this text, put out by Pope Clement VIII in 1592. This edition was declared by edict to be superior to the Greek originals and was used later as the basis of the Douay (Roman Catholic) New Testament.

The oldest manuscript representing Jerome's version of the New Testament was discovered in 1907. It was bound up with a collection of shorthand symbols (tenth century) and a number of short prayers (seventh century); but it dates from the sixth century,

[41] F. C. Burkitt in *Ency. Biblica*, IV., 5008-10.

being thus the oldest large Latin Bible text now in the British Museum. It is a vellum leaf which was once the sixth leaf of an uncial Latin New Testament, in which the gospels were written in their present order. The leaf contains Mark 16: 15-20, representing in general the Vulgate text, and on the opposite side of the leaf are two ecclesiastical lections of the eighth and ninth centuries, containing John 14: 7-14; Luke 24: 49-53. There are a few curious readings, the most interesting being Mark 16: 17, where *"uelute apostoli"* is added to the regular text, thus limiting miraculous signs to such disciples as have the same kind of faith as had the apostles.[42]

The recent study of Jerome's translation has been valuable; but previous to Jerome there had been several other translations or recensions of the New Testament into Latin, and in recent years scholars have been able for the first time to get back with considerable certainty to those texts which antedate the original Vulgate. Fragments of at least eighteen manuscripts of the Old Latin gospels still exist, five of which are of the fourth or fifth century. The advantage of this is incalculable, since the tendency after Jerome was toward an unhealthy uniformity of Latin text. The fine faithfulness of the early Latin copyists makes even short quotations or broken manuscripts of unusual value. The general conclusion of an examination of all the evidence gathered from these hundreds of Latin New Testaments in Africa and Europe, and from the quotations made by the early Fathers of the Latin Church, is to confirm the authority of our present

---

[42] Described in *Jour. of Theol. Studies*, XIII., 369-371. For the changes in the Vulgate text of St. Paul's epistles, see *Revue Biblique*, 1915, pp. 358-392.

Greek text, which we have already seen to lie at the basis of the Coptic and Syriac translations. Such is the settled conclusion of Biblical science.

A young English scholar, however, Mr. E. S. Buchanan, has recently been attempting a quixotic attack upon the Greek manuscripts, affirming that they were all wilfully changed in the second or the third century and that the Latin manuscripts are far more trustworthy. This claim would not be worthy of attention here were it not that a few reputable American magazines have seemingly sanctioned this theory, supposing it in some way to be a "defense of orthodoxy." Instead of favoring orthodoxy it leads directly to out-and-out textual skepticism. Fortunately, it is diametrically opposed to all legitimate conclusions from the many text discoveries of the last quarter of a century. No one doubts that we possess twentyfold more Greek than Latin manuscripts dating from the early centuries. Of the 2,369 Latin manuscripts catalogued by Gregory less than half a dozen date as early as the sixth century. No one doubts that the Latin manuscripts were derived from Greek originals. The Latin manuscripts from which Mr. Buchanan obtains these unique readings—which he believes to be primitive— are late manuscripts dating from the sixth to the tenth century.[43] It is a mere speculative decision on his part that these new readings are primitive, and in most cases his decisions are opposed by other textual scholars.

Mr. Buchanan's basal claim is that the copyists in the second or third century changed the original

---

[43] Mr. Buchanan dates two of the manuscripts he edits early in the fifth century, but those from which he obtains his most sensational variants date from the eighth to the tenth century.

text in the interests of the "hierarchy" against the virgin birth and the deity of Jesus, and the personality of the Holy Spirit; but this is against all historical perspective. The Christian theologians of that era were zealously accepting these doctrines. To suppose that anybody could have introduced at that era changes against the cherished beliefs of the Church and had them universally accepted is simply preposterous. A church of heretics and fraudulent deceivers would have to take the place of the Church of the martyrs in order to give Mr. Buchanan's theory an *a priori* standing. But even if the possibility of changes so vital as these was acknowledged, it would yet be absolutely incredible that such particular changes as many of those which he mentions could be primitive. It is easy to see how such readings could arise at a comparatively late era on the basis of the present Greek text, but impossible to explain how the present Greek text could have arisen from such an original text as Mr. Buchanan's theory presupposes. It is also impossible to imagine original readings of the following nature dropping absolutely out of sight in the primitive Church:

"And they were astonished at the teachings of the Holy Spirit, for the word of the Lord Jesus was powerful" (Mark 4:24).

"Judge not your brethren and ye shall not be judged" (Luke 6:37).

"Holy Father which art in heaven: Give us to-day for bread the Word of God from heaven" (Luke 11:2, 3).

"In him was the life of God, which is the light of men" (John 1:4).

"No man can come unto me except the Father which sent me and the Holy Spirit draw him" (John 6:44).

"He that followeth me shall not walk in darkness but shall have the eternal light of the life of God" (John 8:12).

"If thou art God, tell us plainly" (John 10:24).

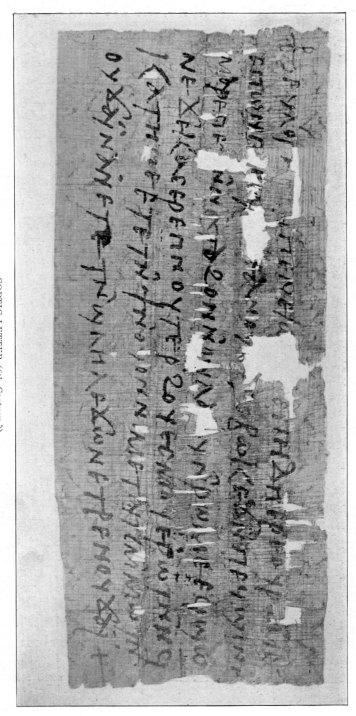

COPTIC LETTER (6th Century ?)

From an unpublished papyrus obtained in Egypt by the author

SELF-COOKER

LOAF OF BREAD

WALL-PAINTING

SURGICAL INSTRUMENTS

LAMPS AND CANDELABRA

RELICS FROM THE APOSTOLIC AGE (1st Century)

"Whatsoever ye shall ask in my name, that will I do, that the Son of God may be glorified" (John 13:14).

"And the word which ye hear is not man's, but the Father's which sent me" (John 14:24).

"These things have been written that ye may believe that Jesus Christ is Son of Man and Son of God, and have life eternal in his name" (John 20:31).[43a]

One might hope that a few of the readings in these Latin manuscripts shall prove to be primitive, such as:

"John did baptize in the wilderness and preach repentance for the remission of sins" (Mark 1:4).

"No prophet is acceptable in David's country" (Luke 4:24).

"Do good to them that curse you" (Luke 6:28).

"I have sinned against heaven and . . . am not worthy to be thy servant" (Luke 15:21).

"Except a man be born of the Spirit, he can not enter the kingdom of God" (John 3:5).

But while the above texts appeal to us as possibly defensible primitive readings, according to the proper canons of criticism, yet this does not prove that they were primitive. It is only by an exhaustive examination of the manuscript testimony that such matters can be decided. It is perfectly clear, however, according to every canon of criticism, that such a reading as the following could not be primitive:

"I say unto thee, upon this rock shall be built by the Holy Spirit his disciples."—Matt. 16:18.

Mr. Buchanan finds this reading in a Spanish manuscript from the library of the late J. P. Morgan. It is a very handsome manuscript containing 110 richly colored miniatures and was copied in the tenth century, tho it dates back to the Presbyter Beatus who lived in the eighth century. It is evident that Beatus

---

[43a] These instances have all been taken from the *Irish Codex Harleianus*, edited by E. S. Buchanan, M.A., B.Sc., 1914.

was rather a remarkable man, for his comments written in the text are noteworthy: "Christians are called after Christ; therefore, the Lord said, 'Upon this rock shall be built by the Holy Spirit his disciples,'" and "This is the first church that was founded at the first by the Spirit upon the rock, Christ"; but to imagine that such a comment represents a primitive reading which has been dropt out in some miraculous or fraudulent way from the Greek text and from all versions excepting this one very late and very gorgeous copy, is to allow one's credulity to take the place of reason.[44]

Text critics are eager to welcome any new reading with a fair probability of truth behind it, but in the interest of solid learning such hasty conclusions as those noticed above are much to be regretted. Whatever may be the outcome of the contention by Merx, Hoskier, Von Soden and others that the Western text, including also the old Latin Syriac, and Coptic Versions, must be given more prominence than has ordinarily been given it by text critics, no such argument as the above can seriously assist this claim. The new discoveries prove that the Alexandrian critics did not even form a new standard text of Homer, as was once supposed certain—the earliest texts being "substantially identical" with the very late texts—and every great text critic now believes that the variations of text, either in the classics or in the New Testament, are due, not chiefly to wilful corruption, but to ignorance.[45] Ignorant as the scribes were who wrote some of the Greek minuscules, few of them can be

<hr/>

[44] *Bibliotheca Sacra*, Oct., 1915; *The Early Revisers of the Gospel*, E. S. Buchanan, 1915; *Search for the Original Words of the Gospel.*, Dec., 1914; *Sacred Latin Texts*, Vols. I.-II., V.; cf. *Jour. of Theol. Studies*, 1917, p. 171.

[45] Cf. F. G. Kenyon, in *Proceedings of Brit. Acad.*, 1903-4, pp. 139-293.

compared in this respect with the Latin scribes. In the *Codex Laudianus,* "church" and "elder" are each spelled in four different ways, and in the *Codex Corbeiensis* Paul is spelled "paulus," "laulus," "paus," "populus."

While we have thus frankly criticized some of the sensational conclusions of Mr. Buchanan, we do not fail to recognize the value of his textual work and of the new viewpoint which would magnify the importance of the old Latin readings. If, further, he shall be proved right in his belief that the gospel of Mark was written originally in Latin, this will give to the study of the Latin manuscripts, especially to the gospel of Mark, a new interest. Mark was anciently called the "interpreter" (*i.e.,* "secretary" or "dragoman") of Peter; and if this gospel were written in Rome it would naturally be put in the vernacular. The native people were undoubtedly talking Latin. It is said that even Cicero did not know Greek until he was over sixty years of age. At any rate, Mark has a Latin background; and as there are forty Latin names of persons and places and thirty other Latin terms, military, judicial, and domestic found in the New Testament (Robertson), all Bible students may well be interested in every new discovery or new theory connected with the Latin manuscripts. If Mark's gospel were written originally in two languages (either Greek and Aramaic or Greek and Latin), the double ending of the sixteenth chapter might also be more easily explained.[46]

A considerable number of other Biblical manuscripts have recently been brought to light, written in Arabic, Armenian, Ethiopic, and other languages, but these have

---

[46] *Cf.* Swete, *Gospel according to St. Mark,* pp. xxiv., xlvii.; Salmon, *Introduction to the New Testament,* p. 151.

added comparatively little to our knowledge of the Bible
text. We may mention, however, a rather surprizing
discovery which Dr. J. Rendel Harris (following
Preuschen) has just made in an Armenian version of
the Acts of the Apostles. He believes that he has found
there the name of the author. This not only assists to
settle the old controversy concerning the correct spelling of Luke's name, but has at least some little bearing on certain more important questions concerning
that much discust work. Scholarship has gradually
come to see that the "we" sections of the Acts can
not be detached from the rest of the book. In language, style, atmosphere, and outlook the book is a
unity. Dr. Harris has convincingly shown that the
Western text differed from the ordinary text just as
widely in the far East as in the near West and now,
in a second century Armenian commentary, he has
found this unique reading: "But [I], Luke (Λούϰιος),
and those who were with me, went on board."

5. A Very Ancient "Harmony of the Gospels"

Tatian, who was an eastern Syrian rhetorician of
Greek education born about A.D. 110—some six or
eight years after the traditional date of St. John's
death,—was an independent thinker. Before his conversion to Christianity he had studied all the learning
of the Greeks and was dissatisfied with it. He says:
"While I was giving my most earnest attention to the
matter" (the discovery of truth), "I happened to meet
with certain barbaric writings too old to be compared
with the opinions of the Greeks and too divine to be
compared with their errors" (*i.e.,* the Old Testament
Scriptures). "I was led to put faith in these by the

unpretending cast of the language, the inartificial character of the writers, the foreknowledge displayed of future events, the excellent quality of the precepts, and the declaration of the government of the universe as centered in one being." [47]

At Rome he met Justin, "the martyr," and was converted to Christianity. Justin was a great man. He had been a pagan philosopher, but had met with Christianity and it had conquered him; he had traveled all over the civilized world and personally knew the men who had known the apostles. Tatian studied with this man and perhaps saw him, with six other Christians, beheaded in Rome A.D. 166. Thus Tatian became a Christian philosopher, and wrote various philosophical treatises against the Greeks. Philosophic discussion, however, is not always a good thing for every man, and very soon Tatian was drawn away from the simplicity of the gospel. He was led in these discussions to feel so keenly the difficulty of acknowledging Christ's humanity while claiming his divinity that he finally gave up the doctrine that Christ was human, declaring that his human body was but an appearance and that only his divinity was real. In connection with this heresy he taught also that the body was an evil thing and everything was evil that gave it pleasure. He became, therefore, an ascetic of a pronounced type, abstaining from all luxurious food and abhorring marriage. He also followed Marcion in distinguishing the Demiurge from the God of the Old Testament; he followed Valentine in his theory of eons, and propounded one or two original unorthodox theories of his own, such as his denial of the salva-

[47] *Address to the Greeks,* chaps. 29-30.

bility of Adam. By the time he died (A.D. 172) he was regarded by the Church as a dangerous heretic and was banished, but it was probably before he fell so far from orthodoxy and yet after he began to scruple concerning the true humanity of the Christ that he wrote his *Diatessaron*.[48]

This *Diatessaron* or "Harmony of the Four Gospels" was an attempt to weave everything in all the gospels into one continuous narrative. It was a difficult task but a very worthy one, and it made a serious impression upon the early Church. Undoubtedly it received criticism, for it was a new and advanced plan for Bible study—and all such plans are criticized—but it nevertheless became so popular that by the third century it was being read in some churches (notably at Edessa) instead of the four gospels at the regular church services. This continued to be such a common custom that when Ephraem Syrus, in the fourth century, wrote his commentary on the gospels, he actually took this "Harmony" as the text on which he based his comments.[49] But when the Peshito was issued, probably by Rabbula the bishop of Edessa, as the "Authorized Version" of the Syrian Church (A.D. 411-435), a crusade began against this Harmony of Tatian, and proved so successful that soon not only had the public use of the work ceased in the Church, but it almost disappeared from private circulation, altho it was occasionally read as late as the middle ages.

The unusual importance of this work may be judged from the fact that certainly the Peshito (fifth century) and perhaps even the Old Syriac translation

[48] Some time between A.D. 153-170, according to Nestle in Hastings, *Dict. of Bible*, IV., 646.
[49] *Dict. of Bible*, Extra Vol., p. 452; *Studia Biblica*, III., 132*ff*.

(*cir.* A.D. 175) had been influenced by it; yet unfortunately the original work was entirely lost and all that remained of it were a few quotations in certain early writings. However, an Armenian translation of a commentary by Ephraem Syrus, who had used the work, one imperfect fourteenth century Arabic MS. which purported to be a translation of the *Diatessaron,* and a Latin codex (*Fuldensis*) of the sixth century, which was thought by some to be a translation of it, were recovered. Notwithstanding the unsatisfactory data, Professor Zahn, in 1881, gathered all the evidence available and attempted to reconstruct the original text—an attempt which was proved to be brilliantly successful by the discovery of another older and better Arabic text which was published by Ciasca with a Latin translation, in 1888, in honor of the jubilee of Pope Leo XIII. While this Arabic MS. was only of the eleventh century, it translated a Syriac text written in the ninth century and showed far less conformity to the orthodox Syriac version than any manuscript previously known. While, of course, a late manuscript such as this could be of no value in settling by its readings the ancient text, yet wherever this manuscript could be tested by ancient quotations it proved its trustworthiness. Its independence was shown by the omission of the last twelve verses of Mark omitted in the oldest Greek MSS., and also by the omission of Luke 22: 43, 44 (the bloody sweat) and 23: 34 (the prayer on the cross), which it was known Tatian had omitted from his "Harmony," tho there was in general a verbal harmonization with the accepted Syriac text.

Only a short time before this discovery, a celebrated foreign critic had declared that if this lost work were ever recovered, it would be seen that Tatian's gospels were not at all our gospels, but very different records, since at that early date (A.D. 160-170) our gospels, as we now have them, with their accounts of miracles and assertion of our Lord's deity and other supernaturalisms, were probably not received as authoritative, even if they were then in existence. The scientific recovery of what is essentially the ancient form of this "oldest life of Christ," compiled from the four gospels, has sufficiently answered such skepticism; and it is a source of considerable gratification that we now possess several English translations of this newly discovered manuscript, one of the best of which is that by Rev. J. Hamlyn Hill, of Cambridge, whose work we shall use freely in the comparisons about to be made.[50]

In appreciating the value of this new discovery it must be borne in mind that Syriac was Tatian's native language and the first language into which our gospels were ever translated, and that scholars generally believe that this translation of our gospels from Greek into Syriac had probably been made either before the Apostle John died or, at farthest, within two generations afterward.[51] Does, therefore, this Tatian manu-

[50] *Earliest Life of Christ*, Edinburgh, 1894.

[51] I am accepting here provisionally the ordinary dating of St. John's death (*cir.* A.D. 100-105), tho it must be admitted that modern scholarship has made this dating quite insecure. See *e.g.*, Moffatt, *Introduction to the Literature of the New Testament*, pp. 602-619. Yet the names of great scholars can still be cited who do not accept the popular modern position. Besides Harnack, Drummond, Stanton, Workman, Lepin, Abbott, J. H. Bernard, and J. Armitage Robinson quoted by Moffat (*op. cit.*, p. 605), add the strong arguments for the old view offered by Zahn, *Introduction to the New Testament*, 1909, III., 178-194; Peake, *Critical Introduction to the New Testament*, 1913, pp. 136-151; and for a non-committal position Sanday, *Criticism of the Fourth Gospel*, 1905, pp. 108, 251*ff.*; and Swete, *Apocalypse of St. John*, 1907, pp. clxxv.-clxxxv.

script make known to us different gospels from those reported to us by the evangelists; gospels in a formative state out of which the gospels which the Church now accepts were evolved toward the end of the second century? Not at all. That was the theory woven with great ingenuity and learning upon German and French spindles some few years ago; but the theory is already dead and buried. This is not a "patchwork," as one learned scholar called it, made up of various primitive traditions very different from our own; but is an amalgamation of our four gospels and of our four gospels only, with not one sentence taken from any "Gospel of Peter" or any other apocryphal gospel however ancient or however interesting.[52] If this eleventh century Arabic text, made from a ninth century Syriac MS., represents truly the original Syriac text of Tatian, as scholars now seem generally to acknowledge,[53] it discovers to us the text of the gospels which over 1,700 years ago was accepted both by the orthodox and the heterodox churches. It is impossible to attempt here a comparison of this text with the ancient Syriac version (the Peshito) and the Greek text. It may be said in general terms that this Arabic translation (representing Tatian's Syriac) does not fundamentally differ from our present Greek text much more than the German or French Testament differs from it. There are, however, a few peculiar readings; e.g., "No man hath seen God at any time; the only begotten God who is in the bosom of the

[52] So Gregory distinctly affirms, *Canon and Text of New Testament*, 1907, p. 128; as to Tatian's manner of using the Gospel material see the remarkably clear and thorough examination by A. A. Hobson in Univ. of Chicago's *Hist. and Linguistic Studies*, 2d Series Vol. I., 841.

[53] *E.g.*, *Hist. and Linguistic Studies*, 2d Series, Vol. I., Univ. of Chicago, 1909, p. 216.

Father, he has declared him"; "Glory to God in the highest and on earth peace, good hope to men"; "Strain out a gnat and adorn a camel," etc. Instead of "pray and not faint" this version reads "pray and be not slothful." On the Mount of Transfiguration instead of the remark: "They saw no man save Jesus only," this version reads: "They saw Jesus even as he was." When Jesus said to the young man "sell all" this version adds, "at this word the young man frowned." Instead of "a hundredfold" this version writes "twice as many." In Gethsemane, instead of "sweating great drops of blood" this version declares it was "a stream of blood"; and when Jesus says to Cephas, "thou shalt catch men," this version adds, "thou shalt be catching men unto life."

In almost all of these readings the text of Tatian follows that of the Old Syriac, but there are some terms of expression peculiar to himself; e.g., "He that hath received this witness hath set his seal to this, that he is truly God"; "Forgive and ye shall be forgiven, release and ye shall be released"; "And many envied him and did not apply their mind to him"; "Even so your Father which is in the heavens willeth not that any one of these little ones should perish, whom, after erring, he calleth to repent"; "That which is exalted among men is small in the sight of God"; "Spitting on his own fingers, he put them on the blind man and healed him," etc. The greatest changes are a few vivid touches at the trial and crucifixion peculiar to this text. When Jesus "went out, Simon Cephas was standing in the outer court warming himself," and going to Calvary "Jesus went on with his cross behind him." The title was written on a "tablet" and nailed to the cross, and the chief priests and scribes "mocked him and laughed to each other saying, The Saviour of others can not save himself."

Such are the most striking of all the differences between this version of the gospels and ours—a scarcely greater difference, so far as fundamental statement of doctrine or fact is concerned, than between the A. V. and the R. V. or between the French and the English Testaments. It ought, perhaps, to be emphasized once more that there is no evidence whatever that Tatian intended his compendium to supersede the four gospels. It seems rather intended to have been a companion to the four gospels, just as our modern harmonies are. This discovery proves once more the care of the gospel text taken by those early Christians who lived within fifty years of the apostolic age.[54] Justin Martyr, the teacher of Tatian, received many accounts from the aged men concerning Jesus and his life, which he regarded as being absolutely reliable— the names of the thieves on the cross, various people who had been healed, etc.,—and Tatian no doubt believed these things, too; but he did not put in one single item of that kind. He stuck close to the thought of the original Greek, which he evidently regarded as the authoritative inspired original, and was so anxious not "to omit the slightest comment of any one evangelist unless it was substantially preserved in the words of another" that often he has been led into undue repetition "by placing one after the other passages of different evangelists that vary but little from one another."

[54] E.g., see Hastings, Dict. of Bible, V., 452; A. A. Hobson, Diatessaron of Tatian and the Synoptic Problems, p. 80; Milligan, New Test. Documents, p. 219.

There were no brilliant "patchwork" additions by the heretical editor. The worst that Tatian did was to omit from his "Harmony" the genealogies of Jesus and other references that "show our Lord to have been born of the seed of David according to the flesh"; yet the book and its author were anathematized. The early Church would not sanction even an abridged edition, much less a mutilated edition of the authoritative historical records. The discovery of this document, and its acceptance by scholars as representing the ancient Syriac text, also buries the theory so popular a few generations ago that the miracles of the gospels were an addendum to the original unmiraculous narrative of the Lord's life. This discovery makes still more certain, what was sufficiently proved before, that the "memoirs of the apostles," which Justin says "contained all things concerning our Saviour Jesus Christ," and were read together with the writings of the prophets in the weekly services of the Christians, were our four gospels and none other; since Tatian, the heretical disciple of Justin, uses these and none other as the authoritative and the only authoritative historical and biographical documents of the Christian Church. Already, only two generations after the death of the last apostle, these four gospels (just these four and no others), altho written in different countries by different persons and at different times, had been so long recognized as Christian Scriptures that they could be used in combination both by heretic and orthodox as the complete and authoritative record of the events related in them. Thus the most scholarly and weighty arguments ever formulated against the Christian faith[55] have been rendered obsolete.[56]

In completing our survey of the discoveries in this most important field of textual criticism we are imprest with the complete and thorough way in which the radical theories of a century ago have been disproved. The text of the New Testament is now fixt more certainly than that of any ancient book. Not even one discovery has been opposed to the overwhelming testimony regarding the antiquity of the text, while the general purity of the text has been established by a mass of evidence a hundredfold greater than that which can be marshalled for any ancient classic. Ninety years ago, when Horne published his *Introduction,* about 550 MSS. of the New Testament had been collated by scholars; a little over thirty years ago, when Westcott and Hort brought out their epoch-making Greek text, some 1,700 MSS. were ready for their use; to-day over 4,200 Greek MSS. have been collated, and they all confirm the integrity and purity of the New Testament text.

The importance of the new discoveries may be vividly appreciated by remembering that 300 years ago, when the King James' version was made, probably not one MS. dating as far back as the sixth century was available for purposes of textual criticism; even when the Revised Version was issued less than a dozen such MSS. were known; but between the years 1900-1912 we find that twelve manuscripts written in uncial form and

---

[55] I refer to the brilliant arguments of Baur and Strauss.

[56] For literature on Tatian's *Diatessaron* see especially Hastings, *Dict. of Bible,* IV., 648; *Ency. Brit.,* III., 882; XXVI., 312; for the story of Zahn's most brilliant restoration of the text see *Hist. and Linguistic Studies,* Univ. of Chicago, 1909.

of very great importance were discovered, ten of these containing substantial parts of the New Testament and two of them containing complete copies of the four gospels; while many fragments of texts containing the Acts, Catholic epistles and Pauline epistles were found, 500 different Bible texts having been discovered during that brief period.[57]

In addition to these Greek texts hundreds of manuscripts in many languages, Coptic, Syriac, Latin, etc., have been collated, representing very ancient translations of the Greek New Testament—some of these being practically as near to St. John as we are to Shakespeare—and these also confirm the integrity of the text. A vast number of these ancient translations, especially in Syriac and Coptic, have been recently discovered. Of the old or Curetonian Syriac our knowledge is due entirely to quite recent discoveries, as "little more than fifty years ago its very existence was unknown" (Kenyon). Until very recently, no MS. of the Memphitic or Bohairic text older than A.D. 1173 was known to exist; while the Thebaic or Sahidic was not known until the end of the eighteenth century. We now possess sufficient fragmentary texts, many of them from the fifth or fourth century, to "compose a nearly complete New Testament."

It is not, therefore, an exaggeration to say that the original text of the New Testament is now fixt at least as certainly as the text of some of Shakespeare's plays.

[57] See Kenyon's *Handbook*, 1901, compared with list given in the same *Handbook* in 1912.

NEW LIGHT ON THE NEW TESTAMENT FROM PRIMITIVE CHRISTIAN DOCU- MENTS RECENTLY DISCOVERED

1. THE LOGIA, OR NEWLY DISCOVERED "SAYINGS OF OUR LORD"

UP to our day the oldest documents of Christianity were the Holy Writings, the MSS. of which dated from the fourth, fifth, sixth or later centuries, at a time when Christianity had become victorious. Not one scrap of Christian writing was known from any pen previous to the Constantine era, and not one smallest fragment of the Holy Scriptures or other literary or private Christian memoranda had survived in its original form nor any autographic account of any act relating to the early Christians.[1]

Most wonderful seemed the discovery of Grenfell and Hunt when, in 1896, they dug up at Oxyrhynchus a collection of "Sayings of Jesus" dating from the third century of our era and purporting to come from the lips of our Lord himself. No one had doubted that Jesus had uttered many words worthy of memory which had not been recorded in the brief memoranda contained in our gospels. St. Paul had quoted one such sentence, "It is more blessed to give than to re- ceive" (Acts 20: 35), and Clement of Alexandria, writ- ing at a time when the early Church still possest a living memory of the apostolic era, had quoted several sayings of Jesus which were most striking: "Be ye

[1] For a most vivid statement of these facts see Wessely, *Les Plus Anciens Monuments du Christianisme Écrits sur Papyrus*, p. 99.

trustworthy money changers"; "Ask great things and the small shall be added to you"; "He that wonders (*i.e.*, with reverent faith) shall reign, and he that reigns shall be made to rest." In the Codex Bezae, too, Jesus was represented as saying to a man working on the Sabbath day, "Oh man, if thou knowest what thou doest, then blessed art thou; but if thou knowest not, then art thou accursed."[2]

When it is remembered that in all the sixteen centuries since Clement there have not been two sayings a century originated by all the thinkers of the earth worthy to be placed alongside the golden sentences of Jesus, it becomes possible (and perhaps more than possible) that several of the above sayings represent a correct memory of the early Christian Church, thus giving to us veritable utterances of our Lord himself. This is even more probable when we consider the "logia" discovered recently.

The papyrus leaf first published in 1897 contained seven or eight sayings, as follows:

1. ". . . And then shalt thou see clearly to cast out the mote that is in thy brother's eye."

2. "Jesus saith, Except ye fast to the world, ye shall in no wise find the kingdom of God; and except ye make the sabbath a real sabbath, ye shall not see the Father."

3. "Jesus saith, I stood in the midst of the world, and in the flesh was I seen of them; and I found all men drunken, and none found I athirst among them, and my soul grieveth over the sons of men, because they are blind in their hearts and see not . . ."

4. ". . . poverty . . ."

5. "Jesus saith, Wherever there are two, they are not without God; and wherever there is one alone, I say, I am with him. Raise the stone, and there thou shalt find me; cleave the wood, and there am I."

[2] For a full list of these "sayings" quoted by ancient authors see J. H. Ropes' "Agrapha," in Hastings, *Dict. of Bible,* V : 343-352.

6. "Jesus saith, A prophet is not acceptable in his own country, neither doth a physician work cures upon them that know him."

7. "Jesus saith, A city built upon the top of a high hill and established can neither fall nor be hid."

8. "Jesus saith, Thou hearest with one ear (but the other ear hast thou closed)."

The saying which seems hardest here is the one which was originally translated "Except ye sabbatize the sabbath, ye shall not see the Father." If this had really meant that no man could see the Father and enter the kingdom of God without observing fast days and keeping the Jewish Sabbath (Bodman, Bacon, James, etc.), then the idea must have been given up that Jesus ever uttered these words. But Prof. J. Rendel Harris of Cambridge and Prof. Adolph Harnack of Berlin, soon after the discovery, indubitably proved that these words were to be taken figuratively, not literally. They gave many instances in the writings of the early fathers in which this form of mystical or symbolic language was used. To "fast to the world" meant, in the early Church, to abstain from worldly lusts and to deny sensual appetites (Clement). By such a fast men died to the world and thus became able to enter the kingdom of God and partake of heavenly food (*cf.* Isa. 18:6). Both Professor Harris and Professor Harnack quoted the words of Justin Martyr: "If there is an adulterer let him repent, and thus he has sabbatized the true and delightsome Sabbath of God." In this passage the very expression was used which is found in the new text; so that the teaching became plain, and it is now universally accepted that the injunction to "sabbatize the sabbath" did not mean that one must keep the seventh day of the week as his rest day, but that he must keep himself pure in heart and in act. The right

way of keeping the sabbath was determined not by
the clock or by the almanac, but by the soul.

When properly understood, this new "saying" seems
an eternal word, a word for all time, and is in beautiful
harmony with the teachings of Jesus recorded in the
gospels. It is true that Professor Harnack thinks that
Jesus would not have antagonized his countrymen by
using this expression, virtually telling them that with
all their strict sabbatarianism they were not really keeping the Sabbath; but this objection loses its force when
we remember that the gospels are full of this criticism
of outward sanctimoniousness without the inward spirit
of holiness. He who spoke so strongly to hypocrites,
scrupulous in their regard of outside observances while
inwardly full of corruption, would not have hesitated
to call those who claimed to be sabbath keepers "sabbath breakers," unless they kept the day of rest "in
the spirit." These words seem to the writer a true
message from the lips of our Lord, a message never
more needed than in this age of sabbath desecration
and worldliness.

In regard to the third saying, Professor Harnack
in a burst of enthusiasm cries out: "We receive this
beautiful word with thanks"; for in this logion Jesus
speaks as a divine being who, tho he was a Son,
"in the flesh," was not to be confounded with the "sons
of men" over whom he grieved. This is very like an
expression often found in John's gospel. It is a significant thing that in all these new discoveries the
nearer we get to the lifetime of Jesus the more confidently is his deity presupposed in every word that
reaches us from those martyr centuries. How like
Jesus also are these tender words: "My soul grieveth

over the sons of men, because they are blind in their heart." The blind heart—that is the worst thing! One other figure used here recalls St. John's gospel: "I found all men drunken and none found I athirst among them" (*cf.* John 7:35; Matt. 5:6). Men had so lost the natural appetites of the children of God that they did not even desire the pure water of life. The world was drunk without even a thirst for holy things![3]

In February, 1903, Messrs. Grenfell and Hunt returned to Oxyrhynchus, and "by a curious stroke of good fortune" their second excavations were, like the first, signalized by the discovery of another fragment from a collection of "Sayings of Jesus." These sayings were prefaced by the statement:

"These are the (wonderful) words which Jesus the living (Lord) spake to . . . and Thomas; and he said unto (them), everyone that harkens to these words shall never taste of death."

The translation of the newly found sayings, as given by Grenfell and Hunt, runs as follows:[4]

1. "Jesus saith, Let not him who seeks . . . cease until he finds, and when he finds he shall be astonished; astonished he shall reach the kingdom, and having reached the kingdom, he shall rest."

2. "Jesus saith, (Ye ask[?] who are those) that draw us (to the kingdom if) the kingdom is in heaven? . . . the fowls of the air and all beasts that are under the earth or upon the earth and the fishes of the sea, (these are they which draw) you; and the kingdom of heaven is within you, and whosoever shall know himself shall find it. (Strive therefore) to know yourselves, and ye shall be aware that ye are the sons of the (Almighty?) Father;

---

[3] We have used in this review: Grenfell and Hunt, ΛΟΓΙΑ ΙΗϹΟΥ, the *editio princeps*, June, 1897; Harnack, *"Ueber die jüngst entdeckten Sprüche Jesu"*; Lock and Sanday, *"Two Lectures on the Sayings of Jesus"*; Oxyrhynchus Papyri, Pt. I., pp. 1-3.

[4] *"New Sayings of Jesus,"* 1903; *Oxyrhynchus Papyri,* Vol. IV., 1904.

(and?) ye shall know that ye are in (the city of God?) and ye are (the city?)." [5]

3. "Jesus saith, A man shall not hesitate . . . to ask concerning his place (in the kingdom. Ye shall know) that many that are first shall be last, and the last first, and (they shall have eternal life?)."

4. "Jesus saith, Everything that is not before thy face and that which is hidden from thee shall be revealed to thee. For there is nothing hidden which shall not be made manifest; nor buried, which shall not be raised."

5. "His disciples question him and say, How shall we fast and how shall we (pray?) . . . and what (commandment) shall we keep . . .? Jesus saith . . . do not . . . of truth . . . blessed is he."

The discoverers declare that these forty-two Greek lines which were found on the back of a survey list of various pieces of land at Oxyrhynchus can hardly be later than A.D. 300. These may, indeed, be the beginning of the collection which later on included the first found logia, yet these words do not seem as striking as those of the former series. Of the first saying, the latter part had been quoted by Clement of Alexandria from the *Gospel of the Hebrews,* and many scholars believe that we have here an excerpt from that gospel; tho Professor Harnack thinks it came from the *Gospel according to the Egyptians,* and still others believe that they came from the *Gospel of Thomas.* Most scholars, however (Sanday, Swete, Rendel Harris, Lock, Heinrici, etc.), believe that both of these sets of "sayings" represent an independent collection, being possibly one of the earliest attempts to write in connected form an account of the teaching of Jesus (and therefore dating back into the first century); or else

[5] See an attempt to reconstruct the text differently in this and the following "saying" in Deissmann, *Light from the Ancient East,* p. 439.

originating very early in the second century, being composed under conditions of thought which had been created by the canonical gospels. The fact that the additions found in these "sayings" were evidently not made in the interests of any sect or heresy is an indication that they contain genuine first century material.

A word may be added with reference to the meaning of some of the sayings most recently discovered. The first (*cf.* Matt. 6: 33; 7: 7; 13: 44; Luke 5: 9; 11: 9) emphasizes the strenuous effort needed to attain the kingdom. Harnack points out that "astonishment" is to be thought of as a sign of joy, not of fear. The parallel to the second saying is found in Luke 17: 21, and the meaning is that, tho the divine element in the world begins in the lower stages of animal creation, yet it rises to the highest stage in man, who has within him the kingdom of heaven; self-knowledge, when profound enough, brings God-knowledge. The third saying (*cf.* Mark 10: 31) emphasizes the fact that the standard of values in heaven differs from the earthly standard. In the fourth saying the revelation of all hidden things in the future is affirmed (*cf.* Matt. 10: 26; Mark 4: 22; Luke 12: 2). The question in the fifth saying concerning the keeping of Jewish ordinances (*cf.* Matt. 19: 16-22) may be compared with the second saying in the earlier collection commented upon above.

The logia found in 1897 were in the form of a handsomely written book; those discovered in 1903 are in roll form, written on the back of a trivial document. In the earlier collection no direct parallel with John's or Mark's gospel could be traced; but this collection has a distinctly mystical and Johannine character, while the third and fourth sayings have closer connections

with St. Mark than with St. Luke.[6]   It can be safely
inferred from the correspondence with John's gospel:
"that the editor of the collection lived in an atmosphere
of thought influenced by those speculative ideas in early
Christianity which found their highest expression in
the Fourth Gospel" (*ibid.*, p. 14).

The very latest date for either collection would be
A.D. 140, tho, according to the learned editors, it probably dates from the first century.   Sir F. G. Kenyon
thinks this may be a collection which St. Luke himself
used.[7]   Professor Petrie suggests that these sayings, like
the Memorabilia of Socrates, might naturally grow up
during the lifetime of the great teacher.   The Sermon
on the Mount may have been originally a collection of
sayings codifying the chief tenets of the "Way" in
thirty clear statements taken down by Matthew, the one
handiest with the pen, long before any elaborate history
was needed.[8]

Several other isolated "sayings" of Jesus, of perhaps
even an earlier date, have been found in mutilated Greek
papyri which may have originally contained a collection of such words.[9]   There is also one new "saying"
which sounds good enough to represent a true tradition in Cod. C. of the *Palestine Syriac Lectionary:*
"Men must give an account of every good word which
they shall not speak."   Another new "saying" in a
Coptic fragment published by Jacoby, in 1900, is more
doubtful: "I have revealed to you all my glory and I
have told you all its power and the mystery of your
apostleship."   We do not mention here the sayings

[6] Grenfell and Hunt, *op. cit.,* p. 11.

[7] *Bible and Ancient Monuments,* p. xvi.

[8] *Athenæum,* Sept. 27, 1897.

[9] See, *e.g.,* Wessely, in *Zeitschrift für Kath. Theologie,* xi : 507-515.

of Jesus found in Mohammedan literature, altho some of these are quite suggestive, as: "Leave the world and meditate over death. To a believer, death comes with good which has no evil after it, but to a wicked man it comes with an evil which has no good after it."

The chief value of these newly discovered "sayings" is that they show the links between the canonic and uncanonic gospels and the relationship of both to the main current of orthodox Christianity. It has an important bearing on the question of sources used in the synoptic gospels and indicates that the mystic elements in early records of Christ's sayings may have been more general and less peculiarly Johannine than hitherto supposed. It may be well to add that these same mystic and speculative elements are found in an even greater degree in the newly discovered *Odes of Solomon,* published from a Syriac version by J. Rendel Harris in 1909, which turns out to be a book of Christian songs from the early years of the second century, incorporating Jewish mystical phraseology from the first century A.D., some of which is remarkably similar to that used by the fourth evangelist. This will be discust later.

2. NEW FRAGMENTS OF LOST GOSPELS, ACTS, REVELATIONS, ETC.

(1) THE GOSPEL OF PETER

In 1885, a long fragment of the Gospel and of the Apocalypse of Peter was discovered at Akhmim in Upper Egypt, which was published by Bouriant in 1892, and subsequently by Lods, Robinson, Harnack, and other scholars. This created a marked sensation because it was the first to be found in modern times of the multitude of apocryphal gospels known to have existed in the early centuries of the Christian era. The manuscript dates from about A.D. 400, but the text from which the manuscript was copied was much older. All scholars agree that this "Gospel" was written a good while before A.D. 190, for by that date it was so well established in one city that Serapion, who was bishop of Antioch (A.D. 190-203), could write:

"We brethren receive Peter and the other apostles even as Christ; but the writings that go falsely by their names we reject knowing that such things as these we never received . . . (though) most of it [the Gospel of Peter] belonged to the right teaching of the Saviour, but some things were additions." (Eusebius, *Ecclesiastical History*, VI., 12.)

This "Gospel" must be dated then almost certainly as early as the first half of the second century; while some scholars, as Dr. Moulton of Cambridge University, would put it a generation before the close of the first century. The little parchment book on which this gospel is written contains also fragments of the Book of Enoch, which is pre-Christian and is quoted by St. Jude; and also the Apocalypse of Peter, the composition of which may go back almost to the end of the first century of our era. The "Gospel according to Peter" begins the book. It reads:

1. "But of the Jews none washed his hands, neither Herod nor any one of his judges, and when they wished to wash them, Pilate rose up. And then Herod the king commandeth that the Lord be taken, saying to them, What things soever I commanded you to do unto him, do.

2. "And there was come there Joseph the friend of Pilate and of the Lord; and knowing that they were about to crucify him, he came to Pilate and asked the body of the Lord for burial. And Pilate sent to Herod and asked his body. And Herod said, Brother Pilate, even if no one had asked him, we should have buried him; since indeed the sabbath draweth on: for it is written

in the law that the sun go not down on him that is put to death on the day before the unleavened bread, which is their feast.

3. "And they took the Lord and pushed him as they ran and said, Let us drag away the Son of God, having obtained power over him. And they clothed him with purple, and set him on the seat of judgment, saying, Judge righteously, O king of Israel. And one of them brought a crown of thorns and put it on the head of the Lord. And others stood and spat in his eyes. And others smote his cheeks; others pricked him with a reed; and some scourged him saying, With this honor let us honor the Son of God.

4. "And they brought two malefactors and they crucified the Lord between them. But he held his peace, as in no wise having pain. And when they had raised the cross they wrote upon it, This is the king of Israel. And having set his garments before him, they parted them among them, and cast a lot for them. And one of those malefactors reproached them, saying, We have suffered thus for the evils that we have done, but this man, having become the Saviour of men, what wrong hath he done to you? And they being angered at him commanded that his legs should not be broken, that he might die in torment.

5. "And it was noon and darkness covered all Judea and they were troubled and distressed lest the sun was going down, since he yet lived: (for) it is written for them that the sun go not down on him that is put to death. And one of them said, Give him to drink gall with vinegar; and they mixed, and gave him to drink, and fulfilled all things, and accomplished their sins against their own heads.

"And many went about with lamps supposing that it was night and fell down. And the Lord cried out saying, My power, my power, thou hast forsaken me. And when he had said it, he was taken up. And in that hour the veil of the temple was rent in twain.

6. "And then they drew out the nails from the hands of the Lord, and laid him upon the earth, and the earth all quaked, and great fear arose. Then the sun shone, and it was found the ninth hour: and the Jews rejoiced and gave his body to Joseph that he might bury it, since he had seen what good things he had done. And he took the Lord and washed him and wrapped him in a linen cloth and brought him to his own tomb, which was called the Garden of Joseph."

In the seventh section the people and priests lament, saying, "Woe for our sins," and later charge the disciples of Jesus with "wishing to set fire to the temple." In the eighth section the scribes and Pharisees and elders ask a guard:

"And Pilate gave them Petronius the centurion with soldiers to watch the tomb. And the elders and scribes came with them to the sepulcher, and having rolled a great stone, along with the centurion and the soldiers they altogether who were there set it at the door of the sepulcher, and they put upon it seven seals; and they pitched a tent there and kept watch."

Section nine describes the resurrection heralded by a great voice in the heaven, and "two men descending thence with great light and approaching the tomb. And that stone which was put at the door rolled away of itself and departed to one side; and the tomb was opened and both the young men entered in."

The tenth section reads:

"When therefore the soldiers saw it, they awakened the centurion and the elders, for they too were hard by keeping watch; and as they declared what things they had seen, again they see coming forth from the tomb three men, and the two supporting the one, and a cross following them. And of the two the head reached unto the heaven but the head of him that was led by them overpassed the heavens. And they heard a voice from the heavens saying, Hast thou preached to them that sleep? And an answer was heard from the cross, Yea."

Section eleven tells of the report of the centurion to Pilate, and Pilate's confession, "Truly he was the Son of God . . . I am pure from the blood of the Son of God." The leaders of the Jews also beseech Pilate to command the soldiers to say nothing of the things which they had seen, "for it is better for us to incur the greatest debt of sin before God, and not to fall into the hands of the people of the Jews and to be stoned."

The twelfth and thirteenth sections tell of the women coming secretly to the tomb fearing lest the Jews should see them, and finding to their surprize that the stone was rolled away. They see an angel in the midst of the tomb, who tells them of the resurrection. "For he is risen and gone away thither whence he was sent."

The gospel ends with the fourteenth section:

"Now it was the last day of the unleavened bread, and many went forth returning to their homes, as the feast was ended. But we the twelve disciples of the Lord wept and were grieved: and each one, grieving for that which was come to pass, departed to his home. But I, Simeon Peter, and Andrew my brother took our nets and went away to the sea; and there was with us Levi the son of Alphæus whom the Lord . . ." [10]

In considering the above account, the hatred of the writer for the Jews is constantly in evidence. Pilate is exonerated. The Jews must bear all the blame. He is also a heretic, for he is not willing to admit the humanity of Jesus who (sec. 4) could not suffer pain until (sec. 5) the "power" (the divine Christ) finally left the human Jesus upon the cross. Considering that this probably represents the earliest of all known apocryphal gospels, it is suggestive to note that it has beneath it every one of our four gospels, in some places referring to particulars only found in John's gospel, and in other places depending definitely upon Matthew, or Mark, or Luke. This is but a fragment of the gospel, and deals only with the death of Jesus; yet it gives testimony to the fact that Jesus lived, was brought

[10] The above translation is given from *"The Gospel According to Peter,"* by J. A. Robinson, 1892.

to death by the Jews on a Friday, was tried before
Herod and Pilate; it tells of the purple robe and crown
of thorns and that he was spit upon and smitten on
the cheek; it gives the names of several disciples, and
says there were twelve in all; it declares that he was
crucified between two malefactors, one of whom repented; it gives the title on the cross and the time of
the death; it tells of the parting of garments, the drinking of gall and vinegar, the cry on the cross, the rend-
ing of the temple veil, and the darkness that was over
all the earth; it reports the begging of the body by
Joseph, who wrapt it in linen clothes and laid it in
his own tomb, and of the guard asked of Pilate by the
scribes and Pharisees for three days; it describes the
rolling away of the stone, the resurrection of Jesus,
the flight of the soldiers, the visit of Mary Magdalene
and other women, and the questions and answers of
the angels. These are a few of the many facts to
which this little independent fragment, not a part of
the Bible, testifies. It also emphasizes in a most
marked way the deity of Christ. This author, who
may have actually been a contemporary of St. John,
or at least lived as near the apostolic age as we do to the
age of Abraham Lincoln, believed so fully in the deity
of Christ that he almost or quite denied his humanity.

This oldest non-Biblical account of Christ's life in
Greek does not contain nearly so many grotesque im-
becilities as the later apocryphal gospels. Many of
these fill up the boyhood of Jesus with silly miracles.
He can carry water in a cloak; he helps his father
in the carpenter shop by stretching timber to the
proper length with his bare hand; he plants one grain
of wheat and threshes eight hundred bushels; he makes

birds out of clay, and by clapping his hands gives life to them; when a boy runs against him on the street Jesus becomes angry and curses him, whereupon he immediately falls down dead; and when the dead boy's parents complain they become blind. Things almost as foolish as this are to be found in all the apocryphal gospels, and even in this earliest one is the fanciful statement about the cross walking and talking, and about Christ coming out of the tomb so tall that his head was above the clouds. How it would have destroyed the dignity of the solemn narratives to which we have been accustomed if any such grotesque incident had crept into our gospels.

(2) THE REVELATION OF PETER

In the same year in which the Gospel of Peter was found and in the same book in which it was recorded, the Revelation of Peter came to light. This is a document constantly mentioned in early writings; yet only eight lines from this famous ancient treatise had been known to scholars previous to this discovery. It had such an enormous influence in early times that it distinctly affected the Sibylline oracles and the Apocalypse of Paul, and even influenced through the latter the Divina Commedia of Dante; yet no scholar in modern times had ever read it. As translated and paragraphed by Montague Rhodes James [11] this document begins as follows:

1. "Many of them will be false prophets and will teach ways and various doctrines of perdition: and they will be sons of perdition. And then will God come unto my faithful ones that are hungering and thirsting and suffering oppression and proving their own souls in this life; and he will judge the sons of lawlessness."

[11] *Revelation of Peter*, 1892.

The second and third paragraphs tell of the Lord and his disciples going to the mountain to pray. The disciples besought the Lord that he show them one of the righteous brethren that had departed from the world, so that they might see what form the dead took in the future life. While they prayed, two of these departed saints stood before them, "their bodies whiter than any snow and redder than any rose . . . and their shoulders like a wreath woven of spikenard and bright flowers, and their raiment so bright that they could not be looked upon."

In paragraphs four and five the Lord showed to the disciples the other world "blooming with unfading flowers . . . and the dwellers in that place clad in the raiment of angels of light."

The remainder of this "Revelation" (paragraphs 7-20) had to do with a vision of the place of the damned. We offer a few quotations:

"And there were some there hanging by their tongues, and these were they that blaspheme the way of righteousness: and there was beneath them fire, flaming and tormenting them."

"And there were also women hung by their hair over that mire that bubbled up: and these were they that adorned themselves for adultery: and the men that had been joined with them in the defilement of adultery were hanging by their feet, and had their heads in the mire: and all were saying, We believed not that we should come into this place."

"And I saw the murderers . . . and there were set upon them worms as it were clouds of darkness. And the souls of them that had been murdered were standing and looking upon the punishment of those murderers and saying, O God, righteous is their judgment."

"And hard by that place I saw another narrow place wherein the gore and the filth of them that were tormented ran down and became as it were a lake there. And there sat women having the gore up to their throats . . . and these were they that destroyed their children and caused abortion."

"And there were other men and women on fire up to their middle and cast into a dark place and scourged by evil spirits and having their entrails devoured by worms that rested not: and these were they that persecuted the righteous and delivered them up."

"And hard by them again were women and men gnawing their lips and being tormented and receiving red hot iron upon their eyes: and these were they that had blasphemed and spoken evil of the way of righteousness . . ."

"And in a certain other place were pebbles sharper than swords or than any spit, red hot, and women and men clad in filthy rags were rolling upon them in torment: and these were the wealthy that had trusted in their wealth and had not had pity upon orphans and widows."

"And in another great lake full of pitch and blood and boiling mire stood men and women up to their knees: and these were they that lent money and demanded interest on interest."

"And others again . . . women and men were burning and turning themselves and being roasted: and these were they that had forsaken the · v of God."

This apocalypse naturally falls into three parts. The first is the eschatological discourse; the second, the vision of Paradise; the third, the inferno. The first is doubtless intended to recall Matt. 24: 24 and Mark 13: 22, and is supposed to be the concluding lines of a speech of our Lord concerning the end of the world; but it also contains a strong resemblance to the second epistle of Peter, a dozen distinct resemblances to this epistle being detected in this and the following paragraphs. Perhaps the greatest importance of these non-canonical visions of heaven and hell is found in the contrast they offer to the reticent statements of the canonical gospels. This new discovery shows very clearly how even the earliest Christians were accustomed in their sermons to picture the future world. It also shows how many of our popular notions are ultimately derived, not from Holy Scriptures. but from the early apocryphal literature.

(3) OTHER FRAGMENTS OF IMPORTANCE RECENTLY RECOVERED

A very much more important discovery was made in 1903 by Grenfell and Hunt in this same town of Oxyrhynchus.[12] It is a fragment of a lost gospel, the manuscript of which dates from the third century, the very words of which recall vividly the language of our own gospels. It reads:

"Take no thought from morning until evening nor from evening until morning, either for your food what ye shall eat or for your raiment what ye shall put on. Ye are far better than the lillies which grow but spin not. Having one garment what do ye (lack)? . . .Who could add to your stature? He himself will give you your garment. His disciples say unto him, When wilt thou be manifest unto us and when shall we see thee? He saith, When ye shall be stripped and not be ashamed . . . He said, The key of knowledge ye hid; ye entered not in yourselves and to them that were entering in ye opened not."

Even Zahn looks with some favor on the genuineness of this fragment which, as Grenfell and Hunt believe, originated earlier than the middle of the second century and is taken from a narrative "which followed more or less closely the version of the teaching of Jesus given by Matthew and Luke."

In December, 1905, a fragment of another lost gospel was unearthed at Oxyrhynchus, consisting of a single vellum leaf practically complete except at one of the lower corners. The leaf was from a book so small that its written surface only slightly exceeded two inches square. On the two pages which we possess are forty-five lines in very small capital letters, the form of

---

[12] *Oxyrhynchus Papyri*, Vol. IV., pp. 23-28.

which indicates a fourth century date. The bulk of the fragment is concerned with a conversation which takes place in the Temple at Jerusalem, between Jesus and a chief priest. The episode, which is of a dramatic character, is preserved almost complete, and in the translation given by Grenfell and Hunt reads as follows:

". . . before he does wrong makes all manner of subtle excuse. But give heed lest ye also suffer the same things as they; for the evil-doers among men receive their reward not among the living only, but also await punishment and much torment. And he took them and brought them into the very place of purification, and was walking in the temple. And a certain Pharisee, a chief priest, whose name was Levi, met them and said to the Saviour, Who gave thee leave to walk in this place of purification and to see these holy vessels, when thou hast not washed nor yet have thy disciples bathed their feet? But defiled thou hast walked in this temple, which is a pure place, wherein no other man walks except he has washed himself and changed his garments, neither does he venture to see these holy vessels.

"And the Saviour straightway stood still with his disciples and answered him, Art thou then being here in the temple clean? He saith unto him, I am clean; for I washed in the pool of David, and having descended by one staircase I ascended by another, and I put on white and clean garments, and then I came and looked upon these holy words. The Saviour answered and said unto him, Woe, ye blind who see not. Thou hast washed in these running waters wherein dogs and swine have been cast night and day, and hast cleansed and wiped the outside skin, which also the harlots and flute girls anoint and wash and wipe and beautify for the lust of men; but within they are full of scorpions and all wickedness. But I and my disciples who thou sayest have not bathed (βεβαπτίσθαι) have been dipped (βεβάμμεθα) in the waters of eternal life, which come from . . . But woe unto thee . . ."[13]

[13] *Oxyrhynchus Papyri*, Vol. V, No. 840. Note here the metaphorical meaning of Βαπτίζω "baptize" (*cf.* Mark 10: 38), which has been also noticed in several other papyri. It may be added that the papyri have shown that where the phrase "baptized into" occurs (*e.g.*, Acts. 9: 16; 19: 5; Rom. 6: 3; Gal. 3: 27) that the person baptized becomes the property of the divine person indicated (Souter).

The contrast of external bathing with inward purity here is very like many words of Jesus found in our own gospels (*cf.* Matt. 15: 1-20; Mark 7: 1-23). The statement that no one could enter the temple without being previously cleansed ritually is sustained by Josephus, and the necessity of putting on white garments is in accordance with the regulations for priests described in the Mishna; but nothing is known about the "place of purification" or the "pool of David" within the temple, while the statements concerning dogs and swine being cast into the "pool of David" seems to be a mere rhetorical invention; and it seems impossible that the "sacred vessels" would be visible from the place where Jesus is represented as standing. "So great, indeed, are the divergencies between this account and the extant and, no doubt, well-informed authorities, with regard to the topography and ritual of the temple, that it is hardly impossible to avoid the conclusion that much of the local color is due to the imagination of the author, who was aiming chiefly at dramatic effect and was not really well acquainted with the temple. But if the inaccuracy of the fragment in this important respect is admitted, the historical character of the whole episode breaks down and it is probably to be regarded as an apocryphal elaboration of Matt. 15: 1-20 and Mark 7: 1-23. In these circumstances the gospel to which the fragment belongs can hardly have been composed before the middle of the second century, after the four canonical gospels had come to be exclusively used in most churches—a process which was complete by the end of the second century." [14] It was probably written in the second century, for altho the style is

---

[14] Harnack, *Geschichte der altchristlichen Litteratur*, II, p. 699.

more redundant than that of the New Testament, the author "is more successful in catching something of the genuine ring than many of the authors of [the later] apocryphal gospels."

In 1903, the Cairo Museum published in the *Catalogue général des Antiquités,* No. 10735, a small uncial (sixth or seventh century) of ten lines which is concerned with the annunciation and flight into Egypt; and in 1906, Wessely, in *"Les plus ancients monuments du Christianisme"* (No. 20), published another fragment of a similar nature; while in 1911 Dr. Hunt edited a small fragment of what may have been a Gnostic gospel (*Oxyrhynchus Papyri,* viii. 1081). It is a leaf from a book dating from the early part of the fourth century, and its chief value consists in one new "Saying of our Lord" which emphasizes the inner insight needed to understand the gospel:

"He who hath hearing beyond his ears let him hear."

Following this logion the gospel continues:

"Everything that is born of corruption perisheth . . . but that which is born of incorruption abideth incorruptible . . . The disciples ask him, How then can we find faith? The Saviour saith, If you pass from the things that are hidden and into the light of the things that are seen, the effluence of conception will of itself show you faith . . . He who hath ears to hear let him hear. The Lord of all is not the Father but the Forefather . . ."

Another uncanonical gospel, found on the leaves of a papyrus book (fourth century) was published by Grenfell and Hunt in 1914,[15] but the text is too imperfect to build upon it with confidence.

In 1915, Grenfell and Hunt published a fragment from still another of these uncanonical gospels. In

---

[15] *Oxyrhynchus Papyri,* Vol. X., cf. *Greek Papyri,* No. 10735.

this papyrus, which dates from the fifth century, the disciples say to our Lord:

"Jesus, what cure is possible for the sick? And he saith to them, I gave olive oil and . . . myrrh to them that believe on the (name) of the Father, and the Holy Spirit, and the Son."[16]

Another fragment found connected with the last shows that even angels were supposed to be sick at times, and to need the divine help supplemented by medicine.

"The angels of the Lord rose up to (mid-) heaven suffering in their eyes . . . The Lord said Why have ye come up, ye holy and all-pure ones?

"Iao Sabaoth, we have come up to receive healing, for thou art powerful and strong."

It is suggestive to notice how the early Egyptian Christians sought in the worship of Christ the bodily healings which were supposed often to occur in the pagan temples of Isis and Serapion.[17]

Still another Coptic fragment published by Julius Boehmer, in 1903,[17a] has been called a parallel to the parable of the Good Samaritan. It describes our Lord and his disciples walking in the country and finding a mule falling under its burden while its master was still beating it:

"And Jesus . . . said, Man, why dost thou beat thy animal? Seest thou not that it is too weak for its burden . . . ? But the man answered and said, What is that to you? I can beat it as much as I please, since it is my property and I bought it for a good sum of money . . . But the Lord said, Do you not see how it bleeds, and hear you not how it laments and cries? But they (the disciples) answered and said, Nay, Lord, we hear not that it laments and cries, and the Lord was sad and exclaimed, Woe to

[16] *Oxyrhynchus Papyri*, Vol. XI, No. 1384.

[17] See Mary Hamilton, *Incubation*, London, 1906, for cases of healing in heathen temples.

[17a] *Neutest. Parallelen und Verwandtes aus altchristl. Literatur.*

you that you hear not how it cries to the Creator in heaven, and cries for mercy. But three times woe to him, of whom it complains and cries in its distress. And he came forth and touched the animal. And it arose and its wounds were healed. And Jesus said to the man, Now, go on and beat it no more, that you also may find mercy." [18]

Some important fragments of two apocryphal "Acts of the Apostles" have also been found at Oxyrhynchus,[19] both dating from the fourth century, the earliest of these (No. 849) is a single leaf from a vellum codex of the "Acts of Peter," the two pages being numbered 167 and 168, respectively. Our fragment belongs to the portion of the Acts concerned with Simon Magus, and represents an original second century manuscript:

". . . (the youths having examined his nostrils to see) whether indeed he was really dead, and seeing that he was in truth a corpse, consoled the old woman saying, If indeed you wish, mother, and trust in the God of Peter, we will lift him up and carry him thither in order that Peter may raise him and restore him to you. While they were thus speaking the prefect looking intently at Peter (said), Behold, Peter, my servant lies dead who was a favorite of the king himself, and I did not spare him although I have with me other youths, but because I desired to try you and the God whom you preach whether ye are indeed true, I wished him to die. And Peter said, God is not to be tried or proved, Agrippa, but when he is entreated, he hearkens to those who are worthy. But since now . . ."

The second fragment (No. 850) was a leaf from the "Acts of John," giving an incident which is of a type very familiar in apocryphal Acts. The apostle is

---

[18] This translation is taken from Bernard Pick's *Paralipomena,* 1908. For a convenient survey of the literature in general see *Encyclopædia of Religion and Ethics,* vi., 346*ff.* For Coptic gospels, where hundreds of Scripture texts are quoted, see *Texts and Studies,* Vol. IV; and for a Coptic "Apocalypse of Paul," etc., see Budge, *Coptic Texts,* 1915.

[19] *Oxyrhynchus Papyri,* Vol. VI., 1908.

represented visiting the brethren apparently at a village near Ephesus, but his passage is barred by a demon in the form of a soldier. Rebuked by John, the demon vanishes and, on reaching his destination, the apostle exhorts the brethren to worship and joins with them in prayer. The back of the leaf represents a more obscure incident in which a person called Zeuxis had just tried to hang himself, but had been miraculously saved by St. John. There is also some question about the eucharist which is obscure. In reading this it may be remembered that the composition of the original Acts of John is assigned by all critics to the second century. When our fragment is compared with other previously known portions of the Acts of John, it, like the Acts of Peter, agrees with them so closely as to show that even these apocryphal works "have not undergone any serious amount of revision" (Hunt). It is noticeable that the proconsul in this account addresses St. John as the "servant of the unnameable One," and that John prays: "O Jesus, Comforter . . . We praise thee and worship thee and give thanks to thee." The narrative then continues:

"After a few days had passed John went forth with several brethren to . . . and wished to cross a bridge under which a . . . river was flowing. And as John was on his way to the brethren a certain . . . clothed in the fashion of a soldier approached him, and standing before his face, said, John if thou (advancest) thou shall straightway engage me in combat. And John said, The Lord shall quench thy threat and thy wrath and thy offence, and behold the other vanished. John then having come to those whom he was visiting and found them gathered together spake, Let us rise up, my brethren, and bow our knees before the Lord, who has made of none effect the unseen activity of even the great (enemy?) . . . he bowed his knees with them . . ."

In another papyrus codex of an apocryphal "Acts" (fourth century) occurs a notable sentence:

"O, Lord Prefect, this man is not a magician but perhaps his god is great." [20]

A particularly curious apocalyptic work dating from the second century, representing another type of composition, is the *Testament of Abraham*.[21] Abraham is represented as going to heaven's gate from which he saw two ways, narrow and broad, and two gates, narrow and broad. He sees Adam laughing and weeping, but weeping far more than he laughed, for only one soul in seven of all the human race was being saved. He saw the angels beating the lost with "fiery thongs," and saw the scales on which souls were weighed before the judge, Abel (*cf.* Gen. 4: 10; Heb. 12: 24), any soul against which was registered one truly good deed being saved.

This is the first apocalypse in which occurs the idea of the weighing of good and evil deeds, tho this is common in Egyptian documents and is found also in Mohammedan eschatology. The author of this work paints death as having seven dragon heads and fourteen faces, among which are fire, darkness, viper, lion, snake, fiery sword, etc.

The Greek Apocalypse of Baruch (3 Baruch) was found in 1896, tho a less complete Slavonic version had been published in 1886. It belongs to the second century of our era, the Jewish original having been worked over by a Christian editor about A.D. 136. The motive of the work is to bring Jews and Ebionites to baptism. It is full of symbolism and pictures. In the extract to be

[20] *Oxyrhynchus Papyri*, Vol. VI., 19.
[21] *Texts and Studies*, Vol. II., No. 2, by J. Armitage Robinson.

given, the angels with full baskets represent Christians;
those with half-full baskets, half-converted Jews; those
with empty baskets, opposing Jews:

"And as I was conversing with them, behold, angels came bearing baskets full of flowers. And they gave them to Michael. And
I asked the angel, Lord, who art these and what are the things
brought hither from beside them? And he said to me, These are
angels who are over the righteous. And the archangels took the
baskets and emptied them into the vessel. And the angel said to
me, These flowers are the merits of the righteous. And I saw
other angels bearing baskets which were (neither) empty nor full.
And they began to lament and did not venture to draw near, because they had not the prizes complete. And Michael cried and
said, Come hither also, ye angels; bring what ye have brought.
And Michael was exceedingly grieved, and the angel which was
with me, because they did not fill the vessel."

"And in that very hour Michael descended and the gate was
opened and he brought oil. And as for the angels which brought
the baskets which were full, he filled them with oil, saying, Take
it away, reward our friends an hundredfold, and those who have
laboriously wrought good works. For those who sowed virtuously, also reap virtuously, And he said to those bringing the
half empty baskets, Come hither, ye also, take away the reward
according as ye brought, and deliver it to the sons of men" (XV).

"And turning he said to those who brought nothing, Thus
saith the Lord, be not sad of countenance, and weep not, nor let
the sons of men alone. But since they angered me and their
works, go and make them envious and angry and provoked against
a people that is no people, a people that has no understanding
. . . punish them severely with the sword and with death, and
their children with demons. For they did not hearken to my
voice . . . but were despisers of my commandments, and in-
solent towards the priests who proclaimed my words to them."

The "Acts of Paul" was discovered by the Germans.
In 1896 Dr. Reinhardt procured at Akhmim a papyrus
codex which turned out to be the "Acts of Paul," a book
so highly reputed in the ancient Church that many, in
the fourth century, supposed that it ought to have a place

in the New Testament. The book originated somewhere between A.D. 160 and 200. Prof. Carl Schmidt
of Heidelberg, after laborious study, succeeded in trans-
lating it in 1904, but as this translation is too long and
too complicated to be quoted here, we will merely give
an abbreviation of Dr. Goodspeed's fine summary of
some of the chief events depicted in this remarkable
manuscript.[22]

The curtain rises at Pisidian Antioch. Paul restores
to life a Jewish boy, and this leads to the conversion of
the boy's parents, but the populace becomes incensed
and drives Paul from the town.

Paul reaches Iconium. Here he meets Thecla and
leads her to conversion. The story romantically re-
lates this conversion, Thecla's refusal to marry her
betrothed, her persecution, baptism, miraculous escapes,
her visit to Paul at Myra, her final retirement to
Seleucia, and her death there. This chapter, giving the
"Acts of Paul and Thecla," was the most popular of
all the narratives, and was widely published in ancient
times as a separate tract.[23]

Paul cures various persons at Myra and Tyre and
suffers great persecution at Sidon, where he is imprisoned in the temple of Apollo, which collapses
miraculously in the night.

The apostle has some adventures in certain mines,
and then is imprisoned, probably at Ephesus, and later
at Philippi. At the latter city he receives from the
Corinthians a letter reporting that two false teachers,

---

[22] See *Biblical World*, December, 1915.

[23] The actual existence and martyrdom of Thecla has just been corrobor-
ated by a first century inscription set up in remembrance "of the martyr
Thecla" recently found at the church of St. Menas in N. Cyprus (*Am.
Journal of Archæology*, 1915, p. 489).

Simon and Cleobius, are disturbing the church, and writes to them the letter which is received as genuine in many ancient Syrian and Armenian churches. From Philippi he goes to Rome, where he is beheaded under Nero, but afterward reappears.

The above represent some of the most important of the early apocryphal stories in Greek which have recently been discovered; however, very many of these early writings in Coptic have been found in Egypt. Among these one of the most interesting happens to be the most famous of all the ancient "Acts," the *Book of the Resurrection,* attributed to the Apostle Bartholomew, recently printed by the trustees of the British Museum. It describes the descent of Jesus into hell; the conquest of death; the defeat of the devil; the destruction of the gates, bolts, and bars of hell; the extinction of its fires; the overthrow of its blazing cauldrons; the liberation of Adam and Eve and all the children of men; the final condemnation of Judas Iscariot; the ascent from hell of the Lord Jesus; his resurrection; his enthronement at the right hand of the Father in his tabernacle of light in the seventh heaven; and the reconciliation of God with Adam and his sons.

The whole Apocryphon exhibits strong Egyptian (Gnostic) influence, and professes to give the actual words of the divine unknown language in which Jesus and the Virgin Mary spoke to each other. The first four or five leaves of the manuscript are wanting. These no doubt contained, in addition to the title of the work, a description of the crucifixion of the Savior. The manuscript continues:

"Now when they had crucified the Saviour they laid him in a

tomb, (and) he arose from the dead upon the third day, (and) he carried the soul of the holy man Apa Anania with him into heaven forthwith, and he ate and drank with our Saviour at the table of his kingdom. And Joseph of Arimathea made ready for burial the body of the Son of God, and when large quantities of most precious scents and unguents had been poured out upon it, he laid it in a new sepulcher; then Death came into Amente (the grave) saying, Where is this soul which hath come forth from the body newly? It hath not been brought unto me to Amente. For behold I have sought for it for two days but have not found it. What then is (the meaning of) this mighty and wonderful thing? I know not, neither do I know what is (the meaning of) this terrible disturbance (which taketh place) this day. The whole world and everything which is therein is in a state of violent commotion. Never before have I known anything like unto this. And Death called his minister, and said unto him: Let us go into every place, and see if we can find this newly dead body, and this new soul which hath hidden itself; for I know not whither it hath departed.

. . .

"Then Death came into the tomb of the Savior and he found it lighted up with the light of life and he went into the back of the tomb and seated himself there with his ministers. Now Abbaton, who is Death, and Gaios and Tryphon and Ophiath and Phthinon and Sotomis and Komphion, who are the six sons of Death, wriggled into the tomb of the son of God on their faces in the form of serpents (?), wriggling in with their great chief in very truth. These robbers and evil-doers were lying in wait for the moment wherein the Saviour would go down into Amente, so that they might enter with him and know what it was that he would do.

"And the Saviour made himself manifest unto them in the form of a dead body in the hinder part of the tomb; he was lying upon the ground in their midst—now it was the second day that he was in the heart of the earth, and there was a napkin bound around his face, and another one bound around his head. And Death said unto his son, the pestilence, Hath this soul which hath died recently been brought unto thee, Amente? Show me, for I am disturbed greatly by this terrible quaking, and I do not know what hath happened this day. . . . The hours have been shortened, the nights have been put out of course . . . Gehenna has gone cold . . . Thou hast disturbed me exceedingly, me who am wont to destroy everything (hast thou) destroyed. . . .

"Then Jesus removed the napkin which was on his face, and he looked in the face of Death, and laughed at him."

The text then recounts how disturbed Death was as he looked on the Saviour, falling down upon the earth with his six sons, and acknowledging him to be "First-born of the Father, the Holy Lamb." It tells how Jesus went down again into Amente, breaking in pieces the doors, smashing their bolts, and dragging away and destroying the door-posts and frames, and extinguishing the fires, putting in fetters the "shameless one." It closes by an address to Judas:

"Tell me Judas, in what way didst thou profit by betraying me? Assuredly I only endured sufferings of all kinds in order to fulfill (the will) of my Father, and to redeem (and set free) my creatures which I had fashioned. As for thee, woe be unto thee with two-fold woes."

With this ought to be compared the recently discovered *Conflict of Severus*, which, however, contains more Scripture quotations. Severus is armed with the "Four Holy Gospels" as David with the four stones, and could cast out devils by merely saying: "The Lord rebuke thee." In the triumph at its end "hell" (Amente) was destroyed; paradise was laid open and the tree of life was revealed; the heavens became the world, the world became heaven; God became man; man became God. A final prophecy is that "Severus shall cut off the head of Satan." [24] This curious work contains the following elaborate declaration of faith:

"We believe in the Holy Spirit, the Saviour Lord, with the Holy Lord, three substances abiding and perfect, three substances equal, undivided in glory and splendor, one likeness, one essence, one power and one worship, one faith; so is it meet for believers to believe."

[24] *Patrologia Orientalis*, Tome iv, Fascicule 6; Edgar J. Goodspeed, *Conflict of Severus*, 1907.

Various other Coptic stories have been even more recently discovered, among which may specially be mentioned an apocryphal Acts, in which Andrew plays an important part.[25] In all of these texts hundreds of Scripture passages are quoted or paraphrased. In the above we have been able to give only a mere suggestion of the wealth of new material recently brought to light.[26]

Among the Syriac apocryphal works perhaps the most important is that which includes Mara's testimony to Christ, first translated in 1872, which Harnack dates soon after A.D. 165. It is a letter written to Marcus Aurelius by Mara, in which he asks what benefit the Jews received by the murder of their "wise king," seeing that from that very time their kingdom was driven away from them, "yet the wise king did not die because of the new laws which he enacted."[26a]

(4) IMPORTANCE OF THESE APOCRYPHAL GOSPELS, ACTS, ETC.

Certain reflections must occur to every one who reads these strange narratives coming out of the early centuries so near to the time of Jesus.

[25] Crum, *Anecdota Oxoniensia*, 1913, No. 14.

[26] See, for example, the exhaustive article, "Gnostic Apocrypha" in *Encyclopædia of Religion and Ethics;* and "Acts (Apocryphal)" in the *Dictionary of the Apostolic Church;* and "Apocryphal Acts," *International Standard Bible Dictionary.*

[26a] Quoted with the correspondence of Abgarus and the sentence of Pontius Pilate, letters of Pilate to Claudius, and all other apocryphal literature known at the time of the book's issue by Bernard Pick, *Extracanonical Life of Christ*, 1903; *Apocryphal Acts of Paul, Peter, John*, etc., 1909. See also on Christian apocryphal literature in general *Encyclopædia Britannica*, ii, 169-182; Hastings, *Dictionary of the Apostolic Church*, i. 478-506; *Ante-Nicene Fathers*, Am. ed., Vol. VIII; and for a more popular treatise, J. DeQuincey Donehoo, *Apocryphal and Legendary Life of Christ*, 1903.

First, every unprejudiced mind must be imprest with the fact that the canonical gospel narratives differ almost as much from these nearly contemporaneous documents as Jesus differed from other men. The difference is that between a religious history and a religious novel.

Secondly, all of these apocryphal narratives are demonstrably later, most of them centuries later, than our four gospels, and rest upon the written or oral gospel teaching as their basis. They contain no new essentials; they are simply additions to the accounts in our gospels and assume the history recounted there. They give incidental testimony to the great leading facts affirmed by the four gospels and take for granted the teaching and doctrines of the New Testament. They witness to the existence of our gospels by multitudes of quotations more or less exact; they witness to the facts of the gospels by their presuppositions; they witness to the truth and inspiration of our gospels by their differences in content and style. In the twenty or more so called gospels referred to in early Christian writings, some of which have now been recovered, there is not one new parable or beatitude, and very few new sentences worthy to be placed by the side of these plain narratives written by the fishermen and other "ignorant and unlearned" disciples from Galilee.

Third, these new discoveries suggest that most of the so-called "false" gospels were not wilful falsifications. They may well have been written by men who trusted to the memory of aged people who had actually heard Jesus speak or had listened to sermons from the apostles or their successors. Some of the statements which are seemingly most ridiculous may have arisen from an honest misunderstanding of the pictorial or allegorical language in which the events were described. No one can think of the Coptic description of the resurrection quoted above as being accepted by any one as a literal account. The author of it accepted the gospels as authoritative. The sermons of the Copts, even to this day, when uttered by men of eloquence and passion, are full of these same vivid allegorical pictures. Native Egyptians do not think or speak abstractly.

Fourth, these discoveries illustrate the material which existed in considerable quantities before our gospels were written and were used by St. Luke (Luke 1 : 1). Men talked as much and wrote almost as freely in the first century as now. The words and acts of Jesus made a great stir, and therefore hundreds of people either took notes on the spot, or in after years talked with those who had seen the events. Local incidents were remembered best and were naturally exaggerated. Let the facts of the gospel narratives be granted, and it is perfectly easy to see how in later years not only notes from private diaries would become important but anecdotes would be told of Jesus not always having a historical basis, and that popular sayings would naturally be attributed to him. Would not the grandsons of the man who was born blind or who had been healed of a withered hand tell about this? Justin Martyr and others may have had good authority when they gave the names of these men and told their trade, and gave also the names of the two thieves on the cross, and of the centurion who had charge of the crucifixion, and of the soldier who pierced the side of Jesus. It is not incredible that the Gospel of Nicodemus may represent a valid tradition when it declares that Pilate "swore by the sun" that he found no fault in him, and that at the trial not only Nicodemus but one of the lepers that Jesus had healed, and even a woman (Bernice) and several friends of Jesus, offered their testimony. When Clement of Alexandria quotes Jesus as saying, "Ask great things, and the small shall be added unto you"; when Origen quotes him as saying, "For those that are infirm was I infirm, and for those that hungered did I hunger, and for those that did thirst did I thirst"; when the Gospel of the Hebrews puts in his lips the words, "Never be joyful except when ye have looked upon your brother with love"; when the Acts of Philip reports him as saying, "If you do not make your low things high and your crooked things straight, ye shall not enter into my kingdom," and, again, "He who longs to be rich is like a man who drinks sea water; the more he drinks the more thirsty he becomes, and never leaves off drinking until he perishes"; these may represent, possibly, valid historical memories carried down by oral tradition from the earliest times.

Fifth, it may be well to add that these apocryphal gospels never were rivals of our four gospels. The new discoveries emphasize the fact that our four gospels were the only gospels ever accepted universally by the early Church, being counted authoritative by Christians, heretics, Jews, and heathen. The discovery of these apocryphal writings only confirms the good judgment of the early Church which set apart these calm, candid, judicious documents as distinctively "Holy Writings" as distinguished from all others. As early as the second century they were accepted as *par excellence* the authoritative memoirs and stood without rivals (Harnack). Nevertheless, supplemental narratives continued to be used in local churches and were sometimes quoted by these churches or their ministers in their controversies with the heathen and the Jews.

3. SOME FAMOUS ANCIENT DOCUMENTS, RECENTLY RECOVERED, WHICH MENTION OR USE THE NEW TESTAMENT

(1) THE APOLOGY OF ARISTIDES

It was in the spring of 1889 that Mr. J. Rendel Harris, later of Cambridge University, after spending several days in one of the libraries of the Convent of St. Catherine, looking over the ancient Greek manuscripts which were thrown indiscriminately into large chests, was taken one morning by Galaktion, the librarian, into another part of the convent, where a door closed by a large rusty padlock was thrown open and a narrow room was reached, the walls of which were lined with oriental books in the Syriac, Arabic, and Iberian languages. Here he found a Syriac translation of the long-lost Apology of Aristides, which previously had been known only by an Armenian fragment published in 1878.[27]

While the Syriac manuscript is only of the seventh century, this new discovery represents a text which in its substance, according to all scholars, dates to the second century. Professors Harris and Harnack believe this "Apology" or argument for Christianity to have been presented to the Emperor Antoninus Pius, who reigned A.D. 138-161; but Dr. J. Armitage Robin-

[27] For other details see *The Newly Recovered Apology of Aristides,* by Helen B. Harris, pp. 8-25. At the time of this discovery Professor Harris was connected with Haverford College, Pa.

son accepts the claim made in the "Apology" itself
(which is confirmed by the Armenian version), that
it was addrest to the Emperor Hadrian who reigned
A.D. 117-138. If the latter be correct, this earliest
extant argument for Christianity came into existence
within a short generation of the apostolic age, and its
author must have been a boy when the Apostle John
died. If the later date is accepted it would have been
written about as far from the death of St. John as we
are from the Lincoln-Douglas debates (see p. 204, note
51). All agree that in either case the "Apology" was
probably written somewhere between A.D. 124 and 140.

Aristides was a philosopher of Athens, and he is
mentioned by Eusebius as a contemporary of Quadratus,
who lived so near to the lifetime of Christ that he
declares some who had been healed by the Savior "lived
on to our own times." [28]

"Aristides the philosopher is a Christian who has
preserved the philosophic manner and probably the
philosophic dress with a view to future service in the
gospel. It seems to have been the practise of not a
few of the famous second century Christians to attract
an audience in this way. Justin certainly did so, and
almost as surely Tatian; and if these why not Aristides?" (Harris.) The settled condition of the Christian
faith at this era is seen from the way Aristides marshals
his argument. "He talks of angels as tho all men knew
them, dashes through the dogmatic statements of the
Church as tho they were perfectly familiar, and without a word of preliminary explanation of terms, makes
a peroration of the impending judgment day." Dr.
Harris in a most ingenious way has restored from this

[28] *Hist. Eccl.,* IV., 3.

document a part of the creed of the Christian Church of that era.[29]

> "We believe in one God, Almighty,
> Maker of heaven and earth:
> And in Jesus Christ his Son
>
> . . . . . .
>
> Born of the Virgin Mary
>
> . . . . . .
>
> He was pierced by the Jews:
> He died and was buried:
> The third day he rose again;
> He ascended into Heaven;
>
> He is about to come to judge
> . . . . . ."

The "Apology" opens:

"I, O king, by the grace of God came into this world; and having contemplated the earth and the heavens and the seas and beheld the sun and the rest of the orderly creation, I was amazed at the arrangement of the world; and I comprehended that the world and all that is therein are moved by the impulse of another, and I understood that he that moveth them is God, who is hidden in them and concealed from them: and this is well known, that that which moveth is more powerful than that which is moved."

He goes on to state certain facts about the Creator:

"He is incomprehensible in his nature . . . is not begotten, not made; a constant nature without beginning and without end, immortal, complete, and incomprehensible: and in saying that he is complete, I mean this, that there is no deficiency in him and he stands in need of naught but everything stands in need of him . . ."

"He has no name . . . he has no likeness nor composition of members . . . adversary he has none, for there is none that is more powerful than he; anger and wrath he possesses not; for there is nothing that can stand against him . . . he asks no

[29] *Texts and Studies,* I., 25.

sacrifice and no libation nor any of the things that are visible; he asks not anything from anyone, but all ask from him."

How much this philosophic statement of the nature of God reminds us of Paul's sermon at Athens which was preached perhaps half a century or less before the birth of Aristides!

He next discusses the four races of men in this world, "barbarians and Greeks, Jews and Christians," and then makes what has well been called "the first attempt at a systematic comparison of ancient religions." Idolators he subdivides into Chaldeans, Greeks, and Egyptians, showing the worship of each of these to be erroneous and absurd. The Jews he mentions briefly (Sec. 2) as descending from Abraham, and later (Sec. 14) he praises them because they say:

"God is one Creator of all and Almighty . . . and they imitate God . . . for they have compassion on the poor and ransom the captive and bury the dead . . . nevertheless they too have gone astray . . . their service is to angels and not to God in that they observe sabbaths and new moons and a Passover . . . and circumcision and cleanness of meats; which things not even thus have they perfectly observed."

Aristides then proceeds in his argument before the emperor to a description of the Christians. He begins (Sec. 2) with a statement which, when purged of glosses by a comparison of the three forms in which it survives, shows a striking correspondence to the second section of the Apostles' Creed:

"Now the Christians reckon their race from the Lord Jesus Christ; and he is confessed to be the Son of God most high. Having by the Holy Spirit come down from heaven and having been born of a Hebrew virgin, he took flesh and appeared unto men to call them back from their error of many gods; and having completed his wonderful dispensation, he was pierced by the

Jews and after three days he revived and went up to heaven. And the glory of his coming thou canst learn, O king, from that which is called among them the Evangelistic Scripture, if thou wouldst read it. He had twelve disciples who after his ascent into heaven went forth into the provinces of the world and taught his greatness, whence they who at this day believe their preaching are called Christians."

After a long discussion, showing to this heathen king the error of the heathen who think sun, moon and stars to be gods, he reaches his climax in ridiculing the gods of Egypt, who worship not only evil deities but beasts and creeping things and even garlic and onions and other plants.

The last quarter of the argument consists in a beautiful statement concerning the Christians who, he says, not only have a purer theology than all others, but live in the world as if they were a different race:

"These are they who beyond all the nations of the earth have found the truth; for they know God as Creator and Maker of all things, and they worship no other God beside him; for they have his commandments graven on their hearts, and these they keep in expectation of the world to come. . . . (They do not commit adultery nor fornication, they do not bear false witness, they do not deny a deposit nor covet what is not theirs . . .) whatsoever they would not should be done unto them they do not to another . . . (they do good to their enemies: and their wives, O king, are pure as virgins and their daughters modest . . . and they walk in all humility and kindness, and falsehood is not found among them and they love one another . . .) he that hath, supplieth him that hath not without grudging: if they see a stranger they bring him under their roof and rejoice over him as over a brother indeed, for they call not one another brethren after the flesh but after the spirit. They are ready for Christ's sake to give up their own lives; for his commandments they securely keep, living holily and righteously according as the Lord their God hath commanded them, giving thanks to him at all hours over all their food and drink and the rest of their good things.

. . . (And if any righteous person of their number passeth away from the world they rejoice and give thanks to God, and they follow his body as if he were moving from one place to another . . . as men who know God they ask from him petitions which are proper for him to give and for them to receive . . . but the good deeds which they do they do not proclaim in the ears of the multitude, and they take care that no one shall perceive them . . . but their sayings and their ordinances, O king, and the glory of their service and the expectation of their recompense of reward . . . which they expect in another world thou art able to know from their writings.")

When we remember the age of this document and its official character, we are amazed at the boldness of the claims made here concerning the moral character of the Christians—the modesty of the women, the kindness of Christians to inferiors, their care of the poor, their assurance in prayer, and their joy at death; and we are also much imprest with this appeal made to the emperor to read the authoritative "writings" and learn for himself concerning the new "way." The writer continues:

"For truly great and wonderful is their teaching to him that is willing to examine and understand it. And truly this is a new race and there is something divine mingled with it. Take now their writings and read in them and lo! ye will find that not of myself have I brought these things forward nor as their advocate have I said them, but as I have read in their writings these things I firmly believe and those things also that are to come."

Our author then tells how the Christians pray for the heathen that they may repent and have their hearts cleansed and their sins forgiven, closing:

"And truly blessed is the race of the Christians more than all men that are upon the face of the earth. Let the tongues of those now be silenced who talk vanity and who oppress the Christians and let them now speak the truth . . . Let all those . . . who do not know God . . . anticipate the dread judgment which is to come by Jesus, the Messiah, upon the whole race of men.   The Apology of Aristides, the philosopher, is ended." [30]

(2) THE SHEPHERD OF HERMAS

Down to 1859 this remarkable apocalypse, which was accepted as divinely inspired both by Irenæus (c. A.D. 115-190) and Origen (c. A.D. 182-251), was known only from translations and quotations.   In that year Tischendorf discovered about one-fourth of the work at Mt. Sinai in a fourth century parchment.   In 1888 twelve more leaves (third century) were found by Professor Lambros.   In 1900 seven more leaves from the sixth century were edited with the *Amherst Papyri* (Vol. II: p. cxc) and several more scraps were excavated by Grenfell and Hunt at Oxyrhynchus, tho the most important discovery was made at Athos when a seventh century manuscript, containing most of the parts omitted by the Mt. Sinai text, was brought to light.[31]   For the first time, therefore, we are able to take a complete and connected view of this ancient work which greatly resembles Bunyan's *Pilgrim's Progress* and was in its day even more popular.

Hermas, who may have lived A.D. 90-100 (Salmon, Zahn) and certainly not later than A.D. 150 (Harnack, Lipsius), had originally been a slave.   After he secured his freedom he succeeded well in business, but was irre-

[30] For full Syriac text and translation of above bracketed portion, see J. Rendel Harris, *Texts and Studies*, Vol. I., pp. 1-64; for a corrected text (represented in unbracketed portion), see J. A. Robinson's "Apology of Aristides," *Encyclopædia Britannica;* and for original Greek text see *Texts and Studies*, 1: 65-112.   The close relation between some portions of this "Apology" and the anonymous Epistle to Diognetus (second or third century), which has been known from the sixteenth century, is very marked.

[31] Facsimiles of the Athos fragments were published by Kirsopp Lake in 1907, and a translation into English was made from these Mt. Sinai and Athos texts by C. Taylor, 2 vols., 1903.

ligious, having evidently no very good influence upon
his family. Having at length lost his property, he was
converted and became intensely religious, as the strong
moral earnestness of the book makes very apparent.
His work is really a "Manual of Religion," tho cast in
an imaginative form. It is a mighty call to repentance
addrest to men who can well remember the days of
persecution, yet have allowed themselves to be swal-
lowed up by business affairs and riches and heathen
friendships and many other affairs of this world.
Man's sinfulness is powerfully depicted, but over
against this is put the power and willingness of the
Good Shepherd to lead his sheep to repentance and a
new life. In order to make forgiveness possible to one
who has sinned after baptism, a most curious explanation is given of Heb. 6: 6; 12: 17, after which the
author hears the "Angel of Repentance" saying to him:

"Go and tell all men to repent and they shall live unto God;
for the Lord in his compassion sent me to give repentance to all,
tho some do not deserve it."

The indwelling of the Spirit in each believer is
strongly strest by this ancient Christian author. Indeed, he does not always discriminate between the
Son and the Holy Spirit, believing that the human
Jesus, because of his goodness and faithfulness, had
been unified with the Spirit and made partaker of the
divine nature:

"The Holy pre-existent Spirit, which created the whole creation, God made to dwell in flesh that he desired (Jesus). This
flesh therefore in which the Holy Spirit dwelt was subject unto
the Spirit. . . . When it had lived honorably in chastity, and
had labored with the Spirit and had cooperated with it in everything, behaving itself boldly, he chose it as a partner with the

Holy Spirit" (Sim. V:6). "For that Spirit is the Son of God" (IX:1).

While this may sound a little like heresy, yet it remarkably resembles Paul's statement: "The Lord (Jesus) is that Spirit" (2 Cor. 3:17). There is no thought of denying the deity of our Lord, but this is one of the first attempts to explain how Jesus could have been completely human and yet have become divine.[31a]

Hermas shows great familiarity with the Book of James. His statement of Christian duty sounds as if it could have been written by that practical apostle. After mentioning the necessity of faith, fear of the Lord, love, concord, righteousness and a perfect fast, "a fast from every evil word and every evil desire," he urges his fellow Christians

". . . to minister to widows, to visit the orphans and the needy, to ransom the servants of God from their afflictions, to be hospitable . . . to resist no man, to be tranquil, to show yourself more submissive than all men," etc.

This book, as several scholars have strongly pointed out, witnesses emphatically to the worldliness of the Church within half a century of the apostolic age—but it must be remembered that the sins which he condemns were also mentioned by Paul, and that they have not yet vanished from the Church. On the other hand it also witnesses to the love and benevolence of some church-members in that era, and proves that the fundamental faith of that earliest post-apostolic period was sincere and thoughtful and fervent. While Hermas

[31a] Compare my explanation of the above text given in Hastings, *Dictionary of Christ and the Gospels*, II., 495; and see the illuminating review of A. Mitchell in Hastings, *Dictionary of the Apostolic Church*, 1916, I., 561-4. Very much of the above discussion and that which is to follow has been adapted from this latter article.

is interested most in experimental religion, yet he gives us some light on the officiary of the Church in his day— mentioning bishops, elders, teachers, deacons, prophets, and ministers.

Perhaps our greatest present interest in Hermas, however, is connected with his confirmation of the authority of Scripture. While he never quotes word for word any New Testament book, yet he "continually uses Scriptural words and ideas," and was certainly acquainted with all the gospels.[32] There are, indeed, several statements in his visions which refer to the gospels as having been "four" by divine ordination, as where he represents the Church as seated on a bench which has four feet and stands firmly "as the world is held fast by four elements."[33] It may be finally added that while the Church is pictured by this ancient believer as a tower, he represents the tower as being founded not on Peter, but upon the "rock of the Son of God."

(3) THE RING OF POPE XYSTUS

This may be the best possible place to mention the above famous book of devotion, which was widely read and highly prized in Christian circles as early as A.D. 250, and was undoubtedly composed "at least a hundred years earlier" (Conybeare). We venture to speak of it as a new discovery because recently for the first time it has been rendered into English.[34]

With the exception of the *Pastor of Hermas,* which

[32] This was proved exhaustively by C. Taylor, *Witness of Hermas to the Four Gospels,* 1892, and in *New Testament in the Apostolic Fathers,* 1905, pp. 105 ff.

[33] Taylor, *Shepherd of Hermas,* p. 33, gives similar statements from Irenæus and Origen.

[34] With critical commentary, by F. C. Conybeare, M. A., London, 1910.

we have considered above, and the Acts of Pilate—with their interesting but unreliable "official reports"—and perhaps two or three other apocryphal works, such as the Acts of Paul and Thecla, no other Christian work equalled this for popularity in the third and fourth centuries.

Its deeply religious tone can be seen from its opening sentences:

"A faithful man is a man elect.
"A man elect is a man of God.
"He that is worthy of God is a man of God.
"He that doth naught unworthy of God is a man of God.
"Wherefore if thou art endeavoring to be faithful, do naught unworthy of God.

.   .   .   .

"Reckon it thy best purification to wrong no man."

(4) LOST WORKS OF EARLY CHRISTIAN FATHERS
RECENTLY DISCOVERED

Many fragments of papyrus and parchment have been found in recent years giving scraps of well-known productions from the various early fathers; but it is a surprize, indeed, to be able to report that at least two lost works from the pens of two of the most celebrated men of ancient Christendom have just come to light after being buried in oblivion for unknown centuries.

Dr. E. J. Goodspeed in *The Biblical World* (December, 1915) has told this fascinating story and we here offer an adaptation of his brilliant and comprehensive summary.

Irenæus, Apostolic Preaching

In 1904 a native scholar found in Erivan in Armenia an Armenian manuscript containing a lost work of Irenæus, *In Proof of the Apostolic Preaching*.

Up to that time only one complete work of Irenæus was known to be extant, his famous treatise *Against Heresies,* written about A.D. 185; but here there was restored to us a large book which no one, previous to this discovery, could ever have hoped to see. Irenæus was born probably at Smyrna, a few miles from Ephesus, within half a century of the traditional date of St. John's death, and enjoyed the instruction of Polycarp, who was a pupil of the holy "presbyter." [34a] He may have accompanied Polycarp on his journey to Rome in connection with the Easter controversy (A.D. 154). At any rate he was a missionary to Gaul and under the persecution of Marcus Aurelius (A.D. 177) he witnessed there the terrible torture and death of many of his fellow presbyters. In A.D. 178 he was elected bishop of Lyons, and for the rest of his life this greatest man and most superb scholar of his generation labored with pen and tongue for Christianity. His writings prove conclusively that in the churches of his day strong emphasis was put upon the New Testament and "Scripture"; upon the Apostolic Creed and episcopal organization. In the work previously known he had made hundreds of quotations from the New Testament in his ardent defense of the "faith delivered to the saints." It ought to be almost awe-inspiring for any devout Christian to read a new literary and religious work from the pen of this "commanding figure" in early Christian literature.

"The newly discovered work," says Dr. Goodspeed, "was evidently addrest to the laity. It sets forth in a

---

[34a] As we have previously stated, it is very doubtful whether the "presbyter John" of Ephesus can any longer be identified with the Apostle John.

simple and telling way the apostolic type of Christianity which Irenæus maintained, and shows its agreement with numerous Old Testament prophecies. Irenæus's usual method is to describe an incident in the gospel story and then quote some prophecy which he thinks is fulfilled in it. The work shows Irenæus at the task of teaching his Gallic flock to defend their Christian faith in all its aspects by appeal to the Old Testament. Many New Testament books are reflected in it, but here, as in the older work of Irenæus, no use is made of Hebrews or Revelations, and it seems clear that these books had no place in his New Testament."

In the second century many theologians looked upon Hebrews as edifying literature but not as inspired Scripture, and Irenæus may have seriously objected to Revelation because of the Montanist controversy which made so much of this work.[35]

Origen on the Book of Revelation

"In July, 1911," still to quote Dr. Goodspeed, "Constantine Diobouniotis, a Privat-Docent in the University of Athens, sent to Berlin a copy he had made of a short work on the Apocalypse which had been found in a tenth-century manuscript in the Meteoron monastery in the north of Greece. The monastery is one of those so picturesquely situated on the summits of the rocky detached pinnacles of the Pindus Mountains, which have to be reached by the aid of basket, rope, and windlass. The commentary was anonymous, but

---

[35] See Moffatt, *Introduction to the Literature of the New Testament,* p. 498. For the testimony of Irenæus to the Fourth Gospel and to John the Apostle as its (indirect) author, see Univ. of Chicago, *Hist. and Linguistic Studies,* 2d Series, Vol. I., Part VII.

Diobouniotis thought it might be the work of Hippo
lytus, one of whose treatises had already been found in
the same manuscript.

"The Berlin scholars at once recognized in it a work
of Origen, the founder of Christian interpretation and
of systematic theology, the leading theologian of Christian antiquity, and the father of ecclesiastical science.
Origen was the most voluminous of ancient Christian
writers. Ephiphanius says that he left six thousand
works, but this enumeration must have included individual sermons, lectures, and addresses, as well as
greater works, like the Hexapla, which was so huge
that it was never copied. Part of Origen's prolificness
was due to his friend and patron, Ambrose, who supplied him with stenographers and secretaries so that
he might have every facility to record the results of
his studies, and so eagerly urged him on in his work
that Origen calls him his 'taskmaster' who left him no
leisure for meals or rest.

"These thirty-seven paragraphs of the commentary
on Revelation are a new and unexpected legacy from
the first great interpreter of the New Testament. It is
true that it had not been known that Origen ever wrote
a commentary or even a set of scholia on Revelation.
But it is an interesting fact that in his commentary on
Matthew he exprest the intention of producing a commentary on it. More than this, the commentary on
Matthew was one of the latest of Origen's works, and
falls between A.D. 245 and 249. It was in A.D. 249 or
250 that the persecution of Decius overtook Origen,
and the tortures he then endured eventually resulted
in his death in his seventieth year. It has been suggested that these comments on Revelation may have

been his last work and that they broke off before the whole book had been covered, because the persecution interrupted Origen in the midst of his task." [35a]

Letters of Ignatius

No one connected with the history of the early Christian Church is more famous than Ignatius. According to early tradition he was the pupil of the Apostle John and for over forty years the contemporary of Polycarp; finally being thrown to the wild beasts in the Colesseum at Rome somewhere between A.D. 105 and 115. Our knowledge of him, however, up to the present generation, has been confined to a few short notices by Irenæus and Origen and to a number of epistles which claimed to be from him but the authorship of which was disputed.

Thanks to the researches of modern scholars, notably Zahn and Harnack, seven (short recension) epistles, written to the Ephesians, Romans, Philadelphians, etc., are now accepted with practical unanimity, being dated by a majority of scholars A.D. 110-117, tho Harnack prefers A.D. 117-125.[36] This brings the words of Ignatius almost within the apostolic age and gives to them a tenfold force. What is it that this earliest post-apostolic teacher believed concerning Jesus Christ? This is his creed:

"Be ye deaf, therefore, when any man speaketh to you apart from Jesus Christ, who was of the race of David, who was the son of Mary, who was truly born and ate and drank, was truly persecuted under Pontius Pilate, was truly crucified and died in the sight of those in heaven and those on earth and those under

[35a] For full Greek text see *Texte und Untersuchungen zur Geschichte der altchristlichen Literatur*, 1911, Heft 3, pp. 4-49.

[36] See R. H. Charles and others in *Encyclopædia Britannica*, II., 189; VII., 393; XIV., 292-294; XXII., 20.

the earth; who moreover was truly raised from the dead, his Father having raised him, who in the like fashion will also raise us also who believe in him—his Father, I say, will raise us—in Christ Jesus, apart from whom we have not true life. . . . There is one only physician, of flesh and of spirit, generate and ingenerate, God in man, true life in death, Son of Mary and Son of God, first passible and then impassible."

Ignatius was the first writer known, outside the New Testament, to mention the virgin birth, but he lays great stress upon this. He describes the holy sacrament as the "medicine of immortality, and antidote that we should not die, but live forever in Jesus Christ." His view of the supremacy of Christ is so clear that he gladly puts him even above the Old Testament itself, saying: "As for me my archives— my inviolable archives—are Jesus Christ, his cross, his death, his resurrection and faith through him."

When we read such words from this comrade of Polycarp, we are glad to find that modern discoveries of new Ignatian texts, as gathered from the *Rainer Papyri* (K9416-9422), corroborate fully the antiquity and essential purity of these ancient epistles.[37]

4. THE DIDACHE OR "TEACHING OF THE TWELVE APOSTLES"

This most important of all recent discoveries that touch Church history and doctrine was made by Bishop Philotheus Bryennios, the "Tischendorf of the Greek Church," in the library of the Jerusalem Monastery of The Most Holy Sepulcher in the *Phanar* of Constantinople, and was announced by him in 1875. What he found was a collection of manuscripts written on well-

[37] So Wessely, *Sitzungsberichte der philosophisch-historischen Klasse der kaiserlichen Akademie der Wissenschaften*, Band 172, Wien, 1913, pp. 1-70.

preserved parchment and bound in one volume containing 120 leaves. This volume includes the only complete manuscript of the first and second epistles of Clement of Rome to the Corinthians and several other works beside the *Didache;* but the latter is by far the most valuable, altho it is less than ten pages in length. Its publication in 1883 created a profound sensation in the learned world. The work was undoubtedly genuine and was dated by all scholars as the oldest church manual in existence. It was written in Hellenistic Greek, and of the 552 different words used 504 were to be found in the New Testament (Harnack). The date at which the manuscript was copied by Leon, the humble "notary and sinner," was A.D. 1056, but the date of the original was variously placed between A.D. 50 and A.D. 160; until the consensus of scholarship has finally decided, with comparatively few dissenting voices, that it was written "before rather than after A.D. 100." [38]

The reason for the special excitement concerning this find was very manifest. Here for the first time could be obtained the long-desired answer to many historical questions concerning the doctrine, ritual, and polity of the earliest Christian Church. What did those earliest Christians believe concerning God and Christ and baptism? Out of the long-forgotten past this earliest ritualistic discipline arose to speak concerning the habits and beliefs of the primitive Church at a time when it was "neither Catholic nor Protestant,

---

[38] So Bartlet in Hastings, *Dictionary of the Bible,* V., 449; Professor Harnack, however, does not date it earlier than A.D. 120 and says it may be later. J. Armitage Robinson, *Journal of Theol. Studies,* XIII., 339-356, has advanced certain arguments to prove that the writer used St. Paul, St. John, and St. Luke, but attempted to conceal his obligations.

neither Episcopalian nor anti-Episcopalian, neither Baptist nor paedo-Baptist, neither sacerdotal nor anti-sacerdotal, neither liturgical nor anti-liturgical"; yet it claimed to convey a genuine apostolic doctrine as received from "the Lord," *i.e.,* the glorified Christ (VIII: 2; IX: 5; XI: 2, 4, 8; XV: 4; XVI: 1, 7*ff*). The best edition of this work in English was published by Philip Schaff in 1886, giving the Greek text and English translation, and from this edition we now quote portions of this most remarkable manuscript interjecting some of the more important scriptural parallels.

THE TEACHING OF THE LORD BY THE TWELVE APOSTLES TO THE GENTILES

Chapter I

THE TWO WAYS—THE WAY OF LIFE

1. "There are two ways, one of Life and one of Death; but there is a great difference between the two Ways.

2. "Now the Way of Life is this: First, Thou shalt love God who made thee; secondly, thy neighbor as thyself; and all things whatsoever thou wouldst not have done to thee neither do thou to another.

3. "Now the teaching of these (two) words (of the Lord) is this: Bless those who curse you, and pray for your enemies, and fast for those who persecute you: for what thank is there if you love those who love you? Do not even the Gentiles the same? But love ye those who hate you, and ye shall not have an enemy.

4. "Abstain from fleshly and bodily (worldly) lusts. If anyone give thee a blow on the right cheek, turn to him the other also, and thou shalt be perfect. If anyone press thee to go with him one mile, go with him two; if anyone take away thy cloak, give him also thy tunic; if anyone take from thee what is thine, ask it not back, as indeed thou canst not.

5. "Give to everyone that asketh thee and ask not back, for the Father wills that from his own blessings we should give to all. Blessed is he that gives according to the commandments, for he is

guiltless. Woe to him that receives. For if anyone receives, having need, he shall be guiltless; but he that has not need shall give account why he received, and for what purpose; and coming into distress he shall be strictly examined concerning his needs, and he shall not come out thence till he shall have paid the last farthing.

6. "But concerning this also it hath been said, Let thy alms sweat (drop like sweat) into thy hands till thou know to whom thou shouldst give."

Chapter II

The Second Great Commandment—Warning Against Gross Sins

It is hardly necessary to quote this in full as it is an expansion of the second table of the decalog with reference to prevailing heathen vices, to which are added points of warning with reference chiefly to sins of the tongue. Some of the most striking commandments are as follows:

"Thou shalt not use witchcraft; thou shalt not practice sorcery; thou shalt not procure abortion; thou shalt not speak evil; duplicity of tongue is a snare of death; . . . thou shalt not hate anyone, but some thou shalt rebuke, and for some thou shalt pray, and some thou shalt love above thy own soul (or life)."

Chapter III

Warning Against Lighter Sins

This chapter emphasizes the fact that anger leads to murder, lust to adultery, superstition to idolatry, lying to theft. It warns against quick temper and filthy talk and astrological practises and vain-glorious ambitions and continues:

"But be thou meek, for the meek shall inherit the earth. Be thou long-suffering and merciful and harmless and quiet and good and trembling continually at the words which thou hast heard . . . the events that befall thee thou shalt accept as good, knowing that nothing happens without God."

Chapter IV

SUNDRY WARNINGS AND EXHORTATIONS

This chapter enjoins duties on Christians as members of the Church, commanding them to honor their minister, who speaks to them the word of God "as the Lord," and continues:

"And thou shalt seek out day by day the faces of the saints that thou mayest rest upon their words.. . . Be not one that stretches out his hands for receiving but draws them in for giving . . . nor in giving shalt thou murmur . . . thou shalt share all things with thy brother, and shalt not say that they are thine own; for if you are fellow-sharers in that which is imperishable, how much more in perishable things."

It commands kindness to slaves that they may fear "him who is God over you both," and commands reverence and fear on the part of bondmen, and adds:

Thou shalt hate all hypocrisy and everything that is not pleasing to the Lord . . . In the congregation (ἐκκλησία) thou shalt confess thy transgressions; thou shalt not come to thy prayer with an evil conscience. This is the Way of Life."

Chapter V

THE WAY OF DEATH

This chapter describes the way of death by a catalog of sins which, as Dr. Schaff says, "faithfully reflects the horrible immorality of heathenism in the Roman Empire" (*cf*. Rom. 1: 18-32). It is significant that the "Synagog Confession" gives the lists of vices in almost the same order. We quote in full the first paragraph:

"First of all it is evil and full of curse; murders, adulteries, lusts, fornications, thefts, idolatries, witchcrafts, sorceries, robberies, false witnessings, hypocrisies, double heartedness, deceit, pride, wickedness, self-will, covetousness, filthy talking, jealousy, presumption, haughtiness, boastfulness."

The chapter closes with a warning against those who are "advocates of the rich; lawless judges of the poor; wholly sinful."

Chapter VI
WARNING AGAINST FALSE TEACHERS AND THE WORSHIP OF IDOLS

This chapter contains a passage often quoted as the foundation of the practise of ascetism.

"For if indeed thou art able to bear the whole yoke of the Lord, thou wilt be perfect; but if thou art not able, do what thou canst."

It also speaks of idol offerings as "a service of dead gods."

This closes the first division of the book—the first "Way" which has to do with moral precepts. Many scholars think that an ancient Jewish work has been used in the composition, modified, however, by the insertion of passages from the Sermon on the Mount, etc. Dr. Schaff finds thirteen distinct allusions and two quotations from the Old Testament in the Didache and forty-six reminiscences of the New Testament, including many parallels to the synoptic gospels and at least three to John's gospel (Did. 10:2; cf. John 1:14; Did. 9:2; cf. John 15:1; Did. 9:2, 3; 10:2; cf. John 15:15). He also sees important resemblances to Jude and 2 Peter, but no acquaintance with the pastoral epistles. Professor Harnack acknowledges five quotations from the gospels and twenty-three citations.

The second part of the Two Ways consists of precepts relating to church life. The first four chapters are intended as "a short sacramental manual intended for the use of local elders or presbyters, tho such are

not named, for they were not yet a distinctive order of
the clergy." This section was probably added to the
Two Ways before the edition of the remainder. It
orders baptism in the threefold name, making a distinction as to waters, which has Jewish parallels, and
permitting a threefold pouring on the head if sufficient
water for immersion could not be had. It prescribes a
fast before baptism for the baptizer as well as the candidate. Fasts are to be kept on Wednesday and Friday,
not Monday and Thursday, which are the fast days of
"the hypocrites." Then follows the Lord's Prayer
almost exactly as in St. Matthew, which is to be repeated three times each day. Next come three
eucharistic prayers, the language of which is clearly
marked off from that of the rest of the book and shows
parallel with the diction of St. John's gospel. They
are probably founded on Jewish thanksgivings, and it
is of interest to note that a portion of them is prescribed as a grace before meat. As in Ignatius and
other early writers, the eucharist, a real meal of a
family character (10:1), is regarded as producing
immortality ("spiritual food and drink and eternal
life"), and none are to partake of it save those who
have been "baptized in the name of the Lord"—an expression which is of interest in a document which prescribes the threefold formula. The next section
(XI-XIII) deals with the ministry of spiritual gifts
as exercised by apostles, prophets, and teachers. Next
comes a section (XIV, XV) reflecting a somewhat
later development concerning fixt services and ministry.
The eucharist is to be celebrated every Lord's Day and
to be preceded by confession of sin. The book closes
(XVI) with exhortations to stedfastness in the "last

days" and to the coming of the "world-deceiver" or anti-Christ, which will precede the coming of the Lord." [39]

We will quote only special sentences from these chapters.

Chapter VII

BAPTISM

1. "Now concerning baptism, baptize thus: having first taught all these things baptize ye into the name of the Father and of the Son and of the Holy Ghost in living water.

2. "And if thou hast not living water baptize into other water; and if thou canst not in cold, then in warm (water).

3. "But if thou hast neither, pour (water) thrice upon the head into the name of the Father and the Son and of the Holy Ghost.

4. "But before baptism let the baptizer and the baptized fast and any others who can; but thou shalt command the baptized to fast for one or two days before."

Chapter IX

THE AGAPE AND THE EUCHARIST

With perhaps one exception the three prayers given in this chapter are "the oldest known Christian prayers after those in the New Testament . . . they furnish together with the Lord's Prayer the elements of a primitive liturgy . . . they are very remarkable for their brevity, simplicity, and high-toned spirituality, but also for the absence of any allusion to the atoning sacrifice of Christ except perhaps in the mystic meaning of the 'vine of David' and the broken bread. Not even the words of institution, 'this is my body,' 'this is my blood,' are mentioned; much less is any theory of the real presence intimated or implied. The prayers are too low for the sacrament and yet too high for an

---

[39] See for further analysis *Encyclopædia Britannica*, VIII., 201.

ordinary meal" (Schaff). The prayer for the cup reads:

"We give thanks to thee, our Father, for the holy vine of David thy servant, which thou hast made known to us through Jesus thy servant; to thee be the glory forever."

The prayer for the broken bread:

"We give thanks to thee, our Father, for the life and knowledge which thou hast made known to us through Jesus thy servant; to thee be the glory forever. As this broken bread was scattered upon the mountains and being gathered together became one, so let thy church be gathered together from the ends of the earth into thy kingdom, for thine is the glory and the power through Jesus Christ forever."

The post-communion prayer is given in chapter X:

"We thank thee, holy Father, for thy holy name which thou hast caused to tabernacle in our hearts; and for the knowledge and faith and immortality which thou hast made known to us through Jesus thy Servant; to thee be the glory forever. Thou, O almighty Sovereign, didst make all things for thy name's sake; thou gavest food and drink to men for enjoyment, that they might give thanks to thee; but to us thou didst freely give spiritual food and drink and eternal life through thy servant. Before all things we give thanks to thee that thou art mighty; to thee be the glory forever. Remember, O Lord, thy Church, to deliver her from all evil and to perfect her in thy love; and gather her together from the four winds, sanctified for thy kingdom, which thou didst prepare for her; for thine is the power and the glory forever. Let grace come and let this world pass away. Hosanna to the God (Son) of David. If anyone is holy let him come; if any one is not holy let him repent. Maranatha. Amen."

Altho the prophets are permitted to pray in any words that they may chose, few modern prophets could do better when administering the sacrament than to use this most ancient communion prayer. An impressive prayer craves the unity of all congregations.

Chapter XI

APOSTLES AND PROPHETS

The "apostles" here are evidently traveling evangelists or missionaries; and the "prophets," tho they may have been itinerants, are more like settled ministers, being entitled to support and being the "chief priests" who officiate at the holy sacrament. The instruction given to these apostles is:

"Let every apostle that cometh to you be received as the Lord. But he shall not remain (longer than) one day . . . if he remain three (days) he is a false prophet. And when the apostle departeth, let him take nothing except bread (enough) till he reach his lodging. . . . But if he ask for money he is a false prophet."

Of the settled preachers it says:

"Not every one that speaks in the spirit is a prophet but only if he has the behavior (τοὺς τρόπους) of the Lord . . . No prophet that orders a table in the spirit eats of it (himself) unless he is a false prophet . . . if he does not practice what he preaches, he is a false prophet . . . Whosoever says in the spirit, Give me money or any other thing, ye shall not listen to him; but if he bid you to give for others that lack, let no one judge him."

Chapter XII

RECEIVING DISCIPLES

"Let everyone that comes in the name of the Lord be received, and then proving him ye shall know him . . . if he wishes to settle among you, being a craftsman, let him work and eat (earn his living by work) . . . No Christian shall live idle among you. And if he will not act thus he is a Christ-trafficker. Beware of such."

Chapter XIII

TREATMENT OF PROPHETS

"Every true prophet who wishes to settle among you is worthy of his food (i.e., "support") . . . therefore thou shalt take and give all the first fruit of the produce of the wine press and threshing floor, of oxen and sheep, to the prophets; for they are your chief priests. But if ye have no prophet give to the poor."

Chapter XIV

THE LORD'S DAY AND THE SACRIFICE

It is noticeable that there is no commandment in this document to keep the Sabbath, and that already at the end of the first century Sunday is the sacred day of worship.

1. "And on the Day of the Lord come together and break bread and give thanks, having before confessed your transgressions, that your sacrifice may be pure."

2. "Let no one who has a dispute with his fellow come together with you until they are reconciled, that your sacrifice may not be defiled."

3. "For this is that which is spoken by the Lord: In every place and time offer me a pure sacrifice, for I am a great King, saith the Lord, and my name is wonderful among the Gentiles."

Chapter XV

BISHOPS AND DEACONS

The early age of our document is seen from the fact that traveling missionaries and prophets are given higher rank than purely local officers, such as bishops and deacons. Presbyters are not mentioned because the word bishop is used in the same sense (as in 1 Tim. 3: 8-13 and Phil. 1: 1); but these bishops and deacons "are not to be looked down upon because their own special functions are of a humble order, but are to rank as associates of their more gifted colleagues" (Bartlett).

1. "Elect therefore for yourself bishops and deacons worthy of the Lord, men meek and not lovers of money and truthful and approved; for they too minister to you the ministry of the prophets and teachers."

2. "Therefore despise them not, for they are those that are the honored (men) among you with the prophets and teachers."

Chapter XVI

WATCHFULNESS AND THE COMING OF CHRIST

1. "Watch over your life; let not your lamps be quenched and let not your loins be unloosed but be ye ready for ye know not the hour in which our Lord comes."

2. "But be ye frequently gathered together seeking the things that are profitable for your souls; for the whole time of your faith shall not profit you, except in the last season ye be found perfect."

3. "For in the last days false prophets and destroyers shall be multiplied, and the sheep shall be turned into wolves, and love shall be turned into hate."

4. "For when lawlessness increases, they shall hate and persecute and deliver up one another; and then shall appear the world deceiver as Son of God, and shall do signs and wonders, and the earth shall be delivered into his hands . . . "

6. "And then shall appear the signs of the truth: first, the sign of expansion in heaven; then the sign of the voice of the trumpet; and the third resurrection of the dead. . . . "

8. "Then shall the world see the Lord coming upon the clouds of heaven."

Such is this ancient synopsis of the official teaching of the Christian Church in Palestine which comes to us from a time as near to the lifetime of those who knew the last of the apostles as we are near to those who personally knew Abraham Lincoln and General Grant.[40]

5. LIBELLI

When Grenfell and Hunt published in 1904 a Greek papyrus in which could be read the actual certificate given by a Christian living about A.D. 250, stating in set form his recantation of Christianity, the Christians all over the world were stirred to a feeling

[40] For an extended and profound analysis of this document with full statement of all the literature connected with it, see especially Hastings, *Dictionary of the Bible*, V., 438-451.

of horror. As early as 1893 Dr. Fritz Krebs had found a similar certificate among the papyri of the Berlin Museum and two others had appeared a little later; yet none of these had made so great an impression, at least upon the English-speaking world. The statement as translated by the discoverers read as follows:

"To the superintendents of offerings and sacrifices at the city. From Aurelius . . . son of Theodorius and Pantonymis of the said city. It has ever been my custom to make sacrifices and pour libations to the gods and now also I have in your presence in accordance with the commandment poured libations and sacrifice and tasted the offerings, together with my son Aurelius Dioscuros and my daughter Aurelia Lais. I therefore request you to certify my statement.

"The first year of the Emperor Cæsar Gaius Messius Quintus Trajanus Decius Pius Felix Augustus. Pauni 20." [41]

Poor Aurelius! His act of apostasy is known now the world over.

From this same reign of Decius (about A.D. 250) have since been discovered a number of others, all having the same set form, showing that a stereotyped official wording was used.

By the time Dr. Charles Wessely published his great work, *Les Plus Anciens Monuments du Christianisme écrits sur Papyrus,* in 1907, five of these libelli had been recovered. The publication in the same year of a *libellus* issued to "Aurelia Ammonous Mystos, priestess of Petesouchos, the great god," threw a new light upon the possibilities connected with the use of these certificates. Was it possible that Christianity had grown so popular that everybody, even the pagan priestesses, were suspected and forced to sign these

[41] *Oxyrhynchus Papyri,* IV., No. 658.

certificates? Or did it mean that this woman who had originally been a priestess had been converted to Christianity, and later under stress of persecution had sacrificed to the gods—or else had bribed some government officer to give her this certificate making use of her former title in order to procure it? The latter seems to the writer a natural explanation, since we know from the statement of the early Christian fathers that if Christians had friends among the government officials or could part with a sufficient financial inducement, it was not impossible to obtain a signed and witnessed certificate without having to go through the damnable ordeal of sacrifice. This newly found libellus suggests also that some of the men who previously signed these certificates may not have been apostate Christians, but may have been heathen falsely accused of being Christians.

In 1911 Dr. Paul M. Meyer [42] published the Greek text of nineteen libelli from Theadelphia, in the Egyptian Fayum, dating from June 12 to July 14, A.D. 250, all being relics of this same Decian persecution. He exprest the judgment that the Roman government in this persecution was less concerned to hurt Christianity than to check what was considered a non-patriotic refusal to adhere to the official Roman religion. We give below translations of the two longest and most complicated of these newly published documents:

"To those chosen to have charge of the sacrifices from Aurelia, wife of (?) Ammonarios, from the village Theadelphia, and who always sacrifices and reverences the gods, together with the children of the Aurelians Didymos and Nouphios and Taat. (?)

"We have ever continued to sacrifice and to reverence the

[42] *Abhandlungen der Berl.-Akademie, Phil. hist. Klasse,* No. 5, p. 34*ff.*

gods with the children of the Aurelians Didymos and Nouphios,
and now in your presence according to the orders we have poured
libations and have sacrificed and have tasted of the sacrifices, and
I demand of you that you witness this with your signature for
me. Farewell. (No. 2.)

(Another hand) "We Aurelians Serenos and Hermas have
seen you sacrificing.

(A third hand) "Erm(a)s has set his seal.

(The first hand) "The first year of the Emperor Cæsar Gaius
Messius Quintus Trajan Decius, Revered, Fortunate, August.

"To those chosen to have charge of the sacrifices from Aurelios
Euprodokios (Euprodoktos?), household servant of Aurelios
Apianos, who has been in charge of the sacred rites of the most
illustrious city of the Alexandrians, and he is engaged in business
in . . . Theadelphia, ever sacrificing to the gods and now in
your presence according to the commands; I have sacrificed and
poured libations and have tasted of the sacrifices, and I demand
that you witness this with your signatures. Farewell. (No. 16.)

(Second hand) "We Aurelians Serenos and Hermas have
seen you sacrificing.

(Third hand) "Hermas (Seal).

(First hand) "First year," etc. (as in other example).

Since Dr. Meyer's list was published Leclercq [43] has
lifted the number known of these strange documents
to twenty-five—twenty of which came from Theadelphia—and three others have just been published (1915)
from the *Catalogue of Greek Papyri* in the John
Rylands Library. The latter all came from Theadelphia. The first of these (No. 112) is the certificate of
A. Souelis, "whose mother is Taïsis," signed as witnesses by A. Serenus and A. Hermas; the second and
third certificates coming from A. Aouteis and A. Iseitos
Anoutos and signed by the same witnesses.

Among those who have made for themselves an

[43] *Bulletin d'ancienne litterature et d'archéologie chrétiennes,* 1914, pp. 57-
60, 126-139, 188-201. An additional *libellus* appears in *Oxyrhynchus Papyri,*
XII. (1916), No. 1464.

eternal infamy by signing other papers similar to the above, the writer has noticed the names of Horion; Charis; Alexandros; Kamis, "who was seen to sacrifice by A. Serenus"; Serenis Herod; Tausis; Thermouthe Melana; A. Diogenes, son of Satabous, "aged about 72 years, with a scar on his right eye"; A. Syrus and Paspes his brother, and Demetria and Serapias, their wives; and A. Demas, whose husband signed for her, "she being illiterate," etc., etc.

A word ought perhaps to be added concerning the Decian persecution from which all these *libelli* have come. Decius was not a monster but a man of high aims. He sought the best good of his people, but his judgment concerning Christianity was wrong. His idea was that Rome in order to be strong must have absolute control over both government and religion; and as this one religion by its intolerance of all rivals was a constant menace to the public peace and authority, he bitterly antagonized it. He recognized its claim of world-wide dominion; and instead of linking the government to it, as its ally, he set out to conquer it. It was the greatest political mistake of his reign. Trajan (A.D. 112) was the first to denounce Christianity as a crime against the State; and under Marcus Aurelius (about A.D. 176) informers against Christians were allowed to take the latter's property when convicted; but under most of the emperors until Decius, the Christian associations were permitted registration as "burial clubs," tho Septimus Severus (A.D. 202) issued a proclamation against proselyting. Previous to Decius it was mostly the people, not the upper classes, who opposed Christianity; but the nobles by this era had become antagonistic to this avowedly democratic propaganda, and Decius greatly pleased the heathen Senate by putting the strong arm of the law against this movement. Doubtless both Decius and his counsellors believed that Christianity was opposed to patriotism, as it refused worship to the national gods.

When this persecution began, most of the civilized world had been evangelized; but success had made the Church luxurious and worldly. Bad as this persecution seems, it was a good thing. The *libelli* weeded out the tares from the wheat. It is certain, however, that many who are affirmed to have sacrificed never actually did this, as it was counted a much smaller sin to bribe an official to give a false certificate than actually to sign such a document. Some of the more ardent Christians greatly objected to the ease with which such certificates could be obtained and the ease with which such cowards were readmitted to communion.[44]

It will be noticed that almost all of the victims of this persecution were members of the Aurelian gens. It is also to be noticed that it was not mere conformity to the Emperor cult which was required, but a positive and public sacrifice made to the "gods" of Rome. A long list of these gods and goddesses comes to us from the reign of Diocletian. The refusal of any Christian to worship any one of these deities assured his death.[45] Dr. Meyer has been understood to suggest, in his fine work which we have previously quoted, that these certificates were required only from Roman citizens; but several instances which he himself gives intimate that no such limitation was made. Certainly servants as

[44] See for further particulars J. A. F. Gregg, *The Decian Persecution*, 1907.

[45] *Anecdota Oxoniensia*, 1913, No. 22.

well as masters were required to give this pledge of
loyalty to the state religion.

6. ANCIENT CHRISTIAN SERMONS

The oldest known sermon was discovered by Bryennios in the Jerusalem Monastery and published in 1875.
It is from an unknown Greek or Roman author of the
middle of the second century and was formerly ascribed
to Clement of Rome. It is an interesting fact that he
read from manuscript and addrest his hearers as
"Brothers and Sisters!" He was an exhorter rather
than a preacher, but had the root of the matter in him,
as is seen from the fervent doxology with which he
closes:

"To the only God invisible, the Father of truth, who sent
forth unto us the Saviour and prince of immortality, through whom
also he made manifest unto us the truth and the heavenly light.
To him be the glory forever and ever. Amen." [45a]

An early Christian fragment of the third or early
fourth century contains what seems like a paragraph
from an early sermon on "The Spirit of Prophecy":

"Man being filled with the Holy Spirit speaks as the Lord
wills; the spirit of the divine nature will thus be manifest. For
the spirit of prophecy is the essence of the prophetic order, which
is the body of the flesh of Jesus Christ, which was mingled with
human nature through Mary." [45b]

It is interesting to note here that Tyconius (fourth
century) seemed to have been the first preacher in the
Western Church who attempted to treat of the meaning
and inspiration of the Bible as a whole. In his "rules"
he tried to lay down a scientific method of interpreta-

[45a] *Patrologia Apostolica*, I., 111-143.
[45b] *Oxyrhynchus Papyri*, I: 5.

tion; and altho many of these, as found in his newly discovered work, are now wholly antiquated, a few of them sound as if they might have been formulated by some ultra-conservative professor of hermeneutics in a modern theological seminary.[46]

Liberius was one of the most celebrated bishops of the Western Church in the fourth century (A.D. 352-366) and one of his sermons seems to have been most fortunately resurrected for us (*Museon,* XX, 1). While Lefort, in the article referred to, does not positively guarantee the authenticity of the homily, there can be no doubt of its antiquity, even if the wrong name was anciently affixt to it. It is suggestive that this preacher of the olden time fills his sermon with Biblical quotations from many books (Zech. 8: 19; Ex. 20: 13-17; Deut. 5: 17-21; Matt. 19: 18; Mark 10: 19; Rom. 13: 9; 2 Tim. 2: 21). He is preaching on the forty days preceding Easter and beautifully says:

> "Lent is the time of fasting, of pardon, of enfranchisement from the corruptions of earth. Let us advance to the struggle determined to rise victorious; the idle may labor, the coward have courage, the peaceful become warlike in these days."

One of the very celebrated preachers of the Eastern Church in the third century was Bishop Gregory Thaumaturgus (died A.D. 270). From his pen we have what may perhaps be called the "oldest extant Christian sermon." [47] It is a Christmas sermon and he calls this anniversary "The Festival of the Birth of Christ our God, which is the Beginning of Festivals." The sermon is too commonplace to be quotable; but in this respect it differs from one on the same theme by

---

[46] See *Rules of Tyconius* in *Apocrypha Anecdota,* F. C. Burkitt, 1904.
[47] See *The Expositor,* III., 392-400.

Ananias of Shirak, who begins his Christmas sermon in the following flowery fashion:

"When I remember the disobedience of Eve I weep; but when I view the fruit of Mary I am again revived. Deathless by descent, invisible through beauty, before the ages Light of Light; of God the Father wast thou begotten . . . with roses and lilies and fragrant wreaths Christ our imperishable Spring hath come unto us and hath filled the fair garden of the churches, even the seed plots of our hearts, from the paradise of God." [47a]

Another sermon by an ancient preacher named Marlochanis (Father John) was found at Mt. Sinai at the same time that the Syriac gospels were discovered. The text seems to have been "Feed my sheep" (John 21:16). Some of the most striking sentences are:

"The sheep are the men, and the ewes they are the women, and the lambs they are the young boys and the little girls. Lo thou seest the priest of the people! With what care the Lord instructed Peter, saying to him, not once but three times, Feed thou the flock."

A far more remarkable discourse on "Peter the Rock" comes from the same place. It is a most elaborate argument that the Church was founded not upon St. Peter but upon Christ the Rock:

"It is our Lord Jesus the Messiah who goeth down amongst the dead, and hath lordship over death, and cutteth the bonds of Sheol, and breaketh the bars of iron, and leadeth captivity captive, and goeth up in glory. And I will show you, my beloved, upon the New Testament and the Old . . . other foundation a man is not able to lay outside that one which is Lord, that which is our Lord Jesus the Messiah . . . after I have built my barns, and gathered my fruits, and given thee the keys; after I have prepared the fold and gathered the sheep—O Petros, thou wast convicted of fault by Paulus thy colleague. How do men say that upon Petros . . . I have built (the Church which) is not shaken . . . O Petros, after that thou didst receive the keys of heaven, and the Lord was seen by thee after he rose from amongst the dead, thou didst let go of the keys, and thy wage is agreed with thy Master when thou saidst to him, Behold we have let go of everything and have come (after thee. What then shall be to us? And he said to him, Ye shall be sitting on) twelve thrones and judging the tribes of Israel, and after (all these signs, O Petros), thou wentest away again to the catching of fish . . . Thou didst deny me!" (*Anecdota Oxoniensia*, 1896.)

A vast number of these ancient homilies have been recently recovered, especially those delivered by the early Coptic preachers; and altho they in general scrupulously avoid new ideas and are rather painfully orthodox, yet a few of these may be quoted to advantage. A large collection of sermon MSS. in Coptic over 1300 years old has just been published by Mr. W. E. Crum.[48] In these sermons mystic numbers and pictorial language are prominent, and much Scripture is quoted. The topics of the sermons are interesting, the "Last Judgment" being particularly popular; but "Charity" and the "Good Samaritan" and "Repentance" are also in evidence. Under the latter topic the preacher gives good advice:

"Hearken unto repentance, she that cleanseth such as are old in wickedness . . . O Repentance, pure bread which nourisheth . . . fellow unto the angels of God . . . But the rich man is like unto a great ship whose freight is heavy."

One sermon is on the death of the Virgin Mary, and the rejoicing among the angels when she reached heaven, still another is a very rhetorical Christmas sermon which emphasizes the baptism of the Holy Ghost (Acts 1 : 3), and the fact that all power was given to the Son.

It is a curious fact that one of these sermons

[48] *Anecdota Oxoniensia*, Semitic Series, Part XII, 1913, No. 10.

FOURTH CENTURY CHURCH AT RUWÊHA, SYRIA
American Expedition (1899-1900)

CHURCH AND BAPTISTRY AT KASR IBLISŪ, SYRIA (A.D. 431)
From Butler, "Ancient Architecture in Syria"

THE CHURCH OF SS. SERGIUS AND BACCHUS AT UMM IS-SURAB,
SOUTH SYRIA (A.D. 489)
From Butler, "Ancient Architecture in Syria"

A ROW OF CHRISTIAN SHOPS IN THE BAZAAR AT BA'UDEH,
NORTH SYRIA (4th to 6th Century)
From Butler, "Ancient Architecture in Syria"

EARLY CHRISTIAN TAVERN OR CAFÉ IN SERDJILLA, SYRIA
(A.D. 473)
From Butler, "Ancient Architecture in Syria"

CHRISTIAN HOUSE AT SERDJILLA, SYRIA
(Late 5th or Early 6th Century)
From Butler, "Ancient Architecture in Syria"

preached in the cathedral church of Alexandria by the patriarch Damianus has much to say of a recent earthquake (A.D. 589), the subject being "The Terror of Death." We possess it only in fragments, but it speaks of Jesus, "The greatness of thy divinity . . . whose is all honor and all blessing . . . the true Shepherd that laid down his life for the sheep." There is one remarkable passage in which the mother of Jesus is eulogized:

"Hail, Mary! Pure meadow wherein is the pearl which is our Lord Jesus Christ. . . . Holy Virgin, adorned with all knowledge . . . Thou didst nurse him that shepherdeth all creation. He that giveth food unto all creation, thou gavest him milk . . . God the Creator is swathed in bandages."

One of the best preserved sermons is by Gregory Nazianzen, having for its text Romans 4: 15. The preacher brings out clearly the truth that transgression grows as knowledge is increased. Our transgression is especially great since not only the prophets but the Son of God have spoken unto us. True repentance comes when one forsakes sin. His yoke is easy and his burden is light. Do not delay repentance, for "thou knowest not that thou shouldst live until thou be old . . . hast thou established a covenant with death in thy youth?" To go to a wizard or soothsayer or to be a fornicator or liar is to give up Christianity.

"A Christian that shall lie in anything is not a Christian. Faith without works is barren. Thou hast received baptism and clothed thee with Christ; if therefore thou strip thyself with him through thy evil deeds then hast thou made thyself barren . . . if thou do not the deeds of baptism thou hast destroyed baptism . . . woe unto thee if the sign of Christ's death be not found upon thee, which is his cross . . . beat thy breast saying, 'I have sinned.'"

Here follows a statement that the clergy, too, have sinned, but that the laity have not been intrusted with the souls of the clergy as the clergy with the souls of the laity; therefore it is not their business to criticize their minister. He closes with' an exhortation to benevolence:

"He that giveth unto a poor man lendeth at usury unto God. Inasmuch as ye have done it unto one of these little ones, it is unto me that ye have done it. . . . Verily, my beloved, unless God forgive us there shall not a single one from this generation be saved from the punishment of the Son of God."

Another sermon on "The Last Judgment," by a preacher equally revivalistic, points out the inability of the parent to aid his child in that day; and, in the midst of a powerful call to repentance, the preacher pictures the doom of the lost soul who in the midst of his torment sees his friends in glory, and cries out as he recognizes his father: "It were good if thou hadst not begotten me!"

Other sermons preserved elsewhere which have recently been brought to light [49] illustrate God's vengeance on sinners by stories of David, Elijah, and Pharaoh, and contain homilies against the "mischief-maker" and clerical "evil-doer." This ancient preacher warns against the man who elicits confidences only to repeat them to an enemy, thus making trouble, declaring that every man that is double-tongued is "estranged from the Father, the Son, and the Holy Ghost until he repent."

In a sermon on "Humility" there is a warning against those who boast of "prayers and fastings and great asceticisms; for every one that exalteth himself

[49] *Coptic Ostraca.*

shall be humbled; but he that humbleth himself shall be exalted. . . . Moreover it is written that Jesus spared not to visit the teachers that were in the temple and to learn, for the end of all this is humility." Another sermon on the present troubles of the world points out that these troubles "do but lightly requite all our misdeeds." One sermon particularly notable, coming as it does from such an early era, urges that Christians should not judge each other in non-essentials; for some Christians are called to celibacy but others to "till the earth and sell what is brought in by labor . . . let each be content with such good works as he is able to perform . . . in which there is not evil."

One of the most beautiful sermons is on "Forgiveness of Injuries":

"For it is no sin to continue being insulted; but it is wholly sinful if thou requite an insult with insult. For is it a sin to bear insult in silence? Does not Christ say, Whosoever smiteth thee on thy right cheek turn to him the other also?"

Dr. E. A. Wallis Budge, of the British Museum, who had previously published very many of these ancient sermons, in 1910 published several more of most unusual interest.[50] These sermons, which were long and well-developed discourses concerning fasting, repentance, the end of the world, the incarnation, the purity of Susanna, continence, etc., were found in Egypt by some peasants in a stone box under the ruins of an ancient Coptic monastery where they had been hidden years ago. Over half of this volume of ancient sermons has been lost, but 175 leaves remain. The book itself dates from the seventh century, the

[50] *Coptic Homilies in the Dialect of Upper Egypt.*

sermons being those of preachers most of whom lived in the fourth and fifth centuries. The book showed evidence of having been read for many years, and no doubt constituted a standard guide to Christian doctrine, being read to the monks evening by evening.

If we except one homily which antagonized the "contemptible dogma" of Nestorius, we have here a body of very ancient pulpit orations that will compare favorably in many respects with any volumes published lately in America. We have heard so much of the ignorance of the ancient Egyptian clergy that it is a surprize to find in these ten sermons over 300 Scripture quotations and allusions from almost all the books of the Old and New Testaments. They also contain many brilliant rhetorical figures. They will appear to many to be extravagantly orthodox, but they are at any rate "Scriptural" and evangelistic in a marked degree. Some of the expressions sound very much as if these were meant for "revival" sermons: "We must weep and wipe away our defilement by tears"; "Because thou canst not be a vessel of gold or silver, do not become a log of wood which is only fit for fuel"; "If the Psalms are in our mouths, they will be guarded against the entrance of the Evil One"; "Abstinence from sin is the only true abstinence," etc.

Among the most interesting of all these homilies is one by St. Athanasius (fourth century) who takes as his text the Parable of the Laborers (Matt. 20: 1-16), strangely interpreting it to mean that the laborers whom the Master hired at daybreak were Moses, Aaron, and Joshua; those hired at the third hour, the Judges, those hired at the sixth and ninth hours were Samuel, David and the other prophets; while those hired at the eleventh hour were the apostles whom the Master found idle the whole day. Why were they idle? Because "the devil found that he could not hire them, for they would not do evil." The sermon closes with the very flowery peroration:

"And now, O man, come and embark in the ship of salvation, which is the faith of the Church. It hath two steering oars wherewith it is guided, and these are the Testaments; whereon if thou shalt meditate they will bring thee unto a good place for tying up thy boat. It hath a mast which is the cross of the Lord; a rudder, which is thy hands stretched out in prayer to God. It hath a sail which beareth it onwards, that is the power of God, which directeth thee into every good course. It hath a guiding pole, which is the bishop in the church. It hath a helmsman to steer it, who is Jesus, who directeth the course of the universe," etc.

Bishop Proclus in the fifth century (A.D. 434) in his inauguration sermon when he was installed as archbishop, and also in a later discourse when it is said Nestorius was present, preaches on the "Deity of Jesus Christ," rejoicing in the mystery of this doctrine:

"Which is the greater miracle? The heavens raining down bread, or God taking upon himself flesh? Which is the greater miracle? The sea which became divided that thou mightest pass through it, or the virgin who ceased not to be a virgin, even after a passage had been made through her? Which is the greater miracle? The rod which made the rock to become a lake of water, or the cross which cleansed the world?"

After quoting the law and the prophets, as well as the evangelists and apostles, to prove Christ's deity, he appealed to the four elements at the time of the crucifixion in support of his doctrine:

"Heaven declareth that he was God; the sun saith, 'Jesus Christ was my Lord'; the earth saith, 'He whom they crucified was the Creator in human flesh'; the sea saith, 'He was not my fellow servant'; the temple saith, 'He who was crucified was God, who was worshipped in me from the beginning'; the grave saith, 'He who came into my domain was the Almighty.' And the angels and archangels and all the hosts of heaven say, 'He who was crucified was the King of Glory.' "

The old Egyptian word "Amente" is the one used in these sermons instead of "grave," and in many cases when the punishment in the future world is described, ancient Egyptian terms and ideas are used.

To the writer the most interesting sermon of all is one by Apa Eusebius, bishop of Cæsarea, upon the Canaanitish Woman (Matt. 15:21ff). This ancient preacher begins by showing how the wickedest could get to Jesus and he could transform them:

"If thou art a tax gatherer, thou hast the power to turn thyself into an evangelist. And if thou art a thief, thou hast the power to enter into the paradise. For there is no kind of sin whatsoever which repentance will not do away."

He continues by pointing out that Jesus is a great physician who loves to get difficult cases so that he can prove his power, and continues:

"If thou hast committed sin, make haste, stand upon thy feet, be sorry and let thy heart eat thee, and pour out thy tears. For did not the sinful woman act in this wise? And did she not pour out her tears and lay hold on repentance?

"Now Jesus came out of the border of Tyre and Sidon, and behold a woman set out to go to him. The evangelist is stricken with wonder and saith, 'A woman,' i.e., the strongest weapon of the devil; the mother of sin; the beginning of wickedness; woman who was cast forth from the paradise! This is woman and such is her nature.

"Oh what strange and wonderful works are these! The Jews fled from him, but the woman fled to him. Consider this woman, who made herself to be a preacher and one who acknowledged the government of God; for she said, 'Lord,' which was the confession of his divinity, and 'Son of David,' which was the acknowledgment of his manhood; 'have mercy upon me.' Is not this act better than every other act in this world? . . . She did not make an appeal to the apostles . . . she said, 'I have no need of men to make him come to where I am.' And why? 'Because he came down, and took upon himself flesh, I will speak with him in the flesh.' . . . She said: 'Have mercy upon me! for this reason hast thou taken upon thyself flesh, and hast come forth, and hast entered into the world for the sake of sinners like unto myself' . . .

"He answered her not a word. The sickness increased, but the Physician kept silence. The blow was sharp and severe, and the Word kept silence. The Physician held his hand. What is this new and wonderful matter? Thou didst run after others and did say, 'Come ye unto me. I will heal you.' Yet from her who ran after thee thou didst run away." . . .

He then quotes the passage that has so influenced modern commentators and their interpretation of this incident: "I was not sent unto any except the sheep which had gone astray of the house of Israel"; but the old preacher sees that this, when properly understood, can not declare that Jesus was not sent to this woman:

"It was for this very thing that thou didst take upon thyself flesh; that thou mightest do good to a certain woman who is going to perish . . . Or didst thou come into this world only for the sake of the Jews? . . . Wherefore then did David say, 'Ask of me and I will give thee the heathen for thine inheritance, and thy dominion unto the end of the earth.' Why then didst thou, O Lover of every soul, say to thy disciples, 'Go ye, baptize all nations in the name of the Father and of the Son and of the Holy Ghost?'"

This ancient preacher points out that Jesus had not refused to go to the Roman centurion nor even to harlots; why then should he speak as if those who were not Jews were dogs? And he properly resolves the difficulty by saying:

"All these words were intended to shame the Jews who called themselves 'Children' . . . Make thou thyself like unto this

Canaanitish woman. And when thou goest into the Church of the Persians, and of the Cuthaeans, and of the Hindoos, and of the Moors, thou shalt hear Christ saying out, 'O thou woman, great is thy faith.'"

It is a most astonishing thing to find this early Christian preacher taking this broad position that the Canaanite woman was not a dog but a child, and that Jesus was trying to teach the disciples this great truth. This sermon alone ought to be enough to bring an increased respect for the thinking qualities of the primitive Christian ministers who preached these sermons nearly 1600 years ago.

A preacher by the name of Alexander who was archbishop in Alexandria A.D. 313-326 has some sentences in one of his sermons which, whatever may be thought of its author's mechanical theology, can rival in eloquence anything by the leading pulpit orators of America:

"And now, O soul, sing thou hymns of praise to thine own imperishable God, because Christ died for us in order that we might live with him forever. Tho he himself was the fabricator of the universe, he endured patiently and allowed himself to be begotten in the womb of a woman. And they wrapped in swaddling bands him that had been arrayed in all the glory of the Father. He who sat on the chariots of the cherubim was laid in a manger. He before whom the seraphim stand in awe, ascribing glory to his divinity, and who sent forth waters from heaven, received baptism in the Jordan by a mortal man. He upon whose word hang the seven heavens was himself hung upon a cross of wood. He gave his soul for the soul of man. He gave man for man and his death for our death. He gave his blood on behalf of all. It was the wicked people whom he loved that put him to death. They pierced the side of him who had created them. They hung upon a tree him that had hung out the earth. He who was the Judge was judged. He through whom the whole universe liveth, died. The grave was perturbed when the Lord went down into it. He despoiled the grave and made himself master of it.

He burst open the gates of brass. He broke through the bolts of iron, and he took the souls which were in Amente and carried them to his Father. Death fell down upon the feet of Christ, and Christ carried him away. One died in order that all might rise from the dead. For having died he put man on himself like a garment, and took him with him into the heaven of heavens; and man became one of one with him. He took him as a gift to his Father. The gift was not gold, neither was it silver, but it was man whom he had created in his own likeness and in his own image. Glory be unto him for all ages of ages. Amen."

From this same collection we give one more example of the manner in which these most ancient preachers speak of Christ:

"He is the Light; therefore is he the Sun of our souls. He is the Life; therefore we live in him. He is Holiness; therefore is he the slayer of sin. He is Salvation; therefore it is he who hath purchased the whole world with his blood. He is the Resurrection; therefore it is he who hath set free those who are in the tomb, and hath made them new a second time by his blood. He is the Way; therefore he is the guide to his Father. He is the Door; therefore he is the guide into paradise. He is the Shepherd; therefore he is the seeker after the sheep which is lost. He is the Lamb; therefore he is the cleanser of the world from its impurity. This is my God; I will ascribe glory unto him, for unto him belong glory and power for all ages and ages. Amen."

In the above references we have not attempted to mention all the newly discovered sermons, but probably a sufficient number of quotations have been given to indicate the wealth of new material and the character of the preaching A.D. 250 to A.D. 600. How impossible it would be in any such work as this to review competently the entire field may be seen from the fact that over forty complete sermons of Chrysostom have been found written in Bohairic, and in the one convent library of St. Michael, dug up in 1910 and now preserved in the J. P. Morgan collection, there are at least forty other sermons, which with Acts of martyrs, Lives of saints, etc., were regularly read to the monks at various times during the liturgical year. This is only one of several collections recently discovered. The early Christians were surely great sermon-tasters![51]

7. Ancient Prayers and Amulets

The oldest written prayer of post-apostolic times was recovered by Bryennios from the ancient monastery in Jerusalem in 1875, being found at the close of Clement's Epistle to the Corinthians. Dr. Philip Schaff, in a very thorough analysis of its contents, says: "It is long and carefully composed and largely interwoven with passages from the Old Testament. It begins with an elaborate invocation of God in antithetical sentences, contains intercession for the afflicted, the needy, the wanderers and prisoners, petitions for the conversion of the heathen, a confession of sin and prayer for pardon (but without a formula of absolution), and closes with a prayer for unity and a doxology. Very touching is the prayer for rulers, then so hostile to the Christians, that God may grant them health, peace, concord and stability."[52] A few sentences from this prayer are all that can be quoted here:

"Grant unto us, Lord, that we may set our hope on thy name, which is the primal source of all creation; and open the eyes of

[51] On the Morgan collection see especially Hyvernat, *Revue Biblique*, 1897, and *Journal des Savants*, X., 174*ff.* Some newly published sermons of interest probably equal to that of any mentioned above are those of Shenoute published by Maspero and Chassnat in their *Coptic Texts*, Vol. IV. (Cairo, 1911); but the writer has not seen this work nor any satisfactory account of its contents.

[52] *Church History*, II., 226; for the Greek text of the prayer consult *Patrum Apostolicorum Opera*, edition by Von Gebhardt and Harnack, III., 517; and for English translation Lightfoot's *St. Clement of Rome*, Appendix pp. 376-379, or Schaff's *History*, II., 228-229.

our hearts that we may know thee, who alone abidest, Highest in the highest, Holy in the holy; who layest low the insolence of the proud; who scatterest the imaginings of nations; who settest the lowly on high and bringest the lofty low; who makest rich and makest poor; who killest and makest alive; who alone art the benefactor of spirits and the God of all flesh . . . Let all the Gentiles know that thou art God alone, and Jesus Christ is thy Son, and we are thy people and the sheep of thy pasture.

"Save those among us who are in tribulation; have mercy on the lowly; lift up the fallen; show thyself unto the needy; heal the ungodly; convert the wanderers of thy people; feed the hungry; release our prisoners; raise up the weak; comfort the faint-hearted."

One sentence concerning the rulers may be added:

"Grant unto them therefore, O Lord, health, peace, concord, stability, that they may administer the government which thou hast given them without failure . . . that, administering in peace and gentleness with godliness the power which thou hast given them, they may obtain thy favor."

This prayer is known from a rather late copy, and was certainly not from the pen of the Clement who was bishop of Rome A.D. 92-101; but as it is found in the oldest extant Christian sermon, which is confidently dated by all experts in the middle of the second century, we possess in it an unrivaled treasure.

A Christian prayer (sixth or seventh century) reads:

"Grant to us in the day of judgment to stand near thee, O worthy One . . . and to hear the voice of the Father saying, Thy sins are forgiven.[53]

About a century earlier than this a Christian woman concluded her written prayer with a quotation of the opening words of the Gospels of St. Luke, St. Matthew,

[53] *Amherst Papyri*, **IX.**

and St. John, and fortunately this prayer has been preserved to us in the original handwriting.[54]

"Extend to me rescue . . . from the horns of one horned. . . . To my brethren in the midst of the Church I will sing thy praise. . . . Good One, protect thy servant . . . her redemption from all weakness that has to do with her spirit through the name of the Lord salvation.✠ Of the living God, inasmuch as many have undertaken to set in order an account concerning the things brought to pass among you, the book of the generation of Jesus Christ. . . . In the beginning was the Word, and the Word was with God, and God was the Word.✠ O holy Phokas, O holy Merkourius, guard thy servant." ✠

Another Christian prayer, the autograph of which is 1,500 or perhaps 1,600 years old, reads:

"O God Almighty, who madest heaven and earth and sea and all that is therein, help me, have mercy upon me, wash away my sins, save me in this world and in the world to come through our Lord and Saviour Jesus Christ, through whom is the glory and the power for ever and ever. Amen." [55]

A Greek papyrus in the Cairo Museum dating from the fourth century which may be from a "Lost gospel," but which is in part written in the form of a prayer, reads:

"Christ . . . the true Word, the God of eternity . . . The blessed Lamb wherefore souls were set free through his blood . . . the earth rejoiced because the enemy departed . . . Thou didst give freedom to the creation-that asked for a Master, Jesus. Thou . . . that forgivest sins . . . we call upon thy holy name."

Another very early Christian prayer from the Fayum is written on the back of an ancient Coptic text:

"I pray that the person named may not be led into falling but to his salvation; but if he cannot hear that which is said for his

[54] Grenfell and Hunt, *Greek Papyri*, No. 10696.
[55] *Oxyrhynchus Papyri*, Vol. III., No. 407.

salvation, may it be for a judgment. Jesus himself taught that his presence was for a judgment, that those who see not might see, and that those who see might become blind. The very word of the gospel taught that Jesus came not only for lifting up but also for falling down. . . . See that these words be not spoken for thy fall." [56]

Gustave Lefebvre has published the Greek text of several Christian prayers which are of deep interest, altho the text is occasionally very obscure:

"The God of the spirits and of the flesh, the one that has abolished death and the grave (Hades), the one that has freely given life to the world, give repose to the soul of thy servant Marianos . . . in the bosom of Abraam and Isaac and Jacob." [57]

"Lord, grant repose to the soul of thy servant Thecla, summon her to the bosom of Abraam and Isaac and Jacob, and feed her upon the tree of life and hearing (*i.e.*, let her hear): 'Come, ye blessed of my Father, inherit the kingdom made ready for you from the foundation of the world.'" [57a]

Another private prayer of unusual value, dating from the fourth century, has just been published by Dr. C. Schmidt:

"Give light in (by) thy consolation, that we may be deemed worthy of the glorious teaching of our Saviour Jesus Christ." [58]

"God the all-conqueror, the one that is, that was, that is to be, Jesus, the Christ, the Son of the living God, remember the sleep and the rest of thy servant Zoneese, the most devout and loving-the-commandments, and deem her worthy to tabernacle through thy holy and light-bearing archangel Michael, in the bosom of the holy fathers, Abraam and Isaac and Jacob, because thine is the glory and the power to the ages of the ages. Amen. She lived blessedly seventy-seven years and her memory . . ." [59]

[56] Bouriant, *Memoirs de la mission arch. française au Caire,* I., 1889, p. 243.

[57] *Recueil des Insc. Chrét. de l'Egypt, Cairo,* 1907, No. 64.

[57a] *Ibid.,* No. 107.

[58] *Neutestamentliche Studien für G. Heinrici,* 1914, p. 71.

[59] Reference mislaid.

While few private prayers, outside of cemeteries, have been preserved, we have many public prayers such as this coming from a very ancient Greek library recently discovered:

"Glory be to the Father and to the Son and to the Holy Ghost. Holy is God, strong and undying; have mercy upon us, save us, Son of God, our Saviour. Alleluia, alleluia, alleluia!" [60]

Many individual prayers from poor people have been found written on pieces of broken pottery, and a few official church prayers, among which is a very ancient invocation used in the primitive Church in preparation for the kiss of peace:

"Cleanse us from all deceit and all malice, and make us worthy to salute one another with a holy kiss, that we may partake without condemnation of thine immortal and heavenly gift." [61]

It is very noticeable that the earliest Christian prayers, many of which will be mentioned later from epitaphs found in Christian cemeteries, quote Scripture more freely and are decidedly more spiritual or, at least, less mixed up with superstitious and magical references than those of later eras. In the most ancient official Christian literature, magic is mentioned only to be attacked as an error of heathendom (*Didache*, II, 2; III, 4; V, 1); but among the lower classes magical expressions probably entered into Christian letters and prayers from the earliest period; and certainly by the fourth century, notwithstanding the fact that the great leaders of Christianity protested against

[60] *Coptic and Greek texts in British Museum*, H. R. Hall, 1905, p. 53. See for another beautiful Christian prayer of third or fourth century, *Greek Papyri in British Museum*, No. 1189.

[61] Crum, *Coptic Ostraca*, No. 5.

the adoption of superstitious means for the regaining of health or the recovery of lost articles, the papyri show that this was very common. This is not at all surprizing. The fear of demons had for centuries ruled the heathen world. A special charm had been arranged against every possible disease and dangerous circumstance. Curative charms, weather charms, love charms, malevolent charms, meet us everywhere in the heathen literature. Christians evidently used these so far as they were not against their religion, tho attempting to exclude everything that connected them with idolatry; yet amethysts were preferred for rings even by Christian nobles and bishops, and herbs were used as charms rather than medicine, and scarabs and other protective tokens were not infrequently placed in Christian graves. The name of Jesus together with gospel texts and certain liturgical formula were early used as amulets, and by the sixth century the sign of the cross and other symbols for Christ had quite widely taken on a magical import. Several of the early fathers speak of the Christian women wearing diamond editions of the gospels round their necks after the manner of Jewish *tephillin,* and the papyri show us the Lord's prayer as one of the most common devices to ward off evil. Wilcken and others have published a goodly number of Christian amulets from the sixth century, in which prayers to God and the local saints are made against the demons of asthma, croup, hydrophobia, insanity, indigestion, witchcraft, and pain. These amulets often end with the Lord's prayer. A beautifully written Christian relic of this character has recently been recovered (1911) from Oxyrhynchus. It is of thin vellum, dating from the sixth century, and contains Matt. 4: 23-24, written in five columns in the form of a series of small crosses.[62]

It ought not to be expected that a man's ignorance shall be wholly cured by Christianity. While the early Christians had lost their faith in heathen demons, they often expected some Bible text or a repetition of the omnipotent "Name" (*cf.* Acts 4: 7, 12) to do for them what magical charms had formerly been supposed to do. The following amulet, published in 1911, shows the piety of an ignorant Christian of the fifth century:

"In the beginning was the Word and the Word was with God and the Word was God. All things are made by him, and without him was not anything made that hath been made. O Lord Christ, Son and Word of that Living God, who healedst every sickness and every infirmity, heal and regard thy handmaid Johannen." [63]

Another amulet of the sixth century, published in this same volume, quotes Matt. 4: 23-24, under the suggestive title, "The Gospel of Healing according to Matthew." Christian amulets of all eras ordinarily consist chiefly of gospel verses strung loosely together.

A magical text of the fourth century, previously quoted, more fully shows the common form of divination at that era condemned by the Christian Church:

"If the abdomen quiver, it denotes something good with adverse talk; . . . if both parts of the hips quiver, a person so affected will stand in the grip of a twofold trouble." . . .

With this may be compared the modern Jewish incantations by means of chanted "Names" in the synagog,[63a] and the following Christian gibberish from the fifth or sixth century:

[62] *Oxyrhynchus Papyri*, VIII., No. 1077.

[63] *Oxyrhynchus Papyri*, VIII., 1151.

[63a] *Journal of Biblical Archæology*, 1916, p. 221.

"Oror phor, Eloi, Adonai, Iao sabaoth, Michael, Jesus Christ help us and this house." [64]

It may be that a very curious papyrus of the third or fourth century, which contains an explanation of some of the most powerful and comforting Biblical names, may have been used as an amulet of protection. We give this, in part following Dr. Deissman's translation: [65]

"Arima, Jesus; Jo, Salvation; Ariel, My light of God; Azael, strength of God; Eli, Eli sabachthani, My God, my God, to what purpose hast thou forsaken me? Judas, Jao confession; Jonathan, Jao gift; Joseph, Jao addition; Jakin, Jao resurrection," etc., etc.

Jews, Christians, and heathen, alike, believed in the power of magical names, and therefore Hebrew archangels, together with Greek, Roman, and Egyptian deities, appear ·most confusedly mixed up in some of these conjurations. In the great magical papyrus of Paris, olive branches are placed before the man possest of demons, and the exorcist standing behind him pronounces over his head:

"I invoke the God of Abraham, I invoke the God of Isaac, I invoke the God of Jacob, Jesus Christ the Holy, the Spirit Son of the Father, above the seven, below the seven. We bring Iao Sabaoth, whom thy power scoffs at (beyond others) until thou hast exorcised this supreme demon Satan who is in him. I exorcise thee, demon, whoever thou art, by this god, Sabarbathiot, Sabarbathiouth, Sabarbathioueth, Sabaraphia." [66]

In the Leyden papyrus the method of making a dream (A.D. 300) is given:

"Take oil in the left hand and repeat formulae . . . then go to bed with the head turned toward the east. Jesus—Anoubis." [67]

[64] *Oxyrhynchus Papyri*, VIII., 1152.
[65] *Light from the Ancient East*, pp. 415, 416.
[66] Wessely, *Les Plus Anciens Monuments*, No. 16.
[67] *Ibid*, No. 18.

An even more elaborate magical formula from the third century gives the method by which supernatural information may be obtained:

"Great is the lady Isis . . . take twenty-nine leaves of a male palm and inscribe on each of the leaves the names of the gods; then after a prayer lift them up two by two and read that which is left at the last and you will find wherein your omen consists." [68]

Another magical formula from the fifth century, quoted previously, reads:

"Fly, hateful spirit! Christ pursues thee. The Son of God and the Holy Spirit have outstripped the . . . in the beginning was the Word (John 1: 1-3 is quoted here). . . . O, Lord Christ, Son and Word of the Living God, who healest every infirmity, heal . . . thy handmaid . . . put to flight all fevers and every kind of chill . . . on thy name, O Lord God, have I called, the wonderful and exceeding glorious name, the terror of thy foes. Amen." [69]

The most curious of all magical prayers has just been brought to light, in which a miserable widow conjures a mummy and its companions against her oppressor, urging them to cry to God the Father, Son, and Holy Ghost, con-substantial Trinity ('Ομοούσιος), until he hear. The widow most fervently appeals to the God of the widow and Father of the orphans, to the God who created Adam and helped Job:

"I adjure thee who sittest upon the chariot, before whom stand a thousand and ten thousand archangels and seraphim with six wings, to do justice against Schenute, son of Pamin, that thou mayest slay him as thou didst slay the 85,000 Assyrians in one night; that thou mayest bring upon him heat and cold and jaundice; and open the mouth of his enemies against him; and when he flees from them, may he flee on the same road which his pursuing enemies take!"

[68] *Ibid*, No. 886.
[69] *Oxyrhynchus Papyri*, VIII., 1151.

Then she invokes the mummy that it call night and day clear across to another land, and with the other mummies cry all together "that which stands upon this paper until God hears and gives us justice in haste, Amen." It closes with an Alpha and Omega, each repeated seven times.[70]

Stars of five, six or eight points, or some other symbol to bring good luck, were as common on the door-lintels in Syria in the early Christian period as now. Characteristic inscriptions found on Christian dwellings in the sixth century are:

"Christ's is the victory. Flee, Satan!" (A.D. 524).

"Of this house the Lord shall guard the entrance and the exit; for the cross being set before, no malignant eye shall prevail." [71]

In order, impartially, to give proper credit to the ignorant Christians whom we have just been quoting, it ought to be remembered, first, that the charms which come from the middle ages in every part of Europe, and even from some sections to-day, are at least as bad as any of these; second, that the differences in favor even of these most superstitious and ignorant Christians, when their prayers are compared with those of the heathen, are far more marked than the similarities.

A prayer which has been common in certain parts of Europe for over three hundred years and is yet in use reads:

"O, Holy Cross of Christ, ward off from me all sharp repeating words. Ward off from me all dangerous weapons. Holy Cross of Christ, protect me from all my enemies." [72]

[70] *Beiträge zur Forschung*, 1915, pp. 96, 97.

[71] *Am. Journal of Archæology*, XXI., 137-141.

[72] *Ancient Egypt in the Light of Modern Discoveries*, Davis and Cobern, p. 255.

The rubric connected with this prayer declares:

"They who shall repeat this prayer every day or hear it repeated or keep it about them shall never die a sudden death nor be
drowned in water, ... nor shall poison take any effect upon
them." [73]

The Jews of Jerusalem are to this day accustomed
to write out prayers and leave them at the so-called
Tombs of the Judges, as the Jews in Hebron leave
similar prayers at the Tomb of Abraham, hoping that
the ancient saints may help them in trouble. A typical
Jewish amulet reads:

"M. M., son of Joseph. May he grow up to a prosperous life
and to peace with male issue continually." [74]

Certainly, as compared with the above, the ordinary
early Christian amulets take on a more dignified appearance, as may be seen from a typical invocation
found in a magical papyrus owned by Dr. Charles
Wessely and dating from A.D. 300.

"I invoke thee, O God of all, whose name is above all power
and authority and dominion and every name; who is seated above
the cherubim; I invoke thee by our Lord Jesus Christ, thy beloved Son." [75]

8. ANCIENT CHRISTIAN HYMNS

The oldest Christian hymn known to scholars up
to the most recent discoveries dates from the early part
of the third century and comes from Clement of Alexandria. It has long been known, and breathes the
most devotional spirit:

"O King of Saints, all subduing Word of the most High
Father, Prince of Wisdom, Support of sorrows that rejoicest in

[73] For additional instances of the same kind, see London *Academy*
1893, pp. 132-150.
[74] *Am. Journal of Biblical Literature*, 1903, pp. 164-186; 1904, p. 97.
[75] Wessely, *op. cit.*, No. 19.

the ages, Jesus, Saviour of the human race, Shepherd, Husband-
man, Helm, Bridle, Heavenly Wing of the all holy flock, Fisher of
men who are saved, catching the chaste fishes with sweet life from
the hateful wave of a sea of vices," etc.

Very recently, however, a number of fragments of
new hymns that are almost or quite as ancient as this
standard hymn of the Church have come to light.
One of the first of these to be discovered—found with
the *Logia* at Oxyrhynchus—proves to be over 1,500
years old, and resembles the hymn of Clement in a
marked way. We transcribe a few lines of this, following Grenfell and Hunt's translation:

"Hold fast the hope which thou hast learned,
    Which the Master determined for thee.

"O the rest of the sorrowful!
    O the leaping of the flame!
    O the fire, fearful for the wicked!

"Glorious are the ordinances of God,
    In all things he suffers as an example
    That thou mayest have glorious life.

"The Father sent him to suffer,
    Who has received eternal life,
    Who has received power over immortality,
    In order that thou mayest see the light of
        eternity," etc.[76]

Another hymn which seems to have been a favorite
of the Gnostics was first published in 1871 by Prof.
William Wright, but has recently been re-edited.[77] It
dates probably from the first half of the third century.
Its pictorial and symbolic language is especially to
be noted.

[76] *Oxyrhynchus Papyri*, Vol. I.
[77] By Mr. A. A. Bevan in *Texts and Studies*, Vol. V., Art. 3.

EXTRACTS FROM THE SYRIAC HYMN OF THE SOUL

"I went down into Egypt
And my companions parted from me;
I betook me straight to the serpent;
Hard by his dwelling I abode
(Waiting) till he should slumber and sleep
And I could take my pearl from him.

"I forgot that I was a son of kings
And I served their king;
And I forgot the pearl
For which my parents had sent me;
And by reason of the burden of their . . .
I lay in a deep sleep."

Then his father, the "King of Kings," sent him a
letter by an eagle, the king of all birds:

"Call to mind that thou art a son of kings!
See the slavery—whom thou servest!
Remember the pearl
For which thou didst speed to Egypt!
Think of thy bright robe
And remember thy glorious toga
Which thou shalt put on as thy adornment
When thy name hast been read out in the
lists of the valiant!

"I remembered that I was a son of kings
And my free soul longed for its natural state.
I remembered the pearl
For which I had been sent to Egypt
And I began to charm him,
The terrible, loud-breathing serpent.

"And I snatched away the pearl
And turned to go back to my father's house,
And their filthy and unclean garb
I stripped off and left it in their country.

"And my toga of brilliant colors
I cast around me in its whole breadth;
I clothed myself therewith and ascended
To the gate of salutation and homage;
I bowed my head and did homage
To the majesty of my Father who had sent
      it to me.
For I had done his commandments
And he, too, had done what he promised.

"For he rejoiced in me and received me
And I was with him in his kingdom."

Another Christian hymn written in the form of an elaborate metrical acrostic comes to us from the fourth century: [78]

"Some come in sheep's clothing who are inwardly wolves,
   .   .   .   .
Seek to live with the saints,
   Seek to receive life, seek to escape the fire.
Hold fast the hope which thou hast learned,
   Which the Master determined for thee.
God came bringing many blessings,
   He wrought a triple victory over death,
Jesus who suffered for this, saying:
   I give my back that thou fall not a prey to death . . .
He washed in Jordan, he washed as an example,
   His is the stream that cleanseth.
God said, Feed the stranger, the stranger and the helpless,
   That thou mayest escape the fire.
Oh, the fire! fearful for the wicked! . . .
   Christ is the crown of the saints, Christ is the fire for the
      wicked . . .
Freely hast thou come under grace, listen to the prayer of the
      poor.
   Speak no more arrogantly. . . .
Singing psalms with the saints . . . knowing these Scriptures,
   Thou shalt never fear death."

[78] *Amherst Papyri*, Part I., No. II.

Another (sixth to eighth century) which seems to us a little more musical, reads somewhat as follows:

"Cherubim and Seraphim, the many-eyed, sing the thrice holy hymn:
　Holy, holy, holy art thou!
Thou who art seated upon the right hand of the Father,
(Image) of the Godhead, take not thy mercy from me." [79]

Another Christian hymn, one or two centuries older than that just quoted, but representing doubtless an ancient form, is an acrostic, having a kind of refrain after every fourth line. It reads in part:

"Let us glorify him singing, Glory to thee, O Lord!
Let us worship him and say, Glory to thee, O Lord.

"The Lord is risen for us, the Word of truth,
　Incarnate of the unwedded virgin,
Let us extol him and say, Glory to thee, O Lord!" [80]

A great many short hymns used in the Eastern Church have come down to us from the fifth, sixth, and seventh centuries. In very many of these the Virgin is mentioned with great honor. Nothing seemed to astonish the early Church as much as the fact that God should deign to come to earth in human form, and the mystery of this incarnation induced a reverence for the "Mother of God"—as the Virgin was commonly called by the sixth century—which was often extravagant in its expression. Yet nothing is clearer from these earliest hymns than that the honor given to Mary was due to the high theological concept concerning the Son. We give a number of short hymns from this early period, showing the thought of

[79] *Ibid.*, Part I., No. IX.
[80] *Catalogue of Greek Papyri in the John Rylands Library*, Vol. I, 7.

that early Church concerning Christ and his salvation.[81]
The opening hymns given here were sung before reading the gospel at the kiss of peace:

> "Sing a song of joy, ye people, that Christ is born,
> Made flesh from a virgin to save us
> And to glorify thy name, O Lord.

> "Blessed art thou upon the throne of thy kingdom,
> And much to be extolled and exalted for ever more."

At another feast, perhaps the purification, these
hymns were used:

> "Hail Mary, favored one!
> The Lord is with thee, and the Holy Spirit.

> "Thy priests shall clothe themselves with righteousness,
> And thy holy ones shall rejoice with much rejoicing,
> Because of David, thy servant, O Lord.

> "Hail Mary, glorious Virgin, gifted with grace!
> The Lord is with thee.
> Blessed art thou among women,
> And blessed is the fruit of thy womb,
> Because thou hast received Christ, the Son of God,
> The nourisher of our souls."

Some of the most impressive among these early productions are the post-communion anthems:

> "Heavenly bread he gave to them,
> And a human being ate the bread of angels!

> "Blessed bread have we received,
> The body of our Lord and his precious blood.

[81] The Greek texts of these hymns can be found in the early pages of
Crum's *Coptic Ostraca*.

"Having received holy bread, let us bless God,
The One doing marvelous things throughout the
whole earth.

"We give thanks to thee, Christ our God,
Because thou hast deemed us worthy to partake of
thy body and blood."

One specially impressive chant preserved in several
Greek texts reads:

"O thou who once spoke to Moses in Mt. Sinai,
Now from a spotless Virgin hast received a form of flesh free
from all sin.

"O thou who didst nourish Israel,
Now thou hast been fed on milk from a mother who knew not
marriage,
O marvelous One!

"Oh thou who once smote kings,
Now in Egypt has thou escaped a king.

"Thou that sittest upon a lofty, exalted throne,
Thou wast laid lowly in a manger tho still living sublimely re-
vealed on high.
Now in faith let us count happy the one who bore thee,
And let us exalt with hymns the One born.

"God who was on high without mother
Was below and was without mother. Glory to thee!

"O God, who humbled thyself to be born as an infant from a
Virgin,
The holy mighty One who was willing to be placed in the arms
of Mary,
Thou holy immortal One who came to lead Adam back from the
grave,
Christ our God have mercy upon us!

"Stainless Virgin, gifted with grace, mother of God,
Thy holy womb hast born Emmanuel,
Thy breasts gave suck to the nurturer of all.
Therefore art thou highly praised and in great honor.
Hail, mother of God, precious treasure of angels,
Thou favored one, proclaimed in the message of the prophets,
The Lord is with thee." [82]

Several copies of the Psalter used in the ancient Coptic Church have recently come to light. One of the most important of these was found by some Egyptian peasants in Upper Egypt hidden in a stone box or coffer. Two books were inside the box, wrapt in coarse linen cloth. They were written upon papyrus but bound in stout leather covers. They were beautifully preserved and consisted of a volume containing ten complete homilies by the Fathers of the Monophysite church and a complete copy of the Psalter in the dialect of Upper Egypt.

This Psalter, consisting of 156 leaves, was edited by Dr. Budge, of the British Museum, who pointed out its unique importance since it was the "only complete copy of the Psalter in the dialect of Upper Egypt, which has come down to us." It dates from the sixth or seventh century, tho rebound in the eleventh or twelfth century.[82a] Another discovery as spectacular as the above occurred in 1908 when Charles L. Freer succeeded in obtaining in Egypt a volume of 700 pages— a volume so small that the pages only measured 2¾ inches wide by 3⅛ inches high—containing a Psalter made of goat skin and dating A.D. 400-700.[82b]

[83] See also Greek and Latin hymns, *Encyclopædia of Religion and Ethics*, Vol. VII., 1914.
[82a] E. A. Wallis Budge, *The Earliest Known Coptic Psalter*, 1898.
[82b] *The Coptic Psalter in the Freer Collection*, ed. by William H. Worrell, 1916.

It may be added that the "Canticles of the Christian Church East and West," as found in all available manuscripts, have recently been published by Dr. James Mearns (1914). Any one who, like the writer, has ever been at the dawn service at Mt. Sinai can quite understand how St. Augustine felt when A.D. 358 he for the first time heard the Scriptures sung or chanted by a choir of monks. In these earliest manuscripts just found we can read the very phrases over which St. Augustine wept when he first heard them. They include the Lord's Prayer, Magnificat, Gloria in Excelsis, Nunc Dimittis, etc. This Dawn Service proves, according to Dr. Mearns, that the "Odes of Solomon," next to be mentioned, were known to their composer.

Many hymns have been preserved, and recently discovered, written in Syriac. Here is one written by Bishop Severus about A.D. 500:

On the Holy Ascension

"Thou God who bowedst the heavens,
The Word who is before the ages,
The Word of God who shone on us
Through the only Son of God, the Word
The hosts of heaven shook with amazement." [83]

By far the greatest discovery, however, so far as Christian hymnology is concerned, was made when Dr. J. Rendel Harris recovered a large Syriac manuscript of 64 leaves and published it to the world in 1909 under the title, *Odes and Psalms of Solomon*.[84] Really the "Psalms" have very little in common with the "Odes," and they should not be classed together. The

---

[83] For many more of these see, *Patrologia Orientalis*, 1911, pp. 1-179, 595-802.

[84] In 1911 Prof. F. C. Burkitt found in the British Museum another MS. (10th century) containing a large part of these newly discovered Odes.

"Psalms" were a collection made by the Pharisees some half-century before the birth of Christ, and had been known (tho in a different version) for many decades. The "Odes," however, now come to light for the first time, and because of their peculiarly mystic thought and phraseology, greatly resembling that of the gospel of St. John, they occupy a uniquely important position for Christian scholars. Professor Harnack in a splendid hundred-word sentence declares the find to be superior to anything ever discovered since the *Teaching of the Apostles,* being "epoch-making for the higher critic of John's gospel," since these odes contain "all-important pieces of the Johannine theology together with their religious tone color."[84a]

Dr. Harnack is certain that we possess here a "Psalm-Book" of the time of Jesus, which was taken over and edited by the Christian community of Palestine about the year 100 (*ibid.,* 3: 5). Dr. Harris and many other specialists regard the "Odes" as the work of a Jewish Christian of the first century, tho some think them to be wholly Jewish, adopted with certain Christian interpolations to form the earliest Christian hymnal. Very many, following Harnack, Kennedy, and Cheyne, think the interpolations numerous, but some—notably Kittel and Abbott—offer strong verbal and stylistic arguments to prove the unity of the book and the interpolations negligible. Bishop Bernard[85] believes them to be hymns of "the newly baptized," which give us the actual form of initiation with which converts were received in the second century,

---

[84a] *Texte und Untersuchungen zur altchristlich. Literatur,* von A. Harnack u. C. Schmidt, Vol. XXXV (1910), Heft 4.

[85] See *Texts and Studies,* Vol. VIII, 1912, No. 3.

into the Christian communion; and he sustains this
view with forceful arguments. Dr. E. A. Abbott prefers to think of them as "Songs of Ascents or Degrees," in which the thought ascends from the Son
of David, husband of Pharaoh's daughter, to that second and perfect Son of David who was hailed from
heaven as the Beloved and who was the Spouse of the
Church.[86] In any case, the exceptional value of these
hymns—which without any question represent Christian doctrine and feeling within a few years of the
death of the "beloved disciple"—throws an unexpected
light upon the Johannine spirit and mystic phraseology
of the early Church at a time previous to the development of Gnosticism.[87]

The interest awakened by this unique treasure of
early Christian song may be seen from the fact that at
least 166 books or important articles concerning this
discovery appeared between the years 1909-1914.[88]
There is a marked literary excellence as well as beauty
of thought shown in these hymns. As Bishop Bernard
says, it would not be easy to find Christian poems of
any age "which strike a higher spiritual note." The
author was evidently a devout Christian—who may
have been a Jew but who certainly did not keep the
Jewish Sabbath (Ode XVI)—having an attitude of
mind possible only to one who has entered into close
fellowship with God.[89]

The Odes are "marked by a vigor and exaltation

[86] *Light on the Gospel from an Ancient Poet*, in *Diatessarica*, Part IX.

[87] See especially the works cited by Harnack and Abbott and the articles
by R. H. Strachan, *Expository Times*, 1910-11, pp. 7-14, and by Dr.
Schweitzer, *Journal of Theol. Studies*, XIII., 372-386.

[88] See full list in Gerhard Kittel's *Die Oden Salomos, Leipzig,* 1914,
pp. 142-158.

[89] Kittel, *op. cit.,* p. 36.

of spiritual life and a mystical insight to which we can find parallels only in the most illuminated periods of the history of the Church" (Harris). They have few, if any, quotations or adaptations from Scripture; but this only suggests their extreme antiquity and that their "inspiration is first-hand and immediate" (Abbott).

No one doubts that we have here a collection of "hymns and spiritual songs" coming from the apostolic age and breathing the deepest thoughts of the New Testament. This, indeed, as one scholar suggests, may possibly be one of the very collections referred to by St. Paul (Eph. 5: 19; Col. 3: 16), having come into existence before the gospels were universally known. While, as we have said, there is no direct mention of any incident in Christ's life, nor any direct quotation from the New Testament, there are oblique references to the dove of the baptism (Ode XXIV), to his yoke (Ode XLII), to the "rock" on which he built the Church (Ode XXIII); and frequent allusions to Christ as the Head, which has a Pauline ring (Eph. 11: 22; 5: 22; Col. 1: 18) and to the living crown which reminds us of other New Testament writers (1 Peter 5: 4; James 1: 12); while there is the most pronounced connection in thought and style between these Odes and the writings of St. John. The author's keywords are love, joy, faith, knowledge, truth, rest, grace, glory; and he urges in Johannine fashion the spiritual necessity of fruit. It is to be noted that the Lord Christ, as Abbott pointed out, is not mentioned as the conqueror, but as the "Redeemer" of the Gentiles. This author finds 132 references to John's gospel suggested by the Odes.

The thought of these hymns is not put in the familiar orthodox form—these Odes were written before orthodoxy had crystallized—but our author clearly states that "Christ is the Word; that he is before the foundations of the world; that he bestows living water abundantly; that he is the door of everything; that he stands to his people in the relation of Lover to the beloved; that they love him because he first loved them" (Harris). We find in this earliest Christian hymn-book, which was in use before the reputed death of St. John, a direct teaching of the doctrine of the Trinity, virgin birth, and descent into Hades, while its Christology gives tone to almost every thought of every Ode: Christ's pre-existence, his preeminence in the Church; spiritual union between himself and believers, his deity as "Son of the Most High who appeared in the perfection of the Father . . . the Word . . . the Messiah who was truly One and was known before the foundations of the world." [90]

We will now give from this very long document, containing over 1,000 verses, a sufficient series of extracts to show the general style and teaching of the various hymns. We will follow Dr. Harris' translation—altho with the omission of many lines and paragraphs—except as this is slightly modified occasionally by the rendering of Johannes Fleming, Abbott, and (most frequently) Bernard:

ODE I (given in full)

"The Lord is on my head like a crown and I shall not be without him. A crown of truth has been woven for me, and it has caused thy branches to grow in me. For it is not like a withered crown which blossometh not, but liveth upon my head, and thou

[90] For this rather elaborate analysis of this remarkable work the writer is wholly indebted to the brilliant and thorough investigations of J. Rendel Harris and E. A. Abbott, referred to above.

hast blossomed upon my head. Thy fruits are full grown and perfect, full of thy salvation."

ODE II

"And on them do I hang, and he loves me, for I should not have known how to love the Lord if he had not loved me (*cf.* 1 John 4: 19). For who is able to distinguish ["discern and interpret," Abbott] love except the one that is loved? I love the Beloved and my soul loves him; and where his rest is, there also am I, and I shall be no stranger, for with the Lord Most High and Merciful there is no grudging. I have been united in wedlock to him, for the lover has found the beloved; and because I shall love him that is the Son, I shall become a son . . . Hallelujah!" [90a]

ODE IV

"Thou hast given thy heart, O Lord, to thy believers. Never wilt thou fail nor be without fruits; for one hour of thy faith is more precious than all the days and years. For who is there that shall put on thy grace and be hurt? . . . distill thy dews upon us, and open thy rich fountains that pour forth to us milk and honey . . . Hallelujah!" [91]

ODE VI

"As the hand moves over the harp and the strings speak, so speaks in my members the Spirit of the Lord, and I speak by his love. . . . For there went forth a stream and became a river great and broad. . . . Blessed then are the ministers of that draught who are entrusted with his water . . . for every one knew them in the Lord and they lived by the water of life forever. They have refreshed the dry lips, and the will that was paralyzed they have raised up, and the souls that were near departing they drew (back) from death."

ODE VII

" . . . He became like me in order that I might receive him; he was reckoned like myself that I might put him on (as a robe), and I trembled not when I saw him because he is my salvation;

[90a] *Harris:* "Because I shall love him that is the Son that I may be a son; for he that is joined to him that is immortal will also himself become immortal."

[91] *Abbott:* "Sprinkle on us Thy sprinklings (of dew) and open Thy rich fountains that pour forth to us milk and honey (of Thy promise)."

like my nature he became, that I might learn him and like my form, that I might not turn back from him; the Father of knowledge is the word of knowledge . . . the Most High shall be known in his saints to proclaim the good news to those who have in their hearts songs of the Lord's coming . . . and they shall bring their songs, and their heart shall be like the day; and like the excellent beauty of the Lord their pleasant song; and there shall be nothing that breathes . . . that is dumb . . . Hallelujah!"

ODE VIII

". . . Keep [or "guard"] my secret, ye who are kept [or "guarded"] by it; keep my faith, ye who are kept by it; and understand [or "know"] my knowledge, ye who know me in truth. Love me with affection [or "fervent love"], ye who love; for I do not turn away my face from those who are mine; for I know them, and before they came into being I took knowledge of them, and on their faces I set my seal; I fashioned their members; my own breasts I prepared for them that they might drink my holy milk and live thereby. . . . Ask and abound and abide in the love of the Lord, and, ye beloved ones, in the Dearly Beloved; and ye shall be found incorrupt in all ages ["aeons"] to the name of your Father . . . Hallelujah."

ODE IX

"Open your ears and I will speak to you. Give me your souls that I may also give you my soul, the word of the Lord and his good pleasures, the holy thought which he has devised concerning his Messiah. . . . Be strong and be redeemed by his grace. An everlasting crown forever in truth . . . blessed are they who set it on their heads. Put on the crown in the covenant of the Lord. And all those who have conquered shall be written in his book, . . . Hallelujah!"

ODE X

"The Lord hath directed my mouth by his word. And he hath opened my heart by his light; and he hath caused to dwell in me his deathless light; and gave me that I might speak the fruit of his peace; to convert the souls of them that are willing to come to him; and to lead captive a good captivity for freedom. . . . And the Gentiles were gathered together who were scattered abroad. And I was not polluted by my fervent love for them. . . . And they walked in my life and were saved and became my people for ever and ever. Hallelujah!"

ODE XI

"My heart was circumcised [or "cloven"] and its flower ["stem"] appeared; and grace sprang up ["budded"] in it; and it brought forth fruit in the Lord; for the Most High circumcised me [or "clove my heart"] by his Holy Spirit and revealed my reins toward him; and filled me with his love. And his circumcision of me became my salvation; and I ran in his way, in his peace, even in the way of truth . . . and I was established upon the rock of truth . . . and speaking waters touched my lips from the fountain of the Lord poured forth without grudging, and I drank and was inebriated with the living water that doth not die. . . . Hallelujah!"

ODE XII

" . . . The mouth of the Lord is the true word and the door of his light; and the Most High hath given it to his worlds . . . for the swiftness of the word can not be expressed, and according to its swiftness so is its sharpness . . . by it the worlds talk one to the other; and in the word there were those that were silent; and from it came love and concord . . . and they were penetrated by the word . . . for the dwelling-place of the word is man and its truth is love. Blessed are they who by means thereof have understood everything and have known the Lord in his truth. Hallelujah!"

ODE XIII (in full)

"Behold! the Lord is our mirror; open the eyes and see them in him; and learn the manner of your face; and tell forth praises to his Spirit; and wipe off the filth from your face; and love his holiness, and clothe yourselves therewith; and be without stain at all times before him. Hallelujah!"

ODE XV

" . . . Death hath been destroyed before my face; and Sheol hath been abolished by my word; and there hath gone up deathless life in the Lord's land, and it hath been made known to all his faithful ones, and hath been given without stint to all those who trust in him. . . . Hallelujah!"

ODE XVII

"I was crowned by my God; my crown is living; and I was justified in my Lord; my incorruptible salvation is he. . . . I received the face and the fashion of a new person; I have entered therein and have been saved; and the thought of truth led me on . . . and I sowed my fruits in hearts and transformed them into myself; and they received my blessing and lived; and they were gathered to me and were saved; because they were to me as my own members, and I was their head. Glory to thee, our Head, the Lord Messiah. Hallelujah!"

ODE XIX

"A cup of milk was offered to me; and I drank it in the sweetness of the delight of the Lord. The Son is the cup and he who was milked is the Father; and the Holy Spirit milked him; because his breasts were full, and it did not seem good to him that his milk should be spilt for naught; and the Holy Spirit opened his bosom and mingled the milk from the two breasts of the Father; and gave the mixture to the world without its knowing it. And they who receive it are in the perfection of the right hand. The womb of the Virgin caught it and received conception and brought forth, and the Virgin became a mother with many mercies; and she travailed and brought forth a son without incurring pain; she brought him forth openly, and acquired him with great dignity, and loved him in his swaddling clothes, and guarded him kindly, and showed him in majesty" (*cf.* 1 Tim. 3: 16).[91a]

ODE XXII

"He who brought me down from on high also brought me from the regions below; and who gathers together the things that are betwixt is he also who cast me down . . . he that overthrew by my hands the dragon with seven heads . . . Thou didst bring thy world to corruption; that everything might be dissolved and then renewed, and that the foundation for everything might be thy Rock and on it thou didst build thy kingdom; and it became (or 'thou wast') the dwelling place of the saints. Hallelujah!"

[91a] Johannes Flemming translates: "And it did not seem proper that this milk should be carelessly spilled . . . and those who receive it in its fullness are on the right hand . . . He embraced the body of the Virgin, and she conceived and became a mother with much grace."

ODE XXIII

"Joy is of the saints! . . . Grace is of the elect! . . . Love is of the elect! and who shall put it on except those who have possest it from the beginning . . . and his thought was like a letter . . . and many hands rushed to the letter to seize it and to take and read it; and it escaped their fingers, and they were affrighted at it and at the seal that was upon it. Because it was not permitted of them to loose its seal; for the power that was over the seal was greater than they . . . and the letter was a great tablet (cf. Matt. 28: 19), which was wholly written by the finger of God; and the name of the Father was on it and of the Son and of the Holy Spirit, to rule for ever and ever. Hallelujah!"

ODE XXIV

"The Dove fluttered over the Christ (Messiah) because he was her head and she sang over him and her voice was heard . . . the birds dropt their wings and all creeping things died in their holes; and the abysses opened themselves and were hidden [92] . . . and they sealed up the abysses with the seal of the Lord."

ODE XXVII (in full)

"I stretched out my hands and sanctified my Lord; for the extension of my hands is his sign; and my expansion is the upright tree (or cross)."

ODE XXVIII

"As the wings of doves over their nestlings, and the mouth of their nestlings toward their mouths, so also are the wings of the Spirit over my heart. . . . I believed; therefore I was at rest; for faithful is he in whom I have believed; he has richly blest me and my head is with him; and the sword shall not divide me from him nor the scimitar . . . immortal life has come forth and has kissed me,[93] and from that life is the spirit within me and it can not die for it lives . . . vainly did they cast lots [or "make attack"] upon me . . . in vain did those who were behind me seek to bring to naught the memory [or "memorial"] of him who was before them; for nothing is prior to the thought of the Most High; and his heart is superior to all wisdom. Hallelujah!"

[92] Harris, "the abysses were opened which had been hidden."
[93] Harris, "Immortal life will come forth and give me to drink."

ODE XXX

"Fill ye waters for yourselves from the living fountain of the Lord, for it is open to you; and come, all ye thirsty, and take the d aught; and rest by the fountain of the Lord . . ."

ODE XXXI

"And they denounced me as a criminal when I showed myself, me who had never been a criminal;[94] and they divided my spoil tho nothing was due to them. But I endured and held my peace and was silent . . . and I bore their bitterness for humility's sake; in order that I might redeem my people and inherit it, and that I might not make void my promises to the fathers to whom I promised the salvation of their seed. Hallelujah!" (*cf.* Luke 1:69-73.)

ODE XXXII (in full)

"To the blest there is joy from their hearts, and light from him that dwells in them; and words from the Truth who was Self-originate; for he is strengthened by the holy power of the Most High; and he is unshakable for ever and ever. Hallelujah!"

ODE XLI

" . . . His word is with us in all our way; the Saviour who makes alive and does not reject our souls, the Man who was humbled and exalted by his own righteousness, the Son of the Most High appeared in the perfection of his Father; and light dawned from the Word that was before time in him; the Christ is truly one; and he was known before the foundation of the world, that he might save souls forever by the truth of his name. A new song (arises) from those who love him. Hallelujah!"

ODE XLII

"I stretched out my hands and approached my Lord; for the stretching of my hands (*i.e.,* the cross) is his sign; my expansion is the outspread tree which was set up on the way of the Righteous One . . . and I lifted up over them the yoke of my love; like the arm of the bridegroom over the bride, so was my yoke over those that know me . . . and I was not rejected, tho I was

---

[94] Harris, "And they made me a debtor when I rose up, me who had not been a debtor."

reckoned to be so. I did not perish, tho they devised it against me. Sheol saw me and was made miserable, death gave me up and many along with me. I was gall and bitterness to him, and I went down with him to the uttermost of his depths . . . and I made a congregation of living men amongst his dead men and I spake with them by living lips . . . let us also be redeemed with thee; for thou art our Redeemer. And I heard their voice; and my name I sealed upon their heads; for they are free men and they are mine. Hallelujah!"

We have made these many quotations from these oldest Christian hymns because of their phenomenal importance in showing the Christian doctrine of that earliest Christian Church and the confidence with which they rested upon the acts recorded in the four gospels. The doctrine of the Trinity was distinctly taught (Ode XIX). The Messiah was the divine Son of God "by whom the worlds were made" (XVI: 20); "who appeared in the perfection of his Father" (XLI); born of a Virgin (XIX); that he might redeem his people (XXXI); who descended into the grave but rose again, and with whom his people can rise (XLII); and have complete victory over death (XLII). The last ode is evidently the climax of the whole collection. There is nothing in it for which the way has not been artistically prepared (tho perhaps rather by a spiritual than by a conscious art) in various preceding stages. There is, for example, almost at the opening, the "stretching out of the hands," mentioned before and now repeated, as the "sign" of the Lord, indicating the triumph of the cross; there is also the bridegroom, no longer merely the Beloved, but with his "arm over the Bride," the wedding being consummated; there is the rescue of the dead, like Israel of old "brought again from the depths of the sea"; lastly there is a "running" of captive humanity toward its Rescuer, and a simultaneous recognition of him as the "Son of God" (Abbott, *op. cit.*, 477). It is a fit close to a series of visions, depicting the purpose of the Father to redeem to the uttermost all who "run" to "the Son of God for help"—for the Christ is Lord even over the grave!

9. PRIVATE AND OFFICIAL LETTERS OF EARLY CHRISTIANS

The writer can never forget the strange thrill of excitement that came to him when he first examined a letter which was supposed to be written by a Christian of the second century. It was a papyrus found by Grenfell and Hunt and published in 1903.[95] The name of the writer was Serenus, and the letter was addrest to his "sister" (*i.e.*, wife) Isidora. It read in part:

"Many greetings. . . . Before all else I pray for your health, and every day and evening I perform the act of veneration on your behalf. . . . I assure you that ever since you left me I have been in mourning, weeping by night and lamenting by day."
. . .

Unfortunately this text, upon closer inspection, proved to be from a heathen.[96] The same editors, however (1909-1911), published the Greek text of several letters which are certainly Christian. One of these is from a sick woman living in the fourth century:

" . . . to our God and gracious Saviour . . . I write this to you in sickness, and very ill and quite unable to rise from my bed." [97]

[95] *Oxyrhynchus Papyri*, II., No. 528.

[96] Dr. Victor Martin of Geneva, Switzerland, who was one of the joint editors of the *Catalogue of Greek Papyri in the John Rylands Library*, writes me that there can be no possible doubt as to the heathen character of this letter.

[97] *Oxyrhynchus Papyri*, VII., No. 1161.

Another is too mutilated to be well read, but it is from a man of the same era and in it certain phrases stand out with distinctness:

"Fullness of joy . . . . I pray for your health in the Lord God. . . . Beloved brothers in the Lord God . . . Emmanuel is my witness." [98]

Certainly these early Christians did not forget their religion when they wrote letters to their friends. Neither did they fail to show themselves to be Christians when they wrote to their superiors. A Christian servant, writing to his master concerning the illness of his mistress (fourth century), writes in this courteous fashion, incidentally illustrating an important New Testament word:

"Please pardon me, my lord, and receive me kindly (ἀποδεξει; cf. Acts 24:3; 28:30; 2:41), tho I unwillingly caused you so much anxiety by writing to you the messages which you received." [99]

In the very latest discovered Christian letter,[100] a father and mother of the third century of our era write to their son thanking God they have recovered health, and adding the strange words: "up to the present time we have not sacrificed the pigs!" This I suppose to allude to a common form of heathen sacrifice, and to be a notice to their absent son that they were standing firm in the faith. In this same collection (No. 13) a son, who almost too prominently emphasizes his religious profession, writes home (fifth century) asking his mother in a badly spelled letter to send him "the

[98] *Ibid.* No. 1162.
[99] *Oxyrhynchus Papyri*, VI., No. 939; *cf.* Moulton and Milligan's *Vocabulary*, I., 61.
[100] *Oxyrhynchus Papyri*, 1914, X., 1299.

rings" and to buy him certain things for winter. It begins:

"To the lady, my most esteemed and virtuous mother, Maria, from your son Peter in the Lord God, Greeting."

Greetings are then added to various "sweetest brethren" whose names are given, and the boy closes with the customary prayers for their health. The opening words of this letter are τῇ κυρίᾳ, almost exactly as the opening words of 3 John; and it is delightful to find this Christian youth in the midst of his letter speaking of his mother most tenderly as "my dearest Maria," "Lady Mother," etc.

From this same century, or a little earlier, occurs this rather formal Christian epistle:

"To my beloved brother blest in God, Paulus, from Apa Johannes. I wish to be found worthy of writing continually to your holiness. . . . I greet you, my brother Paulus, and all those of your house in the Lord." [100a]

One of the most curious of the Christian documents so far discovered (The Epistle of Psenosiris) was published in 1902, with its true explanation by Dr. Deissmann:

"From Psenosiris the presbyter to Apollo the presbyter his beloved brother in the Lord, greeting!

"Above all, I salute thee often times, and all the brethren that are with thee in God. I would have thee know, brother, that the grave-diggers here into the inner parts have brought Politike, who was sent into the Oasis by the government, and I have handed her over to the good and faithful among the grave-diggers until her son Nilos be come. . . . I wish thee welfare in the Lord God."

That is the way one preacher wrote to another in the third century concerning a Christian woman who

[100a] *Amherst Papyri*, Part 2, 1901, No. CXLV.

was banished to the Oasis of el-Khargeh, where prisoners of State were sent. The "grave-diggers" or *fossores* mentioned in the text were the undertakers, who are often mentioned in the Catacombs and elsewhere as having charge of the selling of graves and the setting up of monuments, and were often extortionate in their charges. In this case, however, they may represent fellow Christian exiles in the Oasis. It is a curious thing that the Greek name *politikan* was the term for "harlot" in Byzantine times; tho it occurs also as a proper name. Whether this woman was a converted harlot or had been given by some misfortune this peculiarly ill-odorous name, in any case she must have been a woman of the better class whose property had been confiscated and who had been banished to this desert place.[101] This letter throws a vivid light upon the care which Christians had for each other at that early period.

Other Christian letters show that even in money matters the Christians were expected to help each other, and that the early Christian churches were also expected to be banks which could loan money to deserving brethren.[102]

Numbers of business letters from Christian men have come down to us, among which I would especially mention that of Zacharias and Silvanos, "head men" of the village of Demetrios near Hermopolis, who write to Tyrannos, deacon of the church there, sending him a receipt for "fifty-one thousand talents"—tho part of this debt still remains unpaid.[103] It is noticeable that Sil-

[101] Several of the most celebrated of the early Christians bear this name; see *e.g.*, *Sinaitic Palimpsest*, vii, viii.

[102] *E.g.*, *Amherst Papyri*, II., pp. 28-30.

[103] *Publicazioni de la Societá Italiana*, Vol. I, No. 43.

vanos, notwithstanding his wealth, is unable even to sign his name, and Zacharias—who could write but certainly could not spell—signs his name for him.

In another document (sixth century) Aurelius Ploution, a baker from the city of Oxyrhynchus, rents "the small house" belonging to one of the churches of that city, on the street Ἀκακιός, with its lands, agreeing to pay "to the same holy church . . . yearly of gold coin a third (?) by private scale." This indicates that the church had a special scale of values bʸ which they tested all purchases.[104]

One beautifully written missive is addrest to a Christian soldier stationed in the Fayum about A.D. 346. It is one of a package of some sixty letters written from A.D. 343 to 351, belonging to Flavius Abinnæus, a Roman cavalry officer. This particular note is from a priest who intercedes for a private soldier who is under discipline, very much as St. Paul interceded for Onesimus (Philemon, verses 15-18).

"Greeting! I salute thy children much. I would have thee know, Sir, concerning Paul the soldier, concerning his flight; pardon him this once . . . and if he desist not he will come again into thy hands another time. Fare thee well, I pray, many years, my lord brother."[104a]

A most interesting letter from the fourth century is from Justin to his dear brother Papnuthius Chrestophorus ("Christ-bearer"). It reads:

"It behoved me to write to thy excellence, my dear lord. For we believe that thy citizenship is in heaven; wherefore we regard

[104] *Ibid.*, No. 75. I am much indebted to my colleague, Dr. Wm. A. Elliott, for assistance in working out the meaning of several of the above very obscure letters and for other help in instances too numerous to mention specifically.

[104a] Deissmann, *op. cit.*, pp. 205-210.

thee as our master and common protector. But lest I write and prate too much (for in much talk there is no escape from sin), I pray thee, Master, recall me in thy holy prayers that we may be partakers in the cleansing of sins. For I am of those that sin. . . . Many greetings I send to all our many brethren in the Lord, and may the divine providence protect you long in Jesus Christ, beloved Lord." [105]

The above title, Chrestophorus or "Christ-bearer," was commonly given to bishops in the Coptic period, so that this letter probably suggests how bishops were already honored at the beginning of the fourth century.

This conclusion of Dr. Deissmann may be modified, however, by the next new discovery, which may show that the title "Christ-bearer" was not confined to bishops any more than the title *papa* ("pope") was. The following letter of the sixth century, the Greek text of which was published in 1913 by Dr. Paul M. Meyer,[106] speaks for itself regarding the distinction even then made between "pope" and "bishop"—the latter being the superior title:

"To the beloved and most God-fearing brother . . . Sarapion, a priest *(papa)*, the priest *(papa)* Heron sends greeting in the Lord.

"When I was in the village Aphrodite I was urged by the elders ["presbyters"] there to write to your holiness in regard to one Sansneut, long ago appointed by Phoibadios of blest memory bishop *(episkopos)* . . . of his village. So inasmuch as he is vouched for by his village and by the clergy themselves as being of blameless life, have the goodness to give directions that he be instructed ["regarded"?] as a deacon until he be able by God's help to return to his own village. I and those with me in the Lord address you and the brethren with you in the Lord."

[105] Facsimile and full text in Deissmann's *Light from the Ancient East,* pp. 203-204.
[106] *Griechische Papyri im Museum . . . zu Giessen,* Band 1, Heft 2. No. 55.

This letter was dictated according to the usual custom, and Father Heron adds his greeting in his own handwriting just as Paul was accustomed to do:

"I pray that you are well in the Lord, beloved and most longed-for Father."

Meyer thinks that this letter shows how the ranks of the diaconate in the fourth and fifth centuries were recruited from the lowest classes, particularly the country clergy, who knew very little, often being able not even to write. This point, however, must not be unduly strained. The surprize is to find so few either among the clergy or common people who are unable to write; and at least in some dioceses in Egypt, candidates for orders, as has recently been proved, were required to pass rather severe examinations before being admitted to ordination. Samuel, Jacob, and Aaron, in a letter written to their bishop about A.D. 600, promise that if they do not watch their beds on the days of communion and "learn by heart" the entire gospel of John and "practise it," they will not even apply for ordination.[107]

Another Christian letter from near the middle of the third century—perhaps the earliest of which the original has come down to us—shows that Christians in Alexandria and Rome who were dealing in "barley" and "linen cloth" were accustomed to deliver the money for safe-keeping to "Maximus the pope" (τὸν πάπαν), who is to act as confidential agent in this business engagement. One or two phrases from this letter will show how intimate those early Christians were with their official superiors, and how interested this "papa," who was evidently an ordinary "father" of the church, was in the business success of his parishioners:

[107] See Deissmann, *op. cit.*, p. 211.

"Ye shall do well therefore, brethren, having bought the linen cloth. Then let some of you take the . . . and set forth with it unto Maximus the papas and . . . the lector. And having sold that linen cloth in Alexandria deliver the money unto Primitinus or Maximus the papas, receiving a quittance from him. But the gain, the price of the bread sold by you and the money for the linen cloth, let him commit and deliver it up unto Theonas, in order that I being come with God to Alexandria may find it ready against my charges. . . . Fare ye well, I pray." . . . etc.[108]

Another letter given by Deissmann,[109] tho certainly not Christian, coming from the second century so thoroughly illustrates the parable of the prodigal son (Luke 15: 11-32) that we quote a paragraph from it here:

"Antonis Longus to Nilus his mother, many greetings. And continually do I pray that thou art in health. I make supplications for thee daily to the Lord Serapis. I would thou shouldst understand (cf. Phil. 1 : 12) that I had no hope that thou wouldst go up to the metropolis. And therefore I came not to the city. But I was ashamed to come to Caranis, because I walk about in rags. I write to thee that I am naked. I beseech thee, mother, be reconciled to me. . . . I know what I have brought upon myself. . . . I know that I have sinned."

The verbs "beseech" and "reconcile" are exactly the same as those used in the New Testament, while the phrase "I have sinned" sounds as if it were coming from the lips of the prodigal himself. The letter continues finding great fault with Postumus, who had told his mother of his bad conduct and had, perhaps, suggested that he had badly run in debt, for one of the few remaining sentences that can be deciphered asks in very prodigal fashion, "Knowest thou not that I had rather be maimed than know that I still owe a man an obol?"

---

[108] Deissmann, op.cit., pp. 192-201.
[109] Op. cit., p. 177.

Let us hope for his mother's sake that Antonis did return home as that other prodigal of whom Jesus spoke.

In one particularly interesting note, which some scholars have thought to be Christian, dating from the second century, Eutychides makes complaint to Heliodorus concerning Demetrius and certain other village elders ("presbyters") who have been acting, he says, like "busybodies" (ἐργολάβους) having seized Peteus— probably in order to compel him to pay his taxes.[110]

As Christian letters written in Greek are so rare, and therefore so priceless in interest, we give here a few more which we find scattered through the various publications. One of the most valuable as showing the hospitable Christian "way" in the fourth century reads as follows:

"To the beloved brother Peter:

"Greetings in the Lord. I, Sotas, bid you receive our brother Heracles according to (the usual) custom,[111] through whom I and those with me salute (προσαγορεύομεν) you and all those with you. I pray that you be strong (in good health) in the Lord."[112]

How the style of writing changed for the worse may be seen by another missive which, however, is badly damaged, dating from A.D. 602.

"In the name of the Lord and Master Jesus Christ, our God and Saviour . . . to Flavios Apion, the all-illustrious and most excellent of consuls, possessing land, and to the illustrious city of

---

[110] *Amherst Papyri*, II, CXXXIV; 3. Dr. Victor Martin of Geneva assures me, however, by private letter that there is no substantial reason why this letter should be ascribed to a Christian writer.

[111] Ἔθος, of Acts 6:14; 16:2; 26:3; 28:17; Luke 1:9; Heb. 10:25.

[112] *Publicazioni de la Societá Italiana*, Vol. III, No. 208; No. 209 also contains a few words from Serapion, a Christian, to Herakles (whose name he misspells) about a talent of silver.

INSCRIPTION ON GRAVESTONE OBTAINED BY THE AUTHOR AT CÆSAREA, PALESTINE

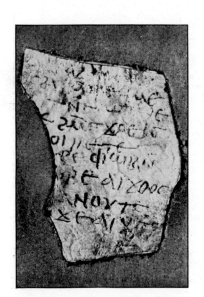

NOTE FROM ABRAHAM ABOUT A HOE SENT TO
HIM BY THE PRIEST SHENUTE

From a previously unpublished parchment in
author's collection

LETTER FROM PARENTS TO THEIR SON, WHO IS THE ADMINISTRATOR OF A CONVENT

From a previously unpublished papyrus in the author's collection

the Oxyrhynchites, through Menas the servant, who requests and procures for his master the all-illustrious . . . Greeting!" [113]

Besides the Greek letters there are a very few known written in vulgar Latin, which seem to be Christian. One of these, dating from the second century, is addrest to a military tribune:

"Greeting! Already aforetime I have recommended unto thee Theon my friend, and now also I pray, Lord, that thou mayest have him before thine eyes as myself (cf. Philemon, verse 17). For he is such a man that he may be loved by thee. For he left his own people, his gods and business, and followed me. And through all things he hath kept me in safety. And therefore I pray of thee that he may have entering in unto thee" (cf. 1 Thess., 1:9). [114]

While so few Christian letters have been found written in Greek or Latin, the results have been much more favorable so far as Coptic is concerned. These Coptic letters are very generally written not on papyrus but on potsherds; but the writer had the good fortune to obtain in Egypt in 1913 a number of ancient Christian letters written in Coptic on papyrus. Of several of these I will append free renderings, being indebted to Dr. Hyvernat of the Catholic University of America for the decipherment and preliminary translations of these texts, which I hope may be edited by him later:

"Bless (us), our Father. Since a man who is ours is sick, we wish to go and visit him. May your mercifulness grant us something for a sick man, so that God may multiply his blessing on you (and) be kind to you, while you give to all who ask you. Be well to us (for our sake) while you pray for us that we may be well."

This shows most vividly the dependence which the

[113] *Ibid.*, No. 179; Lefebvre, *op. cit.*, gives the fragments of a few more Christian letters but they are too mutilated to read.
[114] Deissmann, *op. cit.*, p. 183.

people placed in their religious superiors when they came into trouble.

Among these unpublished letters are several written to Father Shenute, and one very curious letter written by parents to their son who was at the head of a monastery. This may be later than most of the letters given above, as the florid style seems to attest as well as the excessive humility of the parents.

"Before (further) discourse, our humbleness greets your (lordly) sonship, honorable in every manner. In Christ Jesus, greetings!

"Then we make known to you the well-being of our house from the big one to the little one, and the well-being of the whole village from the little one to the big one."

This letter closes by mentioning that the messenger who bore this note "has told us of all the good things that your lordly sonship achieves."

How close such a letter as this brings us to the early Egyptian life!

Multitudes of such letters have come to light written on pieces of broken pottery or on flakes or slices of white limestone, the latter being regarded as the most honorable material. In ecclesiastical letters the limestone was frequently used, an apology seldom being made for it, tho such apologies were often offered when potsherds were used. These *ostraka* contain a vast quantity of business letters, episcopal decisions, petitions to clerics asking for prayers because of illness, and especially begging letters of all kinds. The Church and its ministers were evidently regarded as being open-handed, for here are requests for vinegar, flax, oil, rope, clothing, vegetables, and especially for bread and corn. A common type of the begging letter is that of John to Apa Victor:

"First I greet thee, devout and pious man. May the Lord bless thee and all that thou hast, men and beasts. Be kind and have pity upon this poor man." [115]

A son writes to his mother asking her to send him a blanket, as he has none. In another, Paul promises to provide a blanket for a brother in need. A rather heart-breaking letter from a man whose name is lost, which was written to his "dear and holy father," throws light on the material need of the early Christians:

"Be so kind as to pray for me. Again I have told thee of my misery. I tell thee didst thou know the plight that I am in thy heart would be sorely grieved. It is written 'Get thyself a friend, but not friends of eating and drinking, rather friends in thy need.' Never have I suffered trouble greater than this present. Do not fail to come to me in the trouble that I and my children are in. . . . If thou hast compassion on me, thou wilt have redeemed six souls from death. No man gives me wherewith to cover me. . . . Thy heart will grieve for me if I die with my children. . . . If I can find two loaves a day I shall not die; if I find one I shall not die. I have little ones and they . . . come weeping to me and break (?) my heart." [116]

One letter of a different nature seems equally full of tears:

"Forgive me the sin that I have committed, my Lord, father, and my brethren; for it is great and ye are pitiful. Indeed through shame I am not able to say, Forgive me." [117]

It must be said, however, that there was rather an affectation of sinfulness and humility very common in the sixth century, as some of the expressions in letters from "Peter the little" and "this humble and wretched sinner" show very clearly. A few suggestions as to the

[115] W. E. Crum, *Coptic Ostraca*, No. 75. It is strange that in Wilcken's great work, *Griechische Ostraka*, 1899, giving 1624 documents, there is not a single letter so far as I can find having any Christian interest.

[116] *Ibid.*, No. 254.

[117] *Ibid.*, No. 275.

habits of the early Christians light up the ordinary dulness of these very commonplace letters. One man writes:

"Excuse me that I can not find papyrus, as I am in the country." [118]

In one note one Christian writes another: "Thou knowest that we prayed together."

One parishioner expresses surprize that his pastor had not visited him in his sickness.

Very many of the letters contain requests for books to read. It is probable that it was some book of the Bible that was generally desired, but certainly in one case a medical work was asked for (No. 253). On one piece of broken pot a theological student has given a list of the apostles in which Philip is said to be the son of a charioteer, and on another sherd there is the record of a priest who has been excommunicated—probably for making boys drunk (No. 47).

The general poverty of the times and its financial ruin is seen from the fact that one man promises if he fails in his business agreement he will pay "five baskets of bronze money." It appears that thousands of these bronze coins were received to equal one large silver coin.

It is suggestive to observe that a thousand or more years ago (as two thousand years earlier), in legal documents "word of God" meant the decree of God's ministers or of God's Church:

"Lo here is the word of God to thee; thou mayest come and gather thy dates and no one shall hinder thee." [119]

---

[118] Crum, *op. cit.*, No. 129; See also Nos. 97, 212, 332, 374. Papnoute being unable to write, signs with three crosses.

[119] Crum, *op. cit.*, p. 100.

One ostrakon, which evidently represents a practise exercise for young monks, well expresses the duty of a preacher of the gospel as these early Christians understood it:

"He was sent to all men, to the flock of the faithful, to the dwelling of the Son of God to bring old men to God, little children to the Church, to pasture the sheep of God, to tame the antelope, etc." [120]

Such are samples of the goodly number of Christian letters which have been recovered from the dusty past in our generation. As a whole these private notes speak well for the early Christians. It may be doubted whether the ordinary mail of modern followers of the Man of Galilee would give better testimony to spirituality. It is noticeable that few of these ancient letters deal with theological questions. Only occasionally has there been any autograph preserved to us from a man distinguished in his generation for scholarship or piety, and very few mention any of the great church movements. The ordinary Christian then as now was especially interested only in what touched his own life. Yet a very few letters have fortunately been found which enable us better to appreciate the intellectual struggles of those early days and the splendid leadership which sought to protect that early Church from superstition.

Among such letters attention may be called to one just found, written by Theodore of Egypt, in which he refers to the "Canon of the Books of Holy Scripture" reported to the Church by Athanasius, the archbishop of Alexandria, in the very year in which this letter was written (A.D. 326-328). Theodore praises Athanasius,

[120] *Amherst Papyri*, II., CXXXIV.

calling him "a son of the holy apostles . . . who
taketh care of the flock of the Lord, giving them nour-
ishment in due season" and preserving them from "the
lying waters of which so many drank"—that is, the
apocryphal books to which were falsely given "the name
and age of the holy books." [121]

While we can afford in this era to be more charitable in our judgment of the apocryphal writings, yet it
is a good tonic to sensitive nerves to read these positive
words from a letter written some sixteen centuries ago.

10. Liturgical Fragments and Biblical Quotations

When in 1910 there were published the sixth-cen-
tury litany of the Lord's Supper, in 1911 the new
manuscript containing Origen's comments on the
Apocalypse, and in 1913 the new Armenian text of
Irenæus, it was found that these newly recovered documents were a mass of scripture texts. This is practically
true of all ancient ecclesiastical documents. Whether
one examines the newly found Acts of Paul and Thecla,
or the Passion of St. Perpetua, that "most beautiful of
all the records of Christian martyrdom"; or the newly
found second-century Christian dialog (A.D. 155) between Bishop Athanasius and Zacchæus the Jew, in
which the Christian defends the thesis that "Christ is
God, yet there are not two Gods"; or any other of the
recently recovered church writings from the ancient
past, nothing is more impressive than the multitude of
Biblical quotations or references, which appear everywhere in early Christian literature like the miraculous

[121] *Muséon,* New Series, XI., 205.

draught of fishes.[122]   Sometimes it is impossible to tell whether these fragmentary Greek papyri are leaves of ancient Bibles or whether they are portions of sermons or letters, or church rituals.   We will give a few samples of the way in which these quotations appear.

In 1887, Dr. Charles Wessely published a fragment from the third century found in the collection of Archduke Rainer relative to the denial of St. Peter, which contained an exact quotation of Mark 14: 26.   Its back adhered to a contract of a lease dating from the Emperor Alexander Severus (A.D. 221-235).   The fragment reads:

"You shall all be offended this night, as it is written, I will smite the shepherd, and the sheep will be scattered; but Peter said, Although even all, yet not I, and Jesus saith, Before the cock crow twice thou shall deny me thrice." [123]

In 1906 the same author published an ecclesiastical papyrus (third century) from Akhmim containing two passages from our gospels (Luke 2: 34; John 9: 39), one of these being an exact word-for-word quotation:

"I pray that the named be not lead to his humiliation, but to his salvation.   But when he does not understand this that is said for his salvation, let this be for his judgment (κρίμα).   Jesus himself has taught that his presence is to exercise judgment, in order that those who see not shall see, and those that see shall become blind.   The same words of the gospel show that Jesus has not come only for the rising but also for the downfall: 'Behold he is placed for an occasion of falling and for rising. . . . pay attention that these words be not said for your falling.' " [124]

[122] For these and many other newly recovered works see Armitage Robinson in *Texts and Studies*, Vol. I-VIII, and Harnack, *Texte und Untersuchungen zur Geschichte der altchristlichen Literatur*, Vol. I-XI.

[123] Wessely, *Les plus anciens monuments du Christianisme écrits sur papyrus*, 1906, No. 14.

[124] *Ibid.*, No. 20.

In 1903 Grenfell and Hunt published some Christian fragments from the second and third century, and among them was one which contained a perfect quotation of Matt. 3: 16-17, describing the baptism of Jesus, the words from the heavenly voice being indicated by wedge-shaped quotation marks. Perhaps the most important of all this class of discoveries are the many fragments of the early Fathers and other early writings of the Christian Church specially revered, which are full of Scriptural thought and phraseology. Among these ought particularly to be mentioned the second epistle of Clement of Rome, found by Bryennios in 1875, "probably written in the middle of the second century"; [125] the probably third century Greek text of *Irenæus against Heresies;* [126] and the later but very important and newly discovered *Scholia of Origen on the Apocalypse,* first published in 1911; [127] the lost Commentary of Œcumenius (about A.D. 600) on the same Biblical book; [128] and a sixth century copy of the Nicene Creed. [129] This is nearly the same as our version—variations are slight—and fortunately the scribe writes at the end of it in brown ink, his personal confession of faith:

"This is my creed, and with this language (I shall approach without fear) the terrible judgment seat of the Lord Christ in that dread day when he shall come again in his own glory to judge the quick and the dead and to reign with his saints forever and ever, Amen."

Another papyrus of the fifth century classed as a

[125] Kenyon, *Bible and Ancient Monuments,* Appendix.
[126] *Oxyrhynchus Papyri, cf.* Barnard's "Examination of the Biblical Quotations made by Clement of Alexandria" in *Texts and Studies,* Vol. V., pp. 899*ff.*
[127] Harnack, *Texte und Untersuchungen zur . . . altchrist. Lit.;* see also the new Armenian text, *ibid.,* XXXVI.
[128] See *American Journal of Philology* XXXIV, 1913, 3-301.
[129] *Papyri in John Ryland's Library,* No. 6.

"liturgical fragment," tho it may be from a private book of devotion, reads:[130]

"Suffer the little children to come unto me, of such is the kingdom of heaven. On Thee do I wait all the day. Remember thy tender mercies, O Lord . . . Saviour, keep me, O Lord, as the apple of thine eyes . . . Create in me a clean heart, gracious God, and save me."

"The most unique of all the new ecclesiastical documents is the calendar of church services at Oxyrhynchus A.D. 535-536, discovered in 1905-6, and first published in 1915.[131] This contains a list of the services at the various churches in Oxyrhynchus on Sundays and holy days during a period of five months. Twenty-six different churches are mentioned, and these special episcopal services are given for sixty-two different days, including Christmas and the various Sundays of Lent, the day of St. Peter and St. Paul, etc. It is noticeable that the Virgin and St. Euphemia are the only two female saints honored by special services. A church was also named after the latter saint, as well as after St. Justus, St. Menas, St. Philoxenus, and several lesser martyrs; there were besides churches of St. Mary, St. Michael, St. Gabriel, St. Jeremiah, St. Zachariah, "the Baptist," "the Evangelist" (St. John) and others. The calendar is too technical to be quoted. No Scripture quotations occur in this document because of its character.

One class of works regularly read with the liturgies in the monasteries dealt with the lives of saints and martyrs who died because of their loyalty to the Bible and the Church. A number of these have recently been

---

[130] *Ibid,* No. 8, *cf.* No. 9.
[131] *Oxyrhynchus Papyri,* XI., No. 1387.

recovered. The style of this not altogether commendable literature may be judged from the following:

STORY OF THE MARTYRDOM OF S. CHRISTINA

" 'If you do not go and sacrifice . . . I order heavy penalties, and the one who was put to death by the Jews, whom you serve, shall not rescue you.' "

"And the saint looking up into the sky and laughing strangely, said to Urbarius: . . . you do not know that the Son of the living God, the Light of truth and the Saviour of the world, has come down from the heaven to put away all iniquity from the world in order to save us, and now through him, the Lord who saves me, I endure all these things, so as to overcome your power . . . ' But her father Urbanus . . . ordered the wheel to be brought and the holy Christian to be placed upon it and fire to be kindled under it and oil to be poured to make it burn . . . and when . . . the wheel, turned around, had broken the whole body, the holy Christian . . . prayed saying: I bless thee, thou God in the heaven, and I thank thee, thou Father of the Lord Jesus Christ; do not leave me forever, but stretch out the hand and take hold of the fire and quench . . . that Urbanus the tyrant may never rejoice over me . . . the fire came forth suddenly and slew 1,500 idolaters . . . and the holy Christian was resting upon the wheel as upon a bed," etc., etc.[132]

ACTS OF MARTYRDOM OF PAPNOUTIOS

". . . the maiden said to her mistress, Come out and see . . . the man called Father Papnoutios, who is the one doing wonderful things before the ruler. And . . . she saw Father Papnoutios standing as an angel of God and he struck the . . . she saluted (worshipped) him saying, Truly my life is not equal to the joy that has taken hold of me. And then she took hold of his hand and kissed (it) saying, The Lord be magnified because thou hast come under my roof this day, and she placed for him a chair of silver. But Father Papnoutios laughed and said to her, Daughter, these silver and gold things give me no gain . . . but hear me, daughter, and choose for thyself the life of the angels,

[132] Fifth century papyrus in *Publicazioni de la Societá Italiana*, Vol. I., No. 27.

. . . and her daughter . . . came out from her chamber bringing a costly garment and having a golden diadem upon her head. But Father Papnoutios sat upon the ground and they sat at his feet and he says . . .   Children, forsake vain wealth, for it is written . . ." [133]

While the Scripture references in the above narrative are lost, many documents remain, giving these quotations so voluminously as to prove conclusively that these primitive Christians were great Bible students. One paper whose title seems to have been *Notes on Famous Biblical Texts* (sixth century) refers to Matt. 25: 1ff.; 12: 32; 16: 19—but the "notes" are scant, tho the precious Bible words are written out fully.[134]

While the discoveries of Greek documents have given us such treasures, the finds so far as Coptic liturgical texts are concerned are even greater, many of these being translations from Greek originals. Among these may be mentioned particularly the Acts or Canons of the Council of Nicola (which Hyvernat accepts as genuine); Acts of the Council of Ephesus and Memoirs of Dioscurus, a fragment of a great work by St. Epiphanius; the lost Festal Letters of St. Athanasius; a panegyric of St. George, by Bishop Theodosius; and Encomiums of Severus on St. Michael; and especially an Ecclesiastical History in twelve books—one so early that it was used by Eusebius, the "father of Church history."

Many church disciplines have recently been discovered in Coptic, including the "Ecclesiastical Canons and Canons of the Apostles;[135] the canons of Hippolytus described by Hyvernat but as yet not published; and

[133] *Ibid,* No. 28.
[134] *Papyri della Società Italiana,* I., No. 65.
[135] Eng. translation by G. Horner, 1904.

the canons of St. Athanasius and St. Basil edited by W. E. Crum, 1904.

A complete edition of the Coptic (Sahidic) liturgy was prepared by Dr. H. Hyvernat, with full translation in Latin, in 1909. All of these liturgies are full of Scripture quotations. The J. P. Morgan collection, discovered in 1910, also contains a complete lectionary, breviary, and antiphonary in this same dialect.

These ecclesiastical documents not only quote much Scripture but also throw an enormous light on the life of the Church. Dr. G. Horner has recently published the *Statutes of the Apostles or Canones Ecclesiastici* (1904), from which we give a few suggestions of the early church life as seen from these liturgies. No catechumen could be a painter or sculptor, go to the theater, nor train men for pugilism or war.[136] No Christian is allowed to be a soldier. No Christian could wear lascivious clothes or ornaments, or wear phylacteries, or drink magical potions. All believers are urged to bring bread and wine for the Eucharist. Prayers are made over the bread that it may become the body of the Lord Christ, or according to one recession, the "form of the flesh of Christ." Exorcism and the breathing upon the candidates that they may receive the Holy Spirit is mentioned. All are excluded from "the mysteries" who eat with heretics or adulterers or those devoted "to the world." A long catalog of reasons is given for not working on the Sabbaths—"Sabbaths" presumably including both Saturday and Sunday.

Among the special commandments are:

"Thou shalt not corrupt young children, thou shalt not be a

---

[136] The Jewish Church also opposed painting and sculpture, which was devoted to idol making; and the theater, which was a murderous as well as an idolatrous show. *Texts and Studies*, VIII², p. 27.

soothsayer, star-gazer, or magician, thou shalt not kill young babes, after birth; thou shalt not be a speaker against any, and thou shalt not think about doing evil."

Of bishops it is said that they shall be "without sin, without anger, lovers of the poor, not lovers of the greater share for himself." Widows in limited numbers are permitted ordination (by words, not by the laying on of hands) in order to devote themselves to prayer for those in affliction, and to stay with women who are suffering. Of laymen it is said:

"The lay people shall do the commandment which is told them with cheerfulness, and they shall obey those who devote themselves to the altar . . . and ye shall not have enmity one with another . . . but rather shall each one hasten in his work according as it has been given him from God."

Of baptism it is said: "Candidates shall be baptized naked" (*i.e.*, only with the undergarment), the little children first, "and if they can speak for themselves, let them speak; but if they can not, their parents shall answer for them, or one of their relatives." No adult was allowed baptism until "he had learned the Psalm." The minister prayed concerning the candidate that the Savior might "open the ear of his heart, and enlighten the eyes of his mind, and give to him the light of knowledge and impart to him the washing of regeneration for the forgiveness of sins, making him the temple of the Holy Spirit by our Lord Jesus Christ," etc., etc. The ordinary baptism was by dipping three times, but if the candidate was weak, pouring was allowed. The confession made by the candidate was as follows:

"I believe in one God, the Father Almighty, and in his only son, our Lord and Saviour Jesus Christ, and the Holy Spirit, giver of life to all creation, the Trinity equal in God-head, one Lord and one kingdom; one faith, and one baptism, in the Holy Church Catholic, and life eternal. Amen."

Such was the early Ethiopic liturgy.[137] While few direct quotations are made in some of these ecclesiastical documents, it is plain that they rest solidly upon the New Testament Scriptures, as they interpreted it.

Not only the papyri but also ordinary inscriptions connected with official and private buildings dating from the early Christian era contain many Biblical quotations. M. Gustave Lefebvre, in 1907, published 808 such inscriptions gathered from all parts of Egypt during six years or more of careful work. Of these three of the most ancient (Nos. 34, 35, 54), dating from A.D. 148-159, are doubtfully Christian; but two others of the fourth century, three of the fifth century and sixty-two of the sixth century are almost certainly Christian. Of these 808 inscriptions sixteen are New Testament texts (Matt. 3:3; 5:13; 9:27; 19:18; 25:34; Mark 1:3; 10:19, 47, 48; Luke 18:38; 23:42; John 8:12; 10:25; 14:6), and certain other formulæ are certainly based on expressions used in Corinthians, Colossians, Ephesians, Timothy, and Hebrews. While these texts are on the walls of buildings or portals of churches or engraved on stone tablets or lamps or bronze crosses and are not in any sense portions of ancient Bibles, they vividly disclose the constancy with which the early Christians used their new Testaments.

Altho they may not illustrate this point quite as well as some other examples, we give here a few very recently discovered texts:

"Lord, grant repose to the soul of the servant Thekla, summon

---

[137] For the modern form see *The Ethiopic Liturgy*, Rev. S. A. Mercer, 1915. This entire liturgy should be compared with the *Didache*.

her to the bosom of Abram and Isaac and Jacob and feed her upon the tree of life, hearing Come, ye blessed of my Father, inherit the kingdom made ready for you from the foundation of the world."

"God, the All-Conqueror, the one that is, that was, that is to be, Jesus, the Christ, the Son of the living God, remember the sleep and rest of thy servant Zoneese, the most devout and loving-the-commandments, and deem her worthy to tabernacle through thy holy and light-bearing Archangel Michael, in the bosom of the holy fathers, Abraham and Isaac and Jacob, because thine is the glory and the power to the ages of the ages. Amen, she lived blamelessly seventy-seven years . . ."[138]

We have already mentioned the Biblical references to be found in the ancient sermons.[139]

Many liturgical Greek fragments have been recovered from the fifth and sixth centuries telling of the adventures of Christian saints, condemned to starvation, etc., and a good many texts so broken that one hardly knows whether they are private Christian letters or official church documents.[140]

A great multitude of Christian documents written in Coptic but not strictly liturgical, dating from near A.D. 600, have also recently been published. Here, for example, is a dialog in which different interpretations are proposed of various passages in the gospels, such as the miracle at Cana, the temptation of Jesus, etc. These interpretations aim to be practical; e.g., under John 9: 3, the expositor says: "The pool of Siloam is the Church; the waters are the waters of holy baptism."[141]

---

[138] (A.D. 409.)

[139] Pp. 260ff; and see further *Homily of Pope Liberius,* reported by Lefort (which quotes from Matt., Mark, Rom. and 2 Tim.) in *Muséon* XII., 1.

[140] One, *e.g.,* speaks of the "terrible judgment seat of Christ our God." *Greek Papyri in the John Rylands Library,* Vol. I., No. 8, *cf.* Nos. 10, 11; and another of "Christ the King risen from the dead," *Jour. of Theol. Studies,* 1915-16, pp. 171-3.

[141] Crum, *Anecdota Oxoniensia,* No. 12.

There are many accounts of martyrdom that have recently come to light, one representing Diocletian being inspired by the devil in the guise of a serpent; another narrating with eagerness the tortures of the martyrs crowned with red hot helmets or boiled, after strips were cut from their back, etc.[142] They thought too much of the martyrs in the sixth century, as is shown by many texts such as, "Let us pray the holy martyr of Christ, Apa Moni, that he guide us in this sea that is full of trouble."[143] Yet they talk and write religiously and quote Scripture voluminously. Even the ostraka give us some material of value. A "Confession of Faith," which was written over 1300 years ago, shows the careful theological discrimination attempted in that era:

"We confess a Trinity which is in a Unity, namely the Father, the Son, and the Holy Ghost, three persons ('υποστάσεις), of whom One took flesh for our salvation, namely, the Son. Yet each one of these Persons is a thing apart not in the others."[144]

Compare also the following ancient *Sanctus* in which occurs the passage:

"That he may make them all worship him . . . Thy beloved and holy Son, Jesus Christ our Lord, the First-born of all creation (who is also co-essential with thee), who didst make us heirs of these (good things by his precious blood; we give thanks to thee, the incorruptible, unapproachable, unsearchable,) inexpressible (God Almighty). . . . Before thee stand . . . the many-eyed cherubim and seraphim, each having six wings (and with twain veiling their face, because) they fear to look upon thee, Image of the Invisible . . . shouting and saying, Holy, holy, holy Lord God Almighty, which was and is and is to come."[145]

[142] Crum, *op. cit.*, Nos. 17, 18.
[143] Crum's *Coptic Ostraka*, 1902, No. 1.
[144] *Ibid.*, No. 3.
[145] *Ibid.*, No. 4.

The ostraka used as lesson tables in the schools contain many direct Biblical quotations: *e.g.,* Rom. 16: 10-12, and the story of the woman taken in adultery, John 8: 9-11; 2 Cor. 4: 18; 5: 5; Matt. 5: 13. A very great multitude of "copy-books" and "exercise books" from the early Christian centuries have been preserved to us from Egypt. Most of the literary exercises consist of quotations of Scripture such as the above or of religious sentiments such as:

"The grace of Jesus Christ conquers. Amen."[146]
"Jesus Christ. Alleluia. O Eternal Life."[147]

Among the many spelling books and grammatical and arithmetical exercises in Greek and Coptic have also been preserved a few school-boy compositions which are attempts to copy Bible models. One of these from a boy by the name of Enoch starts in with an attempt to reproduce a religious legend but closes up with a rebuke written in another hand, evidently that of the school master—showing that the copying of a "holy legend" had not kept this lad out of mischief:

"As Jesus went out of the gate of Paradise he saw a vine which wept and was giving forth tears. He spake saying: 'Why does the vine weep and give forth tears?' It spake saying: . . . 'It has pierced my eye . . . I have raised my eyes to heaven' . . . Enoch, don't throw your pen on . . ."[148]

Several documents of excommunication have been discovered, the usual form being:

"M. M. shall be anathema, to the Father, Son, and Holy Ghost and to the Christian community, and his house shall be anathema."[149]

[146] Hall, *Coptic and Greek Texts,* p. 34.
[147] *Theban Ostraka,* p. 211.
[148] *Coptic Ostraca,* p. 149. This is probably a little later than the sixth century.
[149] *Ibid.,* No. 135, *cf.* No. 78.

An episcopal letter is extant which forbids communion to a whole village until one of its leading magistrates shall "pay the man what is his." In other documents litigation among Christians is prohibited under fine.

One edict of excommunication, much more elaborate, is quoted by Deissmann [150] from a bishop named Abraham. The episcopal letter is written to the clergy of his Egyptian diocese and has to do with the sin of a man named Psate who had been oppressing the poor. It is written in Coptic about A.D. 600, on a piece of pottery, and contains several expressions that might make good copy for a modern episcopal address:

"He that oppresseth his neighbor is altogether reprobate; and he is like unto Judas, who rose from supper with his Lord and betrayed him, as it is written, He that eateth my bread hath lifted up his heel against me.

"He that oppresseth his neighbor is altogether reprobate, and he is like unto the man to whom Jesus said, 'It were better for him if he had not been born' (that is, Judas).

"He that oppresseth his neighbor is altogether reprobate, and he is like unto them that spat in his face and smote him on the head.

"He that oppresseth his neighbor, is reprobate, and he is like unto Gehazi, unto whom the leprosy of Naaman did cleave, and unto his seed.

"He that oppresseth his neighbor is altogether reprobate, and he is like unto Cain, who slew his brother," etc.

The phrases used above are evidently stereotyped, so that this was not the only instance in which discipline was carried out in ancient times for this crime— and the language is almost wholly Scriptural.

It is evident that these various official Christian documents which represent not simply the feeling of

[150] *Light from the Ancient East,* 1910, p. 216.

an individual but the thought of the Church are quite as important as private letters, perhaps even more important.

We find coming from the era of Constantine the following beautiful tribute to several Christians who had proved their constancy by a martyr's death:

"Ploution the blessed celibate (παρθένων) having borne witness . . . became a martyr in the nineteenth year and fell asleep aged forty-one. He went to the land of the blessed having two crowns. Similarly Berekon a self-controlled (ἐγκρατής) man (*cf.* Titus 1:8) became a martyr and fell asleep aged thirty-six. Likewise also his son Konon a neophyte." [151]

This inscription is most remarkable, since it is a relic of two heretofore unknown martyrs of the epoch of Diocletian. The text can not be much posterior to the year 300, and M. de Ricci even calls it the most ancient Christian inscription from Egypt. One of the most suggestive features is the mention of the future life in a phrase which was constantly used in the classics, and the further mention of "two crowns" which the Christian was to receive, which must be a reference to 2 Tim. 4:8 and James 1:12, or to Heb. 2:7.

While we will later analyze the multitudes of Christian epitaphs which are to be found in many lands dating from the second to the sixth centuries, it may be well under the present caption to notice the liturgical language and Biblical pre-suppositions continuing in every century through all these Christian epitaphs:

EPITAPH OF MARIANOS (7th-9th Centuries)

"The God of the Spirits and of all flesh who hast abolished death and the grave (Hades), and hast graciously given life to the world; give repose to thy servant Marianos in the bosom of

[151] M. de Ricci in *Revue Epigraphique,* 1913, No. 10.

Abraham, Isaac and Jacob (in the Bright Place, in the Place of Rest)."

EPITAPH OF JOHN THE DEACON (8th Century)

"Oh how dreadful is this separation! Oh departure to the strange land, which removes one for all time. Oh condition of Hades, how do we come to thy gate! Oh death, name bitter in the mouth of all beings, which cutteth off, which sundereth fathers from their children, and children from their fathers. Let all who love to weep for their dead come to this place and mourn greatly."

THE EPITAPH OF HELENE (11th Century)

"With God fell asleep in Christ Jesus the deceased, Helene . . . May the God of the Spirits and the Lord of all flesh give repose to the soul of thy servant in the place of rest. Amen." [151a]

GREEK EPITAPH OF MENA (8th Century or later)

"By the command of God, who ruleth both the quick and the dead, the deceased Mena reached the end of this life . . . Lord Jesus Christ, rest the soul of thy servant in the bright place, in the coolness, in the bosoms of Abraham . . ." [152]

Another Greek epitaph showing perhaps also the influence of Egyptian phraseology reads:

"Eutychousa, who entered into rest . . . in the place of verdure at the water of rest, whence have fled all pain and grief and groaning, in the brightness of thy saints." [153]

These illustrations of the influence which the New Testament had upon early Christian literature might be indefinitely increased. Practically innumerable quotations from the New Testament have been found in Italian, Syrian, and Mesopotamian inscriptions from the second to the sixth century, as well as from Egypt.

[151a] *Coptic and Greek Texts in British Museum,* H. R. Hall, 1905, plates III, VIII.
[152] *Ibid.,* p. 13.
[153] *Ibid.,* page 138.

And while most of these are connected with the ritual services of the churches, or are such texts as are appropriate for epitaphs, yet it would be safe to say that if every New Testament in the world should be destroyed and with them all the writings of the ancient Fathers, such as Tertullian and Justin Martyr, Eusebius and Jerome, a very large collection of the most precious texts of the New Testament expressing every vital doctrine and experience of Christianity might still be gathered from these newly found papyri and other inscriptions written by poor and often nameless Christians of the first six centuries.

And while most of these are connected with the ritual services of the churches, or are such texts as are appropriate for epitaphs, yet it would be safe to say that if every *New Testament* in the world should be destroyed, and with them all the writings of the ancient Fathers, such as Tertullian and Justin Martyr, Eusebius and Jerome, a very large collection of the most precious texts of the *New Testament* expressing every vital doctrine and experience of Christianity might still be gathered from these newly found papyri and other inscriptions, written by poor and often nameless Christians of the first six centuries.

PART TWO

THE MONUMENTS, INSCRIPTIONS, AND OTHER ANCIENT REMAINS

STUDIED WITH ESPECIAL REFERENCE TO THEIR
BEARING ON THE LIFE AND TIMES OF THE
PRIMITIVE CHURCH

I

NEW LIGHT FROM GRAVES AND BURIED CITIES

1. New Light from the Land of Palestine

PALESTINE was the stage on which the drama of the New Testament was enacted. One would naturally expect that from its cemeteries and buried cities a flood of light would have been poured upon the culture and literature of the early Christian centuries. Unfortunately, however, very few authenticated monuments of this period have been found in the Holy Land. Not even one leaf of the Vulgate has been recovered from Bethlehem, the home of St. Jerome; not one certified ancient relic can be found in Nazareth, the home of Jesus—excepting the old well; while scarcely a solitary monument from the first century remains even in Jerusalem except, possibly, the Holy Sepulcher, and a few broken remnants of ancient Roman buildings, roads, and walls.[1] There is no doubt that the location of Herod's temple can be determined with certainty, and some of the valleys, springs, and pools, and the sites of ancient gates can be fixt; but doubt remains even as to the location of the little upper room where the disciples met, and the palaces of Herod and Caiaphas, and the praetorium and other sites connected with the trial of our Lord. Even the eleven cities which have recently been excavated in the Holy Land, while giving much new light upon the era of the kings and the patriarchs, have given us pitifully few

[1] For the far greater discoveries in Palestine illuminating the Old Testament, see the author's *Recent Explorations in Palestine* (3d ed., 1916), Collegiate Publishing Co., Meadville Pa.

remains from the era of Jesus and the Christian community previous to Constantine. Some reasons for this lamentable silence are easily discovered. Palestine has been the battleground of the ages; Jerusalem has been pillaged and destroyed many times, while the destruction wrought by pious pilgrims was almost an equal catastrophe. Even nature has conspired against the archeologist, for the rains of Palestine have rotted all papyri, and the stones are of a character which will not permanently hold inscriptions. History has also been antagonistic to scientific research, because this land for centuries has been at the mercy of the Moslem, and because the most important New Testament sites could not in any case be thoroughly excavated, since they still remain inhabited villages.

Notwithstanding these disadvantages, considerable has been accomplished. Individual surface exploration, which has been going on ever since the time of St. Jerome, reached its climax in the last generation in the person of Dr. Edward Robinson. In 1856 this distinguished American scholar published his three volumes of *Biblical Researches,* and altho he had spent barely five months in his explorations, yet, in that short time, he virtually "reconstructed the map of Palestine" (Bliss). He identified 160 Bible sites, and almost every one of his decisions has been confirmed by modern scholarship. He studied Jerusalem with critical care, being the first to show that the fragment of an arch still in existence had been part of the ancient bridge connecting the temple with Mt. Zion. He was also the first to trace with accuracy the windings of the tunnel leading from the Virgin's Fount to the Pool of Siloam. Other particularly successful explorers in Palestine, in the earlier period, were Lieutenant Lynch, who in 1848 made the first thorough examination of the Dead Sea, and Tobler (1845-68), and Guérin (1852-75), who both made extensive scientific explorations. One of the most remarkable single discoveries ever made in Palestine directly touching New Testament times was that of Clermont-Ganneau, who in 1871 found the Jewish placard which had been posted up in Herod's temple forbidding Gentiles to enter the sacred enclosure. The characters were monumental in size and contained the following inscription in Greek in seven lines:

"No stranger is to enter within the balustrade round the temple and enclosure. Whoever is caught will be responsible to himself for his death, which will ensue."

Dr. Ganneau made many other important discoveries adding to our knowledge of the first century by his recovery of a goodly number of ancient inscriptions, rockcut tombs, and other monuments. One of his most famous "finds" was the "stone of Bethphage" (cf. Luke 19: 29) on which was frescoed a precious ancient picture of the resurrection of Lazarus. Colonel Conder also did specially good work in a private capacity, and as the head of the archeological party under the auspices of the Palestine Exploration Fund reported, in 1880, ten thousand place-names and 172 new Bible sites successfully identified.

The work of the Palestine Exploration Fund, begun in 1865, marked a new era in the work of discovery. It is scarcely too much to say that more advance was made during the first fifteen years of its existence than in all the fifteen centuries before. Perhaps the greatest work, however, done by this society was that connected with the topographical survey of Western Palestine

(1871-77) and of Eastern Palestine (1881-82), resulting in an authoritative map on the scale of an inch to a mile, showing accurately all previous identifications of ancient places. These maps still hold their places among the best published, and when they first appeared, together with eight massive volumes giving full results of the topographical and archeological survey of Palestine, scholars declared with some appearance of reason that this work represented "the most important contribution to illustrate the Bible since its translation into the vulgar tongue." It would be impossible even to hint at the contents of these enormous volumes, with their hundreds of maps and plans of churches, mosques, temples, and tombs from every part of Palestine, and the monographs, rich with learning, which discuss the botany, zoology, geology, etc., of the Holy Land. In 1913-14 a survey of South Palestine was made by Capt. S. F. Newcombe and Lieut. F. C. S. Greig, including the Negeb—from Beersheba to the Egyptian frontier, from Rafah on the Mediterranean to the head of the Gulf of Akaba—but at the present writing (1917) the map based on this survey, tho completed, has not yet been issued.

Jerusalem was also explored by this society with great thoroughness so far as this could be done under a Moslem government, and with the embarrassment to excavation caused by the necessary protection of modern buildings and cemeteries. But tho the remains of seven synagogs and many ancient churches were carefully examined—among which was the ruined church of Justinian on Mt. Gerizim,—and tho a few relics were recovered from the time of Queen Helena and Hadrian, and while much was done to settle disputed questions concerning the ancient walls and pools,

O. Marucchi

Sir William M. Ramsay

Dr. Rodolfo Lanciani

Dr. Agnes Smith Lewis
© Elliott & Fry

Giovanni Battista De Rossi

Dr. Margaret Dunlop Gibson
© Elliott & Fry

Melchior De Vogüé

Dr. J. Rendel Harris

Prof. Howard Crosby Butler

it must be acknowledged that few discoveries were made having any close connection with the New Testament text or New Testament times.

It would be ungrateful, however, not to mention the work of Sir Charles Wilson, Sir Charles Warren, and others who uncovered the temple area of its countless tons of débris, traced its approximate outline, examined underground rock chambers, opened ancient streets, and discovered many thousand specimens of pottery, glass, tools, etc., dating from the Jewish to the Byzantine period. Among other discoveries the thirty-four rock-cut cisterns found on the ancient temple site are impressive. The largest of these has a depth of forty-three feet and a capacity of more than 2,000,000 gallons, while another had a depth of sixty-one feet and a capacity of 700,000 gallons. One can not forget Maudslay (1875), who made a masterly examination of the great scarp; and Guthe (1881), who made fine additional discoveries at Ophel; and the later work of Warren and Conder, who published an elaborate plan of the whole city, twenty-five inches to the mile—a plan which remains the basis of all later maps. Neither can one forget the work done in Jerusalem, 1884-97, by Dr. F. J. Bliss; and that done since then by the Assumptionist Fathers of Mt. Zion and others who have excavated beneath and around their churches, and have brought to light many ancient relics and some remarkable construction, beside tracing the history of the sacred sites quite elaborately.[2] One of the most inspiring of these later discoveries was that of Dr. Bliss in recovering the ancient church which had been built over

[2] See, e.g., P. Urbain Coppin, *Le Palais de Caiphe*, 1904, P. Barnabé, *Le Prétoire de Pilate*, 1902.

the Pool of Siloam (John 9:7); and almost equally stimulating was the discovery by the White Fathers of what is probably the ancient Pool of Bethesda with the ancient church above (fifth century), built in memory of the troubling of the waters (John 5:4). The Assumptionist Fathers found, in 1912, on Mt. Zion what seems to be the remains of an ancient prison and the foundations of an ancient church; also, at a time somewhat earlier, a set of Hebrew measures, enabling us for the first time to be sure that we possess a correct knowledge of the ancient measures of capacity mentioned in the Old Testament and in later Jewish writings.

The Algerian Fathers, in 1912, also made a peculiarly valuable discovery at Jerusalem when they found the standard talent, which was kept in the sanctuary. This was a spherical stone with flattened bottom having a rude inscription at each end and weighing about nineteen pounds.

But the new era in Palestine exploration opened in 1890 when Dr. W. M. Flinders Petrie began to excavate the ancient Biblical city of Lachish at *Tel el Hesy,* in southern Palestine. There had been much surface exploration and some miscellaneous digging at various sites previous to this, but Dr. Petrie was the first to undertake the scientific excavation of an entire town. At the end of six weeks' work he could date approximately some seven successive occupations of this site covering a period of a thousand years, and because of his previous excavations in Egypt this explorer was able to produce a chronological scale by which the age of each city could be definitely calculated from the styles and decoration of the pottery fragments. While no relics of the Christian era were found in this particular city, it was a necessary preparation for the excavation of about a dozen other ancient sites in some of which remains of the Christian era were found.

During 1890-1900 Dr. Frederick Jones Bliss—who had followed Dr. Petrie at Lachish—and Dr. R. A. Stewart Macalister dug up four towns on the borderland between Philistia and Judea, the most important of these being situated at Tell Sandahannah. This town covered about six acres, and the work done was "unique in the history of Palestinian excavations" (Bliss), because at this place was "recovered almost an entire town, probably the ancient Mareshah (Joshua 15:44), its inner and outer walls, its gates, streets, lanes, open places, houses, reservoirs, etc." (Bliss). It was a Seleucidan town (third to second century B.C.), built with thin brick-like blocks of soft limestone. The town was roughly divided into blocks of streets, some of the streets being paved. The houses were lighted from the street and from an open court. Very few rooms were perfectly rectangular, while some were of awkward shape. Many closets were found, and pit-ovens and vaulted cisterns reached by staircases, as also portions of the drainage system. The cisterns had plastered floors and sometimes two heavy coats of plaster on the walls. The houses occasionally had vaulted roofs, but usually the ordinary roof of to-day made of board and rushes covered with clay. The chief importance of this discovery lies in the fact that it shows us a Palestine town just previous to the Christian era. The towns of Palestine two centuries later could not have been very different.[2a]

[2a] The work of Petrie, Bliss, and Macalister was carried on under the auspices of the pioneer society, *The Palestine Exploration Fund.*

The fact that the Holy Land was freely open to foreign immigration is shown from the Sidonian tombs found near Tell Sandahannah. Drs. J. P. Peters and H. Thiersch discovered these strange examples of sepulchral art in 1902. The walls of the tombs were brilliantly painted, showing a bull, panther, serpent, ibex, crocodile with ibis on its back, hunter on horseback, etc., with dated inscriptions, the earliest being 196 B.C. Nothing shows better the interrelations of that age than this Phœnician colony living in Palestine, not only writing in the Greek language but also using Egyptian and Libyan characters in their art. The dress of this period is surprizingly modern, as shown by some of the figures. That they also believed in the future life is shown by their tomb decorations. In a similar tomb which the writer discovered in 1913 the most prominent features of the decoration were a garland of flowers surrounded by a cross and a cock. The cross was probably merely an ornament, but the cock as "herald of the dawn" almost certainly symbolized the hope of a future life. Another painted tomb of the same era has more recently been discovered, and thoroughly described by Warren J. Moulton, but it adds little more to our knowledge of the period.[2b]

The most striking find at Tell Sandahannah consisted of sixteen little human figures dating from the early Christian era. These little "revenge dolls" are bound in fetters of lead, iron, etc., through which the owners hoped to work magic on their enemies. Together with these, forty-nine fragments of magical tablets were found inscribed in Greek on white limestone with exorcisms, incantations, and imprecations.

[2b] *Journal of Roman Studies,* 1915 (Jan.-March).

Nor was belief in magic confined to the Jews and heathen. In a Christian exorcism recently published the ancient writer attempts to put magical bonds upon an enemy who he supposed was working evil through the "spirit of evil whom the angel Gabriel released from fiery chains." The "name" of Jesus and certain "scripture" narrating the power of our Lord in Galilee is "proclaimed" to this evil spirit, and he is bidden to flee to the woods on the mountain top and leave the tormented Christian alone.[3]

It seems a great pity that in the remarkable excavations of Dr. Ernest Sellin at Jericho (1907-9) no remains from the early Christian era were discovered excepting two crosses and two or three other Christian emblems. They did, however, find a large Jewish town (600-400 B.C.), and proved that the Jericho of Jesus' day was a double city spreading itself out on both sides of the wady. They found a rich hoard of Jewish household utensils, and proved that Greek merchants and terra-cotta manufacturers found in Jericho a very good sale for their wares about the days of Ezra. Toys in terra-cotta were common, and fragments of a beautiful animal frieze were found, as well as twelve Rhodian jar handles stamped in Aramaic with the words "To Jehovah." All of this shows that Jericho, the city of priests, was a cultured and religious town several centuries before the birth of Christ.

While Dr. George A. Reisner, with a staff of specialists, made many remarkable discoveries at Samaria, 1908-9, almost all of these refer to a period long before the Christian era. They did, however, trace the road of columns leading to the forum and the great

[3] *Bulletin d'anc. litt. chrét.*, 1911, p. 81, No.1.

outer wall "twenty stadia in circuit" which Josephus
mentions, and uncovered the ornamental gate and
several important buildings. Many inscriptions and
much pottery of the Roman period were excavated, and
the old Roman chariot road leading into the forum,
which Jesus and his disciples must have known well,
was positively identified. Adjoining the forum and
connected with it by a wide doorway was a basilica consisting of a large, open, stone-paved court surrounded
by a colonnade with mosaic floor. An inscription in
Greek on an architrave in the courtyard dates this
A.D. 12-15. The plan of this Herodian temple, which
was built during the boyhood of our Lord, consisted of
a stairway, a portico, a vestibule, and a cella with a
corridor on each side. The staircase was eighty feet
wide, composed of seventeen steps beautifully constructed, the steps being quite modern in style, each
tread overlapping the next lower by several inches.
The roof was arched and the walls very massive and
covered with a heavy coat of plaster still retaining
traces of color. A few Greek *graffiti* were found near
here, 150 stamped jar handles, and many fragments of
Latin inscriptions. A complete inscription on a large
stele proved to be a dedication from some Pannonian
soldier (probably second century) to "Jupiter Optimus
Maximus." Near this was found a torso of heroic size
carved in white marble with such superior skill as to
bring to mind the Augustus of the Vatican. Close to
this statue was a Roman altar (presumably Herodian)
about 13 x 7 feet, rising in six courses of stone to a
height of six feet.

Beneath the Roman city was a Seleucid town (about
300-100 B.C.) with its fortifications, gateway, streets,

one great public building and complex of private houses, in connection with which was a large bathhouse with mosaic floor, containing hot and cold baths, water-closets, etc., which was heated by a furnace. In this connection we ought perhaps also to mention M. Gaster's discovery at Samaria of fifteen ancient phylacteries, the text of which dates back to the first century of the Christian era, being therefore the kind of phylacteries referred to in Matt. 23: 5. They consist of quotations from the Old Testament, and also contain a curious list of the names of male and female sorcerers.[4]

The greatest single excavation ever made in Palestine was that undertaken under the auspices of the Palestine Exploration Fund by Dr. Macalister at Gezer, some twenty miles northwest of Jerusalem, in 1902-5; 1907-9. No explorations have been continued so long on one spot, or have produced more unique discoveries, or thrown more light upon the development of Palestinian culture and religion; and none have been reported as fully. Unfortunately, however, even here the early Christian era is almost a blank. The population had either disappeared in the early Christian period, or the monuments had been broken into dust in some terrible catastrophe. It is something, however, to find here coming from the time of Ezra or a little earlier another complete plan of an ancient Palestine town. Gezer at this era was in appearance like a modern Arab village, a huge mass of crooked, narrow, filthy streets, shut inside a thick wall with no trace of sanitary conveniences, with huge cisterns in which dead men could lie undetected for centuries, and with

[4] Palestine Expl. Fund, *Quarterly Report*, March, 1916, etc.

no sewers. Even in the Maccabean time the only sewer ran, not into a cesspool, but into the ground close to the governor's palace. No wonder that the death rate was exceedingly high, few old men being found in the cemeteries, while curvature of the spine, syphilis, brain disease, and especially broken and unset bones were common.

The houses were generally of one story, and when two-storied the stairs led up from the outside and the lower floor was mostly given up to the cattle. When a chamber was too large to be spanned by a single length of roofing timber, middle posts were used. Tweezers, pins, and needles, bottles containing eye-paint, mirrors, combs, perfume boxes, scrapers for baths, and jewelry of various kinds were common, while a pulley of bronze was also found and an iron hoe exactly like the modern one. During the Maccabean epoch the people of Gezer built reservoirs (one having a capacity of 4,000,000 gallons), used well-paved rooms, favored complex house plans with pillars, the courtyard becoming less important as compared with the rooms, tho domestic fowls were now for the first time introduced. The architectural decorations have all been annihilated, excepting a few molded stones, and an Ionic volute from a palace supposed to be that of Simon Maccabeus because of the reference in Josephus and because of a scribbled imprecation found in the courtyard: "May fire overtake (!) Simon's palace." This is the only inscription from this period excepting one grotesque animal figure on which is scrawled a name looking something like "Antiochus." [5]

[5] The writer has quoted freely in the above summary of results, from

Since the above excavations were finished, a
few other explorations of minor importance have been
made which ought to be mentioned. These have consisted mainly of topographical, geographical, and
meteorological notes; examination of ancient walls,
towers, caves, roads, and springs; a critical study of
the natural products and of the exports and imports
of Palestine; modern manners and customs, religious
ideas, folk-lore, etc. Yet many small objects have been
brought to light, such as seals, glass mosaics, wall
frescoes, ossuaries, osteophagi; Greek, Latin, and Kufic
inscriptions; and other objects too numerous to mention. In the midst of this wealth of small discoveries
it seems almost impossible to mention any without un-
fair discrimination; yet we can not wholly omit from
our review a few of the most recent "finds." No Bible
student could fail to be interested in the two fine rock-
cut tombs containing Jewish sarcophagi found recently
in a sι·bιιrb of Jerusalem, a rolling stone being used for
one of the doors of the tomb. As these are almost the
only Jewish sarcophagi ever found in Jerusalem, it is
of interest to note how carefully the tombs were made,
and that the walls were prepared for paintings, just as
in the best heathen tombs of this period. In connection
with this might be mentioned the discovery of a richly
carved marble sarcophagus (second century B.C.), at
Turmus Aya near Shiloh.[6] It was constructed out of

his article, "Palestine (Recent Explorations)," in the *International Bible
Encyclopedia* (IV., 2222-2235), published by the Howard-Severance Co.,
Chicago, 1915. Thanks for this privilege are hereby returned to the publishers, and the reader is referred to that work for a list of authoritative
publications on this subject. An additional official publication of value
is, *Fifty Years' Work in the Holy Land,* published by the Palestine Exploration Fund, London, 1915.

[6] Described by Mr. Jacob E. Spafford, June, 1913, in the *Journal of the
British Archæological Association.*

fine white marble, the heavy lid being gable-shaped like most of the Greek and Roman sarcophagi, and its sides ornamented with elaborate carvings, little inferior to the best work previously unearthed in Palestine. Among these are fruits and flowers in abundance and several remarkable symbolical figures. The figures represent Bacchus, a horse and rider, a man in the clutch of a dragon, and the four seasons with symbolical figures of the Earth and Ocean. The figure representing Winter is covered with an ample mantle, his right hand is broken, and birds are held in his left hand. By his side is Spring, whose left arm rests on a gnarled branch, the right hand holding a basket of flowers. Next to this is the figure representing Summer, pictured as a winged cupid, whose hair is adorned with ears of wheat and who carries a basket overflowing with the same grain. The Earth is seen at the feet of Winter, wearing a garland of ripe grain upon her brow.

In April and May, 1905, the German Oriental Society excavated a Hebrew synagog of the Roman period at Tell-Hum. It was 78 feet long by 59 feet wide, was built of beautiful white limestone almost equal to marble, and was in every way more magnificent than any ever before found in Palestine, that in Chorazin being the next finest. Its roof was gable-shaped, and it was surprizingly ornamented with fine carvings representing animals, birds, fruits, etc; tho in some cases these ornamentations had been intentionally mutilated. In January, 1907, Macalister and Masterman reported that they had made sufficient excavations at Khan Minyeh to prove that it was not the ancient Capernaum, as it contained no pottery older than the Arab time. This report being accepted, Tell-Hum is left without a rival in its claim to be Capernaum and makes it probable that the synagog excavated there is the very one referred to in Luke 12: 5.[7]

Among the most recent finds we perhaps ought to mention also the heathen temple from the time of Diocletian recently found a little south of the "street called Straight" in Damascus; the inscription (A.D. 318) found east of the Jordan telling of the existence of a Marcionite synagog there; the small, vaulted chapel discovered in 1905 under the traditional site of the house of Ananias; and the Christian mosaic found on the Mount of Olives in 1907, containing the monogram of Jesus Christ and the letters *alpha* and *omega*. The finest mosaic, however, ever found in Palestine was that discovered in 1896 at Madeba by Father Cleopas, librarian of the Greek patriarch.

This proved to be a part of the pavement of a sixth century church (A.D. 527-565) and is a "veritable map of Palestine," showing its chief cities, the boundaries of the tribes, and especially the city of Jerusalem with its walls, gates, chief buildings, including the Church of the Holy Sepulcher, and its chief streets; notably one long, straight street intersecting the city and lined with colonnades. As Madeba lies near the foot of Mt. Nebo, it has been thought that the artist may have intended to represent ideally a modern sixth century vision of Moses. This mosaic was very large and was beautifully laid out in colors. It has just been very pleasingly suggested that this "oldest land-map known" was probably a votive offering to the church by some ancient pilgrim. In 1899 Mr. S. W. Woodward of Washington,

[7] Yet see *Pal. Expl. Fund,* 1916, p. 194.

D. C., obtained in Jerusalem the remarkable drawing of this mosaic, which we reproduce through the kindness of Dr. I. M. Casanowicz and the editor of *Art and Archæology*. It was orientated toward the sunrise and contains about one hundred forty place names, some eighty of which have reference to the Bible narratives.[8]

Another mosaic found recently at 'Ain 'Arrub, between Bethlehem and Hebron, contained an inscription in Greek telling of St. Plesippos, who, "like St. John," had lived to be a hundred years old. Still another described recently by Mr. Willard H. Robinson, Jr.,[9] discovered at Ard el-Muheit near Mt. Nebo, early in 1914, deserves to be more fully described, as it is one of the most beautiful ever found in Palestine. It is part of the floor of an ancient church, and is 36 feet long by 27 feet broad, being richly adorned in colors with figures of men, and animals of various kinds; perhaps the most important is the representation of a man and woman with a serpent coiled about a pole between them. The whole is in an excellent state of preservation. Along the borders there are three Greek inscriptions dating probably from the fourth century, the largest and most valuable of which consists of six lines telling of the prayers of certain devotees to the god of "holy Lot" and "holy Procopias." The designation of Lot as a patron saint seems strange; but an ancient Jerusalem ritual mentions that Abraham and Lot were both reverenced in Galilee in the seventh Christian century.[10]

Many inscriptions have recently been found in

[8] *Art and Archæology*, March, 1916.
[9] *American Journal of Archæology*, 1914, pp. 492-498.
[10] See article of Prof. George L. Robinson, *Harvard Theological Review*, October, 1915, pp. 525-552.

MAP OF PALESTINE AS SEEN FROM MT. NEBO (6th Century)

From "Art and Archaeology," March, 1916

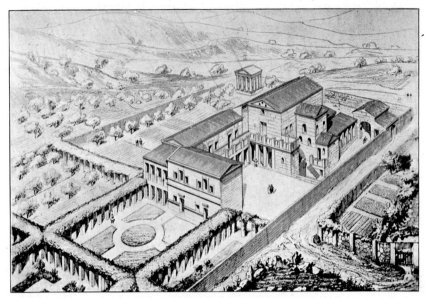

CHRISTIAN VILLA AT EL-BARAH, SYRIA

From De Vogüé, "L'Architecture dans le Syrie Centrale," (Vol. I)

CHRISTIAN HOUSES AT DJEBEL RIHA IN CENTRAL SYRIA (6th Century)

From De Vogüé, "L'Architecture dans le Syrie Centrale," (Vol. I)

Eastern and Western Palestine. One of these, coming from Gerasa, has to do with Hadrian's campaign against the Jews, A.D. 132-133, and proves that eight squadrons of the Royal Body Guard were at Gerasa at that time with the Emperor. Dr. A. Cowley, 1914-1915, found a particularly interesting inscription at Khalasa, about forty-five miles southeast of Gaza, dating from about 96 B.C.:

"This is the place which Nuthairu made for the life of Aretas, king of the Nabateans."

A number of other inscriptions mention Aretas, "who loves his people." One of these dates from A.D. 31, and another from A.D. 37. It was at some time between these dates that Paul escaped from the governor of Aretas in Damascus (2 Cor. 11: 32).[10a]

Mr. M. N. Todd reports a building inscription at Beersheba, dating A.D. 241-242, possibly Christian, and several other funeral inscriptions elsewhere, certainly Christian, dating from the fifth and sixth centuries. One of these gives not only the month and year, but the day and hour of the person's death.

The present writer, in 1913, saw a large grave tablet at Beersheba which he copied, containing the following previously unpublished epitaph (A.D. 589-604):

"Here was deposited Emma Nonna, the deaconess, in the month of Daesius . . . the twenty-third of the first indiction."

This reminds one of the grave inscription reported in the *Revue Biblique* (N.S., Tome II, p. 248):

"Here is deposited the happy Peter, the first day of the month Artemesios in the third indiction."

[10a] For a translation of these texts see Geo. A. Barton, *Archæology and the Bible*, p. 442.

There are also Christian epitaphs for "the late Abraham, a physician, who died May 8 in the twelfth indiction in the year 365," reported from Beersheba, for Father Symmachis, and for "the happy Victorine," etc. But the most important is the following:

"I am George, the son of Theodotus. Fate extinguished me in my youth and I have left to mourn me my father and my uncle, who brought me up and gave me an excellent education . . . indiction. 12 . . . . May the Christ give thee rest, my orphan."[11]

Nathaniel Schmidt has also recently reported twenty-one texts from Ruhêbek (*cf.* Gen. 26:22), all of a similar nature to the more simple epitaphs given above, and three more from Beersheba, one of which is an honorific inscription dedicated to an artist who had evidently just designed and erected some magnificent monument there in the middle of the fifth century:

"Eyes, what marvel is this! Such an ornament, how was it made here? What mortal devised this beautiful thing the world never saw before? Antipater made it, and shewed how Uranus (gracious be he!) holds in his hands the reins of armies dear to Mars."[12]

In 1914 Dr. G. Dalman was able to report twenty Greek inscriptions and a number of Hebrew and Aramaic epitaphs from the fourth to the sixth centuries, coming from Jerusalem, Nazareth, Gadara, and other towns. Perhaps the most interesting of these is that of Oneos, "the high priest," A.D. 539, closing with the ordinary heathen formula, "Be of good courage, no one is immortal." In connection with the latter in-

[11] *Op. cit.,* pp. 249, 250.
[12] *American Journal of Archæology,* 14:67.

scription we would like to mention a small marble slab
which we obtained at Caesarea in 1913, containing the
following Christian epitaph:

"In the month Loos, the priestess passed away . . . on the
eighth day of the year . . . of Christ."

The fact that this is certainly a Christian inscription makes us wonder whether Oneos was a Christian
priest, and whether "the priestess" mentioned above
was a converted heathen priestess or whether this was
a Christian title. It is interesting tho puzzling to find
on the tombstone of this priestess two engraved figures
which seem to be those of a scorpion or spider and a
hare. If properly interpreted the former may be the
heathen symbol representing pain and destruction, as
the hare was certainly the Christian symbol representing escape from danger.[13]

That the spider was sometimes used by Christians
in exorcisms is shown by a very curious Latin text,
recently published, in which the exorcist denounces his
enemy in the name of the Lord Jesus Christ, declaring
that he shall not be able to "cross the river" because
of the "fiery spider." [14]

[13] The carving is so imperfect, however, that it may be possible that a
butterfly was intended instead of the spider. For the other inscriptions
quoted, and many more, see *Zeitschrift des deutschen Palästina-Vereins*,
1914, pp. 135-145. Some Latin inscriptions were also recently found in the
Lebanons by Prof. James A. Montgomery (*Am. Journal of Archæology*,
Jan. 1916). The writer is greatly indebted to Dr. E. J. Goodspeed
of the University of Chicago for help in deciphering several of the above
previously unpublished inscriptions.

[14] Text published by Giulio Bertoni in *Bulletin d'anc. litt. chrét.*, 1911,
p. 81, No. II. Ancient inscriptions are always difficult to read because of
their mutilation, bad orthography, and bad grammar; but magical texts
are also made intentionally obscure. I am indebted to my friend and colleague, Prof. Clarence F. Ross, A. M., for help in unraveling some of
the puzzles in language connected with this and several other Latin texts.
For the detailed interpretation, however, I must alone be held responsible.

In addition to inscriptions, many fine statues and marble bas-reliefs, with a few personal ornaments, have been recently found at Askalon, Caesarea, and elsewhere. One of the most interesting pieces of jewelry was an onyx seal ring of Abbahu, containing a Hebrew inscription dating from A.D. 279-80, found at Caesarea and reported by Dr. P. Schroeder.[15]

While the record of these new discoveries in Palestine has, in a way, been disappointing, yet they have been important in bringing clearly to view the extreme poverty of the poor and the wealth of the rich in the cities with which our Lord was best acquainted. It is now seen that Jesus lived in a luxurious age, coming into close touch daily with the currents of an important world traffic. Jesus and his disciples were poor, but their neighbors were rich. The shore of the Sea of Galilee was a favorite place for the summer residences of Roman nobles. When one thinks of the splendid Greek city of Tiberias, the most prominent object on the Sea of Galilee, built during the early manhood of Jesus, and made capital of Galilee by Herod, and when one examines the magnificent ruins of Samaria, a city which was directly on the route to Jerusalem, and then crossing the Jordan visits Gadara or the even more wonderful ruins of Gerasa in Decapolis (cf. Matt. 4: 25), with its 230 great columns and Corinthian pillars, its triumphal arch, its magnificent baths and temples, its splendid theater, capable of seating 6,000 spectators, and its newly excavated harbor for naval engagements—a Bible student comes away with a new impression of the surroundings of the Founder of Christianity.

[15] Op. cit., p. 177.

2. New Light on the First Century from Pompeii

August Mau, in the great work to which every student of Pompeian life is indebted, has said: "Pompeii, as no other source outside the pages of classical authors, helps us to understand the ancient man."[16]

But even this does not state the complete fact. The classics only incidentally reveal the life of the middle and lower classes; but in Pompeii we see the scribblings and sports of these classes, in which we are now so intensely interested. To the New Testament student as to no other, Pompeii appeals, since we here see a concrete illustration of the civilization contemporaneous with the apostles; for it was in the twenty years preceding the destruction of Pompeii that all the synoptic gospels were written, together with all Paul's great letters, and in fact the entire New Testament with the exception of a few very small pieces and perhaps the gospel of John.

The culture of this country town in Italy was superior in certain respects to the average town of Palestine, Egypt, and Syria; yet the life of the middle and lower classes was fundamentally the same. It must not be forgotten, also, that culture was not confined to Italy, as has recently been very conclusively proved by the excavations. There is no single work of architecture in Pompeii that imprest the writer as much as the ruins of the ancient synagog in Capernaum and those other great ruins at Chorazin and Samaria, or the extraordinary and immense ruins at Timgad in Northern Africa, all of which date from the first century.

[16] *Pompeii, Its Life and Art*, Kelsay ed., 1904, p. 511.

While no palace in Pompeii could compare in elegance with the Villa of Hadrian—out of which came almost all the art treasures of the Naples Museum, contrasted with which our finest palaces would rank as common bungalows—yet the house of the Vettii, of the Silver Faun, or of the Golden Cupids, exceeds in beauty the average residence of modern men of wealth. The best houses may not even yet have been uncovered, for Cicero had a villa near here where he wrote his famous *De Officiis;* and Nero in A.D. 64, murdered one of the officials in order to take possession of his property. The jewelry and ornaments found in Pompeii and especially in Herculaneum were rich and artistic, while one blue glass vase ranks only second to the celebrated Portland vase, the pride of the British Museum; and the hoard of seventy beautiful bowls, in South Gallic style, discovered in one house in Pompeii in 1881, proves that the importation of foreign ware was common.

There was not the same comfort in the home life of Pompeii as is common in modern times, for such comfort is unknown even now in the East; but the plumbing and heating was adequate, baths and fountains were numerous, the marble center-tables and ornamental stands were as beautiful as any to-day, while the kettles and pots and "self-cookers" found in the kitchens prove that the people lived well. There were three public baths, the largest of which covered as much ground as the Houses of Parliament in London. In the Forum baths alone, 1,300 lamps have been found, and there were sixteen independent water-jets in the house of the Vettii.[17] Pictures of the dining-

[17] Alberto Piso and William Mackenzie. *Pompeii,* 1910, p. 120.

rooms show the table surrounded with couches each
made to accommodate three persons. "The diner rested
on his left arm on a cushion at the side nearer the
table and stretched his feet out toward the right.
Hence the first on the upper couch had what was
called 'the highest place.' The one next was said to
recline 'below' him, because lying on the side toward
which the first person extended his feet; the man at
the outer end of the lower couch was said to be 'at the
foot.' When in the gospel of John we read of a disciple 'lying on Jesus' breast,' the meaning is easily explained by reference to Roman usage; John was reclining in the place next below the Master." [18]

The Pompeians loved sports. Their large stone
theater had been built for a hundred years before the
first stone theater in Rome (55 B.C.); and when the
Romans built their first stone amphitheater (about
29 B.C.) the Pompeians had already been enjoying
theirs for some fifty years. The small theater was used
specifically as a music hall, and the barracks of the
gladiators were established in the colonnade of this
theater. The gladiatorial combats were frequent and
on a large scale for so small a town, thirty or forty
pairs fighting each day of the show, the amphitheater
being large enough to accommodate the entire population of 20,000 people. It was not alone the combatants
that were killed at these theatrical exhibitions, for a
record remains of a riot, A.D. 59, in which many of the
populace met their death.

All these public buildings and all the better class
houses were decorated with wall paintings which show
at their best "refinement in the choice of subjects,

[18] Mau, *op. cit.,* P. 263.

fertility in the composition, firmness of touch in the drawing, and exquisite finish in even the smallest details" (Mau). Expert artists can speak of the frescoes in the villa discovered in 1909 as representing a "very natural and noble art," and of the cupids and psyches in the house of the Vettii "as very dainty and charming," "revelling in brilliance and variety of color," "a perfect blaze of harmonic polychromy," expressing "delicacy of touch, fertility of invention, novelty of theme—the blossoming of a new life"—"a living art not a series of mechanical replicas," a style "that passed into early Christian art" and "profoundly influenced the artists of the Renaissance." [19]

Yet the fact is that in some rooms these beautiful cupids, instead of being represented as vine-dressers, goldsmiths, or flower merchants, blacksmiths or sellers of oil, are painted engaged in such evil actions, with such devilish ingenuity of imagination, that ordinary visitors to the ruined city are not allowed to see them. When the present writer was taken, in 1913, through the new street which had just been discovered, he found that the walls of the houses fronting the street were covered with such abominable pictures that the excavator had covered them with sheets so that his working men might not be debauched by them. The street was straight and broad, the houses were well built of brick and concrete, and the balconies covered with tile exactly such as are used for roofs now; but the unblushing immoral tone of the town's life was below anything that can be found in any European or

[19] Gerhart Rodenwaldt, *Die Komposition der pompejanischen Wandgemälde*, 1909; Alberto Pisa, *Pompeii*, 1910; R. A. Briggs, *Pompeian Decorations*, 1911; *Revue archéologique*, 1915, pp. 321-347; *Journal of Hellenic Studies*, XVI., 143-157.

A WINE SHOP OR "SALOON" RECENTLY DISCOVERED AT POMPEII

"Notizie Degli Scavi Di Antichita," 1912, p. 114

BRONZE DOOR OF A ROMAN VILLA
IN POMPEII

"Notizie Degli Scavi," etc., 1910, fig. iv

WALL PICTURE FROM A POMPEIAN
VILLA

"Notizie Degli Scali," etc., 1910, fig. iv

COLOSSAL SEATED STATUE OF TIBERIUS
The Vatican

A BLASPHEMOUS CRUCIFIX
(Third Century)
From Marucchi, "Eléments d'archéologie
chrétienne, I, 38

THE MARK OF THE BEAST
Seal of the "Divine Cæsar" (A.D. 5-6)
From A. Deissmann's "Light from the Ancient
East," p. 345

VIEW OF THE APPIAN WAY

ANCIENT RELICS FROM ROME

American city to-day. In the worst sections of the worst cities such obscene scrawls, dealing with the depths of human depravity, could not remain untouched by the public censor.

Modern civilization is not chiefly a matter of better inventions but of better morals.

In the House of the Surgeon was found a number of instruments exactly such as our best surgeons now use. The bronze bust of Caecilius Jucundus, the banker of Pompeii, whose receipts and legal documents, carefully signed by nine witnesses, have come down to us from A.D. 15, A.D. 27, A.D. 52-62, shows a typical capitalist's face and would not look out of place in the office of any modern captain of industry; while the bar-room, found two or three years ago, with marble counter and with glasses and decanters in place, was almost exactly like a modern bar-room, even to the hot lunches offered with drinks; but behind the veneer of wealth and civilization there was a moral rottenness which no one seemed to care to hide. The people were not all wicked; yet I do not wonder that one man, probably a Jew, scribbled on the wall one day, "Sodom!" "Gomorrah!" Other scribblings reveal the life of the city equally well. One of the most curious of these *graffiti* speaks of Harmonia saying, "The number of her beautiful name is 45." The name Harmonia, of course, suggests the "Muses" and $45 = 1 + 2 + 3 + 4 + 5 + 6 + 7 + 8 + 9$, and is therefore a number of perfection. So 666 (Rev. 13: 17)$= 1 + 2 + 3$ up to 36, and $36 = 1 + 2 + 3 + 4 + 5 + 6 + 7 + 8$.[20] It would seem more likely to

[20] Numerical identifications are never demonstrative. One scholar has actually suggested that the Beast of the Apocalypse was numerically equal to the Gnostic "Wisdom," *Journal Theol. Studies*, XIV., 444.

the writer that 666 would equal the subhuman or demonic as compared with 777, the symbol of absolute human perfection, while 888, the common "number" of Jesus Christ, would represent the superhuman.[21] If 616 is the real "number" of the beast, as it is according to a most ancient text, then there can be no doubt whatever as to its meaning; for it numerically represents Καισαϱ Θεος—the "God Cæsar," against whom the "Lord Jesus" was opposed.[21b]

That this rather mystic method of expressing thought was very common during St. John's lifetime is proved by the fact that even in one of the Pompeian election notices the vowels are distinguished cryptically by numbers.

A favorite actor is mentioned as "darling of the people"; a certain gladiator is spoken of as "the glory of the girls," and a "lord among the lassies." A woman is named in this public way followed by the invocation, "may you sneeze sweetly!" Another amatory verse by an unknown poet reads:

"Good health be with you lovers all;
Who knows not how to love be cursed."

Another effusion from a Pompeian lover may be paraphrased:

"My fair girl has taught me to hate brunettes.
I never love a dark-haired woman except against my will."

Another ne'er-do-well with a different taste has scribbled something which may be feebly paraphrased:

"Dark maidens for me; I always did like blackberries."

[21] If this is a proper explanation, the number 888 must be considered the earlier form, and "Jesus Christ Saviour of Man" its later explanation.
[21b] That is, Καισαϱ Θεος, which in Greek is 666, is 616 in Latin and therefore this must be the original meaning.

One scrawl reads, "He who has never been in love can be no gentleman," and still another, "All lovers come! I purpose to break the ribs of Venus and to smash the small of her back with clubs," and still another placard, whether of warning or praise, it may be difficult to say, reads, "Restitutus has many times deceived many girls." Many of the *graffiti* found in the city are of such a character that they can not be quoted; many more are of a personal nature such as the following:

Samius to Cornelius: Go hang yourself."

"Pyrrhus to his chum Chius: I am sorry to hear that you are dead."

One of the most valuable of the wall-paintings discovered 1911-13, represents a large religious procession carrying a statue of Cybele. The crowd is large and drest in brilliant costume. One woman is noticeable for her blond hair and green dress. A priestess who is inviting the populace to the sacrifice also wears a green dress and green crown. The priest wears a white tunic striped with purple and a white toga. Brown and black shoes and stockings seem most popular.

The most interesting placards are, however, the election notices. There were bulletin boards at the head of the street leading from the forum for notices of all kinds, but besides this the walls of the houses were freely used. One of these on the most public street in letters nearly eight inches high, reads:

"Make Publius Furius duumvir, I beg you; he's a good man."

Another notice, just uncovered, reads:

"Sergius Felix recommends A. Vettium as a strong character."

Another, which may show the interest of women
in politics (as is usually supposed), or may only be an
opponent's suggestion that the corrupt women of the
town were supporting Fuscunas, reads:

"Asetinas and Smyrine say, Vote for Fuscunas as your alder-
man."

So in a text published in 1912, Julius Polybius is
"recommended" by Smyrina and H. Priscus.

About 1600 of these election notices have been
found, the qualifications of the candidates being boldly
set forth, as:

"He is worthy of public office; he is a good fellow"; "He is
an upright young man"; "He will be the watchdog of the
treasury." "This young man is honest and is worthy of election."

Occasionally a man who has recommended a candidate draws a line through his name later, indicating,
probably, that for some reason he has withdrawn his
support.

While most of these recommendations are from
individuals, many of them are from the different guilds
and trade unions, such as barbers, carpenters, laundry-
men, pastry cooks, inn-keepers, masons, bakers, etc.
The muleteers, porters, fishermen, apprentices, ball
players, and even the schoolmasters and their pupils
have their political "say" in this public way, and in at
least a few instances recommendations for a candidate
come from the "late drinkers," the "loafers," the
"sneak thieves," the "assassins," and from "all the
people who are asleep!" These are placards evidently
put up by the opposing candidate. The shops and even
the gravestones are desecrated by these election notices,

which are sometimes painted and sometimes scrawled in charcoal.

The above shows the frivolity and careless sport of the town; yet many were trying to be religious. There is no intention of suggesting that Pompeii was more frivolous than other towns of the first century. Probably Neapolis (Naples), being a watering-place, was more frivolous than Pompeii. This town merely represents the ordinary life of the Roman world. The tendency fifty years ago was to overestimate the frivolity and sin of this era. Scholars have now generally gone to the opposite extreme. Many street altars have been found, one being dug up two or three years ago with the offering still upon it; and in front of many a house can yet be seen painted the symbol of Hermes—a wand with two serpents twisted about it, warning off loiterers from the premises. Very few indications of intellectuality and love for literature have been found in this country town, tho there is a picture of a girl with a writing tablet in her left hand holding the end of a stylus against her lips "as if pondering what to write," and that of a young man with one end of a roll of papyrus under his chin. One wall-painting pictures an elderly man and three younger ones writing in the open air, probably representing an open-air school, since another boy "is receiving his moral instruction in more tangible form upon the bare back" (Alberto Pisa). An Egyptian priest is also pictured chanting before the goddess Bast from a papyrus text (*Ancient Egypt,* 1916, p. 17). While this proves that in Pompeii, as everywhere else in the apostolic era, the people could read and write, it is quite evident that education was not a strong point of its population. A study of all the relics left in this town—whose famous mountain for the first time became volcanic a few months after Paul stopt at its port— leaves the impression that its view of life was the same as that found on a gaming-table at Timgad:[22]

This may not have been the view of life taken by the Jewesses Mary and Martha, who worked for a Pompeian weaver, nor of those other Jews for whom Umbricius Scaurus manufactured the special fish sauce which he marked "Pure" (Casta); but it undoubtedly represented the general spirit of the people.

The town was utterly destroyed a very few years after Paul stopt for an entire week within a few miles of it on his journey to Rome (Acts 28:14). If he visited it, as is very possible, he may have seen the large wall-painting of the Pompeian Venus drawn by elephants in a quadriga, which was dug up three or four years ago, and he may have met some of the very men who were a little later in the bar-room previously mentioned, drinking at the marble counter on the night of the catastrophe. At any rate, the very cash box which was found in its place in the wine room with the bronze and silver coins in it, just as they were received as the fatal eruption began, was probably the same as was being used when the sailors on Paul's ship ran over from Puteoli in order to see the sights of this famous little city in the year A.D. 59 or 60.[23]

---

[22] *Venari, lavare, ludere, ridere—hoc est vivere*—"To hunt, to bathe, to gamble, to laugh, this is indeed to live."

[23] There were five coins of silver and twenty-seven of bronze found in this saloon minted under Augustus, Vespasian and Nero. Besides personal observation, my authority for these most ancient discoveries is the *Nuovo Bulletino die Archeologia Christiana*, 1912, pp. 102*ff*., 185*ff*.

3. New Light on the First Century from the Roman Catacombs

The mass of new material brought to light in Rome in the last forty years is without a parallel in history. The excavations, during which 270,000,000 cubic feet of earth have been displaced, have uncovered pottery, inscriptions, tombs, and private houses in almost incredible quantities. Yet none of these are equal in value for Christian antiquity to the discoveries in the catacombs. In order that the later work may be appreciated a summary of the earlier excavations must be given.[24]

The catacombs represent the most notable monuments of primitive Christianity which have come down to us. They are entirely of Christian construction and did not originate, as was formerly supposed, out of ancient stone quarries, but are hewn out of the tufa rock. The vastness of these labyrinths awakens astonishment when we consider the poverty of the early Christians. "This work of giants was completed by a community of poor men destitute of resources, without talent as without fortune, incessantly persecuted and frequently decimated . . . With one hand they constructed in the bowels of the earth a city more astonishing than Babylon; . . . with the other seizing on the pagan world in the abyss of degradation they raised it . . . and suspended it to the cross" (Abbé Gaume).

[24] Altho the writer has visited the oldest catacombs at Rome, he has no independent judgment concerning them, and the facts and generalizations from the earlier period have been gathered chiefly from the great work of De Rossi (Northcote and Brownlow ed. 1869), and from the summaries of recent excavations given by other specialists. For the more recent excavations he has been mainly dependent upon the reports of Dr. Orazio Marucchi in the *Nuovo Bullettino di Archeologia Christiana,* and his invaluable *Christian Epigraphy* (1912).

These catacombs were dug along several of the principal streets leading out from Rome, and if the galleries were extended in a straight line they would reach, according to De Rossi, at least 550 miles. They are narrow passages with graves on the right and left, the number of which has been estimated at nearly two millions. They were evidently built on Jewish models, the Jews having made such underground cemeteries near Rome in pre-Christian time. Several of these Jewish catacombs remain, containing pictures which represent the olive branch, the dove, the palm, the seven-branched candlestick, and a number of inscriptions, prominent among which may be seen the Hebrew word שלום "Peace." Up to A.D. 70, the early Christians were legally regarded as Jews by the Roman government, and could doubtless be buried in Jewish catacombs or in graves of their own without fear. Burial places, even of criminals, were sacredly respected by the Roman Empire, so that for several generations Christian cemeteries were not disturbed.

By the end of the first century Christianity had already won a number of wealthy heathen converts, and these permitted the poorer Christians to construct burial places in connection with their magnificent private tombs. A characteristic inscription is "M. M. made this hypogeum for himself and his (brethren) who believed in the Lord."

The earliest of the catacombs, those of Domitilla, Priscilla, Commodilla, the crypt of Lucina, etc., are accepted practically by all scholars as dating back to the first century. In the third century these cemeteries were violated during the persecutions of Valerian (A.D. 258) and Diocletian (A.D. 303-305), and in the sixth century by the Goths. De Rossi found in the cemetery of Calixtus a mysterious stairway hanging in mid-air which indicated that at one time this catacomb was used as a hiding-place by persecuted Christians, but it is perfectly evident that they were not often used for this purpose. It is now equally clear that preaching was not ordinarily conducted in many of them, altho the Chapel of St. Priscilla is an exception, a pulpit having been erected there behind the coffin of an ancient martyr; and a baptistry has also been found in the catacomb of St. Pontianus.

In something over 300 years, more than fifty catacombs have been dug up, the greater number of these belonging to the fourth century. The Emperor Constantine set the example of building churches over the graves of the martyrs; but while Christian cemeteries above ground became common, the catacombs were still used and revered, and the old graves during this century were adorned with marbles and inscriptions. The invasion of Alaric A.D. 410, put an end to burial in the catacombs and no inscription is dated later than this. By the eighth century these sacred cemeteries had been deserted, some of them being turned into sheep stables; soon the popes began to transfer the remains of the martyrs to the great cathedrals. From the tenth to the sixteenth century they were almost completely forgotten, excepting those of St. Sebastiano, which continued to be visited by pilgrims. In 1578 one of the catacombs was accidentally discovered by Antonio Bosio, who thereupon spent forty years in studying these hidden ruins, publishing his results in 1632. The "true Columbus" of the catacombs, however, was Giovanni Battista de Rossi

(d. 1894), who "created from the foundations a science of cemetery topography which he based upon solid and unshakeable criteria," publishing his results in three splendid volumes.[25] In 1890 De Rossi made one of his greatest discoveries, finding certain galleries "that had not been touched since they were filled in during the Diocletian persecution." The *loculi* or shelves in the rock used as graves were intact and the epitaphs still in their places, so that "they formed a kind of museum in which the development, the formulæ, and the symbols of epigraphy from its origin to the end of the third or fourth century can be contemplated . . . in the genuine and living reality of their original condition."[26]

Since then Stevenson, Armellini, Marucchi, Wilpert, Lanciani, and others have carried on De Rossi's work. Several thousands of dollars have been expended each year by the Holy See for this purpose, and "there has been dug up a treasure of early Christian epitaphs and paintings, valuable beyond all expectations, which has given much unlooked for information concerning the faith of the early Christians, their concepts of life, hopes of eternity, family relations, etc."[27]

Even as early as 1873 there was found under an ancient basilica a bas-relief representing the martyr Achilleus (A.D. 391-395) receiving his death blow from the executioners. Achilleus was a martyr of the first

[25] *Nuova Roma Sotterranea,* 1864-1877.

[26] *Bullettino,* 1884, p. 68. It was at this time that he uncovered the wonderfully beautiful chamber of Ampliatus, its frescos rivaling those of the Golden House of Nero and so ancient that he identified it as that of the friend of St. Paul (Rom. 16:8).

[27] Anton de Waal, *Catholic Encyclopædia,* III., 417-426.

century and is represented tied to a stake which is sur-
mounted by a cross. The cross is crowned by a
triumphal wreath as a symbol of the immortal recompense which awaits the confessor of the faith. The
picture and inscription dates from the fourth century,
the inscription being erected by Pope Damasus:

"They had enrolled with fearful heart in the army and were
performing their cruel functions prepared to serve . . . the will
of a tyrant looking to his every order. With marvelous faith
they suddenly put aside their madness and turning in flight they
leave the unholy camp of their commander, hurl away their
shields, their breast plates and their bloody weapons and, confessing their faith, rejoice to conduct the triumphal celebrations of
Christ." [28]

Many beautiful inscriptions date from Damasus,
the "poet of the martyrs" (A.D. 366-384), the most impressive being his own epitaph:

"Here I, Damasus, confess that I wished to place my members
but I feared to disturb the holy ashes of the saints. . . . He
who walked upon the fierce waves of the sea and stilled them at
his command . . . who could loose the bonds of death from
Lazarus . . . he, I believe, will make Damasus to rise again." [29]

During 1887 over eight hundred tombs were
opened in nine months, among which was the tomb of
a boot-maker with the tools of his trade pictured on
the gravestone. Even earlier than this the tomb of
a surgeon had been found with his surgical instruments
figured in the marble, and the tomb of a dentist with
his forceps. It is interesting to note that while gold-
plating was excellently done in the first century, few

[28] Latin text in *Encyclopædia Britannica*, V., 498.

[29] For other inscriptions of Damasus, see Marucchi, *op. cit.*, pp. 415-435.
Cf. J. H. Treat, *Catacombs of Rome*, p. 35. The name of his mother—
Laurentia—has recently been discovered. His father, who had been a
shorthand writer, took holy orders early in life, after which his wife took
the vow of chastity, lasting sixty years.

if any instances of gold filling have been preserved.[30]
Many tradesmen appear in the inscriptions—carpenters,
masons, curriers, wool-combers, shoemakers, blacksmiths, weavers, vine-dressers, bakers, gardeners,
cooks, charcoal sellers, stone-dressers, tent-makers, etc.,
often with the tools of their trade. A few physicians
and teachers, many clerks, a few soldiers, and one
racing charioteer were buried as Christians. The
epitaphs of several Christian senators and a number
of ladies who were members of senatorial families
have been found, but none which are so impressive
as this inscription from the grave of a Lycaonian
soldier, Marcus Julius, who writes (earlier than A.D.
311):

"Having suffered many annoyances from the general, I resigned my military commission, holding fast to the Christian
faith."

In 1884 the house and tomb of the Licinii Calpurnii
were discovered, the former being the richest and most
important palace found in a generation, the latter containing the burial urns of these princes of the time of
Nero, but with the urns broken and the ashes scattered
to the four winds.

In 1888 the crypt of the Acilii Glabriones was discovered, a family very famous in the first century. In
1885 a sarcophagus of the daughter of a Christian captain of the ninth battalion of the Pretorian Guard was
dug up, and even earlier than this an entire cemetery
of Christian soldiers was discovered. It may have
been in the barracks of these soldiers that several
graffiti were found, dating from early in the third cen-

---

[30] Lanciani, *Pagan and Christian Rome*, p. 364.

tury, in which ridicule was offered to those who had become Christians. The most famous is the well-known scrawl in which a crucified man is represented with an ass's head and underneath it the sneer:

"Alexamenos worships his god!"

The same occurs again with the sneering epithet, "The faithful!" Another soldier appears, bearing the title, "Libanus the bishop!"

One of the most successful recent explorations was conducted 1897-1900, when a fine double crypt with frescos representing Christ seated between six saints was discovered in the cemetery of Domitilla, and another fine fresco of Christ seated among the apostles on the day of judgment was found in the catacomb of Santi Pietro e Marcellino. To the epitaphs of four popes discovered by De Rossi a fifth was added, found in the crypt of St. Cecilia, his only title being "Overseer" (ἐπίσκοπος).[31] Since that date a number of other inscriptions and frescos and several new catacombs have come to light, but few things have been found of preeminent importance.

In 1908 Professor Marucchi made a particularly thorough study of the Cemetery of Priscilla,[32] finding a pontifical basilica and an ancient baptistry, and making a re-examination of the vast number of inscriptions found there, identifying this cemetery with that of Ostriano. Seven years later he continued these explorations and found in the very oldest part of the catacomb fragments of a great sarcophagus from the time of Damasus (A.D. 366-384), and a theological in-

[31] American Journal of Archæology, XIII., 603.
[32] Nuovo Bullettino di Archeologia, Christiana, 1908, pp. 5-125.

scription containing the phrase, "the divine kingdom of Jesus Christ."

In 1911-12 he excavated in the catacomb of Domitilla, finding a number of wall-paintings and a few inscriptions. This was the cemetery where Boldetti had discovered the remarkable bronze medallion containing the portraits of Paul and Peter (late second or early third century), and much was expected, but very little of importance was found.[33] Another discovery, however, this same year more than repaid the excavator for all his work and more than fulfilled all his hopes, for in March he began to open an old primitive subterranean graveyard which proved to be the cemetery of the Flavii, in which still remained one particularly magnificent sarcophagus covered with bas-reliefs. He also found not far away a small, rude sarcophagus of the fifth century representing the Epiphany and the visit of the Magi, one of the Magi carrying a lamb in his arms as his gift. Another figure held a volume in his hand, and still another picture represented Moses bringing water from the rock. Another very magnificent tomb uncovered this year was that of a presbyter, Dulcitus (early fourth century), in which was an inscription dated November 3, 369, recording the death of the deacon, Gregorus.

In November and December, 1914, and during the early part of 1915, while engaged in repairing the Cemetery of St. Marcellino, Marucchi found some interesting new inscriptions, one of these being written by

[33] Lanciani accepts these "portraits" of the apostles found on this medallion and on many third century glass baptismal cups. He says: "The type never varies; the antiquity and genuineness of both types can not be doubted" (*Pagan and Christian Rome,* p. 212).

Jannarius (third century) in honor of his infant son Africanus, whom he calls his "little lamb." A little later, in the most ancient part of the cemetery of Domitilla, three fragments of a burial inscription erected by Fanius Paulus to his two-year-old "sweetest child," Fanius Leo, was found. The father is recorded as asking his infant son Leo to "pray" for his brethren. The year 1915 brought several other important discoveries, including a previously unknown Christian and a Jewish cemetery, but most spectacular of all, an ancient church, which was found under the basilica of St. Sebastian on the Appian Way—where, according to very ancient tradition, St. Peter and St. Paul were temporarily buried about A.D. 258, during a time of persecution when the vaults of the Vatican were unsafe. In 1915, through the generosity of Mons. De Waal, thorough excavations were made here, near the spot which tourists remember because of the "three springs," uncovering, some six feet beneath the floor of the present basilica, a pagan columbarium of the first century, and near this an ancient building partially destroyed. While most of the walls of this very ancient building were broken down, one remained containing third century paintings and fourth century *graffiti,* the latter referring frequently to Peter and Paul, a reference which proves to Professor Marucchi's satisfaction that this was the authentic site of that ancient famous sepulcher.[34]

A few remarks ought now to be made on the general bearing of the catacomb inscriptions upon our knowledge of the early Christian life. The most

[34] See for the above statement *Nuovo Bullettino,* 1912, pp. 123*ff.,* 169*ff.;* 1914, pp. 95*ff.;* 1915, pp. 57*ff.,* 147*ff.,* 152*ff.;* 1916, p. 516.

ancient of these inscriptions, which are usually written very beautifully, begin as early as the first century and are very brief—*e.g.,* "Peace"; "Peace to thee." The symbols used during the first and second centuries are few and simple, the peacock, the anchor, the trident, and the ship with rigging—the latter, perhaps, representing a hidden form of the cross. During the third century, which was the period of persecution, the dove with the olive branch in its mouth appears, as also the palm branch, crown, and fish. By the close of the third or beginning of the fourth century the cross appears, and the monogram of Christ containing the initial letters of the Savior's name (X and P) and the common Ιχθυς—which was an acrostic meaning "Jesus Christ, Son of God." The crucifix does not appear until the seventh century, the cross, however, often appears previous to this, the cross of the crucifixion being painted green or red, that of the resurrection and ascension blue or white. By the middle of the fourth century appear the symbols of the lion, phoenix, cock, hare, etc., and by the end of this century the glasses or mugs grow common, on the bottom of which are gilded the portraits of Peter and Paul.

These little glasses were probably gifts received at baptism. Eighty of these precious relics contain the portraits above mentioned. They also frequently bear inscriptions such as the following:

"Mayest thou live long."
"A mark of friendship."
"Life and happiness to thee and thine."

With the Constantine era the dead are eulogized as "wholly good," "entirely innocent," etc., and the inscriptions take on a triumphal note: "Living in eternity"; "Living in God Christ forever," etc. With the fifth century the catacomb inscriptions cease, but those above ground grow frequent and sarcophagi begin to appear, the latter having been previously confined to wealthy cemeteries like that of Domitilla.

The new joy of the Christian can be seen to no better advantage than when these burial inscriptions are contrasted with the death memorials of the contemporaneous Romans. While the common people among the Romans were at this time cherishing the hope of a future life, the supposed "better class" held very gloomy and pessimistic views, the grave being called "an eternal home" and death "an eternal sleep." A typical inscription is "Farewell, farewell, farewell forever!" Another inscription reads, "The cruel fates . . . have placed me, snatched away, in the infernal bark," and still another, "I, Procope, lift up my hands against the god who snatched me away (being) innocent"

Even more pathetic are such cynical inscriptions as "What I have eaten and drunk I have with me; what I have foregone I have lost"; or "Drink now to my memory and wish that the earth may be light on me"; or the numerous ones in which life is compared to a play:

"While I lived I lived well. My play is now ended; soon yours will be. Farewell and applaud me."

Many of the Roman epitaphs and a few Christian epitaphs contain warnings to travelers not to violate the grave.

In contrast with the above we transcribe a few Christian epitaphs from the catacombs: "Weep not, my child; death is not eternal"; "Sweet Simplicius

lives in eternity" (second century); "Gemella sleeps
in peace"; "Sweet little daughter, Severa, beloved by
her parents and servants . . . her body rests here
in peace until it shall rise again in God. . . . The
Lord will reclothe her . . . with spiritual glory"
(about A.D. 300); "If I have lived virtuously I have
not repented of it, and if I have served Thee, O Lord,
I will give thanks to thy name" (second century);
"Prosenes received to God" . . . (A.D. 217); "Alexander is not dead but lives above the stars."

Other inscriptions read: "She was borne away
by angels"; "He sleeps but lives"; "He went to God";
"He reposes in the Lord Jesus"; "Here lies Proteus
in the Holy Spirit of God."

Many beautiful tributes to relatives and friends
from Christians of the earliest centuries have been preserved, such as:

"God's little lamb"; "Little dove without gall";
"Sweeter than honey"; "A sweet spirit, gentle, wise
and beautiful"; "Aurelius Ampliatus and his son
Gordian to Aurelia Bonifatia, his incomparable wife, a
woman of true chastity, who lived twenty-five years,
two months, four days and two hours" (second century); "To her sweet nurse, Paulina, who dwells in
Christ among the blest"; "Peter, a most sweet adopted
son *(alumnus)* in God."

The oldest Christian inscription, coming from an
unidentified catacomb, was written A.D. 72. One from
the first century and two from the early second (A.D.
107, 110) came from the catacomb of St. Lucina,
where, according to De Rossi, St. Paul was buried a
few decades before.[35] The earliest of these reads:

[35] *Op. cit.,* p. 66.

"As a resting-place for Titus Flavius Eutychus, who lived nineteen years, eleven months, and three days. His dearest friend, Marcus Orbius, gave this spot. Farewell, beloved."

Before the middle of the fourth century, prayers to martyrs appear:

"Holy souls have in remembrance Marcianus Successus Severus and all our brethren . . . May (they) have a prosperous voyage." [36]

There are many inscriptions coming from the third century, tho the greatest number of all date from the fourth.

The change wrought by Christianity in the social relations of master and slave is plain from the exceedingly small number of Christian inscriptions containing the words "slave" or "freedman," words which are constantly seen on pagan gravestones. Instead of this those formerly slaves appear with a new name, "alumnus," i.e., foster child. As early as the second century, slaves were buried in the catacombs with honor. One text (No. 257) tells of the manumission of seven slaves by one family at the funeral of a little daughter.

Almost as important as the inscriptions are the specimens of the earliest Christian art preserved here. "These first and second century paintings are in the most classical style, and are scarcely, if at all, inferior in execution to the best specimens of contemporary pagan art" (De Rossi).

The earliest paintings of the Savior date at latest from the third century, and represent him in the form of a shepherd, clad like a Roman peasant, usually carry-

[36] De Rossi, op. cit., p. 133.

ing a lamb or kid in his arms or being followed by his flock, or in a few instances with the sheep on one side of him and wild beasts on the other.[37]   By the fourth century the garb and posture of the Divine Shepherd has become stiff and conventional and the face has lost its youthful freshness.[38]   Some wall-paintings, even as late as the fourth century, continue to represent Jesus as a youth and all the disciples as mere children; but others at this era represent Jesus as very old, and the twelve sitting about him at the Last Supper, looking quite like aged Roman senators.[39]   Peter and Paul often appear in the fourth and fifth century paintings, the former with broad face and luxuriant curly hair and close-cropped beard, the latter of much more noble and impressive presence, having a narrow face, bald head, and long Vandyke beard.[41]   It is interesting to notice that sometimes one and sometimes the other of these apostles appears standing in the place of honor on the right hand of their divine Lord.[42]   There was no attempt in the earliest pictures at making a likeness of the Savior, the conception being purely ideal, representing a beardless youth in the serene joy of a noble and divine task.   Toward the middle of the fourth century a new tendency appears in all Christian art, perhaps brought about by the triumph of the Church or by an artistic desire to represent the Redeemer as an oriental.   He is now painted with a beard; the brow is calm, shaded by long brown hair parted in the middle

[37] Giuseppe Wilpert, *Le Pitture delle Catacombe Romane,* 1903, Tav. 5, 106.

[38] See Wilpert, *op. cit.,* Tav. 168.

[39] *Ibid.,* Tav. 193.

[41] *Ibid.,* Tav. 48, 252.

[42] De Rossi, *op. cit.,* 286.

and falling upon the shoulders; the eyes are large and thoughtful. In 1887 the fragment of a marble bust of this type, dating, it is said, from the fourth century, was discovered. The pathetic representation of Christ as the Man of Sorrows does not arise until much later.

Other paintings from the third and fourth century are the Orante (a female figure in prayer) ; the raising of Lazarus, the escape of Noah from the deluge, Isaac escaping the knife of Abraham, Daniel escaping from the den of lions, the three Hebrew children delivered from the fiery furnace, and Jonah escaping from the sea-dragon—all of which represent the Christian's escape from death through Christ; while the appearance of the wise men from the East in adoration of the infant Savior probably receives its prominence because the Magi were the first representatives of heathendom to give honor to Jesus. Wilpert dates one Jonah picture as early as the second century.[43] In the same way pictures of Orpheus taming wild beasts may have symbolized the peaceful sway of Christ, while Odysseus, deaf to the siren's song, may have represented the Redeemer triumphing over the allurements of sensual pleasure.[44]

The Eucharist was probably celebrated at every funeral, and it is very natural to find eucharistic symbols—the vine, baskets of bread, etc.—in the earliest pictures. In most of these pictures the fish is also prominent; in a picture dated by Wilpert to the second century the basket of loaves is placed on a fish.[45]

[43] *Op. cit.,* Tav. 47.

[44] Ludwig von Sybel's *Christliche Antike* (2 vols., 1906-9) shows, in a beautiful way, the pictures on the sarcophagi, mosaics, etc.

[45] *Op. cit.,* Tav. 27, 28.

The fisherman appears in many of the wall-paintings, and in one inscription (not in the catacombs) Christians are spoken of as "the divine children of the Heavenly Fish." [46]

The same pictorial methods of expressing religious truth which were universal among the heathen were wisely utilized by the early Christian artists. As early as the first century (Wilpert) a cupid is changed into a Good Shepherd, probably suggesting that Christ was the true king of love. All the great doctrines of salvation, Christian eschatology and the divine nature of Christ, were taught by symbols.[47]

The oldest picture of the Virgin Mary represents her holding the divine Child on her lap, while the Prophet Isaiah, or perhaps one of the Magi, points to the star overhead. This picture, which De Rossi dated in the second or perhaps the first century, has had its claims to antiquity reinforced by recent discoveries of undoubted second century inscriptions on the same level with it. In these earliest pictures the Virgin does "not appear as the central figure but as accessory to the divine Child." [48]

In the third century the nimbus first appears about the head of our Lord—not far from the same era when a pagan artist placed it on the imperial head in the Arch of Constantine.[48a] In the early fourth century it seems generally reserved for Christ and the angels, but by the end of this century the Virgin and the

[46] De Rossi, Op. cit., p. 219.

[47] American Journal of Archæology, 1911, pp. 507-522.

[48] Withrow, Catacombs, pp. 307-318.

[48a] Cf. Strong, Roman Sculpture, pl. XL, XLI, 1907, and accompanying text. The heads on this arch, originally Domitian, have been reworked or replaced to honor later emperors. I owe this reference to the kindness of Dr. John R. Crawford.

apostles are similarly decorated, and by the fifth century it begins to be used for any of the "saints." [49]

In the 15,000 Christian inscriptions that De Rossi gathered, and in the thousands that have been gathered since, many suggestions can be obtained concerning the social condition and the religious and theological views of those early Christians. Many of them appear bearing Biblical names such as Phoebe, Prisca, Aquilius, Felix, Ampliatus, Epenetus, Olympias, Onesimus, Philemon, Asyneritus, Lucius, Julia, Gaius, Timotheus, Tychicus, Crescens, Urbanus, Hermogenes, Tryphena and Trypho(sa), the last two appearing together on the same stone. A light is thrown upon the religious spirit of early Christian families by the names which they were accustomed to give their children, such as Faith, Constancy, Peace, Amiable, Pure, Light, A Pilgrim, Born of God, God-beloved, Redeemed, Handmaid of God, etc. It is also significant that the burial inscriptions omit the birth years but practically always give the date of burial, presumably because of the feeling of the early Church that death was the Christians' "true birthday," as St. Cyprian exprest it, and therefore the relatives should not wear black but should dress in white at the funeral of believers. So Philete is called a child (*puella*), altho thirty years of age, because she was baptized only a few weeks before she died. It may be noticed also that few, if any, apprehensions of purgatory are found in the earliest inscriptions, but a confident and joyous anticipation of immediate reception into the presence of God. Wedlock is also honored in many inscriptions. Only a very few

[49] De Rossi, *op. cit.*, pp. 193, 194; Wilpert, *op. cit.*, Tav. 116, 141, 207, 209, etc.

among the many ancient epitaphs request the dead in heaven to pray for the living on earth, as (No. 103), "Jannaria, be thou refreshed and pray for us." More often the living friends pray for the dead: "Lord Jesus, remember our daughter," etc.

The oldest baptismal pictures date, perhaps, from the second century, coming from the most ancient part of the catacomb of St. Calixtus. They all represent the baptized standing in a stream with the administrant on dry ground, the former being nude, the latter more or less clothed. The very oldest picture represents the new convert as "coming up after immersion from the river which reaches over his knees, and joining hands with the baptizer, who is drest in a tunic and assists him in ascending the shore; while in the air hovers a dove with a twig in its mouth. . . . As far as they go all of the pictures confirm the river baptism prescribed by the *Didache* as the normal form, in imitation of the typical baptism in the Jordan. . . . From these pictorial representations we have a right to draw the inference that the immersion was as complete as the depth of the accessible stream or fount would admit, and that the defect, if any, was supplemented by pouring water on the head. The baptism of the head is always the most essential and indispensable part of the baptism." [50]

Presbyters are not distinguished from bishops in the inscriptions. There are numerous texts in which presbyters and deacons lament the death of their wives, and there is very early proof that the primitive church possessed a female diaconate for administering charity, caring for the sick, and instructing the young. There

[50] Philip Schaff, *Teaching of the Twelve Apostles,* pp. 36-41.

is little trace in the catacombs of that ascetic spirit which grew up in the fourth and following centuries. It is perfectly certain that those early Christians believed in the Trinity, the deity of Christ, communion of saints, the resurrection of the body, and life everlasting. They also believed in the doctrine of the atonement as preached by St. Paul.[51] They seemed, however, to have had too high an appreciation of the value of the sacraments, and too great veneration for martyrs. Some of the recently discovered doctrinal inscriptions, such as can not be found in the earlier period, deserve mention:

"O thou who hast been born again of water, come with thy fellows hither where the Holy Spirit calleth thee to receive his gifts. . . . Thou hast received the sign of the cross; learn to conquer the temptations of the world." [52]

In a baptistry said to have been built by Fausta, the wife of the Emperor Constantine, the following appears, written by Sextus III (fifth century):

"A race to be dedicated to the heavens is born here from beautiful seed, which the Spirit nourishes with its fructifying waters. The fruitful mother Church bears from the virgin stream sons whom she has conceived by the breath of God. Ye who have been born again from this fountain hope for the kingdom of heaven. A happy life awaits not those born but once. This is the fount of life, which purifies the world, taking its source from Christ, from his wound. Dip, sinner, to be purified in its sacred flood, and though old it will receive you and bring you forth from its waters made new." (No. 78.)

One young scholar, utilizing the new archeological material, has recently offered a very ingenious argument seeking to prove from the pictures of the cata-

[51] See Albert Schweitzer, *Paul and his Interpreters*, 1912, p. 248*ff.*
[52] Marucchi, *Op. cit.*, No. 77.

combs that St. John's gospel was in use in Rome by the end of the first century, or at least by the opening decade of the second, and that it was influencing the wall-paintings in a marked degree before the middle of the second. He shows from the best authorities on art that Biblical themes peculiar to St. John—raising of Lazarus and the woman of Samaria—are each found once before A.D. 180 (one of these almost certainly being as early as A.D. 130), while three or four other pictures of the resurrection of Lazarus must be dated to the end of the first or during the second century. As these themes are not treated in the synoptic gospels, but only by St. John, the inference is drawn that the Fourth Gospel must have become widely influential before such pictures would have been painted on Christian tombs.[53] By a similar argument the influence of Matthew's gospel can be proved from the many pictures of the Magi, while it may also be shown that no influence of the apocryphal gospels is apparent earlier than the fourth century.

4. New Light from Christian Cemeteries in Egypt

Cemeteries of Christian people dating from a comparatively early time have been found in many parts of the world.[54] The most remarkable of those known previous to the most recent finds were at Rome, Naples, Syracuse—where they constitute an entire underground city—at Malta and in Alexandria; but the excavations of Christian graves (1896-1900) at Antinoë and

[53] C. O. Lamberton, *Themes from John's Gospel in Early Roman Catacomb Paintings.*

[54] See summary in *New Schaff-Herzog Encyclopedia,* "Cemeteries".

Akhmim in Egypt outrank most of these in importance, giving to us a flood of new light upon early Christianity and the changes it wrought in religious thought upon the banks of the Nile.

Other recent excavations of ancient cemeteries are important, such as those of Father Delatre, near Carthage, in 1905, when he opened up an ancient Christian graveyard and obtained nearly 1,800 epitaphs from the third century and later, as also the discovery of Christian catacombs at Hadrumetum in 1906, and since then the opening of Nubian cemeteries (first to sixth centuries); but those at Antinoë and Akhmim have almost proved epoch-making. The catacombs of Hadrumetum and Mar Sousse are dated by Harnack as earlier than Cyprian (A.D. 238), and those at Tipasa as perhaps pre-Constantine; but the discoveries of Christian antiquities are not comparable to those now to be mentioned. At Oxyrhynchus also every Christian relic from the Græco-Roman cemetery had perished, unless a little doll-like image resembling the Madonna and Child be an exception. All of this shows the unique importance of the Egyptian cemeteries to be mentioned.

A complete series of tombs were excavated by M. Gayet at Antinoë dating from the time of the foundation of the city by Hadrian, A.D. 120-140, up to the end of about the fifth century; and fortunately many of these graves were Christian. Some of the tombs had brick chapels before them, eight of which were Christian, resembling in their symbolism that of the catacombs, the frescos showing the Good Shepherd, the dove, trees of paradise cross-garlanded with flowers, etc., most of these pictures probably dating to a time anterior to the reign of Constantine. At Akhmim ex-

404 THE NEW ARCHEOLOGICAL DISCOVERIES

cavations were conducted at various times by M. Maspero, director of antiquities in Egypt.[55]

The classical analysis of the results of both investigations was made by Mr. Philip David Scott-Moncrieff, *Paganism and Christianity in Egypt* (1913), and we use his data freely in the following discussion. He shows that notwithstanding the strong Hellenic influence, the old Egyptian religion held its own in Egypt until Christianity came. Indeed, the religious rites became more elaborate in late Ptolemaic time and the early Christian era, the most salient feature being the worship of the gods of the dead, and especially of Osiris, the "god of life in death"—who taught the hope of a new life springing from decay, death having a divinely revivifying power. Renunciation of the world, leading to asceticism and celibacy, was not peculiar to Christians but was common to Jews and heathen in the first two centuries of the Christian era. As the old systems crumbled before Christianity, the ancient gods did not disappear but lived on as demons who could be controlled by sorcery. The demotic papyri of the first century are full of pictures of the other world, grim and wild as those of Dante; but "salvation" for the soul was obtained, according to the ancient Egyptian worshiper, not by wealth or gorgeous funeral ceremony, but by the preponderance of the deceased's good deeds over his evil ones when weighed in the scales of the gods. It is now proved that the Egyptians did not believe in a resurrection tho they did believe in a future life, and much of their old religious symbolism was adjusted to the

[55] These discoveries were reported in *Annales de Musée Guimet,* tome XXX; *Bulletin de l'Institut Égyptien; Die frühchristlichen Alterthümer von Achmim-Panopolis.* The last-named publication the writer has not been able to examine.

new Christian faith. The pictures of Isis nursing
Horus became a forerunner of the Madonna and Child,
while Haroëris, especially when mounted on horseback,
is probably the ancestor of the military saints so dear
to Coptic art. The early Egyptian Christians were
mummified clear up to the Arab conquest and used the
old Egyptian forms connected with the burial rites to
enforce their new doctrine. As the poor man who was
an unconverted native Egyptian had a ticket put around
his neck to take him to the cemetery by boat on which
was written, "May his spirit serve Osiris"; so the
native Christians wore the same kind of a tablet, but
instead of the appeal to Osiris the monogram for
Christ appeared—this symbol probably being employed
as a seal as early as the third century, tho outside of
Egypt it has not been found earlier than the fourth.
One of these burial tickets from a middle-class grave
reads: "Taesai lived twenty-eight years. She has
gone to the Shining (Land)."

Another, almost certainly Christian, speaks of
Satripes Psenmagotos having "gone to rest" at Alexandria (*cf.* Rev. 14: 13).

One of the earliest graves found at Antinoë was
that of a woman named Krispina, whose handsome
oval face, with the hair drest somewhat after the manner of the Antonine empresses, is well shown by the
painted portrait in the coffin of the deceased. The
left hand still clasps the Egyptian symbol of life,
slightly changed to a shape like that found in early
Christian designs. The additional fact that only floral
decorations are represented in the frescos of the tomb,
instead of the typical Egyptian figures, makes it the
more probable that this woman was a Christian. Another

woman (early third century) has the monogram of Christ stamped on the seals of her bandages, and the legend, "Be at peace," embroidered on her shoes. In another grave (fourth century) was a cross flanked by the Alpha and Omega. With this body a wooden symbol of life, the *crux ansata,* was found, together with two reed baskets and a large jar. Did the baskets and jar indicate that the friends of this Christian woman had yielded to the old Egyptian custom of burying food offerings with the dead, or were they only Eucharistic vessels connected with the Christian (or Gnostic) sacraments? The latter is probably correct. It is also interesting to note that the hands of the deceased were grasping a small cruciform flower well-known as a desert plant which ordinarily lies dead and lifeless but on contact with the slightest moisture blossoms into life. This was entirely analagous to the Egyptian custom of placing the Osiris on a bier covered with soil and planted with grain, allowing the mummy to remain there until the wheat sprouted. Both Egyptians and Christians used these nature-symbols of life springing from death to express their faith in a future world. Near this rather luxurious grave was another of quite different character, containing the body of Sarapion, a Christian anchorite, clothed in a coarse brown robe and black mantle, with a cross hung from his neck and iron bands about his waist, ankles, and arms.

Some of the bodies found had been dipt in a bath of bitumen, certain parts being afterward covered with gold leaf. Then the entire body was bandaged and re-bandaged in spiral or interlaced patterns, over which was put a fresh coat of bitumen and a fresh layer of

bandages, the face being finally covered with a fine
cloth, painted and gilded with a plaster mask simulat-
ing the features of the deceased. This was the elaborate method used in the burial of the Christian woman
mentioned above. A slightly later method of burial was
not to envelop the body in bandages or dip it in
bitumen, but simply to clothe it in a tunic or shawl as
Sarapion the ascetic was clothed. Another Christian
body, embalmed according to the earlier method, was
found by Dr. Naville at Deir el-Bahari, the deceased
holding in his right hand a cup containing a red liquid
and in his left something that looks like a handful of
wheat. M. Naville believes these to be emblems of the
Eucharist. On the left shoulder is the swastika (卐)
which was used as a Christian emblem from the earliest
times not only in the Roman catacombs but also in
Egypt. Yet the lower part of the robe covering the
deceased contains a painting of two jackal-headed gods,
probably Anubis and Apuat, adoring the sacred bark
of Socharis. This seems to Scott-Moncrieff as almost
incredible unless the dead man belonged to some
fantastic Gnostic sect which might have employed this
mixed symbolism; but to the writer it seems perfectly
harmonious with the practise of Christians in all lands—
that of using the native symbolism wherever possible to
express their religious ideas. It must be remembered
also that heathen relatives or heathen artists might
have been permitted some discretionary powers in the
decoration of early Christian graves. We see exactly
this same use of heathen mythological motifs in the
frescos of the catacombs, in the ancient Christian
sarcophagi in Italy and North Africa, and in the gravestones from Phrygia. Several ivory objects were

found in the Egyptian Christian graves of the third and fourth centuries which probably had been used for counting the number of prayers recited.

The Christian tombs were decorated with vines painted black, resembling those of Pharaonic tombs, and in one grave was found a little terra-cotta model of several figures reclining at a table spread as if for a banquet. This evidently represented the Christian Agapē, or else was an imitation of the old burial customs of the Egyptians, or, perhaps, as Scott-Moncrieff suggests, it may have had some connection with some fifth century rite for nourishing the soul, which may have been used at Antinoë. Even at that early era the Eucharistic ceremony must have been thought to have some connection with the repose of the dead, for this man in his will expresses the desire that "celebration be made of the holy offerings and funerary repasts for the repose of my soul before Almighty God." When we consider the condition of the Church even in the middle ages, we must not discount too easily the spirituality of the Christians of the fourth and fifth centuries because of their use of semi-pagan symbolism or superstition.

The cemetery at Akhmim was in use from the first to the eighth century of our era. The bodies were mostly laid in a trench without coffins but drest in their richest clothing. The method of preservation, which was not by the use of bitumen but apparently by soaking in natron, was wholly successful, and has brought to us both clothes and bodies in fine condition. "It is due to this cause that we possess the magnificent series of textiles from this site which are a revelation of the skill and artistic knowledge for which the Panopolites were famous."

Worked upon these tapestries of the second and third centuries are designs of nymphs and garlands, of the cross, the fish, the dove, and the hare, the last three being "peculiarly employed in early Christian designs as furtive symbols of the faith"; while another representation of two doves on either side of a cup seems to be even more certainly of Christian origin, the type persisting in Christian tapestry for centuries. In later eras these designs were still employed; but the pagan deities which were used from the first to the third century have been changed into military saints and representations of the Savior. Of course, the Egyptian hieroglyphic of life is always used as one of the principal forms of decoration to represent the Christian cross. A ring from Akhmim, probably of the second century, has incised upon it an anchor and two fishes, while a model anchor comes from a neighboring tomb. From one grave comes a little figure bandaged like a mummy with the hands folded on the breast, which may have represented Osiris or may have been a figure of our Savior represented in the same way as the dead Osiris was pictured. The figure of Osiris found in another Christian tomb may have been, not an amulet as usually supposed, but a symbol expressing to the Christian as to the heathen the certainty of a future life. Scott-Moncrieff well says: "Everything seems to point to the fact that as far as funerary customs are concerned the syncretism of the age is evident not only in early Christian art but also in early Christian beliefs. We must also bear in mind when considering these objects the notorious activity of the Gnostic teachers during the second and third centuries and the conservative character of the Egyptians themselves." It should be remembered that Gnosticism was a system in which all religions found a place; its object was to explain not only the mysteries of the Christian faith but those of the pagan religions as well.

It is also plain that ignorant natives who had, previous to conversion, believed in a magical resurrection through Osiris, the divine man who had risen from the dead and who through magical rites could impart immortality, might without careful instructions confuse this with Christ's death and spiritual resurrection. Such men would also naturally use ancient customs and old artistic designs, not remembering their original meaning or not being philosophically curious; only knowing that Christ, like Osiris, came to life, and that through Christ immortality could be gained. Sometimes, also, a Christian would appropriate a pagan tombstone with all its mythical ornamentation.[56] Very constantly the early Christians in their art were influenced by the forms of artistic representation, with which they were familiar. In the Roman catacombs the decorations, as we have seen, were freely inspired by pagan *motifs,* and nymphs, fawns, Apollo, and Orpheus appear there commonly in the earliest period of Christian art, just as similar old Egyptian designs are used at Akhmim. This does not mean that the artists were unchristian, but only that Christian art was still in the process of birth.

Perhaps the most interesting thing coming from the Akhmin cemetery was the picture of the Savior

---

[56] See a notable illustration in *Paganism and Christianity,* pp. 134-135, and compare De Rossi, *Roma Sotterranea* (Northcote ed.), p. 299.

(fourth century) worked in white on a purple background showing a young man with curly hair, beardless, and wearing a long tunic and cloak. In his left hand he holds aloft a cross, and in his right is a cross-headed lance with which he spears a snake-like crocodile. Two other representations woven into the textile fabrics seem to represent the Good Shepherd and his flock.

A vast number of Christian grave inscriptions have been found in Egypt, the oldest of all, according to De Ricci, being the following:

"Ploution the blessed, a celibate, having borne witness in the nineteenth year fell asleep, 41 years of age, and went to the Land of the Blessed having two crowns; likewise Berekon, the self-controlled, having borne witness fell asleep, (being) 36 years old; and likewise also his son Konon a disciple of the celibate." [57]

Of the persons mentioned at least Ploution must have been a martyr, as the "double crown" plainly indicates. Several Biblical terms occur here. It is just possible that the term "self-controlled" (A.V., "temperate") applied to Berekon may indicate that he was a bishop (see Titus 1: 8). We append two later Christian inscriptions as published by De Ricci, as types of ordinary epitaphs:

A.D. 597.—"There fell asleep our father among the saints(?), Abba Kuriakos the anchorite (father?), of the Abba Nilos the anchorite in the month of Thoth . . ." [58]

A.D. 574.—"O Lord God of righteousness, give rest to the souls of thy servants Euthalios and Maria, for Euthalios was put to rest Phaph 12 . . ., and Maria . . . in the reign of Justinian." [59]

[57] Seymour de Ricci, "Inscriptions grecques d'Égypte," in *Revue conservies epigraphique*, N. S. I., 153, No. 10.
[58] *Op. cit.*, No. 11.
[59] *Op. cit.*, No. 14.

What has imprest us most in this study has been the proved interrelationship between pagan Egyptian and early Christian art and thought, and the new and vivid proof of the extraordinary power of primitive Christianity. The Egyptian religion, as we now see, was able to sustain itself in a surprizing way against the Asiatic and Syrian cults—such as those of Adonis, Atys, Cybele, and Mithra, and perhaps of Buddha also—and remained practically unaffected, except for the renaming of some Egyptian gods, even by the religion of their Greek rulers; but yielded unreservedly to the new ideals and the new theology of Christianity, tho retaining much of its old religious symbolism and some of its external forms of expression.

5. New Light from Second and Third Century Christian Gravestones in Phrygia

It has been just about thirty-five years since the École Française d'Athenes and the Asia Minor Exploration Fund of England began their work in Phrygia, which was the district most thickly populated by Christians in the early centuries, so far as records exist. Even earlier than this Hamilton and others had made important observations there, but detailed and scientific excavation has been confined to the period named.

Sir William M. Ramsay, who first entered Phrygia in 1880, and has visited Asia Minor almost continuously year after year from that time up to the present, is the main authority on this important Christian district, having settled many geographical and topographical points, located some of the celebrated rivers of classic history, and above all gathered vast quantities of antiquities and utilized them, in a peculiarly convincing way, to explain the New Testament.[60]

The story of Sir William Ramsay's "call" to his providential work is fascinating beyond description. He was a young married man of twenty-five with only money enough to pay his debts, when his physician, in his last year at Oxford (1876), ordered him to travel for his health. For several years he rambled in Germany, Switzerland, Italy and England, paying his expenses by teaching, writing for the *Encyclopædia Britannica,* and other such methods. Finally, in 1880, through the efforts of Mr. Stuart Poole, keeper of coins at the British Museum, he was elected to a studentship paying him $1,500 and entitling him to travel for research in Greek lands. His desire was to go to Athens; but instead of this, when he landed at Smyrna he was induced by Sir Charles Wilson, against the judgment of all his friends, to start work in Phrygia. When he entered Phrygia there was not a trustworthy map of the country, either in its ancient or modern state. He undertook to supply this need and also to trace the history of Roman institutions in Asia. He was not at all interested in the bearings of his discoveries upon the New Testament and early Christianity.

In fact, he considered the time lost which he had to spend in copying Christian inscriptions. That seemed

[60] In saying this we do not forget the work of Humann, who made an important journey in 1882, or of Körte in 1899, or of Prof. J. R. S. Sterrett, D. G. Hogarth, J. G. C. Anderson, T. Collender and others who have done splendid work, on the foundations laid by Ramsay; nor are we underrating the previous work reported 1862-1872 by G. Perrot and E. Guillaume, *Explor. de la Galatie,* and later by G. Radet, M. S. Reinach, Le Blant, and others.

outside his province, and besides he was a "worshiper of Wellhausen," and accepted without question the verdict of such critics that the Acts was an untrustworthy work of a highly wrought imagination produced in the second half of the second century. He was first awakened from this illusion by a study of Acts 14: 5, which stated as a geographical fact that one passed from the frontier of Lycaonia in going from Iconium to Lystra. The statement seemed absurd and was opposed to the decision of the most authoritative modern geographers, and seemed to be contradicted by ancient writers; but as Sir William studied the contemporaneous inscriptions, he discovered that the author of the Acts knew more about the ancient geography of Phrygia than any of his modern critics. In all the other statements of this book he also found such surprizing accuracy that he has finally been able to state (1915) as a scientific conclusion from all the data now in our possession that "Luke's history is unsurpassed in respect to its trustworthiness." [61]

We will now look for a moment at this strange district from which so many astounding discoveries have recently come.

Phrygia was the name of a very large country in Asia Minor which had great celebrity in ancient times, not simply because of the fame of King Midas and of the trade routes leading through this land to Boghaz-Keui, one capital of the Hittite empire; but also because of the civilization which could invent money and guarantee its value, thus "placing traffic on a new footing by

[61] See for most of the above facts and for an entrancing examination of late discoveries in Asia Minor *The Bearing of Recent Discoveries on the Trustworthiness of the New Testament,* Sir William Ramsay (2d. ed.), 1915.

regulating exchange." The immense riches of this land in ancient time is seen from the fact that Lydia could offer Xerxes as a bribe 2,000 talents of silver and 3,993,000 gold darics. In Roman time Phrygia was divided into two provinces, Asia and Galatia, called Phrygia Asiana and Phrygia Galatica. Galatic Phrygia extended along the front of the Pisidian mountains and included, according to popular understanding, the cities of Iconium and Antioch. One inscription has long been known mentioning Phrygia as a part of the province of Galatia and two or three others written in poetic phraseology have seemed to mention "Phrygian" Antioch; but in 1911 Sir William Ramsay found another which conclusively proved to him that Luke's geographical terminology (Acts 16: 6) could have been made "no more precise, definite and clear." [62] Racially this region was Phrygian, but administratively it was Galatic. The Phrygian language kept the racial feeling alive, as was confirmed in 1910 by the discovery of two Phrygian inscriptions (A.D. 150-250) at Iconium. Asian Phrygia was much larger; but we are particularly interested in the former because of Paul's travels in that region.

North Galatia in the first century was one of the least civilized corners of the Greek world; road-building did not begin till Vespasian; travel was difficult; the customs were barbarous; there were no literary interests before the fourth century after Christ; and while a few of the people could speak Greek, Phrygian was the tongue generally known, and the laws (e.g., of inheritance) were very different from those of Greece or South Galatia. It

[62] London Expositor, 1911, 263; compare on Luke's grammatical terms Ramsay's Church and the Roman Empire, pp. 74-177.

was certainly not to such people that the epistle to the Galatians was written.[63]

Whether we accept the South Galatian theory or not, there can be no doubt that either through the work of Paul—whom the inscriptions prove to have been thought of with special regard in this region—or through some other early teacher, almost this entire district was converted to Christianity earlier than any other of corresponding size in the civilized world. By the end of the second century Christianity was so dominant that it is against heretics, not against pagans, that the Christians were contending, while by the middle of the third century the population was so largely Christian that local persecution seems to have completely ceased; and when in A.D. 301-312 Diocletian sought to destroy this faith, bringing in government troops for that purpose, he was compelled practically to annihilate the population of Eumenea and perhaps other cities.

That the heathen had tried hard, tho unsuccessfully, to check by other means than persecution the onward sweep of Christianity, is shown by a most valuable inscription (A.D. 300) found in 1882 by Sir Wm. Ramsay, which tells of the "Tekmorian Guest-Friends," an anti-Christian secret society established on the imperial estates of Pisidian Antioch. These "brothers of the sign" spoke of the pagan devotees as "saints" (ἅγιοι), and doubtless sought to rebuild the decayed temples and

---

[63] See Ramsay, *Epistle to the Galatians*, pp. 131-194. It will be noticed that we accept without question Ramsay's South Galatian theory, believing that the archeological facts compel this, notwithstanding certain verbal arguments from Biblical texts which we think have unduly influenced such scholars as Schmiedel, Steinmann, Moffatt, etc., who have opposed it. For full list of the latter see Moffatt, *Introduction to the Literature of the New Test.*, p. 90.

to win new votaries to the old faith in their homeland, which had become wholly Christian, by an imitation of the languages and virtues of the new Way.[64]

One reason for the swiftness with which this district was converted may have been found in the psychology of the native population, who seem to have had a strong leaning toward religious and mystical discussion; but the prevalence of Jews, who had never been taught rabbinically, was probably the chief cause. Jews for several centuries had been granted special privileges, 2,000 families having been brought by the Seleucidan Emperor for political purposes from Babylon into Lydia and Phrygia about 200 B.C.[65] They had populated the district in great numbers and had grown rich and very influential. They maintained much of the old Jewish character, their morality being doubtless much higher than that of their neighbors; yet they had lost connection with their country, having even forgotten their language. According to the Talmud they represented the remnants of the Ten Tribes; certainly they were rather foreign in their sentiments, having a sympathy with non-Jewish thought and manners very unlike their Palestinian brothers. The inscriptions prove that they were complying with many pagan customs, and Ramsay believes that this may account for the fact that Timothy, tho having a Jewish mother, had never been circumcised.[66]

The two chief pagan deities of Phrygia were Cybele, the Great Mother, symbolizing the reproductive and nourishing power of the earth; and Sabazius, the son,

[64] Ramsay, *Studies in the Hist. and Art of the E. Provinces of the Roman Empire*, Chap. ix.
[65] See Ramsay, *Epistle to Galatians*, p. 74.
[66] Acts 16:2; Hastings, *Dictionary of the Bible*, III., 869.

symbolizing the life of nature dying and reviving every year. A drama representing the life and death of the latter was given annually, being characterized by a frenzy of devotion, unrestrained enthusiasm, and wild orgiastic dances. As late as the second century, women of the highest circles in Lydia lived as courtezans before the goddess. One woman records this service in a public dedication. To want to detain one's wife when it was her turn to serve in the temple was accounted a sin. Even after civilization stopt this as a general custom, a class of priestesses kept it up.[67] As the pig was the animal used in religious purification by the Phrygians as well as the Greeks, it is hardly likely that the Jews were reached, excepting very indirectly, by the native Phrygian worship; tho perhaps they, like the early Christians, were influenced somewhat by the universal belief in magic among all classes.

The Christian remains of Phrygia come from three districts, one in the center of the country, one in the north, and one in the extreme southeast and in the adjoining northern part of Lycaonia. A long-continued study of the trade routes convinced Ramsay that all three districts, altho differing widely in local inscriptions, were Christianized through Pauline influence. One line of influences undoubtedly starts from Ephesus, coming up the Maeander Valley and then on to Pisidian Antioch; another from the Pauline churches of Derbe, Lystra, Iconium, and Antioch into Lycaonia, etc. The inscriptions which center in Eumenea are generally very orthodox, those which center in Lycaonia and the adjoining Phrygian district are of a mixed nature; but those in the north of Phrygia, which

[67] *Cities and Bishoprics of Phrygia,* I., 95.

seem connected with the Christianity of the Troad (*cf.* 2 Cor. 2: 12), spreading up through Mysia and Bithynia, are akin to the Montanist heretical type. We shall not discriminate constantly between these districts, but shall use the inscriptions chiefly for the sake of throwing light upon the general condition of the earliest followers of the "Way" and illustrating their religious faith.[68]

The first thing that strikes us in examining these Christian epitaphs is the fact that, except in slight variations, they resemble the pagan epitaphs. This was intentional. However powerful the Christians grew, they were always in danger of governmental interference and felt it prudent to make their declarations of Christianity in a way so inconspicuous as not to rouse the attention of Roman officials. Most Christians did not covet martyrdom, and the greatest Christian teachers discouraged public statements which would bring persecution. It was also easier to follow customary formulas than to invent new ones, so that among some of the less intelligent Christians distinctly pagan abbreviations—which very likely were not fully understood—were occasionally cut upon the gravestones.

A very curious epitaph from a Parthian of high

---

[68] The text used, unless otherwise stated, is that given in the *Cities and Bishoprics of Phrygia*, 1895, 1897, excepting in a very few instances where later examination has given a different reading; Sir William's translations have been used when available. We once more wish to express our constant obligation in almost every paragraph of this discussion, to the various learned works of this distinguished explorer. We have also consulted the later texts published in the *Journal of Hellenic Studies* by Hasluck, Anderson, etc., XXIII., 20*ff.*, 75*ff.*; XXV., 81*ff.*; XXVII., 61*ff.*; XXVIII., 180*ff.*; XXXIII., 97*ff.*; XXIV., 20*ff.* It may be worth while to add that a sample collection of all known Phrygian inscriptions was given by Ramsay in 1905, in the eighth volume of *Jahresbericht des österreichisch-archäologischen Instituts*, pp. 79-110; but many have come to light since.

rank, dating probably from the fourth century, either marks the grave of a Christian who only slightly modified a very usual heathen formula or of a heathen who, during the anti-Christian revival, imitated in a rather imperfect way the moral epitaphs used by his opponents:

"I was not; I came to be; I shall not be";
"This life does not concern me. Farewell, ye passers-by." [69]

On the grave of another man who was certainly a Christian is carved the rather hopeless words:

"Do not weep . . . There is one end that comes to all."

When one died who was, perhaps, a Christian official of the third century, those who had the responsibility of providing for him a proper tribute used very classical terminology but failed to get in much of the Christian joy:

"Here lies Aurelios Trophimos . . . Here the doom of death overtook me, the public teacher of wisdom. I dwell in the house of Pluto . . . The light of the moon does not shine from heaven but there is dark night. . . . I went to the house of Hades, the lightless land, I who was once called teacher of sacred wisdom." [70]

But while occasionally the old fashions in grave inscriptions interfere with the expressions of the new view of the future life introduced with Christianity, ordinarily certain Christian expressions or symbols clearly differentiate the Christian from the pagan grave; altho even the early symbols were chosen from those used by the pagans or were made to resemble

[69] Op. cit., No. 134.
[70] Ramsay, Studies in the Hist. and Art of the E. Provinces of the Roman Empire, 1906, pp. 138, 142.

such. The dove and fish are seldom used in Phrygia, but as Sir William Ramsay points out, the horse, the ship, anchor, palm, etc., were used, as also certain anagrams which presumably had a Christian significance, altho it must be confest, most of these differed but slightly from those favored by their heathen neighbors. Quite often it is only the names which have a Christian meaning, thus indicating the Christian nature of the inscription; or perhaps names given to the Christians in scorn by their opponents, such as Credula, Alogius, Injuriosus, Calumneosos, Malus, Pecus, Fugitivus, etc. Biblical names excepting Maria are rare in Phrygia. Even when the term "deacon" or "bishop" appears, it usually marks the grave of some official of a pagan temple. The Christians here seemingly did not publicly use the title "bishop" until a later era. One distinguishing mark, however, of the Christian epitaph is the "deeper thought" and more "human feeling" displayed. Also when there is more than one body permitted in the grave it is almost certainly Christian. The heathen (and perhaps many Christians, too) believed that the preservation of the grave had something to do with future happiness, and so invoked penalties upon all violators of its sanctity; but the Christian not only often shared his grave with relatives, but in a surprizing number of cases with friend or stranger. One beautiful Christian inscription of the third century (about A.D. 270) shows the good political standing of the Christians at that time:

"Aur. Menophilos, Jr., the (son) of Asklepiades, senator, constructed the enclosure before you for himself and his son Apillonius and his wife Meltine and his grandsons Menophilos and Asklepiades and for whomsoever he himself wishes . . . But if any one else shall attempt to place (herein) another it shall be to him according to Jesus Christ." [71]

One of the formulas quite common is shown in the following gravestone of the fourth century:

"Eutyches son of Eutyches, to his wife Tatia and her father in remembrance, being Christians," etc.

A still more common formula which occurs very often scratched upon the corner of the tombstone:

"Thou shalt not wrong God."

Other Christian expressions are "God help"; "Lord help"; "Servant of God"; "Pardon our sins"; "Sleep"; "Rest," etc. The word which indicates the grave as a "resting-place" (Κοιμητήριον) is "only found in Christian inscriptions" (Hogarth). One such inscription reads:

"Aurelius Asclepiades made this resting-place. Peace to all the brotherhood."

A most common formula in the third and fourth centuries is this:

"Aurelius Zoticus, son of Marcion, to his own parents Marcion and Appe; . . . in remembrance during his lifetime, Chreistians to Chreistians."

The variation in spelling the word Christian is a certain proof of early date. Dating from the year A.D. 333 comes the following:

"CHREISTIANS TO A CHREISTIAN"

"Aurelia Ammia with their son-in-law . . . and grandchildren . . . to her husband constructed this tomb." [72]

[71] Greek text in *Bishoprics of Phrygia*, No. 371.

[72] The above inscriptions are given by Hogarth, *Authority and Archæology*, p. 386.

From the century previous occur similar epitaphs full of Bible names:

"Ioulios, son of Onesimus to . . . A Chreistian to a Chreistian."

"Auxanousa . . . and his son Trophimos . . . Chreistians to a Chreistian."

The title Christian was originally a taunt meaning "Messiah-ites," and very many of the early Fathers preferred, instead of writing "Christus," to write "Chrestus" (the "good" one). This invariably marks a pre-Constantine grave. On one third century stone an open book is pictured, evidently the Bible. Many tombstones are made in the form of altars or in some districts in the form of doors, with the knockers in place and the common utensils of life carved on the lintels—as if all the Christian needed to do was to pause and knock at the door of the grave and then pass through to eternal life. On the door-posts of one door is written the beautiful sentiment:

"They live having escaped great danger."

On another Lycaonian stele, placed above the grave of Dikios, "a measurer of wheat," is written:

"The sarcophagus belongs to him who knocks where the door stands before him."

Many inscriptions quote or paraphrase Scripture. The texts used in four typical grave inscriptions were: Isa. 1: 16-18; 25: 6; 60: 1-3; 61: 1, 10; Matt. 6: 13; 24: 15; Luke 15: 4; Phil. 1: 21.[73]

One of the most pathetic of all these third century

[73] *Op. cit.*, Nos. 674-678.

gravestones is that in which Aurelius Alexander, son of Mark, puts up a memorial to his martyred family:

"To my sweetest children honored by God in the peace of God (here follow five names) who on one single occasion were blessed with the lot of life . . . and whatsoever alien shall injure this tomb may they have children who die young."

This, as Ramsay points out, certainly marks the grave of five martyrs, for there can be no slightest probability that five children would be killed even by the plague in one day. Sir William dates this epitaph to the persecution of Decius or Gallienus, A.D. 249-260. It was quite customary with the Christians, as with the pagans, to call down an imprecation upon any one who would meddle with the tomb. The customary formula was, "He shall have to reckon with Christ"; but the father who had lost five children in one day puts on record a prayer which, under the circumstances, would affect the reader even more powerfully.

Another heroic inscription of a little later date, already quoted, describes the attitude of an officer in the Lycaonian army—Marcus Julius—who when Maximinus issued an order compelling Christians to sacrifice, wrote to his general, Diogenes, "I resigned my military commission, holding fast to the Christian faith." [74]

Mystical inscriptions, the meaning of which is often obscure to us, are not uncommon. Marcus Aurelius of Hierapolis, about A.D. 200, puts his will on his tombstone, leaving a large share of his property in the care of the presiding officers of the "purple-dippers" (or "those bathed in purple"), a part of the estate, under certain conditions, to go permanently to this "Guild of the *Thremmata.*" He also leaves money

[74] Marucchi, *Christian Epigraphy*, No. 379.

for candles to be used on "the wonted day." This enigmatical text seems to most scholars clearly Christian. That it is either Jewish or Christian is pretty certain from a second inscription, which also mentions "the most reverend assembly of the purple-dippers" (*porphyrabaphoi*), where a certain further amount is left to be used "on the feast of Pentecost." [75] Scholars generally agree that this "Ekklesia of Purple-Dippers" was a Christian burial club, the name being chosen because dyeing was one of the leading industries at Hierapolis and a "guild of dyers" was well known. Mr. Hogarth [76] accepts the Christian reference and says "the passers-by would read it as 'purple-dippers,' 'dyers in purple'; but the Christians would know that it meant 'those who were washed in the blood of the Lamb.'"

The most celebrated of all the Phrygian inscriptions is the mystical and allegorical poem found by Sir William Ramsay on the tombstone of a second century Christian named Avircius or Abercius, who places his confession of faith—evidently directed against the heresy of Montanus—in the most prominent way possible upon his tomb. There are in existence so few long inscriptions from the second century that his has an unequalled value. We give Hogarth's translation:

"I, the citizen of a notable city, have made this tomb in my lifetime that I may have openly a resting-place for my body. Avircius by name, I am a disciple of the pure shepherd, who feedeth flocks of sheep on mountains and plains, who hath great eyes looking on all sides. For he taught me faithful writings, and he sent me to Rome to behold the king, and to see the golden-

[75] The Greek text is given in *Cities and Bishoprics of Phrygia*, I., 118; II., 525, 545.
[76] *Authority and Archæology*, p. 383.

robed, golden-slippered queen, and there I saw a people bearing the splendid seal. And I saw the plain of Syria, and all its cities, even Nisibis, having crossed the Euphrates. And everywhere I had fellow worshipers. With Paul as my companion I followed, and everywhere Faith led the way, and everywhere set before me fish from the fountain, mighty and stainless, whom a pure Virgin grasped. At all times Faith gave this to friends to eat, having good wine, giving the mixed cup with bread," etc.

This epitaph can hardly be dated later than A.D. 192, and as at the end of the inscription Avircius says he was in his seventy-second year, this would date his birth A.D. 120, only some fifteen years after the traditional death year of John the Apostle. Another inscription A.D. 216 quotes a portion of this epitaph. Christ is evidently the Good Shepherd whose "great eyes" represent symbolically his prudent care. Avircius had taught his catechumens, he says, from true and sacred books, having been brought up on the writings of the Apostle Paul, who in the spirit was with him in all his journeys. The "fish" was the common symbol for Christ, born of a "pure Virgin," while the "mixed cup with bread" seems a clear reference to the Holy Communion. To allow that the king's daughter, the queen whom he saw at Rome, represents the Christian Church seems a little less certain, tho scholars generally accept it; but it is absolutely clear that Avircius found Christians everywhere he went in the second century from the Euphrates to the Tiber.

In a number of the inscriptions which we have quoted, burial guilds have been mentioned and charitable bequests. So the will of Aristeas, in central Phrygia, leaves a bequest to the "Society of Neighbors" in order that every year they may "cause the grave of my wife Aurelia to bloom with roses." The burial club was almost certainly the first official society established under the auspices of Christianity. It was common among the pagans and the Jews, tho not conducted probably on the same wide lines of charity and brotherhood as among the early Christians. It was the easiest way to get official recognition, as the government respected tombs and burial societies and allowed such clubs legal privileges. So far as charity is concerned mention of it occurs in many inscriptions as, *e.g.,* in one of the fourth or fifth century where on a tombstone the duties of a presbyter are declared to include "the help of widows, orphans, strangers(?) and poor." The name of the presbyter is mentioned who has "charge of the sacred expenditure (?) in remembrance." [77] The inscriptions speak of Christian orphanages for foundlings and of the church funds which were used for the liberation of slaves and for the care of aged people, prisoners, and exposed infants. Throwing the infant out to die or to be picked up by strangers was "a horribly common practise in Asia Minor." It was also common for pagan families to bring up foundlings in order to sell them for immoral purposes; so that this branch of charitable work on the part of Christians differentiated them very clearly in early times from their heathen neighbors; altho later, at the time of the anti-Christian revival, pagans were accustomed to imitate these acts of charity, as they were also accustomed to quote on their tombstones Christian phrases.

Very impressive is a gravestone found near Iconium in 1905, dating from about A.D. 350:

"Koulas to Solon, a stranger, in remembrance."

[77] *Expositor,* XII., 444.

Even now it is not too common for Christians to put up tombstones in memory of dead strangers. One bishop about the middle of the third century is called in his grave memorial, "Friend to all men"; which is even a better tribute than that on another bishop's tomb who is called "the very pure and sweet-voiced"; while an inscription on the tombstone of a priest emphasizes another beautiful quality:

"Here lies a man, priest of the great God, who on account of gentleness gained heavenly glory."

The honor given to women in Phrygia is marked. On a Jewish tombstone, A.D. 60-80, Nicias Lucius and his wife are both called archons or official officers in the synagog (ἀρχισυνάγωγος). Even if this were merely an honorable title so far as the wife is concerned, it still indicates the rank of women in the community.[78] This Jew had both a Greek and a Roman name, tho he was not a Roman citizen; he also acted as priest for the emperor cult, having to do especially with rites in honor of Poppæa, the wife of Nero. Ramsay has shown [79] that the Jews before A.D. 70 constituted a self-administrating community, "the law of the Jews," being, in fact, specifically mentioned on one tombstone. While it is an old tradition, probably untrue, that the Roman government did not discriminate between the Jews and Christians in the first century, yet it is often difficult to determine whether an inscription is Jewish or Christian unless the seven-branched candlestick or some other distinctively Jewish symbol is engraved on the stone.

[78] So in A.D. 200, we hear of a woman *"prophetess"* from the inscriptions, Ramsay, *Cities and Bishoprics of Phrygia*, I., 118.
[79] *Op. cit.*, Chap. XVI.

It is interesting to know that many soldiers and senators were Christians in Phrygia in the second and third century. It is far more interesting to discover that the early Church favored education, and that it was not until after the annihilation of the most prosperous part of the Church that the Christians began to underrate the value of learning.[80] It is supremely interesting to note that in almost all these pre-Constantine Christian inscriptions, which outrank in number those found anywhere in the world—unless we except the catacombs of Rome,—we find not only a firm faith in the fundamental doctrines of primitive Christianity, and a faithful spirit, which did not slacken even in the face of martyrdom, but also a love for the stranger and outcast which is peculiarly Christlike.

In addition to the foundation work which we have described as done by Sir William Ramsay in western Asia Minor, a great deal of supplemental work has been accomplished there and in other sections. Prof. J. R. Sterrett, in 1883-84, made an independent journey, bringing back 390 inscriptions; and in 1885 conducted the Wolfe expedition which obtained 625 texts. Very many more expeditions have been made, such as that of Cornell in 1907, conducted by A. T. Olmstead; the Princeton expedition, and the later expeditions at Cyzicus by several scholars, all of which have yielded an enormous treasure of inscriptions—tho all of these do not seem to have been carried away, as proved by Ramsay's most successful journeys in 1910 and 1911.[81]

[80] *Ibid.*, II., 509.

[81] Ramsay published a complete collection of all known Phrygian inscriptions in 1905 in *Jahresbericht des österreichisch-archäologischen Instituts*, which has since been greatly supplemented. See, *e.g.*, *Journal of Hellenic Studies*, Vol. 31, etc.

As early as 1856-59 His Britannic Majesty's government sent an expedition into S. Asia Minor, examining ancient cities and obtaining a goodly number of Greek sepulchral inscriptions from Halicarnassus, Cnidus, etc.; and these results were much enlarged by the work of C. Lanckoronski, F. von Luschan, K. Humann, and others (1888-1890), altho nothing for our present discussion was discovered more important than Sir Charles Newton's early find at Cnidus of a collection of leaden imprecatory tablets from the temple of Demeter which are remarkably like some later Christian imprecations. In East Asia Minor, G. Perrot and E. Guillaume, whom we have previously mentioned, did a magnificent piece of work (1862-1872), while the art of this district has been treated in a particularly thorough way by Professor Strzygowski, followed by Miss Margaret Ramsay—a strong argument being made to prove that the early art of Asia Minor exercized a strong influence on the development of Roman and Byzantine Christian art.[82]   D. G. Hogarth and other later investigators have added considerably to the knowledge of this section, while from Northern Asia Minor other scholars like J. C. Anderson and F. Cumont have done splendid work. Some of these results will be utilized later.

There is, however, one city, Cyzicus, where the explorations have been so extensive that it must receive special mention. Cyzicus was a town so ancient that its founding is placed by tradition only thirty-four years after Ilium, its king being the central figure in the famous expedition of the Argonauts. In 1902 F. W. Hasluck assisted Mr. Henderson in making a sur-

[82] *Journal of Hellenic Studies*, XXIV, 206*ff.*; Ramsay, *Studies in the History and Art of the Eastern Provinces of the Roman Empire.*

vey of the site under the auspices of the British School
of Archæology, and afterward each year up to 1906
he conducted excavations there, giving important
epigraphic and numismatic results, besides determining
positively many of the ancient roads and giving us the
first and only reliable map of the district. He found
the Roman walls of the city still standing, and was able
to give a good description of the style of buildings from
the first century to Hadrian's time. The substructure
(252 x 150 feet) and "a few gaunt piers" of Hadrian's
temple are still standing, tho the great theater remained but a shapeless remnant overgrown with brush-
wood. A necropolis was found in the east end of the
ancient ruins, and nearby a church where insanity
and all kinds of diseases were supposed to be miraculously cured—a direct perpetuation of the traditions of
the old Cybele worship.

The custom was to remain at least forty days, sleeping each night in the temple, and during this time the
temple physicians treated the disease; so medical
science developed. Investigators tell us that by the
fifth Christian century the medical profession had practically eliminated superstition from their theory and
practise and "stood on the solid ground of scientific
observation and experiment." [83] We shall see later,
however, that at least among the common people these
superstitions were long-lived.

The language of Cyzicus was a mixture of Lydian
and Phrygian. The local religious cult was transformed
into a gorgeous emperor worship, the ruling emperor as
early as A.D. 124 being styled "the New Son," "Olympian Saviour," etc., while the female members of his

[83] Botsford and Sihler, *Hellenic Civilization*, 1915.

family were worshiped as "The New Aphrodite," etc.[84] The mass of inscriptions found here, while exceedingly interesting, are valuable chiefly for their complete corroboration of Sir William Ramsay's previous conclusions concerning the religion and customs of Asia Minor, and therefore need not be quoted.

6. NEW LIGHT FROM THE SECOND, THIRD AND FOURTH CENTURY MONUMENTS AT SALONA, DALMATIA

For an entire century magnificent imperial constructions and vast ruins from the early Christian cemeteries at Salona have been the wonder of all travelers in Dalmatia. This city under the Roman emperors was one of the chief ports of the Adriatic, and the town of Spalato, situated near its site, is still the largest city of the district.

In 1818 the Emperor Francis I visited the ruins of Salona, and to his royal interest we owe the systematization of the explorations and the foundation of the archeological museum. The first excavations were conducted by Dr. C. Lanza, 1821-1827, and were continued by Dr. F. Carrara, 1842-1850, bringing to light the circumference of the city walls and some important buildings like the amphitheater, theater, several splendid gates, an old Christian baptistry, and several cemeteries. These excavations were continued intermittently till 1877, when a subsidy was granted to this work by the Austrian government, since which time annual excavations have been made. In 1870 all the collections previously gathered were housed in the gymnasium near the Silver Gate. After the accommo-

---

[84] See a fascinating account of the entire history of this city, *Cyzicus in Mysia*, By F. W. Hasluck, 1910.

dations provided here were overcrowded, additional sections were added, and finally a new museum of magnificent proportions was projected by the state in 1894.

Mons. Fr. Bulić has been the director of excavations since 1884, and it is from his reports chiefly that we gather the following information. One of the most spectacular discoveries has been in connection with Diocletian's palace. This wonderful building covers nearly ten acres, resembling in outline a Roman camp, tho its architecture is distinctly non-Roman. Portions of the old arched aqueduct still stand, by means of which Diocletian brought good water to the palace from mountain springs five and a half miles away.

Diocletian retired here to private life near his birthplace, about A.D. 300, and at once began the building of this palace, the workmen evidently being imported from Greece, Syria or Asia Minor. In five years it was so nearly completed that he brought his household gods and lived here the remainder of his life, dying about A.D. 313. The wall surrounding the palace is in some places two hundred feet high. There are towers at the extremities with truly imperial portals, many Doric columns adorning the approach. The colossal arched gates, which resemble those of the temple of Isis at Pompeii and the temple of the sun at Baalbec, have been recently cleared at immense expense. Many niches for statues and inscriptions appear, but the latter were all broken to pieces in the fifth century. A fine staircase leads to the most beautiful part of the palace, which contained the imperial apartments. The style of this palace is absolutely unique, representing the death of the old and the birth of modern art. As Dr. Bulić says, "Without the palace of Diocletian we should have been in the dark on the relation between the earliest Christian architecture and the Roman architecture." A noble mausoleum, far superior to the famous mausoleum of Napoleon, was constructed within the palace area and adorned with twenty-five Corinthian columns. Perhaps, however, this never received Diocletian's body, as tradition states that shortly after his death it became a prison for Christians who were martyred there. Their bones have actually been found, in recent years, walled in the niches.

It is difficult to describe the effect which the sight of this ancient palace still produces upon an intelligent traveler. Its size is astounding, for it yet accommodates from fifteen to twenty thousand people within its ancient walls. Its magnificence when new must have been almost without parallel. Even yet it causes all modern mansions and government buildings to appear small and unworthy.

But far more than this is its historic importance to Christian architecture. It can scarcely be doubted that this latest palace produced by Roman imperial art, constructed for the "last really great emperor," furnished the "source and type of the arcaded interiors of the early Christian basilicas built soon after under Constantine, some of which had architraves, while others had their lines of arcades on either side of the nave." [85] The mausoleum, of which we have spoken, built under the center of the palace dome, is undoubtedly "the progenitor of the Christian baptistry."

It will not be forgotten that it was under Diocletian that the Christians were most violently persecuted, and

[85] See A. L. Frothingham, *Roman Cities in Italy and Dalmatia*, 1910, p. 318*ff.*

that this persecution took place at the exact time when this palace was in process of erection. Even after the persecution ceased elsewhere, the emperor personally conducted it in this locality. But he failed in his purpose to exterminate the disciples of the new faith. Christianity had been introduced into Dalmatia probably by Titus (2 Tim. 4: 10), and recently discovered monuments prove that as early as the beginning of the second century it had found adherents among the higher class of citizens and even among the high officials of the palace. Lucius Ulpius, contemporary with the first bishop, Doimus, established at about the end of the second century a large Christian cemetery beside his own monument near his villa, and his descendants continued for a century or more to erect Christian mausoleums near their own family monuments. Even more interesting than this is the fact that in some inscriptions recently found it is proved that among the martyrs of the third century there were even some members of the illustrious family of Valerius, to which ancestry the Emperor Domitian himself belonged.

Instead of being destroyed by Diocletian's persecution, parts of the palace were turned into Christian worshiping places not long after the emperor's death, and the worshipers so multiplied that by the fourth century the Christian cemetery had extended at least over three hundred feet in all directions from the central basilica. Out of this cemetery—"the greatest known open-air Christian cemetery in all the ancient world" (Frothingham)—have come most important inscriptions and monuments. As early as 1894 Professor Bulić could report that the collection in the museum comprised at least twelve thousand small objects, including 2,034 inscriptions, 387 pieces of sculpture, 176 architectural fragments, 1,548 terra-cottas and vases, 1,213 glass objects, 3,184 metal articles, 229 gems, etc. Yet the largest excavation projects have been carried on since this period. In 1902 it was estimated that 60,000 feet of material were removed, and in 1905 a field railway was constructed and the government took part in clearing the débris, using it for the filling of a nearby marsh.

Besides the ruins of very ancient churches which have been uncovered, and many grave inscriptions, some intensely interesting relics from the tombs of Christian martyrs have been recovered. Among the most remarkable discoveries may be mentioned the sarcophagus of the Abbess Johanna, found in 1884, the unique baptistry first discovered in 1842 but more recently described, and the colossal Christian sarcophagus of Julia Aurelia Hilara (sixth century). On the latter is sculptured the remarkable figure of the Good Shepherd in short tunic with hands extended holding on his shoulders a lamb, exactly after the type of that seen in the Roman catacombs. The baptistry is of octagonal shape, its walls adorned by large white marble columns, and its central baptismal font sustained by slender columns of red marble. In 1915 Dr. Jelić described a unique ornamental communion table made of marble and adorned with figures of Christ and the apostles. Instead, however, of thirteen figures, this frieze, strangely enough, has seventeen—the extra saints probably being four of the most celebrated martyrs of Salona. On the table was a figure of Jonah thrown out from the mouth of a strange, elaborately carved monster—this picture symbolizing, of course, the resurrection.

Several remarkable mosaics have been discovered. One of these, reported in 1903, is that in connection with an ancient Christian baptistry (about A.D. 400), representing two stags drinking from a vase, while over them are placed these appropriate words from Ps. 42: 1: "As the heart panteth after the water brooks, so panteth my soul after thee, O God." Another polychrome mosaic, even more impressive, was uncovered July 11, 1902, in the choir of the basilica. In the midst of a very large section of beautiful mosaic pavement the excavators found an inscription, parallelopiped in shape, in honor of some martyrs who lived in the days of St. Jerome and St. Ambrose. The letters were cut into the mosaic and originally filled with colored paste mixed with crystalline powder, the cubes around the letters being of blue indigo color and of a vitreous substance. Each line of lettering was separated by a line of cubes of Venetian red, and the entire inscription was surrounded by seven lines of cubes of various colors. This curious inscription reads:

"A new construction after the old; Escychius his grandson, with the clergy and people, has finished it (in honor of) Synferius. Receive these labors as gratefully given to thy house, O Christ."

The word which we here translate "house," is written in its usual form, *domus,* but means "church." Another inscription recently discovered reads:

"Jesus Christ, King of Kings and Lord of Lords, may thine eyes be open in mercy day and night over thy house."

A funeral inscription dating from the end of the third century shows how even the soldiers and highest

government officials were at this time unashamed of
their Christianity:

"To Quintia . . . daughter of Quintus Germanus, a chief
centurion, a noble woman, who paid the debt of nature at the age
of thirty, Flavius Valens, special governor of Upper Pannonia,
to his beloved wife." [86]

From A.D. 303-305 multitudes of Christians suffered
martyrdom, and as early as A.D. 375 their tombs had
become so sacred that Constantine, ex-proconsul of
Africa, and his wife, Honoria, came back here choosing
for themselves a burial place "near to the martyrs."

Over 600 short inscriptions have been found, mostly
in the large Christian cemetery. This cemetery, as has
been previously indicated, has been a source of incalculable wealth to Christian epigraphy and martyr-
ology. It had been partially opened earlier, but in
1859 a farmer struck with his plow the cover of a
marble sarcophagus having engraved on the top of it
the story of Hippolytus and Phaedra. This roused
great interest, and soon other wonderful sarcophagi
were found, among which was the immense one of the
matron Asclepia, dating from the end of the third or
the beginning of the fourth century, known for its remarkable representation of the Good Shepherd. Several
Christian cemeteries have been found, but the most
important is this Manastirine cemetery, which Dr. Bulić
calls the "most important ever discovered," both because of a long uninterrupted series of monuments
dating from the first Christian generation up to the

---

[86] Jacques Zeiller, *Les Origines Chrétiennes dans la province romaine
de Dalmatie,* p. 85. This book gives many texts; a detailed description of
the early evangelization of Dalmatia, and good illustrations; also the
names of all the known Dalmatian Christians from the Diocletian era to
the sixth century so far as these are found in tradition or in the cemeteries
here.

seventh century, and because of the novelty of its architectural forms, but especially because of its intimate connection with celebrated historic martyrs such as St. Doimus (d. A.D. 107), whose tomb Dr. Bulić believes he has recovered.[87]

One other point should be remembered as showing the importance of the discovery of the ancient episcopal basilica mentioned above, with its surrounding buildings, baptistry, confirmation hall, episcopal palace, and hospice. If at Ravenna and Parenzo we see the early Christian basilica almost untouched in its architecture and the main lines of its decorative mosaics, better in fact than anywhere else in the world, it is to Salona that we must come to study the accessories and surroundings of the early churches."[88] Both the episcopal church, which was the city cathedral, and another suburban basilica (around which was located the large cemetery) have been thoroughly excavated. "In both basilicas numerous columns, capitals, mosaic pavements, cornices, parapets and screens, dating from the fourth to the sixth centuries, have been uncovered, giving us all the necessary elements for reconstructing the artistic appearance of the interior." Dr. Frothingham considers the confirmation hall of the suburban church, which contained the symbolic mosaic representing the stags drinking from the sacred fountain to be "the most perfect known."[89]

[87] With the exception of other authorities mentioned, this description was taken from *Guida di Spalato e Salona,* by Prof. Dr. L. Jelić, Mons. Dir. Fr. Bulić, e Professor S. Rutar, Zara, 1894, and in *Bullettino di archeol. e stor. dalm. a.* 1902, 1903, 1904, 1906; *Revue Biblique* October, 1915. I am indebted to Prof. Amos W. Patten of Northwestern University for first calling my attention to the special importance of these excavations.

[88] Frothingham, *op. cit.,* p. 279.

[89] *Op. cit.,* p. 281.

7. NEW LIGHT FROM FOURTH AND FIFTH CENTURY
CHRISTIAN BASILICAS AND SIXTH CENTURY
CHRISTIAN TOWNS STILL STANDING IN THE
DESERTS OF SYRIA

The Christian monuments of Syria constitute one
of the seventy wonders of modern archeological exploration. The "thousand and one churches" of Kara
Dagh recovered for us only twenty-six Christian
basilicas dating at the very earliest from the fourth century, and in all the rest of Asia Minor and in all European
Turkey, Italy, and North Africa—those rich centers of
primitive Christianity—scarcely an equal number of
equally ancient churches remain in a good state of preservation; yet in northern central Syria, within one hundred and fifty miles of Antioch, in a district measuring
not much more than a hundred miles square, not only
scores of fourth century churches have been found, but
also at least one hundred Christian towns and villages
stand practically uninjured, just as they were left by
their owners over thirteen hundred years ago.

There is no other land where the architectural monuments of antiquity have been preserved to us in such
large numbers, in such perfection, and in so many
varieties. But far better than this, these are monuments
of Christian architecture that show us the ordinary
town life of the Christians from the fourth to the seventh
century in a most vivid way. To the surprize of every
one, it is found that this was a population of wealth and
refinement, the houses being well lighted, well ven-
tilated, and beautifully ornamented. Wall paintings
and mosaics of rare workmanship and vessels of glass
in a hundred different shapes of rare beauty have been
found.

While some early travelers, like Burckhardt, Seetzen, de Laborde, Wetzstein, William Rey, M. Porter, and a few others had reported the existence of strange ghost cities in the trackless wilderness, it was the Marquis Charles Jean Melchior de Vogüé, with Waddington as his colleague, who first drew the attention of the learned world definitely to these architectural marvels. He made an extensive tour in 1861-62, and five years later published the results in two magnificent volumes which at once drew the attention of scholars.[90] De Vogüé reported that he had found over a hundred cities within a territory of seventy-five to a hundred miles, all built in practically the same style and dating from the same epoch, the epoch of primitive Christianity, thus throwing light on the most obscure era of historic art. These towns are in general so well preserved that one must "almost refuse to them the name of ruins." The life which they reveal is not that of the catacombs, hidden, secretive, and sepulchral, but the free and open life of unrestrained development under favorable conditions, "a large, opulent, artistic life, displaying itself in roomy dwellings built of heavy hewn stone, perfectly put together on a palatial plan," while the inscriptions bring to us voices from a previously unknown "Church triumphant." The inscriptions, however, are full of a Christian humility contrasting in a marked way with the bombast of the pagan inscriptions. They are almost universally architectural, not sepulchral, representing the utterances of the owners and architects of dwellings, churches, and other monuments. These Christians were not ashamed of their Christianity, for

[90] *L'Architecture civile et religieuse . . . dans la Syrie centrale,* Paris, 1865-1877.

almost every house was marked by the sign of the cross, while the well-known symbols of salvation were engraved on the doors and the windows, painted on the walls, and embroidered on the garments.

De Vogüé reported that all the constructions in this district earlier than the first century had totally disappeared, either because made of less durable material than was used by later builders, or because previous to the Roman period this part of Syria could not have been policed or made safe for colonists. He also pointed out that these towns represent a line of frontier posts which were then in the most prosperous condition, altho now several days' journey from cultivated territory. By the end of the first century there grew up in all directions "houses, palaces, baths, temples, theaters, aqueducts, arches of triumph, and cities built in the style of all the Roman colonies," a Greek style modified by local interests.[91]

It was nearly forty years after De Vogüé's great journey before any additional work of an equally thorough nature was done in this strange country, but in 1899-1900, 1904-1905, and 1909, the American and Princeton Archeological Expeditions to Syria conducted elaborate investigations under the direction of Prof. Howard Crosby Butler with Dr. William Prentice as his colleague, the latter having special charge of the Greek and Latin inscriptions.[91a] The results of this expedition, worthily published by Professor Butler, in sumptuous double-folios, of which ten volumes have already appeared, represent the finest monument of American

[91] De Vogüé, op. cit., pp. 1-6.

[91a] The expedition of 1899-1900 was not a Princeton undertaking but was called the American expedition.

scholarship in the field of Christian archeology. The writer feels himself wholly unable to give in a brief summary any adequate conception of the magnitude and importance of these discoveries, but in order so far as possible to do this, he will freely use Professor Butler's facts and felicitous phrases.

This first American expedition made an elaborate and thorough search of the entire region previously explored by De Vogüé in north central Syria. The explorers visited every site previously described and discovered many new sites and important archeological remains; they also visited every site described by De Vogüé in the Djebel Hauran with the exception of three. They procured an enormous number of dated monuments, and were able not only to corroborate the general results obtained by De Vogüé but also to correct him in numbers of instances and to add largely to his results in many directions. It was elaborately proved that the architecture used was not Byzantine but an alliance between the Greek style and some hitherto unknown oriental style. The latest dated inscription was A.D. 609. After this building activity seems to have ceased abruptly, probably because of the lack of rain, perhaps due indirectly to the cutting down of the forests, and more directly to the coming of the Persians, A.D. 538, who not only destroyed the olive groves but also practically destroyed the country.[91b] It was found that the people of the northern half of Northern Syria were poorer and were more influenced from Antioch, while those of the southern half were richer and more in-

[91b] Professor Butler writes me that the first invasion of Syria by the Persians in 538 does not seem to have affected the smaller cities or towns of Syria. But the second invasion under Chosroes II. (590-628) seems to have put an end to the Christian civilization here.

fluenced from Apamea; yet strangely enough in the north was found the "most magnificent ruin of early Christian architecture in the world—the church of St. Simeon Stylites at Kal'at Simân." This church was probably not, however, merely a local enterprise, but was built by contributions throughout all Christendom.

The earliest well-preserved Christian churches date from the fourth century, tho the Christians were a considerable part of the population as early as the third century. Previous to this the architects were non-Christians, and the work was in the usual classic style as found in the provinces. Perhaps one most interesting of the pre-Christian ruins consists of the subterranean rockhewn tombs at Il-Maghârah. These are very elaborate and magnificent, but contain no inscriptions nor sarcophagi. The civic buildings of the second century are less grandiose but more refined than the third century ruins at Baalbec.

With the fourth century, as we have said, the dated monuments become numerous and a large majority of these are Christian. It is often only by the inscriptions that certain basilicas can be known as churches, since these are made in exact imitation of the public buildings of the Romans of the previous period. The private houses are often most elegantly built, and the pyramid tombs, such as the mausoleum at Rbêah and the miniature temple at Ruwêhā (A.D. 384), are often "marvels of construction." The pyramid tomb just mentioned was corbelled in, and built without mortar or clamps of metal, and can probably be compared favorably with any pyramid tomb in the world.

We continue to follow Prof. Howard Crosby Butler and read with delighted surprize his description of a

Christian villa at Ruwêhā in the Djebel Rîhā (A.D. 396). The plan is a great square, on the north side of which rises a long two-story building having four compartments in each story and a two-story portico in front. On the west side of the court are two large compartments with the entrance—a triple gateway—between them. The entrance is guarded by a tower, which also doubtless served as a porter's lodge. The ornamentation is fine, and many Christian symbols are carved in prominent places. All the more expensive dwellings have private stables at the back of the courtyard; the more modest houses have these on the ground floor. The stairs of the houses, usually of stone, are always on the outside, usually at one end of the portico.

One of the strangest things connected with these early Christian towns is found in the light thrown on the "captains of industry" at this early era. In some instances whole blocks have been preserved showing the shops of the fourth century. These are a series of small two-story dwellings with only a doorway on the ground floor of each, but with doors and windows on the floor above. Universally there is a long, low, two-story portico in front. The lower chambers were evidently used as storehouses for the merchandise which was displayed during the day in the portico fronting the street. The upper story was undoubtedly the home of the proprietor. Christian inscriptions are found upon many of these shops. Business men of that era were not ashamed of their Christianity. One inscription written A.D. 350 reads:

"One God, one Christ, be a helper to Flavius
Eusebios, buyer and builder."

Between the fourth and fifth centuries there was

some development in architecture, so that strange styles of capitals and a new and rich Christian symbolism appear. In the fifth century classic models of ornamentation are less and less used. The churches of this era, instead of the nine arches on either side of the nave as in the fourth century, now have seven and sometimes five arches, and the central nave becomes much wider and the apse arch much broader, while bands of chain and basket work ornament the moldings. The churches are large and magnificent, often having splendid baptistries in connection with them, and vast inns for the accommodation of pilgrims; they often stand inside of strong forts, whose towers occasionally, as at Kasr il-Benât, rise to six stories in height. The ecclesiastical dwellings around the churches are small and of the simplest rectangular style, almost entirely devoid of moldings. The shops of the fifth century are substantially like those of the fourth, while the houses with restaurants and baths near by prove that luxury and wealth still continued.

The sixth century saw the elaboration and perfection of all the architectural motifs that had been initiated and developed in the two centuries preceding. This was the century that produced the church of St. Simeon Stylites and many others of magnificent proportions and splendid perfection of details. Professor Butler shows that these Syrian Christians were better architects than even those royal engineers of Justinian who designed and executed the famous Saint Sophia in Constantinople. Altho their work was not so stupendous and awe inspiring, it was more symmetrical and beautiful. We dare not attempt to describe the many beautiful churches photographed and minutely described by

Professor Butler in his great volumes, but will merely add that Professor Butler declares too much can not be said of the beauty of the interior decorations and the crisp and graceful carving of the great archivolts, the elaborate and flowing ornament of the chancel arch, the bold treatment of the foliage of the great capitals of the piers of the naves, and the graceful turnings of the slender colonnettes.

So far as domestic architecture is concerned, the sixth century offers to us several very fine palatial Christian residences. One of these at Serdjilla is a double house of imposing appearance, while several at Ruwêhā are real mansions, in some cases so well preserved that they need only roofs and a few minor repairs to make them quite worthy to be used as town residences for wealthy gentlemen of the twentieth century. In the sixth century three-story houses were not uncommon in the cities, and the rear entrances, as well as those in front, began to be made attractive. The beauty of some of the doorways and windows could hardly be surpassed in any modern structure. The wood and bronze doors of ancient times have disappeared, but some very fine doors of black basalt remain. These were hung with such mechanical perfection that they still "swing so easily upon their ball and socket hinges that they can be moved by one finger."

The first Princeton archeological expedition to Syria (1904-5) re-examined certain sites previously explored by the first expedition, and then passed to other regions farther north, which few travelers had ever reached, and where only four or five buildings had been mentioned by De Vogüé, and only a few others by the first American expedition.

The technical diversities of style between the different sections of Syria and between the fourth, fifth, and sixth century architecture in each section are elaborately set forth by the distinguished director of the expedition. Space restrains us from attempting even to hint at these important comparisons.

Perhaps of most popular interest would be Professor Butler's observations concerning the Christian architecture of the fourth century in this district which, as in those previously examined, shows every variety of structure required by a civilized people. Here, as elsewhere, were perfectly developed basilicas of the fourth century; public baths as luxurious as those of pagan times, the best preserved houses of antiquity—not excepting those of Pompeii—and mausoleums of great magnificence. It was found that classical ornament, in the hands of these Syrian architects, was infused with a luxuriant grace unknown at Rome, while some of the most stupendous and some of the richest buildings of the Roman empire were erected here. The Christian period of architecture in Syria did not inaugurate a decline as it did in Europe, but began a new, fresh, and vigorous style that continued in its prime until cut off by Mohammedanism.

The oldest architectural fragment could be dated by inscription to A.D. 73, and similarly the oldest church to A.D. 372. In the mountains of northern Syria the vault was very little used, and then in a style peculiar to this region. The building material here was almost exclusively limestone and produced effects often "unmatched for beauty." In the 'Ala plateau the vault was used more than elsewhere; while basalt was the ordinary building material, houses were occasionally

TEMPLE OF JUPITER (ESCULAPIUS)?
AT SPALATO

From Kowalczyk and Gurlitt's "Denkmäler der
Kunst in Dalmatien," 1910

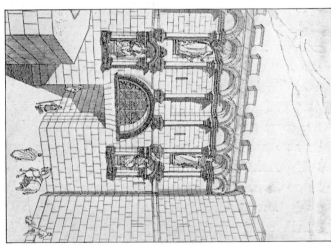

THE GOLDEN GATE AT SPALATO
(RECONSTRUCTED)

From "Jahrbuch des archäologischen Instituts,"
XXIV, Abt. 2, p. 49

DETAIL OF PERISTYLE AT SPALATO

From Kowalczyk and Gurlitt's "Denkmäler der
Kunst in Dalmatien," 1910

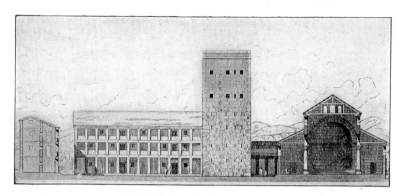

CHRISTIAN CONVENT (A.D. 390-418)
From Butler, "Ancient Architecture in Syria"

OCTAGONAL CHURCH AND RESTAURANT AT MONDJELEIA, SYRIA
From De Vogüé, "L'Architecture dans la Syrie centrale." (Vol. 2)

constructed of quadrated limestone blocks, and towns
built of sun-dried bricks—tho such towns have now
completely disappeared except for mounds of clay. All
the churches were built on the basilica plan, altho sometimes containing unique features, and were usually
roofed with beams of great length. One church, A.D.
582, very nearly anticipates by 500 years the Lombard
and French Romanesque system, which has vaults constructed above the nave and side aisles. The Kasr Ibn
Wardan church, which is situated on the rolling desert
far from contemporary buildings, is the most imposing
of all ancient sites in northern Syria, and is in some
respects the most remarkable of all. Seen from a distance its ruins "loom up like the vision of some great
modern city"; yet it represents a group of only three
buildings, a square domed church, a large palace, and
the military barracks. The bricks of which these buildings are partially composed came from Constantinople
kilns. Tradition declares these bricks were made of
clay mixed with rose water. Professor Butler believes
this church, like those at il-Anderîn and Fálul, may have
been built by an architect from Antioch. A fine-grained
white limestone and rare marbles of various colors were
used in the shafts and capitals of the interior, while the
floors, and possibly some of the walls, were covered
with beautiful mosaics. The local basalt was used for
the foundation, the lintels, and the jambs, and alter-
nated with brick in the walls. The church was sur-
mounted by a dome about sixty-five feet high, and its
great arched windows and the walls of the lower story
still stand almost intact. The palace, which was two
stories in height, measures 162 by 170 feet, and is
almost as handsomely built as the church. Professor

Butler believes that the windows of the palace were glazed, and indeed fragments of flat glass have been found in the ruins. Great churches were usually attached to forts from the middle to the end of the sixth century, and several of these constructions built of this imported brick may represent colonies of princes or ecclesiastical dignitaries banished by the reigning emperor.

The Djebel il-'Ala and Djebel Bārîsha are bordered by the Roman road running from Antioch to Aleppo. Here both American expeditions found and described many ruins. This differed from the Djebel Rihā in having no rich suburban villas, all the town buildings being huddled together evidently for business purposes. These towns ordinarily had gardens in the plaza, two or three churches—finer in most cases than those of Djebel Rihā,—and occasionally a watch tower; but the centers of the towns were exclusively given up to shops. The inscriptions, too, were found in three languages, Greek, Latin, and Syriac, showing that these ancient Christians were in close touch with cosmopolitan business centers.

From this business district twenty-five Christian churches have been examined, two of these dating from the fourth century, seven from the fifth, and fifteen from the sixth. None of these are of the first magnitude, the largest measuring only about eighty feet in length, and the smaller something over fifty feet. The architecture is less dignified than that of the more southern districts; and altho often very rich, there is the over-elaboration which shows lack of culture. In connection with the churches, inns are often found. These have no courtyards nor enclosed gardens as private residences have. They face the street or open square and have no dividing walls in the lower story, the entire space on the first floor being longitudinally divided by a row of mangers. One inn was definitely dated A.D. 436, while the shops and bazaars in Dâr Kìta were erected A.D. 350-354. The funereal architecture here is particularly impressive, some of the fifth century tombs, built out of polygonal blocks of limestone, comparing favorably in technique with the best examples in Greece.

Limestone, as we have said, represents the main building material in the mountains of North Syria; but some doors of imported basalt—for example those at Sêra—are beautiful beyond description, both in their design and execution. In northern central Syria wood and other materials are used more commonly. The largest cathedral known in northern central Syria is found at Kerrātin (cir. A.D. 500), measuring 195 feet long by 85 feet wide. In north central Syria, in the Djebel Rihā, the architectural materials are more varied and the structure and ornament are exquisitely beautiful. Among the thirty ancient towns excavated in this region there are several which show a type having no parallel in any part of the ancient world. Serdjilla is such a town, having no streets, alleys, bazaars, shops, or poor quarter; being composed wholly of elegant residential villas with one or two churches, and some rich ornamental tombs fringing the outskirts.

It betokens advanced civilization and a high degree of public order, as Professor Butler well points out, when people can live in safety and in such luxury as this. These were not powerful lords or millionaires, but well-to-do people of the middle class.

The necropolis of Serdjilla was rifled in ancient times, but a number of very large and beautiful sarcophagi were found. The bath here dates from A.D. 473, and is the most perfect building of its kind in Syria. M. De Vogüé describes this bath, but the American expedition found the many colored mosaic pavement with an inscription giving the date of its erection and the name of the donors, Julianos and his wife, Domna. The bath contains many rooms, was well fitted to give cold, hot, and vapor baths, and was elaborately decorated, the mosaic probably being its chief adornment. It is intensely interesting to notice that this best preserved bath in Syria, and perhaps in the world, dating from a time immediately after Constantine, was found in a Christian community and for the benefit of a Christian population. In connection with the bath was a "café."

At Il-Barah were found a large and a small church and some monumental tombs which are the finest in the entire region. At Ruwêhā many acres were covered with ruins of shops, churches, wonderfully preserved tombs, and splendid villas. This town, like the others we have described, touched its most flourishing period in the fourth century. The north church in this city is the largest in the district. In some respects it is the most important church in north Syria, owing to the T-form of the piers of the nave which supported not only the usual longitudinal arches but two higher transverse arches that spanned the nave, dividing the plan into three equal squares. Transverse arches carrying gables—reducing the number of roof trestles—is a new feature in ecclesiastical architecture, as this church dates from the fifth, or at the latest from the early sixth,

CHRISTIAN TOMB FROM RUWÊHÂ,
SYRIA (A.D. 384)
American Expedition to Syria, 1899-1900

CHRISTIAN TOMB, REBÊFAH
(4th Century)
American Expedition to Syria, 1899-1900

CHRISTIAN TOMB, MARATA, SYRIA (5th Century)
Butler, "Ancient Architecture in Syria," II. B., Part 2, 111, 103

CHURCH OF ST. GEORGE AT ZORAH, SYRIA
American Expedition to Syria

BASALT DOOR OF A CHRIS-
TIAN HOUSE, KHAN SEBIL,
SYRIA (4th or 5th Century)
American Expedition to Syria

A CHRISTIAN CHAPEL AT KFELLŪSIN, SYRIA (A.D. 500-550)
From Butler, "Ancient Architecture in Syria"

CHURCH AND PALACE IN THE DESERT IN NORTH SYRIA (A.D. 561-564)
From Butler, "Ancient Architecture in Syria"

CHRISTIAN HOUSE FROM DILLŌZA, NORTH SYRIA (6th Century)
From Butler, "Ancient Architecture in Syria"

century. The ornamentation is rich, yet reserved and used to the best advantage.

The first American expedition made some of its best discoveries in the Djebel Halakah, which is situated to the northeast of the great plain of Sermedā, through which runs the great road from Antioch to Aleppo. The ruins are very similar to those at Djebel Bārîsha and Djebel il-'Ala. The earliest inscription here dates from Refâdeh, A.D. 73, and the earliest dated house (which is built of polygonal cut stone) from A.D. 207. In general the architecture is the same as formerly described, but the rock-cut tombs of Katura are unique in central Syria. These tombs, which are cut from the solid rock, are carved elaborately and contain remarkable reliefs. Sometimes as many as four seated figures are to be found cut in a tomb, altho in the majority of cases only a single figure is represented. These sepulchers belonged to the pagan forefathers of the Syrian Christians. They must, at the latest, have been cut very shortly after the end of the third century, since Katura became predominantly Christian A.D. 366.

A tower house, five stories in height, was discovered at Serdjibleh, and at Kafr Hauwâr another was found four stories high; what is much stranger, there was a good sewer of original design connected with one of these buildings, the pipe being made of terra cotta and the whole construction furnishing "proof of an advanced state of what might be called sanitary plumbing at this early date." This was not the only locality where sewerage was provided, for Professor Butler says: "The latrinae of many houses in the Hauran have niches or brackets for water jars in their side walls, and others have wash hand basins corbelled out from their walls. If the degree of advance in these particulars which have to do with sanitation and personal cleanliness is to be taken as an index of progress and civilization, we must infer that the civilization of Syria in the fourth and fifth centuries was considerably in advance of that of large parts of Europe at the present day."

In the Hauran—which lies far south of the other districts visited, being close to Galilee—the American expedition examined many important sites. While the Christian buildings here do not look in their ruined condition to be so fine as those in north Syria, this is because of the poor mortar, which when it falls away makes only too visible the rough stones. Originally, however, the buildings were covered with colored plaster, and the churches and private dwellings were really larger and more attractive than those in the north. The stucco was very fine and hard, so that moldings of this material looked almost as fine and beautiful as marble, while the colors—grays, greens, deep reds, pale blues, browns, and soft yellows—must have originally made these towns look more attractive than many modern watering-places. It must be added, however, that the interior ornamentation, while simple and virile, was not as refined and beautiful as in the north. At Umm is-Surab the expedition found a fifth century church which proved to be a true basilica of three aisles separated by two rows of five columns each and having an upper story or gallery over the side aisles. It was the only church found in the Hauran with a gallery. Around the church was just such a group of ecclesiastical residences as may be found about the cloistered courts of the medieval abbeys of north Europe. Several of the churches had heathen temples adjoining them, which had been turned to Christian purposes.

It gives us a new impression of early Christianity to be told by Professor Butler that even some of the stables of these primitive Christians are built of stone carefully drest, handsomely finished, and fitted together with great care, the jambs and all the lintels of the doorways being highly finished. At il-Medjdel a Christian city was found with straight streets containing rectangular blocks of houses, and even boasting of sidewalks on one or both sides. One house (A.D. 431), which stood at the street corner, had two stories of high arched apartments in front and four stories of ordinary height in the rear, and a large stable behind it. This was the residence of a single family, yet the upper story, in true oriental fashion, was completely cut off from the lower, being reached by an outside staircase. There were five rooms in the upper story; this being, according to Professor Butler, the women's quarters.

Umm il-Kuttên is one of the largest of the ruined towns of the southern Hauran. It extended over half a mile from north to south and its streets were broad and straight. On the outside of the town were several reservoirs, one of these being over 200 feet long, 85 feet wide, and 16 feet deep. At Dêr il-Kahf a fortress was found containing 114 rooms dating from the year when Constantine became Cæsar.[92]

Dr. William Kelly Prentice was the expert to decipher the Greek and Latin inscriptions found during

[92] The above description has been taken from the following works: *Architecture and Other Arts,* by Howard Crosby Butler, N. Y., 1903. *The Princeton University Archæological Expeditions to Syria,* by Howard Crosby Butler, 1907; *Ancient Architecture in Syria,* by Howard Crosby Butler, Leyden, 1910; *Princeton University Archæological Expedition to Syria,* 1904-5, Parts I-V, Leyden, 1907-1914.

the first American archeological expedition. Of the
283 inscriptions discovered in north central Syria, over
100 were definitely dated. A large number of these
had to do with the pagan life (A.D. 60-250) which preceded the domination of Christianity in this region, but
our interest centers in the Christian inscriptions dating
A.D. 324-609; altho one text (A.D. 50-100) should be
made an exception since it mentions "King Agrippa,
Friend of Cæsar."

Some of the more interesting liturgical inscriptions
read as follows:

"Holy God, Holy Mighty One, Holy Immortal One, Crucified
for us, have mercy upon us."
"Glory to the Father, and to the Son, and to the Holy Spirit."
(A.D. 369.)

It is thrilling to find painted on a wall of the sixth
century this liturgical hymn:

"Though immortal he endured many sufferings—Jesus the Christ.
Of David's race a heavenly branch—Jesus the Christ.
Extol the Only Begotten, Immortal One in all the earth—Jesus
the Christ.
In compassion he descended from the heavens upon the earth—
Jesus the Christ.
Teacher of true life from everlasting—Jesus the Christ."

The last three words of each line of this hymn are a
cryptogram of three numerals. These cryptograms are
frequently found; in one case the number 8051 being
written upon a door-post; meaning "The Lord shall
preserve thy coming in and thy going out, from now
even for evermore. Amen." (Ps. 121:8.)

The funereal inscriptions are numerous. Sometimes they imitate the pagan formula:

"Ah why, when about to face the dreadful voyage, hast thou
not taken me, but hast left to me, tenderly loving, such a wealth of

woe, bereaving my house, removing to another land? Alas, a miserable lot hath fate to mortals meted out."

"Life is a wheel! Vanity of vanities, all is vanity!"

"Thou runnest, I run—unto where? Unto here."

The Christian epitaphs frequently contain the expression:

"Hail, ye passers-by, and offer ye prayers for him."

On the Bizzos tomb (sixth century) is carved this suggestive word:

"I sojourned well, I journeyed well, and well I lie at rest.
Pray for me."

Another epitaph which may not be Christian but which ends as many Christian inscriptions end, reads:

"Farewell, loved places! Thou joy of enemies, grief of children, expectation of the aged, healer of troubles, anguish of the rich, desire of the wretched, with no respect of persons, making equal all, thee none may escape! An eternal dwelling has Thalabathos, son of Ansos, built for himself and his children and his dependents. Be of good cheer, my soul; no one is immortal."

Occasionally we have an extended theological inscription, as in the case of Eusebios and Antoninos (fifth century):

"Thou who gavest life to the human race and didst enjoin death on account of transgression, and in thine own loving-kindness and tender mercy didst promise a resurrection and gavest us the pledge (the Holy Spirit) . . . Christ, visit with thy salvation thy servant Antoninos . . . and the others who lie at rest here, that they may see the good of thy chosen."

About 1,200 Greek inscriptions were copied by the Princeton expedition (1904-1905). Many of these were dated and some were exceedingly important from a historical or linguistic standpoint. Besides the Greek inscriptions there were 100 Nabatean, 1,300 North Arabic, and several hundred in other languages; but of these we need not speak.

About 100 of these Greek inscriptions came from the 'Ala, eight of them belonging to the fourth century, and over sixty to the sixth century. Often in these sepulchral epitaphs we see the deceased spoken of as "ever-victorious," "care-free," etc. Some of the more noticeable epitaphs read:

Where Christ is gracious every man is happy"; "An eternal place of dwelling, and at least for those who lived piously a gateway of Holy Paradise"; "Be of good cheer . . . no one on earth is immortal."

One epitaph, which immediately strikes attention because of its resemblance to those so often found in old English and American graveyards, reads:

"Verily, I say to thee, I was as thou also art; as I am, thou shalt also be."

On the churches all over Syria, texts of Scripture may be found, and other inscriptions similar to those used at the present day, such as, "Enter into his gates with thanksgiving and into his courts with praise." It also seems natural to see on the lintels of private houses the term, "Good Luck"; but it seems strange to find carved over houses and baths and barracks such words as "Life," "Light," and such expressions as those given below:

"This is the gate of the Lord; the righteous shall enter in it."
"Our Lord Jesus Christ dwells here, the Son and Word of God. Let no evil enter."
"Of this house the Lord shall guard the entrance and the exit; for the cross being set before, an evil eye shall not have power."
"If God be for you, who is he that is against you?"
"What is the name of the bath? Health! Through this entering, Christ hath opened for us the bath of healing."

Sometimes the inscriptions on these civic and do-

mestic buildings are strongly theological, especially in
the sixth century:

"May the Trinity, our God, drive envy far away! O Image of
the Heavenly Word of God, O kindly Light, thou art Christ,
thou who hast built the world, incomprehensible(?), grant me
prosperity, and grant thy grace, unfailing ever! Christ, ever
living, . . . frees from ill; therefore I fear no designs of evil,
no working demon, no hateful and lawless eye of man."

Many of these inscriptions had, without doubt, primary
reference to deliverance from evil spirits; yet there
must have been, nevertheless, a fine spiritual consciousness back of many of these seemingly spontaneous
utterances.

Prayers of dead saints are invoked from the earliest
eras. One text which is unique reads: "Prayers of
apostles, prophets, martyrs for the renewal of the
synagog and people." The Christian kindness of this
early population is everywhere manifest, as in this inscription on a house lintel: "Abraham received the
angels in hospitality" (cf. Heb. 13:2). The modern
Church may well rejoice over these newly discovered
evidences of the character of the early Syrian Church
which reached such unprecedented prosperity so soon
after the martyr period. These ancient towns show
many characteristics which might happily be imitated
by modern Christian villages.[93]

The unique value of these Syrian discoveries begins
to dawn upon us when we note that in all Egypt only
three or four poorly preserved church or ecclesiastical

[93] The above inscriptions have been selected from the multitude which
Dr. W. K. Prentice and his colleagues, Drs. Enno Littmann, David
Magie, and Duane Reed Stuart have published: *Greek and Latin Inscrip-
tions in Syria*, in *Ancient Architecture in Syria*, Division III, Leyden,
1914; *Princeton University Archæological Expedition to Syria*, Parts I-V,
Leyden 1908-12, Div. III.

buildings date from the fourth century; and in all Italy and Palestine very few more can be found. The earliest basilicas in Rome, such as the Vatican, St. Peter's, and St. Paul's, outside the walls, have long since lost their original character; the same thing can be said with equal truth of St. Helena's buildings in Jerusalem; and in Constantinople only one basilica dates as early as the fifth century. Nowhere else on earth can there be found standing, practically unrepaired and uninjured, so many early churches as in this strange desert land of Syria—and nowhere else can we walk through the streets of a well-built Christian town over 1,500 years old.

II

NEW LIGHT FROM FAMOUS CITIES MEN-
TIONED IN THE NEW TESTAMENT

1. Recent Excavations at Ephesus

A PILE of beautiful white marble chips, which I gathered two years ago upon the site of the Temple of Diana, lies on my table as I write. It was difficult to find even this slight evidence that on that spot once stood the most celebrated temple, next to Solomon's, which was ever constructed. It was rightly classed among the "seven wonders of the world"; yet even the real name of the goddess (Artemis) has practically perished from memory, being replaced by the Latinized form Diana, while the little village built on the ancient temple grounds is named in memory of St. John—who according to a very old tradition spent the closing years of his life in Ephesus—and the prominent tower of Astyages is called the "Prison of St. Paul."

The romantic story of the digging up of this ancient temple has been told in a most fascinating way by its discoverer, Mr. J. T. Wood.[1] Twenty years after Wood had finished his researches the Austrian Archæological Institute began work at this famous city, publishing its final results in two magnificent volumes in 1906 and 1912.[2] It was on May 2, 1863, that Mr. Wood began

---

[1] *Discoveries at Ephesus,* 1877; *Modern Discoveries on the Site of Ancient Ephesus,* 1890.

[2] *Forschungen in Ephesos veröffentlicht vom österreichisch-archäologischen Institut,* 1906-1912.

searching for this most famous monument of antiquity. He found the boundary wall of its sacred precincts on May 2, 1869. How he found it is a thrilling story. He had been digging up the ancient city of Ephesus but had discovered no sign of the temple excepting a few inscriptions. But on one of these inscriptions, to be mentioned later, he found a description of one of the temple processions in which it was stated that in carrying the sacred images of the goddess from the theater to the temple the cavalcade passed through the Magnesian gate. This proved that the temple was outside of the city, and the excavator began at once to trace the city walls. He soon found a magnificent gateway with three openings, two for vehicles and one for foot passengers, the deep ruts in the marble pavement showing how much it had been traveled in ancient times. The road was thirty-five feet wide and the paving stones were of fine marble. No one of us who have ever stood upon this pavement and looked back upon the great theater—and at its side the wonderful ancient marble library, more imposing than any Mr. Carnegie has built—can ever forget the sight.

Mr. Wood followed this sacred road for a mile around the mountain uncovering the funeral monuments with which it was lined and taking note of the porticoes built in ancient times to shelter pilgrims on their way to the temple. Then he began, inside of the ancient sacred *temenos,* to hunt for the ruins of the temple itself, and on December 31, 1869, at a depth of twenty feet, he came upon its white marble pavement made of slabs of pure marble three inches thick. For five years longer he worked here, employing from 100 to 300 native laborers digging up the magnificent capitals and sculptured columns and massive blocks in white, blue, red and yellow marble, now to be seen in the Ephesus gallery of the British Museum. He found six or more wonderfully sculptured drums from ancient columns, so huge that it took fifteen men fifteen days to lift one of them from the pavement. These drums were twenty feet in circumference and six feet high, having eight figures, all of life size, sculptured on them. He found some splendid statues, like that of Hercules struggling with the Queen of the Amazons; what was more important, he discovered hundreds of temple inscriptions; so that when his excavations ended in 1874, he had cleared away over 132,000 cubic yards of débris from the ancient site, and was able to report with certainty and fulness concerning this temple so famous in heathen and early Christian history.

The temple was octagonal, and about 160 feet in width by 340 in length; its richness may be imagined when we notice that, instead of mortar, gold is reputed to have been used between the joints of the marble blocks. The *cella,* or Holy of Holies, was seventy feet wide and open to the sky. Here was found *in situ* what the excavator believed to be the foundation of the ancient altar, twenty feet square, close to which must have stood the divine statue. Many fragments were found of the large white marble tiles which covered the roof of the temple and of the double rows of fluted columns in the peristyle. Over 700 inscriptions were also brought to light.[3]

From the ruins and from these inscriptions many facts were learned concerning the history and ritual of

[3] See particularly *Ancient Greek Inscriptions in the British Museum,* part III, section II, by Rev. E. L. Hicks, 1890, to which work we are constantly indebted.

the temple, most of which have been confirmed and supplemented by later excavations. The earliest temple, which took a century in building, was completed 480 B.C., just about the time Ezra was bringing back the exiles to Jerusalem. When the temple was burned on the night Alexander the Great was born, all Asia helped in its restoration. The temple worship was never more enthusiastic, seemingly, than at the era when Paul visited Ephesus. Augustus (5 B.C.) built the boundaries of the temple, within which limits asylum to criminals was promised, and the next year ordered a rebuilding of a large part of the temple. We know that in A.D. 4 the canals leading from the temple to the sea were repaired, and the votive gifts prove that the temple was increasing in wealth during the first Christian century. It was captured by the Goths in the middle of the third century and left desolate; a little later, when the early Christians became dominant at Ephesus, it was completely destroyed. The earliest excavator actually found the kiln in which these Christians turned into lime such marble blocks as they could not utilize in other buildings. It is literally true that, with the exception of a little pile of inferior foundations, not one stone remains above another of this most glorious structure.

Many hundreds, if not thousands, of priests must have been connected with the temple ritual, and many of the priestly cells have been found within the temple area. While honors were paid in the city and even in the temple to Poseidon, Demeter, Dionysos, and other deities, yet Artemis (Diana) was supreme, and her priests ever preceded those who had charge of the cult connected with the adoration of the emperor. In the month Artemision (March-April), dedicated especially to this goddess, the greatest of all the religious festivals was held, during which there were athletic, dramatic, and musical contests in connection with the ritual. These festivals were celebrated with especial glory every fourth year. In a most interesting decree dating from A.D. 162, which Hicks thinks to have represented an anti-Christian demonstration, it is decreed that all the days of that month shall be sacred holidays in honor of the goddess.

The head of the temple hierarchy was the Megabyzus, or chief priest, who was probably a Persian. A multitude of priestesses, who came as virgins to the temple, were dedicated to prostitution in the temple's service.[4] These vestals were presided over, at least in the early period, by a eunuch priest. The bee which is engraved on so many of the temple coins was the symbol of the Ephesian priesthood, perhaps symbolizing its organization, ritual chastity, and beneficent industry; perhaps having a mantic significance, the bee in Greek myth being connected with the foretelling of events.[5] Another important college of the priests was called Essenes (drones), while the priestesses were called Melissae (working bees). One important college of priests, which passed several decrees in honor of the emperor, wore a peculiarly rich dress marking them as engaged in some particularly honorable service of the goddess, and received therefore as their special name

[4] Dr. Percy Gardner, *The Ephesian Gospel*, 1915, believes that altho at Babylon the temple of Artemis was a seat of prostitution, at Ephesus, through Greek influence, her worship was conducted "in far less repulsive guise." Yet he admits that there were "elements of sexual impurity" in her festivals where crowds of priestesses performed "orgiastic dances" in her honor.

[5] See *Journal for Hellenic Studies*, XV, 1-24.

"gold wearers"; still another priestly caste—who probably had to do with the transcribing and interpreting of the sacred legends—were called "theologians."

Music must have had a great part in the service. A boy's choir seems to have been connected with the temple, and one inscription speaks of a golden chaplet being voted to a Bœotian flute player who had won honors during a festival. Like most ancient temples, this sanctuary was a bank of deposit, and the "elders" or "presbyters" are mentioned as having charge of the temple accounts.

The "Asiarchs," "town clerk" and "temple-keeper," mentioned in the Acts (19: 31, 35), are officers well-known from the inscriptions. The Asiarchs were provincial, not municipal, officers, who traveled in great state accompanied by a train of long-haired pages, and had special charge of the great festival in adoration of the emperor, at which time each Asiarch tried to outdo his predecessor in the games which he provided for the people at his own expense. One of his titles was "high-priest of Asia," his wife also being "high-priestess." One monument in honor of one of these Asiarchs mentions the troop of gladiators which had been slaughtered at a particular show. Altho there was only one Asiarch in office at any one time, there must have been many ex-Asiarchs, since this official was changed every quadrennium; so that there is now hardly any need of explaining the Asiarchs of Acts 19: 31 as referring to a problematical "council" of Asiarchs at Ephesus, as Sir William Ramsay does.[6]

The town clerk (γραμματεύς) was a most important

---

[6] Hastings, *Dictionary of the Bible*, "Asiarchs"; *cf. Journal of Hellenic Studies*, 1910, p. 261.

personage, as is known from the inscriptions. He was responsible for the form of the decrees which were submitted to the popular assembly and helped to draft them; he sealed such decrees with the public seal; he often proposed decrees and acted as chairman at popular meetings, which meetings were commonly held in the theater; he had charge of the money bequeathed to the people; in fact, he was so great a man that events are sometimes dated by reference to the year when such and such a town clerk held office.

When the town clerk called Ephesus the "temple-keeper" (νεωκόρος) of Diana he is using the exact expression used in various inscriptions where the city is spoken of as "temple-keeper of the divine emperor." The local color of the Bible narrative can be vividly seen by comparing with Acts 19: 27-35 an inscription recently dug up at Ephesus which speaks of the city as:

"The first and greatest metropolis of Asia and twice temple-keeper of the Emperors, according to the decrees of the sacred assembly and temple-keeper of Artemis," etc.[7]

In an inscription found in the Diana temple, excavated in 1910-13 at Sardis, one of these temple-keepers is mentioned as having been "treasurer of the kingdom." The title *Neōkoros* is the same as that given to the official who had charge of the Jewish synagog in an Egyptian village two centuries before Christ, and is yet the current title in Greece for the sacristan of an orthodox church or Jewish synagog.[8]

There were twelve temple wardens in the Ephesian

[7] Greek text published in *Forschungen in Ephesos*, II, 163.

[8] So Reinach, quoted by Moulton and Milligan under νεωκόρος in their Vocabulary given in the London *Expositor*.

temple, two being constantly in service, the term of office being two months each. One inscription declares that both of these were required to accompany processions in order to see that the sacred images got safely to and from the temple. They were required to be present also when the images were cleaned; they had charge of the sacrifices; they were treasurers of certain temple funds and took the fines due to the goddess; they had general charge of the temple and temple repairs. In addition to this one of these is mentioned as "chairman of the board of corn commissioners." It is an interesting fact that they were elected or confirmed by a state assembly called "ekklēsia." [9] The shout of the mob, "Great is Diana (Artemis)!" is now shown to have been a common formula in the Artemis worship.

Artemis is mentioned in every inscription, being sometimes called the "saviour goddess." Her image, which according to tradition had fallen from heaven (Acts 19: 35), was probably an aerolite which had been roughly shaped into a mummy form, sometimes pictured as a many-breasted, hideous idol. It is better known than almost any other ancient image. She was adored as the mother of life and nourisher of all the creatures of the earth, air, and sea.

During the years 1904-1905, Mr. D. G. Hogarth excavated at Ephesus. On the site of the old temple he found two beautifully carved heads and some minor fragments of sculpture, and below the remains of the sixth century temple he uncovered the foundations of a much smaller temple built of yellow limestone. Over 2,000 small dedicatory gifts were brought to light, as well as the greatest treasure-trove ever discovered here, con-

[9] Hicks, op. cit., DLXXIX.

sisting of some four thousand objects, including brace-
lets, charms, brooches, pendants, and other objects in
bronze, ivory, crystal, glass, paste, enameled wood, iron,
and terra-cotta, besides at least a thousand articles in
gold and electrum.

The story of the finding of this ancient hoard reads
like a romance. Mr. Hogarth had been digging for
many weary months on the temple site without finding
anything worth reporting, the previous excavator having gotten, as it seemed, everything worth carrying
off. But in November, 1904, he came, in the course of
his work, to the small oblong structure which Mr. Wood
had denominated the "great altar," and decided, since
there was nothing else to do, to examine its construction. But almost the first blow of the pick revealed a
most surprizing fact. The supposed altar was not
marble, but was merely veneered with marble, and beneath this was piled countless limestone slabs and beds
of mortar, and in each bed of mortar the most astonishing treasure. Here were earrings of all patterns,
pieces of necklaces, jeweled hairpins and brooches,
primitive electrum coins, and 160 electrum stars, most
of the artistic work being of the finest quality, and the
whole treasure trove evidently coming from the best
era, "the Ionian springtime" of Greek art.

What did this mean? Had these precious things
fallen down, in some way, from the altar where they
had been laid as votive offerings? No; Mr. Hogarth
immediately sensed the true meaning of the puzzle.
These were the ancient "foundation deposit" made
when the temple was first built, and represented the
pedestal on which the divine statue—which the worshipers thought had "fallen from heaven" (Acts

19: 35)—was placed as on a throne.[10] The Egyptians made their foundation deposits under the main threshold of the temple or under the corner-stone or central axis; but this discovery showed that the Greeks made their richest deposits under the pedestal which held the image of deity.

The weather was execrable, but the diggers groped for jewels waist deep in water and slime, beaten with fierce rains and cyclonic winds, while Mr. Hogarth, sick tho he was, rejoiced daily at such discoveries as made the world of scholars gasp as they read of them. About the pedestal three small shrines were found, many broken vessels used in the worship, and vast quantities of votive offerings, together with scores of statuettes in ivory, bronze, and terra-cotta. Perhaps the best prize of all to classical scholars was the discovery of a thin silver plate containing the earliest record of accounts preserved to us in the Greek language (550 B.C.); but to Bible lovers the best discovery was that of the many statuettes of the goddess, representing her (cir. 700 B.C.) not as a loathsome, many-breasted idol but either as a very beautiful woman or more commonly as a mummy. She is usually represented standing stiffly with feet close together, swathed from feet to ankles in mummy-like wrappings, sometimes decorated with figured scenes, sometimes with scales. The whole front, from throat to waist, was usually covered with ornamental pendant breasts (suggesting fulness of life), and the arms were extended from the elbow. Behind the head a sort of nimbus was pictured, and sometimes, tho rarely, stags were placed on either side. As early as the fifth century before Christ the seated Mother and

[10] Compare the foundations of the New Jerusalem, Rev. 21: 10-20.

Child was a common representation. Not one figure
of the many-breasted type was found.[11]

The most important excavations, however, at
Ephesus were those by the Austrians, which began in
November, 1897, and were carried on continuously for
sixteen years. In the great work to which we have
previously referred, Drs. Otto Benndorf and Rudolf
Heberdey, assisted by a large number of distinguished
scholars, give special studies of the topography of the
district, its harbors, mountains, hills, brooks, etc., together with a most thorough examination of the ruins
between the harbor and the mountains, where the old
Hellenic city stood, and especially of the great theater
which Wood had hardly touched. They thoroughly
examined the circular structure called the "tomb of St.
Luke," finding that it had nothing to do with St. Luke,
but was an ancient pagan edifice altered into a Christian church. They also examined the other Christian
monuments, especially the celebrated "double church"—
900 feet long by 100 feet wide,—and found a basilica in
the western part of the ancient building, evidently representing the large church of St. Mary in which a great
church council was held A.D. 431, the edifice, however,
being erected at least a century earlier. They also excavated a smaller sixth century church and found a great
treasure of wonderful bronze lamp stands and a frieze of
"hunting Cupids" so fine and large that an entire room
has been given up to it in the Vienna Museum; in
addition to all this they obtained a large number of
priceless statues, among which was one of the finest
bronze statues of heroic size known to antiquity, being

[11] *Cf.* Hogarth, *Accidents of an Antiquary's Life,* 1910; British Museum,
Excavations at Ephesus, 1908; *Journal of Hellenic Studies,* XXIX, p. 192.

that of a Greek athlete originally dating from the first
century, but the base of which contains a dedication to
the Emperor Constantine.[12] They were also able to
publish ninety new and important inscriptions; their
work representing, therefore, as the editor well says,
not merely a few "sheaves" but a "fresh harvest,"
gathered from the site of this famous city. The third
volume of the Austrian excavator's great work on the
sculptures has not yet appeared, but Dr. W. R. Lethaby
and others have given satisfactory preliminary statements of results in the *Journal of Hellenic Studies*.[13]

They found an arched roadway nearly half a mile
long running from the harbor to the theater, lined with
monumental buildings. From 1864 to 1866 they
thoroughly explored the theater, which was the central
object in the ancient city, and in size and beauty at
least equal to any now used in London or Paris. Set
up against the mountain which was utilized in order
to give grandeur to its architecture, it still seems magnificent even in its ruins, and the acoustics are so perfect that even a whisper can be heard clear back to the
topmost row of seats. The Austrians have minutely
traced the changes in the architecture of the auditorium
and orchestra during the centuries even down to the
smallest detail, the enlarging of a door or the change
in size of a window. The reader can not be expected
to take interest in more than the general statement that
this theater could seat nearly 25,000 people, and that the
orchestra was 80 by 37 feet, and the stage about 20 feet
deep and 80 feet long, being supported by 26 round

[12] *Op. cit.*, I : 181-204; *cf. Journal of Hel. Studies*, XXIII, p. 347-350.

[13] XX, pp. 178-181; XXXIII, pp. 187-196; XXXIV, pp. 76-88;
XXXVI, pp. 25-35.

PAVED ROAD FROM THEATER TO TEMPLE, EPHESUS

SITE OF THE TEMPLE OF DIANA, EPHESUS

ANCIENT DOUBLE CHURCH, EPHESUS

ANCIENT LIBRARY BUILDING, EPHESUS

THEATER AT EPHESUS

pillars and 10 square piers. During the apostolic era (A.D. 40-112) the stage was raised, the ornamentation enriched, and arched entrances constructed, while in the parterre the old wooden ceilings were replaced by beautiful stonework, the footlights were rearranged, and several very artistic façades with elegant frescos were erected in front of the stage. By A.D. 66 the work was practically completed. In the lowest of the sixty-six tiers of seats were twelve wonderful marble thrones, one or two of which still remain almost intact, presumably having been erected for high officials or victors in the games.

In front of the great theater was the Serapion, and on its west side the Odeum, or lyric theater, corresponding to our music hall. Here the medical doctors came together for their meetings, as we know by the four prizes they offered. Here also the guild or college of schoolboys appeared on festival occasions with their teachers. One inscription of the first century mentions the death of a pupil of one of the celebrated teachers of Ephesus, and another was set up in the temple at the expense of his pupils in honor of Soteros, a famous rhetorician. The school of Tyrannus (Acts 19:9), where Paul gave his peripatetic talks, was probably not the hall of a sophist, for the proud sophists would have held aloof from making such an arrangement with a Jew; but must have been the room of an elementary teacher, who according to custom used his class-rooms only twice daily, teaching a few hours in the early morning and a little while in the afternoon. Thus the rooms would be empty and very suitable for such work as Paul wanted to do, especially if, as was customary, these lecture rooms were adjacent to the street.[13a]

The inscriptions give many points which ought to be interesting to the Bible student as he reads the story of Paul's visit to Ephesus. The very oldest inscription of all,[13b] inscribed on a block of blue-veined marble, deals with the rules of augury with reference to the flying of birds:

"If the bird is flying from right to left, if it settles out of sight, it is lucky; but if it lift up the left wing, then whether it rises or settles out of sight, it is unlucky. But if the bird is flying from left to right, should it settle out of sight in a straight line, it is unlucky; but if rearing the right wing it . . ." etc.

How vividly this brings to mind the great bonfire in which Paul's converts that had practised magical arts "brought their books together and burned them in the sight of all; and they counted the price of them and found it 50,000 pieces of silver. So mightily grew the word of the Lord and prevailed." [13c] In this connection it may be well to mention· that a new copy of the apocryphal correspondence of Christ with Abgarus has recently been found by the Austrians inscribed as a charm on the lintel of a Byzantine house.[14]

Amid the multitude of dedications to emperors, honors to the imperial family, to public bodies, and to distinguished private individuals, certain letters appear, written only a few years after the close of the apostolic era, and the names of certain individuals are given who offered votive gifts to Artemis and celebrated the "mysteries of Dionysus" at the very era when the

[13a] Otto Benndorf, *op. cit.,* I, p. 98.

[13b] Hicks, No. DCLXXVIII.

[13c] Acts 19: 18-20; *cf.* also Deissmann, *Light from the Ancient East,* pp. 250-254.

[14] *Journal of Hellenic Studies,* XX, p. 79.

Ephesian church was having its great fight with
paganism. These comparatively small and poor relics
are far more valuable to us than the elaborate inscriptions which were most prized then. Here is one inscription, however, which catches the attention, for it
is dedicated "To Artemis of Ephesus and Emperor
Cæsar Nero Trajan Augustus"; the Asiarch who inscribed it, speaks of Nero as the "high priest, most
mighty father of his country." [15]

Another Latin inscription, tho written in Greek
letters, speaks of "Paullus Fabius, Pontifex of the
brotherhood of Augustus . . . of Tiberius Caesar." [16]

Another interesting dedication is by Hiero, son of
Hiero, "holy, emperor-loving," who during his term in
office built from his own private funds a certain part of
the theater, dedicating it to the people. [17] These gifts
to the people are often mentioned. In one decree three
very rich men who had shown themselves great benefactors to the city in time of famine by selling wheat at
cost are granted citizenship; [18] in another case a golden
crown and front seats at all the games is voted for public services to a Rhodian whose name is unfortunately
gone. [19] In a number of cases a *Dikast* or judge, who
has been called in from another municipality in order
to decide impartially critical cases of justice and has
succeeded in his generous but difficult task, is voted
special honors. Of even more interest to the Bible
student is a list, engraved on a marble slab, of names of
those who in Hadrian's reign had celebrated the pagan

---

[15] Rudolf Heberdey in *Forschungen in Ephesos*, Vol. II, p. 161.
[16] *Ibid.*, II, p. 115.
[17] *Ibid.*, II : 157.
[18] Hicks, No. CCCCLXI.
[19] *Ibid.*, CCCCLXVI.

"mysteries"; a text in which an athlete is said to have fought three fights, for two of which he was crowned;[20] an official inscription in which Julius Caesar is spoken of as the "God made manifest . . . saviour of human life"; and the dedication in which Ephesus is spoken of as "temple-keeper of Diana" (νεωκόρος τῆς Ἀρτέμιδος), thus reproducing the exact phrase used by the town clerk in his celebrated speech.[21]

The "golden crown" so often mentioned in the Bible was one of the highest badges of honor in imperial Rome. Many texts occur in which this is mentioned, one of the most interesting having been found by Prof. A. H. Sayce a few years ago at Antinoë. Palm branches and a Maltese cross appear at the bottom of the inscription, which seems to date from the fifth century:

"The famous, the glorious (*lit.* "golden") Erutheos (?).
"This foremost man is conspicuous to a great degree, in a golden crown. For he has this honor, worthy of his deeds, from the king who sent him afar to Thebes . . . upon a magnificent car as guardian of the younger Rome."[22]

The most important pagan monument is without doubt that which mentions the dedication by a very wealthy Ephesian, Gaius Vibius, in the very year in which St. John is supposed to have died, of a great number of statues which were to be set up in the temple of Diana; a monument which brings us into close touch with the "craftsmen" whose business was interfered with by Paul (Acts 19: 24). It certifies to us at first hand the truth of the statement of Demetrius,

[20] *Cf.* 2 Tim., 4: 7, 8.
[21] Acts 19: 35.
[22] Greek text in *Academy,* Feb. 2, Aug. 22, 1900.

"Sirs, ye know that by this business we have our wealth" (Acts 19: 25).

The Austrians were fortunate enough to find the base of this dedicatory inscription, on which the donor is given all his titles, and the enormous amounts of his benefactions are properly tabulated. Omitting a few sentences we translate this. The top of the inscription is written in Latin:

"Gaius Vibius, prefect of a cohort of the Astures and the Gallaeci, tribune of the XXII legion, deputy of the province of Mauretania Tingitana and of the district of Belgica [Belgium], has at his own expense made a silver statue of Diana and also two silver images, one of the city of Rome and one of the senate, with this stipulation, that in every public assembly (ἐκκλησία) they shall be placed on pedestals, for the dedication of which he has set aside to the senate for allotment 17,000 sestertia."

If correctly transcribed this would report a donation equal to about $850,000; yet this was only one of many gifts. Immediately below this on the same stone is another dedication in Greek, reading much as the above but containing the heading and adding a few more honorary titles:

"TO ARTEMIS OF EPHESUS AND THE EMPEROR-LOVING COUNCIL OF THE ELDERS OF THE EPHESIANS

"Gaius Vibius, son of Gaius Vofentina, salutaris, commissioner of the harbors of the district of Sicily and commissioner of the grain supply of the people of Rome . . . caused to be made out of his own private funds a silver Artemis and silver images, one of Imperial Rome and another of the Senate, which he dedicated to be erected at the place of public assembly [Biblical, "church"] upon the bases as the arrangement there permits.

"He dedicated also for the portion of the council of elders 4,250 denarii. . . .

"In the time of the proconsul Gaius Aquilla Proclus, recorder of Tiberius Claudius Julian, lover of emperor and fatherland."

Many other inscriptions exist recording the gifts of this liberal Ephesian, the most important being the one transcribed by Hicks.[23] This noble memorial consists of a series of public documents in which this Roman knight and naturalized citizen of Ephesus in A.D. 104 dedicates twenty-nine images in the first case and two more later, nine of which, weighing from three to seven pounds apiece, were exceedingly valuable, being either of solid gold or of silver overlaid with gold. Among these the most prominent was a golden image of Diana with two silver stags at her side. In addition to this he donated 20,000 denarii, the annual income of which at 9 per cent. interest was to be spent for gifts to the citizens, temple ministers, etc., on the goddess' birthday. The manner of conveying the images to and from the theater is carefully set forth, and with great definiteness it was specified what should be done with the money, even down to items respecting the powder used to clean the statues. The gifts were to be divided in a manner specifically stated between 1,200 picked citizens, twenty-three choristers who took part in the mysteries of Diana, the temple-keepers, certain priests, a priestess, and forty-nine "boys"—the latter probably representing sons of prominent citizens who were being instructed in the temple school or were candidates for the priesthood. These "boys" certainly held a rather distinguished position, for according to one of the recently discovered texts they had a place reserved for them in the theater. The nine most im-

[23] *Op. cit.*, pp. 127-142.

portant images consisted of the golden Artemis mentioned above, a silver Artemis with torch, silver images of the Roman senate, knighthood, people of Rome, etc. Of course, these votive images have special interest for us because of the mention in the Bible narrative of the "silver shrines of Diana" (Acts 19:24). These "shrines" were not, however, mere statuettes of the goddess, but were probably miniature representations of the temple shrine which were sometimes dedicated to the goddess as votive offerings, sometimes doubtless kept in the homes, or placed in graves by the side of the dead. Almost all of the silver images and shrines have disappeared, having been made of such precious metal that they were all carried off when the temple was captured; but in the old temple ruins at Ephesus some terra-cotta images were found, archaic in style, representing the goddess sitting and holding an infant in her arms, while numbers of marble and terra-cotta shrines still exist where the goddess is seen seated in a niche, sometimes alone, sometimes accompanied by one or two figures. She ordinarily holds in one hand the tambourine, in the other a cup, while beside her are one or two lions; occasionally the lion serves her as a footstool. There is just one silver statuette of Diana in the British Museum, but it did not come from Ephesus.

A few ancient Jewish inscriptions and quite a number of Christian inscriptions have been recovered at Ephesus. One very curious Christian triumphal text which probably dates from the fourth century vividly shows how the Christians were accustomed to treat these Diana images after they came into power. This tablet was found just east of the magnificent two-storied library, and reads:

"Having taken down a deceiving image of the *daemon* Artemis, Demeas set up this symbol of reality (truth) : A God that drives away idols and a cross . . . victorious, deathless symbol of Christ." [24]

By far the most interesting Jewish inscription is that of a man named Julius, a physician. Elsewhere we learn that there were ten of these public physicians supported by the city at Ephesus, tho it is peculiarly interesting to find a Jew among these professional citizens of high standing.

The early Christian churches and tombs, which contrast so modestly with the proud buildings of antiquity, speak a language highly impressive even in their ruins. Standing in the midst of these religious edifices dating from the second to the fifth century, one can better appreciate and feel "how the power of the local goddess was broken and the faith of the Redeemer began its victorious, absolute reign" (Benndorf).

Crosses are everywhere. It is only by the cross on the tombstone that we recognize Prosdokimos, who "with good fortune founded the castle," as a Christian. One ancient Christian prays in a public inscription for the protection of himself and house:

"Oh Lord, help thy servant . . . and his son and all his household. Amen."

Another speaks of "Christian kings" and of the "party of the green." Still another, as early as Justinian, mentions the "house of the apostle at Ephesus." What was probably the most important of all the Christian inscriptions is, unfortunately, entirely

[24] Benndorf, *op. cit.*, Vol. I, p. 103.

lost; but on this fine stele of white marble there are four sunk panels; in the first panel appears a lion rushing upon a man who defends himself with a club, and in the third panel the lion fastening upon the thigh of the man who lies as if just beaten to the earth.[25] Mr. Wood thinks this represents a Christian martyr. It dates from the second Christian century, and it will be remembered that Polycarp, who lived not far from here, was thrown to the lions A.D. 155 at the close of a gladiatorial show.

A number of inscriptions mention the Virgin Mary, and Sir W. M. Ramsay is certain that the worship of the Great Mother at Ephesus led to special reverence for the virgin.[26] The supposed recent discovery in a dream of the House of the Virgin at Ephesus is, of course, absolutely valueless; but the "virginizing" of Christianity is largely due to the influence of Ephesian thought, and Ephesus—"the most important city of Christianity next to Jerusalem"—was affected largely by the ancient reverence for the "Great Mother." It was not so much due to the residence of Mary at Ephesus—which is not very thoroughly proved—as to the ancient cult that the early Christian bishops emphasize the "glory of the female" and give their glowing panegyrics of the "Mother of God." [27]

One inscription of peculiar interest to the Biblical student exhibits a list of Ephesian citizens arranged according to their tribes, two from each tribe, representing the ancient board of magistrates in Ephesus. This list begins as follows:

[25] Hicks, No. DCLXX.

[26] *Expositor*, XI, 413; *Pauline and Other Studies*, pp. 125-158.

[27] So Ramsay, *Expositor*, XI, 401-413; for "Great Mother" see especially H. A. Strong, *The Syrian Goddess*, 1913.

"1. OF THE EPHESIAN TRIBE.

"Demetrius son of Menophilus, son of Tryphon, of the Thousand Boreis; Thoas, son of Dracontomenes, of the Thousand Oinopes.

"2. OF THE AUGUSTAN TRIBE," etc.

Dr. Hicks dates this A.D. 50-60 and thinks it most suggestive that the very man who at this exact date is mentioned by this name as the opponent of St. Paul (Acts 19: 24) is here found as president of this great board of city fathers. Sir William Ramsay thinks Canon Hicks has made out a strong case, altho he himself prefers a slightly later date for the inscription.[28]

2. RECENT EXCAVATIONS AT ATHENS

Modern Athens is more beautiful than our Washington, and the ancient Athens of St. Paul's day was incomparably more glorious. But this outwardly prosperous city was in New Testament times inwardly decadent, living upon the memories of its great past, flippantly pretending to the most eager desire for new truth, yet lacking both the spiritual and intellectual energy of the past which it sought to imitate. A "restless inquisitiveness and shallow skepticism" had taken the place of the ancient love of knowledge and moral earnestness. Nero had just been crowned emperor at Rome when the great apostle came to Athens, and during his reign many of the ancient monuments were carried from this city to the imperial capital. It has been suggested by a recent writer that the cargo of bronze and marble statues found at the bottom of the

[28] *Expositor*, I, 401, II, 1; *Church in the Roman Empire*, pp. 132, 145n; it should be borne in mind, however, that the name Demetrius was a very common name, five occurring in one list of Lycian inscriptions. *Cf. Journal of Hellenic Studies*, 1914, pp. 1-35.

sea by some sponge divers in 1900 may have been destined for Nero's palace.

The richness of discovery at Athens has been so great as to make any adequately impressive sketch impossible.[29]

As early as the middle of the seventeenth century the Parthenon had been well studied and a good description of the ruins of the city had been written; while the topography of ancient Athens had been so thoroughly examined that the works of that period have been taken as the basis of the epoch-making work of Wilhelm Dörpfeld and others. For nearly two and a half centuries Athens, so far as sculptures are concerned, has been the El Dorado of the world. There is not a capital in Europe which has not been enriched by this spoiling of the Greeks; yet there exists to-day in no land of the earth a treasure-trove of art equal to that which is still to be found in Athens.

It is true that Lord Elgin at the beginning of the nineteenth century carried off to England all the art treasures of the Acropolis which he thought worth exporting, but the preservation of the Parthenon, the most exquisitely beautiful building ever erected by man, the remarkable excavation of the Acropolis by Dr. P. Cavvadias, with its astounding results, and the recent restoration of the Propylæa under the direction of M. Balanos, have permitted Greece to save for herself her choicest jewels. The Athens which St. Paul knew has been largely uncovered within the last two genera-

[29] Probably the best brief statement of the modern excavations on the Acropolis is that of Prof. Martin L. D'Ooge, *The Acropolis of Athens*, while a brilliant résumé of the history of the city is given by Prof. Howard Crosby Butler, *The Story of Athens*, 1902. Our plan limits us to such discoveries as illustrate in some way the New Testament era or narrative.

tions. A recent visitor has vividly described the things which we once looked at together—things that Paul also must have seen:

"There is the great ancient outdoor theater of Dionysus built into the south slope of the Acropolis.[30] Would Paul perhaps have gone to see a play by Æschylus? Certainly he could there see one of the ways in which the Athenian people thought about some of the great problems of life. There is the recently rebuilt stadium, which was the scene of the Panathenaic games. Certainly Paul may have gone to this, for he often draws illustrations from games. There is the exquisitely wrought monument of Lysikrates, who once won the tripod in the games of the festival of Dionysus. There is the 'Tower of the Winds,' which accommodated a water clock, a sun-dial, and a weather-vane. It is decorated with figures of the winds, the north wind being 'a cross-looking old man in a heavy cloak,' while the other winds are as suitably represented. Did Paul perhaps get the time of day from this tower in the Roman market-place? There is the platform of the Pnyx, where once the democratic Ecclesia of the Athenians met and made its laws, and where orators brought their causes before the Athenian people.[31] There is the recently excavated street of tombs that led out of the Greek market-place. There is the splendidly preserved Theseum which was probably dedicated to Hephaestus, the divine smith, who was worshiped

[30] This is the most ancient theater in the world. It was here that in the fifth century B.C., the drama developed out of the religious rites used in the worship of the god Dionysus. In Paul's day Nero built a new stage to the theater.

[31] This place of popular assembly was very thoroughly excavated 1882, 1883, 1911.

by artizans, especially by metal workers. There are the ruins of the Asclepieum, a temple to Asclepius, the god of healing. People came and stayed all night in the temple and sometimes were cured of their disease by morning. There are standing several columns of the colossal temple to Olympian Zeus. This temple might specially interest Paul because much of it was built by that Syrian ruler, Antiochus Epiphanes, who had conducted such terrible persecutions in Jerusalem with the hope of inducing the Jews to accept Greek religion and culture. In fact, everywhere one looked there were temples and altars to various gods, and standing up in splendor above them all were the temples of the Acropolis, the chief of which was the Parthenon, adorned with marvelous sculptures and enclosing the colossal statue of Athena, the goddess of wisdom. Among these temples walked Paul, who knew himself to be a temple of God." [32]

Recent excavations, as we have said, have thrown a new and unexpected light on the art, monuments, and topography of the ancient city. Five foreign schools of archeology established in Athens and directed by eminent scholars have assisted the Greek government in a series of extraordinary researches centering in Athens but extending throughout all Greece. The scope of our discussion does not permit mention of the remarkable results obtained by the Germans at Olympia, by the French at Delphi, by the Greek Archeological Society at Eleusis, by the Americans at Heraium, or the other important excavations at Tiryns, Mycenae, Sparta, etc.

Ever since Schliemann, in 1868, began to open to

[32] E. D. Wood, *Life and Ministry of Paul the Apostle*, 1912, pp. 129, 130.

modern eyes these ancient wonders, scarcely a year has passed without some unexpected discovery throwing light upon ancient architecture, art, or religion. All of this assists the modern scholar to get the proper perspective as he seeks to understand the conditions under which Christianity arose—and it is something to know that these discoveries have proved that "man in Hellas was more highly civilized before history than when history begins to record his state." It is something to stimulate historic imagination to be able to read the original report made to the financial Board of Control at Athens concerning the big loan which had been made in order to complete building the Parthenon, or to be able to sit at Eleusis on the very step where those initiated into the mysteries sat when they looked at the sacred drama. It throws light on the New Testament conditions to read the records of cure found at Epidauros in the ruins of the ancient temple of Asclepius as they were written down by grateful devotees, and to find that the priests of that temple also sometimes offered surgical aid to the worshipers and used narcotics or anesthetics in their operations;[33] and it throws light on the triumphs of early Christianity to find the remains of a fifth century church on the site of this ancient pagan temple of Asclepius at Athens.

But it is far more valuable to the Bible student to walk through the street recently uncovered at Athens and look at the ancient Greek houses, very unlike the Roman dwellings uncovered at Pompeii; or to visit the ruins of the ancient Syrian temples, observing how open Athens was to foreign influence; or to walk through the ancient cemetery of Athens and the splen-

[33] Gardner, in *Authority and Archæology*, p. 264.

did "Street of Tombs," where many monuments were
centuries old when Paul saw them, and to copy from one
of these, as the writer did on his latest visit, the inscription of the stranger who moved from Sunium to Athens
and after a life of prosperity carved in elegant and
enduring characters his remembrance of his old home:

ΣΩΣΙΒΙΟΣ
ΣΩΣΙΒΙΟΥ
ΣΟΥΝΙΕΟΣ.

There were other "strangers" in Athens (Acts 17: 21)
who when they came to die did not forget their native
home.

Yonder in the Parthenon you can still see the place
where the shields once hung which were sent here as
a gift by Nero. Yonder at the foot of the Areopagus
is the Theseum, the best preserved antiquity of the
Greek world—the very building which was before the
eyes of St. Paul when, as Luke says, his spirit was
stirred within him. It was in the midst of these countless temples and thousands of graven images that he
spoke to the officials of this university city about the
religious "ignorance" which God had winked at in the
centuries passed, but which now wise men ought no
longer to countenance.

Yonder is the theater of Dionysus, which could hold
30,000 people, the names of the owners of some of the
principal seats still being carved upon them. And
yonder, making our modern stadiums look poor and
cheap, is the ancient stadium, seating 50,000, the
ancient benches having only recently been covered with
marble by a Greek citizen at a cost of $500,000.

And yonder between the Propylæa and the

Parthenon may yet be seen the spot on which stood the great statue of Athena made by Phidias, a statue over 60 feet in height, the point of whose uplifted lance was for centuries the landmark to approaching boats.

Shall we not appreciate the circumstances of Paul's oration better, having thus put ourselves in the midst of the ancient city? If not, the writer has failed of his purpose; for this is one of the chief contributions of archeology, that it permits the exercise of a historic imagination which makes the ancient past to live again.

It is a most suggestive fact that while these un-rivaled discoveries of the monuments and inscriptions of the ancient world have in scores of instances cast discredit upon the accuracy of classical historians and ancient writers, they have served only to put in clearer light the remarkable knowledge and scrupulous exact-ness of the New Testament writers. The account of Paul's visit to Athens sounds to modern scholars who are best acquainted with the Athens of the first century like the report of an eye witness. The statement of Luke that Paul's soul "was irritated at the sight of the idols that filled the city" (Acts 17: 16) has been illus-trated in every extensive excavation there; countless idols were in and about the temples at which he must have looked as he spoke. The reference to "strangers" staying in Athens who "spent their time in nothing else, but either to tell or to hear some new thing" (Acts 17: 21) recalls the fact that the university of Athens was celebrated throughout all the world, and that students gathered there from every civilized land, while the whole population was celebrated for this very trait of loving "novelty of argument." [34]

[34] *Cf.* Thucydides, III, 38.

"The Epicureans were sometimes called the 'garden philosophers' because their lectures were given in the garden of Epicurus; the Stoics frequented the Painted Porch in the Agora, and it was here in the market-place that the students heard the informal debates which occurred when philosophers of different schools met. Into this university circle came Paul with his gospel, and the philosophers 'encountered him' just as they did each other. But they saw that he did not bear the usual university stamp, so they called him a 'babbler' or a 'hanger-on' or a 'picker-up-of-learning's-crumbs.' " The meaning of this strange word *spermologos,* translated "babbler" in our version, has received a curious illustration from a newly recovered papyrus in which it is applied to the crumbs and scraps thrown out in the streets to the dogs. It evidently meant to these learned Athenians that Paul, notwithstanding his claims, was not an original philosopher but was a picker-up of certain scraps of philosophy which had been thrown away by authorized and properly educated teachers. This view seems very superficial when we remember that one of the men most competent to speak has recently declared at Cambridge University that Paul was the only thinker who has added anything substantial in the last 2,200 years to the philosophic system of Aristotle; but it no doubt exprest correctly the views of the university men in Athens who listened to him. Paul was brought for his teaching "unto the Areopagus" (Acts 17: 19). The Areopagus was, in ancient times, a judicial council of Athens which held its meetings on the "hill of Mars," a little west of the Acropolis, which is in full view from its summit. On the top of this hill can still be seen the rock benches on which the Areopagites sat in the open air, and the two great rocks on which the accused prisoners sat. But it is not certain that Paul was officially tried before this ancient court. He may have been taken to this place as the most appropriate spot at which to address quietly an interested audience, or this may have been merely an informal inquiry made by the members of the court concerning his teaching. Yet from all the evidence available it seems certain that this council had the right to pass upon the qualifications of all lecturers either in the university or in the city, and the official arrest of this unauthorized lecturer is by no means impossible. The apostle, who if he stood on the top of the hill could look over the entire city, with the Parthenon and Temple of Augustus so near that his voice might have been heard there, begins his defense with a compliment to the Athenians, who he says were "very religious" (Acts 17:22), since they not only revered the gods whom they knew, but when an unknown deity protected them or bestowed upon them some great favor, they would then put up an inscription in honor of this unknown benefactor. Several of these inscriptions have been found. Such dedications were not peculiar to Athens. Dr. Deissmann has published a picture of an altar recently found at Pergamum containing the inscription:

"TO THE UNKNOWN GODS." [35]

The apostle further compliments his audience by quoting a hymn of Cleanthes, the Stoic philosopher, who had once been a teacher in Athens. The passage

[35] *St. Paul; a study in Social and Religious History*, 1912, p. 262.

from which he quotes is the most beautiful in the entire hymn:

> "Oh God, most glorious, called by many a name,
> Nature's great King, through endless years the same;
> Omnipotence, who by thy just decree
> Controllest all, hail Zeus, for unto thee
> Behoves thy creatures in all lands to call.
> We are thy children, we alone, of all
> On earth's broad ways that wander to and fro,
> Bearing thy image wheresoe'r we go;
> Wherefore with songs of praise I will thy power forth-
> show." [36]

In connection with this the words of that older philosopher, Epimenides, whom Paul elsewhere quotes (Titus 1:12), ought also to be remembered:

> "A grave have they fashioned for thee, O Zeus, highest and greatest—the Cretans, always liars, evil beasts, idle gluttons. But thou art not dead, for to eternity thou livest and standest, for *in thee we live and move and have our being.*" [37]

In the midst of these glories of architecture and art, only just revealed to us, and with the splendid literature of ancient Greece in our memories, it stirs our hearts to see Paul lifting up his hands, which were pricked and roughened with his daily toil, before these representatives of the best learning of the earth; and we rejoice in his confidence that the new gospel of

[36] Translation of Dr. James Adams quoted by Dr. E. D. Wood, *op. cit.,* p. 135. For the further relation of this speech to Greek philosophy, see Carl Clemen, *Primitive Christianity* (trans. by R. G. Nesbit), 1912, pp. 58-60. For the fluctuation of opinion concerning the influence of the Greek world on St. Paul, see Albert Schweitzer, *Paul and his Interpreters,* 1912.

[37] Dr. James Hope Moulton, who quotes this in his *Religions and Religion,* 1913, p. 46, punctuates Paul's words (Acts 17:28) in a new and attractive way: "For in him we live and move and have our being (as even some of your own poets have said), for we are also his offspring."

purity could succeed even in such surroundings. His confidence was vindicated, for there came a time when the temple of Athena and even the Parthenon became Christian churches. Vast numbers of inscriptions have been gathered in and around Athens. In 1896 Mr. Andrews of The American School in Athens deciphered a text, with the help of the nail holes by which the bronze letters had been affixt, and was rewarded for his ingenuity by finding that it was a dedication in honor of Nero, which had been placed in the Parthenon within a few months of the time that Paul had visited the city. Monuments in honor of almost all the emperors of the early Christian centuries have been found, but not many Christian texts of great importance. One of the most interesting recent discoveries is that of a tombstone in the form of a statuette of the Good Shepherd, in which Christ is represented as a boy carrying a sheep upon his shoulders (A.D. 300), the design being an original combination of the two types ordinarily found.[38]

A few Jewish memorials have been recovered, tho Jews were not attracted in as great numbers to Athens, the philosophical center, as to Corinth, the commercial center of Greece. It is known that St. Paul disputed with the Jews in the synagog (Acts 17: 17), and it has been thought by some scholars that the site of this synagog was fixt by a modern discovery; but while this is doubtful, it is interesting to find the modern Jewish synagog and Jewish quarter close to the Agora, and to discover in Athens a number of gravestones bearing Jewish inscriptions. A translation of one of the most valuable of these, which illuminates in a strik-

[38] *American Journal of Archæology*, XX, 624.

PICTURES OF ST. PETER
AND ST. PAUL
From Medals and Early Communion
Glasses

ST. PAUL'S GATE, TARSUS

PICTURE OF ST. PAUL (4th Century)
From the catacomb of Domitilla

OLDEST PICTURE OF ST. PAUL
AND ST. PETER
(2nd or 3rd Century)
From Marucchi, "Elements d'archéologie
chrétienne," I, 330

VIEW OF THE RIVER CYDNUS, TARSUS

RUINS OF THE TEMPLE OF APOLLO AND THE ACROPOLIS, CORINTH

GENERAL VIEW OF LATE EXCAVATIONS AT CORINTH

ing manner the bloody spirit of the age, may close our survey of this famous Biblical city:

"I invoke and implore the most high God, the lord of the spirits and of the flesh, against those who by treachery slew and poisoned the wretched Marthina before her time, shedding her innocent blood unjustly, that it be so with them that slew her or poisoned her, and with their children. O Lord, that seest all things, and the angels of God (*i.e.*, God), to whom every soul humbles itself with supplication, (I beseech thee) that thou avenge the innocent blood and that most speedily."

A pair of hands engraved on this stele is the not unusual symbol of invocation for divine help, even on pagan gravestones.

3. RECENT EXCAVATIONS AT CORINTH

No one who has once taken the journey from Athens to Corinth can ever forget it. The traveler can still see pieces of the ancient road, leading across the isthmus, along which ships were dragged in St. Paul's day, by the side of the great royal highway along which the ancient caravans traveled from the city of culture to the city of commerce. Nero in A.D. 67 began cutting a canal through this isthmus, but the project was abandoned until modern times, when it was finished in 1893. The modern Corinth, which is only some fifty miles by rail from Athens, is an inferior village situated about three miles away from the site of the older town, which was completely destroyed by an earthquake in 1858.

As one views the limestone pavements and marble staircases and fragments of splendid marble ornaments, and especially as he stands amid the mighty pillars of the temple of Apollo and on one side looks out upon the gulf and on the other sees Acro-Corinth rising 1,500 feet above him, and farther off, a higher snow-capped peak on the top of which in the ancient time was the temple of Aphrodite with all its horror of religious prostitution which appealed to every ancient traveler, one is imprest with the courage of that Christian Jew who could establish himself in this great center of wealth and expect to conquer it for the pure but lowly Nazarene. It is suggestive that it was in writing to this most licentious city that Paul most emphasized his teaching that a man's body was the temple of the Holy Spirit and a member of Christ (1 Cor. 3: 16; 6: 15, 16). It appears rather suggestive that Paul did not venture to preach here until he had received a special revelation from God encouraging him (Acts 18: 9, 10), after which he made this his missionary base for nearly eighteen months, succeeding in a remarkable manner in winning some of the leading Jews, including Crispus, the ruler of the synagog; but especially having a multitude of conversions among the non-Jews (Acts 18; I Cor. 1: 14-16; 16: 15).

While Paul was at Corinth, Gallio was appointed "governor" (*i.e.,* proconsul) of Achaia. A fragmentary inscription recently discovered at Delphi contains a letter of the Emperor Claudius, proving that the appointment of this Roman official fell between the summers of A.D. 51 and 52. This shows that Paul came to Corinth early in A.D. 50, and left in the autumn of A.D. 51, and this is confirmed by the edict of Claudius expelling the Jews.[38a] Gallio had the honor of establishing as a precedent the right of the Christians to teach their doctrine without interference from the

[38a] See *American Journal of Archæology,* XXVII, 1912, p. 582,

Roman law, the value of which decision to the early Christians is just beginning to be appreciated.

It was in Corinth that Paul met Aquila and Priscilla, who had been expelled from Rome with other Jews in A.D. 50, and it may have been in part their influence and the influence of this great cosmopolitan center which caused Paul to mature a plan for evangelizing Rome and the West.[39] Modern discoveries have opened up to us the culture and vice of ancient Corinth, and have also given us many monuments mentioning the Isthmian Games which were held at the shrine of Poseidon, a little northeast of the city—from which games St. Paul may have borrowed some of the figures of speech used in his letter to the Corinthians (I Cor. 9: 24-26).

A recent visitor, who has the rare gift of historic imagination, has brought vividly before our eyes those early days, big with promise, spent in Corinth by Paul the apostle. "How long was it before Aquila discovered that he had taken into his shop a man who was active with his mind and spirit as well as with his hands? When did he discover that this fellow tentmaker had ideas that were of the greatest interest? How many talks they then must have had about Jesus, the Messiah, as they worked together cutting out and sewing up the heavy tent-cloth. And in the evening in the home, Priscilla, the Roman wife of Aquila, probably became as deeply interested as her husband, and soon instead of one Christian in Corinth there were three, two tent-makers and a woman. Could they affect the wealthy, wicked city of Corinth?"[40]

As the traveler sits amid the ruins of the temple of

---

[39] Ramsay, in Hastings, *Dictionary of Bible*, I, 482.

[40] Wood, *Life and Ministry of Paul the Apostle*, 1912, p. 140.

Aphrodite, once the temptress of the nations, where a thousand priestesses are said to have sold themselves in the name of religion, and looks out at the bay and tries to locate the ancient harbor of Cenchrea, and climbs the hill from which he can see Salamis, so famous in heroic story, and rides along the seacoast to the medical springs which are yet visited by travelers from distant lands because of the value of the baths, and walks among the enormous blocks and into the underground subways of the ancient city, stopping occasionally to work out the meaning of an ancient inscription, and then turns his eyes upon the wonderful fertile plain which coasts the sea; it is easy to close his eyes and visualize the ancient Corinth in its imposing surroundings as St. Paul knew it—and the difficulty of the task of converting such a city grows upon him.[41] It was a bustling, money-loving city, and St. Paul knew it and all its peculiarities as thoroughly as any of us know the city in which we have spent eighteen months of earnest toil.

Within a few years of the time when Paul visited this city Nero also visited it, as we know by the "advent" coins struck in his honor, and also by an inscription on which a speech which the emperor made is immortalized and he himself given divine homage.[42] How often Nero and Paul—those two best-hated men of the first century—crossed each other's track!

Altho we are nearer relatives of the Greeks than

[41] "At Corinth, besides the female prostitutes who gave their gains to the temple, there were also, doubtless, titled ladies who occasionally offered themselves in the service of the goddess. In Baalbec every maiden was required to offer herself to a stranger at least once in her life in the temple of Ashtarte" (*Ency. Ethics and Religion*, VI, 672-4).

[42] See Deissmann, *Light from the Ancient East*, pp. 358, 375.

of the Semites, yet it is the fact that Paul, a Jew, lived in this place which makes its ruins so impressive. The first tentative excavations on the site of ancient Corinth were carried on by Dr. Dörpfeld in 1886; a little more was done by Mr. Skias in 1892, but the work which proved epoch-making was begun in the spring of 1896 by the American School of Classical Studies under the superintendency of Dr. Rufus B. Richardson, and was continued almost without intermission up to 1913. The excavators were compelled to buy the modern village and displace an immense amount of débris before anything of value could be reached; yet within a year they had dug up for some distance an entire street of the ancient city, and had uncovered the old Greek theater; within two years they had discovered the Peirene, the most famous fountain of the ancient world, and had cleared the hexostyle temple of Apollo which Dörpfeld had discovered ten years before; and within three years their discoveries had taken first rank among all the splendid excavations carried on in Greece during the present generation. In fact, they had been able to bring to light in that time most of the "sights" of Corinth which Pausanias, "the ancient Baedeker," who visited the city about a century after Paul, had put down in his guide-book as the places most worth seeing.

The Greek theater was a large edifice, rather cheaply constructed, semi-circular, with at least thirty-eight tiers of seats, but this was replaced in Roman time by a better one which even Pausanias could admire. The Peirene, which was celebrated five centuries before St. Paul was born—Corinth being called by Pindar the "Peirene city,"—was entirely uncovered. It was placed at the entrance to the Agora in the most prominent place in the entire city, and was so well preserved that the main conduit of the old fountain still supplied water to the modern village.

In 1899 the American excavators cleared the Glauke, another famous fountain, even better preserved than the Peirene, the old marble lion-headed spouts which had been used before the remodeling of the fountain in Roman times being still *in situ*. During the next year they cleared the market-place and entered the Agora, having disclosed its magnificent gateway and found just inside a fine series of colossal statues in Parian marble, part of the ornamentation of the Propylæa, which was practically a Roman triumphal arch. The statues, which probably date from the time of Marcus Aurelius, were of rather poor work, but were, perhaps intentionally, made to look very uncouth, for they represented male and female captives and were clothed in barbarous style.

By 1901 the excavators had been able to uncover a considerable part of the Romanized city; to open out the great Hellenic stoa, over 350 feet long, which was standing in Paul's day, but with its front hidden by a row of vaulted steps; and to pile up such a vast quantity of lamps, pottery, terra-cotta figurines, and old Greek material reaching clear back to the sixth century before Christ, that a museum had to be built at Old Corinth in which to store the new-found treasures.

Of all such finds, perhaps the enormous quantity of terra-cotta figures representing human and animal forms in antique style were the most curious. Over forty-four examples of a horse carrying a rider came from the theater, while sixty-eight standing female figures of

Aphrodite, dating from the fifth century before Christ, were dug up, and many more were found showing the love-goddess reclining or else seated holding a dove to her bare breast. All of these were originally painted and must have stood in brilliant rows as votive offerings in the temple; one life-size statue of Artemis, of much better work, was found. The god of wine also had his temple at Corinth and some suggestive sculptures were recovered—for example, the statue of a nymph struggling to free herself from the embraces of the intoxicated and leering deity.

A few works of art of less importance and many valuable vases of rare type, as well as very rich topographical information, have been some of the other results accomplished during the eighteen years of excavation; but how true it is that our interest in Corinth is almost wholly dependent upon its relations with a maker of tent-cloth whose name was never heard spoken by the aristocrats and rich merchants of the city!

Inscriptions in Corinth did not appear as plenteously as at Athens. Omitting the Byzantine inscriptions, the excavators found only about sixty Greek inscriptions, with an even smaller number of Latin ones, during their first six years of work. Almost all of these dated from the rebuilding of the city by Julius Cæsar 46 B.C. Was this due to the fact that the libraries have been destroyed, or were the people "so busy making money and making love as to ignore learning?" A few words written on vases and jar handles, and oblong stamps are about all that have been recovered. Very few of the inscriptions strike fire from our hearts as we read them; but here is one dating from Roman times that makes our nerves tingle, for it has to do with granting certain honors to "Titus . . . because of his most noble character." [43] On another grave memorial, erected in honor of two artists, Diogenes and Hermolaos—perhaps the very men who made the sculptures for the Parthenon of Agrippa in Rome 27 B.C.,—there is claimed for these men either a very ancient and noble ancestry in the flesh or else the even greater honor that their work reflects the spirit of the Periclean age:

> "I am from the Attic fatherland;
> I inherited the blood of Perikles.
> The son of Hermolaos,
> My name is Diogenes.
> . . . set for me in Ephyre near to
> the spring Peirene."

A distinctly Christian inscription was cut on a large block of white marble found in 1899 at the top of the steps leading to the Propylæa:

"Demetrios, servant of Christ."

The man may have been a bishop, but we do not agree with Professor Powell that his title (δουλος Χριστοῦ), makes this evident. [44] Very few Christian epitaphs were found, but some most impressive inscriptions had to do with the Jews.

While the excavators were clearing the street of shops discovered in 1898 on the main road of the city leading to the port, they found a door lintel on which was written in ancient Greek letters:

SYNAGOG OF THE HEBREWS.

[43] Cf. Titus, 1:4; 2 Cor. 8:23; 12-18.
[44] See *Journal of Hellenic Studies*, XVIII, 64.

This inscription was over eighteen inches long and the height of the letters averaged about three inches. It dates from the Imperial period, and therefore it is "a possibility seriously to be reckoned with that we have here the inscription to the door of the Corinthian synagog mentioned in Acts 18:4, in which St. Paul preached" (Deissmann).

The miserable appearance of this scrawl, which is without ornament of any kind and is poorly engraved, Dr. Deissmann considers to illustrate well the low social position of the people to whom Paul at first preached (*cf.* 1 Cor. 1:26-31). Altho it was found as they were excavating the finest street of the city, and altho another piece of Hebrew writing was found not far away, it seems probable that this block had been moved from its original position, since it would be almost impossible to suppose that a Jewish synagog had been located on such a magnificent boulevard.[45]

When we remember the poverty of Paul's friends in Corinth we can appreciate better the letters to the Corinthians with their emphasis upon eternal values. Dr. Deissmann has well said: "The pæan of love chanted at Ephesus under Nero for the poor saints of Corinth, has not perished with Corinth. Annihilated forever, the magnificence of Nero's Corinth lies buried to-day beneath silent rubbish mounds and green vineyards on the terraces between the mass of the Acrocorinthus and the shore of the gulf; nothing but ruins, ghastly remnants, destruction. The words of that pæan, however, have outlasted the marble and the bronzes of the Empire. . . . The Corinthians, who

[45] In preparing this résumé of the work at Corinth all the reports made in the *Journal of Hellenic Studies* (1897-1914) have been freely used, as also Mr. A. S. Cooley's short article in *Records of the Past*, 1902, pp. 33-88.

suffered other writings of St. Paul to be lost, preserved these." [46]

One recent discovery previously mentioned should,
perhaps, receive additional emphasis. In 1908 there was
found at Delphi a stone in which Gallio is spoken of as
pro-consul, which shows, according to Dr. Deissmann,
that Gallio entered upon his office in the summer of A.D.
51, and Paul had certainly been preaching in Corinth
some time before this. Deissmann thinks, as does O.
Holtzmann, that the text of Acts implies that he had
been in Corinth eighteen months before Gallio came. In
that case Paul must have reached the city at least as
early as the summer of A.D. 50—which is at variance
with most chronologies. Because of this new discovery
Dr. Barton concludes that the Epistle to the Galatians
was written from Ephesus toward the close of the year
A.D. 54, or near the beginning of A.D. 55.[47]

4. RECENT EXCAVATIONS AT ROME

A renaissance of archeological study began in Rome
some 500 years ago, and since then excavations have
been carried on almost without intermission; yet never
have these been more successful than in the last four
or five decades. More than a thousand volumes have
been written based upon the excavations which have
been made since 1870; yet the treasures not found by
the archeologists are much greater than those which
have been found. When Rosa in 1866 uncovered a
lime kiln dating from the middle ages filled to the brim
with the most exquisite works of art, it caused a
shudder in the breast of every one interested in the
golden age of Rome. The discoveries mentioned in a

[46] *Op. cit.*, p. 399.
[47] *Journal of Biblical Literature,* 1914, pp. 120-126.

synopsis like this must always seem to many less wonderful than those which have been omitted. To give even a hint of the marvels which have been uncovered before the eyes of modern archeologists would seem almost impossible; yet while we recognize the impossibility of giving more than an impressionist sketch of these most recent discoveries, we shall attempt the task, and enable the reader to visualize the conditions with which the early Christians were familiar, tho omitting everything which will not assist the historic imagination to reconstruct the ancient past.

In 1870 special excavations began, the most spectacular discovery that year being the remains of the house supposed to be that of Pudens, a famous Roman of the apostolic age and earliest wealthy patron of the Christians. From 1872-1889, over 275,000,000 cubic feet of earth were excavated for building purposes in Rome, and in the course of this civic reconstruction a vast number of antiquities were discovered. Of the newly found articles stored in the capitol the Director mentions 2,360 lamps, 1,824 inscriptions, 77 columns of rare marble, 405 works of art in bronze, 192 well-preserved statues, 266 busts and heads—all masterpieces of art—besides over 700 gems, 36,679 coins, etc. Libraries have been written on the exquisite works of art, paintings as well as sculptures, discovered since 1870. On Christmas Eve, 1874—to mention one instance—Professor Lanciani found lying on the marble floor in one room just uncovered a remarkable portrait bust of Commodus, flanked by two tritons or marine centaurs, and by two beautiful statues representing either the two maiden daughters of Danaos or two of the Muses. He found also the "Venus Lamiana," a head of Diana, a Bacchus of semi-colossal size, with drapery of gilt bronze (missing), and about twenty-five exquisite fragments, legs, arms, hands, feet, etc., belonging to statues whose drapery was likewise of bronze.[48]

During this period the Forum was excavated from end to end, as well as the Sacra Via, baths of Caracalla, stadium of Domitian, and a greater portion of the palace of the Cæsars. Among other famous works of art found in these researches were the two bronze athletes uncovered on the slope of the Quirinal hill, the bronze Bacchus of the Tiber, the Juno of the Palatine, and many statues of the gods and wonderful bas-reliefs.

In 1887 an inscription was found, particularly interesting to students of early Christian history, in which a father had engraved on the tomb of his daughter the statement that she was "a pagan among the pagans and a Christian among the Christians"—perhaps suggesting that she was a Christian married to a heathen. In 1881, when the foundations of the English Chapel were being laid, a remarkable collection of bronze imperial busts was found piled up and concealed in a subterranean passage. Between 1885 and 1887 the house of the Symmachi was again thoroughly searched, yielding a broken Victory, the statue having been smashed into over one hundred and fifty pieces, probably by the Christians who pillaged this palace in the fourth century. About this same date the tombs of the Calpurnii, which had received the bodies of nobles killed by Nero, Caligula, etc., were exhaustively excavated, yielding the richest and most

[48] Rodolfo Lanciani, *Ruins and Excavations in Ancient Rome,* pp. 407-8.

important discoveries for several decades. Within the next ten years Cicero's villa, probably, the house of Pliny the younger, and many wonderful tombs were discovered, including the supposed grave of Seneca on the Appian Way, as well as that of the bald and wealthy shoemaker who had the instruments of his trade carved on his funeral monument; and the grave-yard near the Coliseum dating from the seventh century was uncovered, where one tomb was found on which was carved the warning, "Whosoever shall violate or injure this tomb, may he share the fate of Judas."

Perhaps the most important single discoveries since 1900 have been those connected with the ancient temples of Rome, and of these none were more important than those in the temple of Jupiter Dolichenus, the Syrian Adadus on the Janiculum, the triangular altar of which was found still standing in its central chapel. This chapel was surrounded by five or six others, in all of which triangular-shaped altars were used. One of these altars discovered February 6, 1909, had a rim or raised border as if to prevent the blood of the sacrifices from dripping from it.

It was found that the Mithras worship was closely associated with Jupiter worship at least as early as the fourth century. Under the Jupiter temple above mentioned were found statues of such gods as Bacchus, Isis, etc., hidden under the floor; and in another little receptacle a bronze figure of an unidentified male divinity about which is coiled a serpent. Several egg shells were found with this figure.[48a] There was also discovered right under the feet of Jupiter-Baal

[48a] Dr. John R. Crawford, of Columbia University, writes me: "No connection between this sanctuary of Syrian divinities and Mithras has been proven."

a human skull hidden in a place carefully prepared for it. This may have been one of the emblems used in the "mysteries" or may have been connected with the human sacrifices which were originally a part of the temple consecration. It is interesting to note that in the twenty Mithraic sanctuaries found and explored in Rome recently, the entrance has in each case been carefully concealed.

Another third century temple of Mithras just found under the Baths of Caracalla measured 91 x 49 feet, and contained a circular font and two lavatories, a sacristy, and a marble statue of Venus Urania. Opposite the font were niches for lamps. Mithras was represented in the frescoes with a Phrygian cap on his head and the disc in his hand, and in one fresco his head was crowned with seven rays of light. The pictures showed the god with the raven and lion, and gave the usual relief behind the altar in which he is represented as slaying the sacred bull. On the right of the altar when discovered were found several oblation bowls.[49] The titles of the deity were given on a tablet nearby: "Sungod, the Great, God of the Spirits, Saviour, Giver of Riches, Benefactor," etc.

As the Mithras worship was such a rival of the early Christian worship, it may be added that in 1915 there was opened under the church of St. Clement at Rome, and made accessible to visitors, the foundations of a temple of Mithras built during the reign of Augustus. The sacred font was found, also a part of the altar and the remains of ancient sacrifices which proved to be wild boars.[50]

---

[49] *Journal of the British Association,* 1914, pp. 15-36.
[50] *C. R. Acad. Insc.,* 1915, pp. 203-211.

In 1889-90 a temple of Isis was uncovered, showing the figure of the goddess veiled and crowned with poppies. In connection with this a wonderful figure of the cow Hathor was found cut out of spotted granite. In the sacred place pieces of amethyst columns were found.

The temple of Asclepius, recently excavated, contained a curious inscription dating A.D. 138, which shows the prevalent thought of heathen worshipers at this period.

"To Valerius Aper, a blind soldier, the god gave commandment to come and take the blood of a white cock along with honey, and to mix together an eye salve, and for three days to anoint the eye with it. And he received his sight and came and gave thanks publicly to the god." [51]

Probably no spot has yielded greater treasure than the Forum in connection with these modern excavations. Explorations here had been begun by the popes as early as 1431, and had been continued with intermissions to the beginning of the nineteenth century, when the French Government itself made extensive excavations 1811-14, and Pope Leo XII, 1824-35. But it was in 1870 that the Italian Government began a complete clearing of the Forum. In 1888, Otto Richter discovered the remains of the Triumphal Arch of Augustus; and in 1898 Giacomo Boni began his remarkable series of excavations which have opened to us the past of the ancient Forum as we never had hoped to know it. Perhaps to the classical scholar the most spectacular discovery has been that of a monument very doubtfully recognized as the cenotaph

[51] *London Expositor*, VII: 30.

and national monument of Romulus, the founder of
the city; but to the Bible student, other matters are at
least equally important. It was in this public resort
that the book-sellers, fruit-venders, fishmongers,
usurers, and pickpockets were clustered when Paul
walked through it. Surely the apostle to the Gentiles
must have been interested in what he saw there. It
was on this Palatine hill nearby that St. Paul "undoubtedly came to judgment" (Marucchi).

The first Christian monument to be erected near the
Forum was the Arch of Constantine, after which,
as Marucchi well phrases it, "the cross entered
triumphantly the city of the Cæsars." For the next
century the emperors diligently cared for the works of
art in the Forum; but Christianity soon began to appropriate these, the Church of Santa Maria Antiqua
being established in the library of the temple of
Augustus. This was the first Christian building in
the Forum (Marucchi). Professor Boni in 1898 began
digging on this ancient site and many important discoveries were made. The church was found to have
been divided into three naves by marble columns belonging to the ancient edifice, and its walls were
covered with frescos of the eighth century. Among
the earlier remains was a Christian sarcophagus found
in 1901, dating from the early fourth century. The
figures carved on this sarcophagus are most interesting. Two fishermen, almost naked, hold between them
a net containing fish, which Marucchi believes to
symbolize the apostles as fishers of men.[52] Next to
this the baptism of Christ is represented, John the

---

[52] Yet see Charles R. Morey in *Supplemental Papers of American
School of Classical Studies,* 1905, pp. 148-156.

A UNIQUE SEATED STATUETTE OF CHRIST
AS A YOUTH

Reproduced in "American Journal of Archæology," (1915, p. 491)

HEAD OF THE STATUE OF ANTINOÜS, FAVORITE OF
THE EMPEROR HADRIAN

(Early 2nd Century)

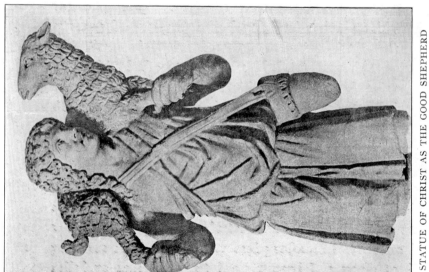

STATUE OF CHRIST AS THE GOOD SHEPHERD

(Early 3rd Century)

Baptist standing on a rock and Christ being shown as a little naked boy standing in the stream, with the heavenly dove above him.

The Good Shepherd is next shown with the ram on his shoulders and two sheep standing at his feet looking up at him. The center is occupied by two figures, the deceased and his wife (the latter represented as an *orans*), the faces of neither being yet finished—the sarcophagus having perhaps been made previous to any knowledge of what Christian should occupy it. Beyond these figures is an extensive and artistic representation of Jonah and the sea monster. At the extreme left is a sea divinity holding a trident, which may be here, as elsewhere, a disguised form of the cross, while before him the sea is lashed into fury and a ship rides the waves with sails unfurled. The latter is a new symbolic suggestion, as on all other sarcophagi the sails are fully set. This is undoubtedly a survival of the catacomb type of symbolism.[53] It may be added that this is the first sarcophagus to show a definite separation of scenes, and probably the earliest to show a picture of the baptism of Christ. Since this important discovery the Forum has yielded nothing for us of marked interest, unless it be a well-preserved private dwelling of the Republican period just brought to light, and the systematic exploration of the houses of Livia and the palace of the Flavian emperors, and several beautiful statues.[54] This may be a good place to mention the discovery in 1907 of the marvelously artistic bas-relief of Antinous found at Canuvium, the famous statue of the disc-thrower found at Castel

[53] *Nuovo Bullettino de Arch. cristiani,* 1901, pp. 206-216.
[54] See particularly *Nuovo Bullettino,* 1914, pp. 73, 74.

Porziano in 1909, and the remarkable statuette of a seated Christ, reported in 1915.

Next to the Forum the baths were places of public resort, and many masterpieces of Roman art have lately been found in the baths of Diocletian and Caracalla. The former of these could accommodate 3,600 bathers at one time and the latter as many as 1,600. There were besides nine other large public baths from as early as A.D. 300 and multitudes of smaller ones.

During 1882-1884 great researches began on the site of the house of the Vestal Virgins, and these have been continued. This very celebrated institution, the restoration of which dates from A.D. 193-212, is now found to have been built of brick. The atrium of the house measured 215 feet long by 78 feet wide. It was elaborately heated by a system of hot-air pipes, and some of the ancient plumbing and a large section of the fine old mosaic pavements, of geometric pattern, dating from the time of Julia Domna, have been discovered, together with many statues, busts, pedestals, inscriptions, etc. Some of the furniture of the house—including the handmill of the cook in the kitchen—was found just where it was left when the house of the Vestals was destroyed in the fourth century by the Christians. Professor Lanciani, who was connected with these later excavations, fortunately found fifteen marble pedestals, and on these were several eulogistic inscriptions celebrating the high priestesses of Vesta. Probably for us the most important of these is the one in which these pagan priests, A.D. 364, eulogized one priestess for her "chastity and profound knowledge in religious matters," but later caused her name to be erased—either because of a moral lapse, or more likely, as Professor Lanciani believes, because she had become a Christian.

The house of the Vestals was situated at the foot of the Palatine Hill, which was the most sacred place in all ancient Rome, on which, from the earliest time, the palaces of the Cæsars stood. In our lifetime these palaces have been dug up and it is thought that at least the foundations of the house of Augustus have been found. We can now examine in detail the plans of the palaces of Augustus, Caligula, Nero, Domitian, and the Cæsars who followed. It is true that what has been found poorly represents the "Golden House" of Nero, filled with hundreds of statues from Greece and Asia Minor, with its world-famous zoological and botanical gardens, whose waterfalls were supplied by an aqueduct fifty miles long; yet some important relics of these ancient wonders have been discovered. The throne-room of Domitian, the great persecutor of the Christians—a throne-room measuring 160 x 120 feet, the wall-paintings of which show its ancient splendor— has been brought to light, and a beautifully frescoed treasure room. It is even more remarkable that in con- nection with the palace of Domitian (or Nero) Dr. Boni found salt water fish-tanks, where unique varieties of fish could be cultivated for the royal table; and also three "elevators" by which luggage could be lifted from the bottom to the top of the palace.[55] This palace was originally filled with the costliest works of art, and many exquisitely cut columns and capitals, in many colored marbles, have come to light, while in

---

[55] See *Journal of Roman Studies*, 1914, p. 244*ff.* Some scholars believe these strange constructions to be connected with the palace sewerage; but Boni's view seems very plausible.

1888 remarkable frescos were discovered in the dining-hall, representing the butlers and waiters leading guests to the banqueting chambers over fifteen hundred years ago. It is interesting to remember that Domitian's palace received its water supply by means of a powerful syphon, the pipe of which was made of solid sheets of lead and measured about a foot in diameter. This remarkable work of engineering, bringing water across a valley over 130 feet deep, was put into the palace by the brother-in-law of Titus, A.D. 73. Many fragments of this ancient construction have been found, and in the palaces of Domitian and Caligula many pictures and inscriptions particularly interesting for the light they throw upon the early Christian era have been discovered. In one of the so-called "school-rooms" attached to Caligula's palace there was found long ago a remarkable vignette representing a donkey turning a mill, with the writing of the supposed school-boy above it, "Work, work, little donkey, as I have worked myself."

Attached to the palace of the Cæsars was a "stadium" used as a great sunken garden—redecorated after the great fire A.D. 191—which was dug up 1892-3, on the walls of which a considerable number of scribblings have been found, most of which come from the soldiers stationed there. These *graffiti* are traced with a pointed instrument and interspersed with rough drawings, among which a helmet and a boat are most recognizable. Several of these rough barbaric scrawls are comical, and several represent individuals, probably athletes; but the most interesting to us is a rough sketch of the head of Nero with his name under it. Some of the scribblings are too obscene to be quoted, but one, rather longer and better than the rest, reads:

"I desire to give all things to beautiful girls, but no girl from the common people ever pleases me." [56]

Another reads:

"May a bear eat him on the trackless mountains."

It should be remembered that even in the first century "members of Cæsar's household" had become Christians, and there can not be the slightest doubt that there were Christians among the royal pages when these scribblings were written.

The Colosseum, which in magnificence can be compared only with the pyramids of Egypt, and could seat somewhere between 45,000 and 87,000 spectators, was known from the earliest times and was rather carefully excavated by Testa, 1864-5, and by Rosa, 1875-8. In 1878 Professor Lanciani discovered here the bones of the animals which had been used in the gladiatorial shows of the sixth century. The shows of that time, however, were tame affairs compared with those of the apostolic era. There have actually been discovered traces of the more ancient dungeons in which the wild beasts were kept which tore the early Christians to pieces; and in 1874-5 the floor of the old arena was uncovered, together with the sockets to which the windlasses and capstans were fixt by which the cages were raised to the level of the trapdoors of the arena. The funeral monuments of the gladiators which have been found show the fierceness of the fighting in the earlier eras. The shows were so pop-

[56] See Latin text of this and others in Marucchi's *Roman Forum*, pp. 322-357.

ular that even the Emperor Constantine was not able to stop them, and as late as A.D. 384-392 a statue was erected near here to John, a champion fighter of Jewish or Christian origin, by the Emperor Theodosius. Several mosaics have been found giving fighting scenes and many inscriptions eulogizing the gladiators.

No picture of the gladiatorial combats and races in the circus has come down to us which shows in such detail the surroundings of the race-course as a colored mosaic from Carthage (first century) discovered in 1915, which depicts a typical race with four chariots each drawn by four horses and all going at tremendous speed, the whole picture being brilliantly conceived and executed. We can see here dimly outlined the tiers of seats occupied by the common citizens, but the official stalls are plainly indicated. One official is also represented holding out to the successful contestant the grand prize. Whether St. Paul ever saw such a race as this or not, there can be no question about his interest in the race-course, as proved by his many references to it in his description of the Christian life.[57]

It may be added that no amphitheater in Rome is as well preserved as the one lately dug up at Pompeii (1914). It was buried by what seems to have been a gigantic landslide, and is almost intact. Professor Spinazzola reports that even the celebrated Greek theater at Syracuse is nothing when compared with this. "Every seat, every wall, the actors' rooms, the subterranean passages, the wild beasts'

[57] For a very full and accurate examination of the Roman theater (auditorium, stage, costumes, actors, etc.), see *Art and Archæology*, 1915; for the picture referred to above see *Revue Archéologique*, 1916, p. 249.

ANCIENT CHARIOT RACE
From "Revue Archéologique," (1916, p. 249)

CHRISTIAN BAS-RELIEF
Musée du Bardo

PAGAN PRIESTESS
Musée Lavigerie

FRAGMENTS FROM THE ANCIENT TEMPLE OF PERGAMUM
From Julius Lessing

dens, are all in perfect preservation. The frescos adorning the walls and the epigrams of witty visitors carved on the marble rails of the balconies are now coming to light." As a villa of Cicero was nearby, he must have attended plays in this theater. St. Paul on his way to Rome stopt for a week within a short walk of the town where this theater was located.

Many Christian inscriptions have been found at Rome, but most of these came from the catacombs which we have previously described. De Rossi knew of forty-eight inscriptions earlier than Constantine and about one hundred and forty which dated from the Constantine era;[58] but since his day many hundreds have been discovered and some very remarkable Christian monuments. One of the most interesting of these is an ancient crypt dedicated to Gabriel, the archangel, covered with frescos representing Gabriel with his hands in the attitude of prayer, and showing the Redeemer among hosts of angels. This, however, is rather late in date and can not be compared in value with the earlier discovery of a cubiculum covered with paintings of Biblical scenes. The Good Shepherd, Moses striking the rock, the raising of Lazarus, the feeding of the five thousand, Daniel in the den of lions, and Noah and the ark are among the narratives illustrated. This was the place in Rome where foreigners were buried, and Lanciani believes that the crypt adorned with Christian paintings must date as early as the third century.

The Jewish inscriptions in Rome are very numerous. The one best-known monument representing the Jews is probably the Arch of Titus, which shows in its bas-

---

[58] *Inscriptiones christiani Urbis Romae*, 1857-1861.

reliefs the triumphal processions in which they
marched as captives, and here the seven-branched
candlestick is prominently delineated among the objects
captured. The Jews in Rome, however, from the second
century before Christ to the time of their expulsion by
Claudius, represented an influential section of the population.[59] The richer Jews lived in aristocratic quarters
of the city, but the poor people clustered mostly in the
southwest across the Tiber on the outer edge of the
city among the slums of the Trastevere. A considerable district here was given up to foreigners, and in
it all kinds of religious worship were permitted. The
ghetto was in the vicinity of the harbor, a ward in-
fested by foreign sailors and pickpockets. There were
landings in the harbor set apart for dealers in marble,
wine, oil, fish, timber, iron, salt, brick, cattle, etc. In
1892 a tablet was discovered which had been erected in
memory of a man named Terens, who is said to have
been a "most famous importer of pigs and sheep."
There was a special wharf for the Egyptian grain
fleet running between Rome and Alexandria. Grain was
one of the chief monopolies of the government, and it
transported annually 144,000,000 bushels of this
precious necessity of life. A bas-relief lately discovered
represents the unloading of one of these ships. In this
disagreeable ghetto—celebrated in classical literature
for its narrow, muddy streets and numerous beggars
and its wreaths of violets and countless little lamps
which on feast days dropt grease and soot on the
passers-by—the Jewish schools, law courts, and central
synagog were situated. There were, however, nine

[59] See especially Max Raden, *The Jews Among the Greeks and Romans,*
1915, chap. xvi; and Jean Juster, *Les Juives dans l'Empire Romain,* 2 vols.,
1914.

other synagogs in different parts of the city, one of these being located, as we know from its name, in the Campus Martius.[60]

The cemeteries also prove that the Jews overflowed from the Trastevere not only along the wharfs where the boats from Ostia were being unloaded (Martial), but out into the Appian Way, for as many as three cemeteries have been found on or near this central highway. Indeed, while these Jewish peddlers and rag-pickers and dealers in broken glass and cast-off clothing itinerated everywhere, they must especially have enjoyed mingling with the throngs on this great thoroughfare; and we also read in the classics of the bazaars which they had built on the Via Portuensis. It must have been in one of these poorer centers, full of low-priced lodgings, where his fellow Jews were working at cobbling and tent-making and the manufacture of scourges, that St. Paul obtained his "hired house," joining with these day laborers in eating "mouldy bread and ill-looking cabbage soaked in lamp oil and drinking poor wine from a cracked glass" (Abbé Fouard).

St. Paul may have known the fathers and mothers of some of the people whose inscriptions have come to us from the cemeteries. There are 119 of these inscriptions coming from the one cemetery in the Via Portuensis, which was carefully explored through the generosity of Pellegrini Quarantotto, the owner, in 1904-5. Pictures of the seven-branched candlestick and of the dove are carved on the tombs, and the names of

[60] For a very thorough discussion of the Jewish quarters in ancient Rome see Signor Pietro Romanelli in *Palestine Exploration Fund Quarterly Report,* 1914, pp. 134-140; compare also Abbé Constant Fouard, *St. Peter and the First Christians,* pp. 249-259.

Jacob, Judas, Anna, Rebecca, Marian, Titania, Eutropius, Fortunatus, Antipas, Glukus, Alexander, Euodia (*cf.* Phil. 4: 2), and many more, the sound of which must have been most familiar to the apostle. Some of the Jewish tombs are large, one recently discovered measuring 18 feet wide by 17 feet deep, being built by Julius Justus "for himself and his wife, his freedmen and freedwomen and their descendants."

Several times the "synagog of the Hebrews" is mentioned, and once Tychicus the "head of the synagog" (*cf.* Acts 20: 4; Eph. 6: 21); Julianus is also mentioned as "Gerusiarch of the Sanhedrin," and a Macedonian is spoken of whose father came from "Cæsarea in Palestine." Perhaps the most interesting, however, is the epitaph which reads:

"Here lies Prokleina, 18 years and 50 days old. Her mother Aquileina erected this."

The name of Aquila, the friend of Paul, is closely associated with Rome (Acts 18: 2), and Giorgio Schneider Graziosi thinks Aquileina is merely the feminine form of Aquila.[61]

The Palestine Exploration Fund has lately published some very interesting Jewish inscriptions recently discovered in Rome. The largest and most impressive of these concerns a lady whose wifely qualities and religious faith are thus eulogized by her husband:

"Here is buried Regina concealed in this fair tomb which her husband built as a mark of his love for her, who had lived with him twenty years and four months, lacking eight days. She is sure to live again, and again return to the light (of life); for she can have hope of this, because she shall rise for a promised eternity, which is the unfailing faith of the worthy and pious.

[61] *Nuovo Bullettino di archeologia cristiani,* 1915, pp. 13-56, 152-157

She deserved to have an abode in the Blessed Country. This will be assured thee by thy pure life, thy love for thy people, thy fidelity to law, the worthiness of thy wedded life," etc.[62]

Joseph Offord points out that the mention of the resurrection and Paradise is rather novel in a Jewish epitaph.

If just one little sentence could be found on some relic which St. Paul himself had written, it would be worth, sentimentally, more than all these many other Jewish inscriptions; but no such autograph has been preserved, neither can we be absolutely sure even of the place where he lived during his residence in Rome. Lanciani is very certain that it could not have been at the spot pointed out under the Church of St. Maria in the Via Lata, because this at that era was not private property, a public monument standing on this site; neither should it be sought near the Church of St. Paolo della Regola, for almost certainly the rich Jews living in the Campus Martius would not have attracted the apostle to this official district. He favors the site recommended a few years ago by Padre Germano, this being a well-built apartment house of three stories situated near the ancient ghetto, in the Via degli Strengari, where Roman tradition locates it.[63]

[62] Latin Text in *Quarterly Statement*, 1914, p. 47, and July, 1916, p. 146; also this and many others in *Nuovo Bullettino di arch. crist.*, 1915, Nos. I and II, where a catalog is given of all the Jewish inscriptions now placed in the new hall recently set apart for Hebrew records in the Lateran Museum.

[63] Except where other works are quoted or the writer has personal information, the statements in this section are all made upon the authority of Rodolfo Lanciani in his remarkable series of books, *Wanderings in the Roman Campagna* (1909); *New Tales of Old Rome* (1901); *Pagan and Christian Rome* (1893); *Destruction of Ancient Rome* (1899); *Ancient Rome in the Light of Recent Discoveries* (1889); and especially *The Ruins and Excavations of Ancient Rome* (1897); compared with and supplemented by Orazio Marucchi, *Christian Epigraphy* (1912); and *The Roman Forum and the Palatine* (1906); and especially his illuminating reports in the *Nuovo Bullettino*.

An ancient tradition identifies the dungeon in which both St. Peter and St. Paul were incarcerated with the horrible Mamertine prison in which Lentulus and the Catiline conspirators, as well as Jugurtha and other important state prisoners, were killed or starved to death, altho this identification is by no means conclusive; but that the burial place of St. Paul has been found Marucchi does not doubt. In 1915 Mons. De Waal gave a great sum to carry on excavations in the Basilica di S. Sebastiano. About six feet beneath the floor a pagan columbarium of the first century was found and some frescos of the third century; but, far more important than either, *graffiti* were discovered scribbled upon the walls of the nearby crypt, proving that in the fourth century this was regarded as the cenotaph of the two apostles. This confirms the ancient traditions which declare that the bodies were taken here for protection in the third century.[64]

Another even more certain ancient relic commemorating the two great apostles are the gilded glasses, dating from the second half of the second and the beginning of the third century, on many of which pictures of Peter and Paul are executed on the flat bottom in gold leaf. Out of 340 of these glasses published by Garrucci these pictures are found on eighty. They also contained such mottoes as: "Mayest thou live long!"; "A mark of friendship"; "Life and happiness to thee and thine." These were evidently gifts for festival occasions, and Marucchi believes, since there is a uniformity of type in the pictures, that they originated from real portrait pictures.[65]

---

[64] *Nuovo Bullettino,* 1916, pp. 5-61, 159-191, 231-2, 238*ff.*
[65] See also T. Livius, *S. Peter, Bishop of Rome* (1888), pp. 132*ff.*

Excavations at the church of San Clemente begun fifty years ago have recently yielded some important results. Below the eleventh century church a fourth century basilica was dug up "filled with matter of greatest interest to the Christian historian." Underneath this church a Roman house of the imperial period came to light, one chamber of which was evidently regarded as a holy shrine. There is considerable reason for believing that this was the house of St. Clement of Rome; but the strange thing is, that not only a Christian shrine was found there but also a shrine of Mithras—a pathetic relic of the later years when this mystic religion made so many converts from the Christian faith.[66]

5. Explorations in Various Galatian Cities

The discoveries in Asia Minor rival any in Egypt or Italy in their value in illuminating the New Testament. The French were the pioneers in scientific work here, and the publications of the *École Française d'Athénes* have done more than any other to aid the student of Asia Minor.[67] F. V. J. Arundell, in 1832, succeeded in discovering Antioch of Pisidia and brought back to England a number of texts from its ruins, the most impressive being those in which he mentions an official who is called:

"High priest for life of the most glorious god Bacchus."

And on the pedestal of a statue:

"To Titus Claudius Paulinus, the heroic philosopher."

Mr Arundell suggestively remarks that the near relatives of these men or their successors in office may

[66] See London *Expositor*, Feb., 1915.
[67] Ramsay, *Historical Geography of Asia Minor*, p. 9.

have "heard the words of life from the priests of the Most High God." [68]

W. J. Hamilton published valuable researches in 1834 with 455 Greek inscriptions gathered in a two years' journey;[69] and Philippe Le Bas and W. H. Waddington issued a much larger and more important work embodying their researches, 1843-44, and containing many hundreds of short inscriptions.[70] Some other scholars issued important volumes; nevertheless Asia Minor was practically an unknown land to Europe until MM. Duchesne and Collignon in 1876 plunged into this *terra incognita* and made detailed investigations and learned reports of such popular value that soon the entire scholastic world was interested in this country, which was historically the "bridge" between Europe and Asia.

Sir William M. Ramsay, however, has done more than any other man or group of men to investigate thoroughly the antiquities particularly of Anatolia (western Asia Minor), and to apply the results in a very brilliant manner to the illustration and confirmation of the New Testament records. In company with Col. C. W. Wilson he made his first long journey into this country in 1881 and 1882; later with J. R. S. Sterret, D. G. Hogarth, and others, he, as the chief representative of the Asia Minor Exploration Fund, liberally supported by the Royal Geographical Society of England, has visited the country periodically every few years up to the present time (1916), and has gathered vast numbers of inscriptions and much topographical information which have completely

[68] *Discoveries in Asia Minor*, I: 272-290.
[69] *Researches in Asia Minor* (2 vols., 1837).
[70] *Voyage archéologique en Grèce et en Asie Mineure* (5 vols.), 1870.

changed the views of scholars concerning the geography and history of Asia Minor in New Testament times, and in many respects have changed the current views concerning the religious cults of that period.

An enormous body of Christian inscriptions from the second, third, and fourth centuries have thus been brought to light, especially in Phrygia and Lycaonia, some of which have already been made use of in this work. The education of these early Christians, as contrasted with that found in certain later centuries, is set into fine relief when we remember that the Crusaders who marched through Asia Minor to Palestine left not one written memorial.[71]

Sir William M. Ramsay's discovery that the term Galatia, as used in the New Testament and on certain popular non-Biblical inscriptions, did not refer to the northern district but to South Galatia (which district included the well-known cities of Antioch, Iconium, Derbe and Lystra), resolved more New Testament puzzles and eliminated more supposed Biblical "mistakes" than perhaps any other one discovery made in the last half century. There are grammatical objections to this explanation of the term;[72] but such objections are purely verbal, the historical and geographical facts compelling archeologists with practical unanimity to accept Ramsay's theory. While the evidence does not amount quite to a demonstration, it is nearer to it than that offered for many other universally accepted hypotheses; and the difficulties which it raises are very few compared with those met by the opposing theory.

[71] Ramsay, *Seven Churches of Asia,* p. 110.

[72] See *Ency. Bib.*, pp. 1592-1616; Moffatt, *Introduction to the Literature of the New Testament,* pp. 90-94, for literature and argument; and add Robertson, *Grammar of the Greek New Testament,* p. 863.

External history, antiquities, and geography are wholly in favor of the South Galatian view, and the fact that it removes contradictions from the New Testament narrative ought not to be considered as militating against its truth. Sir W. M. Ramsay began his studies in Asia Minor holding to the old belief concerning the meaning of the term Galatia and accepting the view, which was current fifty years ago, that the mistakes in the book of Acts were due to the fact that the book was fabricated in the middle of the second century; but his researches finally drove him to the conclusion that the author of the book wrote with such admirable knowledge that he could not have lived in the second century and that Luke and Paul spoke about these provinces of Rome in the same natural and non-technical way that the Romans themselves spoke and wrote, as was proved by the inscriptions.[73]

If Paul made a missionary journey to North Galatia he almost certainly visited the great cities Ancyra, Pessinus, etc.—altho he never mentioned them afterward,—and it is interesting to note that according to Eusebius the very earliest reference to Christianity in North Galatia is at Ancyra (*cir.* A.D. 192) in an anti-Montanist treatise (*Hist. eccl.,* V, 16). But while the Northern Galatian antiquities are not insignificant, we are concerned alone with Southern Galatia and with the recent discoveries especially at Lystra, Derbe, Antioch, Iconium, and Pisidian Antioch.[74]

---

[73] See *Church in the Roman Empire*, pp. 74*ff; Expositor,* 1911, p. 258; *Pauline and Other Studies,* pp. 199*ff.*

[74] The skeleton of the following discussion is taken from Ramsay's *The Cities of St. Paul,* 1907, and *The Bearing of Recent Discovery on the Trustworthiness of the New Testament,* 2d. ed., 1915, supplemented from the recent Biblical encyclopedias and especially from the *Journal of Hellenic Studies.*

(1) LYSTRA

Professor Sterrett settled the site of this city in 1884-5, and from an inscription found there not only identified *Khatyn Serai* as Lystra but proved that it was a Roman colony. It was situated about eighteen miles southwest of Iconium, and was probably made a Roman colony 6 B.C. No excavation of any great extent, so far as the writer knows, has ever been carried on here, and very few remains of the old city are now visible above ground. It was off the main road, being situated in a secluded, charming spot among the hills, and was therefore well fitted as a place of refuge, as was also Berœa (*cf.* Acts 14: 5 with 17: 10). Modern discovery has shown a particularly strong influence of the old native language here, so that it is most natural to find that this was the only city where Paul came in contact with an uneducated native population that did not naturally use the Greek vernacular (Acts 14: 11). Since Lystra was the seat of a Roman colony and situated near a Roman road, the Latin influence was great. The coins prove that the art of Tarsus influenced this town in no small degree. In a neighboring village two architects named Titus and Gaius, who were brothers, mention their native place in an inscription, showing that in the ancient days, as truly as now, civic pride touched all classes of citizens.

As the Jews usually settled in cities which lay in the line of commerce, it is natural that no synagog is mentioned in the narrative of Paul's visit to Lystra. The general tone of Acts 14: 8-19 suggests, as Ramsay well says, that the surroundings were more thoroughly pagan and less permeated by Jewish bias than in Iconium or Antioch. The few Jews who lived here were probably influenced by their surroundings, and perhaps this accounts for the circumstance that Timothy, altho his mother was a Jewess, had never been circumcised (2 Tim. 3: 10, 11). However, the fact that a Jewess would marry him indicates, as Ramsay points out, that the father of Timothy was a Greek occupying a position of some importance.

One of Sir William Ramsay's latest discoveries, made in 1909, throws light on the conduct of the natives of Lystra who called Paul, Mercury and Barnabas, Jupiter (Acts 14: 12); for he found in a nearby ruin an inscription by native Lycaonians recording the dedication of a statue to Zeus (Jupiter) and Hermes (Mercury). This shows that these two gods were classed together in the local cult, and again illustrates the accurate local knowledge of St. Luke.

(2) DERBE

It was Professor Sterrett who in 1885 fixt the site of Derbe, altho the identification is not absolutely conclusive. This city was most probably situated where a great artificial mound appears just north of the Taurus mountains on the edge of the Lycaonian plain. The remains are so extensive that almost certainly there were two ancient towns at different dates connected with a road which in Paul's day was lined with sepulchers. The surface of these mounds is covered with fragments of pottery of all periods from pre-Hellenic time onward. With the exception of a few hours of digging by a few workmen no excavations have been made. Unfortunately, the Derbe where Cicero was entertained and Paul found refuge is still underground.[75] On the northwest, Derbe was bordered by the Iconium territory, and on the northeast by the district of Barata, from which it was separated by a long line of boundary stones erected at intervals of about 150 feet. An imperial road, built 6 B.C., as proved by the milestones, ran between Derbe and Antioch. Just as there is a peak near Iconium which the early Christians named in remembrance of St. Philip and one near Ephesus named for St. John, so here there is one which bears a name probably reminiscent of its connection in history with St. Paul.

Derbe was the frontier town of the Roman province, and therefore when Paul reached this town he retraced his steps to Lystra. An inscription, probably of the third century, was put up by Nounnos and Valerius in honor of "Paul the Martyr." This was recently found in a ruined church nearby. The tombstone had been purchased ready made and the inscription does not fit very well; but it is a most pathetic reminder that altho Paul is not said to have suffered any persecution here, later disciples of the Nazarene did not escape.

(3) ICONIUM

This city still retains the name Koniyeh (*Konia*), and is well described by Hamilton as an "oasis in the desert."[76] All travelers notice its similarity to Damascus, being surrounded by deserts but situated in the midst of gardens. In each case also a river flows down into the city, tho here the stream is soon lost in the sand. It has always been thought of as one of the

---

[75] *Cities of St. Paul*, p. 396.

[76] *Op. cit.*, II, 146.

most ancient cities of the world, its legendary history beginning "before the flood."

Iconium in the first century controlled the fertile district around it for a distance of 200 square miles, and its mines and great furnaces were very impressive to the ancient mind. It was surrounded by villages which were fragments of the central city, each of these having as its chief officer a "first man." There is now no doubt that Iconium was a province of Galatia during the first three centuries, as this has conclusively been proved by milestones and grave-stones.[77]

The Romans naturally spoke of Iconium as lying in the half barbaric Lycaonia; but the people always distinguished themselves from the Lycaonians, preferring to think of themselves as citizens of a Phrygian-Hellenic city. Even the cities farther from North Galatia spoke of themselves as "Galatian" and enjoyed being addrest thus. The city was strongly Roman and was given an imperial name A.D. 41; so that, as Ramsay suggests, it is now plain that Paul was complimenting the city when he addrest a letter intended for it: "To the Galatians." Luke is also correct when he speaks of an important part of the inhabitants as Hellenes (Acts 14:1) as compared with other Galatian cities, such as Lystra and Antioch; for the latter were Roman *coloniæ*, but Iconium had not received that honor in Paul's day, tho it did receive this title about 100 years later, after which Latin became the official language. On one of the coins of Iconium—perhaps struck while Paul was alive—

[77] Ramsay, *Cities of St. Paul,* pp. 335, 341, and *The Bearing of Recent Discovery,* pp. 37, 45; and especially *Expositor,* 1911, p. 257; *Journal of Hellenic Studies,* 1911, pp. 161-214.

Poppæa, the wife of Nero, is represented as a figure of Good Fortune seated on a throne after the fashion of the Great Mother.

All that we have said above illustrating St. Luke's exact knowledge of local phrase and popular geography may at first seem rather unimportant; but when we remember that when Sir William Ramsay first went to Asia Minor every authoritative geographer in the world supposed that Luke's statements to which we have just referred proved him to be unacquainted with the conditions around Iconium in Paul's lifetime, we may then appreciate more fully the importance of the excavations which have proved the geographers to be wrong and Luke to be right.[77a] Indeed, it was the unexpected discovery by Sir William Ramsay that the book of Acts was correct in its statement that Paul crossed the frontier into Lycaonia in going from Iconium to Lystra, which awakened this distinguished explorer to the possibility that perhaps, after all, the Bible historian might have firsthand information beneath his narrative. It was not until 1910 that Ramsay found the now famous monument proving that Iconium was so thoroughly Phrygian that even well-to-do citizens of wealth and standing were still using the Phrygian language in dedicatory inscriptions as late as A.D. 150-250.[78] It may have been, as Ramsay suggests, because it was the frontier that Luke happened to mention the district, for just as soon as the fugitives had reached this milestone marking their

[77a] These inscriptions prove that from one point of view (*i.e.*, racially) Iconium could be spoken of as Phrygian, while from another point of view (*i.e.*, administratively) it could be spoken of as Galatic.

[78] For full description of this remarkable text see Ramsay's *The Bearing of Recent Discovery on the Trustworthiness of the New Testament*, 2d ed., 1915, p. 45*ff*.

entrance into a new district they were safe from pursuit.

Sir William Ramsay had his headquarters at Iconium each year from 1901 to 1910, but of all his discoveries none were so important as the above unless it was the finding of the inscription, published in 1911 in the *Journal of Roman Studies,* which conclusively proved that Iconium, and indeed all Phrygia, was thought of as a part of Galatia.

The inscriptions show that a tremendous Christian influence spread far and wide from this city of Iconium. Its magistrates were supreme during their term of office and could whip and expel without trial any supposed criminals, if the people who gave them their office did not object; but this expulsion would not necessarily be permanent after public opinion changed or new magistrates came into office. It is an interesting fact that this is the one place in Asia Minor where early Christian (Byzantine) ceremonial can still be seen much as it was carried on before Islam overrun the country. The earliest Iconium saint was a woman (Thekla), a fact which may possibly, as Ramsay thinks, suggest the influence of the ancient Great Mother worship, which was the popular cult here, altho the Greeks worshiped Athena and the Romans adored the emperors. A great number of inscriptions have been found in Iconium and in almost all the villages surrounding it, forty-nine new texts being reported as late as 1910. These inscriptions show prosperity, much interest in good roads, and a real response to imperial favor. Names often occur on the Christian inscriptions which sound very familiar to the Bible reader, such as Publius, Paula, Luke, Rufus, etc. A particularly interesting text is on a monument dedicated to "a good man" who may have been a Christian presbyter:

"Gourdas, a good man, lies here. He was as a dove among men, a priest of the Most High God. (This) stone Trokondas, his successor and follower, prepared, and adorned his grave for the sake of his memory." [79]

(4) PISIDIAN ANTIOCH

This site is now deserted and while the ruins are extensive there is only one rather large building, probably an ancient temple or music hall, which seems imposing. Excavations are much needed here. Great arches, which were once part of the fine aqueduct, and a few broken marble columns are all that now indicate the richness of this celebrated ancient city which was made a Roman *colonia* by Augustus and continued for years to be a great administrative and military center in Phrygia. During the first and second centuries, as the inscriptions show, Latin was used in the official dedications and also in private inscriptions. It was geographically a Phrygian city but politically a city of Galatia, as was quite satisfactorily proved by a group of milestones in 1905. A very large number of inscriptions have been found upon or near this site.

That the Jews were an important element of the population is rendered certain by a most curious fact. While these people did not often write their public inscriptions in Hebrew and were careful not to mention their race in their epitaphs, yet that they held an important place here is proved by the funeral monument

[79] *Journal of Hellenic Studies,* XXII: 124, Gk. Text No. 58.

of a Jewess dating probably from the first century of our era:

"An Antiochian (by race) sprung from ancestors who held many offices of state in the Fatherland, by name Debbora, given in marriage to a famous man Pamphylus (I am buried here), receiving this monument as a return of gratitude from him for my virgin marriage." [80]

Debbora is the ordinary Greek spelling of the Hebrew Deborah. The public proclamation of this intermarriage proves both the prominence of Deborah's family and the breaking down of Jewish exclusiveness. The men of Deborah's household, being in such close touch with heathen officials, must necessarily have acquiesced in much idolatrous ritual; otherwise they could have had neither political nor social recognition. "When Paul visited Antioch, the original Jewish colony had been for three centuries and a half exposed to the influence which such practises exert on the characters of men, and a profound effect must have been produced on a race naturally receptive and progressive." [80a]

There was a native Phrygian element in Antioch, but the Greek was predominant. The city lay on a great commercial highway, and was closely connected with other Greek cities, the population being better educated than at Lystra or Derbe. The Roman element of the population doubtless constituted the chief aristocracy—composed probably, in large part, of descendants of military men who were thrown into the town when it first became a Roman city—and visiting Roman princes were given great honor; but the city as

[80] Ramsay, *Cities of St. Paul,* p. 256.
[80a] Ramsay, *ibid.,* p. 258.

a whole was Greek in feeling tho Roman in government, and Paul appealed most probably to this element.[81]

Men was the chief god of Antioch. On the coins he stands with one foot on a bull's head and wears a Phrygian cap.[82] He was the god of prophecy and healing. The cock, a figure probably used to avert evil, is also seen on the coins. But the most popular deity was Cybele, the Great Mother, who was the leading deity in all Anatolia. She is usually represented in a modest dress with two lions by her side. A cave which was sacred to her, centuries before St. Paul visited the city, is now held sacred in memory of the Virgin Mary. It must not be forgotten, however, that the Romans at Antioch, as elsewhere, worshiped the emperors as their leading cult.

From the more educated among the middle class—to which class it is now seen primitive Christianity chiefly appealed—Paul got a quick response, so that by the second Sabbath he had caught the ear of almost the entire city. He particularly attracted the Gentiles to his teaching; perhaps because in his first address he called them "brethren." Sir William Ramsay believes that the reason this sermon is given in such detail in Acts is because it was here that an epochal step was taken in the proclamation of the gospel, when Paul opened a "door of the Gentiles directly into the Christian Church instead of having them pass first, as previously, through the synagog" (Acts 13: 46). Mr. Hamilton eighty years ago exprest this same

---

[81] For a description of the city and general conditions at Antioch see W. M. Ramsay, *Epistle to Galatians* (1900), pp. 197 *ff.*

[82] For the coins of Pisidian Antioch, see G. F. Hall, *Num. Chron.*, 1914, pp. 299-313.

thought, saying, "From Antioch of Pisidia as from a sacred Jerusalem we may date the first preaching of Christianity to the heathen and can not but look upon the deserted site and fallen ruins with a feeling of respect and veneration." [83] This was a city where the Greeks and the Jews were particularly friendly, and therefore was a good point at which to introduce this new method of evangelism. The Romans, who included the women of rank, would naturally be the class of population least interested at first in the preaching of St. Paul, and naturally it was this class which the offended Jews stirred up against the preacher. They held the reins of government and were quite ready to please the Jews by stopping such novel and riot-provoking utterances.

The sanctuary of Men-Askænos in Antioch was fully excavated 1910-1913 by Sir William Ramsay; the colossal altar, 66 by 41 feet, was found *in situ* within the sacred area, the latter measuring 241 by 136 feet and being surrounded by a wall five feet thick. A fourth century church nearby had been built of the stone from this ruined sanctuary. It is suggestive that no temple of Men was found, but only this holy High Place on the top of the mountain, open to the sky, in the center of which was the ancient hall of initiation, and the high trough or baptismal font where purifications were made by the worshipers. There is no doubt whatever that we may see in this newly discovered sanctuary the famous hall of Phrygian mysteries. The hall proper was, doubtless, the central closed chamber. The soil above the stone floor of this chamber was full of animal bones and teeth, and beneath the floor the

[83] *Researches*, I : 476.

teeth of pigs and wild boars were found. Emblems of Men, a horned bull's head, and many engraved tablets were excavated.[84]

Sir William Ramsay was able to locate the throne of the deity in the northeastern corner of the sanctuary, and also the very spot in the center of the room where the initiate by a mystic rite entered into the "new life" where he could be called "holy and blessed . . . god instead of mortal." Close to this place Sir William found three of the feet of the "holy bed" used for the mystic marriage ceremony between the god and his goddess—in which service, according to immemorial tradition, Anatolian ladies, even those of highest rank, were expected to take part.

The god Men at Antioch was paired with Demeter and closely associated with Artemis (Diana), who was a Hellenized form of Cybele, also sometimes represented here in the form of Hekate, with six birds prest to her breast, as is also the case with Artemis at Ephesus.[84a]

The discovery of this sanctuary is particularly interesting because these Phrygian mysteries were so well known to the early Christians (*cf.* Col. 2: 18), and because they were centers of widespread influence during the first and second centuries. High ecclesiastical dignitaries doubtless visited this shrine at Antioch, as the priest of the Pythian Apollo came from Laodicea to see the mysteries at Klaros, and applicants for initiation and visitors to the oracle must have come from long distances. The ritual was doubt-

---

[84] *Journal of Hellenic Studies,* 1912, p. 111*ff.*

[84a] For discussion of Men see H. R. Hall, *Ancient History of the Near East,* pp. 330, 331 (1913); especially A. B. Cook, *Zeus; A Study in Ancient Religion,* Vol. I., consult Index under Men (1914).

less most impressive, as the chorus at Klaros is known to have been large and made up of singers brought from afar.

The earliest inscription found was that of a freedman of Claudius; the earliest portrait statue also dated from the first century.[85] Sixty-eight inscriptions were brought away from this shrine, the one which is most impressive dating from A.D. 250-315, in which the worshiper of Men and Artemis confesses that he has sinned and needs atonement or expiation. The concept of sin, as exprest here, is so decidedly Christian that it suggests either that the Christian idea is imitated by this heathen or else that the penitent is publicly repenting of the sin of having profest Christianity. The former seems more likely, as this was the era when paganism was making its last desperate fight against the new religion of Jesus, and many of the inscriptions show this tendency to imitate Christian phraseology. In at least a dozen of the votive tablets obtained here by Ramsay in 1911 the strange word Τεχμορεύσας was found—evidently an anti-Christian word reminding one of the pagan *libelli*.[86] It looks as if these heathen, who for more than a century had been coming in contact with the Christians, were finally beginning to imitate Christian phraseology, calling themselves "witnesses" and lauding their departed friends as those who had "borne witness," just as in India to-day the natives sing:

> "Buddha, Lover of my soul,
> Let me to thy bosom fly."

---

[85] *Journal of Hellenic Studies*, XXXII, 1912, pp. 111-142, *390ff*.
[86] *Expositor* (London), 1911, pp. 251-275.

TWO GRAVESTONES FROM BLAUNDOS, NOW AT USHAK

From Sir William Ramsay, "The Bearing of Recent Discovery on the Trustworthiness of the New Testament," (2d. ed., p. 358)

TOMBSTONE IN THE FORM OF AN ALTAR WITH
EPITAPH IN THE ICONIAN GRAECO-
PHRYGIAN PATOIS

From Sir William Ramsay, "The Bearing of Recent
Discovery on the Trustworthiness of the New
Testament," (2d. ed.)

BASE OF THE FIRST STATUE ERECTED IN PISIDIAN ANTIOCH

Probably 8 B.C., in honor of Caristanius, prefectus of Quirinius, honorary duumvir
of the Colony while governor of Syria. The stone is now lying on its side

From Sir William Ramsay, "The Bearing of Recent Discovery on the
Trustworthiness of the New Testament," (2d. ed., p. 284)

One Antiochan text reported by W. M. Calder in
1912 [87] illustrates this tendency, since the wording is
such that one can not be sure whether it was written
by a heathen or a Christian:

"Ailios . . . an elder (πρεσβύτερος), to the freedman Ailios
. . . a freedman most highly honored for his memory."

During this revival of paganism, as it made its last
battle against the Nazarene, Christian benevolence was
also imitated, and heathen worshipers not only began to
use in their public inscriptions the higher spiritual
terms introduced by the New Way, but gave their
children religious names and began to speak of the
deity and of the future life as the Christians did. An
inscription (early fourth century) speaks of one
"glorified by the immortal gods (for she) redeemed
many from evil torments. . . . Truly I received the
gift prophetic of truth in my own city." Other pagan
inscriptions use the expressions so common in Christian literature: "slave of God"; "he was perfected,"
etc.[88]

Sir William Ramsay found in connection with the
heathen sanctuary at Antioch the verb εμβατεύω used
in describing how a neophyte (*cir.* A.D. 150) had "entered in" and "seen" the sacred symbols and had heard
an explanation of religious mysteries which could come
only to an "initiate." This would suggest that in
Col. 2: 18, where the same word is used, the apostle
may be warning the young Christians against this
secret teaching of heathen "wisdom" when he says:
"Let no man rob you of your prize by . . . dwelling

[87] *Journal of Roman Studies,* II, 79-109. But see note 127, page 576
[88] See for other examples Ramsay, *Pauline and Other Studies.*

on the things which he hath seen, vainly puffed up." [89]

Probably the most important of all the new inscriptions found at Antioch is the one which gives additional confirmation to the view that Quirinius (Luke 2:2) was twice governor, once 6-4 B.C. and once earlier, probably 16-12 B.C. There are several ancient inscriptions that relate to the prefectorate of Quirinius, but this is the most important. A member of the family of the Caristanii at Antioch was his representative, and must have filled the place well, for he is recorded to be the first man to whom a statue was ever erected in Antioch at the public expense.

But the facts that this distinguished officer of state who officially represented Quirinius had a wife named Sergia Paulla, and that the governor of Galatia visiting Antioch at this time was named Sergius Paullus, Jr., add immeasurably to the value and interest of this remarkable document.

This brings very near to one the Sergius Paulus of Cyprus with whom Paul had such a dramatic relationship, and who was, according to Sir William's view, the father of this great man of Antioch who, altho but a little past thirty years of age, had won such distinction as president of the Board of Road Commissioners that he had a monument of honor erected to him by the city, Sergia Paulla being his sister. [90]

It will be noticed that either Luke or the city scribe made a mistake in spelling the name of Sergius Paullus (Acts 13:7)—unless, indeed, the ancient governor, like Shakespeare, was independent enough to spell his

[89] In addition to the references given see especially Sir William Ramsay, *Annual of the British School at Athens,* 1911-12, pp. 37-71.

[90] See *Journal of Roman Studies,* 1913, pp. 262ff; 1914, pp. 254ff

name differently at different times. However, Luke was not with Paul at Cyprus and in any case he would be very likely, let us hope, to favor phonetic spelling.[91]

The block of stone on which the above-mentioned memorial was engraved was found at Antioch by Sir William Ramsay in 1912, and reads as follows:

"To Lucius Sergius Paullus, the younger, one of the four commissioners in charge of the Roman streets, tribune of the soldiers of the sixth legion, styled Ferrata, questor," etc.[92]

The other text referred to, which mentions Sergia Paulla—whose name was correctly read only in 1913— joins with the other in bringing the drama of early Christian history very close to us:

"The most excellent Sergia Paulla, daughter of Lucius, wife of Gaius Caristanius Fronto, legatus of the Emperor Cæsar (Domi)tian Augustus, with praetorian rank of Lycia and Pamphylia. (This monument erected by) Gaius Caristanius Fronto, son and grandson of Gaius." [93]

All of these most fortunate discoveries when carefully compared with each other have enabled Sir William Ramsay to draw certain stimulating conclusions with reference to the thoroughness of the proconsul's conversion related by Luke. The statement that he "believed" (Acts 13: 12) does not necessarily mean much more than his intellectual acceptance of Paul's victory over Elymas; but if his descendants

---

[91] Sir William Ramsay is the supreme authority on Antioch and its religion, and all who wish to continue this study must consult his *Cities of St. Paul* and *The Bearing of Recent Discoveries on the Trustworthiness of the New Testament,* 2d ed., 1915.

[92] Sir William Ramsay, *The Bearing of Recent Discoveries on the Trustworthiness of the New Testament,* 2d ed., 1915, p. 157.

[93] *Ibid.,* pp. 154, 155.

were Christians, the content of the statement may be much fuller and richer than this.[94]

We know that the son of the proconsul was probably not a Christian, for the inscriptions show that he had an official career which required him to participate in the pagan ceremonies. This son was probably at Rome, carrying on the studies proper to his rank, when Paul was in Cyprus (*cir.* A.D. 47) and as immediately after the completion of his education, he would soon have left home to take up official duties, any change in his father's religious views might not have affected him very powerfully. But his sister, Sergia Paulla, must have been only a child, or perhaps not yet born, at the time of Paul's evangelistic visit, so that she would have been all her life under the new Christian influence, if the father had whole-heartedly accepted Christianity.

Sir William Ramsay thinks that the new inscriptions give at least an additional hint that Sergia Paulla was a Christian and that she trained her children to be Christians. This hint is found in the fact that while her husband, Gaius Caristanius Fronto, began a senatorial career (*cir.* A.D. 73-74)—probably being advanced from the equestrian order through the influence of his noble wife and her brother, the governor of Galatia—yet from this time forward the Caristanii drop out of office, presumably because they have become Christians. Whatever may be thought of the force of this argument, it is at any rate a great satisfaction to obtain this new light upon the family and descendants of a Biblical character like Sergius Paulus.

[94] For a complete examination of the exact meaning of the leading theological terms in the early Christian vocabulary, see Sir William Ramsay, *Teaching of Paul in Terms of the Present Day,* 1914.

6. Side-Lights from Other Cities Visited by St. Paul

(1) Tarsus

Tarsus imprest the writer as much as Damascus or Rome. The nearby seacoast and the mountain within walking distance where, in ancient as in modern times, the well-to-do families had their summer houses close to the famous Cilician Gates; and the river Cydnus with its enticing swimming-pool flowing so close to the city—all these things were as familiar to Paul in his boyhood as to the eighty-eight students in "St. Paul's Collegiate Institute" of Tarsus, who in 1913 were preparing for life under the wise and brilliant leadership of President Christie.

The ancient Tarsus had a far larger and more famous institution of learning than this modern college, for to its university students were drawn from all parts of the learned world. It was very young and neither as rich nor large as the universities of Athens and Alexandria; yet it almost rivaled even those great schools in the fame of its faculty and in its reputation for doing thorough work. Athenodorus of Tarsus (74 B.C.-A.D. 7) influenced Seneca so powerfully that this may account for the resemblance so often noticed between Seneca and St. Paul.[95] Tarsus in the reign of Augustus was the one example known in history of a state ruled by its university and, as Ramsay has so often pointed out, it was a providential place for an apostle to the Gentiles to be born (cf. Gal. 1: 15). It could not be ranked in size with Rome or Alexandria, nor in trade with such centers as Ephesus, Corinth, or

[95] So Ramsay, The Cities of St. Paul, 1907, 222ff.

Puteoli; but it was a place of importance and it was an old city having a noble history behind it. A recently found text of 740 lines, now in the British Museum, tells how it had been captured by Sennacherib, during the lifetime of Hezekiah and rebuilt by him after the model of Babylon and given a new name Tarsus (Tharsu). From that time on it could be called "no mean city" (Acts 21: 39), and Xenophon could speak of it as a "joy of heart."

Paul was by nation Jewish but by family Tarsian. From childhood he had been a member of the aristocracy of the city. He had the Jewish nature but came into such close contact from earliest boyhood with the Graeco-Roman world at its best that he learned how to make the religion of the Jewish race intelligible to Gentiles. There was no anti-Semitic crusade in Tarsus as in so many other Greek cities, but Greek qualities were guided by the Asiatic spirit. Every citizen was proud of his city and knew well its ancient history. The coinage goes back to the sixth century before Christ, and on her coins Tarsus was proudly called:

"LOVELIEST GREATEST METROPOLIS."

The so-called tomb of Sardanapalus—which may have actually been a Roman temple—must have been familiar to every citizen in the first century, as well as the ancient legend said to have been sculptured upon it: "Eat, drink, and play; for everything else is not worth the snap of one's fingers." But this maxim did not well represent the religion of the average Tarsian. Sandon-Heracles and Baal-Tarz were the leading deities. The former was practically associated in the peasant mind with the same ideas of death and resurrection as pervaded the worship of Adonis, Tammuz, and Osiris. Baal-Tarz—preeminently "Lord of Tarsus,"—who often holds in his hands corn and grapes, is the giver of vegetation and every other good gift, and his picture as seen on the coins of the fourth century before Christ looks as noble as the Greek Zeus whom he so greatly resembled in character. Lic. Hans Böhlig in his recent work has made it perfectly clear that while St. Paul adopted none of the heathen conceptions, he nevertheless at times adapted his terminology and perhaps his method of unfolding the redemptive scheme of a deified Christ to the needs and pre-conceptions of his Gentile fellow citizens, who from childhood had been taught the mystic religion of Sandon. At any rate Paul certainly learned here to recognize even in the pagan religion an element of truth.

Modern investigation has indicated that the Jews, some two centuries before St. Paul's day, were brought into Tarsus under special charter and with special rights. St. Paul was probably descended from these Jews and his citizenship may have been in the family for generations.[96] Certainly Paul's idea of Christianity was an imperial idea. He thought of it as a world religion with Rome as its center. It was as a Roman citizen in the free city of Tarsus that he obtained this vision of an imperial world religion, as also his great emphasis on freedom.

The Tarsian women always drest modestly, being deeply veiled. The veil was the woman's crown and protection, and this early education may have affected

[96] Ramsay thinks it began with Pompey's rule 64 B.C.; *ibid.*, 205.

St. Paul's teaching (*e.g.*, 1 Cor. 11:3-10). Roman citizens always had three or four names, so that their full name is seldom used. Sir William Ramsay emphasizes the fact that Paul certainly had both a Roman and a Jewish name from childhood. Work upon linen and the making of tent-cloth constituted one of the most celebrated industries of ancient Tarsus, and while no Jewish tent-maker could be found in Tarsus when the writer visited there, it is a fact that up to within a few years this business was continued by Jews in modern Tarsus. Every Hebrew, however rich and whatever his profession, had to learn a trade, and Paul took the trade which was most common in his own city.

A Palestinian Jew could never have become the evangelist and teacher of the Greek-Roman world. He could not have touched its heart or even felt its pulse as Paul could do.[97] It was also in Tarsus that Paul so mastered the Greek philosophy as to be able to mix on equal terms with educated men, so that he could be counted a friend of the Asiarchs of Ephesus and talk as an equal to a Roman centurion or a Syrian governor. Let it also be remembered that it was here or near here that Paul began his missionary career and preached his first evangelistic sermons (Acts 15:28; Gal. 1:21).[98]

(2) DAMASCUS

Because of Paul's early acquaintance with this city it probably ought to be mentioned in this list, altho

[97] See Ramsay, *Teaching of Paul in Terms of the Present Day*, 1914, pp. 32*ff.*

[98] For a striking summary of the influences of Tarsus upon Paul see Lic. Hans Böhlig, *Die Geisteskultur von Tarsos*, 1913, 67*ff.*

its poverty of antiquities is remarkable. However, some of the walls are ancient; some of the Roman gates are well preserved; the "Street Straight" still runs through the city from the eastern to the western gate; while the large church of John the Baptist, which was constructed by Arcadius about A.D. 400, still shows at one point, notwithstanding the fact that it was turned into a Mohammedan mosque in the eighth century and has several times been burned, the following famous inscription:

"Thy kingdom, O Christ, is an everlasting kingdom, and thy dominion endureth throughout all generations." [99]

Another interesting inscription (A.D. 318-319) discovered near here reads:

"The meeting house (Συναγωγή) of the Marionists, in the village of Lebanon, of the Lord and Saviour Jesus Christ. Erected by the forethought of Paul the presbyter." [99a]

(3) PHILIPPI

When Paul crossed into Europe the first important city that he came to was Philippi. From both coins and inscriptions it is well proved that this was a Roman colony. But how does Luke dare to speak of this city as being "the first of the district"? Even Dr. Hort [100] thought the author of the Acts had made a mistake here, using a well-known Greek word in an impossible sense, since μερίς never means "region." Dr. Hort

[99] As the writer remembers this inscription it does not read exactly as quoted here, but Dr. R. A. S. Macalister is responsible for the quotation as given.

[99a] Quoted by Harnack, *The Mission and Expansion of Christianity in the First Three Centuries*, 1908, Vol. II, p. 124.

[100] Appendix to his *New Testament in the Original Greek*, p. 96.

was right so far as any text known at that time could throw light upon this word. But recently in the Fayum a number of documents have been found showing that Luke was better posted on the technical names for the local divisions of territory in the first century than even the greatest experts on the Greek language a generation ago. All scholars are now agreed that this word was actually used here "in a legitimate sense and one particularly associated with Macedonia." [101]

But in the Bible narrative there is still another difficulty. Luke calls Philippi "the first" city of the district, whereas ancient historians name Amphipolis as capital of this geographical division of the country. Has the Bible author made a mistake or is the text corrupt, as Blass supposed? Probably neither. Luke being a native of Philippi would naturally claim for his own town the precedence over this other rival city which his townsmen were doubtless claiming then, which claim was acknowledged a little later universally. [102] This incidental proof of the local partialities of the author of the Acts gives better testimony to the fact that he was a companion of the apostle in his journeys and not a second century historian than any number of direct assertions could do if made in the narrative.

The title given by Luke to the officials of Philippi—"praetors"—adds to the above argument. The term was not technically correct, but the inscriptions have proved that it was "employed as a courtesy title for the supreme magistrates of a Roman colony; and as usual Luke moves on the plane of educated conversa-

[101] See Hogarth, *Authority and Archæology*, pp. 349-350.
[102] *Ibid.*, p. 250; and Ramsay, *St. Paul the Traveller*, p. 206.

tion in such matters, and not on the plane of rigid technical accuracy." [103]

(4) THESSALONICA

From Philippi the apostle went to Thessalonica, which was not a Roman colony but a free Greek city, and here again he was supposed, up to a very recent period, to have made a curious blunder when he referred to the "rulers" of the city. He twice calls them πολιτάρχης "politarchs" (Acts 17: 6, 8), a title which is used nowhere else in the New Testament and does "not appear in any other place in Greek literature" (Haverfield).

But some years ago a visitor at Salonika, which now marks the site of the ancient Thessalonica, saw a marble slab built into one of the mud houses, and when he had examined it, found it to be part of an ancient arch which contained engraved upon it certain remarks about the "politarchs" of the city! Since that time sixteen other texts from the same site have been found containing the same confirmation of the local accuracy of the Lukan narrative.[104]

Several other illustrations showing indirectly the unexpected accuracy of the author of the Acts, as proved by modern discoveries, are given in Hogarth's work already mentioned: "The whole aspect of what happened at Thessalonica, as compared with the events at Philippi, is in perfect harmony with the ascertained difference in the political condition of the two places. There is no mention of the rights and privileges of

---

[103] Ramsay, op. cit., 218; quoted approvingly by Hogarth, Authority and Archæology, p. 352.

[104] See especially American Journal of Theology, 1897, p. 598.

Roman citizenship; but we are presented with the spectacle of a mixed mob of Greeks and Jews, who are anxious to show themselves to be Cæsar's friends. No lictors with rods and fasces appear upon the scene; but we hear something distinctly of a *demus* or free assembly of the people. Nothing is said of religious ceremonies which the citizens, being Roman, may not lawfully adopt; all the anxiety, both of people and magistrates, is turned to the one point of showing their loyalty to the emperor. And those magistrates by whom the question at issue is ultimately decided are not Roman *prætors,* but Greek *politarchs"* (Conybeare and Howson).

"It is well known that the visit to Philippi is described in the first person plural, while in that to Thessalonica we get back into the ordinary narrative in the third person. That is usually held to mean that in the one narrative we have the evidence of an eyewitness, whether worked up or not, in the other we have not. And the further question arises, Is the author of the Acts the eyewitness who falls naturally into the first person when he is describing occasions at which he was present with St. Paul, or is he a later writer, who, in an extremely inartistic way, incorporated the fragment of a diary with other information? On this we have only one observation here to make. The narrative of the visit at Philippi is accurate and full of local coloring. That, it is said, is owing to the fact that the author had good material here. But when we pass to Thessalonica, we have the same evidence of local knowledge, and the same accuracy in constitutional points. Does not this suggest that we have here the work of the same hand in both cases? If St. Luke were a native of Philippi, he would know the constitution of the neighboring city of Thessalonica; and altho he was not present, his narrative, based on various information that he received, would be accurate, and the local circumstances would naturally become prominent. The hypothesis that the author was the same is surely more natural than to imagine two sources, both the product of authors with good local knowledge, worked up in the same style by a *tendenz* writer of the second century." [104a]

(5) ANTIOCH IN SYRIA

Of this ancient city little now remains except some colossal ruins of aqueducts and Roman walls; yet it must be mentioned because it was the cradle of Gentile Christianity and one of the most important centers of Christian life from the third to the sixth century. Here it was that the disciples were first called Christians and it was to this center that Paul and Barnabas reported their missionary work. It was called "Antioch the Golden," and only Rome and Alexandria surpassed it in population and wealth, while it was regnant in politics, philosophy, and the arts. Many races met within its walls, the somber cults of the orient being mellowed through contact with the elegant rites of Greece. The Jews were especially well received at Antioch, and the feeling was reciprocated, the Jewish king giving a portico to the city. Being the seat of the first Christian patriarchate of the orient, it rivaled Alexandria in its theological influence, its schools being more stable and sober than those of Egypt. Its society was rich, polished, and refined, and Chrysostom became

[104a] D. G. Hogarth, *Authority and Archæology,* pp. 352-354.

vainly angry against the luxurious dress, false hair, perfumes, and painted faces of its women, and against the love of the circus displayed by its supposedly Christian men. Yet every Christian house was marked by the sign of the cross, and numerous philanthropic institutions arose, more than three thousand widows and orphaned maidens being supported at one time by the church. This city was the home of great engineering enterprises, and its architects were renowned the world over, ordinarily following the Greek tradition, tho adopting the arch and vault from Rome.[105]

The original city was laid out, as was Alexandria, with two great colonnaded streets intersecting at the center. Tiberius built several colonnades and enlarged the theater. A little before Paul's day a large temple to Jupiter Capitolinus was erected and a magnificent forum. A little later Titus, it is said, set up the cherubim captured from the Jewish temple over one of the gates. About an hour's walk from the city was the famous grove of Daphne where Artemis was worshiped with choruses of music, licentious rites, and every extravagance of luxury. It was in this city, which even excelled Corinth in its temptations, that Christianity made its greatest impression in the early centuries. Ten great synods of the Church were held at Antioch in the third century, and it was here that Simeon Stylites practised asceticism on the top of his pillar.

A remarkable discovery made at Antioch was that by some well-diggers in 1910, who found seven silver objects, probably on the site of the ancient church. Of these the most important was a silver chalice, con-

---

[105] Cf. a brilliant description by De Vogüé, *Syrie Centrale*, pp. 13-16.

CHRISTIAN SARCOPHAGUS IN S. MARIA ANTIQUA

From Nuovo Bullettini di Archeologia Cristiana." (1901)

FRAGMENT OF A RE-
CENTLY DISCOVERED
JEWISH
SARCOPHAGUS

From "Nuovo Bullettino di
Archeologia Cristiana,"
(1915)

JEWISH MEASURES OF THE FIRST CENTURY RECENTLY FOUND ON OR NEAR THE
HOUSE OF CAIAPHAS, THE HIGH PRIEST, AT JERUSALEM

("Revue Biblique," April, 1914)

sisting of a silver communion bowl, covered with a silver sheet of beautiful ornamentation, dating, it is said, from A.D. 57-87. This date is possible, as the chased decorations of grapevines, bunches of grapes, birds, etc., are done in so exquisite a manner as to prove that the work was executed by a Greek artist of remarkable skill. But the chief wonder is yet to be told—"portrait figures" of Christ and ten of his apostles are worked out in this beautiful design! But even more remarkable is the fact that these portraits should have been affixt to such a poorly executed inner bowl. Dr. Eisen's explanation is that the inner bowl was regarded as the most valuable part of the chalice, otherwise the artist who made the figures would have improved the bowl to harmonize it with the rest.

Dr Gustavus A. Eisen, who in September, 1916, reported in detail the particulars of the discovery, and described the decorations, says: "The face of the Christ seems divine; no subsequent artist has succeeded in imparting that sweetness and gentleness which tradition gives to the Saviour's features and which we here for the first time see realized. The heads of the apostles are equally remarkable. We seem to read the character of each of them; the very soul of man is here portrayed in the metal as perhaps never before or after in Christian art." [105a]

Every other critic who has seen this truly wonderful artistic creation seems to be almost equally enthusiastic over its technique, it being, as Prof. Geo. W. Gilmore judges, "The best piece of work from the standpoint of execution of any early Christian piece that we have; and certainly the figure which is recog-

[105a] *Am. Jour. of Archæology*, Oct.-Dec., 1916, and April-June, 1917.

nized as that of Peter appears to be the one which has set the model for subsequent alleged portrait-drawing of that apostle." [105b]   If, indeed, scholars shall accept a first century dating for this chalice—thus pushing its age back to a point practically contemporary with that of the Holy Grail—no enthusiasm can be extravagant, since in that case we would probably possess here a genuine portrait head of Jesus coming from the apostolic age.   A final decision on this point must be reserved.

(6) CYPRUS

Since Cesnola, the United States consul at Cyprus, gathered his remarkable collection of precious things in that island, nothing has been discovered there of equal interest, altho excavations have been carried on at many points and a vast amount of material has been gathered by archeologists, especially from the pre-historic era.   When St. Paul came to the island the great shrine of Aphrodite was glorious, and as we now know, the high priest of the goddess had at least as much authority as the proconsul.   Many inscriptions from Paphos have recently been published.[106]   Among these one of the most interesting is a marble block copied by Cesnola but recently recopied with more care:

"Apollonius to his father . . . and to his mother . . . consecrated the enclosure and this monument . . . having filled the offices of clerk at this market, prefect, town-clerk, and high priest, and having been in charge of the record office.   Erected on the 25th of the month Demarchusius, in the year 13.   He also revised the Senate by means of assessors in the time of the pro-consul Paulus." [107]

[105b] Extract from a private letter received in January, 1917.
[106] *Journal of Hellenic Studies*, Vol. IX.
[107] *Ibid.*, pp. 114, 115.

There is no good reason for doubting that this proconsul was the Sergius Paulus mentioned in Acts 13,
he being the only governor of that name, so far as
known, who ever held office in Cyprus. The lettering
is of the first century, being dated by scholars about
A.D. 55. This inscription shows that the name of the
proconsul was actually spelled in Cyprus as Luke
spelled it. It may be mentioned in conclusion that the
embalmed body of Spyridion, a shepherd bishop of
Cyprus who attended the Council of Nicæa, is to this
day carried twice a year about the streets in procession, so that "one may still look upon the hands which
signed the Nicæan creed." [108]

(7) ASSOS

Important excavations were carried out in 1881-
1889 in Assos by the Archæological Institute of
America. It was found that around the sides of the
Acropolis—which is located in the crater of an extinct
volcano—ran narrow paved streets rising tier upon tier
in terraces. Upon the top of the Acropolis the temple
of Athena was located. The market-place is the most
complete and interesting Greek agora known. A Greek
bath in three stories was uncovered, and the remains of
a Christian church were found on the site of an old
Roman bath which had been built A.D. 14-37. Dr. A.
G. Clark remarks that Assos became Christian at an
early date "perhaps in some measure as a result of the
visit of St. Paul and St. Luke . . . but more probably
from the proximity of the seven churches in Asia."

The temple of Assos, Doric in type like that of the
temple at Pergamum, was dedicated to Athena Polias.

[108] George Hodges, *The Early Church* (1915), p. 131.

Among the inscriptions is a decree dating from the accession of Caligula A.D. 37. The oath of the pagan citizens is well worth recording:

"We swear by the Saviour and God, Cæsar Augustus, and by the pure Virgin (*i.e.,* Athena Polias), whom our fathers worshiped, that we will be faithful to Gaius Cæsar Augustus and all his house."

Another inscription of the Roman period found at Mitylene in 1880 gives a curious funereal monument to a dog:

"Parthenope his dog, with whom in life it was his wont to play, Anaxeos here hath buried, for the pleasure that she gave bestowing this return. Affection, then, even in a dog possesseth its reward such as she hath whoever in her life kind to her master now receives this tomb. See, then, thou make some friend who in thy life will love thee well and care for thee when dead "

Another inscription, of sufficient interest to be mentioned, tells of Eutyches, who was elected, by a guild of linen weavers, "director of the market" three terms in succession; another, A.D. 153, gives the name of the victor that year in the "boxing contest and race in armor." [109]

(8) MILETUS

Sir Charles Thomas Newton nearly sixty years ago did some excavating in this city, finding the ruins of the celebrated temple of Apollo, which was connected with the port on the north of the Sacred Way, flanked on each side by a row of tombs and statues. He took ten statues from this sacred street, and a lion and a sphinx. These statues were seated in chairs, and it was discovered that the citizens of Miletus dedicated them as

[109] For many other inscriptions see *Papers of the Archæological Institute of America,* Classical Series, 1882, 1885, 1890, 1898, 1902.

a tithe to Apollo. This temple was the chief sanctuary of the island, and Dr. Wiegand, during a long and successful series of excavations, begun in 1899 and continued for eleven years, found that the public treaties and official records of Miletus were kept here.

Five hundred years before St. Paul landed, this was the chief city of Greece, celebrated for its literature, especially in history and philosophy, but in the Roman age it dwindled to a commonplace commercial town. The poet Timotheus (446-357 B.C.) lived here, and also Aspasia, the famous literary woman who became a friend of Pericles. There can still be seen the magnificent ruins of a Roman theater, excavated by Wiegand, as large as the largest in Asia Minor, having 450 feet frontage, and a nymphæum of the age of Titus, also a number of other important Roman buildings which must have come under Paul's eyes.

A Jewish inscription in the theater reads:

"Place of the Jews, who are also God-fearing."

The secularization of the Jews is shown in a most interesting way by this inscription which was put up in a pagan theater by worshipers of the one God or put up for them by the theater authorities.[110]

In the same theater was a late Christian protective charm written, in a strange symbolic manner in which the seven vowels are arranged as would be natural in incantations, after which comes the prayer:

"O Holy One, keep the city of Miletus, and all that dwell therein."

At the bottom is written in large letters:

"Archangels, keep the city of the Milesians and all that dwell therein." . . .

[110] See Deissmann, *Light from the Ancient East,* pp. 446-455.

This is probably a Christian memorial of the period when the theater was converted into a citadel.

(9) RHODES

Much light has been thrown on Rhodes in late years. Some 350 inscriptions have been discovered since Mr. Hamilton found the first in 1837, and a large number of statuettes, vases, coins, gems, etc., have been deposited in various museums. These inscriptions show that the labor and social guilds were open to all, women as well as men, slaves and foreigners included. Helios was the great god of Rhodes, to whom horses were sacrificed. The Rhodians also sacrificed to the god of good luck before setting out upon a voyage, so that Paul and his party may have witnessed this act. When Tiberius lived in the island there were many Chaldeans here. The Jewish influence was also very strong. An ancient tradition declares that Paul stopt here just before he wrote his pastoral epistles.[111]

(10) CÆSAREA

Vast remains showing many buildings dating from Paul's day existed here as late as 1884, since which time they have suffered much mutilation. There can still be seen, however, remains of a temple dedicated to Cæsar, a theater, a hippodrome, an aqueduct, and a gigantic mole built of stones fifty feet long to protect the harbor, on the edge of which is a remarkable ruin which, tho it may not represent the dungeon where Paul spent several years, suggests, at least, the kind of a prison in which he was incarcerated. We have previously given a Christian epitaph which the writer brought from this site.

[111] See for a fine description, *Rhodes in Ancient Times,* by Cecil Torr.

(11) CRETE AND MELITA

Nothing needs to be added to the proof furnished by Mr. James Smith fifty years ago of the nautical accuracy of Luke's narrative so far as Crete and Melita and the entire voyage to Rome are concerned. He proved by admiralty charts and a study of the tides the remarkable accuracy of the narrative. Modern excavations have had chiefly to do with prehistoric or early historic civilization, showing beyond question that Homer's stories of Achæan splendor were no idle tales. In the harbor extension works of 1865, workmen brought up from a depth of fourteen feet two fragments of white marble columns, and the torso of a statue of Artemis; another fragment was excavated 1877. The chief ancient building near the harbor was the temple of Astarte (later, Juno). It has been fully proved that the official title of the leading official in the Roman era was "chief man" (πρῶτος). Local tradition fixes the site of Paul's landing on the northeastern portion of the island, where the bay as well as a little church bear his name.

(12) SYRACUSE

St. Paul's relations with this city were so brief and comparatively unimportant that we can no more than mention a very few facts concerning it, notwithstanding the enormous number of antiquities which remain here. The cathedral, which was erected about A.D. 640, is built into a noble Doric temple dating from the fifth century before Christ, which was probably a temple of Athena; the length of the temple must have been at least 160 feet, and its breadth 70 feet. Some of the majestic columns still remain to testify to its ancient splendor. Imposing ruins remain of a temple dedicated to Apollo of even greater magnificence, as well as remains of the largest ancient theater in Sicily—about 440 feet in diameter—and of an amphitheater cut out of the living rock by Augustus. A wonderful fortress dating from the fifth century before Christ, representing probably the most imposing of all known Greek fortresses, shows the complicated system of underground passages sometimes connected with such buildings.

However, the most interesting constructions in Syracuse to the Christian visitor are the early Christian catacombs—"the Grottos of St. John." They really represent an entire underground city with several stories of streets and squares and circular halls cut out of the solid rock, with arched tombs and large funeral chambers, closed by locked doors, lining the streets. Christian frescos adorn the walls, much resembling those of Rome; tho as a whole these catacombs are much superior, showing a degree of wealth and architectural elaborateness unknown elsewhere.[112]

(13) PUTEOLI

From the hill close to Puteoli St. Paul would have obtained his first view of Vesuvius and the most beautiful bay in the world; by a short ride or long walk he could have reached either Pompeii or Herculaneum. However, this city especially deserves notice because it was probably the end of St. Paul's sea voyage on his way to Rome.

This was, indeed, the port of Rome, Ostia being a rival port tho not so popular because its harbor was

---

[112] See especially E. Manceri, *Siracusa*, 1904.

not so good. When St. Paul landed here, A.D. 61, it was a beautiful city surrounded by villas, of which Cicero's is the most noted, and containing great sanitariums connected with the mineral springs located here. Part of the massive artificial mole connected with the harbor is still in existence, together with the fine ruins of a large amphitheater, the market hall, which was surrounded by a colonnade of thirty-six columns of marble and granite, a circus, tombs, a temple of Augustus in which the cathedral of St. Proculus was built, and a number of other ancient monuments. The amphitheater was very large, being comparable to the Colosseum at Rome, and the subterranean parts were found intact, even to the holes which contained the trapdoors by which the wild beasts were let into the arena. This magnificent building was probably erected in the reign of Vespasian, but another large amphitheater has just been found, perhaps the very one in which Nero fought.[113] This newly discovered building shows the upper apertures of entrances and exits, together with many fragments of the gilded and colored stucco from the walls, thus proving the former magnificence of its decorations. In Paul's day Puteoli (now Pozzuoli) was one of the most famous commercial ports of the world. The Puteoli pottery was almost equal to the best made in Italy. But besides local wares this was the center from which wheat from Egypt, and iron from Elba, and other products from far distant lands were distributed. Sulphur, alum, perfumes, mosaics, earth for ceramics, and glass cups with views of Puteolian scenery were among the chief objects of local trade.

[113] *Art and Archæology,* 1916, p. 179.

The Eastern merchants found it necessary to establish residences here, and one text which has been found is a letter (A.D. 174) from local Phoenician merchants asking the senate of Tyre to undertake the payment of the rent of their factory. The fact that the senate agreed to this shows the value of this trade internationally. The docks in Paul's day were so large as to accommodate not only the big grain ships but also the larger boats which carried the obelisks of Egypt to this port.

(14) FROM PUTEOLI TO ROME

It was 170 miles from here to Rome, and Paul probably went by the ordinary route, which was to leave Puteoli by the Via Consularis, striking the Appian Way at Capua, twenty miles farther north. Two days after leaving Capua the party would arrive at Terracina, about seventy-five miles from Rome, and pass from here through the celebrated Pontine marshes, the boat being towed by mules through the canal—a long, dreary journey, of which several ancient travelers complain. They must all have been glad to reach the Appii Forum, forty-three miles from the capitol. From here, with some fellow Christians who came to meet them, they passed on to the Three Taverns, where they again broke their journey. Both of these places are well known. The only thing that now remains, of ancient date, at the Appii Forum is the old milestone; but we remember that Cicero records that he wrote a letter from here, and Horace tells how he stayed over night with a surly landlord at the Three Taverns, the whole place being "stuffed with sailors." Some of the tombs which line the highway from here to Rome still catch the eye of the traveler, for here were the sepulchral monuments of Rome's richest and noblest— tombs such as those of Gallianus, Pompey, etc. About four miles from the city they must have passed the villa of Seneca in which he committed suicide five or six years later, and at the third mile the well-known tomb of Cicilia Metella, which yet impresses all observers; and one mile from the gates the newly erected tomb of Drusus, brother of Tiberius.

7. Side-lights from Cities Mentioned in the Book of Revelation or Influential in the Early Church

(1) EPHESUS

The remarkable excavations on this site have already been recounted.

(2) SMYRNA

No excavations worthy of the name have as yet been made here; but visitors can still make out the plan of the ancient stadium and a few other ancient buildings, and every visitor is shown the traditional spot where Polycarp, the friend and neighbor of St. John, was martyred (A.D. 155), saying: "Eighty and six years have I served him, and he hath done me no wrong. How then can I speak evil of my King who saved me?"

It was a very ancient city, claiming to be the birthplace of Homer. It was on the highway between Lydia and the West, and so was a commercial city of prominence. Above everything else it prided itself upon its beauty and its faithfulness to all treaties. Every traveler even yet is imprest with the sparkling beauty of the bay and the crown of buildings encircling the hill, which is the most prominent part of the view from the harbor. In ancient times this hill was encircled by a street so glorious that it was called "the Golden," and this street was lined by palaces and temples and crowned by the acropolis, while the temple of Cybele, the tutelary goddess, situated in the east, just outside the city proper, was the brilliant pendant to this necklace or crown of architectural jewels. Sir William Ramsay quotes Aristides, who compares this to the crown of Ariadne in the heavenly constellation; and he believes the Revelator had this aspect of the city in mind when he promised to the faithful in Smyrna a "crown of life."

Apollonius of Tyana refers to this popular pride when he advises the citizens, "It is a greater charm to wear a crown of men than a crown of porticoes and pictures and gold." [114]

For centuries before the Christian era Smyrna had been celebrated for its trustworthiness. Cicero calls it the "city of our most faithful and most ancient allies," and he who knew better than any other the struggle of the little primitive Christian church here had no word of rebuke for it, but only says, "Continue to be faithful" (Rev. 2: 10).

The reference to the "synagog of Satan" with which the early disciples had to contend reminds Sir William Ramsay that altho Polycarp was martyred on the Sabbath day, the Jews broke the law in order to bring faggots for this human bonfire.

[114] Ramsay, *The Letters to the Seven Churches*, 1906, pp. 251-280.

(3) PERGAMUM

Of the seven cities mentioned in Revelation the only ones distinguished for their architectural and artistic remains are Ephesus, Sardis, and Pergamum. No one of the seven cities could be compared with Pergamum in the matter of art. In the second century before Christ a new school of sculpture arose here which rivaled in achievement anything ever done before or since in this world. A vast quantity of these art treasures have been excavated; but, unfortunately, with the exception of some important remains from the Church of St. John the Theologian, almost all of the larger monuments are pagan, not Christian.[115]

Excavations begun here by the Berlin Museum as early as 1878 have been carried on with little interruption ever since, the later work being done under the auspices of the Imperial German Institute of Archeology. The decorations of the "Great Altar" of Zeus almost rival in strength and artistic power the famous frieze of the Parthenon. The Battle of the Giants is perhaps the most terrific scene ever represented in marble.

The ruins of the temple of Asclepios "the Saviour," to which royal patients came for healing from every land, was magnificent beyond all possible description. Dörpfeld, in 1910, reported finding what was probably a shrine where the "mysteries" were celebrated under this temple.[116] The city was devoted to the Roman emperors, and was the first provincial city to establish the imperial cult. A large temple in Corinthian style has been

[115] It will be remembered that Pergamum was also the place where parchment was invented, receiving its name from this city.

[116] Felix Sarteaux, *Villes mortes d'Asie Mineure,* 1916, pp. 43-45.

found dedicated to the worship of Trajan and Hadrian, and another honoring Caracalla. The early Christians were opposed here by the most brilliant form of paganism. Many of them favored compromise with the old religion and outward observance of the forms of worship which would permit them to take their places in business and social life; but St. John declares in the strongest way against these Nicolaitans. Sir William Ramsay thinks that when the altar of Zeus was dug up here a few years ago the excavators were actually looking upon the very "seat (or throne) of Satan" of which the book of Revelation speaks. The four leading deities of the municipality were Zeus, Athena, Dionysos, and Asclepios. In order to show the reader something of the splendor of these temples we give photographs of some recently discovered works of art.[117]

(4) THYATIRA

This was, as Sir William Ramsay has pointed out, a garrison city whose strength lay in its position between the rival powers of Syria and Pergamum. The coins represent the god of the city with a battle-ax upon his shoulder; but in reality the city was not properly symbolized by a sword or battle-ax, but very appropriately by a blacksmith's bar, since it was famous for its bronze work (cf. Rev. 2: 27). The smiths of Thyatira were united in a rather celebrated guild or labor union, and doubtless this was true also of the manufacturers of garments and of the dealers in purple cloth such as Lydia sold (Acts 16: 40); for there were

[117] For fine plans and reproductions of the Agora, altar of Zeus, and temple of Athena Palias, see *Pergame*, by E. Pontremoli and M. Collignon, 1900, and especially *Königliche Museum, Altertümer von Pergamon* (I-III).

more trade guilds in this city than in any other in Asia. The famous purple garments in which Lydia dealt were not made with Phenician dyes, as was once supposed, but rather, without doubt, with a Thyatiran product, probably the "Turkey red" made from the madder root. The unusual liberty given here to women is indicated not only by the position attained by Lydia but also by the tremendous influence in religious affairs exercised by Jezebel (Rev. 2:20). This woman teacher seems to have had a good moral character, but she believed in compromising with paganism and, probably as a Gnostic, taught that the material world was merely a false claim of the senses. As no citizens could cultivate art or music or mingle in political or social life without accommodating themselves to pagan ritual, her position must have seemed well taken to many educated, broad-minded people. But as Sir William Ramsay says, Christianity would have disappeared if it had not been brave and outspoken in its opposition to the popular beliefs and customs.

(5) SARDIS

The very recent discoveries at Sardes (Bible, "Sardis") have thrown brilliant and unexpected light upon the Diana worship mentioned in the New Testament (Acts 19:24-35). The excavations began in March, 1910, being conducted by Prof. Howard Crosby Butler of Princeton, and were examined by the writer in 1913 when the work was well under way. The ancient Lydian necropolis on the mountainside across from the temple, with its multitude of Lydian inscriptions, particularly the bilingual text from the tenth year of Artaxerxes written in Lydian and Aramaic, may for the historian be the most important of all Professor Butler's discoveries at this ancient capital of Lydia; but to the Bible student the majestic temple of Artemis stands supreme. It will be remembered that Pergamum, Smyrna, Ephesus, and Sardis were neighboring cities, the three former each claiming in the first century the title of "First City of Asia"; but Sardis indisputably held the highest position of honor in the ancient history of Lydia. The worship of Diana or Artemis occupied the same central position and followed the same cult here as at Ephesus. A few of the mighty pillars of this ancient temple had been always visible, but the American expedition cleared the site completely, finding a marble octastyle building, 320 by 150 feet, with twenty columns on either side, thirteen of these columns still standing to a height of thirty feet and two others to the height of sixty feet. The architectural details have surprized all observers with their beauty. The specimens of Ionic ornament dating from the fourth century before Christ are equal to anything the writer knows outside of Greece.[118] The temple was roofed and in use 300 B.C., but in A.D. 17 was badly damaged by the earthquake which destroyed the city, the calamity being so great that Tiberius remitted all its taxes for five years and made a gift to the city of $500,000 for its rebuilding. When the temple was finally destroyed, it was undergoing repairs and a number of the carvings were only blocked out when the worship ceased. It was in July, 1910, that a mortgage-deed was found dating from 300 B.C., which first made known to the excavators the fact that

---

[118] Even the splendid columns laid bare by the Germans at Baalbek do not equal these.

the building they were examining was a temple of Artemis. This mortgage was on real estate, and was given because "the temple wardens are demanding from me the gold lent on deposit and belonging to Artemis." The enormous size of these transactions is indicated by the number of villages near Sardis, including slaves, which the mortgager, Mnesimachus, turns over to the temple as collateral.

The "temple wardens" supervised all details connected with the rental and cultivation of the temple land; they had charge of the records and acted as guarantors of mortgaged land which was foreclosed and sold by the temple. The "temple-keeper" is also often in evidence. Timarchus, who served in this office (second century before Christ), had been royal treasurer for the entire kingdom. It is a question whether the high priest was a eunuch, as at Ephesus; but as the priestesses at Sardis were vestals, who were not allowed to marry until their term of office expired, this is probable. The high priestess of Artemis was, however, the highest official in the Sardis temple and must have been a woman of superior rank and great wealth, for she paid at her own cost for the public sacrifices performed each month by the city.[119]

Among the many remarkable inscriptions is one on a block of bluish marble found in 1910 dating from the first century before Christ, upon which it is declared that Iollas, son of Iollas, is entitled to "two golden wreaths with a golden portrait-effigy, three marble portrait images, four painted portraits," etc. The probability seems to be, however, that the city did not furnish these portraits and wreaths, but merely

[119] See *Am. Journal of Archæology*, XVII, 31, 355*ff*; XVIII, 321, 425*ff*.

gave to this honored citizen the right to buy them and display them. It is also interesting to note that inscriptions celebrating the temple cook as well as the singers and harpists of the temple have been discovered in the ruins. It is found that a singer in the temple was paid better than the teachers of literature and it is entirely possible that the cook received as much as either.

It ought to be added that a very early Christian church of brick was found at the east end of the temple entirely preserved excepting for the loss of its wooden roof. There came great awe, at least to one visitor, as he entered this little primitive Christian church with its ancient altar still standing and looked out through its three modest arched windows at the magnificence of the paganism which it had supplanted. The altar "consists of a crudely cut block of sandstone set upon a short section of a column about 30 centimeters diameter. It is a true table altar with a single support" (Butler). It has been suggested that the rough block was perhaps a relic of a martyr's death.

It is an interesting fact that on the doorpost of the ancient pagan temple were written certain words (φῶς, ζωή) which afterward became favorite terms in the mysteries and in Christian literature, notably in the gospel of John. Even then the term "light" meant spiritual illumination and the term "life" was used in the higher sense. An inscription which was found in 1912 on the tomb of Artemas, a physician, probably of the first century of our era, but possibly of the first century before Christ, closes with the statement, "He is living." [120]

[120] *American Journal of Archæology*, XV: 401*ff*; XVI: 465*ff*; XVIII (1914): 35*ff*, 325*ff*; XVII (1913): 29*ff*, 353*ff*.

VERY EARLY CHRISTIAN CHURCH AT SARDIS
From "American Journal of Archæology," (Vol. 16, p. 476)

TEMPLE OF ARTEMIS (DIANA) AT SARDIS
From "American Journal of Archæology," (Vol. 17, p. 471)

MOSAIC FROM A CHRISTIAN BATH, SERDJILLA, SYRIA

American Expedition, 1899-1900

CHURCH OF ST. SIMEON STYLITES AT KALAT-SEMAN, SYRIA (6th Century)

American Expedition, 1899-1900

(6) PHILADELPHIA

No excavations of importance have been made on this site. However, Sir William Ramsay with rare skill has pointed out certain peculiarities in the ancient city, previously overlooked, to which references are certainly made in the address to this church reported in Revelation 3: 7-13. This was not a military center but, because of its situation, preëminently a missionary city, an "apostle of Hellenism," carrying education and civilization to the surrounding country. The Jewish national party must have been particularly strong here, as also in Smyrna, since it is in these two cities only that this opposition to Christianity is mentioned. In A.D. 17, as Sir William points out, a terrific and long-continued earthquake struck the city, which entirely unnerved the population and caused multitudes to leave their homes (*cf*. Rev. 3: 12). Tiberius sent help and a temple was then erected for his worship and a new name was taken by the city in his honor. To consent to the city becoming his namesake was one of the highest favors the emperor could confer. Yet this new name disappeared from use presently, and about twenty-five years before the book of Revelation was written the city took another "new name" in honor of another emperor! It is to this city that the imperial Christ, who has the "key of David that openeth and no one can shut," says, "Him that overcometh will I make a pillar in the temple of my God, and he shall go no more out, and . . . I will write upon him my new name."

The praise given to this city and to Smyrna is noticeable, and they have well deserved it throughout the centuries. "Those are the two cities which have been the bulwark and the glory of Christian power in the country since it became Mohammedan; they are the two places where the Christian flag floated latest over a free and powerful city, and where even in slavery the Christians preserved cohesion among themselves and real influence among the Turkish conquerors." [121]

(7) LAODICEA

Hundreds of acres are covered with the ruins of this ancient metropolis. Two theaters and the stadium are yet in a fairly good state of preservation, but no extensive excavations have yet been made here. The church at Laodicea is supposed to have been founded by Epaphras (Col. 1:7; 4:12), and Paul wrote a letter to this church which was unfortunately lost (Col. 4:16), unless, indeed, it is to be found imbedded in the Ephesian letter, as is now generally believed.

The prosperity of Laodicea began in Roman time, and the city grew rapidly rich, largely because it was situated at an important junction of the imperial road system. It was a marked administrative and banking center. Some of its manufactories were also famous, especially those which produced a particularly fine and glossy black garment from the wool of a certain peculiar breed of black sheep cultivated here. The Jewish population was quite influential, as is shown from the fact that Flaccus, the governor of Asia, seized in 62 B.C. twenty pounds of gold which had been collected in and around Laodicea to be sent to the poor Jews of Jerusalem (cf. 1 Cor. 16:1). In close connection with the city there was a famous school of medicine which

[121] Sir William Ramsay, *Cities of St. Paul,* p. 403.

was especially renowned for its ear ointment and its "Phrygian powder" to cure weak eyes—the latter being mentioned with respect as early as Aristotle's day. It can hardly be doubted that these facts influenced the phrases used concerning this church in the book of Revelation: "Because thou sayest I am rich . . . I counsel thee to buy of me gold tried in the fire . . . and white garments . . . and anoint thy eyes with eye salve that thou mayest see."

8. OTHER CITIES SPECIALLY INFLUENTIAL IN EARLY CHRISTIANITY

One naturally thinks first of Constantinople since, for several centuries, it was preeminently the dominant metropolis of Eastern Christianity; but unfortunately no serious excavations have been conducted here. Indeed, the archeological results here important to Christianity are confined to certain ancient walls and fortifications and a few ancient relics such as the pedestal of the Eudoxia statue and a few churches, such as those of S. Sergius and S. Bacchus, and especially the church of St. Sophia, which is the finest existing sixth century monument of church architecture, originally "the most beautiful building in the world."

In Asia Minor, in addition to the cities already mentioned, Aquileia, Nicomedia, and Cyzicus may seem to demand further mention. Excavations in the former city have revealed one street and part of the town walls, while the local museum contains over 2,000 inscriptions, besides statues and other antiquities illuminating ancient life. Nothing whatever of importance has, to the writer's knowledge, been reported from Nicomedia, excepting some fifth century columns, a fifth century crypt, and the outline of an ancient church. Cyzicus has yielded a much larger treasure, but the excavations have already been mentioned sufficiently. Few fine monuments have been recovered, probably because Constantine and Justinian carried off the rarest and most costly marbles to Constantinople. It is an interesting theory, recently proposed, that the beautiful clinging and wind-blown drapery, which came into use in the middle of the fifth century, originated in Cyzicus.[122]

It may be added that the Apology of Aristides, if delivered upon the dedication of Hadrian's temple, as usually supposed, can now be exactly dated, since Hasluck's researches have shown that this temple was dedicated A.D. 139.

One of the most interesting texts gives a hymn to Serapis and Isis in a lyrical meter and "excessively crabbed Greek."[123] All that we know about the religion of Cyzicus has been carefully systematized by Sir William Ramsay. This distinguished scholar also believes that St. Paul passed close to Cyzicus on his way to Troas; but this part of the apostle's route is too obscure to be fixt with certainty.[124]

Two other cities in Italy ought to be mentioned—Milan and Ravenna. The church of S. Ambrogio at Milan, built by Ambrose, still shows the pillar where the Lombard kings were crowned, and its wooden doors probably date back to the fourth century. At Ravenna we can see, better than any place else in the world, the early Christian basilica of the finest type almost un-

[122] *American Journal of Archæology,* 1915, p. 475.
[123] *Corpus inscriptionarum Grecarum,* No. 3734.
[124] See especially Ramsay, *Bishoprics of Phrygia,* "Hierapolis"; F. W. Hasluck, *Cyzicus in Mysie,* 1910.

touched in its architecture and mosaic decorations. The tomb of Galla Placidia, built A.D. 450, is probably the earliest building here, a small cruciform structure with a dome on pendentives over the center. The baptistry of St. John, dating almost as early, is a plain octagonal building, forty feet in diameter, containing paintings, stucco reliefs, and mosaics dating from the fifth century. Three churches date from the sixth century, one of which (San Vitale) has a curious dome built of hollow pots, the other two, tho small, are of especial importance, since they were originally built of new materials, and not from more ancient constructions; so that the Christian architecture of the sixth century can be examined here without fear of confounding it with earlier work. It must be acknowledged, however, that comparatively little remains of the untouched original buildings.

In Africa the two chief centers of early Christianity were Alexandria and Carthage. So far as Alexandria is concerned the ancient city lies either beneath the sea or under modern edifices, so that nothing of great value can be reported as recently discovered here;[125] but ancient Carthage has been resurrected in modern times. Some one has said that if Palestine may be called the cradle of early Christianity, Carthage was its nursery. It was here that Tertullian was born and Cyprian was martyred; and it was here that Augustine, who controlled the theology of Christendom for nearly 1500 years, was educated. The beauty of the short ride from Tunis to the site of ancient Carthage can never be forgotten, and as the writer can testify, the

---

[125] For a statement of what has been done see the author's article, "Alexandria," in the *International Standard Bible Encyclopædia*.

view from the Brysa hill, the citadel of Dido, is
positively intoxicating. The ruins of the ancient
amphitheater are plainly visible, and in the center is
a marble pillar in memory of the many martyrs who
there suffered death, and also a small chapel in special
memory of the martyrdom (A.D. 203) of St. Perpetua,
St. Felicitas, and their companions. Père Delattre,
who, representing the White Fathers of Carthage, has
made remarkable excavations here during the past
generation, has found an ancient inscription near this
palace specifically mentioning these martyrs by name.

Three cemeteries have yielded rich treasure to the
White Fathers. Unfortunately the best preserved
sepulchral monuments are those from the most ancient
period of Carthage's history. Yet it is something to
dig up the life history of this place in the era of
Salammbo and Hannibal, especially as it is now found
that many of the ancient customs were carried over
into the Christian era. So the priests with tonsured
heads—and the sacred razors with which they were
shaved; the golden necklaces and pendants and signet
rings; the rouge boxes, of the era of Jezebel, the disc
of Tanith and the crescent of Astarte, and many other
ancient relics, find their duplicates in North Africa
even in the twentieth century.

The necropolis of St. Louis was first touched as
early as 1880, but the main work there was done
1889-90. The necropolis of Douïmes is the oldest of
all. It was in 1892 that an Arab brought to Père
Delattre, arch-priest of Carthage, some small remains
which led to the first excavation here. By 1893 he had
opened 60 tombs, and by 1894 as many as 150. In 1897
the richest necropolis of all, Bord-el-Djeded, was opened.

It is absolutely impossible to describe in any detail the wealth of rich material found at Carthage. Perhaps one of the most exciting moments in the life of Père Delattre was when he brought to light an ancient Carthaginian priestess buried in a superb anthropoid sarcophagus, with the painted representation of its distinguished owner engraved upon it. The priestess' beauty was a revelation. The brilliancy of coloring and the fine raiment does not impress the observer as does the noble dignity and beauty of this ancient high-priestess. At her right hand was buried a priest, represented as clad in a long tunic, reaching to his feet, which were shod with red sandals; his right hand was raised; his left hand held a sacred vessel, while his toga fell gracefully from his left shoulder. Another priest in a tomb not far away had his purse around his neck—as is yet the custom—and wore a gold ring on which was engraved his own profile

But the Jewish and Christian remains, tho comparatively few, are to us the most interesting. The story of finding these is entrancing. One day a little negro child, who was in the Roman Catholic orphanage, noticed some Arabs about to destroy a subterranean catacomb in order to make lime from the marble sarcophagi and inscriptions. One of the inscriptions especially struck the attention of the little negro— *in pace*—and he hastened to tell the father-director of what was being done.

Père Delattre hurried to the place and found that this tomb, which had been the dwelling-place of hyenas for centuries, was in the midst of an ancient Jewish cemetery, where Columbo and Fortunata, Alexander and many other Hebrews had been buried, with the seven-branched candlestick and other Jewish emblems carved on their tombs. Some Christian graves were also found, and the museum contains scores and perhaps hundreds of lamps just such as are found in the catacombs of Rome, some stamped with the cross, others with the dove. Representations are also found of Jonah and the whale, the Hebrew children in the fiery furnace, Daniel in the lion's den, Christ bearing his cross, etc.

We have already mentioned a mosaic of a chariot race discovered at Carthage, March, 1915, and will now add that many magic spells written on metal discs were found, which represent the incantations of jockeys or gamblers who sought in this way to injure the wind and speed of their opposing horses. Another exceedingly curious discovery was that of a terra-cotta figurine showing an organist and organ of the second century—the organ having many pipes of graduated length, stops, sound-board, case, etc.[126]

Many of the later excavations at Carthage have been paid for by Cardinal Lavigerie out of his own private purse.

[126] The authority for this latter statement is Douglas Sladen, *Carthage and Tunis*, 1906, Vol. I, pp. 94-7; for the excavations in general, Mabel Moore, *Carthage of the Phœnicians in the Light of Modern Excavation*, 1905; compare Graham Petrie, *Tunis, Kaironam and Carthage*, 1908; René Cagnat, *Carthage, Timgad, Tebessa*, 1912.

[127] Sir William Ramsay in a letter dated Sept. 17, 1917, gives the following additional information regarding the important texts furnished pages 537, 539: "The text from Antioch which you quote from W. M. Calder was not correctly published by him. The word 'elder,' presbyter, does not occur in it. In his published text most of the abbreviated word, 'presb' is a restoration. ([ΠΡΕ]CB). The correct reading is 'freedman ([C]EB. ΑΠΕΛΕΥΘΕ- of the emperor' (Sebastos). The whole inscription is now quite certain and clear, and has obviously no possible Christian character or reference. We found another interesting inscription relating to a lady, probably the niece of Sergia Paulla about whom you speak on p. 539. The niece was not Christian, as she shows no sign of religion."

III

NEW DOCUMENTARY AND OTHER EVIDENCE THROWING LIGHT UPON THE EARLY CHRISTIAN CENTURIES

1. THE ENVIRONMENT OF THE HOLY LAND IN THE FIRST CENTURY

THE Holy Land is not, as Renan thought, the Fifth Gospel; but it is the best existing commentary on the four gospels. It has long been known that the gospel narratives and the sermons of Jesus lose many of their most beautiful meanings to one unfamiliar with the natural scenery and native customs of Palestine. The language of Jesus, his illustrations and figures of speech, all show the influence of his surroundings. Much deeper than this is the undoubted fact of the psychological influence of these surroundings upon the disciples and the Master. The ancestry and home of the early teachers of Christianity affected them intellectually and spiritually. As Dr. Dale has said, we can not isolate the life of Jesus from the preceding history of the Jewish race. Many people seem to suppose that they may approach the subject as if the Lord Jesus Christ had appeared "in Spain or China instead of Judea and Galilee." [1]

Jesus' mission would have had another character if

[1] Dale, *The Living Christ*, p. 89.

he had "grown up under the oaks of Germany instead of the palms of Nazareth." So also, it is indisputable that for Jesus himself the "facts of his consciousness were given him under those forms of viewing things in which Jewish thought in general was cast!" [2]

To be a "son of Abraham" meant something even to the Son of Man, and Jewish history and literature were the best part of his early education. From the hill above Nazareth he could see scores of historical sites, and in all his boyish wanderings he and his companions were met with reminiscences of David and Elijah and Judas Maccabeus and other heroes of Israel. The modern explorations fixing ancient sites and the recent valuable studies of the physical features of Palestine have brought much more vividly to us the historic and geographical influences which must have affected every thoughtful Galilean youth.

But these investigations have done much more than this. It is now seen as never before that Christianity "at its depths rests upon oriental foundations." Jesus was an oriental. His religious presuppositions, his style of argument, his picturesque language, his thought of nature and of politics, his view of religious truth and his methods of presenting truth were all oriental. The modern excavations in Palestine have given to us a better appreciation of the oriental poverty and comfortlessness of the little adobe houses in which Jesus and his contemporaries of the poorer and middle classes lived.

But perhaps the new discoveries have been most

---

[2] See *History of New Test. Times*, II: 225, quoted by Kelman in his valuable article "Palestine" in *Dictionary of Christ and the Gospels*.

important in bringing clearly to light the fact that the district in which Jesus lived was one which came into close touch with the currents of a world civilization.

Tho it has been well said that the ordinary travels of Jesus were limited to a district scarcely larger than Chicago and its suburban towns, yet one of the great highways of commerce leading from Egypt to Damascus passed up through Galilee by the way of Nazareth, and from the home of Jesus it was only forty miles to Tyre, the celebrated Phœnician capitol, and less than fifty to the great Roman city of Cæsarea Philippi, where the ground is yet covered with the remnants of ancient palaces which in the days of Christ were more imposing than any mansions now owned by New York millionaires.

It must be remembered, too, that the influence of traffic was greater then than now, since travel was slow and every good-sized town and village became a stopping place for caravans which contained not only merchants and soldiers but often foreign scholars and princes. We have said that the travel was slow, but the Roman roads in the first century were really better than our best State highways; and while the ordinary day's travel of a caravan was not more than twenty or twenty-five miles, special imperial messengers were accustomed to make from 100 to 150 miles in cases of emergency.

But it was the Mediterranean which was the swiftest and best highway of the entire civilized world, and it must not be forgotten that the ocean borders Palestine and can be seen from the hills of Nazareth. Those ships were primitive but were often of good size. St. Paul speaks of his ship carrying 276 passengers (Acts 27:37), and Josephus tells of being wrecked on a voyage from Palestine to Italy while on a ship carrying some 600 persons; and there were war ships at that time which could carry as many as a thousand soldiers, and other ships capable of carrying from 250 to 1,500 tons of freight. Pictures of the ships of this era, perhaps painted within twenty years of the time of Paul's journey, are common at Herculaneum and Pompeii, and a vivid description of one of them comes to us from a Syrian who was born about fifty years after Paul's shipwreck. Describing one of the Alexandrian grain ships, such as the one on which St. Paul sailed, he speaks of the long, rising sweep of the prow and the figures of her name—Isis—on either side (cf. Acts 28:11), and continues:

"As to other ornamental details, the paintings and the scarlet top sail, I was more struck by the anchors and the capstans and windlasses and the stern cabins. The crew was like a small army. And they were saying she carried as much corn as would feed every soul in Attica for a year. And all depends for safety on one little atom of a man who controls that great rudder with a mere broomstick of a tiller!" [3]

It is suggestive that the route of this grain ship was exactly the same as the first stage of Paul's voyage and that it also encountered adverse winds. The nautical terms used by St. Luke in his description correspond very exactly with ancient lists, excepting in one place where in speaking of the ship being broken by the waves he says that they needed to bandage it (Acts 27:17), using here a medical term which must have made any sailor smile who heard it or read it. A long

[3] Cf. James 3:4, and see Biblical World, XXXIV:339; and for general information see Cecil Farr, Ancient Ships.

list of medical terms used in the Acts of the Apostles by "the beloved physician" (Col. 4:14) has been known to scholars for many years, and these have been increased through a recent critical study of the text by Professor Harnack; moreover, a celebrated classical scholar not long ago pointed out that the formal introduction to the Third Gospel (Luke 1:1-4) is so nearly like that with which Dioscorides began his great work on *materia medica* that it is quite probable that Luke had this work in his library and imitated it.[4]

As we study these strange conditions and literary coincidences that illuminate Scripture, we are reminded of the beautiful bas-relief of a female head found some years ago in excavations at Athens which was pronounced by M. Kavadias, the archeologist in charge, to be a fragment of the frieze of Phidias on the Parthenon near by. Other archeologists exprest doubt. After a good deal of discussion it was recollected that among the Elgin marbles in the British Museum belonging to the Parthenon frieze there was a figure of Iris, the goddess of the rainbow, lacking the head. A cast was taken of the newly discovered head and sent to England. This was placed on the part of the frieze from which the head had been broken away, and fitted it exactly. No argument was needed. The demonstration was perfect that it was the head of Iris.

The priceless jewel, the New Testament, has been shown by history and archeology to fit its setting as perfectly as the head of Iris its place on the frieze.[5]

[4] W. K. Hobart, *Medical Language of St. Luke*, 1882; A. Harnack, *Luke, the Physician;* Blass, *Philology of the Gospels*, p. 34.

[5] *Cf. Transactions of the Victoria Inst.*, XLV:29.

2. SOME LITERARY HABITS OF THE FIRST CENTURY ILLUSTRATED IN THE PAPYRI

Twenty-five years ago no scholar had ever recognized a "profane" document written in the language of the New Testament. Thousands of such documents now exist, proving that the New Testament was essentially written in the language used by the common people of the first century. The Attic Greek in which the classical literature was written was "an artistic language which nobody spoke." [6] It was as different from the common speech as the writings of Shakespeare from the common speech of his day. The New Testament language, as we have previously pointed out, was the vernacular of the world during the apostolic era. It was not the literary Greek but the language of social and business intercourse which the colonists, merchants, and soldiers, who mingled together all over the world, wrote and spoke. Alexander's conquest had made the world small and changed the babble of tongues into a world language which was to be heard in the first century of our era not only in Greece but also in Egypt, Italy, Palestine, and Asia Minor. It was in this language that the New Testament was written. It was not Wycliffe who first gave the New Testament to the world in the language of the market-place; it was Mark and Matthew and Paul who did this—altho Paul in some of his writings, as also Luke and the author of the Hebrews, used a literary style higher than that found in the papyri. We may now know precisely how the New Testament documents

[6] Jannaris, *Hist. Greek Grammar*, p. 3.

were written, for we possess many specimens of papyrus writings which originated at exactly the same time and were written exactly in the same way.

The poorer classes commonly used ostraka (potsherds), or wrote their letters on the back of some old papyrus which they had found or from which they could wash out the ancient writings (*cf.* Col. 2:14). As papyrus breaks easily, the beginning and ending of every papyrus book is usually much frayed and worn; this would naturally account for the mutilated verses at the end of Mark's gospel and at the opening of the Epistle to the Hebrews. Mark's gospel, in the best copies, closes with a conjunction (16:8) which would have been impossible, of course, in the original. Dr. Milligan, an expert on papyri, says of this: "We may not unreasonably conjecture that the last leaf of the original manuscript was lost at a very early date, and that the additional twelve verses with which we are familiar in our ordinary version and the shorter ending which other authorities offer as an alternative, as well as the expanded account of the newly discovered Freer manuscript, were all added later at different times and by different hands to round off the mutilated Marcan account of the resurrection."[7]

When finished, the papyrus roll was usually fastened with a thread and often sealed (Rev. 5:1). Letters were transmitted to their destination by private messengers, unless through some influence they could be placed in the royal mails or in that of some large business firm.

[7] Swete, *Gospel of Mark*, 1905, CIX, thinks the present ending dates to the second century or earlier. F. C. Conybeare in 1891, in an ancient Armenian MS. of Mark (A.D. 989), found the authority given for these additional verses to be "the presbyter Ariston."

Once more we must call attention to the fact that dictation of letters was almost as common in the first century as among business men of to-day. Not only ignorant persons did this, but likewise men who could write were in the habit of having scribes do this drudgery for them. If a man was not rich he might have a young friend or pupil who would be ready to wield the pen for him. This is in accordance with the dignity of age in the East. "The old man strokes his beard and dictates his words to the scribe. That is what Paul did, altho I do not know whether or not he had the beard which Christian art gives him." [8] It is entirely reasonable to suppose that this common oriental method of letter writing was followed by the New Testament writers as by other literary men and letter writers of the first century.

Shorthand was used not uncommonly in legal cases and by private literary men, at least three different systems being in vogue, one contract from A.D. 155 speaking of a two years' term during which the student is to be taught to read and write these signs faultlessly. It is plain that the same author might have a style and vocabulary, when his letter was dictated, very different from that which was used when he allowed more freedom to his amanuensis in the words and phrases employed. It will also be seen that two different writers might favor each other in style if they employed the same amanuensis. "The form which Peter took and the many Pauline echoes it contains may be due to the fact that Peter employed as his scribe Sylvanus [Silas], who had already acted in a similar capacity for Paul . . . and it is at least possible that

[8] Gregory, *Canon and Text of New Testament*, p. 300.

in the dictation and revision of the Fourth Gospel we may have a partial key to some of the vexed questions that have arisen regarding its authorship." [9]

The fact that the letter is dictated is not ordinarily stated in the papyri, but is proved by the difference of handwriting seen in the signature. It was the authenticating signature of St. Paul which was necessary to prove even to his friends that the writing they received had been made from his own lips (2 Thess. 3: 17, 18; 1 Cor. 16: 21; Col. 4: 18). As the letter to the Galatians was especially severe, this may have been written by the apostle's own hand (Gal. 6: 11). It is possible that the loving paragraphs with which the letter closes, after the reprimand, were written by the apostle's own hand "in large characters" in order to pay a delicate compliment to the church which he had criticized.

It will be remembered that the rough breathing was not commonly used until the eleventh century of our era, while the interrogation mark and the accent arose respectively in the ninth and seventh centuries, and no parentheses and very few punctuation marks ever appear among the papyri of the first century. These ordinary facts of penmanship, illustrated in all ancient documents of the first century, account doubtless for many of the different readings of the New Testament texts which have previously been assigned to carelessness or wilfulness on the part of copyists. It is also now known that the ordinary penman of that era interchanged the long and short vowels almost at will, and that certain consonants were often used interchangeably.

[9] Milligan, *New Testament Documents*, p. 30.

In the sixty or more very ancient New Testament manuscripts recently brought to light there are almost innumerable mistakes of spelling. These mistakes may have been originally made by the Biblical writers or may have been later phonetic blunders; for it was the custom of the classical writers, in the first and second centuries of our era, to have fifty or a hundred copyists who wrote their book as some one read it aloud. So copies of the New Testament may have been multiplied. It is far more likely, however, that the copyist usually did the work privately with an ancient manuscript before him; but some of those scribes knew their New Testament so well that they would only glance at the original and then write an entire sentence or more without looking at their model—giving the sense correctly but committing the same kind of errors in eyesight and memory that a college class would make if assigned a similar task.

A comparison of the New Testament letters with the private correspondence of contemporaries shows that St. Paul used the customary polite form which was universal among the middle classes at that period. There is an opening address or greeting, followed by a thanksgiving and prayer for the one to whom he writes, followed by the special message which has caused the letter to be written, the whole being closed by salutations and perhaps a word of prayer. This polite epistolary phraseology was stereotyped.

Almost universally the letter which is written in good form begins with greetings and closes with good wishes. A recent writer has analyzed several of Paul's letters showing how carefully he observed the polite form, except when pulled from it by special stress of feeling,[11] and gives a number of private letters written not far from the same era, showing a marked similarity in style and even occasionally in phrase. One of these from the first century reads:

"Hermocrates to Chaeras his son, greeting. First of all I pray that you may be in health . . . and I beg you . . . to write regarding your health, and whatever you wish. Already indeed I have written regarding the . . . and you neither answered nor came, and now if you do not come, I run the risk of losing the lot (of land) which I possess. . . . Your sister Helene greets you and your mother reproaches you because you have never answered her . . . I pray that you may be well."

Another beautiful letter from the second century, given by Dr. Milligan, well illustrates this point:

"Ammonous to her sweetest father, greeting. When I received your letter, and recognized that by the will of the gods you were preserved, I rejoiced greatly. And as at the same time an opportunity has presented itself, I am writing you this letter, being, very anxious to pay my respects to you. Attend as quickly as possible to the matters that are pressing. Whatever the little one asks shall be done. If the bearer of this letter hands over a small basket to you, it is I who send it. All your friends greet you by name. Celer greets you and all who are with him. I pray for your health."

Another just published in 1914 is addrest "To the sweetest Apa Domne," and closes:

"Above all I repeatedly salute name by name both Apa Domne and all those in the household from small to great."

Even as late as the eighth century we find the common people in Egypt beginning their letters:

"First I greet thee and all those that are with thee by their names."

[11] Wood, *Life and Ministry of St. Paul*, p. 18.

At this late date, however, the expressions had ordinarily become more effusive and a very common opening sentence is: "I salute the footstool of thy feet."

The postscripts of St. Paul in several epistles, where he adds some specially loving word or mentions by name a list of choice friends, is paralleled in many letters which are practically contemporaneous. Dr. Milligan has published one private letter (second century) containing thirty-one lines of Greek text, thirteen of which are taken up with the closing greetings, and another of fifty lines in which about half of the letter is given up to salutations "to members of the household" mentioned by name.[12]

Every one who has personally examined the papyri arises from the study with a new appreciation of the truth that the literary style and method employed in the New Testament are cut after the pattern most common and popular among the middle classes of the first century.

Perhaps as we end this part of our study we may again remind the reader that in almost every one of these ancient documents Biblical words catch the eye of the New Testament student. Here lying on the table before the writer are many unpublished papyri which he obtained a few months ago in the Fayum. The date upon one of them is December A.D. 182, and the missive is from a goldsmith by the name of Sabirius who writes to Serapias, daughter of Philip, stating that he has paid her 15 minae of "standard gold"—the Greek word being precisely the same as that used in Jas. 1:3 and 1 Peter 1:7.

[12] *Selections from the Greek Papyri*, 1910.

Here is another, of a little later date, beginning:

"Above all I pray for the merciful N——."

The term used here is precisely the same as in the beatitude, "Blessed are the merciful." In the margin is written at right angles to the text: "Mother mine, do write to me immediately." That word (ἐξαυτῆς) is the very one that Luke uses four times (Acts 10: 33; 11: 11; 21: 32; 23: 30).

Here is another papyrus very hard to decipher, tho the name of the writer seems to be Dioskoros, who writes a little note to Hermes, and in the midst of it speaks of an acquaintance saying: "We can not endure the man!" The pen of this old letter writer made here exactly the same strokes which Paul's amanuensis made when at the apostle's dictation he wrote out the sentence (1 Cor. 10: 13): "God . . . will with the temptation make also the way of escape, that ye may be able to endure it."[13]

Only one of these letters quoted above is Christian, and even that is doubtful; but everybody at that era was using Biblical words. Among the 1,624 ostraka published a few years ago by Wilcken[14] not even one was Christian, yet these little texts are full of New Testament words and idioms. In just one letter sent by a prodigal son to his mother there are at least thirteen Biblical terms used (quoted p. 327).

We close this section by pointing out that private letters such as those St. Paul wrote would in that era not only be read by the persons receiving them, but

[13] The writer wishes to acknowledge his obligation to Prof. Edgar J. Goodspeed, of the University of Chicago, who has given valuable help in making out a number of these scrawls, which seemed at first absolutely indecipherable.

[14] *Griechische Ostraka aus Aegypten und Nubien,* 2: 1899.

would also naturally be copied and sent to other bands of believers, if they were thought to contain anything of special interest, as is shown by a letter published in 1914:

"To my lady mother, Germania, greetings: Since I came away from you yesterday without telling you about the pot, take and copy my letter and give it to my mother Apaxris for my sister Hagia. Well, do not forget. I pray that you are well." [15]

3. A New View of the First Century from a Re-examination of the Classical Texts in the Light of New Discoveries

It can hardly be doubted that the new views of the development of Roman history, as given by Ferrero, and the brilliant descriptions of Roman society in the time of Nero by several other scholars, have been largely influenced by the mass of newly found papyri and inscriptions, which have thrown a vivid light not chiefly upon the intrigues of the royal palace but upon the currents of popular life. We can no longer talk about the wars of the Emperors without examining the causes of these wars found in the life of the people and their results in affecting financial and social conditions.

It is now plain that a social revolution was in progress in the first century. The nobles had lost their wealth and prestige, and the whole Roman Empire was being shaken by the grumbling of the "common people," who for ages had felt their wrongs but were at last beginning to speak and make themselves heard. Within two generations of the death of Christ vast mobs, amounting to hundreds of thousands of the unem-

[15] *Oxyrhynchus Papyri*, X: 1349.

ployed, burst into Rome and surrounded the imperial palace howling for bread. The freedmen, whose ancestors had been slaves but who were now the richest of the populace, had also become a tremendous political factor. They had not only money but also trade experience and a practical education superior to the nobles.

The fact that princes and senators were forbidden by law to increase their fortunes by commerce, and the further fact that honest toil even in such professions as pedagogy and medicine was despised by the "best families," had produced this sad condition. The Roman nobles had scorned the drudgery of education, so that it was the slave who had been taught in the schools and had become the expert accountant as well as the poet and literary man of this era. Neither Juvenal nor Quintilian nor Martial came of "good blood." In order to make the slaves who carried on their financial plans more energetic in seeking success their owners had offered them emancipation, so that the active commercial work of the first century was being carried on by this recently servile class, and these despised people had suddenly become the heavy capitalists of the realm. More than this, because of their training in practical affairs, they had fitted themselves for high positions in the imperial service; and a number of these, like Callistus, Narcissus, and Pallas, had risen to the rank of great ministers and were practically masters of the world.[16] Many of these men, who had begun life without a dollar but through industry or intrigue had obtained immense fortunes, were building themselves palaces, almost

[16] For a most interesting résumé, see Dill, *Roman Society from Nero to Marcus Aurelius*, 1905, p. 106.

rivaling the Golden House of Nero, and trying in every vulgar way to imitate the more refined but equally evil excesses of their former masters. They gave gorgeous banquets at which there were unmentionable orgies, and displayed their vulgarity and ignorance and lack of refinement in a way which made them hated and despised by the cultured poor as well as by the titled nobility. No one can understand the work of the primitive Christian Church among the freedmen without bearing these facts in mind.

But the freedmen with whom the early Christians chiefly worked were not of this wealthy class. The proportion of poor to rich in the Roman Empire was much greater than in the world to-day, and the contrast between rich and poor was more startling. Poverty was practically universal, and for almost the first time in history the poor man had become dangerous. The Emperor could no longer spend $15,000 for a vase or $20,000 for a table or $200,000 for a Babylonian carpet; or waste, as Nero did, $175,000 upon Egyptian roses for a single feast and squander $90,000,000 in a few months, without the "people feeling the sting" of their own poverty.[17]

Corporations and monopolies had so taken possession of all the foodstuffs that about half a century before the birth of Christ nearly 300,000 persons were compelled in one year to ask gifts of corn from the State in order to survive. Every successful politician coaxed the citizens to support his administration by giving such gifts and attempting to please the populace

---

[17] W. S. Davis, *Wealth in Imperial Rome* (1910), tells how Claudius dissolved a pearl worth $40,000 in vinegar and drank it; Cæsar, 59 B.C., bought two pearls for $700,000; Lucius Verus gave a feast costing $700,000; Publius Octavius paid $65 a pound for a rare fish (pp. 165-181).

with free shows. The case had become so desperate by A.D. 300 that Diocletian, in an effort to bring down prices to a normal level, not only attempted to suppress combinations in restraint of trade but actually fixt by law the maximum price at which the necessities of life could be sold, any violation of the law to be visited with the penalty of death. Specific prices were fixt upon over 700 articles. The highest price allowed for wheat per bushel was $3.36; beans or salt, 75c.; oil per quart, 30.25c.; honey, 30.3c.; pork per pound, 7.3c.; beef, 4.9c.; ham, 12c.; lamb, 7.3c.; butter, 9.8c.; sea fish per pound, 14.6c.; second quality, 9.7c.; river fish, 7.3c.; salt fish, 8.3c.; oysters by the hundred, 43.5c.; sardines, 9.7c.; dry cheese, 7.3c.; fresh cheese per quart, 6c.; sheep's milk per quart, 6c.; peasants' boots without nails, 53c.; soldiers' boots, 43c.; women's boots, 26c., etc. Transportation was also fixt—one person one mile, 9c.; rent for wagon one mile, 5c.; freight charge for camel load of 600 pounds per mile, 3.5c.; freight charge for wagon containing up to 1,200 pounds per mile, 8.7c.; hay and straw three pounds, 9c. Wages were also fixt by law—the "keep" of the workman being included—as follows: manual laborer, 10.8c.; bricklayer, 21.6c.; carpenter, stone mason, wagon-maker, blacksmith, baker, shipbuilder, elementary teacher, 21.6c.; marble worker, master shipbuilder, 26c.; first-class tailor, 26.1c.; wall painter, 32.4c.; figure painter, 64.8c.; maker of statues, 32.4c.; barber, 9c.; veterinary surgeon, 2.6c.; document writer for record of 100 lines, 4.3c.; writer, 100 lines best writing, 10.9c.; elementary teacher or writing teacher per month per pupil, 21.6c.; teacher of arithmetic per month or of stenography, 32.6c.; teacher of Greek,

Latin or geometry, 87c.; teacher of rhetoric, $1.09; advocate or counsel for presenting a case, $1.09; for finishing a case, $4.35.[18]

Comparing the ordinary income of normal American families with their normal outlay for food, Dr. Abbott finds from the report of the Commissioner of Labor on the "Cost of Living and Retail Prices of Food" (1903), and by Bulletin No. 77 of the Bureau of Labor (1908) that American laborers, however bad their present condition may be, are far better off than the Roman laborer at the above era, since the ancient laborer received only a ninth or a fifteenth as much as the modern while the average price of food was about a third of the average of the same articles to-day.[19] If the Roman laborer bought half a dozen geese for a New Year's feast, it took almost the entire month to pay for them. If he bought a quart of honey, it cost him a day and a half of hard work; while a bushel of beans or barley cost about half a week's income; a pair of boots two and a half days' wage; and if he purchased a pound of purple silk, it took nearly an entire year to pay for it. He would be compelled to give over a fourth of his daily wage for a dozen of eggs, and his wife quite as much for a dozen sewing-needles; if he bought a pound of pork it cost nearly half a day's wages, and three and a half pounds of beef took a whole day's income; while three pounds of ham took two days' wages.[20]

Nevertheless many distinguished scholars believe

[18] Original document given in *Corpus inscriptionum Latinarum*, Vol. 3, pp. 1926-1953; lengthy extract given in translation by Abbott, *Common People of Ancient Rome*, 153-178.

[19] *Op. cit.*, p. 176.

[20] These prices are taken from Diocletian's list formerly mentioned; probably they did not differ greatly from the average in the days of Jesus.

that Jesus of Nazareth in pity for the poor was attempting to inaugurate a new social system where the horror of the old economic system of "grasping"—which originated in the jungle—should give place to the comfort of the new Christian economics which had beneath it the divine principle of "giving." [21]

The brutality of that ancient world has long been recognized. The gladiatorial shows, offered to the people in order to keep them from dwelling upon their miseries, were prize-fights in which hundreds, perhaps thousands, of people were killed annually. These were not simply governmental exhibitions, but were expected of every rich man at every possible opportunity. Even the kindly Pliny applauded his friend for giving a gladiatorial show in honor of his deceased wife, and wrote sympathetically: "I am sorry the leopards did not come in time."

In those ancient theaters the actors were killed frequently in awful agony and under the most grotesque and horrible surroundings, while the Roman ladies laughed and applauded. One of Nero's most popular exhibitions of this kind was carried on at Rome with Christians in the center of the stage. [22]

War is a mild thing compared with murder in the midst of gaiety. The apostolic age was one of intense cruelty. Of the first twelve Cæsars seven died violent deaths. Thirty thousand slaves were crucified under Augustus. Any slave could be crucified at the whim of his master, tho these slaves were often treated as trusted friends, like Rhoda the doorkeeper (Acts

[21] See especially A. N. Craft's *Exodus from Poverty*, 1914, edited by Rev. W. H. Talmage, Flandreau, So. Dakota.

[22] See M. Renan, *English Conferences*, pp. 62-65, for a most vivid description.

12: 13). Under Claudius (A.D. 41-54) 19,000 men
were surrounded and compelled to butcher each other
and fight thousands of wild beasts. Nero assassinated
friends and relatives without number, brutally killing
both wife and mother. An idea of the age may be
gathered from the fact that the Roman Senate thanked
him for the murder of his mother. Yet while Suetonius
called him "a wild beast," and Paul called him a lion
(2 Tim. 4: 17), Domitian (A.D. 81-96) was so much
worse that it is said the populace brought flowers in
sorrow to put upon Nero's grave!

Such was the frightful picture of the first century
offered to the world previous to the new discoveries.
The papyri could not contradict the above facts; but as
we shall see a little later, they furnish material from
another stratum of the population, showing that the
middle classes even in these most frightful reigns retained self-respect and honor and family love and a
sense of sympathy with the poor and opprest. It may
seem an exaggeration when Dr. Dill suggests a doubt
whether private benefactions under the Antonines were
less frequent and generous than in our own day [24] and
when Duruy can hint that the morality of women was
"as high as the morality of any age"; [25] yet we can not
deny that Pliny's gifts—$45,000 for a town library
with an annual endowment of $4,000 to maintain it;
$20,000 for the support of poor children, $20,000 for
public baths, $40,000 to his freedmen, etc., etc.—
formed a larger percentage of his estate paid out in
charity than most public men of to-day can equal. So
the Pompeian inscriptions show many public buildings

[24] *Roman Society,* p. 191.
[25] *History of Rome,* Vol. 5, p. 673.

as being the gift of private citizens, and thousands of tombstones all over the Roman empire testify that the common people still retained kindness of heart and some of the old standards of morality. Of Dionysius, the physician, it is said: "To all the sick who came to him he gave his services free of charge"; of Sofroniola the loving husband records "purity, loyalty, affection, a sense of duty, a yielding nature and whatever qualities God has implanted in woman"; of another the husband Valerius inscribes the tribute, "Pure in heart, modest, of seemly bearing, discreet, noble-minded, and held in high esteem." [26]

It must be remembered, however, that tombstone testimony can not always be received in court; and altho Plutarch's ideal of marriage might "have satisfied St. Paul" [27] and altho Seneca suggests "the single standard" as his ideal of the marriage state; and altho even Ovid, notwithstanding his indecent verses, wrote tenderly to his wife; yet the living testimony coming from innumerable papyri, while modifying the old conception which would make the age absolutely heartless, does not confirm the too optimistic decisions of recent scholars. The morals of the common people were not as degenerate as those of the "smart set," but they were the morals of a heathen people who possess few high ideals of purity even in their gods, and had few impulses to moral self-restraint either from their heredity, education, or environment.

The religion of the first century must be grasped in outline before any one can understand intelligently the

---

[26] Bucheler, *Carmina Latina epigraphica,* Nos. 765, 843, 1414, quoted in Abbott's *Common People of Ancient Rome,* pp. 85-87; *cf.* Dill, *Roman Society,* 76-87.

[27] Dill, *op. cit.,* p. 77.

work done by Christianity or appreciate the revelations of the home life found in the papyri. It has often been said that St. Paul's terrific arraignment of the heathendom of his day and Christ's charges of irreligion upon the Jewish officials of his generation were the productions of empassioned rhetoric rather than the keen and critical diagnosis of diseased conditions; and a few writers in recent times have ventured to affirm that the highest realization of religion as well as of civilization was achieved by that same pagan world at a somewhat earlier period, while several distinguished Hebrews have thought themselves able to prove not only that the Sermon on the Mount was merely a re-utterance of rabbinic platitudes, but also that the religious life of the Pharisees, in its humility and spirituality and self-devotion to God and man, was equal to anything pictured by the great Nazarene or lived out by his disciples.[28]

The papyri are a sufficient answer to the one claim, while answer to the other may be had from the Talmud where the minute stipulations concerning the ceremonial washings and the keeping of the Sabbath prove that, even according to this ancient Jewish record, the words of Jesus were an understatement rather than an overstatement when he charged the religionists of his day with mistaking minutiæ of ritual for the real essentials of religion. The Jews were doubtless better than any other people of the ancient world both in life and religious doctrines, yet the difference between the cosmic view of Jesus and the universal Jewish view of that era is well shown in the new Talmud Dictionary where the

---

[28] Yet against this see *Jewish Encyclopedia*, "Jesus" and "St. Paul"; and Montefiore, *Synoptic Gospels* (1909), II : 57, 593, 1098.

Hebrew word "stranger" grows to mean "idolatry" and "swine."

No heathen religion of the first century could compare with the religion of the Hebrews in purity of doctrine or in the purity of life enforced. The Hebrew view of God brought a hope and the spirit of song and a sense of holiness into the domestic and religious life absolutely foreign to heathendom. Even the legalistic ritualism observed by the Pharisees was not as cold and heartless a formalism as the ancient religion of the Romans.[29]

It is true that in the first Christian century the old Roman religion had improved. The doctrine of the brotherhood and equality of men had been taught by the Stoics, and in some of the philosophers, such as Seneca, there may even be heard a note of pity for the miserable and helpless, while in others there is a recognition, in theory at least, of the mental and moral equality of the sexes; but the doctrine of brotherhood and of mercy was preached as an unattainable ideal.[30] More than this, the introduction of oriental religions with their mystic impulses and rites and hope of immortality had caused better thoughts of God and of prayer than even philosophy had encouraged; and especially the Mithras worship with its purifying sacrifices and its narrative of a divine life, instinct with human sympathy, was making a very strong appeal in the first century, particularly to the poorer classes, stirring through its worship some of the best instincts of human nature.

But Stoicism was fatalistic and therefore pessi-

---

[29] Cf. Cumont, *Oriental Religions in Paganism* (1911), Chap. ii, viii.
[30] Cf. Carter, *Religious Life of Ancient Rome* (1911), p. 85.

mistic, and by its neglect of emotion and sympathy it failed to rouse any "enthusiasm of humanity." [31]   On the other hand the mystic oriental cults—including even the superior synthetic religion of Mithras—were mixed up with monstrous fictions and extravagances which outraged the common sense of enlightened Romans. The mysteries of Mithras were frankly astrological and mythological, tho with certain saving esoteric explanations. [32]   The sense of sin, the ascetic systems of penance, the bath of purification in the blood of the sacrificed deity, the oriental symbolism and mystic rites— pictorial representations, many of which were used also by Christianity—could not save even Mithraism from annihilation before a better religion. Its strength lay in the fact that it was a vast improvement in its religious conceptions upon any faith that had preceded it. With other oriental cults it "made straight the way." [33] It was not an entirely unworthy religion, else would our faith in the divine warrant of Christianity be diminished; but it could not conquer because it was separated from Christianity by "an impassable gulf. . . . In place of the narrative of a divine life, instinct with human sympathy, it had only to offer the cold symbolism of a cosmic legend."

These recent studies by classical students have shown clearly that no exceptional conditions were created to help Christianity conquer. It appealed to the same human nature as the other religions, and was victor because of the spiritual and historic truth be-

[31] See especially Fowler, *Religious Experience of the Roman People* (1911), chap. xvi.

[32] Cumont, *Mysteries of Mithra*, pp. 120-148

[33] Cumont, *Oriental Religions in Roman Paganism*, chaps. xi, xii; *cf.* Paul Carus, *The Pleroma.*

hind it. In the worship of the Magna Mater the worshiper, bathed in sacrificial blood, was said to be "born again into eternity"; but this "new birth" was very different from that which the teacher of Galilee encouraged. All of these heathen religions offered salvation by reason, ritual or magic; the Christ offered salvation by faith—a faith which produced moral and spiritual transformation.

We have delayed to the end a consideration of the most important of all the cults of the first century— Emperor worship. This is the only pagan religion which constantly meets us in the New Testament, and it was Emperor worship, not Mithraism, which the Christian Fathers thought of as the rival of Christianity. Augustus established Emperor worship as the state religion 12 B.C. and it soon became "the only universal form of religion in the Roman empire." It is difficult to realize its power. When first introduced it produced an effect almost equal to that of the Protestant Reformation. It not only revived the ancient forms, but taught impressively that morality and prosperity depended upon religion. "By its sacrifices and prayer, thanksgivings and rhythmic hymns it brought a revival to the religious life; in its brotherhood feasts it encouraged a community of religious fellowship; in its agricultural bearings it taught that practical success depends upon the will of the gods; in its nightly ceremonies and prayers it sought to give expression to certain feelings and ideas not far removed in kind from those which in our own day we describe as our religious experience." [34]

[34] W. Warde Fowler, *Religious Experience of the Roman People* (1911), chap. 19.

And yet, as Dr. Fowler well says, "all this taken together, so far from explaining Christianity, does not help us much in getting to understand even the conditions under which it grew into men's minds as a new power in the life of the world. The plant, tho grown in soil which had borne other crops, was wholly new in structure and vital principles. I say this deliberately after spending so many years on the study of the religion of the Romans and making myself acquainted in some measure with the religions of other peoples. The essential difference, as it appears to me as a student of the history of religion, is this, that whereas the connection between religion and morality has so far been a loose one—at Rome indeed so loose that many have refused to believe in its existence—the new religion was itself morality, but morality consecrated and raised to a higher power than it had ever yet reached. It becomes active instead of passive; mere good nature is replaced by a doctrine of universal love; *pietas,* the sense of duty and outward things, becomes an enthusiasm embracing all humanity, consecrated by such an appeal to the conscience as there never had been in the world before—the appeal to the life and death of the divine Master. . . . The love of Christ is the entirely new power that has come into the world; not merely as a new type of morality but as 'a divine influence transfiguring human nature in a universal love.' " [35]

[35] *Op. cit.,* pp. 466-467.

4. New Light on the Jewish Literature (Non-Biblical) which Chiefly Influenced the Theological and Ethical Thought of Palestine in the First Century

There have been few surprizes of modern times greater than that connected with the re-examination and rediscovery of ancient Hebrew apocryphal and apocalyptic works dating from 200 B.C. to A.D. 200. From the times of the primitive Church until a very recent period it was accepted without question that the era between Malachi and John the Baptist had been voiceless so far as any prophetic message was concerned. It was noticed that the New Testament showed a vast divergence from the Old Testament in its treatment of the kingdom of God, the Messiah, general judgment, future life, Holy Spirit, and other fundamental doctrines. But this was counted merely a divine inexplicable mystery. The new examination of well-known Jewish books dating from this "period of silence," and the recovery of others long lost, have made it perfectly plain that this period, hitherto practically neglected by Christian students, was one of eager intellectual inquisitiveness and splendid theological and ethical development. While it is altogether possible that Professor Cheyne and others may have pushed too many portions of the canonical scriptures into this *terra incognita,* no scholar now doubts that this was an era of intense activity out of which have come some most brilliant religious and ethical works. Indeed, Dr. R. H. Charles, who is the highest living authority on this subject, has dared to say that the two centuries immediately preceding the Christian era were "in many

respects centuries of greater spiritual progress than
any two that had preceded them in Israel." [36]

Some of this ancient literature deals wholly with
Jewish history, and therefore does not appeal to us;
while other works, such as Ecclesiasticus (Sirach) and
The Book of Wisdom, Tobit, Judith, etc., had long
been known from ancient versions and had been accepted as "Scripture" by the Roman Church. It is
evident that we need not dwell on the contents of these
books, tho *Ecclesiasticus* was brought into new
prominence a few years ago by the discovery of the
Hebrew text, which had been lost for eight centuries,
and it is "positively invaluable" as exhibiting the religious views of a cultured Sadducee and priest of
Jerusalem, 200-175 B.C. [37]

Tobit throws light on the religious and ethical condition of the Jews in Egypt 225-200 B.C., being a work
of "singular esthetic beauty and remarkable liberal
sympathies," while *Judith* gives us a unique example
of a Jewish work of historical fiction, the author being
a Palestine Jew whose theology was strongly Pharisaic.

The Book of Wisdom (written *cir.* 50 B.C.) is a
most attractive work. It was probably composed
originally in Alexandrian Greek (*vs.* Margoliouth). Its
glorification of the Jewish people and its praise of
wisdom must have been deeply interesting to all Jews

---

[36] *Religious Development Between the Old and the New Testaments*
(1915), p. 8; *cf.* Schechter, *Studies in Judaism* (second series), p. 43.

[37] Professor Margoliouth, in 1899 called into question the authenticity of
the newly discovered Hebrew fragments, believing that they represented
merely a re-translation into Hebrew from a Persian version by way of
the Greek and Syriac; but altho Professor Nestle in part accepted this
hypothesis, competent scholars in general have not favored it, and Professor Margoliouth's far-reaching conclusions concerning "higher critical"
questions have not been confirmed.

of the first century while its discussion of the future world even yet appeals to us:

> "God made not death;
> Neither delighteth he when the living perish:
> For he created all things that they might have being:
> And the products of the world are healthsome,
> And there is no poison of destruction in them:
> Nor hath Hades royal dominion upon earth;
> For righteousness is immortal.
>
> The souls of the righteous are in the hand of God,
> And no torment shall touch them.
> In the eyes of fools they seem to die;
> And their departure was accounted to be their hurt,
> And their going from us to be their ruin:
> But they are in peace.
> For though in the sight of men they be punished,
> Their hope is full of immortality;
> And having borne a little chastening they shall receive
>   great good,
> Because God tested them and found them worthy of
>   himself."

Enoch is a work not so well known as the above. It was lost for nearly fifteen hundred years, and altho an Ethiopic version was then found, the remarkable value of the book was not appreciated until this generation. It is of "immeasurable value" as giving to us "practically the only historical memorials of the religious development of Judaism from 200 B.C. to A.D. 100 and particularly of that side of Judaism to which historic Christendom in large measure owes its existence" (Charles). In the days of Jesus this was regarded as an inspired work by many holy men. There are five places in Jude where this apostle shows undoubted verbal connection with Enoch. There are at least nineteen places in the Book of Revelation, thirteen in Paul's epistles and thirteen in the gospels where there are connections in thought or phrase.[38]

Even this statement does not express fully the obligation of early Christianity to this great work. There can be no longer any doubt that the title, "Son of Man," which our Lord so constantly used, while it occasionally connected itself with Daniel's concept of the Messiah (Matt. 24:30, 26:64), in most instances reflected the usage of the Book of Enoch. By adopting the current title it is now clear that our Lord "made from the outset supernatural claims"; tho he broke entirely from certain external Judaistic conceptions with which the title is often connected in the Book of Enoch. In the "Parables" three other titles are applied in Enoch for the first time in literature to the personal Messiah: "Christ," "The Righteous One," "The Elect One."

Besides this close verbal connection there are equally close connections of thought between Enoch and the gospels in the discussion relating to the Messiah, the resurrection, and the future life (Sheol). This makes clear to us, what had previously been obscure, how our Lord could take for granted in his hearers knowledge on these points not to be found in the Old Testament. He was in fact setting the seal of his approval on the general spiritual teaching of this well-known Book of Enoch, tho—as our quotations will prove—by no means approving everything. The following quotations will suggest Enoch's position regarding the future world and the kingdom of heaven:

"Then will all the righteous escape and will live until they beget a thousand children and all the days of their youth and old

[38] R. H. Charles, *Apocrypha and Pseudepigrapha of the New Testament* (1913), Vol. II, pp. 180*ff*; in his *Book of Enoch* (1893), pp. 41-49, Dr. Charles traces 26 connections with Revelations, 21 with Paul, etc.

age will they complete in peace . . . and I came to a river of fire, the fire of which flows like water . . . and from thence I went to another place which is still more horrible than the former, and I saw a horrible thing; a great fire was there which flamed and blazed, and the place was cleft as far as the abyss . . . and Uriel spake to me, This place is the prison of the angels, and here they will be imprisoned forever . . . and I saw the spirits of the children of men who were dead . . . the souls of the righteous (being) separated from the rest . . . the souls (of sinners) are placed apart in this pain till the great day of judgment and punishment torture the revilers forever . . .

And the Lord of Spirits seated him (*i.e.*, the Messiah) on the throne of his glory, and the spirit of righteousness was poured out upon him, and the word of his mouth slew all the sinners . . . and those who rule the earth will fall down on their faces before him and worship, and set their hope on that Son of Man, and will petition and will supplicate for mercy at his hands. . . .

Fear ye not, ye souls of the righteous, and be hopeful ye that die in righteousness. And grieve not if your soul descends into Sheol and that in your life your body has not fared as your goodness deserved. . . . Now therefore I swear to you, the righteous . . . that all goodness and joy and glory are prepared for them, and are written down for the spirits of those who have died in righteousness, and manifold good will be given to you in recompense for your labor and that your lot is abundantly beyond the lot of the living."

While the use of this work by New Testament writers can hardly be doubted in view of the many parallelisms, we can not fail to admire the fine reserve and self-restraint shown by them in handling this well-known material.[39]

The Testaments of the Twelve Patriarchs were originally written in Hebrew 109-106 B.C., by a very religious Pharisee. This work is of supreme importance because of its high ethical teaching, which "has ob-

[39] Compare Jude, 6:17; Rev., 2:7, 3:5, 8:38, 9:5; 1 Cor., 6:11; 2 Cor., 4:6; John, 5:22, with 1 Enoch, chaps. 12, 25, 37, 38, 48, 60, 61, 69, 77, 78.

tained a real immortality by influencing the thought
and diction of the writers of the New Testament and
even the Sermon on the Mount" (Charles). While
this book was used freely in the first century of our
era, it shortly afterward disappeared and remained for
many centuries unmentioned. In the thirteenth century a manuscript of the work was recovered but its
value has been properly recognized only in this generation. Its author looked for the speedy coming of the
Messianic kingdom and believed in the resurrection of
the body and a new transformed life after death.
Verbal correspondences have been traced with Matt.
18: 15, 35; 22: 37-39; 25: 35, 36; Luke 2: 19, etc.,
while St. Paul "seems to have used the book as a *vade
mecum.*" It may be well to quote some of these great
utterances:

> "Then shall the Lord raise up a new priest,
> And to him all the words of the Lord shall be revealed;
> And he shall execute a righteous judgment upon the earth for
>   a multitude of days,
> And his star shall arise in heaven as of a king . . .
> And there shall be peace in all the earth . . .
> And in his priesthood the Gentiles shall be multiplied in
>   knowledge upon the earth,
> And enlightened through the grace of the Lord:
> In his priesthood shall sin come to an end. . . .
> And he shall give to the saints to eat from the tree of life,
> And the Spirit of holiness shall be on them.
> And Beliar shall be bound by him,
> And he shall give power to his children to tread upon the
>   evil spirits" (*Test. of Levi*).

"And now, my children, I say unto you, be not drunk with
wine; for wine turneth the mind away from the truth, and inspires
the passion of lust, and leadeth the eyes into error, (and) it dis-
turbeth the mind with filthy thoughts . . . but if you would live
soberly, do not touch wine at all, lest you sin in words of outrage

and in fightings and in slanders and transgressions of the commandments of God, and you perish before your time."

"And after these things shall a star rise to you from Jacob in peace.

"And a man shall arise like the Son of Righteousness, walking with the sons of men in meekness and in righteousness, and no sin shall be found in him and the heavens shall be open unto him, . . . and he shall pour out the spirit of grace upon you" (*Test. of Judah*).

"But love the Lord and your neighbor,

"Have compassion on the poor and weak." . . . (*Test. of Issachar*).

"And now, my children, I bid you to keep the commands of the Lord, and to show mercy to your neighbors, and to have compassion towards all, not towards men only but also towards beasts . . . and if you have not the wherewithal to give to him that needeth, have compassion for him in bowels of mercy. . . . for in the degree a man hath compassion upon his neighbors, in the same degree hath the Lord also upon him." . . . (*Test. of Zebulun*).

"Love the Lord through all your life . . .

"And one another with a true heart." . . . (*Test. of Dan*).

"Hatred therefore is evil, for it constantly mateth with lying, speaking against the truth; and it maketh small things to be great, and causeth the light to be darkness, and calleth the sweet bitter, and teacheth slander and kindleth wrath, and stirreth up war and violence and all covetousness; it filleth the hearts with evil and devilish poison. . . .

"Love ye one another from the heart; and if a man sin against thee speak peaceably to him and in thy soul hold not guile; and if he repent and confess, forgive him. . . . If a man prospers more than you do not be vexed, but pray also for him that he may have perfect prosperity" (*Test. of Gad*).

"If you work that which is good, my children,
Both men and angels shall bless you;
And God shall be glorified among the Gentiles through you,
And the devil shall flee from you,
And the wild beasts shall fear you,
And the Lord shall love you." . . .

"Blessed is the man who does not defile the Holy Spirit of God, which hath been put and breathed into him, and blessed is he who returneth it to his Creator as pure as it was on the day he entrusted it to him" (*Test. of Naphtali*).

In a few instances Christian additions have been made to this Jewish apocalypse, as can be seen, for example, in the following:

"In thee shall be fulfilled the prophecy of heaven (concerning the Lamb of God and Saviour of the world) and that a Blameless One shall be delivered up for the lawless men, and a Sinless One shall die for ungodly men (in the blood of the covenant) for the salvation of the Gentiles and Israel, and shall destroy Beliar and his hosts of servants. . . .

"And the twelve tribes shall be gathered together (in the temple), and all the Gentiles, until the Most High shall send forth his salvation in the visitation of an only begotten prophet (and he shall enter into the temple; and there shall the Lord be treated with outrage, and he shall be lifted upon a tree, and the veil of the temple shall be rent, and the Spirit of God shall pass on to the Gentiles as fire poured forth, and he shall ascend from hades and shall pass from earth into heaven)" (*Test. of Benjamin*).

The Book of Jubilees, an Ethiopic version of which was published 1895, contrasts greatly with the *Testaments of the Twelve Patriarchs*. It was written about the same period (135-105 B.C.), but emphasizes the supremacy of the law more after the manner of the Jews against whom Paul directed his scathing dialectic. It shows how great was the gulf which divided the legalistic wing of the Pharisees from the branch represented by such works as *1 Enoch* and *The Testaments of the Twelve Patriarchs*. The author urges that the law is the complete and ultimate authority of mankind, being of everlasting validity. He condemns unsparingly the Hellenistic spirit, believing that the Gentiles must be eternally reprobate, no Gentile being even allowed to keep the Sabbath. The law being the expression of absolute truth, there was, according to this writer, no room for further revelation, not even for prophecy. He thought of the Sabbath in much the same way as the Pharisees against whom Jesus directed his epoch-making word that the Sabbath was made for man and not man for the Sabbath; while those who were not circumcised became by divine predestination "children of destruction." His priestly sympathies were so great that he taught that the coming Messiah should spring, not from David, but from Levi. The spirit of the book is well shown by the prayer,

"May thy name and the name of thy sons go forth and traverse every land and region.
Then shall the Gentiles fear before thy face,
And all the nations shall quake."

The Psalms of Solomon, often called *The Psalms of the Pharisees,* were written 70-40 B.C. Some of the authors believed in a Messiah springing from the royal line of Judah; others expected him from the priestly line of Levi. The hope for the Messiah was very intense, and shows the eager expectation of the people. Altho the work doubtless had considerable influence in the century preceding Christ's birth, it made little permanent impression on Christian thought and soon passed into an oblivion which continued for some sixteen centuries. A new Greek version came to light in 1908, and a Syriac version in 1909. The spirit of the book can be seen from the following quotations:

"The nations reproach Jerusalem, trampling it down;
Her beauty was dragged down from the throne of glory;
She girded on sackcloth instead of comely raiment;
A rope was about her head instead of a crown.

Thou art our God and we the people whom thou hast loved;
Behold, and show pity, O God of Israel, for we are thine . . .
For thou didst choose the seed of Abraham before all the
   nations.
Let the sinners perish together at the presence of the Lord,
But let the Lord's pious ones inherit the promises of the Lord.
The pious of the Lord shall live by it (the law) forever;
The paradise of the Lord, the trees of life, are his pious ones.
Behold, O Lord, and raise up unto them their King, the Son
   of David. . . .
He shall have the heathen nations to serve him under his
   yoke . . .
Nations shall come from the end of the earth to see his
   glory . . .
'All nations shall be in fear before him. . . .
For God will make him mighty by means of his Holy Spirit."

The above clearly shows the popular expectation as
to the coming Messiah, which Jesus had to combat
during all his life. The Gentiles were not wandering
children whom God, the All-Father, was seeking to
bring back to repentance; neither was it possible for
heretic Jews to be forgiven for their heresy.

It is suggestive to note that *The Story of Ahikar*,
found by Dr. Rubensohn in his excavations at
Elephantine in 1906-1908,[40]—which had been popular
among the Jews for 400 years [41] before Jesus—gave the
story of the Prodigal Son, and tells in a most vivid way
how a wicked boy maltreated his father and wasted his
living; but instead of the father's offering him forgiveness he put him in chains, gave him a thousand blows
on the shoulders and a thousand and one blows on his
loins, and fed him on bread and water. Nadan, the

[40] Published by Sachau in 1911, in *Aramaische Papyri und Ostraka aus Elephantine*, and translated by Charles in his *Apocrypha and Pseudepi- grapha*, II : 715-784.
[41] See for early dating, Charles, *Apocrypha and Pseudepigrapha*, II : 715-716.

repentant youth, cried bitterly to his father for forgiveness, saying that he indeed was no more worthy to
be called his son, but that he would gladly be his
servant and tend his horses and feed his pigs; but the
father sternly replied: "To him that doeth good, good
shall be recompensed; and to him that doeth evil, evil
shall be rewarded." The influence of this story and its
recognized connection with our Lord's parable is seen
from the words put into the lips of the prodigal son in
the Syriac version: "Forgive me this folly; I will tend
thy horses and feed thy pigs which are in thy house." [42]
It may be added that while the spirit of Ahikar was
very different from the father whom Jesus pictured,
some of his moral maxims are well worth remembering:

> "My son, it is better to remove stones with a wise man than
> to drink wine with a fool."
> "My son, draw not near to a woman that is a whisperer, nor
> to one whose voice is high."
> "My son, the beating of a boy is like manure to a garden."
> "My son, the flock that makes many tracks becomes the portion
> of the wolves."
> "My son, sweeten thy tongue . . . for the tail of a dog
> giveth him bread, and his mouth gets him blows."
> "Better is one sparrow in thy hand than a thousand on the
> wing."
> "My son, if thou hear an evil matter, put it seven fathoms deep
> under ground."

Altho the above story of Ahikar was very popular
in the days of Jesus, it must be remembered that it
originated at an early period (420-400 B.C.) before the
great ethical reformation out of which came the literature which we have been describing. Very different in

---

[42] See Charles, *Apocrypha and Pseudepigrapha*, II:775, column 1, first
paragraph, and *cf.* Luke 15: 19.

spirit is *The Letter of Aristeas* (originated 130-70 B.C.,
but issued in the present form about the commence-
ment of the Christian era). This is the first book in
which the law is described as "Scripture" and as the
"Oracles of God," and in it is to be found what may
well be called a negative version of the Golden Rule:

"As you wish that no evil should befall you, but to be partaker of all good things, so you should act on the same principle towards others."

We have now mentioned the more influential works
written in the years immediately preceding the Christian era, with the exception of the *Fragments of a
Zadokite Work* which has recently been brought to
light by Dr. Schechter.[43] This strange Hebrew book
(which Dr. Charles believes to have been written 18-8
B.C. by certain reformed Sadducean priests, but some
other scholars, notably Prof. G. Margoliouth, believe
to have been written very early in the first century by
poorly instructed Christians who regarded John the
Baptist as the Messiah and Jesus as the "Teacher of
Righteousness") deserves close inspection, tho its meaning may yet remain obscure.

The author evidently was a priest of the Temple and
belonged to a party called "the penitents of Israel,"
who accepted as leaders "the Star" and "Law-giver"
and had entered into a "New Covenant" and "Covenant
of Repentance," which involved a great moral and
spiritual change. He hated the orthodox Pharisees,
declaring that they made void the written law by raising a body of oral tradition as a "wall" about it. But
he was almost equally opposed to his brethren the
Sadducees, declaring the Prophets as well as the Law

[43] *Documents of Jewish Sectaries,* ed. by S. Schechter, 1910.

to be a religious authority, teaching a blessed immortality, the existence of angels, the advent of the Messiah, a high moral code, and the wickedness of divorce. We will try to give sufficiently lengthy quotations to represent fairly the best teachings of this strange old document, which almost certainly was written within the generation in which Jesus appeared. Even if the scholars are mistaken who think of the writer of this work as a Christian, there can be no doubt, as Dr. Charles well says, that such a soul would eagerly have accepted Christianity when it was offered (*cf.* Acts 6: 7).

> "Because of the trespass of those who forsook him
> He hid his face from Israel and from his sanctuary
> And gave them over to the sword. . . .
> And he raised them up a Teacher of Righteousness
> To lead them in the way of his heart.
> And now hearken unto me, all ye who have entered into the
> Covenant. . . .
> Long-suffering is with him,
> And plenteousness of forgivenesses,
> To pardon those who repent of transgression. . . .
> And through his Messiah he shall make them know his holy
> Spirit.
> And he is true, and in the true interpretation of his name
> their names. . . .
> But God remembered the covenant with the forefathers. . . .
> And he made them to hearken
> And they digged the well. . . .

"The well is the Law, and they who digged it are the penitents of Israel who went forth out of the land of Judah and sojourned in the land of Damascus, all of whom God called princes . . . and the nobles of the people are those who came to dig the well by the precepts, in the which the Law-giver ordained that they should walk throughout the full period of the wickedness. And save them they shall get nothing until there arises a Teacher of Righteousness in the end of the days. . . .

"This is the word which Jeremiah spake to Baruch, the son of Neriah, and Elisha to his servant Gehazi. All the men who entered into the New Covenant in the land of Damascus (and yet turned backward and acted treacherously and departed from the spring of living waters), they shall not be reckoned in the assembly of the people and in its register they shall not be written, from the day when there was gathered in the Unique Teacher until there shall arise the Messiah from Aaron and from Israel . . . and when his deeds become known in accordance with the Midrash of the Law, in which walk the men of the perfection of holiness, no man shall consent to be with him in wealth and labor, for all the saints of the Most-High have cursed him . . . and there shall not come unto them or unto their families a share in the house of the Law. . . . And on the Sabbath day no man shall utter a word of folly and of vanity, no man shall lend aught to his neighbor. None shall dispute on matters of wealth and gain. None shall speak on matters of work and labor to be done on the following morning. . . . No man shall eat on the Sabbath day aught save that which is prepared or is perishing in the field . . . he shall not draw out into any vessel . . . no man shall put on garments which are filthy or were brought by a Gentile unless they were washed in water or were rubbed with frankincense. . . . No man shall carry anything from the house to the outside, or from the outside into the house. . . . Let not the nursing father take the sucking child to go out or come in on the Sabbath. . . . No man shall help an animal in its delivery on the Sabbath day. And if it fall into a pit or ditch, he shall not raise it on the Sabbath. No man shall rest in a place near to the Gentiles on the Sabbath. And if any person fall into a place of water, he shall not bring him out by a ladder, or a cord, or an instrument."

This completes our examination of the apocryphal works published previous to the Christian era. There are a few, however, arising during the first Christian century deserving of special attention.

The Sibylline Oracles (160 B.C.-A.D. 400) have been so long known, and it is so impossible to arrange their obscure statements chronologically, that they must be omitted entirely from this brief summary.[44]

The Assumption of Moses was probably written A.D. 7-29 in Hebrew. We possess only one manuscript of this work, a Latin palimpsest of the fifth century, discovered and published by Ceriani in 1861. It was so popular that a Greek version appeared in the first century, of which a few phrases are preserved, in Acts 7: 36; Jude 9, 16, 18. The work was written by a Pharisee, a quietist, during the lifetime of our Lord. The author's hero was not the great soldier Judas Maccabæus, but the obscure group of unknown martyrs who in each age offered themselves to Jehovah. His conception of spiritual religion and his opposition to the alliance of religion and politics was very much like that held by his greater contemporary, Jesus of Nazareth. He was in favor of the simple life, and was directly opposed to those impious men who are "self-pleasers, dissemblers . . . lovers of banquets . . . gluttons, gourmands . . . devourers of the goods of the poor." He thoroughly believed in the coming of a conquering Messiah.

"And then his kingdom shall appear throughout all his creation,
And Satan shall be no more,
And sorrow shall depart with him. . . .
And the horns of the sun shall be broken, and it shall be
    turned into darkness;
And the moon shall not give her light, and shall be turned
    wholly into blood. . . .
For the Most High shall arise, the eternal God alone,
And he will appear to punish the Gentiles, . . .
And thou shalt look from on high and shalt see thy enemies
    in Gehenna,

[44] The first and most beautiful translation of this work was by Dr. Milton S. Terry, 1890, 2d ed. (much enlarged), 1899.

And thou shalt recognize them and shalt rejoice,
And thou shalt give thanks and shalt confess thy Creator."

Second Baruk, of which a Greek fragment was published from Oxyrhynchus in 1903, was written in the latter half of the first century (A.D. 50-90) by an orthodox
Jew who was a "good representative of the Judaism
against which Paul's dialectic was directed" (Charles).
With the exception of the last nine chapters, this work
was lost sight of for twelve hundred years. A Syriac
version (sixth century) was published by Ceriani in
1883. This book, coming as it does from the very generation out of which the New Testament writings
originated, gives the arguments of a Jewish contemporary of St. Paul who refused to accept Christianity
and attempted by this document to uphold his declining
faith. This fact certainly gives great interest to the
words which we now quote:

"Then all who have fallen asleep in hope of him shall rise again.
. . . And it shall come to pass that when that appointed day has
gone by that then shall the aspect of those who are condemned
afterward be changed and the glory of those who are justified;
for the aspect of those who now act wickedly shall become worse
than it is, as they shall suffer torment. Also as for the glory of
those who have now been justified in my law . . . they may be
able to acquire and receive the world which does not die, which is
then promised to them. But . . . above all shall those who
come then lament that they rejected my law.
"But those who have been saved by their works,
And to whom the Law has been now a hope . . .
They shall be made like unto the angels
And shall be made equal to the stars . . .
For lo! we see now the multitude of the prosperity of the
    Gentiles . . .
But they shall be accounted as spittle. . . .
For though Adam first sinned
And brought untimely death upon all,

Yet of those who were born from him
Each one of them has prepared for his own soul torment to
    come.
And again each one of them has chosen for himself glories
    to come . . .
Each of us has been the Adam of his own soul.

"And Zion has been taken from us
And we have nothing now save the Mighty One and his
    Law . . .
For the youth of the world is past,
And the strength of the creation already exhausted . . .
And the pitcher is near to the cistern
And the ship to the port . . .
And life to its consummation."

Fourth Ezra was completed about A.D. 120. This
work has been known from the eighteenth century, but
the publication in 1875 of a new manuscript was epoch-
making, changing the whole standpoint of the discussion. The work is a Jewish defense of the law, the
acceptance (not observance) of which is the standard
of judgment, the author recognizing the inherent weakness of the law as a redemptive power (*cf*. Rom., chap.
7). There are a number of resemblances to the New
Testament in form and diction, but no direct dependence:[45]

"And I said: O Lord my Lord, out of all the woods of the
earth and all the trees thereof, thou hast chosen thee one vine;
out of all the lands of the world thou has chosen thee one plant-
ing ground; out of all the flowers of the world thou hast chosen
thee one lily; out of all the depths of the sea thou hast replenished
for thyself one river; out of all the cities that have been built
thou hast sanctified Sion unto thyself; out of the birds that have
been created thou hast called to thyself one dove . . . out of
all the peoples, thou hast gotten thee one people; and the Law
which thou didst approve out of all laws thou hast bestowed upon
the people whom thou didst desire. . . . For my Son, the

[45] Yet see, for Paul's familiar acquaintance with this book, *Expository
Times,* 1916, pp. 551-556.

Messiah, shall be revealed, together with those who are with him, and shall rejoice the survivors four hundred years. And it shall be after these years that my Son, the Messiah, shall die and all in whom there is human breath. Then shall the world be turned into the primeval silence seven days, like as at the first beginnings; so that no man is left . . . and the Most-High shall be revealed upon the throne of judgment; and then cometh the end. . . .

> "Think not upon those who have walked in devious ways be-
> fore thee . . .
> But regard them who have gloriously taught thy law;
> Be not wroth with those that are deemed worse than the
> beasts,
> But love them that have always put their trust in thy glory."

The Book of the Secrets of Enoch (II Enoch) has been preserved to us only through two Slavonic manuscripts which came to light in 1880 and 1884. It was written by a Hellenistic Jew in Egypt A.D. 1-50. It often exhibits striking parallelisms with New Testament diction and thought, and clears up several dark Bible passages. It was lost for twelve hundred years, but was much admired both by Christians and heretics in the first centuries. The author sees a blessed immortality for those who "avert their eyes from iniquity and make righteous judgment and give bread to the hungering and cover the naked with clothing and raise up the fallen and help injured orphans"; but terrific tortures in fiery rivers and mountains of ice for those who "seeing the poor, take away their goods and themselves wax rich; who being able to satisfy the empty, made the hungering to die; being able to clothe, strip the naked." One beautiful command is:

> "If ill bequitals befall you, return them not neither to neighbor nor enemy because the Lord will return them for you and be your avenger on the day of Great Judgment, that there be no avenging here among men."

Another beautiful passage is:

"Blessed is he who turns back from the changeable path and walks along the straight path. . . .

"Blessed is he who sows the seed of righteousness for he shall reap sevenfold. . . .

"Blessed is he in whom is truth, that he may speak truth to his neighbor. . . .

"Blessed is he in whose mouth is mercy and gentleness."

In considering the above works produced by the Jews in the two centuries nearest to the birth of Jesus, we are struck by the fact that many of the best productions were written in Galilee, which is here proved to have been the home of the religious seer and mystic. The disciples of our Lord were brought up in an atmosphere created by these books, and were doubtless themselves acquainted with many of them, as were the other writers of the New Testament. In many directions these writings show an advance upon the religious and ethical teachings of the Old Testament. Especially do we find the rather hopeless and gloomy outlook of the faithful concerning the future world to be transformed into one of joy almost equal to the New Testament vision. We now see that the Christian doctrine did not leap full grown into existence without any preparation for it, but that the God of the centuries had been providentially preparing the hearts of men for this new teaching. We see here in some books the legalism in its full maturity which Jesus condemned; but on the other hand, we find some beautiful teachings from a little group of mystics who, when they heard the words of Jesus, must have rejoiced with unspeakable joy as they gladly accepted the words of grace that fell from his lips.[46]

[46] Excepting where otherwise mentioned the translations of the above

We have now considered all the most influential Jewish works published before the end of the Apostolic age, excepting Josephus, Philo, and the Talmud.

We must omit more than a cursory mention of *Josephus* and *Philo,* tho the former throws more light upon the social, religious and political conditions of the first century than any other extra-biblical book, and the latter, as the greatest Hebrew philosopher of the first century and the chief exponent of the allegorical method of interpreting the Old Testament, had without doubt an enormous influence on the development of early Christian theology and hermeneutics. But the large influence of these two writers upon Christianity was pretty fully understood centuries ago.

It may be appropriate, however, to note that modern criticism, while generally condemning as an interpolation the passage in Josephus which speaks of Jesus as "a doer of marvelous works" and closes with the words so impossible from the pen of an orthodox Hebrew, "This was the Christ" (*Ant.,* XVIII: 6, *3f.*); yet accepts as genuine the passage in which he speaks of "the good man," John the Baptist (*Ant.,* XVIII: 116-119), and also accepts with almost equal certainty the genuineness of the notice of the death of James, "the brother of Jesus who was called Christ" (*Ant.,* XX: *200f.*).

The only new thing that need be mentioned concerning Philo is that the theory, once so popular, which claimed that the Fourth Gospel could not have been written by St. John because it was full of Philo's later

---

works have been taken from the authoritative work of R. H. Charles, *The Apocrypha and Pseudepigrapha of the Old Testament,* Oxford, 1913. The judgments ventured concerning these works have ordinarily been those approved by Dr. Charles in his *Religious Development between the Old and the New Testaments,* 1915.

neoplatonism, has received a severe shock. The strength of the theory lay in the fact that the favorite philosophic terms of Philo, such as life, light, logos ("word"), truth, paraclete ("comforter" or "strengthener"), only begotten, firstborn, etc., were also favorite terms with the author of the Fourth Gospel (who in this respect wholly differed from the Synoptics) just as they were favorite terms with Barnabas, Justin Martyr, and Origen. But modern critical study—including a thorough analysis of the Stoic doctrine of the Logos and of the ancient literature of Gnosticism, at Alexandria and elsewhere—has proved that there was a much greater divergence in vocabulary and thought between Philo and the Fourth Gospel than had previously been supposed.[47] It now seems reasonable to conclude, after a study of the literature of the first Christian century and the one preceding, that most of the resemblances found are "due to the common stock of ideas which belonged to thoughtful men at that period" (Drummond). Even Dr. Moffatt, who still holds to certain "reminiscences and adaptations" of Philo's language in the Fourth Gospel, acknowledges the contradiction in thought between the two—Jesus Christ, the supreme Logos, being set over against the many "powers" and "words" of the philosophers.[48]

Finally, the discovery of rare old non-Christian works, such as we have described above, has shown that the religious notions and mystic expressions of certain previously unknown Jewish writers of Palestine

[47] See especially Siegfried, *Philo von Alexandria* (1875); F. Legge, *Forerunners and Rivals of Christianity* (2 Vols.), 1915, and a good statement of the present state of the controversy by James Drummond, Hastings, *Dict. of Bible*, Extra Vol., pp. 197-208.

[48] *Introduction to the Literature of the New Testament*, 1914, pp. 320-325.

or Egypt, of the first century or earlier, resemble in an unexpected degree that of John's gospel.

The Talmud ought undoubtedly to be mentioned as perhaps the greatest of all the literature influencing the thought of the first Christian century.

This mammoth work, much larger than the *Encyclopædia Britannica,* has no logical beginning or end, but is merely a collection of miscellaneous remarks by ancient Rabbis, mostly concerning theology, ethics, synagog laws or Jewish civil rights and jurisprudence, with some gossip about distinguished rabbis. Its composition may have begun possibly as early as the Exile and certainly several centuries before the Christian era, and ended not earlier than A.D. 500; yet the first century, in which the great schools of Shammai and Hillel opposed each other, is the center of its interest. Its contents consist of the Mishna (oral "teaching"), which include sixty-three tractates embodying the interpretation of Scripture and rabbinic decisions from A.D. 10 to A.D. 220; and the Gemara, or interpretation of those earlier decisions by later rabbis who lived from A.D. 220-500. It was in two recensions, the Palestinian and Babylonian, the former being written in Hebrew and Western Aramaic and being more precise; and the latter in Eastern Aramaic, and filled with obscure and discursive remarks, often very slightly connected with the text which they are supposed to explain. The latter recension, however, shows a broader world sympathy than the former, and we shall hereafter confine ourselves to its consideration.

It is very easy for a Jew, who loves everything connected with Jewish thought, to exaggerate the value and breadth of interest shown in this national miscellany. Thus a well-known rabbi has recently declared not only that the Talmud contains poetry which surpasses the Iliad of Homer, but that its writers come from almost every land and walk in life. "You will find a contribution from a plain, modest, unskilled laborer who made his livelihood as a burden-carrier, next to an essay of the great Rabon Gamaliel; a homiletic explanation from a rabbi next to a story of a mermaid by an old experienced tar; a sketch of plant life by a simple farmer arrayed in line with an essay about medicinal anatomy by a famous medical sage. . . . Jesus and Jewish Christians and even pagans have acquired some place among its contributors, for there are extracts by Sadducees, Epicureans, Romans, Persians and Chaldeans whose opinions are published, even tho not in harmony with the Talmudic faith or creed." [49]

This gives quite an incorrect view of the facts. Dr. Goldschmidt gives an accurate statement of the real value of this work in the Preface and Introduction to his edition of the Talmud. He says wisely that it should neither be counted sacred nor a book of the devil; it is as false to claim that it contains all the treasures of science and religion and to read a high moral meaning into every foolish story as it is to select a few places in such a gigantic work for criticism and ignore its more noble teaching. "The Talmud is a collection of debates, doctrines, sentences, stories, and anecdotes of which the greater part were and are instructive; many, however, remaining, according to our conceptions, foolish and silly." [50]

[49] Naphtali Herz Imber, in *Report of the Commission of Education for 1894-5*, Vol. 2, Washington, 1896.

[50] *Der Babylonische Talmud*, von Lazarus Goldschmidt (8 vols.), 1896-1909, p. xvi.

The fact is that the Talmud was written wholly by
Jews, for Jews, and about Jews. The contributions on
medicine, history, philology, agriculture, etc., are
merely illustrative, while Gentiles and Christians are
mentioned only to be condemned; but in spite of all
this it is a vast and noble work and worthy of our profoundest admiration.[51] Altho, as Goldschmidt says,
this vast work until very recently was hidden in an
obscurity more mysterious than any Egyptian hiero-
glyphics, yet it is now open to scholars. There is to-day
no written record nor oral tradition known to any
Hebrew rabbi which is not known by some Christian
scholar.[52]

A very fine edition of the Talmud in fifteen volumes,
giving variants, has recently been published by Rab-
binovicz; an excellent translation in German by Goldschmidt; a translation of the Mishnah by Hoffman and
Baneth, and an English translation with a good introduction and short "History of the Talmud" by Michael
L. Rodkinson (20 vols.).

While the German translation is much more
minutely critical than the English and also more complete, Mr. Rodkinson having used the ordinarily accepted text and having also omitted many phrases and
sections which he believed to be interpolations or un-
necessary,[53] yet for our purpose the latter is entirely
sufficient to give a vivid and novel impression of the

[51] It should always be remembered that the Talmud, like the Bible, was
a book of religion. Almost every item tabulated by Dr. Samuel Krauss, in
his immense *Talmudische Archäologie* (1910), concerning food, dress,
care of body, games, festivities, schools, family life, burial, etc., might be
put under a religious sub-heading. It was in no true sense a book of
history, biography, or science.

[52] Compare especially the wise remarks of Dr. Hermann L. Strack,
Einleitung in den Talmud, Leipzig, 1908, p. vi.

[53] See Goldschmidt's criticism, *op. cit.,* p. xvi.

Jewish religious teaching in the apostolic age. The fact that Mr. Rodkinson is an orthodox Jew opposed to Christianity, who finds fault even with the Golden Rule, makes it perfectly plain that his translation of the Talmud may be trusted as one absolutely fair to Jewish interests and therefore of particular apologetic value to the Christian. The light which this new translation throws upon the times of Jesus and the centuries which immediately follow is impressive, as also its confirmation of the New Testament.

It tells many curious things about the Temple and the priestly ritual, asks and attempts to answer many questions which to us seem foolish, e.g., "Why has an ox a long tail?" "Why has an ass a short tail?" "What is the reason that the lower eyelids of a hen turn up?" It has much to say of the ceremonial purification before each meal; the kind and amount of water that must be used; which hand must be put first in the basin; the place to put the napkin, etc. There is much said also concerning unleavened bread; how the dough must be kneaded; how it must be baked, etc.

But perhaps to the New Testament student nothing else is more interesting than the Talmudic instructions in regard to keeping the Sabbath. Here are prescriptions as to what oil and wicks may be used in the lamps on the Sabbath day; whether a light may be extinguished for fear of accident or to afford rest for the sick; whether a chair may be dragged across the floor; whether victuals left in the oven, having been forgotten and therefore cooked on the Sabbath, ought to be eaten; how long steps one can take when he goes out for his Sabbath walk; may a man with a wooden leg go out at all? Would he not be "carrying his burden with him?" Is it permissible to pare the finger-nails or to make beds or tie knots or to bathe a sore hand in vinegar on the Sabbath day? Is it wrong to rend one's garments when he hears of the death of a relative on the Sabbath; or to close the door on an evil animal that tries to get into the house? How should bread be cut and is it lawful to cover a pot on the Sabbath, or to cover a chest with a goatskin to keep it from burning? What assistance (if any) may be given a woman about to give birth to a child on the Sabbath, and what may be done in the event of an animal falling into the water? Is it allowable to close the eyes of the dead or to move a corpse to save it from the fire? Is one allowed to take a bath on the Sabbath day or only to wash each limb separately? Is it lawful to use soap on the Sabbath? May one warm himself by a hearth fire?

Various answers were given by different rabbis to these questions; but there seems to have been a general agreement that no tailor was allowed to go out with his tools even on Friday evening; nor should one so late in the week sell anything to a Gentile or lend him money. No Jew could heat water on the Sabbath, altho a Gentile cook was allowed to do this for him.

A woman could wear a small golden hairpin, but could not go out with a seal ring on or carry a perfume bottle or a key without being liable to a sin offering; as for the false tooth of metal or of gold, some rabbis allowed it, but the sages generally forbade the gold tooth or filling, tho a silver tooth was generally permitted. Amulets were usually permitted, one celebrated rabbi stating explicitly that one could carry with him on Sabbath "eggs of grasshoppers" (a remedy for toothache), "the tooth of a fox" (to cure sleeplessness), or "a nail from a gallows" (remedy for tumor).

When one reads these voluminous questions and answers he gets a new view of the freedom of Jesus and of the novelty of his new doctrine concerning the Sabbath day.

Some of the answers are as strange as the questions. You may not chop ice on the Sabbath, but you may put chopped ice into a pitcher; a woman can wear hairpins, since these are ornaments, not burdens; but a man can not wear iron-riveted sandals unless his foot is sore; an Israelite can not light a lamp on the Sabbath, but he can use it after a non-Israelite has lighted it. Non-Israelite nurses may be procured for the sick. If an animal fall into a cistern or lake, an Israelite must not pull it out, but he can push something in for it to climb out upon.

Some interesting things may be noticed concerning the relations existing between the Jews and the Gentiles:

"If an Israelite says grace, say Amen to it; but if a Gentile says grace, be careful. (He may be attempting to cause you to blaspheme.) If a Gentile shaves you, keep your eye on the mirror."

Who are meant by "the idiots" is asked, and the answer is, "The Samaritans."

In the midst of these narrow and foolish words there are some beautiful ethical statements that throw a new light upon the religious sentiments of non-Christian Jews. We quote a few notable sentences:

"He who raises his hand to strike his neighbor is already considered wicked even before he has smitten him."

"The name of the Lord shall be loved (Deut. 6:4) through thy treatment of thy fellow man."

"Do God's will as thy own will, submit thy will to his will."

"Do God's will as if it were thine own, that he may do thy will as if it were his."

"Be not like servants who serve their master for the sake of reward."

"Thy neighbor's honor must be as dear to thee as thy own."

"Keep aloof from grumbling."

"Do not hate the one who reproves thee."

"Be afraid of a light sin."

"If you humble yourself the Lord will lift you up."

"Everything is foreordained by heaven except the fear of heaven."

"What is hateful to thee do not to thy neighbor; that is the law. All else is but commentary."

"Pass not judgment upon thy neighbor, until thou hast put thyself in his place."

"One who is tipsy can not pray; he is blaspheming."

"For him who says, I will sin and the Day of Atonement will atone for my sin; the Day of Atonement does not atone."

There are also many good words concerning the certainty of the future life and the happiness of the righteous and the duty of taking care of the poor. One rabbi said as his last word: "Make my funeral sermon impressive, for I shall be present."

The first question asked of a man by the divine Judge is, "Hast thou traded in good faith?"

In the tract on idolatry occurs also this striking statement: "He who occupies himself with the Torah (Law) but does not observe bestowing of favors, is similar to him who denies God."

It is distinctly taught that the "appointed times" for the appearance of the Messiah have already ceased, and that repentance and good deeds are essential.

One striking statement is, "The measure with which man measures will be measured out to him." [54]

[54] Many more gems could be given, gathered from the works of men who have spent years in the study of the Talmud; but the writer has preferred to give those which struck him most as he read the translation referred to.

Jesus is often mentioned in the Talmud. The references have been shown in detail by many scholars, and the fact is acknowledged by Mr. Rodkinson, tho he does not translate these passages (XIX: 106). He is never mentioned by name excepting perhaps once or twice, *e.g.*, where he is said to have been an idolator who worshiped a brickbat (*Sanh.*, 107B); but he is called "that man" or "Son of Stada" or "Son of Pandera," "dead dog," and "the hanged one" and "the sorcerer," "Balaam" and "Seducer." His mother also is mentioned with bitterness; "the hinge of hell's gate fastened in her ear."[55]

There is one instance where it is related that a rabbi hearing that a relative sick unto death was about to be cured by the name of Jesus, hoped that the sick man would die before healing could come to him. The wonderful works of Jesus were not denied, but it was said he had learned sorcery in Egypt. The gospel is referred to not as an *evangel* or good news but as an *avengil* ("blank paper"). Several of the disciples are mentioned by name, and the death of Jesus by crucifixion at the time of the Feast of the Passover is referred to.[56]

The trial of Jesus is illuminated by a study of the Talmud. The tract entitled "Sanhedrin" gives the entire procedure necessary to a legal Jewish trial on a

[55] *The Jewish Encyclopedia* tabulates the places where Jesus is mentioned in the Talmud, saying that it is a mere "subterfuge" to attempt to escape these references as applying to Jesus of Nazareth. It says the Talmud specifies his healing the halt, blind, and leprous, and mentions his walking on the sea. Laible in *Christus im Talmud* (Eng. transl., 1893) also gives a full list of the references to the Virgin Mary, while J. Rendel Harris (*Expositor*, London, 5th series, II: 193) explains certain obscure anagrams so that Pandera becomes equal to the Greek *parthenos* (virgin), etc.

[56] See Dalman, *Jesus Christ in the Talmud*.

capital offense. Many writers have tabulated the illegalities connected with the trial of Jesus and therefore we shall pass that.[57] But no one can read this tract without being struck with the care the Jewish law took to protect an innocent man from unjust conviction. Every member of the Sanhedrin was pledged to impartiality and kindness of thought. There must be a distinct majority of two in favor of conviction, and the vote for conviction must be repeated the next day in order to be effective. If the vote of condemnation was unanimous, the accused went free, this being taken as a proof of personal enmity. Gamblers, usurers, taxgatherers and government contractors were disqualified as witnesses. A herald must go before the convicted one proclaiming his name, the charges upon which he was condemned, and crying aloud that any one who knew anything in his defense should speak it out at once. The procession to the place of execution had to stop at least twice to give opportunity for such late testimony, and if it were offered the trial must be taken up *de novo*.

There were only four kinds of capital punishment known to Jewish law: decapitation, burning, strangling, and stoning. Decapitation, which was the most common method of execution by the Romans, was reserved for murderers, rebels, etc. Burning was the penalty for gross sexual crimes, the penalty originally being carried out by pouring melted lead down the throat, but later a lighted string was used after the man had been partially or wholly strangled. Strangling was the

---

[57] The trial by night on the eve of a great festival; in a private house instead of the hall Gazith, the conviction occurring on the same day as the trial; etc., etc.

penalty for adultery, striking a parent, stealing a living soul of Israel, giving a false prophecy, prophesying in the name of an idol. The criminal was choked by a twisted scarf which was wound around his neck. Stoning was the penalty for blasphemy, and the method of administering the penalty was minutely prescribed.

It is a singular and suggestive fact that in this greatest trial in the history of jurisprudence the supposed criminal did not suffer the penalty of the crime of which he had been convicted; but was punished by a foreign power by a penalty unknown to the laws of his own land. Crucifixion was a penalty unknown to Jewish law, as the Talmud witnesses. It was used by the Romans for piracy, highway robbery, assassination, forgery, false testimony, high treason and rebellion, as also for slaves who had murdered their master; but it was never prescribed by a Jewish court. Yet modern criticism is sure that the teaching of Jesus had the cross as its central theme.

The papyri have given us some important new knowledge concerning the trial of Jesus. These prove that the legal procedure of the Roman government in criminal cases differed in the provinces from what was universal in Italy. In the provinces a preliminary hearing by the local authorities—exactly corresponding to the action of the Sanhedrin—was customary, after which the case was handed over to the prefect for formal trial. Richard Wellington Husband, after a very thorough study of all the data involved, is able to find in the New Testament narratives of the trial a strong new proof of their extraordinary fidelity to fact. He says: "The course of trial in the Roman court . . . harmonized with the procedure shown in the sources to be that pursued by governors of provinces in hearing criminal cases." [58]

We might add as another curious confirmation of the New Testament narrative—a fact omitted by Mr. Husband—the newly discovered decision of an Egyptian governor, A.D. 85, in the case of Phebion, in which he renders his sentence in a way to strikingly remind us of Pilate: "Thou hadst been worthy of scourging . . . but I will give thee to the people." [59]

Pirke Aboth.—Altho this is the most celebrated part of the Mishna as we have it to-day, it is a chapter which we can not be sure was originally in the Babylonian Talmud. [60] It was written by many authors 30 B.C.-A.D. 300. It is to-day part of the authorized Prayer Book of the orthodox Jewish Church and many of its mottos are well worth remembering by all:

"All my days I have grown up among the wise and I have not found anything better than silence; not study is the chief thing, but action, and whoso makes many words occasions sin." . . .

"Talk not much with thy wife. . . . So long as the man talks much with the wife he causes evil to himself and desists from words of Torah and his end is that he inherits Gehennah." . . .

"A rude man fears not sin, and no vulgar person is pious . . . not he that hath much business becomes wise. In a place where there are no men strive to be a man" (R. Hillel). "Be not easily wroth, and repent one day before thy death" (R. Eleazar). "Let the wealth of thy associate be dear to thee as thine own" (R. Jose). "The day is short, and the work is great, and the laborers

---

[58] *The Prosecution of Jesus*, 1916, pp. 281-2. Mr. Husband gives a complete bibliography of works on the Trial of Jesus, pp. 283-295. From astronomical data fixing the full moon each year from A.D. 27 to A.D. 33, he concludes that the crucifixion occurred April 3, A.D. 33, since only in that year did the Passover supper (fourteenth of Nisan) come on a Friday. He decides that the charge against Jesus was treason—treason in Roman law meaning anything done "inimical to the welfare of the Roman people."

[59] Deissmann, *Light from the Ancient East*, p. 267.

[60] H. L. Strack, *Pirqe Aboth* (1915), p. 424.

few, and the hire is much, and the master of the house is urgent"
(R. Tarhon). "When ten are seated and occupied with Torah,
the Shechinah is among them" (R. Halaphta). "Every one whose
wisdom is more than his deeds, his wisdom does not endure" (R.
Heinena). "Every one whose wisdom is greater than his deeds
to what is he like? To a tree whose branches are many and
whose roots are few; and the wind comes and roots it up" (R.
Eleazar). "At five years old one is fit for scripture, at ten for
Mishna, at thirteen for the commandments, at fifteen for the
Talmud, at eighteen for marriage, at twenty for retribution, at
thirty for power, at forty for discernment, at fifty for council,
at sixty for elderhood, at seventy for gray hairs, at eighty for
strength, at ninety for decrepitude" (R. Judah).

Other rabbis offer wise sayings from which we
select the following:

"There are four types of men: (1) He that says what is mine
is mine, and what is thine is thine. This is the average type; some
say it is the type of Sodom. (2) What is mine is thine, and what
is thine is mine. This is the word of the vulgar. (3) What is
mine and what is thine are thine. He is pious. (4) What is thine
and what is mine are mine. He is wicked."

"There are four types of men who sit before the wise: a
sponge, a funnel, a strainer, and a sieve. A sponge, because it
sucks up everything; a funnel, because it receives at one end and
lets out at the other; a strainer, because it lets out the wine and
keeps back the dregs; a sieve, because it lets out the coarse meal
and keeps back the fine flour."

"Great is Torah because it gives them that practise it life in
this world and in the world to come."

5. Intellectual, Social, and Religious Life of the First and Adjoining Centuries as Seen in the Papyri, etc.

The early Christian centuries were creative. The
whole civilized earth throbbed with a sudden liberated
energy. It seemed as if a new intellectual dynamic had
been injected into the blood of the race. Pioneers of

science like Strabo were inventing geological theories which strangely resemble those of modern times; scholars like Tacitus and Livy were writing histories of such elegance and philosophic insight that they are yet classics of their kind; educators like Quintilian were originating methods of pedagogy which are only now in the twentieth century being carried into effect.

The astronomers in Alexandria were calculating eclipses, determining the equinoctial points, solstices, etc., much as is done to-day, and were reaching decisions concerning the size of the earth and the moon and the distance of the earth from the sun which were not far removed from those obtained by modern scholars. The sphericity of the earth was taught and illustrated in the schools, as we know from a fresco on which a terrestrial globe is represented, recently found in Rome. Nero had a pipe-organ worked by machinery, a circular dining-room which revolved like an astronomical dome with the sun, and a bronze hydraulic engine—found only recently in the ruins of his palace; and Dr. Boni has just discovered an elevator 120 feet high connected with the emperor's palace.[61]

The inventions of the mechanical engineers of that era have been famous ever since, and it is plain that they had been struggling somewhat successfully to master the problems connected with the power of sunlight and of confined steam which have been solved only within the last century. Hero of Alexandria is said to have constructed during the apostolic age the

[61] *Journal of Roman Studies*, IV: 251. Some scholars believe this was a latrine rather than an elevator, but the probability is that the distinguished Italian excavator was right in his decision.

first hydraulic engine and the earliest penny in the slot machine. The gage of our modern railroad tracks is almost in exact conformity to the wheel tracks of the Roman chariot, while the Director of Public Roads in the United States has lately declared that if modern road builders were to reproduce a highway like the Appian Way, it would cost over $50,000 a mile.

Even in medicine something was done. While there was usually much magic mixed up with ancient medicine, it is suggestive that Hippocrates admitted no superstition into his practise; that he correctly made hygiene the proper basis of medicine; that he discust the quality of the water supply; and that he set down critical records of cases of fever—typhus, puerperal, malarial, and the like.[62]

Many remains of fine surgical instruments have long been known to archeologists. The medical profession was divided into many branches, in each of which specialists were doing a good business. An oculist's seal of the first century, recently found at Este, gives the specialist's name; the seal is so cleverly constructed that four different remedies can be marked with it. In a papyrus, dating A.D. I, a man puts in an order for drugs, with the very modern postscript: "No stale stuff accepted!" In another papyrus of the third century mention is made of "medicated lozenges"; in one of the second century a prescription for sore eyes and a recipe for tooth powder are given; while a fragment now in the British Museum almost certainly represents an ancient work on dentistry.

Music was one of the common accomplishments of the first century. Some of the best poems ever written

[62] Mahaffy, op. cit., 179.

date from this era, and Statius (A.D. 45-96) even wrote memorial elegiac verses in honor of his parrot!

We have already mentioned Nero's pipe-organ, pictured on a monument, and it is interesting to note that he was conducting a cantata in the Music Hall of Naples when the great earthquake interrupted the performance (A.D. 63).

That the Jews were a music-loving people is shown not only by the poetry in the gospels, but also by the many fine specimens in uncanonical gospels (for example in the newly studied *Protevangelium of Jacob*), where some good specimens of true poetry are recorded.

One piece of music dating as early as the fifth century before Christ has been made known to us through a papyrus—the Orestes of Euripides, the first Greek writer who set his poetry to popular tunes;—and Wessely in 1889 had the good fortune to decipher the ancient system by which such tunes were recorded, so that we now possess the musical notes to several ancient pieces of music. These ancient tunes—with which our Lord may have been familiar—very much resemble the older Arabic and Hebrew melodies, being written in a key which is not naturally appreciated by Europeans. We make a difference between majors and minors; but the Greeks had eleven scales and had quarter as well as half tones in their music.[63]

While Suetonius tells us that among the Romans teaching, as a profession, was despised so that a pantomime actor or boxer might turn teacher, yet we also remember that, occasionally at least, a Roman knight

---

[63] See Carl Wessely, *Aus der Welt der Papyri*, pp. 53-57; for the instrumental music of the Roman Era see *Journal of Hellenic Studies*, XXIII:160ff; and for ancient Hebrew music see, *Jewish Encyclopedia*, *passim*.

entered this position; and Persius (A.D. 34-62) writes
to his teacher:

> "It is my joy to show, O sweet my friend,
> To you, how a large part of me is yours."

There were twenty flourishing grammar schools at
Rome when St. Paul visited the city, and for over a
hundred years girls as well as boys had been allowed
the privileges of the schools. In many lands women
had become fascinated with Greek studies, and occasionally they were employed as professors in the
grammar schools. Dr. Petrie in 1889 found at Hawara,
under the head of a learned woman, a fine copy of the
second book of Homer's Iliad, thumb-marked by careful study and with various critical readings marked in
the margin.

It is noteworthy that Pliny the elder quotes a
woman author among the two thousand authorities
mentioned in his celebrated "Natural History"; and the
wife of Pliny the younger set his poems to music. Even
Martial ranks culture as one of woman's charms, tho
Juvenal condemns a blue stocking as hotly as he does
the wife who delivers curtain lectures to her lord or
elopes with a gladiator.

It must be acknowledged, however, that the larger
part of cultured society agreed with Juvenal in that
judgment. The women were supposed to be the eaves-
droppers and gossips of the world:

> "They know what Juno chatted of with Jove.
> What never was or is—they know it, though!"

Menander was quite in fashion when he wrote that
to marry was "taking arms with no good reason against
a sea of troubles"; for while three out of every thirty

ships that went to sea were wrecked, "scarcely one poor husband escaped." Another poet wails:

> "O, wretched are we, husbands who have sold
> All liberty of life, all luxury,
> And live as slaves of women, not as freemen."

In view of this, it is not surprizing that all the papyri which have to do with the schools speak only of the boys and do not mention the girls. While women of the upper class might sometimes be well educated, the common working girls had not the slightest opportunity for education. And it must be remembered that it is almost exclusively the working people who have left to us these papyrus letters. Most of these poor people seem to have had little difficulty in getting papyrus or in using it after it was obtained, altho one poor man of the third century writes:

> "Do please send me some unwritten papyrus that I may be able to write you."

A boy (third century) writes to his father: "Do not be anxious about my mathematics; I am industrious"; and a most interesting letter (second century before Christ), that of a mother to her student son, has been preserved in which she congratulates him on having completed his education, saying, "You will have now a maintenance for your old age"; while in another letter a boy's father expresses regret because his teacher (διδάσκαλος) had left him, but gladness because his trusty old servant (παιδαγωγός) was with him and would take him to find another worthy instructor (cf. Gal. 3:24).

The British Museum possesses many school exer-

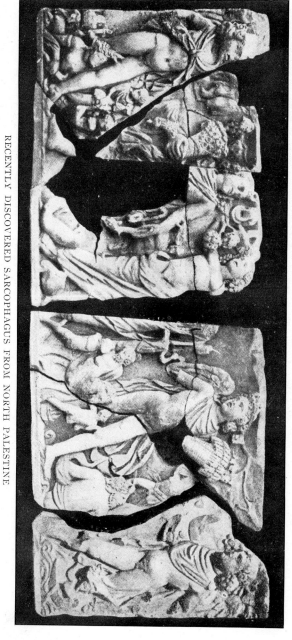

RECENTLY DISCOVERED SARCOPHAGUS FROM NORTH PALESTINE

From "Zeitschrift des deutschen Palästina-Vereins," 37, Taf. xviii

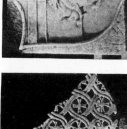

SCULPTURES FROM ASCALON

1. Hellenistic Grave Relief.   2. Piece of an Old Christian
Altar.   3. Crusader's Coat of Arms.

From "Zeitschrift des deutschen Palästina-Vereins,"
XXXVII, 1914, Table XVI

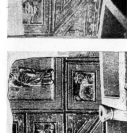

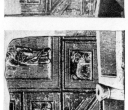

ART FRAGMENTS

Recently recovered at Ascalon

From "Zeitschrift des deutschen Palästina-Vereins,"
XXXVII, 1914, Table XV

cises coming from the second century, which still show the hard usage they received from their ancient owners. Some of these contain the alphabet, the order of letters being imprest by a catalog of familiar names. Then there are syllable lists, each letter being combined with different vowels; then there are lists of polysyllables. There are various copy-books in which the same epigram or sentence is copied six or seven times. Two very fine grammatical tablets of wood about as large as the modern American slate and also a wooden school book of eight tablets containing verbal declensions have recently come to light, as well as a trilingual "Conversation Book."

In one of the school exercises the student has written at the end:

"Good luck to the writer!" [64]

Practically all the letters and most of the school exercises are written in Greek. Latin, however, was also widely used. Indeed, colloquial Latin was probably almost as widely used, geographically speaking, as colloquial Greek. While in India only a hundred in every ten thousand can read and write English—tho this country has been occupied by the English for 150 years,—yet Latin, which in 400 B.C. was spoken in a district of less than a hundred square miles, had expanded until at the beginning of the Christian era it had overspread all countries almost as completely as the Roman arms. Not only in Italy but in most of the provinces all

[64] We do not know much about the prizes offered for excellence in study and contests of endurance, but the *sickles* received in Sparta by boys from ten to thirteen years of age who were victors in athletics and contests of endurance, have come down to us, these having been dedicated as votive offerings. Xenodes and Lochares were each three times victors. (*Jour. of Brit. School at Athens,* 1905-6, p. 314; 1908-9, p. 45.)

government business, all military, legal, and large
monetary affairs were conducted in Latin; all imperial
proclamations and formal addresses were in Latin.
Even Constantine, when he presided at the Council of
Nicæa, addrest the assembly in Latin, and the Emperor
Claudius cancelled the Roman citizenship of a Greek
because he had proved himself unable to write in good
Latin.[65]

Not only Paul and every other Roman citizen would,
of necessity, understand this language, but as native
Roman traders and soldiers were covering Palestine,
Syria, and Egypt during the early Christian centuries,
the common people also must have generally had some
understanding of the Roman tongue—and this is shown
by many Latin inscriptions in every land, tho doubtless
ordinary domestic correspondence and local business
were commonly carried on in Greek.[66]   There is one
letter, however, written in Latin (21-18 B.C.), which
fortunately comes to us from Egypt, enabling us to see
exactly how the original manuscripts of Vergil and
Horace looked.   Macedo in this letter is told by a friend
of some scandal reported in the home of his acquaint-
ances Jucundus, Dido, and Nireus; but far more
valuable than this bit of local gossip is the appearance
of this ancient letter, where the writing shows scarcely
any separation of words, no capital letters, and no
punctuation marks.[67]

But we must not overrate the importance of our

[65] For many other illustrations of this see Abbott, *Common People of Ancient Rome*, 1911, Chap. 1.

[66] M. Seymour de Ricci has just published an important Latin will, almost certainly written for an Italian, from Egypt, *Ancient Egypt*, 1916, p. 18.

[67] For many examples of Roman script from A.D. 55 to A.D. 572, see Wessely, *Aus der Welt der Papyri*, 148*ff*, and references.

few Latin scripts.[68]   Of all the hundreds of letters
written from one end of the Roman world to the other,
only a very few were ever written in Latin.   Everybody was writing; but everybody was writing in Greek.

We possess several bundles of official letters from a
military prefect and other officers of government in
Egypt; a large package of personal notes from a keen
old farmer; a marriage contract in which the amount
of the bride's adornment is given and the statement
that if she shames her husband she shall forfeit all she
has brought, while if the husband brings a mistress
into the house he shall repay the dowry and add to it
a thousand drachmas; an affectionate letter to a child
containing the impressive remark, "Be sure the reason
why I and the rest love you so much is that you obey
them in all things"; a letter of a son to his father closing, "Write to us that we may not be anxious (*cf.* Luke
22:44).   Take care of yourself . . . and come to us
in good health"; a letter of a wife to her husband who
says she is in the last extremity, "because of the high
price of corn," yet complaining that he has "never even
thought of returning"; and multitudes more of the
same sort.

The papyri show us the home life of the common
people of the first century even better than the *graffiti*
of Pompeii.   The latter were scribblings in public places,
but these private letters and business documents show
the hidden thoughts and home occupations of the
people.   They are written carelessly and impulsively,

[68] Dr. Victor Martin of Geneva, in a private letter, kindly warns me
that "all official business in Egypt was conducted in Greek, with the only
exception of matters concerning the army.   The number of Latin papyri
compared to Greek is very small and the people ignored Latin, and the
fact that best proves this is that the New Testament was spread over the
world not in Latin but in Greek."

often in barbarous grammar and without literary charm, but they open out to us the social and religious conditions of the middle and lower classes as could be done in no other way. Alciphron, a Greek author of the second century, published some 1,700 years ago a "Model Letter-writer," containing a hundred or more letters supposed to be written by fishermen, country folk, parasites, and courtezans. It is interesting reading; but it is instructive to compare his artificially constructed letters with those we are about to read. Take, *e.g.*, the description supposed to be written by a farmer concerning his neighbor, "smelling of raisins and dust." It is a cleverly formed sentence, but no farmer would ever have written it. In the papyri we see how farmers really write. A bundle of fourteen letters has come down to us from an old man born about A.D. 14, written probably to his nephew in a shaky and almost illegible hand, telling him in words very badly misspelled, "I blame you greatly for having lost the two little pigs," etc., and intimating very positively his surprize that young folks are such poor farmers nowadays as compared with the time when he was a boy.[69]

Among these scraps of ancient papers picked up miscellaneously from many collections are monthly meat bills; wedding invitations; a marriage contract (A.D. 200), in which "a white striped frock" and "a white veil with purple border" and several pieces of jewelry are mentioned as part of the dowry; the watchman's contract, pledging himself to be honest and not let

---

[69] On the model letter writer see H. W. Smyth, *Harvard Essays on Classical Subjects*, 1912, Essay III. We will not indicate the location of the papyri quoted excepting in extraordinary cases, as they are gathered from scores of collections.

thieves enter the storeroom; a farce and mime from
the second century, full of coarse wit, with the musical
and stage directions in shorthand; a second century
almanac, containing directions too gross to be quoted;
a poll-tax register from the first century; a legal ac-
cusation against a husband affirming that he had "applied fire to his foster daughters, having stript them
quite naked"; salutations in a private letter to Theonis'
children, "whom the evil eye shall not harm"; lease of
a dining-room (A.D. 173), with explicit contract that
the key must be given back and the room left "free
from dirt and filth"; question to an oracle (first century), "Shall the son agree with his father or not?";
other questions (second century), "Shall the slave be
bought or not!" "Is it granted to me to marry?" etc.,
etc.

One rather comical note from a school boy urges
that his teacher be fed well, so that he may be better
natured. Some very modern methods of primary instruction have recently been brought to light, as for
example a "Nursery Acrostic" (probably first century),
in which the loss of a garment is told in short lines beginning with successive letters of the alphabet:

"Alion it was who took it: a fool who lost it," etc.

The ordinary Christian boy at this early era seems
to have been able at least to read and write. This
may seem at first sight a small accomplishment, but
will appear more surprizing when we remember that
not a single letter or inscription remains from
the crusaders who marched through Asia Minor
(Ramsay).

We can now see clearly that the Christians of the

first three or four centuries encouraged learning and
that the new teaching appealed with special force to
educated people, tho later the average of education was
lower. The commonplace and trifling nature of the
ordinary correspondence in the early Christian centuries is sufficient proof of the common and easy use
of the pen at that time. Among the unpublished documents obtained by the writer in Egypt are two letters
written almost entirely about a hoe which, it seems, one
of the parties had taken and the other thought he had
not returned. Shenute writes:

"I let you know about the hoe which I gave them. They sent
to me another time about it . . . remember so they do not
bother me about it."

Abraham answers this note on the opposite side of
the parchment:

"As to the matter of the hoe, I told N—— that I received
it," etc.

It may seem, however, as if the above notes may
possibly have had some necessity of business behind
them and there may be some business excuse also even
for the list of donkey boys scrawled on an ostracon
(first century), and an excuse equally valid for the love
letter of the second century, in which the disappointed
lover sighs:

"Ah me! You have left me alone in my misery!"

But what can be said of this letter (second or third
century)?

"Having spoken, he smote three times and laughed seven
times Ha, Ha, Ha, Ha, Ha, Ha, Ha. And when he had laughed,
seven gods were born!"

It not only shows that the ancients laughed as we do, but it also shows that they wrote easily and carelessly as we do.

The ancient sense of humor is also quite often seen in the papyri, and even occasionally in the tomb inscriptions. In one will, recorded 23 B.C., it looks as if a father had allowed his satiric wrath against his two sons, presumably prodigals, to follow him to the grave, for he wills each of them "a bed"—as if that were all either of them were capable of using to good advantage.[70] On one gravestone appears this satiric injunction: "Lawyers and the evil eye, keep away from my tomb." In a papyrus letter (second or third century) a man sarcastically writes: "It was good of you, you sent me a gift, such a beauty—just weeds!" Was this a young man's anger aroused at receiving an unacceptable wedding present? In a memorandum of the first century Hirax mentions some thirty-six different items that he must not forget, marking an oblique stroke in the margin as each matter is attended to. When one reads among other items that he must not forget to "get a license," to go to "a meeting," to see Philona, to "get some leeks and sandals," etc., one at first might imagine that this was the private domestic record of a young husband; but the mention of an "aqueduct" and "wheel" shows that this was a business memorandum.

How very modern the tone of the following letters: a note from one man to another instructing him to get a better file, "one that would file iron," as the one he had brought in would "file only wood"; a medical papyrus of the second century in which the doctor dis-

[70] See Wilcken, *Archiv für Papyruskunde*, 1:63.

sents from the ancient dictum that ripe fruit was harm-
ful, saying that he believed it was certainly "good for
digestion"; a complaint made by an "unpaid policeman"
concerning a priest, who struck him with a stick and
"tore his shirt"; a will made by Pekysis in Hadrian's
reign written (as usual then and now) "in the street"
by a street notary, in which this Egyptian lawyer starts
out with the declaration that the testator is "sane and
of sound mind"; and another careful legal document
in which a firm of embalmers, of the guild of
Cholchytæ, take a lien on certain mummies—proving
that the undertakers of that era were prudently guarding against unpaid bills!

There are many begging letters addrest to members of the clergy, in one of which Paula, a widow, is
urged for charity on the ground that "she and the
children, each one of them, have pains in the neck, and
I know that thou lovest the poor." Pious ejaculations
are very frequent in these begging letters, as "The
Lord shall bless thee and thy cattle. Kindly have
pity."

The series of twenty-one letters which Dr. Deissmann has recently given, dating from the early centuries, illustrates in a beautiful way the correspondence
between the New Testament writings and the writings
of non-Christians who were contemporaries of the
apostles.[71] In one of these, which was written on a
leaden tablet found near Athens, the man writes home
saying, "Send me some covering . . . as plain as you
have and not broidered with fur" (cf. 2 Tim. 4: 13).
Another from a broken papyrus tells of a festival that
is soon to come, and asks Ptolemæus to send quickly

[71] *Light from the Ancient East*, pp. 148-217.

"the piper Petoys with the Phrygian pipes and the others" and "Zenobius the Malakon" (*cf.* 1 Cor. 6:9), "with tablet and cymbals and rattles; for the women have need of him at the sacrifice. . . . And send us also cheeses, as many as thou canst, and new earthenware and herbs of every kind, and delicacies if thou hast any. Farewell." Another private letter written on a potsherd is really a receipt in which occurs the formula, "I have received from thee the fruit that falleth to me" (*cf.* Luke 15:12). Still another, dated September 13, A.D. 50, is a papyrus in which Mysterion says, "I have sent unto you my Blastus (*cf.* 1 Cor. 4:17 and Acts 12:20) for forked sticks for my olive garden (*cf.* Acts 1:12). . . . See then that thou stay him not for thou knowest how I need him every hour. Farewell."

In another letter of July 24, A.D. 66, a farmer swears that he has had only seven lambs born in the flock since the previous enrolment; this is autographed with the signature of an official, and the date is given in the handwriting of the official: "In the twelfth year of Lord Nero"—exactly the same title of deity being given to the Emperor which the New Testament constantly gives to Jesus. An Egyptian soldier in the Roman army writes to his father in the second century saying:

"Many greetings: Before all things I pray that thou art in health, and that thou dost prosper and fare well continually, together with my sister and her daughter and my brother. I thank the Lord Serapis that when I was in peril in the sea he saved me immediately. . . . I beseech thee . . . father, write unto me a little letter firstly of thy health, secondly of that of my brother and sister, thirdly that I may do obeisance to thy hand because thou hast taught me well, and I therefore hope to advance quickly if the gods will. . . . I am sending thee by Euctemon a little picture of me. Moreover my name is 'Antonis Maximus.' "

In addition to the opening formula here, which reminds us of St. Paul's greetings and prayers in all his letters, there is a true touch of life in the pride which this young soldier shows in his new Roman name and in the picture, perhaps in his new uniform, which he sends back home. The piety of the day is shown by a note from the shipmaster Irenæus written to his brother (second century), saying he has arrived safely with his cargo of corn at Rome, "and the place welcomed us, as God wills." [72]

Many other examples in the social and religious history of the first century might be given from the new texts illustrating the New Testament. Several inscriptions speak of the sparrows sold in the market in packages of ten (Matthew 10: 28; Luke 12: 6).

So the phrase "Deliver unto Satan" (1 Tim. 1: 20) corresponds exactly to the formula in a magical papyrus which attempts to render the cursed one unable to speak: "Dæmon of the dead . . . I deliver unto thee N. N., in order that . . . "; while the "bond of his tongue was loosed" (Mark 7: 35), is exactly illustrated from a magic spell which reads: "Bound and fast held through the mouth and fast held the tongue." The phrase used by Mark is one often used in the magical texts, and shows that the writer of the gospel supposed that in this miracle demonic fetters were broken and a work of Satan undone. [73] So the "marks of the Lord Jesus" (Gal. 6: 17) probably referred to the brand of freedom placed upon the slave when he was

---

[72] Milligan, *Greek Papyri*, No. 41; Deissmann, *op. cit.*, pp. 167-171.
[73] See for full discussion, Deissmann, *op. cit.*, pp. 304-310.

sold to the temple and thus liberated from his master. The usual formula for this reads:

"N. N. sold to the Pythian Apollo a male slave named ——— at a price of ——— minæ for freedom."

In another inscription the god is said to have "bought with a price 'this slave' for freedom." [74]

Everywhere the belief in magic meets us in the papyri in connection with the religions of the first and adjoining centuries. The heathen had always trembled before these demonic powers. A charm recently published well represents a common form:

"Get thee back, thou enemy, thou dead man or woman, who dost cause pain. . . . Thou hast no power over his toes, legs, arms, spine, head." [75]

Another even more lately published reads:

"I give thee (queen of Hades) his ears, nose, nostrils, tongue, lips, and teeth, so that he may not speak his pain; his neck, shoulders, arms, and fingers, so that he may not aid himself; his breast, liver, heart, and lungs, so he may not locate his pain; his bowels, belly, navel, and flanks, so he may not sleep the sleep of health; his thighs, knees, legs, shanks, feet, ankles, heels, toes, and toe nails, so he may not stand of his own strength. . . . Mayest thou irrevocably damn him that his eyes may never see the light of another month." [76]

Above an ancient structure has recently been found this curious curse:

"Whoever steals the nails from this structure, may he thrust them into his eyes!" [77]

---

[74] Cf. 1 Cor., 6:20, 7:23; Gal. 5:1, 13: Deissmann, op. cit., pp. 303, 325, 334.

[75] Theban Ostraca, 1913, C1.

[76] Art and Archæology, 1915, p. 206.

[77] In a recently discovered magical text the word "gospel" is inserted, showing the thought of its power even by its enemies (J. G. Milne, Hawara Papyri, pp. 338-397).

But such curses were not confined to heathen writers. It is very common to find upon Christian tombs a curse upon the man who shall disturb the bones, and in early Christian literature this belief in demons seems almost as universal, among the uneducated classes, as among the opponents of the gospel.

Nor was this confined to the grossly ignorant. The Hermetic books—which throw precious light on pre-Christian times—were so famous that in the early Christian centuries many writings grew up, under the same title, seeking to provide an acceptable substitute for Christianity by "combining the Neo-Platonic philosophy, Philonic Judaism and cabalistic theosophy." [78] The credulous faith in occult and demonic power meets us everywhere in these works. The early Gnostics, tho professing earnest allegiance to Christianity and claiming to adhere in a superior way to philosophic method, were equally superstitious. Their most renowned work, *Pistis Sophia,* was first fully translated in 1850, and in 1891 a papyrus was published by Amélineau, containing two documents disclosing more perfectly the secrets of this esoteric system. The Gnostics brought with them into the new faith "the use of pictures and statues, of incense and of all the paraphernalia of the worship of the heathen gods" (F. Legge), including this firm belief in magical powers. The *Pistis Sophia* pretends to give the secret teaching of Jesus to his disciples during eleven years which he spent with them after the resurrection, and certain other revelations made after his ascension. The five most mysterious

[78] F. L. Griffith; for the Egyptian elements in these writings and their influence on early Christianity see W. M. Flinders Petrie, *Personal Religion in Egypt,* 1909, and other literature given by S. J. Case, *Evolution of Early Christianity,* 1914, p. 192n.

words which he explains and makes the basis of this esoteric teaching are zama, zama, ôzza, Rachama, ôzai. The character of this teaching may be seen from a quotation in which the author explains the glory of the "first mystery," which is as the two vestures of Christ:

"In the first is the glory of all the names of all the mysteries and of all the emanations which are in the ranks of the two receptacles of the First Mystery. And in this vesture . . . is the name of the Recorder who is the First Precept, and the mystery of the Five Marks, and the mystery of the great Legate of the Ineffable One who is the same as the Great Light, and the mystery of the Five Prohegumeni, who are the same as the Five Parastatæ." [79]

The influence of this mystical and magical teaching upon Christianity was immeasurably great. All these synthetic systems taught that it was through the secret knowledge of hidden names and through the performance of certain sacraments, known only to the initiated, that the highest rank could be obtained by the believer, in this world and in the next. This idea was very prominent in all the religions which were popular in the first century. The Mithras worship, which was the most popular of all, contained much astrology and much magic, tho the pictures connected with its shrines doubtless showed to the initiate divine secrets concerning the nature of God and his relation to man and salvation. One of the most surprizing single discoveries of this generation connected with this ancient cult is that of Dr. A. Dieterich, who in 1903 published, with learned notes, what he considered to be substantially "an entire liturgy of Mithras," the "only one which we have re-

[79] For a very learned attempt to explain the exact meaning of all these terms and of the system as a whole, see F. Legge, *Forerunners and Rivals of Christianity*, 1915, 2 vols.

ceived essentially entire" from the ancient past.[80] This document, written according to Dieterich about A.D. 300 and arising not later than A.D. 200, clearly proves to us that tho these ceremonies and beliefs were mixed with many magical names and much senseless superstition; yet they presented in a really spiritual way the "raising of the soul to the divine light and into union with God," actually using in this effort some of the same symbols in which the Christian church has embodied its highest thoughts." [81]

In his struggle for the knowledge of the truth the disciple of Mithras seeks a new birth:

"If it indeed seems good to you, permit me, though now held down by my lower nature, to be reborn to immortality . . . that I may become mentally reborn, that I may become initiated, that the Holy Spirit may breathe in me." [82]

These words, which have become so familiar to Christian worshipers, must not, however, blind us to the vast difference in meaning between the two teachings. This "new birth" is to be accomplished largely by magic ceremonies and comes in any case through a mystic knowledge, not through a transformation of the moral personality. The expectation of the future also is as different from that of the Christian as can well be conceived:

"Hail to thee, lord, ruler of the water;
Hail to thee, lord, establisher of the earth;
Hail to thee, lord, disposer of the spirit.
"Lord, I that am born again take my departure, being exalted on high, and since I am exalted, I die; born by the birth which

[80] *Eine Mithrasliturgie*, Leipzig, 1903.

[81] Dieterich, *op. cit.*, pp. 26-29.

[82] Dieterich, *op. cit.*, p. 4; Case, *Evolution of Early Christianity*, p. 329.

engenders life, I am redeemed unto death, and go by the way which thou hast appointed, as thou hast made for a law and created the sacrament," etc.[83]

Whether this be in reality an original Mithraic liturgy, as Dieterich supposed, or only a Mithraic charm, as others have since affirmed, in either case it shows the religious influences molding the early Christian centuries.

Even the Jews, who for many centuries had been the chief exponents of one omnipotent God, were caught in the swirl of magical beliefs—just as were the Roman Catholics and Protestants of the middle ages. They depended for power over disease, etc., largely upon books of magic and magical spells.[84] In the recently published *Book of the Key of Solomon* (1914), which was the ancient authority on magic rites, is an injunction to guard the secrets of the book as one "would guard his own soul"—which shows how fearful the power of these secret names were supposed to be. The phylacteries dating from the first century recently found by M. Gaster—which represent the very same phylacteries that St. Matthew mentions (23: 5)—testify to the same dread, as seen in the combinations and permutations of the letters of the alphabet in representing the divine name.[85] In Phrygia, where the Jews were very rich and influential in the early Christian centuries, Sir William Ramsay found in May, 1914, two gravestones, each about five feet high and finely

---

[83] See for this quotation, Albert Schweitzer, *Paul and His Interpreters,* 1912, p. 187; for a full discussion of the Mithras religion, F. Legge, *Forerunners and Rivals of Christianity,* 1915, II: 224-276; and W. J. Phythian-Adams, *Mithraism,* 1915; and for a summary, *New Schaff-Herzog Encyclopedia,* VII: 419*ff.*; *cf.* literature previously referred to, pp. 505*ff.*, 600.

[84] See Schürer, *op. cit.,* III: 151-5.

[85] *Society of Biblical Archæology, Proceedings,* March, 1916, etc.

ornamented, on one of which (A.D. 220-250) was inscribed the following unique curse:

"If any one after their burial . . . shall inter another corpse
or do injury in the way of purchase, then shall he bring upon him
the curses written in Deuteronomy." [85a]

The owner of this tomb is said to have "filled all
municipal offices," having been "strategos, steward of
the market-place," etc.

It is interesting to note that this influential Jew
wrote worse Greek than even his Christian contemporaries; yet no one can doubt that the Jews in Phrygia
at this time were rich and powerful. Indeed, it would
be hard to find a place in the Roman Empire where
the Jews were not influential; tho they were probably
more favored in Egypt than anywhere else. In considering the social and religious influences of the first
century, historians must give the Jew a prominent
place.

It has long been known that Alexandria in
Ptolemaic times was the home of the largest Hebrew
population in the world, one of its four chief quarters
being inhabited exclusively by Jews. It was here that
the financiers of this race received their initial education as the bankers and money lenders of the civilized
world. At Oxyrhynchus, Grenfell and Hunt found a
number of fragments of an official letter (*cir.* A.D. 400)
which mentions the "heads of the congregation" and
"elders of the synagog"; and another legal document
of perhaps the fifth century to which several Jews
had fixt their signatures. The *Jewish Quarterly Review*, October, 1915, fills thirty pages with the names
of the towns in the Roman Empire in which the Jews

[85a] *Expository Times*, 1915, p. 170.

are known to have lived and prospered in the first century, and about fifty places can be mentioned in Egypt where they are known to have flourished. That they were organized in Egypt as a religious community as far south as Abydos as early as the third century before Christ is proved by a will in which the testators, who were "heads of the congregation," left as one of their most important legacies a valuable manuscript of the Torah, specifying that it should be divided among certain relatives or friends.[86]

Under Vespasian the temple of Onias, which had been founded several centuries before, was closed. In Trajan's reign because the Jews rose and massacred the Greeks they were practically exterminated in Alexandria; but at a later period they repopulated Egypt and recovered many of their ancient privileges.[87]

An interesting illustration of the influence of the Jews within half a generation of the apostolic age has just been published—a third century papyrus telling of a delegation of Greeks and Jews who came opposing each other in a case before the Emperor Trajan (cir. A.D. 114). One of the chief men against the Jews was "Paulus," a Tyrian by birth but by profession a lawyer, from Alexandria. Both Jews and Greeks are said to carry "their gods" with them to Rome. The Jewish representatives were from Antioch in Syria—where the disciples of Jesus were first called Christians,—and

[86] Society of Biblical Archæology, Proceedings, 1915, pp. 217-220.

[87] The classical work discussing the condition of the Jews in the early Christian centuries is Schürer, History of the Jewish People, tho this has now been largely supplemented by the great work of Juster, Les Juifs dans l'empire Romain, 2 vols., 1914. For comprehensive information concerning Christianity in the early centuries see Harnack, Mission and Expansion of Christianity in the First Three Centuries, 2 vols. (2d ed.), 1908; also G. H. Box, London Expositor, July, 1916.

were named Simon, Glaucon, Theudas, Onias, Colon, Jacob, and Sopater. Trajan is represented as favoring the Jews at first because of his Hebrew wife Plotina; and when one of the Greek advocates says, "We are distrest that your council chamber has been filled with godless Jews," the Emperor replies in wrath, "You are studying how to die, being so contemptuous as to answer me insolently." But the Greek replies, "Then help your own people and do not defend the godless Jews"—and as he speaks the sweat, according to this papyrus, breaks out on the bust of Serapis which the envoys carried; whereupon Trajan marveled greatly and a tumult of fear followed!

Another most interesting notice referring to the Jews was published in 1912, telling of the ransom by the Jewish synagog of a middle-aged Jewess with her two children, the younger of whom was named Jacob. Another very different reference comes from a private letter written A.D. 41 by a man in money difficulty, who urges his friend to borrow some money for him if possible but adds, "Beware of the Jews!"

Signor Dr. E. Breccia, director of the Alexandrian Museum, reported in 1912 a Greek inscription which is not only of some importance for the history of the Jewish residents in the Delta in Ptolemaic times, but is interesting because of the famous names mentioned. It is engraved on a block of marble, and informs us concerning a new site of a Hebrew settlement and synagog:

"In honor of the King Ptolemy and of Queen Cleopatra, his sister; and of the Queen Cleopatra, his wife, the Jews of Xene-phyris (have consecrated) the portal of the Synagogue, the presidents being Theodorus and Achillion." [88]

[88] *Palestine Exploration Fund, Quarterly Statement,* January, 1914.

Many Hebrew manuscripts have recently been recovered from the Ezra synagog in Cairo. While the Genizah in this synagog was discovered by a learned traveler as early as 1864, and was visited by Dr. E. N. Adler in 1888, it was not until later that its treasures began to appear in European collections. Prof. A. H. Sayce obtained some important fragments from it, and Mrs. Lewis and Mrs. Gibson bought from some officer connected with it a valuable ancient copy of Sirach; but it remained for Dr. S. Schechter, in 1896 and 1897, to obtain permission from the synagog authorities to remove to Cambridge University whatever he thought to be valuable in those millennium-old closets. He has told in a fascinating way his experience in doing this.[89] He obtained not only some 12,000 Arabic documents, but a vast quantity of Hebrew manuscripts of a value beyond all price. He carried away only MSS. which he felt sure were over 400 years old; yet obtained as many as 100,000 fragments of these ancient documents. He found "rationalistic works denying the existence of either angel or devil glued to amulets in which God and angels are besought to protect the bearer from demons"; he uncovered from the dust of ages a whole series of Hebrew psalmists hitherto unknown, together with fragments of both Talmuds, many autobiographic and medical works; some very ancient Hebrew liturgies, and a very large collection of Biblical texts, some of which are earlier than any Old Testament MSS. hitherto known. It was such a hoard of ancient documents as no other man had ever been permitted to examine, and we may expect for the next generation

[89] S. Schechter, *Studies in Judaism*, 2d series, 1908.

annual news of unlooked-for treasure dug out of this pile of as yet unedited documents.[90]

Of course, a number of ancient schoolbooks were among the material found by Dr. Schechter in the old synagog at Cairo. The Jews were always near to the front so far as child instruction was concerned. An ancient Jewish maxim reads: "The school teachers are the city's watchmen"; and a distinguished rabbi is reported as once saying: "The world is upheld by the breath of the children in the school house; their instruction must not be interrupted even for the rebuilding of the temple"; while Jehovah is represented as saying: "Dearer to me is the breath of the school children than the savor of sacrifices."

At the very beginning of the Christian era the young were instructed systematically in the schools of Jerusalem, and this was extended to all parts of Palestine shortly after the lifetime of Jesus. Everybody learned to read and write and studied the history of the Jewish people; but foreign languages or foreign histories were not taught, and very little mathematics.

Every Jewish child had to be taught a trade, for the rabbis said: "He who does not teach his son a trade virtually teaches him to steal." [91]

During the first half of the first century the Jews, as the New Testament indicates, were in many places of influence throughout the entire Roman world. After

[90] Even Dr. Schechter did not, however, get all that was of value. Either another synagog has given up its Genizah or else some valuable things were strangely missed in the Ezra synagog, for in 1913 the present writer obtained in Cairo, a considerable part of one of the oldest Hebrew liturgies known. This will soon be edited by Dr. R. Butin, of the Catholic University, of Washington.

[91] Cf. besides Schürer, op. cit., especially, Ency. Religion and Ethics, V; 195ff; Max Radin, The Jews Amongst the Greeks and Romans, chap. xvi; Jester, op. cit., and Krauss, Talmudische Archäologie, 1910, III: 230ff.

the shock of Jerusalem's destruction had somewhat abated, we find them still holding high positions at court and distinguishing themselves in many dignified callings; but after Justinian's reign (A.D. 527-565), tho they continued to be celebrated as physicians, they were debarred from official position and even from all the more honored professions, including that of the army.

The papyri have given us most valuable information concerning the trades and professions of the early Christians. Lefebvre, who has cataloged the employments of all the Christians who have left inscriptions,[92] finds, to our surprize, that while there were many very humble men among the early Christians, such as blacksmiths, gardeners, and bakers, there were also architects, sculptors, writers, and an unusual number of physicians. There were not, however, many soldiers, there being only 545 epitaphs of soldiers in all the 10,050 Christian inscriptions.[93] This was probably because of the idolatrous oath which every soldier was required to take, recognizing the Emperor as divine.

In the wealthier districts of the Roman Empire, slave labor, as Wilcken has shown, monopolized almost all trades, so that all the fishermen, farmers, shepherds, hand laborers, and artizans in bronze, iron, and wood, and even the merchants, money-changers, bankers, physicians, manuscript writers, and teachers were slaves. This, however, does not apply to the fishermen and shepherds of Galilee.[94]

---

[92] *Recueil des inscriptions grecques-chrétiennes d'Egypte.*

[93] Lefebvre, *op. cit.*, p. xxxv.

[94] Among the Jews the tanners, perfumers, butchers, camel drivers, and publicans were generally recognized as being engaged in "unclean" trades, and sometimes the physicians were included, as their profession led to materialism and loss of reverence for the human body.

It would be interesting to know with absolute certainty that the trade unions which were so common in other parts of the empire were equally popular in Palestine. At least 2,500 inscriptions and other documents have come down to us dealing with these. Almost every trade had its guild or union. From Thyatira we hear of the organization of the tanners (who were also sometimes cobblers), leather workers, slave dealers, etc. From Italy and Egypt about a hundred different occupations have been found connected with these secret societies, among which we can reckon the guild of shepherds, the highest official of which was called the "chief shepherd" (*cf.* Heb. 13:20). Each trade union was under some particular patron deity, Bacchus being naturally favored by the innkeepers, and Hercules, quite as naturally, by the cabmen. There were certainly doctors' unions, but probably no lawyers', the lawyer giving his services gratuitously in the first century. These societies made no provision for the widow or orphans, neither did they have a sick benefit connected with them, nor did they ever make the useless attempt to get an increase in wages, so far as we know. They were influential mainly as social organizations.

They first originated as "burial clubs," but soon grew into more complex trade organizations. The only way even a hard-working laborer could be sure of a decent burial in the first century was by joining one of these clubs. They were common both among Jews and heathen, and the first Christian legal organizations were probably formed under this guise. These "unions" were authorized by law 22 B.C., after which they spread rapidly during the first and second centuries of our era, and with these "all that was best in the life of the common people was bound up." [95] The entrance fee, so far as can be learned, was about four or five dollars, and besides this there were monthly assessments. These clubs provided not only for a decent burial, but gave a new impulse to life to their members, who here could breathe as nowhere else the atmosphere of freedom and self-respect. When an extra fee was paid a memorial feast was held by the club on the anniversary of the brother's death.

Corporations of capital, which monopolized every possible industry and food product, had been general for hundreds of years, but by the end of the first or middle of the second century, labor was quite at the mercy of unscrupulous "trusts," which controlled prices and the transmission of food products. Even as early as 191 B.C. a play speaks of the "mountains of grain" which the dealers had in warehouses; and a papyrus some centuries later speaks of the high price of meat as due to the fact that the butchers were in league with the city fathers. Josephus tells of 18,000 laborers out of work in Jerusalem and in danger of dying with their families, so that the treasures of the temple were drawn upon in order to support them; but this was no unusual condition. Hundreds of thousands were forced to receive gifts of corn from the State in order to live during the first century, and it was not in every city that the officers acted as generously as in Jerusalem, where the authorities made provision for a living wage for all artizans. [96]

[95] Pelham, *Essays on Roman History*, p. 701*ff*.

[96] In Oxyrhynchus, also, superintendents of food supply were constantly on duty (second century) guarding the distribution of grain so that the people could get bread at a moderate price, *Journal of Egyptian Archæology*, 1915, p. 43.

The poor people, both in Palestine and Egypt, were ground to the earth by excessive taxation. The tax collectors had so evil a reputation that few decent men could have been willing to hold the office. Many papyri and ostraka contain complaints against the illegal "bleeding" of these publicans. So numerous and violent were these charges that a little before the days of Jesus an official letter was sent by the imperial authorities to these publicans:

"Do not all the time be on the point of levying blackmail, nor of slandering, but carry on your business according to the laws." [97]

The Jewish authorities had the same low opinion of the men engaged in this bad business. The rabbis universally class publicans with robbers and men without honor. No Jew in good standing was allowed to get money changed from a publican's cash box, since, presumably, it contained stolen property. Intercourse with these men was sternly forbidden as with "sinners." [98] It is noticeable that the publicans were more severely censured by the rabbis than the knights to whom the tax was "farmed out" by the Romans.

The ostraka which come from the first and adjoining centuries throw a vivid light upon the conditions of taxation at that time. Everything was taxed. Here are receipts for the bath tax, the olive oil tax, the natron tax, the land tax, the grain tax, the tax on ferryboats and ferrymen, the dyke tax, the salt tax and the tax on bricks (both of which were royal monopolies and must have yielded a handsome income), the crown tax, the wine tax, and the tax on cobblers, strangers

[97] See texts and important comments in Wilcken's *Ostraka*, I: 568-9.
[98] Krauss, *Talmudische Archäologie*, 1910, Vol. II, pp. 374ff.

and weavers. Many receipts from weavers have been found, and there need be no doubt that St. Paul had to pay some tax such as this.

Unfortunately the tax upon many commodities, such as vegetables, clothes, cattle, etc., could not be standardized, so that the amount of such taxation was left to the judgment of the individual publican—this leading to constant injustice and recrimination.

Very many of the ostraka are receipts for the poll tax. One of these which was given to Psemmonthes and his wife Talhoulis, July 29, A.D. 68, is dated in the fourteenth year of Nero—which seems to indicate that these poor people at Thebes had not heard of Nero's death seven weeks after it had occurred.[99]

The only business which was not taxed in Palestine seems to have been the fishing.[100] If Peter carried on his trade in other lands, as tradition affirms, he probably found the conditions less favorable than in Galilee.[101]

The tax upon wine shops is almost as much in evidence as the poll tax. Religious organizations were also compelled to pay a tax; indeed, the place of prayer (προσευχή) was taxed higher than either the manufactories or "saloons." Was this because the religious corporations were more honest in reporting the value of their property? Almost the only business which had to pay a larger tax than these churches or "places of prayer" were the houses of prostitution. Dr. Petrie found at Koptos a tax re-

---

[99] For many such examples see *Theban Ostraka,* Toronto, 1913.

[100] Delitzsch, *Jewish Artisan Life,* p. 47.

[101] For the extraordinary accuracy of the New Testament terminology where it mentions the fishing industry, see *Expository Times,* 1917, pp. 229-31.

port in which seamen were taxed five drachmae, skilled artizans eight, prostitutes one hundred and two.[102]

The life of the common slave was unspeakably hard. While the first century was one in which the tombstones record many gifts from wealthy men—gifts to cities and schools—there were no gifts to establish hospitals and almshouses for the needy, and no one seems ever to have thought to make provision for the comfort of the slave population.

We are not denying that in that age, as now in Turkish countries, the attractive slave was sometimes treated with tenderness. Lady Ramsay has just shown in an interesting discussion that occasionally it is almost impossible in Asia Minor to distinguish now between the daughter of the house and some trusted female slave;[103] and a few papyrus letters have come to us confirming this judgment. Among these the following is the most satisfying:

"Ta-ys to her master Apollonios, heartiest greetings. Before all I salute (with a kiss) you, Master, and I ever pray for your good health. I was not a little distressed to hear that you have not been feeling well, but thanks to all the gods that they keep you without stumbling. I pray them to send you to us, if it seem good to you; otherwise we are dying because we do not see you daily. I would that we were able to take wings and come and greet you. . . . Farewell, Master," etc.

Beautiful as this letter is, it must not be forgotten that notwithstanding special favors that might be proffered by the master or mistress to slaves who for some reason had won momentary esteem, yet the life

[102] In the third century before Christ certain officials at Crocodilopolis built up the doors of their houses and set altars against them to avoid having crown officials billeted on them. Taxation was so high it hardly paid a farmer to plant an orchard—as now under Turkish rule.

[103] See *Expository Times*, February, 1916.

and limb of every slave was wholly at the mercy of
their proprietors, and slaves were ordinarily regarded
as being on "the level of the brute." [104]   It was not expected that they should be either moral or religious
and, without any question, Plautus has exprest their
ordinary moral condition when he writes:

> "A wedding among slaves?
> A strange thing this to play, that's nowhere done!"

Nor are we able to accept certain modern scholastic
conjectures that morals in general in that era might
have compared unblushingly with the present. It is
true that spotless and high-minded women were sometimes to be found, as Ovid allows, and that certain
philosophers, like Seneca, demanded of the husband an
equal faithfulness; but even the religion of the masses
encouraged impurities, and the most popular poetry
and novels were too vile to be legally sent through our
mails. While the papyri have little, if anything, to say
on the subject, it can not be doubted from other evidence that the temples were houses of assignation, and
that even the priestesses of Isis were known to be the
mistresses of certain men of letters in the Augustan
age; it was actually counted a sin for a husband to
object to his wife taking her turn in offering her body
for hire in the name of the goddess.[105]   It is true that
Mithraism with its blood purification, its hope of immortality, and its belief in future punishments and re-

---

[104] Marucchi, *Christian Epigraphy*, p. 11. The ordinary feeling is well
expressed in a recently discovered inscription when during a four-days'
show eleven slave gladiators were killed, whereupon the master sets up
this tablet saying: "Noble fellow citizens, you will remember this in my
honor."

[105] For the low moral standards of paganism see especially Hastings,
Dict. of Bible, Extra Vol., pp. 109-155.

wards, centering around the miraculous birth and
ascension of Mithras, may have offered a moral tonic
to the devout believer; similarly the Emperor worship
was doubtless a moral advance on what preceded;
nevertheless the rapid growth of Christianity was undoubtedly due to its moral and religious superiority to
the religions which it superseded.[106]

That the common people had a strong religious instinct is, of course, perfectly evident from their faithfulness to the religious ceremonial in which they trusted
and from their immense gifts to the temples;[107] yet it
would seem almost in spite of the religious influences of
that era, rather than in response to them, that so much
of the common life was tender and worthy. Certainly
the papyri have proved that the love of husband for
wife and parents for children was often tender and
devoted. One mother, for example, in the third century writes in illiterate Greek, sympathizing with her
boy because of the splinter that had injured his foot,
and saying in mother language:

"Do not forget, my child, to write me regarding your health,
for you know the anxiety of a mother for a child. Your children
greet you."

Many such pathetic letters could be quoted. So
a wife writes to her husband concerning their child
(second or third century):

"I fear he may die while you are not here."

[106] See J. F. Carter, *Religious Life of Ancient Rome*, 1911, pp. 90*ff*; and
Harnack, *Spread of Early Christianity*, II: 29-177, 325.

[107] These temples were ordinarily much larger and finer than either that
of Solomon or Herod. The Parthenon only measured 228 by 100 feet;
but the temple at Sardes was 300 feet long, and that at Miletus, 359 by
171 feet. All of these were more elaborately decorated than the Hebrew
temple, and were literally crowded with votive offerings.

And a little girl writes to her father:

"Ammonous to her sweetest father, greeting. Now that I have got your letter and have learned that by the will of the gods you have been kept safe, I have been made very glad. And finding opportunity the same hour I have written you this letter hastening to greet you. All yours individually send greetings to you. . . . I pray that it be well with you."

RECAPITULATION

BECAUSE of their importance it may be well to repeat a few of the main facts brought out in the last few sections of our discussion, adding a few new illustrations.

Making a broad examination of the papyri gathered from the rubbish heaps and comparing them with other material, we are now able to throw a flashlight upon the early Christian centuries such as was never possible before.

For the first time modern historians are able to read references to Jesus and the early Christians centuries older than have ever before been known. It is true that from a late manuscript of Lucian, a writer of the second century, we had learned of Peregrinus Proteus (A.D. 165), who is described as a rather unworthy follower of the "crucified sophist," and from a second or third century Syriac document, first made known in 1865, we had received the testimony of Mara, who compares Christ to Socrates and Pythagoras, calling him the "Wise King" and speaking of his "new laws," and from various Roman writers such as Tacitus and Pliny we had received most valuable information concerning the early Christians; but none of these had given us the autograph testimonies concerning early Christianity which have in such multitudes been dug up in recent years. The names of Jesus and Paul have met us very often in the course of our study, while multitudes of the documents which we have examined were written by early Christians, and many others mention Jews or heathen who were contemporaneous with the primitive Christians.

A document just discovered mentions Nero the famous contemporary of St. Paul. This infamous ruler, whom some modern scholars have attempted to eulogize as the champion of domestic reform and universal benevolence, may not have "fiddled while Rome was burning," but he certainly followed wherever passion led him and had in his blood the ferocity of a wild beast;[1] yet in the autograph copy of the notification of his accession, written November 17, A.D. 54, he is spoken of as follows:

"The Cæsar who had to pay his debt to his ancestors, god manifest, has joined them, and the expectation and hope of the world has been declared Emperor, the good genius of the world and source of all good things, Nero, has been declared Cæsar. Therefore ought we all wearing garlands and with sacrifices of oxen to give thanks to all the gods."

A new light has also been thrown upon literary conditions among the poorer classes.

It has never been doubted that the "Augustan age" which gave to us the classical literature now studied in our colleges was an age of mental power. No more celebrated professors can be found in any university of the world to-day than could then be found at Alexandria and Athens and Tarsus.

Pliny in his "Natural History"—which was completed A.D. 77—consulted 2,000 volumes. Vespasian in this golden age of Latin literature founded the university of Rome with immense libraries and originated the "Carnegie endowment" idea, establishing pensions

---

[1] See e. g., Pelham, *Essays on Roman History*, 1911, pp. 43ff.

for professors of the liberal arts. Quintilian, the man first pensioned, in a great work still valuable for its pedagogical teachings, argued for the superiority of public schools over private education, condemned corporal punishment, taught that amusements should be turned to account as a means of education, argued that children should begin early with a foreign tongue, emphasized the fact that different natures demanded different treatment on the part of the teacher, and in fact gave "the first scientific statement of the problems of education." [2]

Yet notwithstanding this, and the further fact that Epictetus had told us that every second woman in Rome might be seen reading Plato's *Republic,* the new discoveries concerning the practical universality of reading and writing among all classes of the population has come upon us as a great surprise. It is, on the whole, comparatively rare to find a man unable to sign his name to a legal document or to find it stated in a papyrus that the sender of the letter can not write.

Shorthand, as we have seen, was used in taking notes by literary and professional men such as Cicero, Pliny, and Galen—experts in the art being named as a class, *"notarii,"*—but it would be an almost equal surprise to many to know that "letter books" were in use in antiquity containing copies of letters sent and letters received, portions of at least three of these having come down to us. Every class of people could write, even those who were so poor that they could not afford a sheet of papyrus, but had to write their notes on scraps of broken pottery. Numbers of students write home to their parents telling of their studies. In one of these

[2] See Monroe, *History of Education,* 199-208.

(third century), the text of which was published in 1914, Aurelius, Jr., writes to Aurelius, Sr.:

"My sweetest father, many greetings: I perform the act of veneration for you every day before the gods of this place. Do not be anxious, father, about my studies. I am industrious and take relaxation. All will be well with me."

Another letter (fourth century), the text of which was published at the same time, tho full of misspelled words, seems also to be from a schoolboy, tho perhaps one in the lower classes, for one of his most urgent requests in the letter is:

"Bring the milk cakes when you come. . . . Not the papyrus."

A contemporary of the above, who was evidently a better student, writes to his teacher Gonatus calling him "My incomparable master" (*despota*), "the consolation of all his friends." So a father writes to his son (first century), "I have received the boxes with the books," and tells him that he will soon receive "the variegated wrist bands."

As we read these many documents from the first and adjoining centuries, written in the language of the New Testament, we are imprest with the truth of the apostolic statement, "To us the toll of all ages has come as our inheritance" (1 Cor. 10: 11).[3]

Much new light has been thrown upon the economic and social conditions among the poor of the first century. While one court physician in the days of the elder Pliny had an income of $25,000 a year, and a successful charioteer was able to leave his children a

___

[3] This is the translation of Drs. Rendel Harris and James Hope Moulton, *Egyptian Rubbish Heaps*, p. 30.

legacy of $1,400,000, and while fortunes were so common among the rich that Augustus (A.D. 6) laid a tax of 5 per cent. on bequests of $4,000 or over, and numbers of millionaires put up inscriptions telling of their benevolent gifts, and splendid funereal monuments on which they show themselves counting their money; yet the poor were so poor that thousands of them were compelled to go without burial, thrown into pits like dogs and cattle, while those of the middle classes, farmers and artizans, were compelled to pay enormous taxes, and when they ran in debt were compelled to pay 12 per cent., 18 per cent., and 22 per cent., and occasionally 48 per cent. interest per annum.[4]

It must be remembered that altho there were eighty different trade unions in Rome alone, yet these made no effort to raise wages or improve wage conditions— these being considered beyond hope. Such unions were organized solely for social companionship and to give a little help in some cruel emergency such as death; yet even burial expenses were forfeited if the member failed to pay his dues for six months. These were not charitable organizations, but were for social and convivial enjoyment. It was the social feature which was most important, even the slaves having guilds of their own in which the officers held pompous titles.

Wherever Paul traveled he could meet other weavers of tent cloth in fraternal fellowship, while Luke would naturally go with the physicians.[5]

The superstition of the first century has been constantly evident. Not only amid the orgies of the

---

[4] Lanciani, *Ancient Rome*, chap. iii; Kenyon, *Greek Papyri*, ccii.

[5] However, it is possible that in the first century the best physicians, like teachers, felt it a disgrace to charge for their services, and therefore may not have joined together in a "trade" fraternity.

oriental worshipers can it be said the "air thrilled with demonic terror, [and] witches and lewd sorceresses abounded"; but in all classes of the population the fear of demons was a constant terror. No texts are more numerous than those which have to do with incantations and charms. There were few medical recipes that did not include "the blood of a white cat" or some other magical ingredient. Altho Augustus burned 2,000 books of unlicensed divination, yet even he believed in the astrologers, while Tiberius used the sacred lot, Cicero consulted the Pythia, Nero used magic to protect him from the ghosts of the women he had murdered, Domitian seems to have been literally scared to death by an astrological omen, and Marcus Aurelius consulted a charm doctor in order to cure his wife's infatuation for a gladiator.[6]

If the best educated were thus controlled by superstitious terrors, we must not wonder at the common people nor be surprized if we find some Christians, notwithstanding their faith in the Christ, whose "Name was above all names," yielding sometimes to superstitious fear. Von Dobschütz, however, believes that magic had very little hold upon the Christian Church previous to the fourth century, when martyr worship and the use of relics encouraged this; and he shows conclusively that "the morality of early Christianity, notwithstanding its imperfections, was unmistakably higher than all the Greek civilization could achieve."[7] This judgment we believe the study of the papyri has confirmed.

Previous to the fourth century, the poorly educated

[6] Dill, *op. cit.*, pp. 446-450.
[7] *Ency. of Religion and Ethics,* "Charms and Amulets"; and "Christian Life in the Primitive Church," IX: 363-379.

Christians naturally used such local charms as were not against their religion, but made war on everything that seemed connected with the adoration of demons. While after that time Bible texts and the name of Jesus and the sign of the cross are used as protective charms, it is quite possible that the multitude of magical texts discovered in which Isis and Horus are mentioned side by side with Jewish archangels, and other imprecations and spells in which Christian and Jewish and heathen sacred names occur together, may generally have been of Gnostic origin, adopted by heathen magicians after they began to acknowledge the power of Jewish and Christian deities.[8] In any case no one can fully understand Christianity's battle as the conquering "religion of the spirit" without recognizing the universal dominance of these fleshless "world rulers of this darkness" against which the Christians wrestled (Eph. 6: 12).

It must not be denied that appeals to magic became very frequent in and after the sixth century, and that morality was correspondingly affected in some instances. A Coptic text of about A.D. 600, which correctly speaks of the current "madness of idolatry" in Egypt and asks, "Who shall be able to persuade the people to despise demons?" mentions in the same connection healing by "spittle" and by the "Word" of Jesus.[9] The common people then were much as the common people are now in Palestine and Egypt. The modern Arabs who visit the excavations to-day wear charms against fever and ophthalmia; so, like their contemporaries, many ignorant Christians in the early

[8] See *Zeitschrift für Archäologie*, XXXII: 47.
[9] *Anecdota Oxoniensia*, 1913, No. 15.

centuries sought charms against the demons asthma, croup, hydrophobia, insanity, and indigestion.

An interesting, altho rather obscure love-charm reads:

> "Kronos who holds in check the spirit (breath) of all men, hold in check the spirit of Hori. O Lord whom Mary bore, do not permit him to speak to him whom Taises bore; because I conjure thee by the finger of God not to open your mouth to him, because Krinoupelike is subject to Kronos. Do not permit him to speak to him neither night nor day. . . ." [10]

Yet the ministry, even down to the sixth and seventh centuries, altho in some cases very ignorant, were, as we have previously seen, compelled in some cases to have a better knowledge of Scripture before ordination than many of our theological students receive now. This is abundantly proved from various ostraka where Samuel, Jacob, Aaron, and others promise "to master the gospel of John" and Papas and another bind themselves to learn by heart either the gospel of John or the gospel of Matthew; and still another agrees in the same way to memorize the "gospel according to Mark." [11] So Ammonius (cir. A.D. 390) is said to have been able to repeat the Old and the New Testament by heart.

The religious condition of the common people in the first century has been fully exposed by the revelations in the papyri. That the pagan world has been painted too dark by earlier Christian scholars all historians now acknowledge. The crimes and abnormal wickedness of the court circles made known to us in the classics do not appear in the same prominence among the

[10] Greek text in *Coptic Ostraca*, No. 522.
[11] Crum, *Coptic Ostraca*, Nos. 29, 30, 34-39.

middle and lower classes made known to us through the papyri. The world into which the gospel came was really "very religious" (Acts 17: 22). The people as a whole believed not only in God, but in many gods; they had, too, a sense of sin and a desire to escape from a just judgment which they feared. The following specimen, found ready for use in an ancient model letter writer, shows how in private life this sense of sin against one's neighbor sometimes exprest itself:

"I know that I erred in that I treated thee ill. Wherefore having repented I beg pardon for the error. But for the Lord's sake delay not to forgive me. For it is just to pardon friends who stumble, and especially when they desire to obtain pardon" (cf. 1 Cor. 4: 10; 2 Cor. 4: 11; Phil. 3: 7-8; Luke 17: 4).

There is no doubt that many, even among the common people, were, however, losing their faith in the gods they were taught to worship. In one papyrus recently published, a man writes:

"Come at once. If you neglect this, as the gods have not spared me, so will I not spare the gods." [12]

How very different from this is the joyous statement of the New Testament that "faith is the title deed of things hoped for" (Heb. 11: 1).[13]

The Christian seriousness of faith and love for God and fellow man must have been surprizing and almost amusing to their contemporaries. One papyrus shows a certain Pamphilus (sixth century) borrowing twelve pieces of gold at 33⅓ per cent. interest for the sake of

[12] *Oxyrhynchus Papyri*, VII, No. 1065.

[13] This is the meaning of the Greek text, *cf.* Moulton, *From Egyptian Rubbish Heaps*, p. 28.

distributing these among the poor! Such an act would have been impossible until the new doctrine had taken deep hold upon society. We had known, before the papyri gave up their testimony, something of these Christian benefactions of the early centuries; but these autograph memoranda add to our respect for the "brotherhood" sentiment among the early followers of Jesus.[14]

These early believers also show a higher average type of morality than could have been expected. Among all the cases of church discipline opened up in the papyri, no single instance of a grave charge is now remembered by the writer, except one case of "blasphemy" and another of "ill-using the poor." It is certainly suggestive of a rather high ideal to find even as late as the sixth century that a man who divorced his wife, except for adultery, was excluded from communion, together with the man writing the divorce; and that one who marries a brother or sister's daughter could not have communion "be he alive or dead"; neither could any one come to communion who was at "enmity with his neighbor."[15]

The heathen thought of God differed so diametrically from that of the Christian that it was impossible for them to have the same divine ideal of purity, righteousness, and humanity, as that which came with the faith that the meek and holy Jesus was the highest

---

[14] In a house in Algeria—used as a church during the reign of Diocletian—has been found in connection with the chalices of gold, silver, lamps, etc., used with the ancient church ritual, thirteen pairs of men's boots, forty-seven pairs of women's shoes, sixteen male tunics, and eighty-two female tunics—*Pagan and Christian Rome*, p. 42. Were these used in the church services, or were they for distribution to indigent Christians?

[15] Crum, *Coptic Ostraca*, Nos. 71-73; a most curious case of church discipline is that in which, when Onesimus is late for service, his ox is chastised (Ramsay, *Bishopricks of Phrygia*, p. 149).

conceivable representative of the heart and personality of God. While the ordinary Roman of the first century had advanced morally to a point where he could no longer accept unspeakably wicked deities as his models, yet he was still accepting Osiris and the Emperor as divine ideals. The Emperor worship, was very different in Egypt from the Ptolemaic "Kaiser-cult;"[16] yet in most parts of the empire it was more deep and serious, and certainly more popular, than that of any other deity. But the Emperors were not leading ideal lives and did not possess characters which could encourage morality. It was in spite of such worship that many noble virtues lingered among the middle classes.

Many, perhaps most, of the people whom Paul met had fairly good moral character and were honestly desirous of living upright lives. It is a fact emphasized not only by the papyri, but also in the literary works of the first century, that almost all of the vices enumerated by Paul (1 Cor. 6: 9-10) were recognized as evil by the pagans, while most of his virtues, such as temperance and faith, were being praised. God had not left himself without a witness even among those who had lost faith in written revelation.

While we must read Ovid and Petronius in expurgated editions and while many of the epigrams of Martial "should be effaced from human memory," comparatively few of the papyri and inscriptions show the same putridity of imagination. The common people in every age have represented the best morality of the age. Juvenal's description of the women he knew as "lewd, petulant, and reeling, rife with wine," does not repre-

---

[16] See especially F. Blumenthal, *A. f. P-F*, V, 317*f*.

sent the women whom we meet in these texts, which sprang out of the life of the common people. Everywhere we find husbands and wives praying for their friends and leading useful and hard-working, dependable lives, caring lovingly for their families, and giving amazing gifts out of their poverty in votive offerings to the temples.

Nevertheless, when we remember the wall-paintings and public inscriptions of Pompeii and recall the character of the shows which were most popular among all classes in the first century; when we remember the way in which the slaves were treated, and notice that in almost every slave contract published scars are mentioned, and that the guaranty must be included against epilepsy or some worse disease; we must acknowledge that heathen civilization in the first century, at its best, does not compare very favorably with Christian civilization at its worst.

It would be instructive to a certain class of historians to be compelled to live for a while in the atmosphere of ancient heathendom and study the ancient letters and plays and court records and life. The most beautiful pagan letter of consolation coming from ancient times is perhaps the following, from the second century:

"Irene to Tacunophria and Philo, good cheer! I was much grieved and wept over the blessed one, as I wept for Didymus, and everything that was fitting I did, and all who were with me. But truly there is nothing any one can do in the face of such things. Do you therefore comfort one another. Good-bye." [17]

Compare such a letter with Paul's tender words (2 Thess. 4: 14-18), and notice the infinite difference.

[17] Milligan, *Greek Papyri*, No. 38.

While undoubtedly most of the Romans of the first century believed in an existence of some sort in the world beyond—a belief due in part, it may be, to the Jews but chiefly to the teaching of the oriental religions,—yet the common funereal inscriptions were not joyous:

"Into nothing from nothing how quickly we go."
"Once we were naught, now we are as we were."
"I was not, I was, I am not, I care not."

The last expression (*non fui, fui, non sum, non curo*) was so commonly used that it is sometimes indicated merely by the intial letters *"n.f.f.n.s.n.c."* Even at the best the hope of such a future life as the heathen of the first century accepted could not bring the helpful sympathy in hours of bereavement, and the joyous certainty of future blessedness which was the unique possession of the Christians.

The grossest sexual crimes are publicly referred to without shame in the witticisms written upon the walls, in the private letters, and in the dramatic plays. A farce coming from the second century is not only full of the coarsest allusions, but the plot hinges on the base proposal made to a slave by his young mistress, leading, after the proposal is declined, to an order for his crucifixion along with the female slave whom he is supposed to love. To this same century belongs the speech of an advocate who affirms publicly in court that the chief judge has had improper relations with a seventeen-year-old boy.

But no text the writer has ever seen has so imprest upon him the difference between the ancient and modern civilization as the letter from Hilarion, an Egyptian laborer, written to Alis, his wife, June 17, 1 B.C., concerning his own child and concerning a babe probably about to be born to his daughter:[18]

"Hilarion to Alis, his sister. Many greetings. . . . Be not distressed if at the general coming in I remain at Alexandria. I pray thee and beseech thee take care of the little child. And as soon as we receive wages I will send them to thee (?). . . . If . . . is delivered, if it be a male baby let it live, if it be a female, expose it."

Look at that awful Greek word, ἔκβαλε, "cast it out," "expose it!" What could put in stronger relief the horrors of that age in which the lover of little children came preaching the "Good News" than just the letters which form that commonplace word, written with such utter indifference and without the slightest apology or excuse to that far-off mother.

But this is not the only case of child exposure made known to us in the papyri. It was such a common thing that a large number of documents have come to us from Alexandria, dating near the birth of Christ, all of which prove to be contracts with women who acted as nurses for these little babies picked off the rubbish heap, to be kept for slaves or used for immoral purposes.[19]

As we compare even the best teaching—not to speak of the practise—revealed in these ancient heathen writings, with the New Testament gospels and letters, we

[18] *Oxyrhynchus Papyri,* IV: 744.

[19] Menander's chief comedy is based on the story of an exposed child which a shepherd has found in the wilderness, with which was found also a necklace and ring. Onesimus finds the ring and recognizes it as the property of his master, and then the fun begins!

appreciate as never before the words of Athanasius (A.D. 367) in his recently recovered Festal Letter:

> "THESE ARE SPRINGS OF SALVATION, SO THAT HE
> WHO IS ATHIRST MAY BE FILLED WITH THE ORACLES
> IN THEM. IN THEM ALONE IS THE TEACHING OF
> PIETY PROCLAIMED AS GOOD NEWS. LET NO ONE ADD
> TO THEM, OR TAKE AWAY AUGHT FROM THEM." [20]

[20] Zahn, *Geschichte des neutestamentlichen Kanons*, II : 210.

SCRIPTURE TEXTS ILLUSTRATED
AND
INDEX

SCRIPTURE TEXTS ILLUSTRATED

[687]

INDEX